D0212180

William Shakespeare

A Literary Reference to His Life and Work

VOLUME II

CRITICAL COMPANION TO

William Shakespeare

*A Literary Reference to
His Life and Work*

VOLUME II

CHARLES BOYCE

☑®

Facts On File, Inc.

Critical Companion to William Shakespeare:
A Literary Reference to His Life and Work

Facts On File, Inc.
132 West 31st Street
New York NY 10001

Library of Congress Cataloging-in-Publication Data
Boyce, Charles
Critical companion to William Shakespeare: a literary reference to his life and work / Charles Boyce. — Rev. ed.
p. cm.
Rev. ed. of: Shakespeare A to Z. 1990.
Includes bibliographical references and index.
ISBN 0-8160-5373-1 (hc: alk. paper)
1. Shakespeare, William, 1564–1616—Dictionaries. 2. Dramatists, English—Early modern,
1500–1700—Biography—Dictionaries. I. Boyce, Charles. Shakespeare A to Z. II. Title.
PR2892.B69 2005
822.3'3—dc22   2004025769

Facts On File books are available at special discounts when purchased in
bulk quantities for businesses, associations, institutions, or sales promotions.
Please call our Special Sales Department in New York at
(212) 967-8800 or (800) 322-8755.

You can find Facts On File on the World Wide Web at
http://www.factsonfile.com

Text design by Joan M. Toro
Adapted by Erika K. Arroyo
Cover design by Cathy Rincon

Printed in the United States of America

VB Hermitage 10 9 8 7 6 5 4 3 2 1

This book is printed on acid-free paper.

CONTENTS

PART II

Works

T–Z

Taming of a Shrew, The

Anonymous play first published in 1594, probably a BAD QUARTO of *The Taming of the Shrew* but once thought to have been the principal source of that play. *A Shrew*, as the play is conveniently known, differs most strikingly from *The Shrew* in having a simpler SUBPLOT. *The Shrew* features a contest among three suitors for the hand of the younger of two sisters; *A Shrew* adds a third sister and matches each sister with a suitor, eliminating the rivalry. This subplot is equally filled with romantic intrigue, as the suitors of the younger sisters conspire to outwit the father of the girls, but it lacks the comical confusions of Shakespeare's work. The main plot is the same, and the dialogue corresponds closely throughout much of the play.

A Shrew is, however, a generally inferior drama, and this, combined with the difference in subplots, used to be taken to indicate that Shakespeare had used *A Shrew* as his chief source for *The Shrew*, unless both were derived from an earlier, subsequently lost play, designated the UR-SHREW. However, close examination of the two texts offers convincing evidence that *A Shrew* was compiled from the recollections of actors who had performed in *The Shrew*—that is, that the former is a bad quarto of the latter.

Although similarities in wording occur throughout the two plays, including their subplots, *A Shrew*'s versions of particular passages are consistently garbled or misinterpreted renderings of the corresponding lines in *The Shrew*. Even the introductory moments of the subplot of *A Shrew* bear signs of its derivative nature; it appears that its complexities were not well remembered, so the compilers fell back on a more conventional love plot. Further, *A Shrew* contains echoes of other plays, especially *Tamburlaine* and *Doctor Faustus*, by Christopher MARLOWE. This is characteristic of reconstructed texts, reflecting faulty memories on the part of the actors. And some scenes in a bad quarto are invariably closer to the original text than others, indicating that the principal compilers played the characters whose roles are most accurately recollected and appeared on stage during the best-rendered scenes. It thus seems likely that much of the text of *A Shrew* was the work of the actors who had played Christopher Sly and Grumio in *The Shrew*, probably William SLY and Alexander COOKE, respectively. The title page of *A Shrew* asserts that it had been performed by PEMBROKE'S MEN. This acting company toured the provinces for most of the period 1592–94, when the LONDON theaters were closed by a plague epidemic, and the actors probably produced the text for that tour.

One of the most striking differences between the two texts is the presence in *A Shrew* of four INTERLUDES and an EPILOGUE dealing with Christopher Sly, whereas *The Shrew* abandons the tale after one interlude. It is assumed that the editors of the FIRST FOLIO (1623), in which *The Shrew* was first published, used a manuscript that reflected a production that cut these episodes due to a shortage of actors. Thus, *A Shrew* apparently presents a version of Shakespeare's original interludes and epilogue, and this material is sometimes included in editions of *The Shrew*.

Marlowe's *Doctor Faustus* was probably written in the spring of 1592, and a compiler of *A Shrew* had acted in it, or at least seen it, so that the text of *A Shrew* must have been assembled between the summer of 1592 and the spring of 1594, when it was registered for publication. It was published by Cuthbert BURBY, who also published QUARTO editions of several of Shakespeare's other plays. It was reissued in 1597, and Nicholas LING published a third edition in 1607.

Taming of the Shrew, The

SYNOPSIS

Induction, Scene 1

Christopher Sly drunkenly falls asleep on the ground. As a practical joke, the local Lord decides to take the unconscious man into his home and have him awaken in the lap of luxury. He orders his servants to inform Sly that he is a gentleman who has been insane for many years, believing himself a poor drunkard. A traveling company of Players arrives, and the Lord directs them to perform for Sly. He further arranges for his Page to pose as Sly's wife.

Induction, Scene 2

Sly awakens in a bedroom of the Lord's house, and the servants offer him delicacies. His "illness" is explained to him by the Lord, but Sly denies it and briefly describes his true place in the world. The Lord and his servants offer the gentlemanly pleasures they insist are properly his, including a beautiful wife, and Sly accepts their version of his life. The Page appears, dressed as a woman. Sly's lusty instincts are laid to rest by the assertion that sex will produce further delusions of poverty. The Players' performance is announced, and Sly prepares to enjoy it.

Act 1, Scene 1

Lucentio, accompanied by his servant Tranio, has just arrived in PADUA. They observe Baptista telling Hortensio and Gremio that their courtship of his daughter Bianca is inappropriate, for he will not permit her to be wed until her older sister, Katherina, is married. The suitors state that this is an unlikely prospect, as Katherina is a notorious shrew, unacceptable to any man. Katherina's aggressive response seems to justify their remarks, while Bianca demurely accepts her father's order. Baptista asks the suitors to help him find tutors in music and poetry to keep Bianca happy, and he and his daughters depart. Hortensio and Gremio agree to try to find a husband for Katherina so that they can resume their rivalry for Bianca, and they, too, leave. Lucentio tells Tranio of his immediate and intense love for Bianca. The two devise a plan to permit him to court the girl: Lucentio shall disguise himself as a scholar and become Bianca's tutor, and Tranio shall pretend to be Lucentio. Lucentio's other servant, Biondello, arrives and is told of the plan. In addition, Lucentio decides that the disguised Tranio shall declare himself a suitor to Bianca and convince Baptista to accept him. Christopher Sly, who has been dozing, is awakened by the Page and another servant, and he readies himself to watch more of the play.

Act 1, Scene 2

Petruchio arrives in Padua and calls on his old friend Hortensio. He announces that he has come in search of a wife, and Hortensio suggests Katherina, while warning that she is intolerable. Petruchio is undaunted, for he says he knows how to deal with shrews; he insists on meeting Baptista

immediately. Hortensio decides to masquerade as a music teacher, to be recommended by Petruchio as Bianca's tutor. On their way to Baptista's, they encounter Gremio and Lucentio, who is dressed as a scholar. Gremio declares that he will ingratiate himself with Baptista by presenting Lucentio as a language teacher for Bianca. Tranio, disguised as Lucentio, appears and reveals, in his master's name, his intention to court Bianca.

Act 2, Scene 1

Katherina torments Bianca until Baptista stops her, and the sisters go their separate ways. Gremio, Petruchio, and Hortensio arrive. Petruchio introduces himself as a suitor for Katherina's hand and proposes Hortensio as a music teacher to entertain his prospective bride; similarly, Gremio presents Lucentio as a language teacher, intended for Bianca. Tranio arrives, calling himself Lucentio, and declares himself a suitor of Bianca; he bears a gift of a lute and several books. Baptista distributes these to the appropriate tutors and sends the teachers to their pupils. Petruchio, saying that he is in a hurry, arranges a marriage agreement with Baptista, contingent on Katherina's acceptance. Hortensio reports that Katherina has broken the lute on his head in a fit of anger. Petruchio praises Katherina's spirit and wants to meet her. The others leave, and Petruchio reveals his plan in a soliloquy: He will assert Katherina's sweetness, no matter how shrewish her behavior, and treat their wedding as agreed upon, whatever her protests. She appears, and he immediately takes a familiar tone, addressing her as Kate and complimenting her effusively. They engage in a bantering battle of wits, but he ignores her insults; even when she hits him he responds with moderation. She calls him a fool, but he insists that she shall marry him and he shall tame her. Baptista, Gremio, and Tranio return, and, despite Katherina's protests, Petruchio insists that she has agreed to their marriage and has been very affectionate to him. She calms down as Petruchio confirms with her father his plan to marry her on the next Sunday, and Petruchio takes her with him to get a ring. Baptista asserts that the wealthiest of Bianca's suitors shall marry his younger daughter, and they attempt to outbid each other. Tranio, speaking as Lucentio, offers far more than Gremio, citing the vast fortune of his father,

Vincentio. Baptista agrees that he shall have Bianca once his parent comes to Padua and substantiates his claim. The older men leave, and Tranio plans to recruit a stand-in for Lucentio's father.

Act 3, Scene 1
Lucentio and Hortensio refuse to leave each other alone with Bianca. Lucentio pretends to construe a passage in Latin and reveals his identity and purpose to Bianca. She is demurely wary, but she does not dismiss him, telling him not to despair. Hortensio gives her a love note couched as a lesson in the musical scale, but she rejects him altogether.

Act 3, Scene 2
Petruchio, dressed in ridiculous clothes, arrives very late for his wedding to Katherina and goes in search of her. The wedding guests follow, and Tranio has a chance to tell Lucentio of his plan to find a substitute Vincentio. Gremio tells of Petruchio's obnoxious behavior at the wedding. The rest of the wedding party appears, and Petruchio announces that he is leaving immediately with Kate, rather than staying for the banquet. Furious, Katherina resists, but he carries her off.

Act 4, Scene 1
Petruchio's servant Grumio arrives at his master's house in bitter cold, having been sent ahead to arrange for the newlyweds' reception. He tells Curtis, another servant, of the unchivalrous behavior of Petruchio, who has allowed Katherina to lie in the mud after falling from her horse and has beaten Grumio needlessly, to his bride's horror. The couple appear. Petruchio orders dinner for Katherina, but he rails at the servants for not presenting it properly, throwing the food at them; his wife gets none. He ignores her pleas for patience and takes her off to bed. A servant reports that Petruchio continues to rant and rave, disconcerting Katherina completely. Petruchio returns, and the servants flee; in a soliloquy he describes his plan: He will continue to insist ferociously that nothing is good enough for his wife so that she will get no food, no drink, and no rest. He likens his strategy to the taming of a wild falcon.

Act 4, Scene 2
In Padua, Hortensio brings Tranio, whom he thinks is Lucentio, to overhear Bianca's loving conversation with the real Lucentio. Tranio pretends to be affronted and joins Hortensio in criticizing Bianca as frivolous and unworthy. Hortensio vows to marry a Widow who has pursued him, and he leaves. Tranio encounters the Pedant, a newcomer to Padua, and, after learning that he is from MANTUA, tells him that an outbreak of hostilities has resulted in a new law condemning to death any Mantuan found in Padua. He offers to protect the stranger if he will agree to pose as Vincentio. The Pedant gratefully accepts.

Act 4, Scene 3
Petruchio brings food for Katherina, but she won't speak to him. He refuses to give it to her until she thanks him. She thanks him, but, before she can eat much, he brings in a Tailor and a Haberdasher to provide her with fine clothes. Petruchio rejects these garments, although Katherina likes them. He asserts that she shall have a gentlewoman's clothes only when she is gentle, and, raging, he drives the Tailor and Haberdasher away. Planning their journey to a feast at her father's house, he asserts that it is seven o'clock; when Katherina responds that it is only two, he insists that she must stop contradicting him.

Act 4, Scene 4
Tranio and the Pedant, as Lucentio and his father, call on Baptista. The Pedant asserts his willingness to provide a dowry, and Baptista agrees to the betrothal of Bianca and Lucentio; they leave to sign a marriage contract at Lucentio's house. The real Lucentio, who is present in his role as the tutor, is sent to fetch Bianca. Biondello informs him of Tranio's plan: A priest is ready at a certain church, and Lucentio may now elope with his beloved.

Act 4, Scene 5
On the road to Padua, Petruchio remarks that the moonlight is very bright. When Katherina observes that it is daylight, he threatens to cancel the trip if she does not stop disagreeing with him. She gives in to him, calling the sun the moon, and he says it is the sun. She concurs and states that she will agree to whatever he says. Petruchio asserts that things are now as they should be. When an elderly man approaches, Petruchio calls him a lovely maid, and Katherina, true to her promise, addresses the old gentleman as though he were a girl. Petruchio then changes his mind, and Katherina begs the man's

pardon for her mistake. As they travel together, the older man identifies himself as Vincentio.

Act 5, Scene 1

Bianca and Lucentio enter a church to be married. Petruchio, Katherina, and Vincentio arrive at Lucentio's house, where the Pedant poses as Vincentio. Petruchio and Katherina withdraw to witness this development. The clamor brings Baptista and Tranio. Tranio continues to brazen it out, and Vincentio is about to be arrested as an imposter, when Lucentio and Bianca arrive, married. Lucentio identifies himself and explains what has happened. Baptista's anger is cooled by Vincentio's assurance that he will approve Lucentio's marriage. The discussion becomes more cordial and moves indoors. Petruchio wishes to kiss Katherina before following the others inside, but she is embarrassed to kiss in the street. He speaks of returning home, and she kisses him. Affectionately, they go to join the others.

Act 5, Scene 2

A banquet celebrates the marriages of Lucentio to Bianca, Hortensio to the Widow, and, belatedly, Petruchio to Katherina. The Widow shrewishly argues with Katherina. The ladies withdraw, and the men gamble on whose wife is the most obedient. Bianca is sent for, but she sends word that she is busy and cannot come. Similarly, the Widow sends the message that, suspecting some joke, she will not come. Petruchio sends Grumio to "command" that Katherina come, and she does. Petruchio sends her back to fetch the other women. When the women return, the Widow says she is glad not to be so compliant as Katherina, and Bianca calls Lucentio a fool for having bet on her obedience. At Petruchio's order, Katherina lectures the other women on the virtues of submissiveness. She says that the natural order of things places men in authority and that a woman's virtue and beauty are marred by revolt against nature. A husband takes risks in the world to maintain a home, whereas a woman lives in relative comfort, owing no more for her situation than obedience. She compares a woman's proper devotion to a husband with the allegiance that a subject owes a prince, and she observes that she has rebelled herself and has learned that nothing is to be gained from it. She makes a formal gesture of submission, placing

her hand beneath Petruchio's foot. Petruchio, exulting in his fine wife, takes her off to bed; the others marvel at the taming of the shrew.

COMMENTARY

The Taming of the Shrew is sometimes seen as an account of the tyranny of man over woman, but this is a misinterpretation stemming from our distance from the assumptions of Shakespeare's day. In Elizabethan England it was almost universally agreed that it was a God-given right, confirmed in the Bible, for a husband to dominate his wife in all things, just as a king could dictate to a citizen or a human being could control an animal. Katherina's famous speech in 5.2.137–180 expresses this belief quite plainly. However, it is a mistake to think that the story of Katherina and Petruchio is intended to make this point; rather, it takes the point for granted. Instead, the play's main plot concerns the development of character and of love in a particular sort of personality.

Shakespeare's version of the "battle of the sexes" is a striking advance on its predecessors. In treatments of this classic theme both before and since Shakespeare, a woman is commonly beaten into submission or is tormented in some more sophisticated manner. The violence in _The Shrew_—except for conventional beatings of servants, a staple of theatrical humor dating back to Roman drama—is limited to Katherina's own assaults on Bianca and Petruchio, which demonstrate her shrewishness. Petruchio "tames" Katherina by means of a clever strategy that startlingly resembles modern behavior-modification therapy.

In fact, the psychology of _The Taming of the Shrew_ is highly evolved, evidence that, even early in his career, Shakespeare had the capacity to delineate personalities. Acts 1–3 contain a convincingly familiar portrait of a highly defensive young woman who shields herself from criticism by attacking others first, and she is strong enough to make her father and sister regret any effort to reform her. The portrayal of the deceptively demure Bianca, who slyly taunts her sister in 2.1 and who displays her own willfulness when she is alone with her suitors in 3.1, suggests that Katherina has been compared to her younger sister too often for her temper to tolerate.

Petruchio understands this, and although he is motivated to marry for mercenary reasons, he values Katherina's high spirits. Thus he can maneuver her into abandoning her shrewishness, and his technique, although comically overdrawn, is psychologically sophisticated.

Petruchio persistently assures Katherina that she is a rational and loving person. On the other hand, he himself behaves terribly, throwing tantrums and flying in the face of good sense—in fact, he exaggerates the behavior by which she has distinguished herself. She finally succumbs to him and adopts conventional wifely behavior, represented by the humorous tests she passes in 4.5. Her transformation comes about not because Petruchio has forced her to feign acceptance of a repugnant role, but because she has seen in his antics the ugliness of her own shrewish behavior and has also come to recognize the emotional rewards for herself in being a dutiful wife. He has understood her, and now she understands both herself and him.

That Katherina and Petruchio are in love before the play ends is sometimes disputed on the grounds that she becomes too servile to allow any relationship between them other than master and slave. However, her servility exists only in the minds of observers from another age, our own; for Shakespeare's audience, and for Katherina herself, her new position is simply a conventional one. It does not at all preclude love. Petruchio and Katherina demonstrate their growing affection, rather than declare it outright, but it is no less real. At the end of 5.1 they express affection for each other for the first time: She kisses him, and she calls him "love"; he responds by calling her his "sweet Kate," an epithet he has earlier used only sarcastically.

The "submission" speech is not delivered in slavish resignation to a demand, but as a duty, carrying with it the rewards of a solid place in the world, a place described with approval in the speech itself. Petruchio has not tried to humiliate Katherina, and she is not humiliated. Instead, he has asserted her superiority to other wives and offered her a podium from which to lecture the Widow. He has not asked her to speak of her own relationship to him; it is entirely her idea to assert that her own experience of rebellion has been barren and pointless. To close

the speech, she freely offers a symbolic enactment of her acceptance of the traditional wifely role. Flabbergasted, almost at a loss for words, Petruchio can only sputter, "Why, there's a wench" (5.2.181), and kiss his bride. Shakespeare consistently gives his heroines the last word in his comedies, and in *The Shrew*, as always, that word confirms the triumph of love, specifically conventional married love.

It is ironic that Petruchio's frankly mercenary interest in marriage yields a love match, whereas Lucentio's rapture for Bianca lands him with a shrew. This twist reinforces the contrasts between the main plot and the SUBPLOT. Petruchio's tactics and their happy outcome are juxtaposed with the more conventional romancing of Bianca. The subplot consists of an assemblage of traditional dramatic situations: Youth is pitted against age; the romanticism of intrigue and disguise is compared to courtship conducted in business terms. These comparisons are familiar ones, deriving from Italian and ancient Roman models, and the participating characters are mere stereotypes, with the single exception of Bianca, who is humanly complex. Lucentio and Hortensio are stock young men of Italian romances; Tranio is part of a tradition of cunning servants that dates back to ancient Greek comedy; Baptista is a standard father-of-the-girl; and Gremio is referred to several times as a "pantaloon," the comic old man of the COMMEDIA DELL'ARTE. These predictable characters make the eccentric individuality of Petruchio and Katherina particularly attractive.

The conventionality of the majority of the characters is just one of several features of the play that intentionally stress its artificiality. The Induction asserts that the tale is a fiction, intended for light entertainment. The final scene serves a similar function. By 5.2 the strands of the plot have all been woven together, and all that remains is a formal summation of the play's themes. The ritualistic setting of a wedding feast and the presence of most of the play's cast strengthen the element of magic in the thrice-repeated summons of the wives and their triple responses, and in the crowning gesture of Katherina's statement of proper martial relations. While it does not do so as explicitly as the Sly plot, the ceremonial nature of this scene also emphasizes the artificiality of the fantasy it closes.

The Taming of the Shrew relies heavily on accepted dramatic conventions, and it approaches traditional farce in many respects. It lacks the depth of Shakespeare's later comedies, but it also foreshadows them; Katherina in particular anticipates Beatrice in *Much Ado About Nothing*. In its presentation of several psychologically resonant portraits, as well as in its strong organization and thoughtfully developed themes, it is a remarkable early work.

SOURCES OF THE PLAY

No specific source is known for the main plot of *The Taming of the Shrew*. Folk tales and songs about a husband disciplining a troublesome wife have been common in most cultures, and many were well known in Elizabethan England. A doggerel ballad, *A Merry Jest of a Shrewde and Curste Wyfe*, printed in 1550, is often cited as a possible source, and it resembles the play in that its shrew is the elder of two sisters; in most such works, she is the youngest of three. However, it differs from *The Shrew* in other respects. The playwright will have known many such tales and ballads, and it is unlikely that any one of them was his specific source. His own version is significantly less brutal than all of its antecedents, and it seems most likely that he simply devised a story line from his recollections of a common popular theme.

Similarly, the Induction's tale of a poor man placed in a rich man's world had widespread currency. Like the shrew theme, this was also the subject of a number of 16th-century English ballads, and a version was published in a London jest book in 1570. The details of Christopher Sly's existence are plainly taken from the young playwright's own WARWICKSHIRE background, and it seems clear that, again, Shakespeare created his own version of a widely recognized story.

For the Bianca subplot, the playwright turned to the play *Supposes* (performed 1566, published 1573, 1587), by George GASCOIGNE, a translation of an Italian drama, *I Suppositi* (1509), by Ludovico ARIOSTO, who was in turn indebted to the ancient Roman play, *The Eunuch*, by TERENCE. Knowledgeable members of Shakespeare's audience doubtless enjoyed the coy reference to "supposes" in 5.1.107.

Various other works have been suggested as sources of certain features. The names Grumio and Tranio appear in *The Haunted House*, by PLAUTUS. Gervase MARKHAM's writings on falconry may have contributed to Petruchio's elaborate description in 4.1.175–198. Gerard LEGH's book on heraldry, *Accedens of Armory* (1562), to which Shakespeare would refer in writing *King Lear*, contains a story similar to that of the Tailor in 4.3. In 1484 William CAXTON translated and published a French tale that might have inspired the husbands' wager in 5.2. However, such bets often appear in the folklore of marital relations. In fact, although literary sources may have provided various details, Shakespeare might just as easily have derived any of the play's minor episodes from some popular tale or ballad now lost.

TEXT OF THE PLAY

It is difficult to determine when *The Taming of the Shrew* was written, as it is for all of Shakespeare's early plays. Estimates have ranged from the late 1580s to 1600, although the later dates reflect an assumption that Shakespeare used *The Taming of a Shrew* as a model. Most scholars now regard *A Shrew* as a BAD QUARTO of *The Shrew* and accordingly conclude that the original play must have been written before the summer of 1592, when *A Shrew* was compiled. The numerous references in the Induction to the playwright's native Warwickshire suggest that the work may have been written not long after his arrival in London, probably in 1588 or 1589. *The Taming of the Shrew* is sometimes cited as Shakespeare's earliest work, but this proposition is unprovable.

The Shrew was not published until it was included in the FIRST FOLIO (1623). The first QUARTO edition was published in 1631. The Folio text appears to be derived from Shakespeare's FOUL PAPERS, as transcribed by a scribe hired to make a copy for the use of an acting company. It has served as the basis for all subsequent editions, although, beginning with Alexander POPE in 1723, some editors have included the interludes and the epilogue from *A Shrew* to complete the tale of Christopher Sly.

THEATRICAL HISTORY OF THE PLAY

Little evidence of early productions of *The Taming of the Shrew* has survived. However, Shakespeare's play was certainly popular at least into the 1630s. In about 1611 *The Woman's Prize, or the Tamer Tamed* by John FLETCHER, offered a sequel to Shakespeare's work. This play depicts Petruchio's second marriage, following Kate's death, to a woman who applies to him the treatment he had meted out to his first wife. This could have had point only if Shakespeare's play were in vogue at the time. Moreover, the appearance of a quarto edition of the play in 1631 implies a continuing public interest, and its title page tells of the play's performance by the KING'S MEN at both the BLACKFRIARS and GLOBE THEATRES. The play was also acted at the court of King Charles I in 1633.

After a revival in 1663, no performance of Shakespeare's play was recorded for almost 180 years. *The Taming of the Shrew* was replaced by a series of adaptations, none resembling the original very closely. The first of these, John LACY's *Sauny the Scot*, appeared in 1667. A crude farce, it was extremely popular for a century. It stimulated its own spin-off—a musical entitled *A Cure for a Scold* (ca. 1735)—which was itself performed until the 1760s. The episode of Christopher Sly, deleted from *Sauny*, was used in *The Cobbler of Preston* (1716), by Charles JOHNSON, a political play about the Jacobite Rebellion of 1715. Its popularity stimulated another, nonpolitical, play with the same title in the same year, also based loosely on the Induction.

Sauny was finally replaced on the English stage by David GARRICK's *Catherine and Petruchio* (1754), an abbreviated version of Shakespeare's play, eliminating both the Induction and the Bianca subplot. This popular play was staged regularly for more than a century and Frederick REYNOLDS made an OPERA of it in 1828. An even shorter version, by John Philip KEMBLE, competed with Garrick's production in the late 18th century and introduced a piece of stage business—Petruchio cracking a horsewhip—that became standard in subsequent productions and was probably the public's strongest image of the play into recent times.

It was not until 1844 that Shakespeare's text was revived, in a historic production by Benjamin WEBSTER and J. R. PLANCHÉ that established the use of legitimate Shakespearean texts as a norm. By the end of the 19th century, Shakespeare's version of

The Shrew was well established on both sides of the Atlantic. Ada REHAN was particularly acclaimed as Katherina. The play continued to be popular in the 20th century. Notable production included a modern-dress version by Barry JACKSON in 1928 and two Joseph PAPP stagings: a 1978 presentation starring Raul Julia and Meryl Streep; and a 1990 production, starring Morgan Freeman, set in 19th-century America's "Wild West."

The Taming of the Shrew has been made as a FILM 11 times, six as a silent movie. Two of the talkies are in English. The first, which featured Mary Pickford and Douglas Fairbanks, was long remembered chiefly for a credit line that became a favorite show-business joke: "Written by William Shakespeare with additional dialogue by Sam Taylor." Franco ZEFFIRELLI's 1966 film starring Richard Burton and Elizabeth Taylor was a box-office success. Also, the play has been produced for TELEVISION twice, most recently by Jonathan MILLER in 1980.

CHARACTERS

Baptista Character in *The Taming of the Shrew*, father of Katherina and Bianca. Baptista is an ineffectual elderly gentleman, a comic figure in a tradition going back to ancient Roman drama. He is frequently the butt of Katherina's outbursts of temper. He insists on marrying off his elder daughter first, aggravating Katherina's already shrewish nature. In 2.1, once assured that Katherina is betrothed. Baptista literally auctions Bianca to the highest bidder; his calculating behavior stands in pointed contrast to the infatuation of Bianca's lover, Lucentio. These are standard attitudes and actions of a conventional father-of-the-girl figure; otherwise, Baptista has virtually no personality.

Begger Term used to refer to Christopher Sly of *The Taming of the Shrew*, in speech headings and stage directions of the FIRST FOLIO edition of the play. The use of this designation, so spelled, is part of the evidence that the Folio text of the play (its first publication) was derived from Shakespeare's own manuscript FOUL PAPERS. Sly's name was first employed in these directions by Nicholas ROWE in his 1709 edition of the plays.

Bianca Character in *The Taming of the Shrew*, a young woman courted by three men—Lucentio, Hortensio, and Gremio—in the SUBPLOT of the play. At first Bianca seems simply a demure and dutiful foil for her shrewish older sister, the title character, Katherina. Katherina's stubbornness prevents Bianca from marrying, since their father, Baptista, has ordered that the elder must be wed first. Bianca's sweet submissiveness also seems to make her a perfect object for the stereotypical romantic rapture of Lucentio, who elopes with her at the climax of the subplot.

However, Bianca is more complex than she initially appears. She is catty and self-righteous when she resists Katherina's violence in 2.1, not only declaring her own virtue but also twitting her sister about her age. Furthermore, Bianca draws attention to her supposed moral superiority over Katherina, as when she admonishes her sister to "content you in my discontent" (1.1.80). Her ambiguous sweetness may help to explain Katherina's generalized belligerence, which has presumably flowered after frequent comparison with her sister's apparent virtue.

When alone with her tutors (not yet revealed to be suitors in disguise), Bianca is decidedly willful, insisting, "I'll not be tied to hours nor 'pointed times, / But learn my lessons as I please myself" (3.1.19–20). She is haughtily flirtatious with Lucentio ("presume not . . . despair not" [3.1.43]), and she rejects Hortensio with curt brutality. We are not surprised to find Bianca shrewish herself in the final scene, holding Lucentio up to ridicule for believing in her wifely obedience. This revelation emphasizes the ironic contrast between the two sisters' marriages. Katherina has found true love after an explicitly mercenary courtship, whereas Bianca's union with Lucentio, the product of a conventionally idyllic romance, seems likely to be unhappy.

Biondello Character in *The Taming of the Shrew*, servant of Lucentio. Biondello acts as servant to his fellow employee, Tranio, who is disguised as their master. His mischievous delight in the situation lends humorous force to his only important passage, the description of Petruchio approaching the wedding (3.2.30–83).

Cambio In *The Taming of the Shrew*, the name Lucentio takes when disguised as a scholar of languages in order to be appointed tutor to Bianca.

Curtis Minor character in *The Taming of the Shrew*, a servant of Petruchio. Curtis, who has been in charge of the household in his master's absence, greets the returning Grumio and engages him in comical repartee at the beginning of 4.1. Later in the scene he is one of the servants whom Petruchio abuses as part of his program to demonstrate to Katherina the ugliness of shrewish behavior. Curtis's name is thought to be that of an actor who played him, possibly Curtis GREVILLE.

Gremio Character in *The Taming of the Shrew*, an elderly suitor of Bianca. Gremio is referred to as a "pantaloon" (3.1.36), the humorous figure of a greedy old man in the COMMEDIA DELL'ARTE, and he is indeed simply a character type with little real personality. He is comically cowardly, fearful that the assertiveness of Petruchio will offend Baptista, Bianca's father. His own style is offensively humble; approaching Baptista, he refers to himself as a "poor petitioner" (2.1.72), in the obsequious language of a minor courtier. He lies about his wealth when Baptista promises his daughter to the wealthiest suitor, but to no avail. Gremio is absurdly ineffective; in fact, in his attempt to win Bianca's hand he actually introduces the successful suitor into her presence, for in 2.1 he hires the disguised Lucentio as a tutor for the girl, hoping to impress her father.

Grumio Character in *The Taming of the Shrew*, servant of Petruchio. Grumio is a distinctly English comic figure in all respects except his name. At 1.2.28, he even fails to recognize Italian. Grumio represents a long theatrical tradition—the comical servant whose nonsense masks shrewdness. His wily foolishness is a vehicle for humor when, in 1.2, he remarks sharply on the mercenary marriage that his master is pursuing. It can also be a means of manipulating others, as when he feigns incomprehension—first with Katherina and later with the Tailor—in 4.3. His name comes from a character in an ancient Roman play, *The Haunted House*, by PLAUTUS.

Haberdasher   Minor character in *The Taming of the Shrew*, an artisan whom Petruchio abuses. The Haberdasher, who has been commissioned to make a hat for Katherina, speaks only one line before being driven away by his client, who is demonstrating the ugliness of shrewish behavior to his bride.

Hortensio   Character in *The Taming of the Shrew*, a suitor of Bianca. A bland young man who is outsmarted in his campaign to win Bianca, Hortensio is an appropriate character to enter, ludicrously pale "for fear" (2.1.143), to report Katherina's assault on him with a lute, thus providing an image of the "shrew" of the title at her worst. After losing Bianca, Hortensio turns to a Widow who has pursued him. He visits the country house of Petruchio to observe that character's shrew-taming techniques, but it is unclear at the play's end whether Hortensio will be strong enough to use them when he needs them, for the Widow proves, in 5.2, to be a formidable shrew herself.

Hostess   Minor character in *The Taming of the Shrew*, the proprietor of the tavern from which Christopher Sly emerges at the beginning of the INDUCTION. Sly may be referring to her, in Ind.2.21–22, as "Marian Hacket, the fat ale-wife of Wincot," believed to have been a real person who lived in a hamlet near STRATFORD and whom Shakespeare presumably knew as a boy. In any case, the brief appearance of this angry but businesslike barmaid contributes to the believable rural atmosphere of the Induction.

Huntsman   Either of two minor characters in the INDUCTION to *The Taming of the Shrew*, servants of a local landowner, the Lord. In Ind. 1 the Huntsmen assist the Lord in his practical joke on Christopher Sly, which is the business of the introductory scenes. The Huntsmen's role in the plot could have been filled by servants of any sort, but the Lord's conversation with them on the merits of his hounds contributes to the rural atmosphere of the Induction.

Joseph   Minor character in *The Taming of the Shrew*, a servant of Petruchio. Joseph is one of the servants whom Petruchio abuses in 4.1, as part of his demonstration to Katherina of the ugliness of shrewish behavior.

Katherina (Katharina)   Title character in *The Taming of the Shrew*, the ill-tempered young woman courted, married, and "tamed" by Petruchio. Katherina is sometimes thought of as a representative oppressed woman, dominated by a selfish man and trapped in a loveless marriage. But this point of view is based on modern notions of marital relations (see "Commentary"), and it obscures the real nature of the character. Katherina undergoes a positive transformation during the play: She is freed from an unhappy emotional state, and she enters a happy marriage.

In Acts 1–3 Katherina is presented as a volatile and distinctly unhappy person. She is a familiar type, a young adult who resents the rejection she receives, yet in an effort to feel immune to the opinions of others, she simply makes herself less likable by belligerently taking exception to everything. In addition, she has clearly been compared to her younger sister—the deceptively sweet Bianca—too often for comfort. The psychological pressure within Katherina bursts forth in violence, both threatened and actual. Not content with curtly dismissing the rudeness of Hortensio, for example, she goes on to express a desire to "comb your noddle with a three-legg'd stool" (1.1.64). Corrected by a music teacher (Hortensio again, in disguise), she assaults him with a lute. Her envy and suspicion of Bianca drive her to physical abuse in 2.1.22, 29. When she first encounters Petruchio, knowing only that he is a suitor, she repeatedly insults him (2.1.195–259), and she slaps him to "try" (2.1.217) his gentlemanliness.

In Acts 4–5, however, Katherina changes, under the forceful guidance of Petruchio. His "taming" consists of demonstrating that she need not continue to be an outcast, disliked and shunned, and that there is indeed a place in the world that she can occupy happily. His persistent references to her calm and sweetness—initially fictitious—make her realize the psychological benefits that such attributes could bring: acceptance and a sense of moral worth. His own behavior shows her the ugliness of shrewishness.

She chooses to reject her bristly defensiveness and assume the role of an ordinary wife. She will admit that the world is not hers to control; in return, she will have the emotional security of a prescribed place in it.

The submissiveness that Katherina accepts, and that troubles modern readers, was simply held to be a conventional attribute of a wife. Shakespeare and his contemporaries of both sexes believed that the Bible, as well as long-hallowed tradition, prescribed hierarchical relationships among humans: Husbands ruled wives, as parents ruled children, as monarchs ruled commoners, and as God ruled all. Katherina voices this belief in her banquet speech in 5.2.

Katherina loves Petruchio. She indicates as much in the grace with which she kisses him at the end of 5.1, and her speech in 5.2 is an implicit expression of her love. At the banquet she has already demonstrated her obedience and need not do more; Petruchio has merely asked her for a statement of principle, as much to aggravate the Widow and Bianca as anything else. She goes far beyond his intent, specifically referring to her own experience and stating that she is grateful for inclusion in the system she describes. The entirely spontaneous physical act of submission that closes her speech symbolizes the wifely duty demanded in this system, but it is also directed to her husband, as an expression of her gratitude. That this gesture is loving is confirmed by his affectionate response to it. Katherina has found not only comfort in an assured position in society but happiness in a loving marriage. She is thus the vehicle for an elaboration of two of Shakespeare's persistent concerns: the virtue of an ordered, hierarchical social system and the value of marriage as a venue for love. Her psychological transformation also reflects his fascination with the mysteries of the human personality.

Katherina's is a small part, for all its importance, and, while boldly drawn, she lacks the subtlety of later Shakespearean heroines who resemble her, such as Beatrice in *Much Ado About Nothing*. It is noteworthy that Katherina shares with several of the playwright's most lovingly developed female characters, as well as with the "Dark Lady" of the *Sonnets*, a sharp temper and a dark complexion (see 2.1.248–249). It seems possible (though altogether

unprovable) that these characters share the traits of a woman (entirely unidentifiable) who was romantically important to Shakespeare. The thought certainly adds resonance to his portrait of a shrew.

Litio (Licio) In *The Taming of the Shrew*, the name Hortensio takes when he disguises himself as a music teacher in order to be appointed instructor to Bianca.

Lord Character in *The Taming of the Shrew*, a country gentleman who appears in the INDUCTION. The Lord takes in the besotted and unconscious Christopher Sly and, as a practical joke, installs the rustic tinker in his home as a gentleman. The Lord is not a three-dimensional character, but he offers a plausible picture of a country gentleman amid his pleasures.

Lucentio Character in *The Taming of the Shrew*, the successful suitor of Bianca. Lucentio, aided by his servant Tranio, disguises himself as a tutor of languages and thus gains access to Bianca, against the wishes of her father Baptista. Eventually he elopes with his lover. His wealthy father Vincentio assures Baptista that he will provide an adequate financial settlement on the couple, and Lucentio is forgiven, only to find, in the final scene, that Bianca is not the ideally demure young bride he had anticipated.

Although the romance of Bianca and Lucentio is contrasted to the mercenary calculations of her father, Lucentio is a rather bloodless lover. He is simply a stereotype—the handsome young male romantic lead—representing a tradition as old as ancient Roman drama. However, in earlier plays, this character tended to marry for money and extend romantic love to mistresses and courtesans; Shakespeare's alteration reflects his concern with love in marriage, a major theme of *The Taming of the Shrew*.

Messenger Minor character in *The Taming of the Shrew*, the announcer, in the INDUCTION, of the performance by the Players that begins the play proper. In Ind.2 he informs Sly of the coming presentation and recommends viewing it as a healthy pastime. Various editions of the play have assigned his part to the Lord or one of his Servants.

Nathaniel Minor character in *The Taming of the Shrew*, a member of the household staff of Petruchio.

Nathaniel is one of the servants whom Petruchio abuses in 4.1 as part of his demonstration to Katherina of the ugliness of shrewish behavior.

Nicholas   Minor character in *The Taming of the Shrew*, a member of the household staff of Petruchio. Nicholas is one of the servants whom Petruchio abuses in 4.1 as part of his demonstration to Katherina of the ugliness of shrewish behavior.

Officer   Minor character in *The Taming of the Shrew*, a constable. The Officer is summoned in 5.1 to arrest Vincentio, who is thought to be an imposter. The matter is settled shortly after his entrance, and he does not speak.

Page   Minor character in *The Taming of the Shrew*, servant of the local Lord, who directs him to masquerade as the wife of the deluded Christopher Sly in the INDUCTION. He humorously discourages Sly's sexual advances, and his performance as a wife foreshadows the ideal of womanly obedience that the main play advocates. His instructions are to request, as a real wife would, "What is't your honour will command, / Wherein your lady and your humble wife / May show her duty and make known her love?" (Ind.1.113–115), and he presents himself to Sly as "your wife in all obedience" (Ind.2.108). These attitudes are precisely those prescribed for wives by the converted Katherina in 5.2.

Pedant, the   Minor character in *The Taming of the Shrew* who impersonates Vincentio. The Pedant has no personality; he serves merely to fill out the plot of deception and disguise. He flees when his imposture is discovered and is not mentioned again.

Peter   Minor character in *The Taming of the Shrew*, a servant of Petruchio. Peter is one of several servants whom Petruchio abuses in 4.1. The servants realize that their master's oppressive behavior is part of his strategy for taming his shrewish bride, Katherina, and Peter delivers a succinct analysis of it in the longer of his two lines: "He kills her in her own humour" (4.1.167).

Peter is not named in any of the several lists of Petruchio's servants that are recited in the scene.

This fact, combined with the mute appearance in 4.4 of a servant of Lucentio identified as Peter in a stage direction, suggests that his name may be that of an actor who took both small parts, the second of which appears to have been cut. However, no scholar has been able to identify the actor, and there is nothing inherently improbable in the existence of two Peters.

Petruchio   Character in *The Taming of the Shrew*, the suitor, bridegroom, and tamer of Katherina, the shrew of the title. Petruchio is sometimes seen as a tyrannical male, selfishly dominating a woman who cannot escape him. However, this view reflects certain modern attitudes toward marriage and ignores both the world in which the character was created and the actual text of the play. Petruchio does not physically abuse or humiliate Katherina, and in "submitting" to him, she merely assumes the conventional role of a wife. At the end of the play she is quite evidently grateful for the change that he has wrought in her life. Theirs is a love story, though this is a subtle element set among the play's several comic plots.

Bluff and hearty, Petruchio is a humorous figure—seen in ludicrous clothes while indulging in spectacular tantrums, he provides laughs in an age-old fashion—but his primary role in the play is more serious. Although his attitude toward marriage is distinctly mercenary—"I come to wive it wealthily in Padua," he says (1.2.74)—he is also attracted to Katherina. He is unafraid of her shrewishness, and he sees that the high spirits that underlie her terrible temper may be a positive character trait. His ironic response to the account of her assault on Hortensio (2.1.160–162) reflects a willingness to deal with such a person; he is attuned to Katherina even before he has met her. After the "taming," when they enjoy their first loving kiss (5.1.137–138), his sentimental reaction reflects his real affection for her. His response to her wholehearted commitment to a wifely role, in her banquet speech in 5.2, is simple delight, better expressed in a kiss than in words.

However, Petruchio's importance is not as Katherina's lover but as her "tamer." He is the instrument of the personality change that is the central event of the play. He overrides her outbursts with his insistence that she is actually gentle

In this early 20th-century production of *The Taming of the Shrew*, Petruchio (Frank Benson) terrorizes the servants before an unimpressed Katherina. *(Courtesy of Culver Pictures, Inc.)*

and mild, and he behaves with all the virulence any shrew could ever summon. He perceptively senses in Katherina both her desire for appreciation and her instinctive distaste for shrewish conduct, and he induces her to assume the role of a normal Elizabethan wife. He does not simply bludgeon her into submission—as is common in the literature of shrewish wives, before and after Shakespeare's time—but rather functions as a teacher and guide. For much of his time onstage, Petruchio is explicitly playing a part—like many of Shakespeare's protagonists—and only pretends to be a comical tyrant. It is significant that his most important actions in this role occur offstage and are described by other characters; in 3.2 Biondello describes his outrageous appearance on his wedding day, and then Gremio describes his outlandish behavior at the ceremony; in 4.1 Grumio tells of his intemperate behavior on the journey from Padua, and Curtis recounts his ranting delivery of an immoderate lecture on moderation. This forces the audience to think about Petruchio's ploys rather than simply watch them and emphasizes that Petruchio's shrew-taming is a kind of education: he teaches Katherina that her evil-tempered ways are not desirable and that another behavior pattern is superior. He is training Katherina as he would a hawk, as he describes in 4.1.175–198, and the conceit, although comically grotesque, becomes a metaphor for the socializing process.

Petruchio carries out his functions somewhat mechanically—he states his purposes and accomplishes them, and as a lover he is simply sentimental—but he nevertheless possesses a distinct personality. A genially self-confident aristocrat, he delights in the good life. He understands the appeal of excellent food and fine clothes, and in the final banquet scene he is clearly at home amid the pleasures of merry company. Petruchio doubtless incorporates traits of Elizabethan gentlemen who had hosted the young Shakespeare.

Philip Minor character in *The Taming of the Shrew*, a member of the household staff of Petruchio. Philip is one of the servants whom Petruchio abuses in 4.1 as part of his demonstration to Katherina of the ugliness of shrewish behavior.

Players Group of minor characters in *The Taming of the Shrew*, a traveling company of actors. In the INDUCTION the Players are hired by the local Lord, who is amusing himself by providing gentlemanly amenities to a drunken tinker, Christopher Sly. The Players perform "a pleasant comedy" (Ind.2.130) for Sly; this play is *The Taming of the Shrew*.

One of the Players, identified in various editions as "A Player," "First Player," and "Second Player," is designated by the name of a real Elizabethan actor in a speech heading in the FIRST FOLIO edition of the play; the part was played by John SINCKLO in an early production. In Ind.1.86 he speaks of a role he had played, naming a character in a play by John FLETCHER that was written in about 1620. This is probably a late insertion into Shakespeare's text, not long before its publication in 1623, but it may be original and refer to an otherwise unknown play of the 1580s or early 1590s that served Fletcher as a source.

Servant Minor character in *The Taming of the Shrew*, a worker in the household of Baptista. The Servants escorts the disguised suitors of Bianca in 2.1 and, in 3.1, brings Bianca a message about the imminent wedding of her sister, Katherina.

In the FIRST FOLIO text of the play, the name "Nicke" designates the Servant in the speech heading at 3.1.80. Scholars recognize a reference to the actor who played the part, perhaps Nicholas TOOLEY.

Servants Several minor characters in *The Taming of the Shrew*, workers in the home of the Lord who takes in Christopher Sly in the INDUCTION. On the Lord's instructions, the Servants offer Sly the pleasures of gentlemanly life, encouraging him to believe that he has been insane in believing himself a poor drunkard.

Serving-man Minor character in *The Taming of the Shrew*, a servant of the country Lord who informs his master of the arrival of the Players in the INDUCTION.

Serving-men Several minor characters in *The Taming of the Shrew*, servants at the banquet in 5.2. The Serving-men do not speak.

Sly, Christopher Character in *The Taming of the Shrew*, a drunken tinker and the principal figure of the INDUCTION. In these two scenes, Sly is found asleep outside a tavern by a local landowner, the Lord, who decides to play a practical joke and has him installed as a gentleman in his home. Sly awakes to find himself treated like an aristocrat and told he has been insane to imagine himself a poor drunkard. As part of the joke, a troupe of Players performs "a pleasant comedy" (Ind.2.130) for Sly; this drama is *The Taming of the Shrew*. Sly is last seen dozing in an INTERLUDE (1.1.248–253).

Sly is a boldly drawn minor figure, full of drunken pretensions and country sayings, comically ready to assume his new life of ease, though insisting on his poor man's taste for ale over the gentry's wine. His succinct autobiography—"by birth a pedlar, by education a cardmaker, by transmutation a bear-herd, and now . . . a tinker" (Ind.2.18–21)—gives representation to a multitude of obscure lives among the 16th-century poor. Sly makes numerous explicit references to people and places in the STRATFORD area, and this portrait of a rustic sot clearly derives from the young Shakespeare's recollections of his old home.

Although Sly's story ends abruptly after 1.1 in the oldest edition of *The Taming of the Shrew*, in the FIRST FOLIO of 1623, it is complete in *The Taming of a Shrew*, believed to be a BAD QUARTO of Shakespeare's play and to contain Shakespeare's original rendition of Sly's adventure: In three further interludes. Sly remarks on the play, eating and drinking all the while. In a fifth episode he has fallen asleep, and the Lord orders him returned to the spot where he had been found. In a 23-line EPILOGUE to *A Shrew*, Sly is discovered by the tapster of the tavern, who remarks that Sly's wife will be angry with him for staying out all night. Sly replies that he need not fear his wife, for he has had a dream that has taught him how to deal with her. Sly was probably played by William SLY.

Tailor Minor character in *The Taming of the Shrew*, an artisan whom Petruchio abuses. Commissioned by Petruchio to provide a gown for Katherina, the Tailor is driven away by his client in 4.3. Petruchio's mistreatment of this innocent man is simply part of his demonstration to his bride of the ugliness of shrewish behavior. Although the Tailor defends himself before being routed, he otherwise has no distinctive personality.

Tranio Character in *The Taming of the Shrew*, a servant who impersonates his master, Lucentio. In 1.1 Tranio proposes that Lucentio disguise himself as a humble tutor in order to approach Bianca, and when he is assigned to take Lucentio's place and maintain his household in PADUA, Tranio is entirely at ease in the role. He plays a smooth young nobleman with education and wit enough to cite classical authors while ingratiating himself with Baptista, Bianca's father. His initiative propels the SUBPLOT: he launches Lucentio's courtship; in 2.1 he outbids Gremio for Bianca's hand in his master's name; he conceives (2.1) and carries out (4.2, 4.4) the impersonation by the Pedant of Lucentio's father, Vincentio; and he arranges for Lucentio and Bianca's elopement (4.4). And he is sufficiently bold to carry on with his plot even when the real Vincentio appears (5.1). However, for all his cleverness, he has little personality; he is a stock character, a comically deceitful servant deriving ultimately from ancient Roman drama. In fact, Shakespeare took the name Tranio from *The Haunted House*, by PLAUTUS, where it is given to a witty and resourceful slave who tells inventive lies on his master's behalf.

Vincentio Minor character in *The Taming of the Shrew*, the father of Lucentio. Vincentio, described as "a sober ancient gentleman" (5.1.65), arrives in PADUA to find himself impersonated by the Pedant and Lucentio by his servant Tranio. He is understandably angry, but otherwise he has no distinctive personality traits.

Widow Minor character in *The Taming of the Shrew*, the bride of Hortensio. The Widow first appears at the banquet in 5.2. She is unwilling to obey her new husband, although he believes he is able to control her, having watched Petruchio handle the shrewish Katherina. When the men bet on the obedience of their wives, the Widow flatly refuses Hortensio's mild request, and Katherina gives her a lengthy lecture on a wife's proper duties. The Widow has no developed personality; she serves simply as a foil for the newly obedient Katherina.

Tempest, The
SYNOPSIS

Act 1, Scene 1
On a storm-wracked ship, the Boatswain exchanges curses with two arrogant passengers, Antonio and Sebastian, who are traveling with King Alonso of Naples. The king's counsellor, Gonzalo, remains calm, however, as the ship goes down.

Act 1, Scene 2
On a nearby island, Miranda is upset by the shipwreck, but her father Prospero, a magician, assures her that the seamen will be safe. He reveals to her that he was once the Duke of MILAN. He studied magic in preference to governing and was deposed by his brother, Antonio, who was aided by King Alonso. The conspirators put Prospero and Miranda, then two years old, in a small boat and abandoned them at sea, but the kindly Gonzalo had given them supplies, including Prospero's books of magic. They then found the island and have lived there since. Through magic, Prospero has raised the storm to bring his old enemies to the island. He magically puts Miranda to sleep and summons his servant, a sprite named Ariel. Ariel reports that he has entranced the vessel's passengers and dispersed the people around the island, taking particular care, as instructed, with Ferdinand,

the son of King Alonso. When he complains about his tasks, the magician sternly reminds him that he must work in exchange for his rescue from magical imprisonment in a tree trunk, imposed by the now-dead witch who formerly occupied the island. Prospero promises that if his present scheme is successful, he will release the sprite. He then instructs Ariel to wear a cloak of invisibility, so that he can be seen only by Prospero, and report for further duty. After Ariel leaves, Miranda awakes and Prospero summons Caliban, his half-human slave, son of the late witch. Ariel returns, invisible to Miranda, and is sent away again with whispered orders. The surly Caliban reluctantly appears and complains of his slavery, but Prospero declares that he has earned it, for after being taken in and educated by the magician, he attempted to rape Miranda. Caliban is sent to gather wood. Ariel returns, leading Ferdinand by singing fairy songs. Miranda is amazed and delighted by this, the first young man she has ever seen. Ferdinand is equally charmed to encounter her. Prospero observes in an aside that they are already in love, as he has planned. However, to ensure that Ferdinand will not take Miranda lightly, he adopts a stern attitude and pretends to distrust the young man. Despite Miranda's pleas, he imprisons him.

Act 2, Scene 1

Gonzalo attempts to cheer King Alonso with assurances that Ferdinand has survived, but he is mocked by Antonio and Sebastian. Ariel appears, invisible to the men, and puts Gonzalo and the king to sleep. Antonio suggests to Sebastian, who is the king's brother, that they should kill the sleeping men and make Sebastian king. Sebastian agrees, but as they draw their swords, Ariel reappears and awakens Gonzalo and the king. The four men go off in search of Ferdinand.

Act 2, Scene 2

Caliban tries to hide from Trinculo, a FOOL who has survived the shipwreck, but Trinculo sees him. Frightened by thunder, Trinculo takes refuge under Caliban's cloak. Another survivor, Stephano, appears, drunk on salvaged wine. Seeing Trinculo and Caliban, he decides they are a single, two-headed, four-legged monster. He feeds Caliban wine, hoping to tame the monster. Trinculo identifies him-

self, and the two friends rejoice at their reunion. Caliban is delighted with his first taste of wine and tipsily volunteers to serve the two men as though they were gods, if they will give him more. They agree and leave with him. Caliban sings drunkenly of his pleasure at leaving Prospero.

Act 3, Scene 1

Ferdinand, forced by Prospero to move a large pile of logs, reflects that though his princely nature rebels against such labor, the work seems joyous because he knows his master's daughter sympathizes with him. Miranda appears, and they confess their love for each other, agreeing that they will marry. Prospero, overhearing them, is pleased.

Act 3, Scene 2

Caliban, Stephano, and Trinculo are drunk and squabble comically. Caliban proposes that Stephano kill Prospero, stealing his magic books and taking possession of Miranda. Stephano decides to do so, envisioning himself as king of the island, with Caliban and Trinculo as viceroys. Ariel leads them away with fairy music.

Act 3, Scene 3

Prospero causes a magical banquet to appear. Alonso, Sebastian, and Antonio step forward greedily, but the banquet disappears. Ariel, disguised as a Harpy, declares that they are evil men and that destiny has therefore stranded them on this island and taken Alonso's son. They shall be tormented until they atone and adopt a sin-free life. Alonso leaves, declaring that he will find his dead son and die beside him. Sebastian and Antonio go with him, angrily intent on fighting the spirits of the island. Gonzalo, believing that their guilt has made them crazy, follows them, to keep them from harming themselves.

Act 4, Scene 1

Prospero consents to the engagement of Miranda and Ferdinand. He calls on Ariel to provide entertainment to celebrate the bethrothal, and several sprites impersonate the goddesses Iris, Ceres, and Juno in a MASQUE. Prospero, recalling Caliban and Stephano's plot, sends Ariel to gather some fine clothes he has prepared, which are hung in full view. Caliban, Stephano, and Trinculo arrive, still drunk. Trinculo and Stephano, seeing the fine clothes, cannot resist trying them on, despite Caliban's warnings that Prospero will catch them. Spirits disguised as hunting dogs chase the comical villains away. Prospero reflects that his enemies are now all at his mercy. Soon his task will be complete, and Ariel can be freed.

Act 5, Scene 1

Ariel reports that the captive Alonso, Sebastian, and Antonio are insane, while Gonzalo is grief-stricken. Ariel says he feels sorry for them, and Prospero declares that he will be merciful to them, despite the losses he has suffered at their hands. After sending Ariel to fetch them, he asserts in a soliloquy that he will renounce magic once he has cured his victims. He exchanges his magician's robes for the garments he wore as Duke of Milan, and as the victims recover their senses they recognize him. He forgives their offenses, and they concede him his duchy. Alonso still mourns the loss of his son, and Prospero reveals Ferdinand and Miranda. Miranda is delighted to see so many humans, Ferdinand is reunited with his father, and the future succession of the engaged couple to the throne of Naples is proclaimed. Ariel appears with the Boatswain and Master of the king's ship; they report that the vessel has been miraculously restored to shipshape condition. Ariel fetches Caliban, Stephano, and Trinculo—still drunk—and Prospero sends them to restore the stolen clothes to his closet. He then invites the king and his followers indoors, to hear the story of his time on the island. He gives Ariel a last order—to prepare auspicious winds and weather for the return to Milan—and sets him free.

COMMENTARY

With *The Tempest* Shakespeare reached new heights in a recently developed genre, the ROMANCES; indeed, some commentators find it the greatest accomplishment of his career. After progressively more successful attempts—in *Pericles, Cymbeline,* and *The Winter's Tale*—at mingling elements of TRAGEDY and COMEDY within a framework of magic and exoticism taken from literary romances, the playwright created in *The Tempest* a stunning theatrical entertainment that is also a moral allegory of great beauty and emotional power. Unlike the tradi-

tional medieval MORALITY PLAY, Shakespeare's work does not merely present symbols of already understood Christian doctrines; rather, it offers a vision as complex and ambiguous as human nature itself. Such is the inclusiveness of Shakespeare's sensibility and the power of the play's characters as emblems of humanity that *The Tempest* cannot be pinned down by any particular interpretation but must instead be taken as the embodiment of a variety of propositions. The themes of *The Tempest* are multifarious and mingled, but nevertheless the various elements come together in a traditional comedic happy ending of reconciliation and regeneration.

The Tempest has very little actual plot: The love of Ferdinand and Miranda meets only token—and feigned—opposition, and the proposed assassinations of Alonso and Prospero are never plausible, due to Prospero's overwhelming mastery of the situation. However, Shakespeare makes up for the lack of suspense with bold theater. Bizarre characters and extravagant effects abound in a spectacular presentation that plainly reflects the influence of the courtly masque, an increasingly popular form in the early 17th century. Striking tableaux figure in almost every act: the shipwreck in 1.1, the supernatural banquet in 3.3, the formal betrothal masque and the spectral hounds in 4.1, and the sudden appearance of Ferdinand and Miranda in 5.1. These elements are almost independent of the dialogue, but their visual imagery adds meaning to the story.

Magic is a vital ingredient of *The Tempest*. The supernatural qualities of Caliban and Ariel are particularly impressive on stage—Caliban is usually costumed to resemble a sea monster, and Ariel sometimes flies on cables. The text describes a number of remarkable feats of magic that add to our sense of wonder, as do Ariel's appearances with goddesses and as a harpy. Music is another strong component of the play, which incorporates many songs and several dance numbers. Indeed, music is part of Prospero's magical repertoire, as all of the visitors to the island are manipulated at some point by Ariel's tabor and pipe. The island itself seems haunted by "sounds and sweet airs [of] a thousand twanling instruments" (3.2.134–135).

Another unifying feature of *The Tempest* is the way the conspiracies that compose the action reflect each other. Before the time of the play, Antonio stole Prospero's dukedom; on the island, that original crime is reenacted as Antonio offers Sebastian the prospect of a kingdom if he murders Alonso and as Caliban recruits Stephano against Prospero. Each of these conspiracies is finally defused by Prospero, as order is systematically restored. Just as important, they all lead to the reconciliation with which the plays closes.

Yet another important theme is the contrast between Art and nature. Prospero rules through his magical "Art" (1.2.1), consistently spelled with a capital A in the conventional 17th-century usage associated with the RENAISSANCE image of the magician as philosopher. Such a mage, as they were called, attempted to elevate his soul through arcane knowledge of the divine, whether through alchemy, the lore of supernatural signs, or communication with spirits. Although Prospero's goal was originally to transcend nature, he gains control of nature as a by-product of his magic. This, then, provides for his command of the island.

The contrast of Art and nature is furthered by the comparison of Prospero, whose learned sorcery is Art, and the "natural" Caliban, with his lust and his beastlike resistance to education. Caliban's naturalness leads him to attempt rape—he would have "peopled . . . this isle with Calibans" (1.2.352–353)—whereas Prospero and Ferdinand, with civilized sensibilities, believe in celibacy before marriage. They understand marital happiness to depend on discipline; the satisfactions of sex are to be preceded by a formal declaration of intention, in the "full and holy rite" (4.1.17) sanctified by tradition. Put another way, we must intelligently assert what we are doing and not simply plunge. Ferdinand, Miranda, and Prospero all exercise the self-discipline that Caliban lacks, and their success and happiness are compared with his misery. Nature is insufficient and must be built upon by civilization.

When Prospero arrived on the island, he found it in a state of barbarity; Ariel was imprisoned, and the amoral beast Caliban ran free. At the close Ariel is liberated as Caliban returns to the bondage he briefly evaded. The contrast between these two characters spans the play. Both are supernatural, and they are

similar in their dislike for being under an obligation to mortals, but otherwise they are antithetical creatures—one airy and beautiful, pleasant, and allied with good; the other dank and ugly, sullen, and inclined to evil. Ariel is a spiritual being, composed of air, uninhibited by normal physical restraints, while Caliban is utterly material, confined to the earth, without the power to resist even the "urchin-shows" (2.2.5) of Ariel's minor underlings. Explicitly nonhuman, Ariel and Caliban are essentially allegorical, representing human possibilities. Ariel embodies our potential spirituality, Caliban our propensity to waste that potential in materialism or sensual pleasure.

Ariel is Prospero's analogue and like him is rather isolated; except as a seeming hallucination, he has no contact with anyone but his master. Caliban, however, is pointedly compared to many other characters; he is the baseline from which all else is measured. As we have seen, his conspiracy

A scene from *The Tempest*. A stunning mix of tragedy, comedy, and magic, *The Tempest* is considered by some to be Shakespeare's greatest accomplishment. *(Courtesy of Culver Pictures, Inc.)*

parallels Antonio's. His inability to learn more than curses contrasts with Miranda's high moral sensibility, even though they were educated together. His response to Miranda's beauty contrasts with Ferdinand's. Caliban resists carrying wood in 1.2, while Ferdinand rejoices in his similar labor in 3.1. When Miranda judges her admirers, she finds Caliban "a thing most brutish" (1.2.359) and Ferdinand "a thing divine" (1.2.421).

As already suggested, the ultimate comparison is between Caliban and Prospero. The evil work of Caliban's long-dead mother, "the foul witch Sycorax, who with age and envy / Was grown into a hoop" (1.2.258–59), is vividly evoked by Prospero in 1.2.258–280. Her black magic contrasts with Prospero's employment of sorcery for a good end, after which he abjures it. Caliban wishes only for "a new master" (2.2.185) and even encourages murder to get one; Prospero pits his "nobler reason 'gainst [his] fury," seeking "the rarer action [that] is / In virtue" (5.1.26, 27–28). The ineducable monster can only approach the least of humanity's capacities, while the learned magician aspires to high moral accomplishment.

Caliban represents the "natural man" that enthralled Europeans as the New World was opened up and its natives became known. He is pointedly associated with the New World through allusions to the Patagonian god Setebos, the island of Bermuda, and such familiar anecdotes of exploration as the reception of explorers as gods and their offering liquor to the natives. With these associations, Shakespeare raised an issue that concerned thinking people throughout Europe: the relative merits of nature and civilization. Many of Shakespeare's contemporaries viewed "natural man" as a healthy counter to the ills of civilization—an attitude that has survived to the present day—but the playwright disagreed. One of the chief spokesmen for the admiring view of natural man was Michel de MONTAIGNE, and Shakespeare gave his position a place in *The Tempest*—a passage from Montaigne's essay "Of Cannibals" is echoed in Gonzalo's remarks on an ideal commonwealth in 2.1.143–164, but only as a foil to the play's point of view. The ineffectual Gonzalo envisions "all men idle [and] women . . . innocent and pure" (2.1.150–151), but Caliban,

whose name is a pointed anagram of "cannibal," has in his idleness attempted to rape Miranda and thus represents a standing refutation of Montaigne's thesis. Caliban cannot, like Ferdinand, make the commitment of a "patient log-man" (3.1.67), and his undisciplined lust is naturally rejected by Miranda. Similarly, Prospero's learning, the key to his power, is rejected by Caliban, and the monster is accordingly powerless. His slavery is a function of his defects as well as of Prospero's magic.

That Caliban and Ariel are nonhuman is part of the play's masque-like spectacle, but their supernatural quality also serves another function. The role of providence in human affairs, an important idea throughout Shakespeare's romances, is particularly emphasized by the prevalence of magic in *The Tempest*. Moreover, the references to the New World, along with the unspecific location of Prospero's island, add a sense of exotic climes in which the supernatural is to be expected. The eeriness of the play's world—"as strange a maze as e'er men trod" (5.1.242)—virtually requires divine intervention. Action by a specific divinity (provided in the other romances) is lacking here, but it is alluded to in the betrothal masque with its goddesses. They are merely portrayed—although by supernatural creatures—but their capacity to bless is evoked in striking fashion. When all has been resolved, it is natural for "Holy Gonzalo" (5.1.62) to attribute the outcome to the gods in 5.1.201–204, and for Alonso to cry, "I say, Amen" (5.1.204).

Prospero's magic leaves both characters and audience unclear about what is real and what is not, and the boundaries of reality constitute another important theme of the play. Mistaken beliefs abound: Ferdinand and Miranda each mistake the other for a supernatural being, and Caliban takes Trinculo and Stephano for gods. Alonso and Ferdinand each believe the other dead. Stephano thinks Caliban and Trinculo a two-headed, four-legged creature. (These three buffoons befuddle their senses with liquor and are then led astray by Ariel, so their capacity to recognize reality is doubly damaged. In a remarkable passage that encompasses both sorts of unreality, 4.1.171–184, Ariel relates his supernatural effects on the trio in a delightfully naturalistic description of drunkenness.) Most strikingly, the audience shares the difficulties of Prospero's subjects. We see Ariel when the characters do not, but other illusions are designed to take us in, too. At the outset we are fooled by the supernatural storm and shipwreck. The sudden appearance of the banquet in 3.3 is obviously supernatural, but like Alonso and his party, we believe it is for eating until Ariel's harpy makes it disappear. The king and his party, surprised to have survived the shipwreck, remain baffled throughout, until Prospero finally permits them to shed the "subtilties o' the isle, that will not let you / Believe things certain" (5.1.124–125).

Prospero's "subtilties" are manifested in several miniature plays, each itself a pretense of reality, reflecting Shakespeare's interest in this aspect of theater. Prospero stages the banquet of 3.3, the masque of goddesses in 4.1, and the tableau of Ferdinand and Miranda in 5.1. After the masque he points out to his audiences—both on stage and in the theater—that a masque is an illusion. He then adds, in one of Shakespeare's most famous passages, that reality is too: We ourselves, we are told, "are such stuff / As dreams are made on" (4.1.156–157). The number of levels of reality exposed here is startling to contemplate: The goddesses we have just been delighting in are supernatural, but they are merely portrayed by actors presenting a masque. However, those actors are themselves supernatural, Ariel's cohorts. Yet in reminding Ferdinand of this, Prospero reminds us that these sprites are themselves actors, in *The Tempest*. Then Prospero goes on to dissolve that reality as well, along with "the great globe itself" (4.1.153). Although we are not permitted to dwell on this proposition—Prospero immediately dismisses it as merely a "weakness" (4.1.159)—the point has been made, and the many veils of illusion that have been evoked remain to tantalize us.

The shifting realities of *The Tempest* are appropriate, perhaps even necessary, to its presentation of a multiplicity of themes. Comparisons of art and nature, imagination and reality, discipline and laxity, civilization and savagery combine to yield a powerful image of the moral nature of humankind. At the same time the play's extraordinary complexity permits quite differing interpretations of what

that nature is. For example, Prospero's total control over the events of the play, combined wtih Ariel's and Caliban's desire for freedom from his rule, has suggested political readings to many commentators, especially in the 20th century, with its concern for oppression and imperialism. Another modern interpretation, influenced by the advent of psychology, sees the characters as representing various aspects of Prospero's unconscious enacting an internal conflict. A related, less-scientific idea is that the play is an allegory of Shakespeare's own life, or at least of his artistic career. A large body of interpretation has been devoted to religious readings: The play has been seen as a work of Christian mysticism or as an explication of ancient pagan mystery cults or of the cabala. The 20th-century poet W. H. AUDEN's *The Sea and the Mirror* presents a different, less-esoteric Christian reading. Specific interpretations have ranged widely; among other things, *The Tempest* has been said to be about Neoplatonism, 16th-century French politics, Renaissance science, the creative impulse, and the discovery of America.

Obviously, not all of these interpretations can be correct—possibly none of them are—but whether psychological or political, religious or secular, all reflect an underlying quality of the play. *The Tempest* is about the inner nature of human beings revealed in circumstances of crisis and change. The characters are subject to startling personal transformations: Miranda, Alonso, and Gonzalo are magically put to sleep and awakened; for much of the play, Alonso is stricken by a grief that is based on an illusion; Ferdinand, faced with Miranda, finds that his "spirits, as in a dream, are all bound up" (1.2.489), and he forgets his own false mourning. All of the island's visitors are subjected to a purging experience of some sort: Ferdinand is put to carrying logs, Stephano and Trinculo find themselves in a "pickle" (5.1.282), the king and his followers are rendered "distracted" (5.1.12). Prospero's "insubstantial pageant" (4.1.155) is a fitting metaphor for the play's fluid, transitory world. Not for nothing does Gonzalo rejoice at the end that "all of us [found] ourselves / When no man was his own" (5.1.212–213).

Even Prospero, the agent of transformation in others, is not immune to change, although his occurs largely before the time of the play. His decision that "the rarer action is / In virtue than in vengeance" (5.1.27–28) implies a temptation to avenge himself from which he has refrained. We recognize that he has undergone a series of changes: from a student of magic, he became a seeker of revenge through it, and finally he has found his way to a transcendence of it. At the end he abandons his godlike status on the island and, embracing his own humanity, returns to Milan and his proper position as duke. Like the others, he is subject to alteration in the depths of his being. These processes of transfiguration enact human possibilities; while *The Tempest* points out the clay of which we're made, it also insists on our divine potential.

Strikingly, however, one character, Antonio, is not transfigured. Shakespeare never accepted a single, simple point of view on life's complexities, and *The Tempest* does not provide a clear and unambiguous conclusion. Prospero does not entirely succeed in effecting his reconciliation, for Antonio remains silent (except for one snide witticism). The defeat of evil is not complete; perhaps Prospero's dry response to Miranda's "O brave new world" (5.1.183)—"'Tis new to thee" (5.1.184)—reflects his awareness of this. And while Prospero brings happiness to others, he himself remains melancholy. As in the other late plays, Shakespeare in *The Tempest* acknowledges that an evil once committed can never be entirely compensated for; there are Antonios who will refuse virtue, and Prosperos who cannot forget injustice.

Nevertheless, *The Tempest* has the traditional happy ending of comedy. Prospero is reconciled with his old enemies—he forgives Antonio despite his intransigence—and reassurance is thus offered that redemption is possible in a sinful world. The marriage of Ferdinand and Miranda is especially significant in light of this reconciliation: The daughter of the victim of an injustice marries the son of its perpetrator. The auspiciousness of the marriage is strengthened by the declaration that the couple will inherit the crown of Naples. The focus on the future suggests the rebirth of the world.

SOURCES OF THE PLAY

The general situation in *The Tempest* may derive from the plays of the Italian COMMEDIA DELL'ARTE, several of which depict seamen shipwrecked on islands inhabited by magicians. However, Shakespeare's play is much deeper than these farcical entertainments, and the features that make it so— Ariel and Caliban, Prospero's relationship to and forgiveness of his enemies, and the importance of philosophical themes—are the playwright's inventions. Although various themes in *The Tempest* were treated in earlier works, no specific literary or theatrical sources can be associated with the central material of the play.

Nevertheless, there are various minor sources for particular elements within it. The exploration of the New World inspired Shakespeare and his contemporaries in many ways, and one event in particular probably stimulated the playwright's adoption of a remote island for his drama's setting. A shipload of Virginia-bound colonists was wrecked at Bermuda in 1609; a survivor, William STRACHEY, described his experience in a letter—circulated in manuscript—that Shakespeare read and exploited for *The Tempest*. The shipwreck in 1.1, Ariel's description of St. Elmo's fire in 1.2.196–206, and some other details derive from this document. It was supplemented by two public accounts of the same disaster, *The Discovery of the Barmudas* (1610) by Sylvester JOURDAIN and *A True Declaration of the state of the Colonie in Virginia* (1610), possibly by Dudley DIGGES. Besides offering historical details, these accounts all emphasize the providential survival of everyone aboard the vessel and the fact that Bermuda, previously notorious as an abode of devils and other evil spirits, turned out to be a pleasant and productive island. Both themes are paralleled in Shakespeare's depiction of Prospero's realm.

Another essay on the New World was exploited by Shakespeare, though in a different way. As already mentioned, Montaigne wrote about the native societies being discovered abroad in his essay "Of the Cannibals," describing them as utopian societies free of the defects of civilization. Shakespeare apparently respected Montaigne's clarity of thought, and it finds expression in Gonzalo's remarks on ideal government (2.1.143–164)—although Montaigne's ideas are rejected in general by the play. A passage in another Montaigne essay, "Of Crueltie," probably inspired Prospero's praise of reconciliation in 5.1.25–30. In both cases Shakespeare used John FLO-RIO's translation of Montaigne, *Essayes on Morall, Politike, and Millitarie Discourses* (1603).

Other minor sources supplied additional material. OVID's *Metamorphoses*, either in the original Latin or as translated by Arthur GOLDING, provided much of Prospero's catalogue of supernatural beings in 5.1.33–50. Robert EDEN's *History of Travaille* (1577) also provided several details, including the name of Caliban's god, Setebos. Ferdinand's delight in the pain of worthwhile labor, in 3.1.1–14, may owe something to a similar passage in the *Confessions* of St. Augustine (A.D. 354–430). MUCEDORUS (ca. 1590), a comedy revived by the KING'S MEN in 1610 (and later wrongly attributed to Shakespeare), features a "wild man" (a traditional medieval figure) whose savage nature may have influenced the creation of Caliban. Caliban may also reflect Shakespeare's reading of ARISTOTLE's *Nicomachean Ethics*. Contemporary demonology and spirit lore, from common opinion as well as literary sources, are evident throughout; in particular, Reginald SCOT's *Discovery of Witchcraft* (1584) may have provided hints for Ariel's nature.

TEXT OF THE PLAY

The Tempest was written in late 1610 or 1611, for several of its sources were not available until at least the late summer of 1610; a performance—not necessarily the first—occurred on November 1, 1611. Some scholars believe that *The Tempest* may be a revision of an earlier work by Shakespeare—perhaps from as early as the 1590s—but the evidence for this theory is highly tenuous, and most modern commentators assume that the play was written in a single effort.

The play was first published in the FIRST FOLIO (1623). The copy used in printing it was a transcript of either a PROMPTBOOK or Shakespeare's FOUL PAPERS. The transcript—probably made by Ralph CRANE, whose idiosyncratic spelling and punctuation are present in the printed text—was probably made expressly for the FOLIO printing. As the only early version of the play, the Folio text has served as the basis for all subsequent editions.

One peculiarity of the Folio text may be suggestive of the circumstances in which the play was writ-ten: commentators have speculated that the play's elaborate stage directions may indicate that Shakespeare wrote the play in STRATFORD. Distant from the workaday world of the theater, where the desired behavior on stage could be established at rehearsals, Shakespeare may have felt compelled to be more specific than in earlier plays. On the other hand, these directions are like those of the courtly masque, and Shakespeare may have merely intended to stress the resemblance between masques and his play. It is also possible that the stage directions were not written by Shakespeare but were added later.

THEATRICAL HISTORY OF THE PLAY

The earliest recorded performance of *The Tempest* was at the court of King JAMES I on November 1, 1611, and it was also staged as part of the festivities surrounding the marriage of the princess ELIZABETH STUART in February 1613. (Some scholars believe that the masque of goddesses in 4.1 may have been added to the play for this performance.) No early performances in public theaters are recorded, although John DRYDEN remarked—in the preface to his adaptation of the play—that it had been performed at the BLACKFRIARS THEATRE early in the century. It is believed that Richard BURBAGE originated the role of Prospero.

Dryden's adaptation, in which William DAV-ENANT collaborated, was called *The Tempest, or The Enchanted Island* (1667, publ. 1670). Dryden added many characters—including siblings of the opposite sex for Miranda and Ferdinand, a female monster for Caliban, and a female sprite for Ariel—and little of Shakespeare's language was retained. Also, the additions were in good part plagiarized from the Spanish playwright, Pedro Calderón (1600–81). Though modern commentators unanimously condemn it, *The Enchanted Island* was very popular. In 1674 Thomas SHADWELL turned it into an OPERA, with music by several composers, including Matthew LOCKE; this work inspired a burlesque, Thomas DUFFET's *The Mock-Tempest, or The Enchanted Castle* (1674). In 1690 Henry PURCELL composed a new score for *The Enchanted Island*. This opera remained popular for a century and continued to influence later adaptations of *The Tempest* until well into the 19th century. It was revived in London in 1959, on the tercentenary of Purcell's birth.

In 1745 a brief revival of Shakespeare's play failed, and the Dryden-Davenport version reappeared the following season. David GARRICK produced another operatic version, *The Tempest* (1756), with words by himself and Shakespeare (though very little of the original text was used) and music by John Christopher Smith (1712–95). Immense dance numbers—one involving 60 children—were a prominent feature of this production. However, perhaps repenting, Garrick also staged Shakespeare's text in 1757, with Hannah PRITCHARD as Miranda. John Philip KEMBLE revived the Dryden-Davenant version in 1789, but he included some additional Shakespearean passages and in 1806 restored much more of the original text.

In 1821 Frederic REYNOLDS produced a new version of *The Enchanted Island,* with William Charles MACREADY as Prospero and with music from miscellaneous works by seven composers, including Purcell, Mozart, and ROSSINI. The vogue for such musical pastiches of Shakespeare was past, however, and this production was not a success. Macready also played Prospero in another revival of the Dryden-Davenant *Tempest* in 1833, and then in 1838 he staged his own revival of Shakespeare's play. He cut the dialogue from 1.1 to emphasize a spectacular scenic rendering of storm and shipwreck but was otherwise reasonably faithful to the text, establishing a tradition that has not lapsed. He again played Prospero, opposite Helen FAUCIT as Miranda. Charles KEAN staged a less complete but still wholly Shakespearean text in 1857, playing Prospero in a very elaborate production involving complex "scenic appliances," as he called them, necessitating more than 140 stagehands. In the same fashion, Samuel PHELPS presented the play in 1871, with himself as Prospero, in a production featuring a proliferation of peacocks and dancers, with music by Thomas Augustine ARNE and Purcell. In 1900 F. R. BENSON's *Tempest* helped introduce a more modern restraint in staging, although Beerbohm TREE continued with 19th-century extravagance in his 1904 staging, in which he played Caliban.

Among 20th-century actors, John GIELGUD was particularly associated with *The Tempest,* playing Prospero in four noteworthy productions: two at the OLD VIC THEATRE (1930, 1940), a STRATFORD staging by Peter BROOK in 1957, and a London production of 1974. James Earl JONES was acclaimed as Caliban in Joseph PAPP's New York Shakespeare Festival presentation (1962). Peter HALL made his directorial debut at London's National Theatre with a *Tempest* production in 1973 and ended his tenure there with another, in 1988. Michael BOYD and the ROYAL SHAKESPEARE COMPANY produced an acclaimed staging in 2001.

In an early experiment with FILM, the opening scene of Tree's production was filmed in 1904, and the silent screen saw two full-length presentations of the play (1911, 1912). However, *The Tempest* has only once been made into a movie with sound—a purposefully bizarre version by Derek Jarman (1942–94), set in an abandoned church (1970)—although a famous science-fiction film, *The Forbidden Planet* (1954), was based on it. Peter Greenaway's 1991 *Prospero's Books,* an elaborate adaptation starring John Gielgud (who played Prospero but spoke the lines of all the other characters, until the final scene), used much of Shakespeare but with much more of a great deal else. In contrast the play has been made for TELEVISION six times, including a 1960 offering with Maurice EVANS as Prospero and Richard Burton as Caliban. *The Tempest* is the Shakespeare play that has been most frequently adapted as an opera, beginning in 1674 with the first Shakespearean opera, the Shadwell production mentioned above, though most of them were unsuccessful and have been performed only rarely. However, the play has inspired a number of other musical creations, including symphonic fantasies by Hector BERLIOZ (1830) and Peter Ilyich TCHAIKOVSKY (1873), and a setting by Ralph VAUGHAN WILLIAMS (1951) of Prospero's "revels" speech and Ariel's SONG, "Where the bee sucks" (4.1.148–158; 5.1.88–94).

CHARACTERS

Adrian Minor character in *The Tempest,* a follower of King Alonso of Naples. Adrian hardly speaks; in 2.1 he briefly supports Gonzalo in his optimism, which is mocked by Antonio and Sebastian, and in 3.3 he speaks only half a line, closing the scene.

Adrian, with Francisco, has been seen by some scholars as evidence for the existence of an earlier version of *The Tempest*, in which his role was more substantial, for there seems no reason to include him in the play as it stands. He may have been intended for scenes that Shakespeare originally planned but then discarded in the course of composition. In any case, minor attendants help establish the high status of royal figures throughout Shakespeare's plays, and Adrian has this function for Alonso; moreover, his reiteration of Gonzalo's position focuses attention on it and helps maintain our sense that a remnant of goodwill survives among villains.

Alonso, King of Naples Character in *The Tempest*, father of Ferdinand. In 2.1, when Alonso and his followers are shipwrecked on the magician Prospero's island, Alonso believes his son has drowned and his grief overwhelms him. In 3.3 Prospero's sprite Ariel, disguised as a Harpy, declares Alonso, Antonio, and Sebastian to be "three men of sin" (3.3.53) and reminds the king that he helped Antonio depose Prospero as Duke of Milan (before the play began). Ariel cites the loss of Ferdinand as Alonso's punishment. The three are made insane by Prospero's magic and must be revived at the play's end, in 5.1. Faced with Prospero, Alonso willingly surrenders Milan to him and begs his pardon. When Prospero reveals the surviving Ferdinand, Alonso is overjoyed; his "I say, Amen" (5.1.204) offers a religious reference that reinforces the play's point that providence can restore human happiness.

Alonso symbolizes several of the play's themes. His story demonstrates the Christian pattern of sin, suffering, repentance, and eventual recompense, thus supporting the play's presentation of moral regeneration and contributing to the final aura of reconciliation and forgiveness. His fall into madness and subsequent revival as a purified man is an instance of another important theme, transfiguration. Finally, his innate goodness—exemplified by his grief for Ferdinand and his admission of guilt—contrasts tellingly with the villainy of those around him, especially Antonio.

Antonio Character in *The Tempest*, villainous brother of Prospero. Before the play begins, as we learn in 1.2, Antonio deposed Prospero as duke of MILAN with the help of King Alonso of Naples. Fearful of Prospero's popularity, he staged a natural death for the duke, abandoning him and his daughter Miranda in a small boat at sea. In the play Antonio, along with Alonso and others, is shipwrecked on the island that Prospero rules in exile. He continues to display his villainy in large and small ways, derogating the optimism of Gonzalo and encouraging Alonso's brother Sebastian to assassinate the king and assume the throne of Naples. His manipulation of Sebastian in 2.1.197–291 is a striking demonstration of Macchiavellian villainy, and for this Antonio has been compared to Shakespeare's great villains Richard III and *Othello*'s Iago.

Antonio, Alonso, and Sebastian are all captured by Prospero, who casts a spell of witless insanity on them; when he releases them from the spell, he takes back his duchy and forgives them their crimes in an atmosphere of reconciliation. Antonio, however, refuses to accept this reconciliation, remaining silent when even the bestial Caliban assents. He thereby represents an important qualification to the play's sense of good's triumph: evil cannot be entirely compensated for in a world of human beings, for there are always Antonios who simply will not accept good.

Ariel Character in *The Tempest*, a sprite, or fairy, who serves the magician Prospero. Ariel is invisible to all but Prospero, whom he assists in the schemes that form the plot. He is capable of assuming fantastic disguises and of luring mortals with supernaturally compelling music. He is also something of a theatrical producer, arranging the spectacular tableaux that Prospero is fond of, including the magical banquet of 3.3 and the betrothal MASQUE of 4.1. He performs in both, playing a Harpy at the feast and either Ceres or Iris (depending on one's reading of 4.1.167) in the masque. Ariel is eager to please, asking, "What shall I do? say what; what shall I do?" (1.2.300). To his question "Do you love me, master?" (4.1.48), Prospero replies, "Dearly, my delicate Ariel" (4.1.49), and when Prospero returns to MILAN and resumes his role in human society, he regrets departing from the sprite, saying "my dainty Ariel! I shall miss thee" (5.1.95). A cheerful and intelligent being, Ariel embodies the power of good and is thus an appropriate helper in Prospero's effort to combat the evil represented by Antonio. In this respect he contrasts strongly with the play's other major nonhuman figure, Caliban, whose innate evil complicates Prospero's task.

Freed by Prospero from a magical imprisonment in a tree trunk, imposed by a witch before the time of the play, Ariel must serve Prospero until the magician releases him. But though he fulfills his tasks cheerfully, he yearns to be free again. Almost as soon as he first appears, he reminds Prospero of his "worthy service . . . without grudge or grumblings" (1.2.247–249) and requests his liberty. Prospero—more of a grumbler than his supernatural servant—reminds him forcefully of his former torment, and Ariel agrees to continue serving and "do [his] spriting gently" (1.2.298). He does so, but both he and Prospero frequently mention his coming release. Ariel sings of the future. "Merrily, merrily shall I live now / Under the blossom that hangs on the bough" (5.1.93–94), and his mingling of nostalgia and fresh spirits is touching. In his last lines before the EPILOGUE, Prospero bids Ariel "to the elements / Be free, and fare thou well!" (5.1.318). This theme, Ariel's captivity in the human world—along with Caliban's slavery and Antonio's remorselessness—helps maintain a tragic undertone as Prospero's schemes for a final reconciliation are achieved. Shakespeare does not ignore the inexorability of evil, even in a fantasy world, though he can create a charming sprite to combat it.

Boatswain Minor character in *The Tempest*, a crew member of the ship that is wrecked on Prospero's island. In 1.1 the Boatswain curses the arrogant Sebastian and Antonio, who insist on interfering during the great storm that threatens the vessel. Prospero's sprite Ariel magically preserves the ship and its crew, and in 5.1, as the play closes, the Boatswain is brought to Prospero by Ariel and reports on the ship's miraculous restoration. The Boatswain is a plainspoken working man whose contrast with Sebastian and Antonio helps establish their villainous natures at the outset and whose reappearance at the close suggests the everyday world to which the play's characters will soon return.

Caliban Character in *The Tempest*, the beastlike slave of the magician Prospero. Before the time of the play, Prospero and his daughter Miranda took Caliban, the illegitimate son of a witch and a devil, into their home and taught him to speak and function as a human, but his response was to attempt to rape the girl. In the course of the play, he and Stephano attempt to murder Prospero. Though Caliban is powerless to effect his schemes, his villainous nature is an important element in *The Tempest*'s scheme of things. At the play's close a chastened Caliban declares, "I'll be wise hereafter, / And seek for grace" (5.1.294–295) as part of the general reconciliation engineered by Prospero.

Caliban is only partly human. He is a "monster" (2.2.66), a "moon-calf" (2.2.107), a "born devil" (4.1.188), and a "thing of darkness" (5.1.275). Because his father was a devil, Caliban is supernatural like Ariel, but unlike that airy spirit, he has no supernatural powers. He is more like a debased human than like any other supernatural creature in Shakespeare. He has intelligence enough to learn language, but he is seemingly incapable of moral sense; reminded of his attempted rape, he merely asserts his animal drive to procreate. Caliban serves as a foil for the other characters: His foolish credulity in accepting Stephano as a god contrasts with Prospero's wisdom; his viciousness with Miranda's innocence; his amorality with the honorable love of Ferdinand; and, most significantly, his finally regenerate state with the intransigent evil of Antonio.

Caliban's human qualities illuminate another of the play's themes and, in doing so, shed light on Shakespeare's world, which was just becoming aware of the natives of America (see EPENOW). As Prospero's "slave" (1.2.310) Caliban is linked with America: His mother's god, Setebos, was known by Shakespeare as a South American deity; in finding Stephano divine and in responding greedily to his liquor, Caliban behaves like the American natives of early explorers' accounts.

The discovery of native American societies in the early 17th century stimulated debate on an ancient question: Is "natural man" a savage whose life is governed only by animal drives, or is he in a blessed state, unspoiled by the manifold corruptions of civilization? Although the idealism of the latter view is reflected in Gonzalo's praise of primitive society in 2.1.143–160 (drawn from remarks on America by the French essayist MONTAIGNE), Caliban's nature contradicts it. He represents "natural man," but his very name, an anagram of "canibal" (a legitimate 17th-century spelling of "cannibal"), lends a negative quality to the connection.

It is precisely his naturalness that condemns Caliban. He is confined to brute slavery because he has refused to accept a civil role in Prospero's household. Prospero says that "on [his] nature / Nurture can never stick" (4.1.188–189). In a telling comparison, Caliban's resistance to his wood-carrying chores is contrasted with Ferdinand's philosophical delight in similar labors. The young man knows that "some kinds of baseness / Are nobly undergone; and most poor matters / Point to rich ends" (3.1.2–4). Miranda expressly judges both Ferdinand and Caliban: the first is "a thing divine" (1.2.421), the second "a thing most brutish" (1.2.359).

Yet Caliban has some positive attributes, which qualify Shakespeare's condemnation of "natural man." Though he proclaims that his education has merely taught him "how to curse" (1.2.366), his use of language is in fact quite impressive, and he rises to lyrical poetry—revealing an aesthetic sensibility—in describing his dreams of "a thousand twangling instruments" (3.2.135). He can imagine a level below himself to which he does not want to descend, for he fears he and his companions will be "turn'd to barnacles, or to apes / With foreheads villainous low" (4.1.248–249). Though he is foolish enough to follow Stephano and Trinculo, he is more sensible than they and scorns their frivolous absorption with mere "luggage" (4.1.231). His proposed revolt is both repulsive and ineffectual, but Caliban's dislike for his enslavement is one with which we instinctively sympathize. His initial statement of grievance is compelling; he helped Prospero and Miranda survive and is now enslaved. Only then do we learn of his crime, but even afterward, Caliban is permitted his say on his status: His elaborate complaint of Prospero's harassment in 2.2.1–14 casts his master in a bad light, and his comical enthusiasm for "Freedom, high-day! high-day, freedom! freedom, high-day, freedom!" (2.2.186–187) is infectious.

For all his villainy, Caliban contributes to the general sense of regeneration with which the play closes. He recognizes his folly and expresses his intention to improve himself in a religious metaphor—he will "seek for grace" (5.1.295). His earlier behavior certainly makes us wonder if reform is really possible, but Shakespeare pointedly elevates this beastlike character's moral stature before he exits forever. However appalling Caliban's fallen state, he offers the hope for restoration to grace that is part of Shakespeare's sense of human possibility.

Ceres Pagan goddess and minor figure in *The Tempest*, a character in the MASQUE presented by the sprite Ariel, at Prospero's orders, to celebrate the engagement of Miranda and Ferdinand. Ceres, goddess of harvests, is presented by IRIS but declares she will not participate unless she can be assured that Venus and Cupid will not be present. This reminds us of Prospero's insistence on Miranda's virginity before marriage, part of the play's theme of moral discipline. Once reassured, Ceres joins Juno in singing a hymn of blessing, wishing "Earth's increase, foison [abundance] plenty" (4.1.110) for the couple.

In ancient mythology, Ceres—from whose name comes our word *cereal*—was a pre-Roman corn goddess. She became identified with the Greek goddess Demeter, who governed all fruits of the earth, especially grain. According to a central myth of the classical world, Ceres's daughter was stolen by the god of the underworld; the goddess responded by withholding her bounty until a compromise was achieved: Her daughter spends half the year in the underworld, during which time Ceres resumes her grief, and winter rules. In *The Tempest* Ceres blames Venus and Cupid for her daughter's theft, following the account given in OVID's *Metamorphosis*; the same incident is referred to in *The Winter's Tale*, 4.4.116–118.

Ferdinand Character in *The Tempest*, the lover of the magician Prospero's daughter, Miranda. Prospero arranges the match between Miranda and the son of his old enemy, King Alonso of Naples, as part of the atmosphere of reconciliation and forgiveness with which he resolves his own exile. Prospero pretends to distrust Ferdinand and puts him to forced labor, but when the young man's love survives this trial, Prospero blesses the future marriage of the couple. Ferdinand's ardor is important to the play's scheme of things, for he and Miranda symbolize the healing value of love. Ferdinand is accordingly a stereotypical romantic leading man, though his role is relatively small.

Ferdinand is tellingly compared with Prospero's bestial slave, Caliban. Miranda explicitly judges the two, in pointedly contrasting terms: Caliban is "a thing most brutish" (1.2.358) and Ferdinand "a thing divine"(1.2.421). Caliban has attempted to rape Miranda, but Ferdinand vows to respect her virginity until they are married. Caliban truculently resists his chore of delivering firewood with whines and curses; Ferdinand is assigned a similar task—carrying logs—but he rejoices in the labor, for it is associated with his love. Ferdinand's mourning for his father, whom he believes drowned, is also part of the play's depiction of goodness and helps (with Alonso's similarly mistaken grief over his son) to ameliorate the king's earlier crime against Prospero.

Francisco Minor character in *The Tempest*, a follower of King Alonso of Naples. In 2.1.109–118 Francisco attempts to reassure the king that Prince Ferdinand has survived their shipwreck. This passage is an extension of Gonzalo's efforts to cheer the king, and Francisco speaks only three more words, in 3.3.40, so there seems little reason for his presence in the play. In some editions, in fact, he is deleted and his lines given to Gonzalo. Some scholars have taken him and Adrian as evidence of an earlier version of *The Tempest*, in which they played a greater part. He may have been intended for scenes that Shakespeare originally planned but then discarded in the course of composition. In any case, royal figures are conventionally endowed with unimportant attendants throughout Shakespeare's work.

Gonzalo Character in *The Tempest*, adviser to King Alonso of Naples. Gonzalo is a kind and charitable, if ineffectual, figure who is a foil to the cynical villainy of Antonio, Duke of MILAN, his master's ally. Gonzalo's goodness is an important element in

the play. He persistently takes a generous and optimistic point of view, as in his fantasy of an ideal society in 2.1.143–164 (see also MONTAIGNE, MICHEL DE). At the play's close, when Prospero's schemes result in a final reconciliation and the seemingly miraculous restoration of the king's son, Ferdinand, it is the aging adviser—called by Prospero "Holy Gonzalo, honourable man" (5.1.62)—who cries out, "O, rejoice / Beyond a common joy!" (5.1.206–207).

In 1.1, as the king's ship sinks, Gonzalo's calm acceptance of fate contrasts with Antonio's arrogant fury and helps establish our sense of the moral polarities with which the play is concerned. In 1.2 we learn that Alonso assisted Antonio in deposing his brother, Prospero, and abandoning him and his infant daughter Miranda at sea, but that Gonzalo helped the victims by providing them with supplies. The contrast between Antonio and Gonzalo remains throughout the play. In 2.1 Gonzalo is mocked by Antonio and Sebastian for his attempts to cheer the king, and Antonio proposes to kill Gonzalo along with Alonso in his scheme to place Alonso's brother Sebastian on the throne of Naples. At the close, Gonzalo's hearty participation in the aura of reconciliation points up Antonio's refusal to accept it.

Harpy Supernatural creature in whose guise Ariel appears in 3.3 in *The Tempest*. Prospero's sprite accuses the "three men of sin"—Alonso, Antonio, and Sebastian—and his disguise makes him more terrifying. The harpies, three mythological monsters, sisters, were woman-headed birds. They stole things from mortals—especially food (appropriate to the banquet setting of Ariel's appearance)—and defecated vilely as they left. Apparently wind-gods in origin, these semidivine beings may have derived in part from rumors reaching Greece of an actual creature in India, a large, fruit-eating bat noted for its excrement.

Iris Pagan goddess and minor figure in *The Tempest*, a character in the MASQUE presented by the sprite Ariel to celebrate the engagement of Miranda and Ferdinand. Iris—goddess of the rainbow and messenger of the greater deities—functions as the "presenter" of the masque, which features Ceres, goddess of harvests; Juno, queen of the gods; and a dance of Nymphs and Reapers. Iris's beautiful invocation to Ceres in 4.1.60–75 establishes a tone of serene power appropriate to divinity. Ariel subsequently declares that he "presented Ceres" (4.1.167), indicating that he played the part of either Ceres or Iris, the presenter; most commentators believe Shakespeare intended the former, with Iris's initial speech providing time for Ariel to costume himself.

In Greek mythology Iris is a hazy figure and was never the object of a cult of worship. Originally simply associated with the rainbow, she was perhaps considered a messenger of the gods because rainbows seem to connect sky and earth. In classical literature—as distinct from mythology—Iris was particularly associated with Juno, and Shakespeare draws on this tradition when Ariel's masquer speaks of Juno as "the queen o' th' sky, / Whose wat'ry arch and messenger am I" (4.1.70–71).

Juno   Pagan goddess and minor figure in *The Tempest*, a character in the MASQUE presented by ARIEL to celebrate the engagement of Miranda and Ferdinand. After an introduction by Iris, Juno joins Ceres in singing a hymn of "marriage-blessing" (4.1.106) to the couple. Though queen of the gods, Juno has the smallest role in the masque. However, in Shakespeare's hierarchy-conscious world, Juno's rank gave her a greater importance than she seems otherwise to have. As a queen, her presence—her "sovereign grace" (4.1.72)—gives the masque a particularly dignified air appropriate to the betrothal of Prospero's daughter. If, as some scholars believe, the masque was added to the play when it was performed as part of the 1613 marriage festivities for the princess Elizabeth Stuart, this feature would have had even greater import. Juno's entrance is accordingly a spectacular one. The stage direction at 4.1.72 reads "Juno descends," indicating theatrical practice in Shakespeare's time, at least in the new BLACKFRIARS THEATRE: the goddess was lowered from the ceiling above the stage, probably seated on a throne decorated with peacocks, as mentioned by Iris in 4.1.74. (Nineteenth-century productions of *The Tempest* often featured live peacocks.)

Mariner   Any of several minor characters in *The Tempest*, the crew of the ship that is wrecked on Prospero's island. As the play opens, the Mariners receive orders from the Boatswain—"Heigh, my hearts! . . . yare, yare! Take in the topsail" (1.1.5–6). A little later several of them cry out in unison, "All lost, to prayers, to prayers! all lost!" (1.1.51), signaling the close of the scene, as the passengers prepare for death. These characters are extras, providing a sense of hysteria aboard the doomed vessel.

Master   Minor character in *The Tempest*, captain of the ship that is wrecked on Prospero's island. The Master speaks only two lines, at the play's opening, when he instructs the Boatswain to see that the men act swiftly or they will go aground. In 5.1 he reappears with the Boatswain, who reports on the miraculous restoration of the vessel, but he does not speak himself. He is an extra, helping to provide a realistic depiction of a ship's company.

Miranda   Character in *The Tempest*, daughter of the magician Prospero. Miranda, exiled with her father at the age of two, has lived 12 years with him on the island he rules through sorcery. It is uninhabited except for the supernatural creatures Ariel and Caliban, so when Prospero's magic brings people to the island, Miranda sees her first young man, Ferdinand, with whom she falls in love—and he with her—in 1.2. Prospero has planned this. Ferdinand is the son of his old enemy, King Alonso of Naples—but he pretends to oppose the couple's love to ensure that Ferdinand does not take Miranda lightly. Prospero takes the young man captive, but Miranda contrives to visit him, and they confess their love and plan to marry in 3.1; in 4.1 Prospero declares his approval. As part of Prospero's arrangements for a conclusion of forgiveness and happiness, in 5.1 Miranda and Ferdinand are revealed to King Alonso, who believed his son had drowned. Miranda's marriage plans are confirmed, and Alonso declares that she and Ferdinand will inherit the kingdom of Naples.

Miranda does not speak often or at length, but she is established as a paragon of maidenhood. She displays a touching compassion—fearing for the shipwreck victims, she says, "O, I have suffered / With those that I saw suffer!" (1.2.5–6). She also shows a capacity for delighted wonder; on first seeing Ferdinand, she cries, "I might call him / A thing divine; for nothing natural / I ever saw so noble" (1.2.420–422). Her angry disdain for Caliban, who once attempted to rape her, displays the moral sensibility she has learned from her father, but her innocence of society gives her a simplicity that in a less overtly fantastic context would be disconcerting. She ignores the fact that Ferdinand is the son of her father's enemy, and at the play's close she is filled with pleased admiration for all of the king's party, even though some of them are arrant villains, saying, "How beauteous mankind is! O brave new world, / That has such people in 't!" (5.1.183–184).

Miranda represents the compassionate, forgiving, and optimistic potential in humanity. She is the only human character in the play who does not undergo some sort of purging transformation, for she does not need to. Innocent of life's difficulties and compromises, she repudiates evil and responds to nobility and beauty. She is most pointedly contrasted with the evil Caliban. Both were raised together by Prospero, but she has become a person of moral sensibility, while he is a would-be rapist who declares that his only use for language is to curse. Their responses to the arrival of strangers on the island are also contrasting: She is filled with demure awe, he with crass fear.

Though innocent, Miranda is nonetheless mindful of sexual propriety, speaking of her "modesty, the jewel in [her] dower" (3.1.53–54) and declaring that if Ferdinand will not marry her, she will "die [his] maid" (3.1.84). Her virginity—stressed repeatedly by the men, as in Ferdinand's first declaration of love and in Prospero's emphatic concern about sex before marriage—link her to an ancient archetype, the fertile woman, producer of new generations. The goddesses at her betrothal MASQUE sing of "Earth's increase" and "plants with goodly burthen bowing" (4.1.110, 113), making it clear that the occasion concerns reproduction. They also stress Miranda's virginity, for a sure knowledge of paternity has traditionally been very important to the orderly continuation of society. This is especially true among rulers, and Miranda's future as a queen is frequently pointed up. At the play's close, after Prospero's reconciliations have been effected, Gonzalo blesses the moment and delights in the prospect that Prospero's "issue / Should become Kings of Naples" (5.1.205–206). Miranda thus helps fulfill that most ancient of necessities for human societies, continuance into the future. She and Ferdinand embody the regeneration that is the theme of the play's close.

Miranda's name—Latin for "admirable" (literally, "to be wondered at")—was coined by Shakespeare. It reflects not only her qualities as an example of innocent womanhood but also her own admiring nature and the extraordinary sense of wonder that the play as a whole conveys. It is punned on by Ferdinand when he calls her "Admir'd Miranda!" (3.1.37) and, more subtly, when he exclaims "O you wonder!" (1.2.429).

Prospero Character in *The Tempest*, the magician-ruler of a remote island. Prospero, once the duke of MILAN, lives in exile with his daughter Miranda and two supernatural inhabitants of the island, Ariel and Caliban. Through magic, Prospero controls this world completely, and he is the central figure of the play, simultaneously the sparker and spectator of its various SUBPLOTS. He has freed Ariel from a magic spell in exchange for his service as an assistant; he also befriended Caliban at first but enslaved him after he attempted to rape Miranda. Though embittered by his exile, Prospero has gained wisdom through his sorcery, and when chance places his onetime enemies in his power, he uses his magic to create an atmosphere of reconciliation and forgiveness, providing for the future in the union of Miranda with Ferdinand, the son of his enemy.

Having accomplished these things, Prospero sacrifices both his dominion over the island and his love of magic, choosing to return to Milan. In doing so, he restores a measure of justice to human society, for he had been unjustly deposed from authority before the play began. He also restores himself to a sound moral footing, for he had earlier placed a private concern—his study of magic—above his duty as a leader of society, with disastrous results. However, Prospero's success is not complete; he remains a melancholy figure at the play's end, haunted by Caliban's enmity and his evil brother Antonio, who refuses regeneration. Thus Prospero brings out an important subtheme of *The Tempest* and of the ROMANCES in general: that life is an admixture of good and evil and that good cannot completely eradicate bad.

Prospero is a philosopher as well as a ruler. His magic is referred to as his "Art" (1.2.1), consistently spelled with a capital A; this is a conventional allusion to Neoplatonic doctrines of the occult, familiar ideas in the 17th century. The Neoplatonic philosopher/magician attempted to elevate his soul through arcane knowledge of the divine, whether through alchemy, the reading of supernatural signs, or communication with spirits. If these efforts led to a magical manipulation of the real world, it was only as a by-product of the search for spiritual knowledge. Prospero's original goal was to transcend nature, not control it. Nevertheless, it is clear that the pursuit of this goal was culpably selfish, for it resulted in his exile and the disruption of sound government in Milan, as he recounts in 1.2. He had insisted on studying magic rather than governing and as a result had been deposed by Antonio. Conscious of his failing, regretful at leaving Ariel and the beauties of "rough magic [and] heavenly music" (5.1.50–52), distressed by his evident failure to educate Caliban, and, most important, frustrated by the intransigence of Antonio, Prospero returns to Milan at play's end without the satisfaction the conclusion brings to most of the other characters. Though restored to power, and though he has provided a hopeful future for others, he is a partial failure, and he knows it.

Prospero is not a pleasant character. He is a distant and uncommunicative father and a tyrannical master. His unjustified complaints that Miranda is not listening to him in 1.2 and his anguished disruption of the MASQUE in 4.1 are evidence of his temperamental nature. Only in his affection for Ariel is he a pleasant figure, but he is also capable of rounding vituperatively on the sprite—"Thou liest, malignant thing!" (1.2.257)—and threatening him—"I will . . . peg thee [to a tree] till / Thou hast howl'd away twelve winters" (1.2.294–296). His program of petty harassments of Caliban, recounted in 2.2.1–14, is equally repellent.

Prospero's exploitation of the island's inhabitants is a clearly established element of the play. Ariel, a free spirit by nature, is restive in his service, and Caliban even attempts a revolt. Some modern commentators go so far as to make this exploitation a central concern, and *The Tempest* has been presented as an allegory of colonialism and oppression. However, it is clear that Prospero's control has been employed for good, for he has undone the dominance of evil that he found on his arrival, when the villainous Caliban prevailed, and Ariel, a good spirit, was imprisoned by Caliban's mother. The inhumane treatment of Caliban and Ariel's dissatisfaction provide evidence of the inexorability of evil; good ends must often be compromised by morally unsatisfactory means.

A central theme of the play is transfiguration, as the characters undergo transformations that suggest the varying human capacity for improvement. Prospero's magic effects these alterations in the others, but he himself also undergoes a highly significant change. His transformation occurs largely before the time of the play, but evidence of it remains. His decision that "the rarer action is / In virtue than in vengeance" (5.1.27–28) implies a temptation from which he refrains. We recognize that he has grown: First a scholar of magic, he became a seeker of revenge through supernatural means, but finally he has transcended magic altogether. Once he could say "my library / Was dukedom large enough" (1.2.109–110), but at the play's end he returns to Milan to resume his proper position as a leader of society. In so doing, he renounces his magical powers and discards his semidivine status as the island's omnipotent ruler. Prospero accepts his humanity and comes to terms with the prospect of his own death, to which he will devote "every third thought" (5.1.311). He leaves the future in the hands of Ferdinand and Miranda.

Prospero's "Art" fittingly takes the form of drama, the art practiced by Prospero's creator. Assisted by Ariel, Prospero produces three distinctly theatrical illusions—the Harpy's banquet of 3.3, the betrothal masque of 4.1, and the presentation of Ferdinand and Miranda at chess in 5.1. As producer of these spectacles, Prospero comments on their nature at the close of the masque, in his famous speech beginning "Our revels now are ended" (4.1.148). He points out the illusion involved and goes on to equate such an "insubstantial pageant" (4.1.155) with life itself, which disappears once it is performed. "We are such stuff / As dreams are made on," he concludes, "and our little life / Is rounded with a sleep" (4.1.156–158). Many commentators have regarded Prospero's remarks as Shakespeare's personal valedictory to a career in the theater. While this notion is imprecise, in that Shakespeare continued to write for the theater after *The Tempest*, the passage does seem to reflect the experience of an artist whose long career has led to the belief that art's inherently illusory nature is analogous to, and probably related to, the impossibility of understanding life. Here we have a clue to the philosophy underlying a prominent feature of Shakespeare's work, his persistent attention to ambiguity.

Shakespeare may have taken Prospero's name from Prospero Adorno (active 1460–88), a deposed duke of Genoa, of whom he could have read in William Thomas's *History of Italy* (1549). However, this is uncertain, for another source was nearer to hand: Ben JONSON's *Every Man in His Humour* (1600). This play, in which Shakespeare acted, contains a character—though not a deposed duke—originally named Prospero (the name was later changed to Wellbred, as it appears in modern editions).

Sebastian Character in *The Tempest*, brother of King Alonso of Naples. Sebastian is led by Antonio, the villainous deposer of Prospero, into greater crimes than he would otherwise have contemplated. In 1.1 Antonio and Sebastian arrogantly curse the seamen of their storm-wracked vessel, and after they are shipwrecked on Prospero's magical island, they are equally offensive in ridiculing Gonzalo's attempts to cheer Alonso, who believes his son is dead. However, Sebastian demonstrates no more than crude offensiveness until Antonio suggests that they kill the sleeping Alonso so that he, Sebastian, may inherit the crown of Naples. Sebastian accepts the idea greedily, but Antonio's primacy in evil is demonstrated in their plan: Antonio will stab Alonso, while Sebastian takes on Gonzalo. This is Sebastian's moment of greatest

involvement. Prospero's sprite Ariel prevents the assassinations and reduces Sebastian and the others to madness. In 5.1, free from the spell, Sebastian has one more significant line. When Prospero restores Alonso's son, Sebastian cries, "A most high miracle" (5.1.177). In acknowledging the spiritual power of the moment, Sebastian contrasts with Antonio, who remains unmoved. Thus, Sebastian, like Alonso, finally comes to exemplify humanity's capacity for redemption.

Stephano (Stefano) Character in *The Tempest*, the drunken butler of King Alonso of Naples and the ally of Caliban in his plot to kill Prospero. Stephano is a loutish fellow who is drunk throughout his time on stage, bullies Caliban and Trinculo, and is ludicrously ineffective in carrying out the plot. In 3.2, when Stephano accepts Caliban's suggestion that after killing Prospero he take Miranda for himself, we see that a supposedly civilized man is capable of villainy as deep as that of a bestial savage (for Caliban had already attempted to rape the young woman). Stephano's bluff—and drunken—courage distinguishes him from his companions, but when he is comically distracted from the assassination by the trivial vanity of fancy clothes in 4.1, he seems inferior to even the subhuman Caliban, at least in discipline. He offers an interesting sidelight on one of the play's themes, the relative merits of civilized and natural humanity; in his drunken foolishness, Stephano demonstrates the potential for evil inherent in civilization's pleasures.

Nevertheless, Stephano is basically a comic villain, contrasting with the more seriously evil Antonio in the play's network of comparisons. When he is finally punished, Stephano is reduced to punning on his name, Neapolitan slang for "belly," by saying, "I am not Stephano, but a cramp." (5.1.286). This jest has seemed to some scholars to confirm speculation that Shakespeare found inspiration for *The Tempest* in Italian COMMEDIA DELL'ARTE scenarios, while others point to the appropriate definition of "stefano" in John FLORIO's Italian-English dictionary, *A Worlde of Wordes* (1598).

Trinculo Character in *The Tempest*, a jester to King Alonso of Naples and a follower of Stephano and Caliban in their plot to kill Prospero. Trinculo is a buffoon, drunk most of the time, and alternately servile and presumptuous. He is ridiculously terrified of the weather when he first appears in 2.2 and is a butt for humor when Stephano sides with Caliban against him in 3.2, especially when the invisible Ariel imitates his voice and makes him seem argumentative when he is in fact entirely docile. In 4.1 Trinculo is comically obsequious toward Stephano, in a parody of the relationship between courtier and king. When the trio of would-be assassins is finally punished, Trinculo can only observe ruefully, "I have been in such a pickle . . . that, I fear me, will never out of my bones" (5.1.282–283).

Trinculo is less vicious than Stephano; he is a follower in a conspiracy he could not have conceived himself. Stephano and Trinculo are thus, respectively, like Antonio and Sebastian, within the play's various parallels and oppositions. As a professional jester, Trinculo is technically a FOOL, but in his buffoonery, his cowardice, and his lack of conscious irony, he more nearly resembles the rustic CLOWN.

Timon of Athens
SYNOPSIS

Act 1, Scene 1
In ATHENS a Poet, a Painter, a Jeweller, and a Merchant expect payment from the generous nobleman, Timon, for their efforts to please him. Timon arrives and promises a Messenger that he will pay the debts of Ventidius, which will free him from prison. He promises a fortune to his servant Lucilius so that he may marry the daughter of an aristocratic Old Athenian. The philosopher Apemantus appears, and the company prepares to be insulted by his heavy wit. Indulged by Timon, Apemantus denounces each of them as a dishonest flatterer. Alcibiades arrives, and Timon invites them all to dinner.

Act 1, Scene 2
At Timon's great banquet, Ventidius, whose father has left him a fortune, offers to repay Timon the money he had lent him, but Timon refuses to accept it. Apemantus criticizes Timon's greedy followers who consume his banquet, but Timon praises them for the help he knows they would give if it were needed. A MASQUE is performed, and Apemantus rages against the vanity of such things. Timon offers expensive gifts to his guests. His Steward worries that such generosity has put Timon deep in debt. Apemantus refuses to seek gifts from Timon because it would be sinful to encourage the nobleman's fondness for flattery.

Act 2, Scene 1
A Senator who knows of Timon's excessive generosity decides to send his servant, Caphis, to collect the debt Timon owes him before it is too late.

Act 2, Scene 2
Caphis, Varro's Servant, and Isidore's Servant accost Timon when they arrive to collect debts from him. He is astonished, and his Steward has to point out that he has refused to oversee his accounts despite all urging, and that now the debts caused by his generosity cannot be paid because even his lands are already mortgaged. Hoping to borrow money from his friends, Timon sends Flaminius, Servilius, another Servant, and the Steward to Lucius, Lucullus, Sempronius, and Ventidius, respectively.

Act 3, Scene 1
Lucullus refuses to lend money to Timon and offers to bribe Flaminius if he will say he could not find him to request the loan. Flaminius curses him.

Act 3, Scene 2
Lucius hears of Lucullus's behavior and swears that he would have loaned Timon the money, but when Servilius arrives to ask him for a loan, he refuses and claims to have no funds available. Two Strangers and Hostilius witness this and marvel at such ingratitude.

Act 3, Scene 3
Timon's Servant tells Sempronius that his master's other friends have refused to lend money, whereupon Sempronius claims to be offended that he was not asked first and therefore refuses to help.

Act 3, Scene 4
Lucius' Servant meets Titus, Hortensius, Philotus, and the Servants of Varro, all of whom hope to collect money from Timon. They regret the thanklessness of their masters, who have benefited by

Timon's generosity and now will not forgive him his debts. Timon appears in a rage and insists that they will have to cut up his body as payment; the servants realize they will get no money, and they leave. Timon tells the Steward to send out messages to all of his friends inviting them to an immense banquet.

Act 3, Scene 5

Alcibiades seeks mercy from the Senators for a friend who has killed someone in a fight. They refuse, but he continues to argue, and claims that his friend should be spared because he has served as a soldier. Offended that he will not accept their decision, the Senators banish Alcibiades from Athens. He vows to take revenge on the city with his army.

Act 3, Scene 6

Timon's friends assemble at the banquet and make excuses for not having assisted him. They hope to receive expensive gifts, as before. Timon formally curses the guests and drives them away.

Act 4, Scene 1

As he leaves Athens, Timon maliciously wishes evil on all elements of society.

Act 4, Scene 2

Timon's Steward and several of his former Servants part sorrowfully. The Steward soliloquizes on the pointlessness of wealth and the foolishness of man. He vows to find Timon and to continue serving him.

Act 4, Scene 3

Timon, alone in the wilderness, denounces humanity. As he digs for roots, he finds gold. He curses it as a great evil and decides to distribute it and thereby destroy society. Alcibiades appears with his concubines Phrynia and Timandra. Timon rejects Alcibiades's offer of friendship but is pleased to hear of his plan to conquer Athens, and he urges him to be brutal. Alcibiades departs, and Apemantus arrives. He offers food, but Timon refuses it with curses, and Apemantus observes that Timon is as extreme in his disgust as he once was in his generosity. The two misanthropes remark on the faults of humanity and then fall into an exchange of insults. As Apemantus leaves, a group of thieves arrives. Timon sarcastically praises them for taking

what they want and compares them with thieves who purport to be good citizens. He gives each Bandit gold. They leave as the Steward arrives. His compassion moves Timon to relent and concede that one honest man lives, but he refuses to be served by him and drives him away.

Act 5, Scene 1

The Poet and the Painter have heard that Timon has gold, and they seek him in the woods. They intend to promise him great works so that he will give them gifts. Timon overhears their plans and pretends to trust them. He gives them gold as he denounces them and drives them away. Two Senators arrive and ask for Timon's help against Alcibiades. They offer to restore his wealth if he will return to Athens. He refuses and grimly delights in the atrocities he anticipates Alcibiades will visit on the city. He advises Athenians to hang themselves, and declares that he will leave a gravestone with further advice.

Act 5, Scene 2

Some Senators hear of Alcibiades's approach with a large army and then of Timon's refusal of support.

Act 5, Scene 3

As he seeks Timon with a message from Alcibiades, a Soldier finds a bitter note that announces Timon's death. He also sees a gravestone inscribed in a language he cannot read. He makes a copy of it to take to Alcibiades.

Act 5, Scene 4

A delegation of Senators seeks mercy from Alcibiades, and he promises that he will take revenge only on the few people who had offended him. The Soldier arrives with the gravestone text, which restates Timon's hatred of humanity. Alcibiades mourns for his friend's state of mind at death as he enters the city and vows to make a lasting peace in Athens.

COMMENTARY

Timon of Athens, possibly a collaboration and almost certainly unfinished, is an experimental and ambiguous play—so much so, in fact, that this bleak picture of misanthropy is sometimes classed as a COMEDY by editors and commentators. Though its presentation of a grand figure whose downfall results from his own shortcomings is chiefly tragic, *Timon* is also like a comedy in its final statement of reconciliation and in its considerable dose of social satire. In his attempt to combine such different themes, Shakespeare was continuing a line of experiments that included the PROBLEM PLAYS and was to culminate in the ROMANCES. *Timon* is an important step in this development, though its own contradictions remain unresolved.

The play reflects a 17th-century enthusiasm for social satire. Its crass Athenian money-grubbers, who coolly resort to preposterous excuses when they refuse to return Timon's generosity, resemble the Londoners of Ben JONSON's more overtly satirical comedies. Shakespeare's Athenians are very bitterly drawn—Alcibiades illustrates the play's tone when he solemnly calls the city a "coward and lascivious town" (5.4.1). The critique of Timon's false friends is often straightforward and uncompromising, as in the First Stranger's remarks in 3.2, but sharp comedy is nonetheless present.

In particular, Apemantus's speeches are full of crude jokes, as when he counters the insult, "Y'are a dog" with "Thy mother's of my generation" (1.1.200–201). Though the level of his humor is low, he is a typical ill-tempered buffoon of the 17th-century stage and is clearly intended as a comic figure. In fact, Apemantus's viciousness is often so exaggerated that it is comical in itself, which is characteristic of *Timon*, for the play's humor resides more in its situations than in its dialogue. Apemantus closely resembles Shakespeare's Thersites, of *Troilus and Cressida*. In Act 3 the sequence of hypocritical excuses offered by Timon's supposed friends as they refuse him assistance is amusing; we appreciate these men as comic misers. Timon's story was well known in Shakespeare's time, and he knew his audience would gleefully anticipate the absurd refusals of these familiar character types. Timon's mock banquet in 3.6 is likewise comic in its use of surprises anticipated by the audience but not by the guests. The hypocrisy of his miserly friends as they make excuses to each other for being unable to help their host—though they can find time to dine with him—is broadly humorous. Even in the midst of Timon's grimly inhuman transformation in Act 4, we see humor when Phrynia and Timandra

encourage gross insults about themselves, so long as those insults are accompanied by gold. This behavior was traditionally associated with a comic stage figure, the greedy whore.

Timon's humorous aspects serve a serious purpose, and Shakespeare emphasized this by fashioning the drama to resemble the medieval MORALITY PLAY, which was intended to educate by combining moral lessons with vibrant, often comical entertainment. Because of this resemblance, *Timon* would have reminded 17th-century audiences that such a lesson was being offered. Following the morality tradition closely, *Timon* presents a hero who is totally involved in the material world and only realizes its deficiencies when he encounters catastrophe and is rejected by his materialistic friends. Also like a morality, the play features many allegorical characters who symbolize particular vices and virtues. Timon symbolizes two: ideal friendship at first and misanthropy later. It is even thought that the most famous morality play, *Everyman*, may have particularly influenced the creation of *Timon*. However, in contrast with morality plays—a contrast much more obvious in the 17th century than it is today—*Timon* does not end with the hero's triumphant return to a proper appreciation of spiritual values, but rather with his decline into despair and a miserable death.

Timon can also be classed as a comedy because it culminates in a spirit of reconciliation. The traditional comedy ended in a spirit of wholesale reconciliation usually represented by a marriage, for, like the morality play, it was intended to impart a sense of moral worth. Though *Timon* contains no hint of romantic love, it does nevertheless end in reconciliation and is therefore comedic in this most basic sense. With Alcibiades's ultimate rejection of vengeance when he declares he will "use the olive with my sword, / Make war breed peace, make peace stint war" (5.4.82–83), the play offers a final contrast with Timon's story. Alcibiades's response to the cold ingratitude of Athens is to take action in the real world rather than to dwell in helpless rancor. All along, this response inspires our sympathy more than Timon's monstrous misanthropy, and Alcibiades's story culminates on a fittingly positive note. Timon's decline has ended tragically, but the playwright gives us a final statement that demonstrates the play's ultimate theme: the greater importance of mercy as opposed to justice.

Nevertheless, *Timon* is also distinctly tragic. The protagonist is elevated above his fellow Athenians by his conspicuous kindness and generosity, and he comes to his downfall through the same traits. We are made aware of the fateful vulnerability of human existence, as we are in such greater tragedies as *King Lear* and *Othello*. However, unlike in *King Lear*, with which *Timon* is commonly compared, compassion is seemingly defeated, as Timon rejects the efforts of the loyal Steward to offer comfort and turns instead to brooding exile. Alcibiades's reconciliation at the play's close comes too late for Timon. Like Coriolanus, Timon insists on a world of moral absolutes—he prides himself first on his ideal generosity and then on his extreme bitterness—and he is unable to accept that moral absolutes are not reliable guides to social behavior. He is isolated from the realities of the world, and his retreat into misanthropy is a psychologically plausible response to his disillusion—from one extreme, he can only leap to another. His moral sensibility is arguably noble in that it is superior to ordinary life, but this is also his tragic failing, for he cannot understand the practicality and compromise on which social behavior rests.

Significantly, it is a Senator, one of the governors of Athens, who first decides to call in Timon's debts, in 2.1, for the role of the state in *Timon* is crucial. In 3.5 the Senators banish Alcibiades when he seeks mercy for a deserving veteran. Here they demonstrate a basic failing, a legalistic and uncharitable demand for absolute obedience. In this absoluteness they parallel Timon; also, their ingratitude to the veteran is like the ingratitude that they (and others) show to Timon. Later, their hypocrisy when they attempt to recruit Timon to help defend the city against Alcibiades reminds us of the Lords who flock to Timon's banquet in 3.6 after they have refused to help him. Thus, the evils of the play's world are summed up in the behavior of its leaders. This is highly important, for the callousness of the Senators and the other aristocrats produces a potential civic disaster—Alcibiades's threatened sack of the city—and thus demonstrates one of

Shakespeare's favorite lessons: the immorality of a ruling class leads to catastrophe for the society as a whole. This theme is central both to the comedic tale of Alcibiades's exile and return, and to the tragic story of Timon's psychological collapse.

Like the problem plays, *Timon* addresses public issues with a disconcerting combination of humor and villainy. With its tragicomic mingling of themes, combined with its seemingly old-fashioned allegorical quality and the startling bitterness of its main plot, *Timon* was definitely an experimental play. For centuries, commentators have generally felt that the experiment was a failure, despite the play's many fine moments. (However, 20th-century readers tend to find its ambiguities—often the focus of earlier criticism—more intriguing than faulty.) Because it is centered on a character whose shallowness is evident both before and after his catastrophe, the play does not achieve the grandeur of the great Shakespearean tragedies. Timon's madness is not resolved through any final self-awareness, as in the cases of the other tragic heroes. A lesser figure, Alcibiades, provides the reconciliation at the end, and though his mercy extends to the "faults forgiven" of "noble Timon" (5.4.79, 80), Timon himself is excluded from it. Finally, the excesses that define Timon—his belief first that humanity is worthy of ideal friendship and then that it is only capable of evil—prevent him from having any meaningful interaction with his fellow human beings, to the detriment of the play. The hero is initially aloof, and when brought low, his response is essentially withdrawal rather than opposition; such a moral and psychological progression is perhaps better illuminated in an essay or novel than on the stage.

Shakespeare presumably shared such misgivings, for it seems probable that he abandoned the play before it was complete (see "Text of the Play"). However, the experiment was not wasted, for *Timon* marks a stage in the evolution of the playwright's work. The romances, soon to come, treat the same themes—exile and return, the deficiency of moral absoluteness, the transcendent value of mercy—and they do so in a fashion that may reflect lessons learned from *Timon*. The inhuman response of an aggrieved protagonist is no longer the dominant element in the plot; instead, attention centers on the innocent victims of such inhumanity, who typically are driven to the exile that Timon chooses for himself. Even so, the exile is not the crucial phenomenon that it is in *Timon*. In the romances, Shakespeare expands his concerns and explores communal attitudes with a focus on many characters. The somewhat esoteric, allegorical figures of *Timon* evolve into the symbolic yet lifelike caricatures of injured innocence and vague, impersonal villainy that animate the later plays. Moreover, the effect of change on behavior, an imperfectly developed aspect of *Timon*, becomes increasingly important, for the world of the last plays is powerfully charged with changeability.

The Tempest is a partial exception to some of these ideas, but it is there, in Shakespeare's final triumph, that a theme from *Timon of Athens* is displayed most spectacularly. In *Timon*, the humane and conciliatory attitude of Alcibiades is presented late in the play and only modestly developed, while in the later play the theme he represents—conciliation and forgiveness as necessary elements in human interactions—is central to the work from the outset. Thus, this flawed work retains its interest—aside from its many fine passages and strong theatrical presence—as an excellent demonstration of Shakespeare's continued growth as a playwright late in his career.

SOURCES OF THE PLAY

Shakespeare (and possibly his collaborators) employed several sources in writing *Timon of Athens*. Numerous elements of the plot come from a Greek comic dialogue of the second century A.D., *Timon the Misanthrope*, by LUCIAN. While Shakespeare may have known this work in Latin, French, or Italian translation, no English version existed in his day. He may merely have been told of its features, for actual echoes of Lucian in the play are obscure, if present at all.

Alternatively, he may have used another source based on Lucian, the so-called old *Timon*, an anonymous English play of uncertain date (ca. 1580–1610). This work, which has survived in manuscript, contains material that is found only in itself and the later *Timon*—such as the mock banquet of 3.6 (which may not have been written by

Shakespeare)—and thus it appears to be a source. However, it may be *later* than Shakespeare's *Timon* and is in any case very different, being a farce. Scholars think that if it is earlier than Shakespeare's play, both works are based on a yet earlier work, now lost, derived from Lucian.

The authors certainly knew Timon's story from the "Life of Marcus Antonius" in Thomas NORTH's translation of PLUTARCH's *Lives* (1579), the chief source for *Antony and Cleopatra*. Mark Antony after losing the battle of ACTIUM is compared to the famous Athenian misanthrope, whose story is briefly recounted. Some details appear in *Timon*. Plutarch's "Life of Alcibiades," though it contains nothing specifically reflected in *Timon*, may have provided some ideas for that character as well. Also, many of the incongruously Latin names of *Timon*'s Athenians come from elsewhere in Plutarch. Lastly, Shakespeare may have taken minor elements from another version of Timon's story, that in *Palace of Pleasure* (1566) by William PAINTER.

Another possible source for some details and perhaps an overall concept is the morality play *Everyman* (ca. 1500). This work contains passages that correspond to the introductory observations on prodigality by the Poet, in 1.1.53–90, and to the triple rejection of Timon by his friends in 3.1–3. Also, *Timon* reflects the morality play's overall theme of a representative sinner who is urged to reform by various figures that correspond to Apemantus, the Steward, and Alcibiades, with the important difference that in *Everyman* the hero does reform, while Timon dies in despair. This was perhaps intended as a purposeful contrast, for the morality play model was extremely familiar to Shakespeare's audience.

TEXT OF THE PLAY

The many flaws of *Timon*—irregularities of verse, confusion as to the names of many minor characters, the presence of a GHOST CHARACTER, and so on—inspire the hypothesis that the play was written collaboratively. Many possible coauthors have been suggested—including George CHAPMAN, John DAY, and George WILKINS—but scholars have generally come to the conclusion that Thomas MIDDLETON wrote parts of *Timon*, probably Scene 1.2 and

Act 3. These episodes focus on the treacherous behavior of Timon's debtors but also feature striking speeches by Apemantus and Alcibiades. Others believe that Shakespeare may have rewritten parts of a play originally by Middleton. Whether sole author or not, Shakespeare seems certainly to have written most of the play as it exists and to have been responsible for the presentation of its central themes. The matter cannot be ascertained with certainty, but in any case, scholarly opinion unites in observing that the play is incomplete. Its difficulties are evidence that no one fixed up anyone else's text: the play is not fixed. In fact, among the play's fascinations are a number of passages in which we can see Shakespeare's drafts for BLANK VERSE, with many lines still metrically irregular but carrying their information (e.g., 1.2.190–202). Shakespeare had not yet polished this work to his usual standards when he stopped working on it.

Just when he did so cannot be determined at all precisely, but scholars assign *Timon* to ca. 1606–08. It contains no datable references to the real world, and there are no surviving references to it prior to its publication, which came after Shakespeare's death. However, its stylistic and thematic similarities with the later tragedies favor the idea that it was written around the same time as those works. The common source with *Antony and Cleopatra* (1606–08) seems to narrow the date still further.

Timon was first published in the FIRST FOLIO (1623). The varied speech headings and obviously literary stage directions make it clear that the text was taken from FOUL PAPERS, perhaps as transcribed for the purpose. As the only early text, the First Folio's *Timon* has been the basis for all subsequent editions.

THEATRICAL HISTORY OF THE PLAY

No record of any early performance of *Timon* has survived, and since the play seems unfinished, it was probably never staged in Shakespeare's day. It has indeed been very infrequently performed in any period and has always been one of the least popular of Shakespeare's plays. Thomas SHADWELL presented an adaptation, *Timon of Athens the Man-Hater* (1678), that incorporated a love interest and made other great changes. This production, in

which Thomas BETTERTON played Timon, was reasonably popular and was restaged several times until 1745. At different times, Barton BOOTH played both Alcibiades and Timon in this version, and James QUIN was a notable Apemantus. It is believed that Shakespeare's text was staged in Dublin in 1761, though little is known of this production. Unsuccessful adaptations that combined Shadwell and Shakespeare and new material in various proportions were produced by James DANCE, Richard CUMBERLAND, and Thomas HULL, in 1768, 1771, and 1786, respectively.

Another version, close to Shakespeare's play but incorporating some of Cumberland's text, was devised by George LAMB and produced in 1816 by Edmund KEAN, who was acclaimed in the title role. The original Shakespearean text was not finally staged until 1851—its earliest known production in England—by Samuel PHELPS, who likewise triumphed as Timon. This extremely popular presentation was revived in 1856. In 1892 F. R. BENSON offered a three-act version at the SADLER'S WELLS THEATRE.

The play has continued to be unpopular, and it was performed only rarely in the 20th century. Perhaps the best-known production starred Ralph RICHARDSON as Timon at the OLD VIC THEATRE in 1956. In 1974 Peter BROOK directed a French production noted for its severely plain staging in a physically decaying theater building in a working-class district of Paris. *Timon* has never been a movie and has only been produced for TELEVISION once, by Jonathan MILLER in 1981, as part of the British Broadcasting Corporation's complete cycle of Shakespeare plays.

CHARACTERS

Alcibiades (ca. 450–404 B.C.)   Historical figure and character in *Timon of Athens,* an Athenian general and friend of Timon. Alcibiades is faithful to Timon in adversity and thereby counteracts the play's theme of false friendship. He is most significant as the central figure in a parallel plot in which he is pitted against the coldhearted, legalistic aristocracy of ATHENS. Like Timon he is the subject of ingratitude and a heartless application of the system and its laws. However, Alcibiades takes action and avenges himself. Thus he is placed in sharp contrast with Timon and his passive withdrawal into misanthropy and madness. Then, at the play's close, his humane nature permits a reconciliation, an ending that offers the central lesson of the play: the superiority of mercy over justice in human affairs.

Unlike Timon, Alcibiades realizes that good can exist in a world that is evil, and that mercy is a greater corrective for society than revenge. In his final tribute to "noble Timon" (5.4.80), Alcibiades extends his mercy to the misanthrope himself. Though Timon, as a suicide, cannot participate in the play's ultimate spirit of reconciliation, his extreme hatred is forgiven and finally countered.

For the first half of the play, Alcibiades is clearly an honest friend amidst a group of obviously insincere and hypocritical courtiers that surround Timon, but he is a minor figure. He assumes importance in 3.5, the pivotal scene of the play, when he pleads with the Athenian rulers for mercy on behalf of a veteran soldier sentenced to death for murder. Alcibiades argues that "pity is the virtue of the law" (3.5.8). This reflects a central concern not only of the play but of Shakespearean drama in general. Banished from Athens because he has questioned authority, he promises revenge, and in 5.1 he threatens to sack the city. Thus, he is clearly in opposition to callous ingratitude while at the same time he threatens disaster for the entire city. Such a catastrophe—though here only potential—demonstrates how immoral behavior among the ruling class leads to trouble for the entire society, a lesson Shakespeare repeatedly offered in the HISTORY PLAYS, the ROMAN PLAYS, and elsewhere. Alcibiades is both opponent and savior for the "coward and lascivious" Athens (5.4.1).

Alcibiades is the only character in *Timon of Athens* who is at all fleshed out. He prefers his profession, soldiering, to the banquets of Timon's world, and his controlled anger in his encounter with the Senate is impressive. He knows himself—"I speak like a captain," he says (3.5.42)—and he can plead for a friend. He also understands the self-exiled Timon—as Timon himself cannot—and sees that "his wits / Are drown'd and lost in his calamities" (4.3.89–90). In these respects Alcibiades seems somewhat at odds with the rest of the play, which relies heavily on the bold symbolism of allegorical characters. Perhaps this unresolvable contrast contributed to Shakespeare's decision to leave *Timon* unfinished.

The fascinating career of the historical Alcibiades is only faintly reflected in Shakespeare's character. Alcibiades was a brilliant though unstable young aristocrat who led an ostentatiously decadent life but nevertheless became an influential general and leading politician. However, despite his political power, he faced banishment for his part in a sacrilegious mutilation of icons. He fled to avoid trial and joined Athens's enemies, the Spartans. They mistrusted him and he moved on and joined their allies, the Persians, whom he tried to win to an alliance with Athens. From exile he maintained contact with the turbulent Athenian political world and was thus able to assume command of the Athenian fleet over the government's objections.

Shakespeare's source, PLUTARCH's *Lives*, states that Alcibiades refused the navy's demand that he attack the city; this is the germ of Shakespeare's account. Actually, though on his return Alcibiades was supported by a revolutionary government that arose in Athens at that time, there was no question of his attacking the city. He fought the Spartans and Persians with such success that the Athenians gave him total command of the armed forces. However, a minor loss permitted his enemies to revive popular resentment against him, and he again left Athens and took refuge with Spartan allies in Phrygia. There he was murdered by agents of conservative Athenians who had returned to power and made peace with Sparta. Alcibiades was a byword for treachery in the ancient world, though it was also recognized that the Athenians were foolish to follow political loyalties and discard a military genius when they most needed him.

Apemantus Character in *Timon of Athens*, an angry, misanthropic philosopher. Apemantus's vulgar insults and remarks offer a strong critique of both the gullible Timon and the Athenians who sponge off him. In this he resembles a Chorus, and he provides a running commentary on the action of the main plot. Like such similar figures as Jaques and Thersites (in *As You Like It* and *Troilus and*

Cressida, respectively), Apemantus is distinctly unlikable. This quality ensures his isolation from the other characters and thus assures audiences that his observations are impartial. His cynical attitude, condemned by various characters, proves to be the one adopted by Timon himself in the end. Apemantus disappears after 2.2 and returns in 4.3 to exchange insults with Timon once the former nobleman has retreated to a life of rage and despair in the woods near ATHENS. Though unlikable, Apemantus still has right on his side, and when he tells Timon, "the middle of humanity thou never knewest, but the extremity of both ends" (4.3.301–302), he pinpoints the major defect in Timon's personality. Apemantus refuses to alter his opinions or personality to suit the circumstances of his patron, and this gives him great moral stature compared with Timon's false friends. When this is combined with the honesty of his insults, Apemantus counteracts the play's atmosphere of bleak despair. He helps makes it clear that Timon's misanthropic attitude is not that of the play or the playwright.

Bandit (Thief)   Any of three minor characters in *Timon of Athens*, thieves who hope to rob Timon. In 4.3 after Timon has withdrawn from ATHENS to the woods in rage and despair because he has been abandoned by his friends, the Bandits learn that he has found gold and they accost him. They don't know that he intends to give it away in an attempt to corrupt hateful humanity. He ironically praises them for being obvious thieves and compares them to those who pretend to be good citizens. He gives them gold and encourages them to commit more crimes. "Cut throats. / All that you meet are thieves. To Athens go . . ." (4.3.448–449), he says. As they leave, the Bandits remark on Timon's misanthropy. Two of the three contemplate giving up thievery since it is advocated by so malicious a man. As the Third Bandit puts it, "H'as almost charm'd me from my profession, by persuading me to it" (4.3.453–454). Collectively called "banditti" in the stage direction that introduces them, at 4.3.401, the Bandits are designated as Thieves in many editions.

Caphis   Minor character in *Timon of Athens*, servant of a Senator. In 2.1 the Senator sends Caphis

to collect a debt from Timon, who he fears will soon be bankrupt. The servant barely speaks and serves simply as a vehicle for the Senator's greed. In 2.2 he joins other servants in asking Timon for payment on their masters' behalf.

Cupid   In *Timon of Athens* the name taken by a Lady who leads the MASQUE in 1.2. Her disguise as the Roman god of love demonstrates both the fashionable neoclassicism of such aristocratic entertainments and the slightly lascivious quality that enlivened many of them.

Flaminius   Minor character in *Timon of Athens*, a servant of Timon. In 2.2 Flaminius is told to ask Lord Lucullus for a loan to assist his master, whose extravagant generosity—to Lucullus, among others—has led him to bankruptcy. However, in 3.1 Lucullus refuses and tries to hide his ingratitude by bribing Flaminius to say he could not be found, but the loyal servant is outraged and flings the offered coins at Lucullus. He follows this gesture with a heated condemnation that helps emphasize one of the play's major themes: the appalling ingratitude of the Athenian aristocracy. Flaminius's major function is to further the unfolding of Timon's abandonment by his friends.

Fool   Minor character in *Timon of Athens*, a professional jester. This FOOL accompanies Apemantus in 2.2 and exchanges witticisms with Varro's Servant and others. He is apparently employed by a courtesan who is the subject of two jests about venereal disease, but his circumstances and qualities are not developed. His major speech (2.2.112–118) contains a pithy condemnation of ATHENS, which furthers an important theme of the play. However, most commentators believe that he may represent a false start for the playwright, who introduced him with the intention of developing a SUBPLOT around him and then did not do so before he abandoned this incomplete play.

Hortensius   Minor character in *Timon of Athens*, the servant to a creditor of Timon. In 3.4 Hortensius and other servants unsuccessfully dun Timon and his Steward for payment. The servants regret their assignment, for their greedy masters have benefited from Timon's generosity. Hortensius is especially vocal, and he says, "I know my lord hath spent of Timon's wealth, / And now ingratitude makes it worse than stealth" (3.4.27–28). He thus stresses one of the play's important themes, the callousness of the aristocracy of ATHENS.

Hortensius appears with Titus, Philotus, Lucius's Servant, and two men who are each designated as Varro's Servant. Since the latter three are addressed as "Lucius" and "Varro" (3.4.2, 3), it is assumed that Shakespeare intended the names of the first three to refer to their masters as well, perhaps reflecting a casual linguistic practice of the early 17th century.

Hostilius (Second Stranger)   Minor character in *Timon of Athens*, a visitor to ATHENS. With his companions, the First and Second Strangers, Hostilius witnesses the callous rejection of Timon's request for assistance by the miserly Lucius, in 3.2. Lucius has just insisted to Hostilius that he would always help his generous former patron. Like his friends, Hostilius represents a detached judgment on the selfish citizens of Athens—the First Stranger explicitly makes the case. This is an episode of a type familiar from the medieval MORALITY PLAY that serves to fix the play's moral point of view. In some editions Hostilius, who is named in 3.2.64, is designated as the Second Stranger.

Isidore's Servant   Minor character in *Timon of Athens*, an employee of Isidore, a creditor of Timon. In 2.2 Isidore's Servant, with Caphis and Varro's Servant, solicits Timon and his Steward for payment of debts, but they are put off. These servants of greedy masters are pawns of plot development; Isidore's Servant speaks even less than the others.

Jeweller   Minor character in *Timon of Athens*, a flatterer of Timon. As the play opens, the Jeweller proposes to sell a jewel to Timon, confident that the nobleman will pay a good price. Later in 1.1 he flatters his potential client. The Jeweller is simply a representative greedy flatterer.

Lady   Any of several minor characters in *Timon of Athens*, presenters of a MASQUE at Timon's banquet.

In 1.2 the Ladies, led by one who is disguised as Cupid, perform a masque and dance with Timon's guests. They present an elaborate aristocratic entertainment that suggests Timon's extravagant lifestyle. Lucullus's fatuous remark to Timon that the masque demonstrates "how ample y'are belov'd" (1.2.126) suggests further that the Ladies are among the many spongers off Timon's hospitality.

Lord   Any of several minor characters in *Timon of Athens*, flatterers of Timon. In 1.1 two Lords—designated First and Second Lords but indistinguishable from one another—are criticized by Apemantus as dishonest flatterers whose intent is to profit from Timon's generosity. As soon as he departs, the Lords laugh over their good fortune in knowing Timon, and it is clear that Apemantus's judgment was correct. In 1.2 a Third Lord joins them, and their flattery is again mocked by Apemantus; all are rewarded with expensive gifts. In 3.6 four Lords gather to receive more bounty, even after they have given patently self-serving excuses why they cannot make loans to the newly impoverished Timon. However, Timon curses them and throws them out, and we see no more of them. The Lords have one personality trait between them: They are greedy hypocrites. They talk about their generosity but are actually misers. Some commentators have identified these characters with Timon's faithless friends, Lucius, Lucullus, Sempronius, and Ventidius.

Lucilius   Minor character in *Timon of Athens*, a servant of Timon. When an Old Athenian complains to Timon that the socially inferior Lucilius is courting his daughter, Timon promises Lucilius a fortune and thus makes him acceptable. The episode helps establish Timon's generosity and extravagance. Lucilius speaks very little and serves merely to further the plot.

Lucius   Character in *Timon of Athens*, an ungrateful friend of Timon. In 3.2 Lucius hears that Lucullus has refused to assist Timon with a loan after Timon has impoverished himself by showering gifts on his friends. Like Lucullus, Lucius is also the beneficiary of Timon's excessive generosity, and he proudly declares to Hostilius and two Strangers that he would never turn away a friend. However, when Timon's servant Servilius appears and asks for help, Lucius brazenly declares that he cannot make a loan. The hypocritical Lucius helps demonstrate—with Lucullus and Sempronius—the callousness of the Athenian aristocrats, one of the play's important themes.

Lucius' Servant Minor character in *Timon of Athens*, the employee of Lucius, a former friend and creditor of Timon. In 3.4 Lucius' Servant joins a group of colleagues who unsuccessfully dun Timon and his Steward for repayment of loans. He and his fellows regret the necessity of serving greedy masters who once benefited from Timon's generosity. However, Lucius' Servant is somewhat more aggressive in demanding payment. He observes that Timon's has been a "prodigal course" (3.4.12), and rejects an excuse of ill health, offered by Timon's servant, when he says, "Methinks he should the sooner pay his debts / And make a clear way to the gods" (3.4.74–75). He thus reflects the atrocious behavior of his master, who in 3.2 hypocritically refuses to assist the impoverished Timon after he has declared that he would help a friend in need.

Lucullus Character in *Timon of Athens*, an ungrateful friend of Timon. In 1.2 Lucullus is among the guests at Timon's banquet. In 2.2, when Timon finds that his extravagant hospitality has bankrupted him, Lucullus is among those he assumes he can count on for assistance. However, when Lucullus is approached by Timon's servant Flaminius for a loan, he declares that he had warned his friend. With unconscious irony, he says, "Many a time and often I ha' din'd with him, and . . . come again to supper to him of purpose to have him spend less" (3.1.23–25). He sums up his position when he observes that "this is no time to lend money, especially upon bare friendship, without security" (3.1.41–43). He then tries to hide his ingratitude by bribing Flaminius to say he could not be found. Like Lucius and Sempronius, whose similar responses occur in the next two scenes, Lucullus helps demonstrate the heartlessness of the Athenian aristocrats, one of the play's important themes.

Mercer GHOST CHARACTER in *Timon of Athens*. The Mercer is listed in the opening stage direction of 1.1, but he does not appear. Shakespeare apparently listed a number of characters he thought he would make use of in the course of writing the scene, and then when he did not in fact employ a mercer, he did not bother to delete the reference. Many such minor inconsistencies are found in the plays; *Timon*, as an unfinished play, is naturally subject to them.

Merchant Minor character in *Timon of Athens*, a flatterer of Timon. In 1.1 the Merchant and his friend the Jeweller discuss Timon's free-spending nature and intend to profit from it. The Merchant speaks little and serves chiefly as a sounding board for his colleague. Both of them are representative greedy flatterers.

Messenger Any of several minor characters in *Timon of Athens*. In 1.1 two Messengers bring Timon news, first of the imprisonment for debt of Ventidius and later of the approach of Alcibiades. In 5.2 a Messenger reports on Alcibiades's march on Athens. These may well be different men—servants of Ventidius, Timon, and an anonymous Senator, respectively—but they are indistinguishable and serve to inform the audience of offstage events.

Old Athenian Minor character in *Timon of Athens*, a citizen of ATHENS. In 1.1 the Old Athenian asks the wealthy nobleman Timon to protect his daughter from the courtship of Timon's servant Lucilius, who is socially inferior to his intended bride. The magnanimous Timon solves the problem by providing Lucilius with enough money to be considered eligible. The episode helps establish Timon's extravagant generosity. The Old Athenian is a crude caricature of a social type; the snobbish minor gentleman willing to marry his daughter off for money.

Page Minor character in *Timon of Athens*, an illiterate messenger who asks Apemantus to read the addresses on letters he is to deliver. The Page is an employee of the same courtesan as the Fool and has no place in the play's plot. His brief appearance is sometimes taken as evidence of a non-Shakespearean hand in the composition of the play.

However, the episode closely resembles that of the illiterate Servant in *Romeo and Juliet*, and most scholars now conclude that the Page is Shakespeare's invention. He was probably part of a SUBPLOT that remained undeveloped when the playwright abandoned this incomplete play.

Painter Minor character in *Timon of Athens*, a flatterer of Timon. In 1.1 the Painter and his friend the Poet anticipate that they will profit from Timon's generosity when they present him with examples of their art. The Painter speaks much less than his friend but shares his pride and false modesty. He agrees with the Poet that though Timon is now prosperous, this can change, and the "quick blows of Fortune" (1.1.93) may reduce their host to poverty and friendlessness. Though the Painter is not among the disloyal friends depicted in Timon's downfall, he is not unlike them. In 5.1 he joins the Poet in an attempt to resume their approach to their onetime benefactor in the belief that his fortunes have again improved. "Therefore," says the Painter, "'tis not amiss we tender our loves to him" (5.1.12–13). He is unconcerned that he has never painted anything for Timon. He imagines that a promise of future work is as "Good as the best. Promising is the very air o' th' time . . . To promise is most courtly and fashionable" (5.1.22–27). However, Timon understands what they are up to, and he drives them away. The Painter, like his friend the Poet, is a satirical emblem of the greed and hypocrisy of courtiers.

Philotus Minor character in *Timon of Athens*, the employee of a usurer who duns Timon for payment of a loan. In 3.4 Philotus joins other servants when they approach Timon and his Steward for repayment, but they are put off. They regret that they must solicit for their greedy masters, who have benefited from Timon's generosity but are now merciless when he is in need.

Philotus appears with Hortensius, Titus, Lucius' Servant and two men designated as Varro's Servant. Since the latter three are addressed as "Lucius" and "Varro" (3.4.2, 3), it is assumed that Shakespeare intended the names of the first three to refer to their masters, as well. This may reflect a casual linguistic practice among servants of the 17th century.

Phrynia and Timandra Minor characters in *Timon of Athens*, concubines of Alcibiades. In 4.3 Phrynia and her colleague Timandra are traveling with Alcibiades and encounter Timon in the woods. They generally speak in unison and are entirely indistinguishable from each other. In his misanthropic fury, Timon has decided to corrupt humanity by distributing the gold he has found. He gives some to the courtesans and accompanies the gift with vicious insults. They laughingly encourage his abuse so long as it is accompanied by gold. This mildly humorous passage satirizes greed and also provides a slight respite from Timon's grim misanthropy. Both women represent a stock comic figure, the greedy whore.

Poet Minor character in *Timon of Athens*, a flatterer of Timon. In 1.1 the Poet and his friend the Painter discuss Timon's generosity, which each hopes to exploit when he presents the nobleman with an example of his art. Pompously self-satisfied, the Poet congratulates himself on being a poet from whom art "oozes" (1.1.21). He anticipates the play's truths when he tells that the poem he is writing, in which Timon is shown as a favorite of the goddess Fortune, contains the warning that when Fortune changes, her ex-favorites are abandoned by their seemingly loyal followers. Though the Poet is not mentioned in Timon's downfall, he is presumably among the deserters, for in 5.1 he and the Painter attempt to reingratiate themselves with him because they have heard that their onetime benefactor has found gold. Timon overhears him planning "what I shall say I have provided for him" (5.1.32), though in fact he has written no poems for him. When he and the Painter fawningly assure Timon of their friendship, he mocks them and drives them away. The Poet is an emblematic character, satirically representative of the greed and hypocrisy of courtiers.

Sempronius Minor character in *Timon of Athens*, an ungrateful friend of Timon. Sempronius is among the friends to whom Timon sends for assistance when he faces bankruptcy after he has showered his friends—including Sempronius—with expensive gifts. However, when Sempronius is approached by one of Timon's Servants, he pretends to be offended that Timon has gone to other friends first, and he refuses to lend him money. "Who bates mine honour shall not know my coin" (3.3.28), he declares. Sempronius—with Lucius and Lucullus, who have similarly rejected Timon's request in previous scenes—helps demonstrate the hypocrisy and coldheartedness of the Athenian aristocracy, one of the play's important themes.

Senator Any of several minor characters in *Timon of Athens*, the aristocratic legislators of ATHENS. The Senators benefit from Timon's hospitality, but in 2.1 a Senator begins the process of the protagonist's downfall. He recognizes that Timon is losing his wealth in reckless generosity, and he decides to dun his onetime benefactor for a debt before "Lord Timon will be left a naked gull" (2.1.31). The Senators' cold ingratitude is made vivid by Timon's Steward, who tells that they refused aid for his master "in a joint and corporate voice [and] . . . After distasteful looks . . . and cold-moving nods, / They froze me into silence" (2.2.208–217). In 3.5 this hardheartedness is displayed in a different way when the Senators refuse to accept Alcibiades's argument for mercy toward an honorable veteran. Instead they banish the pleader, who in response vows to conquer the city. In Act 5 the Senators unsuccessfully attempt to win back Timon as an ally against Alcibiades, and in 5.4 they are reduced to begging for mercy. The avenging general Alcibiades grants them mercy in the play's closing atmosphere of reconciliation. Thus, the Senators' callousness has informed both of the play's plot lines, and helps to demonstrate a favorite lesson of Shakespeare's plays: that the immorality of the ruling class can produce disorder and potential ruin for the society as a whole.

Servant Minor character in *Timon of Athens*, worker in the household of Lucullus. In 3.1 the Servant greets Flaminius, who has come from Timon to borrow money from Lucullus. Lucullus ignobly refuses to make the loan. The Servant, who brings

wine and speaks one line when he reappears, serves to indicate the affluent life of his miserly master.

Servants Several minor characters in *Timon of Athens*, workers in Timon's household. In 4.2 the Servants, under the Steward, remain faithful to Timon when his false friends desert him. Though they must leave the bankrupt household to find other work, they remain "fellows still, / Serving alike in sorrow" (4.2.18–19), as one of them puts it. In their loyalty they contrast tellingly with Timon's unfaithful aristocratic friends, and they emphasize one of the play's main themes: the callous heartlessness of ATHENS' ruling class. The Servants are mostly anonymous, though two of them, Flaminius and Servilius, are named in 2.2 and Act 3 and may be present in 4.2. Also, a Third Servant—as he is designated in the stage direction at 3.3.1—distinguishes himself with a scathing monologue criticizing the miserly hypocrite, Sempronius, in 3.3.29–43.

Servilius Minor character in *Timon of Athens*, a servant of Timon. In 2.2 Servilius is sent to ask Lord Lucius to assist Timon with a loan, but in 3.2 Lucius refuses, though he has benefited from the extravagant generosity that has created Timon's money troubles. The episode serves to demonstrate the miserly ingratitude of the Athenian aristocracy, an important theme of the play. Servilius, though he appears briefly elsewhere, simply serves to further the plot.

Soldier Minor character in *Timon of Athens*, a messenger for Alcibiades. In 5.3 the Soldier, sent with a message to Timon, discovers Timon's grave. Unable to read the inscription on it, he decides to copy it and bring it to Alcibiades. He does this in 5.4, and thus inspires the play's final passage, in which Alcibiades translates Timon's last statement and remarks on it.

Steward Character in *Timon of Athens*, the manager of Timon's household. The Steward cannot make Timon refrain from the extravagant generosity that finally bankrupts him, but he nevertheless remains loyal to his master when he loses all. In 4.2 the Steward leads Timon's employees as they regret their master's fate, and in 4.3 and 5.1 he visits his exiled master, who has withdrawn to the woods outside ATHENS. Timon is misanthropic in his mad despair, but he must make an exception for this faithful servant. He declares, "I do proclaim / One honest man," and adds, "How fain would I have hated all mankind" (4.3.500–501, 503). The Steward's virtue counters Timon's absolute hatred of humankind. The Steward is thus very important to the play, for it is through this character that Shakespeare most clearly demonstrates that Timon's bleak view of humanity is not the vision of the play. Like most of *Timon*'s characters, the Steward is not a complex human being, but is rather an emblematic figure who embodies the virtues of pity and loyalty.

Strangers   Two minor characters in *Timon of Athens*, visitors to ATHENS. In 3.2 the Strangers accompany Hostilius, who is also a visitor, and they witness the callousness of Lucius, who refuses to assist his former patron, Timon. The First Stranger's appalled remarks capture the play's condemnation of the heartless greed of Timon's faithless friends. "I never tasted Timon in my life," he says, "Yet I protest" (3.2.79, 81). Because he is detached, he assumes the position of a judge. He protests against "the monstrousness of man" (3.2.74), and declares "Men must learn now with pity to dispense, / For policy sits above conscience" (3.2.88–89). The Second Stranger speaks only half a line, but its quiet condemnation—"Religion groans at it" (3.2.78)—powerfully reinforces his companion's critique. The episode resembles scenes found in medieval MORALITY PLAYS. It stresses the play's moral point of view and also helps the audience recognize that *Timon*'s characters are at least as much didactic models as they are psychological types.

The Strangers are sometimes considered to be three in number. In the FIRST FOLIO text of the play and some other editions, Hostilius is designated as the Second Stranger, in which case the religious remark in 3.2.78 is given to a Third Stranger.

Timandra   See Phrynia and Timandra.

Timon   Title character of *Timon of Athens*, a benevolent nobleman of ATHENS who is abandoned by his false friends when he is bankrupted by his extravagant hospitality and gift giving. He then sinks into rage and despair. He withdraws to the wilderness, where he rages against humanity and dies in abject misery, an apparent suicide. He is the victim of his own excesses of both goodness and hatred.

Timon's excessive generosity is based in misplaced pride, for he attempts to embody an unrealistic ideal of friendship. When he refuses to be repaid for a debt, he says irrationally that "there's none / Can truly say he gives, if he receives" (1.2.10–11). This absoluteness is unhealthy, for it leaves no room for a sensitive and intelligent approach to life. Timon is blind and gullible, and he ignores the sound, if unpleasantly put, advice of Apemantus. When he is rejected by his so-called friends he assumes an extreme degree of misanthropy, a response that is excessive even given his great provocation. Timon assumes that all of humankind is greedy and dishonest, but this is clearly contradicted by the virtues of his own household, especially his Steward. He refuses to accept this evidence, however, and drives himself to a death as unnecessary as his financial losses were. At the play's close, the reconciliation effected by Alcibiades cements our awareness that Timon has tragically wasted his life.

Nevertheless, Timon is a noble figure, for he tries to live up to an ideal conception of humanity. Before his collapse he desires the finest in human relationships, and while this has the effect of insulating him from reality, it also exalts him. It is both symbolically and psychologically appropriate that when he becomes disillusioned, Timon succumbs to another excessive vision of humanity. Obsessive by nature, he can only go from one extreme to another. In both cases, the position he takes is grandiose, capable of inspiring awe along with dismay.

Like most of the characters in the play, Timon is not a fully fleshed-out human being. He is more like an allegorical figure, similar to those of the medieval MORALITY PLAY, a probable influence on Shakespeare's creation of this work. In fact, Timon assumes two such roles in the course of the play, first representing ideal friendship and then extreme despair. As a misanthrope, Timon had been a famous figure for many centuries before Shakespeare's time, but the playwright attempted to demonstrate the defects of the character both before and after his catastrophe, and thus make a profound moral statement of the sort presented in the morality plays. Although *Timon* is an unfinished play, we can still recognize in its title character the representation of a human truth: that we are susceptible to vain and prideful extremes of behavior.

Titus Minor character in *Timon of Athens*, the employee of a creditor of Timon. In 3.4 Titus and other servants dun Timon and his Steward for repayment of various loans, but they are put off. Titus introduces the theme of the episode when he observes that their masters, who solicit Timon for money, wear jewels that Timon had given them before he went bankrupt. The other servants join him, and together they regret that they must serve such greedy men, who were once the beneficiaries of Timon's generosity but are now his merciless creditors.

Titus appears with Hortensius, Philotus, Lucius' Servant and two men designated as Varro's Servant. Since the latter three are addressed as "Lucius" and "Varro" (3.4.2, 3), it is presumed that Shakespeare intended the names of the first three to refer to their masters as well. This perhaps reflects a casual linguistic practice of the early 17th century.

Varro's Servant Either of two minor characters in *Timon of Athens*, employees of Varro, a creditor of Timon. In 2.2 Varro's Servant joins two colleagues, Isidore's Servant and Caphis. Together they approach Timon and his Steward, hoping for repayment of the debts Timon owes their masters, but they are put off. In 3.4 two of Varro's servants—distinguished in speech headings as First Varro's Servant and Second Varro's Servant—join Lucius' Servant, Hortensius, Philotus, and Titus on the same errand, again without success. In the latter scene the Servants express their reluctance to solicit for their greedy masters who have benefited in the past from Timon's generosity but are now merciless.

Ventidius Minor character in *Timon of Athens*, an ungrateful recipient of Timon's generosity. In 1.1 Timon sends the money needed to free Ventidius

from debtor's prison, and in 1.2 Ventidius thanks him and offers to return the money, but Timon refuses repayment. Ventidius observes: "A noble spirit!" (1.2.14), and he does not speak again. However, when Timon has bankrupted himself through extravagant generosity, he sends to several friends for help, and Ventidius—who has in the meantime inherited a fortune—is among them. Act 3 begins with Timon being repudiated by a series of his miserly friends, in the course of which it is mentioned that Ventidius has also denied assistance. Ventidius does not reappear after 1.2, and he is simply an emblem of the callous greed that permeates the aristocracy of ATHENS.

Commentators have often remarked on the oddity of Shakespeare's having so dramatically established Ventidius's indebtedness, only to omit, onstage, his refusal to help his benefactor. In fact, this peculiarity has been offered as evidence that the authorship of the play is divided: Shakespeare may have introduced Ventidius's story and another playwright disposed of it too casually, or vice versa. However, if this is an error—and a case can be made that the omission is effective because it represents the unreliability of Timon's supposed friends—then it may simply reflect the fact that *Timon* is an incomplete work, as most scholars believe.

Titus Andronicus
SYNOPSIS

Act 1, Scene 1
Saturninus and his brother Bassianus both claim to succeed their father as Roman Emperor. Titus Andronicus, a vastly popular general and patriot, is expected to return shortly from a successful war against the Goths. Titus appears, mourning the loss of several sons in the campaign. A surviving son, Lucius, declares that their religion demands a human sacrifice, and he nominates Alarbus, a son of Tamora, the captive Queen of the Goths. Tamora's plea for mercy is ignored, and Alarbus is killed. Titus is asked to choose the new emperor. He declares in favor of the technically legitimate successor, Saturninus, the elder of the two brothers. In gratitude, Sat-

urninus declares that he will marry Titus's only daughter, Lavinia. Titus then turns his prisoners over to Saturninus, who comments lyrically on Tamora's beauty. Bassianus claims Lavinia as his own betrothed, as had earlier been arranged, and Titus's sons back him. Titus accuses them of treason for opposing the will of the new emperor. The sons and Bassianus take Lavinia away by force, and Titus kills one of his own sons in the skirmish. Saturninus, however, seizes on the chance to reject Titus, whose popularity he fears, claiming him to be associated with his family's treason. The emperor then declares his intention to marry Tamora. Tamora purports to defend Titus, but in an aside to Saturninus, she recommends that he take revenge later, when his throne is more secure. She assures him that she will see to it herself to avenge her son's death. Saturninus therefore pretends to forgive Titus and his family. A double wedding is proposed, and a festive hunt is planned for the next day.

Act 2, Scene 1

Aaron, a Moor in Tamora's court, exults in his mistress's newly exalted position, from which he will profit, for he knows she loves him completely. Tamora's sons Demetrius and Chiron enter, arguing over Lavinia, whom each desires. Aaron suggests that they may both have her; he proposes that they rape her during the next day's hunt.

Act 2, Scene 2

Titus and his sons and Saturninus and his court go festively to the hunt. The two couples, Saturninus and Tamora, and Bassianus and Lavinia, are married.

Act 2, Scene 3

Aaron arranges an encounter in which Demetrius and Chiron kill Bassianus and carry Lavinia off to rape her. Then, with the help of a forged letter, he frames Martius and Quintus, sons of Titus, for the murder. Titus pleads for mercy, but Saturninus decrees that the sons shall be executed.

Act 2, Scene 4

Chiron and Demetrius taunt Lavinia, whose tongue and hands they have cut off, and then abandon her. She is discovered by Marcus Andronicus, Titus's brother, who responds with elaborately rhetorical grief.

Act 3, Scene 1

Martius and Quintus are marched across the stage on their way to be executed. Titus describes his grief to Lucius in extravagant terms. Marcus appears with the ravished Lavinia, and more expressions of woe ensue. Aaron arrives to announce that the emperor has declared that Titus's severed hand will be accepted as ransom for the lives of the two sons, and Titus lets Aaron cut it off and take it away. Titus's paroxysms of rhetoric are interrupted by the delivery of the two sons' heads, accompanied by his own hand, and he realizes that Aaron has viciously tricked him. Titus's grief turns to a thirst for revenge; he sends Lucius to the Goths to raise an army with which to wreak vengeance.

Act 3, Scene 2

At dinner, Titus rants of the injuries his family has suffered. Marcus kills a fly with his knife, prompting an effusive speech against murder by Titus, but, when Marcus observes that the fly resembled Aaron, Titus seizes the knife and rhapsodizes about slaying the Moor. Marcus remarks sadly that grief has unbalanced Titus.

Act 4, Scene 1

Mute Lavinia conveys to Titus and Marcus that she wants them to consult a book. It is Ovid's *Metamorphoses*, and she directs them to the tale of the rape of Philomel. They deduce that her case is the same, and they get her to write the names of her attackers in the sand with a wooden staff. She does so, and new vows of vengeance are sworn.

Act 4, Scene 2

Chiron and Demetrius receive a gift of weapons from Titus, with verses that hint at vengeance, though they do not realize it. A Nurse, sent by Tamora, seeks Aaron. She holds the black infant just born to Tamora, and she tells Aaron that the empress wants him to kill it so that no one knows of her adultery with the Moor. Aaron refuses. He kills the Nurse to ensure her silence, and sends Chiron and Demetrius to buy a white baby and take it to Tamora to be passed off as the child of Saturninus. They depart, and Aaron plans to take his own child to friends among the Goths.

Filled with barbaric crimes and horrible slaughter, *Titus Andronicus* was the first tragedy Shakespeare wrote. Titus is an admirable patriot, but his overdeveloped sense of honor causes him to kill his own children. *(Courtesy of Billy Rose Theatre Collection; New York Public Library at Lincoln Center; Astor, Lenox and Tilden Foundations)*

Act 4, Scene 3

Titus, seemingly mad, insists that his family shoot arrows into the sky, each bearing a message to the gods seeking justice for his wrongs. Marcus suggests that the arrows be aimed so as to land in the emperor's courtyard. A Clown appears, carrying two pigeons. Titus persuades the Clown, for a fee, to deliver the pigeons as an offering to the emperor, and Titus includes with the birds a message wrapped around a dagger.

Act 4, Scene 4

Saturninus, who has received several of the message-arrows, asserts that Titus's madness is feigned and threatens to punish him. The Clown arrives, bearing the pigeons and Titus's message. Saturninus orders the Clown hanged and vows to execute Titus personally. Aemilius appears, reporting that a Gothic army under Lucius is approaching. Tamora proposes to trick Titus into halting his son's onslaught. Aemilius is sent to arrange a parley with Lucius at Titus's house.

Act 5, Scene 1

Aaron, who has been captured with his child, is brought before Lucius, who decrees that both be hanged. Aaron says that he will confess the truth about all his misdeeds if Lucius will spare the child. Lucius agrees, and Aaron insolently brags of his evil actions, regretting only that death will keep him from doing more. Aemilius arrives with the offer of a parley, and Lucius accepts.

Act 5, Scene 2

Tamora and her sons, in disguise, approach Titus's house, where she plans to delude the old man that she is Revenge, a spirit sent to aid him. Titus recognizes them, but he pretends to be taken in. Tamora proposes to bring Saturninus to a banquet, where Titus can wreak his vengeance. She goes, leaving Chiron and Demetrius, whom Titus promptly has bound and gagged. He reveals his plan to cook them and serve them to Tamora at the proposed banquet. He then cuts their throats.

Act 5, Scene 3

Lucius, arriving at Titus's house for the parley, turns Aaron over to Marcus. Saturninus and Tamora arrive with their noble retinue, and all are seated at the banquet table. Titus welcomes them, dressed as a cook. Referring to a famous legend of a father who killed his raped daughter to remove his family's shame, he kills Lavinia before the horrified guests. He declares that she had been raped by Chiron and Demetrius. He reveals their heads baked in a meat pie, which Tamora has already sampled, and then he stabs Tamora to death. Saturninus promptly kills him and is himself immediately dispatched by Lucius. The assembled nobles declare Lucius to be the new emperor, and Titus is formally mourned. Aaron is brought forward and sentenced by Lucius to be buried to his neck and starved. He responds with a last boastful refusal to repent.

COMMENTARY

Although *Titus Andronicus* is certainly the least satisfying Shakespearean TRAGEDY, it was also his first attempt at the genre, and it has features that suggest the grander achievements to come. Although it is inferior to later work, it is a fine play by the standards of 1590; the young Shakespeare was already a successful professional playwright. (Note that many modern scholars believe that Shakespeare may have collaborated on *Titus* with another writer. See "Text of the Play.")

The play is based on ancient Roman drama; its format and general character were taken from SENECA. The violence and degradation to which the characters are exposed stand in marked contrast to the highly decorous language in which these excesses are depicted. Also, references to classical literature, especially to OVID, abound. All this was very much in the manner of academic drama that dominated the pre-Shakespearean stage, a tradition that the playwright was soon to outgrow. At the time, still learning his trade, Shakespeare applied the tenets of Senecan drama in a polished and professional manner, using grand rhetoric and precise plotting. He was content to attempt a standard melodrama, plainly geared to box-office success, and he had two recent, immensely popular predecessors to model his work on. One was *The Jew of Malta,* by Christopher MARLOWE, which had created a vogue for exotic villains that the character of Aaron clearly exploits. The other was Thomas KYD's *The Spanish Tragedy,* the first great Elizabethan REVENGE PLAY, a favorite genre of the day; *Hamlet* was to be the greatest of them. In fact, *Titus* and *The Spanish Tragedy* remained among the most popular English plays for the rest of the 16th century and into the early 17th.

Glimpses of later, greater plays may be found in *Titus.* For instance, the combination of shrewdly feigned lunacy with some degree of real insanity, applied rather baldly and unconvincingly in the depiction of Titus, is a profoundly compelling trait in Hamlet. Titus also anticipates Othello in being a simple man out of his depth, a successful but easily manipulated military leader. Titus also foreshadows King Lear in that he commits crimes in the name of honor, but Titus never becomes aware of his errors, as does Lear. The villainous Aaron plainly prefigures such paragons of malevolence as *Othello's* Iago and Richard III. Most important, *Titus* reveals Shakespeare's concern for political ethics. It opens with a question of hereditary succession to a throne, the crux of most of his later HISTORY PLAYS, and concludes with the restoration of orderly rule after disruptions caused by human frailties. Though dealt with very crudely here, these themes suggest the mature presentation to come.

However, *Titus Andronicus* in no way generates the powerful responses we associate with Shakespeare's great works. For one thing, there is no development toward a climax, but rather an assemblage of episodes, all rather similar in tone. Also, the extremely rhetorical dialogue inhibits the development of the characters, who do not reveal their feelings so much as describe them. In any case, the extremely melodramatic plot makes character development all but impossible; for one thing, more than half of the play's characters are killed, often on stage (including a prodigious three in four lines in the final scene).

This combination of academic formalism and blatant gore has appealed to few theatergoers since the 17th century. Scholarly opinion used to deny Shakespeare's authorship of the play on the grounds that it was clearly beneath the sensibility of a great writer. However, modern scholarship has rejected this assertion and reminds us that the young Shakespeare's taste was naturally that of his time. *Titus Andronicus* may be seen as roughly equivalent to today's horror movies. As such, it was a major success; it appealed to its audience, and it established the playwright as superior to most, if not all, of his contemporaries.

SOURCES OF THE PLAY

No source for the story of *Titus Andronicus* is known, although it has been suggested that an older play, now lost, was rewritten by Shakespeare. The tale itself, although presented as historical (in accordance with a standard convention of Elizabethan tragedy), is fictional, and Shakespeare may have invented it. However, scholars have noted an 18th-century chapbook, of which only one copy exists, that contains a version of the same story that seems not to be based on Shakespeare's play. It may reflect pre-Shakespearean material that the playwright knew. If so, Shakespeare made notable alterations, emphasizing the political issues, especially in adding the role of Lucius and asserting the restoration of Roman authority at the conclusion.

Ovid's tale of the rape and mutilation of Philomel is obviously a forerunner of Lavinia's fate in the play; this story is expressly referred to several times. *Thyestes*, by Seneca, probably influenced the general atmosphere of horror pervading *Titus Andronicus* and may have provided certain details as well. While the chapbook has a character analogous to Aaron, another source, a story by the 16th-century Italian author Matteo BANDELLO, features a Moor whose crimes are similar and whose delight in his own evil is much more like the Shakespearean character. Shakespeare may have known the Bandello tale in François BELLEFOREST's French translation or in the English of Geoffrey FENTON; also, the tale is known to have been rendered in a popular English ballad. Shakespeare's conception of Aaron surely owes something to Marlowe's *The Jew of Malta* (1589). Lastly, the feigned madness of Titus may derive from that of Hieronymo in Kyd's *The Spanish Tragedy* (1588–89).

TEXT OF THE PLAY

Titus Andronicus has been said to be Shakespeare's first play; although this cannot be proved, it is certainly among his earliest. The precise date of composition is unknown; estimates have varied from 1588 to the year of its initial publication, 1594. The play appeared in three QUARTO editions (Q1, Q2, and Q3) before being included in the FIRST FOLIO (F) in 1623. Q1 was printed in 1594 by John DANTER for publishers Thomas MILLINGTON and Edward WHITE; only one copy is known to exist. Although sloppily produced, it contains a seemingly accurate text, and it is the ultimate source for the other early texts and thus for all modern editions. Q2, printed in 1600 by James ROBERTS for White alone, was apparently taken from Q1, but from a damaged copy, for it is missing lines in a number of places. Two copies of Q2 are known. Q3, from 1611, was taken from Q2 and provides a small number of corrections to it, but with a much larger number of errors. Unfortunately, this corrupt text, printed for White by Edward ALLDE, was the basis for F, which became the best-known Shakespeare edition for centuries. F contains several lines and one whole

scene (3.2) that are in no other edition. These were presumably written, perhaps not by Shakespeare, after the play had been in production for some time.

Contemporary scholars have tended to believe that some of Shakespeare's earliest work (as well as some of his latest) was collaborative, and attention has focused on *Titus*, especially given its uneven quality. Parts of the play have been attributed to a number of Elizabethan playwrights, but recent studies of word choice and syntactic preferences have led many to believe George PEELE probably had a part in the play, especially in Act 1, at least to the extent of having written a text that was later improved upon by Shakespeare. Yet both the Folio editors, who knew Shakespeare and were part of his theatrical world, and Francis MERES, a contemporary writer on theater, ascribed the play to him, and *Titus Andronicus* has a secure place in the Shakespearean CANON.

THEATRICAL HISTORY OF THE PLAY

Titus Andronicus was immediately popular; the title page of its first edition boasted that it had been performed by three different companies: DERBY'S MEN, PEMBROKE'S MEN, and SUSSEX'S MEN. For about 30 years it remained among the most popular English dramas and was performed repeatedly. For three and a half centuries thereafter, however, it was among the most neglected of Shakespeare's plays. It was not produced at all between 1721 and 1852, nor again between 1857 and 1923; the brief revival was due to the popularity in Britain of a black American actor, Ira ALDRIDGE, who played Aaron. Several 20th-century productions—including a notable 1955 staging by Peter BROOK, featuring Laurence OLIVIER as Titus—helped revive interest in the play, but it remains an oddity. *Titus* has only been made as a FILM once, with Anthony Hopkins as Titus and Jessica Lange as Tamora, in 1991. It has also only once been produced for TELEVISION, in 1985.

CHARACTERS

Aaron Character in *Titus Andronicus*, the chief villain, a vicious criminal who loves evil for its own sake. Aaron, a Moor, is the lover of Tamora, the Queen of the Goths, and carries out her revenge on

Titus Andronicus, who has permitted her son to be killed. Although Aaron is in the retinue of the captured queen in Act 1, he is silent. Only in 2.1 does he begin to reveal his character, rejoicing in the advancement of Tamora, who is to marry the Emperor, Saturninus, because it will also benefit him. Tamora's two sons lust after Lavinia, Titus's daughter. Aaron plans their appalling rape and mutilation of the girl, which is the centerpiece of the revenge upon her father. Lavinia's new husband, Bassianus, is also murdered, and two of Titus's sons are charged with the crime. Aaron tells Titus that his severed hand is required as ransom for the two sons' lives. Titus submits to the amputation, only to have the sons' heads, and his own hand, delivered to him on a platter. This excessive piece of brutality delights Aaron, and he gloats to himself: "O, how this villainy / Doth fat me with the very thoughts of it!" (3.1.202–203).

Aaron's blackness was a common symbol of evil in Shakespeare's day, but even in this early work, Shakespeare doesn't settle for simple conventionality. Later in the play, a Nurse delivers to Aaron Tamora's newborn black infant, his child, calling it "as loathsome as a toad / Among the fair-faced breeders of our clime" (4.2.67–68). She bears Tamora's orders that Aaron is to kill it to protect her reputation. He refuses and defends the baby at sword's point against Tamora's sons. The black man's proud defiance of society reflects Shakespeare's awareness that villainy can have ingredients in common with heroism, regardless of race. Although the irony of this extraordinarily evil man cooing over his infant son was probably intended as humorous, it is also a good instance of the playwright's respect for the full humanity of all his characters, even one intended as a demonstration of cruelty.

Aaron's villainy is certainly still active, for he proceeds to kill the Nurse and send the two sons out to buy a white child for Tamora to claim as her own. Aaron attempts to deliver his infant to friends among the Goths, but he is captured, and Lucius sentences both father and son to hang. Aaron offers to confess all in exchange for the baby's life. Lucius agrees, and Aaron takes the occasion to boast of his evil, declaring, while detailing his crimes, that in his delight with himself, he "almost broke my heart with extreme laughter" (5.1.113). After the grisly banquet scene in which Titus's revenge is accomplished, Aaron is brought forth to be sentenced. He is to be buried to the neck and starved to death. This fate only provokes a last outburst. "If one good deed in all my life I did, / I do repent it from my very soul" (5.3.189–190).

Aaron is the first of Shakespeare's flamboyantly malevolent villains, foreshadowing the likes of Richard III, Edmund (in *King Lear*), Lady Macbeth, and, most spectacular of all, Iago (in *Othello*). A less-developed personality than the later characters, Aaron more clearly represents the conventional figure from which they all descend, the MACHIAVEL. At the time when Shakespeare was writing, *Titus*, *The Jew of Malta* by Christopher MARLOWE ranked as one of the most successful offerings yet presented in the new world of English theater, and it featured two very popular Machiavels—Barabas and his assistant Ithamore, racially exotic evildoers who exult in their criminality. These characters surely influenced the young creator of Aaron. However, some historians of drama see Shakespeare as influenced here by earlier, more purely English theatrical traditions, with Aaron as a descendant of the VICE figure in the medieval MORALITY PLAY. The two propositions are not at all mutually exclusive; the idea of the Machiavel doubtless was influenced by the well-known Vice figure. It is likely that Shakespeare was aware of both and in Aaron he simply combined them.

Aemilius Minor character in *Titus Andronicus*. Aemilius delivers messages between Saturninus and Lucius and helps acclaim Lucius the new Emperor at the end of the play.

Alarbus Minor character in *Titus Andronicus*, the eldest son of Tamora. In 1.1, Titus Andronicus permits the ritual sacrifice of Alarbus, who is killed despite his mother's pleas for mercy. This sparks the cycle of vengeance that comprises the plot of the play.

Bassianus Character in *Titus Andronicus*, brother of the emperor, Saturninus. In 1.1 Bassianus relinquishes his claim to the throne when Titus

Andronicus declares in favor of his brother, but he will not surrender his fiancée, Lavinia, to him. The first victim of Aaron's plots, Bassianus is killed by Chiron and Demetrius, prior to their rape of Lavinia in 2.3.

Caius Minor character in *Titus Andronicus*. Mentioned only in stage directions, Caius does not speak. He is present for the shooting of arrows to the gods in 4.3, and he helps to capture Chiron and Demetrius in 5.2.

Captain Minor character in *Titus Andronicus*, the officer who announces the arrival of Titus Andronicus in 1.1 and praises his virtues as a general.

Chiron Character in *Titus Andronicus*, son of Tamora. Chiron and his brother Demetrius murder Bassianus and then commit the horrible rape and mutilation of Lavinia, the daughter of Titus Andronicus; they are encouraged and abetted by Aaron. Titus's counterrevenge includes the killing of the two brothers, who are baked in a meat pie and served to their mother in the final scene.

Clown Minor character in *Titus Andronicus*. The Clown appears in 4.3, carrying two pigeons in a basket. After some conversation—in which the Clown reveals himself to be a comically naive rustic, a traditional dramatic type (see CLOWN)—Titus offers him a fee to make the pigeons an offering to the Emperor Saturninus. Titus includes a taunting message of his own, wrapped around a dagger. When, in 4.4, the hapless Clown delivers his birds and Titus's message to Saturninus, the infuriated emperor orders him killed. He is led away, exclaiming, "Hang'd, by 'r-Lady! then I have brought up a neck to a fair end" (4.4.48–49). This insignificant addition to the play's roster of victims is one of Shakespeare's earliest clowns, and his realistic, if dim-witted, voice provides a simple, earthy moment of relief from the savagery that dominates the play.

Demetrius Character in *Titus Andronicus*, a son of Tamora. Demetrius and his brother Chiron murder Bassianus and then commit the appalling rape and mutilation of Lavinia, the daughter of Titus

Andronicus; they are encouraged and abetted by Aaron. Titus's counterrevenge includes the killing of the two brothers, who are baked in a meat pie and served to their mother in the final scene.

Goths Barbarian European tribe known to the ancient Romans. In *Titus Andronicus* Shakespeare uses the Goths as the enemies of Rome whose forces are necessary to restore order within the empire, which has been disrupted through the villainy of Aaron and Tamora. This device anticipates several later occasions, notably in *Hamlet* and *Macbeth*, when forces from outside the affected society must take charge, thereby heightening the playwright's emphasis on the catastrophic results of social disorder.

Lavinia Character in *Titus Andronicus*, the daughter of Titus Andronicus, whose brutal rape and mutilation are the centerpiece of Aaron's revenge against her father. After murdering Lavinia's husband, Bassianus, the villainous Chiron and Demetrius rape her and then cut out her tongue and cut off her hands so that she cannot testify against them. Directed by Aaron, they have improved upon OVID's tale of Philomel's rape by Tereus, who removed his victim's tongue but not her hands; she wove a tapestry that told the tale and exposed her attacker. Lavinia's plight is repeatedly compared to Philomel's. In fact, Lavinia exposes Chiron and Demetrius by inducing Titus to look in a copy of Ovid's tales and find the example. She then spells out the villain's names in the sand with a wooden staff. When Titus kills the two, Lavinia is a witness, and she goes with him to cook their bodies into the meat pie that is to be presented to their mother as revenge. Then, in a climax to her trials, her father himself stabs her to death at 5.3.47, emulating an old legend of a man who killed his raped daughter to expunge the family's dishonor.

With very little to say even before she is so cruelly muted—most of it in elaborate pleas for mercy from her attackers, in 2.3.142–178—Lavinia is little more than a victim. She has almost no personality, though as an exercise in pantomime the role can be an interesting challenge to an actress.

Lucius Character in *Titus Andronicus*, a son of Titus Andronicus. In 1.1 Lucius demands the ritual sacrifice of Tamora's son, thus triggering the cycle of vengeance that drives the action. Later he is banished from Rome, and he joins the Goths. He returns in Act 5 at the head of the Gothic troops, and in that capacity he sentences the captured Aaron to death. Continuing to Rome, he is present at the grisly finale, as is his son, Young Lucius. Following the deaths of Saturninus and his father, Lucius is acclaimed the new emperor.

Marcus Andronicus Character in *Titus Andronicus*, the brother of Titus Andronicus. Marcus proposes his brother as a candidate for the vacant imperial throne in 1.1, though he accedes to Titus's determination that Saturninus should reign. He sides with Bassianus and Titus's sons in the dispute over Lavinia, but a reconciliation is soon effected. In 2.4 Marcus discovers Lavinia in her ravished state, and his seemingly incongruous response—distant and rhetorical despite the extremity of her plight—often puzzles modern readers. It is a good instance of a mode of formal discourse, intended to promote a sense of strangeness and unreality, that was highly prized in Renaissance times but is now quite unfamiliar. In 3.2, which Shakespeare may not have written, Marcus kills a fly, provoking so manic a response in Titus that he seems unbalanced by grief. Such mania is an important theme in a REVENGE PLAY, which *Titus Andronicus* is. In the rest of the play, Marcus seconds his brother's sentiments of grief and plans for revenge, and he mourns Titus at the end.

Martius Minor character in *Titus Andronicus*, a son of Titus Andronicus. Martius, with Quintus, is framed by Aaron for the murder of Bassianus in 2.3. After the two are executed, their heads are delivered to Titus, in 3.1.

Messenger Minor character in *Titus Andronicus*. In 3.1 the Messenger brings Titus a grisly package—the severed heads of his two sons and the general's own severed hand—that Aaron has sent in mockery. The Messenger is sympathetic, remarking on the injustice with a personal note that is rare in this play.

Mutius Minor character in *Titus Andronicus*, a son of Titus Andronicus. In 1.1 Mutius is killed by his father during the dispute with Bassianus over Lavinia. His murder is symptomatic of a flaw in Titus, whose sense of honor can lead him to such a crime.

Nurse Minor character in *Titus Andronicus*. In 4.2 the Nurse delivers to Aaron his infant son by Tamora. Aaron kills the Nurse to ensure her silence about the birth.

Publius Minor character in *Titus Andronicus*, the son of Marcus Andronicus. Publius participates in the seemingly mad Titus Andronicus's plan to shoot message-laden arrows to the gods in 4.3, and he helps capture Chiron and Demetrius in 5.2.

Quintus Minor character in *Titus Andronicus*, a son of Titus Andronicus. Quintus, with Martius, is framed by Aaron for the murder of Bassianus in 2.3. The two are executed, and their heads are delivered to Titus in 3.1.

Saturninus Character in *Titus Andronicus*, the villainous emperor. Saturninus becomes emperor through the support of Titus Andronicus but turns against him, fearing his popularity. He becomes a willing accessory to the plots against Titus spun by the empress, Tamora, and her lover, Aaron. He sentences Martius and Quintus to death without a trial in 2.3, and in a fit of temper he has the Clown killed in 4.4. In the final scene he kills Titus and is himself killed by Lucius. Saturninus is an early depiction by Shakespeare of an evil ruler who violates the ethics of kingship, an important issue for the playwright.

Sempronius Minor character in *Titus Andronicus*. Sempronius is present at the shooting of arrows to the gods (4.3), but he does not speak, though his name is mentioned by Titus Andronicus in 4.3.10.

Tamora Character in *Titus Andronicus*, the villainous queen of the Goths. Tamora, her three sons, and her lover, Aaron the Moor, have been captured by the Roman general Titus Andronicus before the play begins. When, in 1.1, her captor permits her eldest son to be ritually sacrificed despite her eloquent plea for mercy, Tamora vows revenge, and the play's bloody cycle begins. Tamora find her chance for vengeance when the new Roman emperor, Saturninus, falls in love with her and marries her. Saturninus fears Titus, who is very popular, and wishes to break with him, but Tamora advises her new husband to make peace with the general until his own hold on the throne is more secure. She will see to Titus's downfall herself, she adds.

After this flamboyant introduction, Tamora recedes from the forefront of the play for a while. Her revenge is implemented largely by Aaron, though she helps him frame two of Titus's sons for a murder, and she is particularly villainous in refusing Lavinia's pleas for mercy in 2.3. Later, in 4.4, when she and Saturninus learn of an approaching army under Titus's son, her husband is stricken with fear, but she reproves him, in a well-known speech emphasizing the power held by rulers (4.4.81–87). She goes on to boast that she will "enchant the old Andronicus"—that is, Titus—and prevail upon him to cancel his son's invasion.

With her sons, Tamora goes to Titus in disguise, pretending to be Revenge, a spirit from within the earth come to help the mad old man achieve his vengeance. In her impersonation, she anticipates later Shakespearean witches and ghosts. She believes that Titus is mad, but he is sane enough to see through her plot and pretend to be taken in. Thinking she has won, she leaves her sons with Titus, but he kills them and serves them to her at the banquet in the last scene, before killing her as well.

Titus Andronicus Title character of *Titus Andronicus,* a Roman general and the central figure in the cycle of vengeance that comprises the play. Titus is initially presented as an admirable patriot whose life has been spent largely in the service of his country, but his inflexible pride and overly developed sense of honor cause him to kill one of his own sons in a dispute over loyalty to the Emperor. In 1.1 Titus permits the ritual sacrifice of the son of Tamora, who consequently seeks revenge against him and his fam-

ily. Tamora's vengeance (implemented primarily by her lover, Aaron) results in the false conviction of two of Titus's sons for the murder of his son-in-law Bassianus and the horrible rape and mutilation of his daughter, the newly widowed Lavinia. Further, Titus is tricked by Aaron into having one hand chopped off, and then, when his two sons have been executed, their heads are brought to him, along with his own severed hand, on a platter. His grief turns to madness, though when Tamora attempts to take advantage of his apparent lunacy by posing as the spirit of Revenge, he shows that he has retained enough sanity to turn the tables on her. However, Titus's own revenge is anything but sane. He kills Tamora's two surviving sons, Lavinia's attackers, and bakes them into a meat pie that he serves to their mother at a banquet. First, however, he kills Lavinia herself, citing a legend in which a father kills his raped and dishonored daughter. Titus then slays Tamora and is killed himself. His only surviving son, Lucius, becomes the new emperor.

It is thought that the name Andronicus may suggest a remote origin for the tale, although Shakespeare will not have known of it. The 12th-century Byzantine emperor Andronicus Comnenus, famous for his cruelty, was killed by a mob after having had his right hand cut off. Perhaps the playwright's unknown source derived ultimately from medieval accounts of this ruler.

Tribune Either of two minor characters in *Titus Andronicus,* officials of the Roman Empire. The Tribunes are present throughout much of 1.1, largely as mute witnesses to the foolish pride of Titus Andronicus. In 1.1.220–222 they speak in unison, their only lines, and declare that they will honor Titus's achievements in war and permit him to choose the successor to the deceased emperor. They represent the pomp and splendor of ROME, while at the same time demonstrating the inadequacy of the society to prevent the tragedy that Titus will unleash. The tribunes of the ancient Roman government were always two in number, though neither the text nor the stage directions of *Titus Andronicus* indicate this.

Valentine Minor character in *Titus Andronicus.* Mentioned only in a stage direction, Valentine helps to capture Chiron and Demetrius in 5.2.

Young Lucius Minor character in *Titus Andronicus*, son of Lucius and grandson of Titus Andronicus. Young Lucius attends Titus in his grief and as he plans his revenge. In 4.2 Young Lucius delivers to Chiron and Demetrius a gift of weapons containing a cryptic message, the first of Titus's taunts to Tamora's family. He also participates in mourning Titus at the end of the play.

Troilus and Cressida
SYNOPSIS

Prologue
A Prologue, dressed in armor, states that the scene of the play is TROY. The Greeks have invaded by sea and pitched camp outside the city. The play omits the first battles, he adds, and begins in the middle of the TROJAN WAR.

Act 1, Scene 1
Troilus, a Trojan prince, is sick with love for Cressida and declares he cannot join the fighting against the Greeks. He rebukes Cressida's relative, Pandarus, who speaks of her beauty and thus aggravates his pain. Pandarus replies that he will no longer carry messages for Troilus if he is to be reprimanded, but he continues to remark on Cressida's virtues. He observes that Cressida's father has deserted to the Greeks. Troilus regrets that he must depend on Pandarus to approach Cressida. A Trojan general, Aeneas, reports that Troilus's brother Paris has been wounded by the Greek Menelaus. This shames Troilus into returning to the battlefield.

Act 1, Scene 2
Cressida's servant, Alexander, tells her that the Trojan crown prince, Hector, wounded by Ajax the previous day, is raging for a fight on the battlefield. Alexander comically describes Ajax as a brute though a valiant warrior. Pandarus arrives; he and Cressida watch the Trojan warriors returning from the field while Pandarus praises Troilus. Cressida denounces Pandarus as a procurer after he leaves, but confesses that she is attracted to Troilus. She decides not to reveal her feelings, however, declaring that a man will cease desiring a woman once he knows she loves him.

Act 1, Scene 3
Agamemnon, the Greek commander in chief, counsels the other Greek leaders not to be discouraged by Troy's survival after seven years of warfare. The Greeks' failure to conquer, he insists, is a test imposed by Jove, who supports them. Ulysses asserts that Troy stands only because the Greeks are weakened by disorder and faction. He sees this as a consequence of a lack of respect for rank. This is what preserves a society, he says, just as the cosmos would be weakened by insubordination of one of the planets. As an example, he points out the disrespectful behavior of the warriors Achilles and Patroclus, who amuse themselves with insulting imitations of their superiors. Nestor adds that Ajax and Thersites, his jester, or FOOL, do the same. Aeneas arrives from Troy bearing a challenge from Hector daring any Greek to fight him in hand-to-hand combat the next day. Ulysses proposes a plot: Although Hector's challenge is clearly directed at Achilles, the most renowned Greek warrior, the leaders should instead select another combatant, Ajax, through a fixed lottery. This might teach Achilles a lesson.

Act 2, Scene 1
Thersites subjects Ajax to witty but crude insults. He mocks him for envying Achilles' reputation. Too slow-witted to retort, Ajax beats the jester, who taunts him for it. Achilles and Patroclus appear and intervene, and Thersites insults them too, to their amusement. Achilles tells Ajax that Hector's challenge is to be met by a warrior selected by lottery.

Act 2, Scene 2
Hector recommends to the Trojan leaders that Helen—whose abduction by Paris from her husband Menelaus was the cause of the war—be released and the war ended. He says she is not worth further loss of life. Troilus counters that this would sully the Trojan honor. The princess Cassandra appears, hysterically predicts disaster for Troy unless Helen is released, and leaves. Troilus states that Cassandra should not influence them, because she is insane. Paris argues for keeping Helen in the name of his honor. Hector criticizes Troilus and Paris for their immaturity. He then goes on to observe that while absolute right demands that they return Menelaus's wife, he will concede that

their honor is a proper issue, and concludes that they must continue fighting. He tells of the challenge he has issued to the Greeks.

Act 2, Scene 3

Thersites, alone, rails against Ajax and Achilles and then insults Achilles and Patroclus when they arrive. When the Greek leaders and Ajax appear, Achilles enters his tent and refuses to see them. After rejecting several messages, he sends word that he refuses to fight the next day. Ajax criticizes Achilles for his pride, while in humorous asides the other Greeks remark on Ajax's own. They then flatter him extravagantly to his face.

Act 3, Scene 1

Pandarus calls on Paris and Helen and gives Paris a message from Troilus requesting that he make an excuse for him to King Priam for missing dinner that night. Paris assumes that Troilus intends to visit Cressida, but Pandarus denies it. This conversation is held in asides so that Helen does not hear it. Helen prevails on Pandarus to sing, and he delivers a song about love.

Act 3, Scene 2

Pandarus brings Cressida to Troilus, and they kiss passionately. Troilus swears undying love, and Pandarus promises the same on his niece's behalf. Cressida confesses that she has loved Troilus for a long time. He observes that although he distrusts the fidelity of women, he is himself by nature faithful; she insists that she will be also. Pandarus declares himself the formal witness to their vows and takes them to a bedroom.

Act 3, Scene 3

Cressida's father, Calchas, asks the Greek leaders to reward him for having deserted to their side by exchanging Trojan prisoners for his daughter. Agamemnon agrees, and Diomedes is told to conduct the exchange. Ulysses suggests that the Greek leaders pointedly ignore the arrogant Achilles to create an occasion for Ulysses to deliver a lecture he has prepared. They agree, and Achilles receives a lengthy talk on honor and reputation from Ulysses. A person's value can be defined only in terms of other people's applause, Ulysses says, adding that Achilles is becoming less valuable since

the applause is going to Ajax. Although still relatively unknown, Ajax will now become famous through fighting Hector. Patroclus seconds the lesson, observing that Achilles' refusal to fight has diminished his reputation. Thersites arrives and comically describes Ajax's strutting pride. Achilles wishes to meet Hector and tells Patroclus to ask Ajax to arrange a meeting. Patroclus rehearses this message with Thersites playing a ludicrously inarticulate Ajax. Achilles decides to write Ajax a letter instead.

Act 4, Scene 1

Paris escorts Diomedes and Antenor, the captured Trojan who is to be exchanged for Cressida, and they encounter Aeneas. Aeneas and Diomedes exchange chivalrous challenges. In asides, Paris tells Aeneas to go ahead of them and get Troilus away from Cressida's house. Talking with Paris, Diomedes denounces Helen as the cause of a pointless war.

Act 4, Scene 2

Troilus bids farewell to Cressida at dawn; she unhappily begs him to stay. Pandarus appears and teases his niece about having lost her virginity. Aeneas arrives and tells Troilus that Cressida is to be exchanged for a prisoner and will depart immediately. Shocked and aggrieved, Troilus goes with Aeneas to meet the deputation as if by chance. The horrified Pandarus breaks the news to Cressida, who vows never to leave.

Act 4, Scene 3

Paris sends the heartsick Troilus ahead of the deputation to bring Cressida out to be delivered to Diomedes.

Act 4, Scene 4

Troilus assures Cressida that he will try to visit her secretly in the Greek camp. They exchange tokens of love: He gives her a sleeve, and she gives him a glove. He asks her to be faithful, and she assures him she will be, but he cautions her that the Greeks are seductive men. Diomedes arrives to accompany Cressida to the Greek camp. Troilus and Diomedes exchange rather sharp courtesies as the group leaves for the city gates. Paris and Aeneas hurry to accompany Hector to the battlefield.

Act 4, Scene 5
Diomedes arrives with Cressida as the Greeks assemble to view the combat of Ajax and Hector. They greet her merrily, kissing her and engaging in witty repartee and sexual innuendo. After Diomedes takes her to her father, Nestor praises her wit, but Ulysses calls her sexually provocative. The Trojans arrive. Hector says he does not wish to fight to the death because Ajax, part Trojan and part Greek, is his cousin. After a brief fight he chivalrously declines to continue. Ajax introduces Hector to the Greek leaders. Achilles insults him, and the two exchange challenges and agree to a hand-to-hand combat the next day. Troilus asks Ulysses to guide him to the tent of Cressida's father.

Act 5, Scene 1
Achilles tells Patroclus that he intends to get Hector drunk so he can defeat him more easily the next day. Thersites arrives with a letter for Achilles and engages Patroclus in an exchange of insults. Achilles announces that the letter, from his lover in Troy, has reminded him of an oath he made to her that he will not fight. He and Patroclus leave to prepare for the banquet. A number of the Greeks arrive for the banquet with Hector and Troilus. Diomedes excuses himself, and Troilus follows him accompanied by Ulysses, with Thersites following them.

Act 5, Scene 2
Diomedes meets Cressida, spied upon by Troilus and Ulysses from one direction and Thersites from another. Diomedes reminds Cressida of a promise she has made, but she tries to revoke it and beseeches him not to tempt her further. He insists on taking from her the sleeve she had been given by Troilus. She refuses to tell him who it was from, but she finally gives it to him and agrees to a later rendezvous. Thersites comments keenly on these developments; Ulysses quiets Troilus's growing anger. Diomedes leaves, and Cressida, thinking herself alone, laments her unfaithfulness to Troilus and her susceptibility to romance. After she leaves, Troilus mourns the collapse of his world and swears he will kill Diomedes in the next day's fighting.

Act 5, Scene 3
Hector's wife Andromache, King Priam, and Cassandra attempt to persuade Hector not to fight on a

day of terrible omens, but he insists he will. Troilus vows he will kill mercilessly. Pandarus brings Troilus a letter from Cressida, but he tears it up.

Act 5, Scene 4
Thersites watches the fighting and describes it in disrespectful terms. Diomedes and Troilus appear, fighting, and continue offstage. Hector challenges Thersites, but he claims he is a coward and is left alone.

Act 5, Scene 5
Diomedes tells his Servant (2) to take Troilus's captured horse to Cressida. Agamemnon arrives with news of Trojan triumphs on the battlefield. Nestor appears with the corpse of Patroclus, which he sends to Achilles. Ulysses reports that Achilles, inflamed by the death of Patroclus, is arming for battle. Ajax, Diomedes, and Achilles arrive and immediately go to join the fighting.

Act 5, Scene 6
Troilus fights Ajax and Diomedes simultaneously, as they disappear offstage. Achilles and Hector fight; Achilles is winded, and Hector chivalrously offers him a respite, but Achilles insults him and leaves, vowing to return. Hector fights an anonymous Greek, the One, in splendid armor. He swears to capture his fine equipment.

Act 5, Scene 7
Achilles instructs the Myrmidons to accompany him but to fight as little as possible. They are to save their strength for an encounter with Hector, when they are to surround him and kill him. Thersites watches a running skirmish between Menelaus and Paris, cheering them on with vulgar remarks. The Trojan Margarelon identifies himself as a bastard son of Priam and challenges Thersites to fight, but the jester flees, saying that he too is a bastard and a coward to boot.

Act 5, Scene 8
Hector, having killed the Greek warrior, starts to exchange sets of armor and is thus unprotected when the Myrmidons appear. They kill Hector as Achilles looks on. As night falls, the armies separate, and Achilles announces that he will drag Hector's body behind his horse as he returns to camp.

Act 5, Scene 9

The Greek leaders, including Diomedes, reflect that if Achilles has truly defeated Hector, then they have finally won the war.

Act 5, Scene 10

Troilus announces Hector's death to Aeneas and other Trojans, but he insists they continue to fight the next morning. Pandarus arrives, but Troilus spurns him and leaves with the other soldiers. Pandarus delivers an EPILOGUE in which he bemoans that the fate of the procurer is to be despised. He declares that the audience are pimps too and asks their sympathy for his venereal diseases. He says that in two months he intends to draw up his will and bequeath them his ailments.

COMMENTARY

Although *Troilus and Cressida* contains humorous material and is conventionally classed as a COMEDY, its bleak ending and its bitter picture of love and power place it among the PROBLEM PLAYS. These works are troubling and ambiguous in their treatment of society and sexuality, and they lack the clear triumph of love that is usually associated with comedy. *Troilus and Cressida* offers an extravagantly corrupt and artificial world. A venomous parody of a classic legend, it satirizes the glamorous attitudes people often have toward sex and/or war. Pretensions to romantic love and to military glory are thoroughly deflated.

The basic satirical technique employed in *Troilus and Cressida* is the use of character types. The dim-witted and prideful oaf, the deluded lover, the cruel and ambitious noble, the voyeur, the coward, the abusive critic—all are presented boldly in Shakespeare's play as (respectively) Ajax, Troilus, Achilles, Pandarus, and, combining the last two, Thersites. Shakespeare makes these character types interesting, but the depiction of personality was of secondary importance as the playwright's purpose in this play was not psychological but philosophical.

Another device that helps establish the satire is the skewed presentation of familiar material. As presented by Shakespeare, the heroes of the TROJAN WAR and the figures in the famous tale of Cressida's betrayal are seen inhabiting a corrupt world.

They are either agents of corruption or deluded and ineffectual victims of it. The contrast between the familiar heroic legends and Shakespeare's satire is so great that the comic intent of the work is obvious. In addition, the role of Thersites resembles that of the traditional CHORUS and boldly emphasizes the satire's critique.

The two plot lines interact very little, but they echo each other and are thematically related, for both illustrate foolish self-deception and emotional dishonesty. The human tendency to succumb to illusions about life is isolated and exaggerated by the play. The two lovers proclaim great emotional involvement, but Cressida's infidelity is hinted at from the outset, and Troilus's self-deception does not hide the true nature of their purely sexual affair. It offers no hint of the fulfilling mutual enjoyment of real love. It seems more tawdry because it is dependent on Pandarus as procurer. Though she undeniably betrays her lover, Cressida is not portrayed harshly. Rather than being a vicious breaker of hearts, she is seen as a representative of human, or perhaps feminine, weakness—"Ah, poor our sex!" (5.2.108), she cries. Troilus is the principal object of satire. His self-deception is extensively developed in both the love story and the warriors' plot, in which he is also a major figure. Just as he deludes himself about romantic love, calling Cressida a "pearl" (1.1.100), he also deludes himself about the pointless war for Helen on the ground that *she* is a "pearl" (2.2.82) and the Trojans doers of "valiant and magnanimous deeds" (2.2.201) in their defense of her.

The warriors talk of honor and glory, but they too are self-deluded. However, the Trojans and the Greeks are gripped by different illusions. Troilus and Hector believe the war is a chivalric game and the stakes are the personal reputations of the warriors—though in the end both succumb to other motives. Ulysses, on the other hand, believes that an orderly social hierarchy can be maintained through clever reasoning, such as he attempts to employ with Achilles. He too abandons his own truth and eventually argues to Achilles that the only merit is in the fleeting glory of reputation. He thus takes a position rather like Hector's, and this ironically reinforces the play's emphasis on human error. The Greek failure to observe Ulysses' ideal of social organization leads to internal squabbling and a collective inertia that is broken only by Patroclus's death; the Trojans have a false idea of honor that leads to their utter defeat at the play's close. By the end of the play, neither honor nor reason controls the warriors; only greed, injured pride, and revenge motivate the action.

Both Troilus's violent despair and Hector's death are results of their illusions. These two idealistic, if foolish, characters represent the traditional codes of romantic love and military honor that are being deflated by the play's satire, and in the end they find themselves completely at the mercy of ugly reality. Troilus, unable to accept the reality that his romance was only a sexual encounter, takes refuge in violence, to the point of comically forgetting what he is fighting about when he demands of Diomedes "the life thou ow'st me for my horse" (5.6.7). Hector, who insists on the worth of chivalric honor, dies because Achilles does not observe the code. His own behavior, however, is just as important, for he is only vulnerable to Achilles because he has abandoned his ideals long enough to pursue a rich piece of booty, the Grecian armor that he is about to don when he is attacked.

Considered alone, the warrior plot amounts to a scathing indictment of warmongers—Hector and Ulysses serving to point up the wickedness of the others—and the play is often taken as an antiwar manifesto. However, the depiction of war serves a more general purpose. War in the play has an equivalent function to that of sex—in the 17th century it was a commonly glamorized human activity—and as such is a telling venue for satire.

The delusions and misjudgments that plague the characters stem from a simple yet inexorable factor: the passage of time. The characters are aware of this, though usually unconscious of its particular effect on themselves. In 4.5, just before the warrior plot begins to build to its bloody climax, Agamemnon stresses the value of the temporary peace in terms of its impermanence: "What's past and what's to come is strew'd with husks / And formless ruin of oblivion . . . [by contrast with] this extant moment" (4.5.165–167). This emphasis on the value of things as they are at the present moment,

without respect to what they were or will be later, echoes Ulysses' claim that "Love, friendship, charity, are subjects all / To envious and calumniating Time" (3.3.173–174).

The audience's familiarity with the legendary tales on which the play is based strengthens the irony. For instance, we are startled by a stark truth when Helen, intending only an idle pleasantry, observes that "love will undo us all" (3.1.105). And when Pandarus unwittingly predicts the lovers' fate to become symbols of the betrayed and the betrayer (with himself the panderer), we can only hold our breath as each affirms, "Amen" (3.2.203–205). These ironies are not only powerful theatrical moments, they also contribute to our awareness that the characters are undone by a process—time—over which they have no control.

Time also changes the value placed on things or people. Cressida observes that "Things won are done; joy's soul lies in the doing" (1.2.292), suggesting that the value of a goal diminishes as it is achieved. Further, Ulysses proposes to Achilles that time brings the destruction of glory through forgetfulness: "good deeds past . . . are devour'd / As fast as they are made, forgot as soon / As done" (3.3.148–150). Troilus argues that circumstances over time determine worth: once a woman becomes a man's wife, his evaluation of her must rest on that relationship, which once did not exist but is undeniable once it does (in the age before divorce). Therefore, he declares, Helen is valuable enough to fight over simply because, as "a theme of honour and renown" (2.2.200), she has been fought over already. "What's aught but as 'tis valued?" (2.2.53), he says, but he doesn't apply this argument to himself: Cressida will, at another time, value him differently, placing him below the more available man.

The idea that values can change is extremely troubling because it contradicts the stabilizing belief in a constant reality. The development of this difficult theme over the course of the play prepares us for the emotional tone of its chaotic culmination in Act 5. In 5.1 Achilles is reminded of his lover in Troy and decides his reputation is less important than she and refuses to fight. In 5.2 Troilus learns of Cressida's revaluation of him and is driven to berserk combat. Forecasts of disaster in 5.3 remind us of the effect time will eventually have on Troy, and the remaining scenes present brutal fighting where all is devalued. Reversing his decision of 5.1, Achilles goes to battle, the raging Troilus attaches Cressida's value to his horse, and Thersites rejects all honor. Most distressingly, perhaps, Hector is betrayed by his own chivalric values, which lead him to courteously refuse his advantage over Achilles in 5.6, who then kills him in 5.8. Worse, Hector betrays his vision himself in chasing after loot, which leaves him vulnerable to Achilles.

The play's relativism strikes a responsive chord in modern sensibilities, and this may contribute more to its popularity in the 20th century than does its reputation as an antiwar piece. It may also account for its origins, for when it was written, England was undergoing unprecedented change as it entered the 17th century; massive revolution and civil war were only 40 years away. A changing economic world generated great uneasiness (as is especially reflected in *The Merchant of Venice*). The Reformation was only a few generations old, and religious tensions still pervaded society; moreover, religious beliefs placed England at odds with the two most powerful nations in Europe, FRANCE and Spain. Though the Spanish Armada had been defeated in 1588, the threat of war still loomed, particularly in light of the imminent death of Queen Elizabeth I. Though old and in poor health, the queen refused to name a successor; the possibility of civil war or invasion by opportunistic foreign monarchs was widely discussed. This atmosphere of crisis—combined with the appearance of George CHAPMAN's translation of the *Iliad*—generated a vogue for tales of Troy, and several plays on the subject were written before Shakespeare's. The English identified with the Trojans (see TROY), and the legend was regarded as a clear example of disaster. The disturbing quality of *Troilus and Cressida* is thus part of England's catharsis; the nation's uneasiness found an outlet in the reenactment of an ancient battle.

Some critics find the play to be an assertion that life is essentially meaningless and that chaos is the inevitable outcome of humanity's futile endeavors. However, this point of view ignores what Shakespeare does in the play to undercut this. For instance, the idea that Cressida is representative of all women is introduced by Troilus, who insists that the fact of her betrayal must be denied "for [the sake of] womanhood" (5.2.128). However, his raving is effectively countered by its senselessness in denying what is obviously true, and by the deprecating remarks of Ulysses and Thersites. And elsewhere the tendency toward outright misanthropy is checked—the Greeks and Trojans fraternizing in the peaceful "extant moment" (4.5.167) of their truce; Ulysses evoking a world without the "envious fever / Of pale and bloodless emulation" (1.3.133–134); Hector's commitment, however flawed, to an ideal of chivalry—such images, woven into the play's general critique of human society, collectively offer an idea of what man might be in a better world than that of the play. Ulysses and Hector, spokesmen for sanity, map out principles for such a world in their famous speeches in the war councils of the Greeks and Trojans. Ulysses advocates a social order like that of the "heavens themselves" (1.3.85), and Hector cites the "law in each well-order'd nation" (2.2.181). Each leader fails to institute such principles or even to be true to them himself, but they stand as ideals against which their conduct is measured by the audience. It is an essential characteristic of satire that its critique of human failings implies the possibility of improvement. Though honor and love are corruptible, they can still exist.

While it is a harshly critical work, *Troilus and Cressida* contains much humor and sympathy. For instance, the vicious anger of Thersites and the sly lewdness of Pandarus may not be likable, but they are inventive and undeniably funny characters. Helen presents a humorous caricature of a thoughtless society hostess, and Ajax is a comical buffoon, especially as impersonated by Thersites in 3.3.279–302. Also, a number of the characters are, at times, humanly sympathetic: the lovers in their aspirations to happiness; Hector in his chivalric idealism; and Ulysses as a commonsense, reasonable man. Even the abrasive Thersites can be respected for his capacity to see through the pretensions of the Greek warriors.

The epilogue highlights the play's essentially positive intentions. Pandarus's flippant insults make an obvious distinction between the real world of the audience—which of course is not composed of "traitors and bawds" (5.10.37)—and the fictional world of the play. Shakespeare's comical pairing of the audience with the pander serves as a release from the bleak last moments of the play. The satire is thereby stressed a last time, contrasting the existence of human virtues—our own, at least—to the vices that have been depicted on the stage.

Thus, despite its bleak and bloody denouement, the play shares the essential optimism of all comedy. The characters are defeated by the imperfections of themselves and their world, but most playgoers and readers care less about their fate than they do about the more general picture of human folly that the satire has so convincingly presented. *Troilus and Cressida*, like all satire, is to some extent educational, and we find ourselves more thoughtful and aware, perhaps in some sense morally elevated, through our experience of the play.

SOURCES OF THE PLAY

Three chief sources—George Chapman's translation of HOMER's *Iliad* (where the Trojan War was first recorded) and two other English renderings of the story, by William CAXTON and John LYDGATE, each of a different version—inspired Shakespeare's presentation of the war in *Troilus and Cressida*. The tale of Cressida's betrayal came from Geoffrey CHAUCER's great poem *Troilus and Criseyde*.

The incidents from Homer in *Troilus and Cressida* tend to be those covered in Chapman's translation (1598), and several verbal echoes confirm that Shakespeare used this work, though nine translations were available to him—five Latin, two French, and two English. Some scholars believe that the play may have been intended in part as a satire against Chapman, whose great admiration for the Greeks, rooted in Homer, was counter to the ordinary English reader's identification with the Trojans.

Homer was not the immediate source for English knowledge of the Trojan War. Traditionally, another work was regarded as more authoritative than the *Iliad* because it was supposedly written by a Trojan eyewitness to the war, Dares Phrygius (Dares the Trojan), himself a minor character in the *Iliad*. This Latin prose account was actually

written in the fifth or sixth century. It inspired a 12th-century French poem by Benoît de SAINTE-MAURE, which in turn was rendered into Latin prose by Guido delle COLONNE, a Sicilian. His *Historia destructionis Troiae* (1270–87) was the standard work on the subject for centuries.

A French version of Colonne's *Historia* was translated by Caxton as *The Recuyell of the Historyes of Troye* (1475; 5th ed., 1596). Lydgate's long poem entitled *Troy Book* (1420, publ. 1512, 1555) was inspired directly by Colonne. Caxton provided much of the detail in Shakespeare's account of the war, while Lydgate drew attention to the chivalric aspects of the warriors' encounters.

The story of Cressida and Troilus first appeared in Saint-Maure's poem, where Diomedes and Troilus are rivals for the love of Briseis, the original of Cressida; all of them are only minor figures in Homer. BOCCACCIO's poem *Filostrato* (1338) was inspired by Saint-Maure; here Pandarus was first given prominence. *Filostrato* in turn inspired Chaucer's *Troilus and Criseyde* (written ca. 1375; published ca. 1482), which provided Shakespeare with his version of the story, though the playwright eliminates many incidents to achieve a fast-paced plot.

One of Shakespeare's favorite works, OVID's *Metamorphoses*, in the translation by Arthur GOLDING, probably inspired a number of passages, especially parts of Ulysses' speeches. Also, several ideas and incidents—especially in the debate among the Trojans in 2.2—may owe something to *Euphues his Censure to Philautus* (1587) by Robert GREENE, a work consisting of philosophical dialogues ascribed to Greek and Trojan warriors meeting during a truce.

TEXT OF THE PLAY

Troilus and Cressida was registered with the STATIONERS' COMPANY by James ROBERTS in February 1603, but it was not published then. Such a blocking action was commonly used to prevent piracy of a new play, so *Troilus and Cressida* was probably new in early 1603 and written in the previous year. However, the play contains considerable evidence of rewriting before publication. It was finally published in 1609 by Richard BONIAN and Henry WALLEY, in a QUARTO edition (known as Q) printed by George ELD. Q appeared in two versions, the second of which has a different title page and an attached "Epistle" preceding the text of the play. These alterations were apparently made in the course of printing the edition, though sometimes the two versions are referred to as separate editions. Q is thought to have been printed from a scribal copy of Shakespeare's FOUL PAPERS, or possibly from the manuscript itself; the evidence is obscure and disputed.

In 1623 *Troilus and Cressida* was included in the FIRST FOLIO, and this text (known as F) was based on Q, but it incorporates numerous minor corrections and adds the prologue as well as about forty other smaller passages. The manuscript used for F had probably been prepared for the KING'S MEN, the acting company that produced the play, for the Folio has many more and markedly superior stage directions.

What the manuscripts were that were used for Q and F, and how they differed, remains uncertain; subsequent editors of the play have been forced to regard both as authoritative, adopting specific readings on a case-by-case basis.

THEATRICAL HISTORY OF THE PLAY

The early history of *Troilus and Cressida* is quite mysterious. The registration of the play in 1603 states that it had been staged by the CHAMBERLAIN'S MEN (soon to become the King's Men), indicating at least one performance in 1602 or 1603. However, while the first title page of Q (1609) observes that the play had been acted by the King's Men, the second omits this claim, and the Epistle expressly denies it. These contradictions, combined with the play's philosophical themes, its high-flown rhetoric, bawdy humor, and legalistic jokes, have sparked a theory that the play was commissioned for a private performance at one of the INNS OF COURT, or that an early version was altered for this purpose and Q was occasioned by this performance. In any case, the play seems to have been unpopular with 17th-century audiences, for the claim that it had not been publicly staged could not have been made if it had been widely performed. In fact, no records of any early performances of *Troilus and Cressida* have survived.

Indeed, no English production is recorded until 1907 (though it was staged in German at Munich

in 1898). However, in 1679 John DRYDEN produced an abridged *Troilus and Cressida*, generally known by its subtitle, *Truth Found Too Late*, which featured a faithful Cressida and a conventionally tragic ending in which Cressida, Troilus, and Diomedes all die. This version, in which Thomas BETTERTON played Troilus, was popular for a few years, and several editions of the text were published before it disappeared from the stage.

Troilus and Cressida was popular in the 20th century; its criticisms of war and its relativistic values seem natural to modern audiences, and a number of distinctive productions resulted. William POEL first produced an uncut text, with Edith EVANS as Cressida (1912–13). In 1938 Barry JACKSON emphasized the play's antiwar message by costuming the Greeks as Nazis; similarly, Tyrone GUTHRIE's 1956 staging was set early in the 20th century in an imaginary Central European country, and his Greeks wore the spiked helmets of 19th-century Prussian soldiers. In 1960 Peter HALL produced the play on an abstract set, while John BARTON used many startling properties and costumes—along with some near-nudity—in a notorious production of 1976. The play continues to intrigue audiences. Michael BOYD's 1998 ROYAL SHAKESPEARE COMPANY staging at STRATFORD and Trevor NUNN's controversial London production of 1999—in which the Trojans and Greeks were portrayed by black and white actors, respectively—led the way to the 21st century and a New York staging by Peter Hall in 2001. *Troilus and Cressida* has never been a FILM, but it has been produced for TELEVISION three times.

CHARACTERS

Achilles Legendary figure and character in *Troilus and Cressida*, a Greek warrior in the TROJAN WAR. Though acknowledged as the greatest Greek warrior, Achilles refuses to fight because he feels he is insufficiently appreciated; he is also motivated by a treasonous desire to please a Trojan lover. Not until Act 5, after his close friend Patroclus is killed, does Achilles, enraged with grief, return to the battlefield. Then he underhandedly has his followers, the Myrmidons, kill the chivalrous Hector, thereby ensuring the defeat of TROY in the climactic battle. In 5.8 he further discredits himself by declaring that he will mutilate Hector's body by dragging it behind his horse.

Achilles scandalizes the Greek camp by ridiculing his superior officers, Agamemnon and Nestor. Ulysses, in a significant passage, holds Achilles' attitude responsible for the Greek failure to defeat Troy despite seven years of fighting. Societies fail, he says, when hierarchical rankings are not observed. Moreover, Achilles' insubordination has spread, and Ajax is behaving similarly. The prideful warrior thus represents a social defect that is one of the targets of the play's satire—the evil influence of morally deficient leadership. Achilles' selfish, traitorous, and brutally unchivalrous behavior is the centerpiece of the play's depiction of the ugliness of war and the warrior's life, in principle dedicated to ideals of valor and honor but in fact governed by immorality.

Personally, Achilles is rude and uncivil for the most part, and he falsely claims the honor of having defeated Hector, whom he has merely butchered. His villainy is underlined by the obscene and vicious raillery of his jester, Thersites, whose remarks include the accurate observation that Achilles has "too much blood and too little brain" (5.1.47), and the imputation that he keeps Patroclus as a "masculine whore" (5.1.16).

The Achilles of classical mythology, recorded first in the *Iliad* of HOMER, is an outsider, the son of a sea nymph and the leader of a semicivilized tribe in remote Thessaly—what is now northeastern Greece. He is disliked as the only Greek leader who still makes human sacrifices, and his treatment of Hector's body is associated with his barbarian ways. He is noted for his uncontrollable anger and his merciless rage in battle. He withdraws from combat during a dispute with Agamemnon over a concubine, Briseis (the original of Cressida), returning, as in the play, upon the death of Patroclus. Apparently under the influence of Homer, cults venerating Achilles as a demigod were established in several distant regions of the classical world. A later tradition, dating only from Roman times, states that Achilles' mother dipped him in the sacred river Styx, rendering him invulnerable except on the heel by which she had held him. He was later killed by an arrow—fired by Paris—that struck that heel. This legend gives us our name for the tendon attached to the heel: the Achilles tendon.

Aeneas   Legendary figure and character in *Troilus and Cressida*, a leader of the Trojan forces in the TROJAN WAR. Aeneas serves as a herald, carrying the challenge of Hector in 1.3, accompanying the visiting Greek delegation led by Diomedes in 4.1–4, carrying a warning of their arrival to Troilus in 4.2, and announcing Hector's arrival for his duel with Ajax in 4.5. Aeneas, a stiffly correct model of knightly manners, represents the Trojan concern for chivalric honor. His exchange with Diomedes in 4.1 of courteous declarations of intent to kill is a bleakly humorous picture of mindless warriors who can reduce the horrors of war to an exercise in etiquette.

In the *Iliad* of HOMER, Aeneas is a more important figure; he is a cousin of King Priam who is notably favored by the gods. The sea god Poseidon predicts that Aeneas shall be a ruler someday. Later tradition developed this forecast into Aeneas's leadership of the Trojan exiles who wandered the Mediterranean world after the fall of their city, and VIRGIL's *Aeneid* makes him the founder of Rome. Shakespeare and his contemporaries saw Aeneas as an ancestor figure because his great-grandson Brut was thought to have settled England and founded London as New Troy. This is reflected in the anti-Greek bias of the play.

Agamemnon   Legendary figure and character in *Troilus and Cressida*, the leader of the Greek forces in the TROJAN WAR. Although Ulysses calls him "Thou great commander, nerves and bone of Greece" (1.3.55), Agamemnon is in fact an ineffectual leader. He preaches ponderously, but Achilles can safely ignore his orders; the Greek forces are accordingly stymied in their siege of TROY. Much of what Ulysses calls the absence of "degree" (1.3.83, 101, 109, etc.)—a dissolution of the hierarchy on which Greek society has been based—can be attributed to Agamemnon's recurrent weakness. At the play's close, Agamemnon still lacks authority; in the last line spoken by a Greek, he sends a messenger to submissively request the presence of Achilles, just as he has had to do all along.

The Agamemnon of classical myth and legend probably derives from a historical king who ruled in the Argive, a region of Greece near Corinth, during the Bronze Age. His post as commander of the

Greek forces at Troy is recorded in the *Iliad* of HOMER, as are his lack of resolve and his inability to control Achilles. Homer's *Odyssey* and later plays by Greek dramatists continued his tale after the war: upon his return home, he is killed by his wife, Clytemnestra, and her lover. This murder impels Orestes, his son, to kill his mother in revenge. This event and Orestes' subsequent torment by supernatural spirits constitute the *Oresteia,* the subject of works by all the major Greek dramatists and many other writers, into modern times.

Ajax Legendary figure and character in *Troilus and Cressida,* a Greek warrior in the TROJAN WAR. For the most part, Ajax is a variant on the ancient MILES GLORIOSUS character type: a braggart soldier, a laughable buffoon who is not to be taken seriously. He presents a comic variation on an important theme: the vanity of the warrior's lust for military glory. At the same time, he has notable redeeming features that offer a counterpoint to the play's generally acerbic tone.

Before he appears, Ajax is humorously described by Alexander as a valiant warrior but a beastlike churl with uncontrollable emotions. (Some scholars believe that this passage [1.2.19–31] is a satirical description of Ben JONSON, though the point is extremely disputable.) When he does appear, Ajax is laughably stupid, incapable of responding to Thersites' teasing except by hitting him. Selected by Ulysses as a substitute for Achilles, Ajax displays ludicrous pride in his undeserved position, especially since he criticizes Achilles for *his* pride, and elicits the amused asides of the other Greeks in 2.3.201–224. One of the play's funniest passages is Thersites' imitation of Ajax's ego in 3.3.279–302. Ajax issues a preposterous parody of a chivalric challenge as he directs his trumpeter to summon Hector for their duel, saying, "Now, crack thy lungs, . . . stretch thy chest, and let thy eyes spout blood" (4.5.7–11).

However, Ajax proves a brave soldier who behaves with valor and chivalrous generosity when he actually faces Hector, getting the better of the fight (according to the cries of the spectators in 4.5.113–115) but accepting the truce his opponent desires. Strikingly, when Thersites describes Ajax as "a very land-fish, languageless, a monster"

(3.3.262–263), we see that this brutish fellow resembles a later Shakespearean figure—also sympathetic in spite of his defects—Caliban, the fishy monster of *The Tempest.*

Ajax (Latin for the Greek Aias) is the name of two characters in the *Iliad* of HOMER; Shakespeare combines them. The opponent of Hector corresponds to Aias Telamon, described by Homer as the bulwark of the Greek forces, a courageous warrior who is slow of speech but repeatedly a leader in assault and the last to retreat; he successfully duels Hector, as in the play. Otherwise, Shakespeare's character corresponds to Aias Oileus, often called Aias the Lesser, also a fine warrior but notorious for his pride, rudeness, and blasphemy. In the *Odyssey,* he is drowned by the seagod Poseidon for cursing the gods while escaping a shipwreck. In a later tradition, he raped Cassandra on an altar during the sack of TROY, a misdeed whose punishment accounted for a custom by which his descendants were annually required to provide two virgins who ran a gauntlet of the townspeople and, if they survived, served for life in the temple of Athena. The end of this barbaric practice around A.D. 100 was reported by PLUTARCH, who said it had lasted 1,000 years.

Alexander Minor character in *Troilus and Cressida,* a servant of Cressida. Alexander appears only in 1.2, where he tells his mistress that the Trojan prince Hector is furious because he has been humbled in battle by the Greek warrior Ajax. He describes Ajax in humorous terms as a beastlike man. This brief episode introduces the rivalries of the warriors in a fashion that signals the play's satiric intent.

Andromache Legendary figure and minor character in *Troilus and Cressida,* the wife of Hector. In 5.3, disturbed by dire omens, Andromache unsuccessfully tries to persuade Hector not to fight. The episode humanizes the warrior by showing that he has a loving spouse, and it also stresses his fatal destiny. According to classical mythology, Andromache became the slave of Achilles' son after the fall of TROY, later marrying Helenus.

Antenor Legendary figure and character in *Troilus and Cressida,* a Trojan warrior captured by the Greeks and exchanged for Cressida. This exchange is crucial to the development of the play's love plot, but Antenor's role is otherwise insignificant. He appears in five scenes but never speaks, serving merely to swell the ranks of the Trojan aristocracy.

However, Antenor has a hidden importance, for, in the version of the legend known to Elizabethan England, he later betrayed TROY to the Greeks. Shakespeare does not mention this, presuming that his audience would know it; the knowledge makes evident a striking piece of dramatic irony. When Calchas, a Trojan deserter to the Greeks, proposes the prisoner exchange in 3.3, the audience knows, although the characters do not, that he has thus laid the groundwork for two more betrayals besides his own, that of Troilus by Cressida and, more important, that of Antenor against Troy. This irony is signaled by the remarks made about Antenor. He is seen as a very important Trojan—Pandarus praises him as "one o'th'soundest judgements in Troy" (1.2.194), and Calchas says that "Troy holds him very dear . . . their negotiations all must slack, / Wanting his manage" (3.3.19, 24–25).

Boy Minor character in *Troilus and Cressida,* a servant of Troilus. In 1.2 the Boy summons Pandarus to his master's house. The incident leaves Cressida alone to soliloquize on her love for Troilus.

Calchas Legendary figure and character in *Troilus and Cressida,* the father of Cressida. Calchas, a Trojan priest, has foreseen the defeat of TROY in the TROJAN WAR and has deserted to the Greeks before the play begins. In 3.3.1–30 he proposes a prisoner exchange: The Greeks can repay him for his treason by trading the newly captured Trojan prince Antenor for his daughter. Thus Cressida is removed from her lover, Troilus, just as their affair has begun, and she is exposed to the temptation that leads her to betray Troilus in favor of the Greek warrior Diomedes. Aside from triggering this development, Calchas's role in the play is insignificant.

In the *Iliad* of HOMER, Calchas is a Greek prophet who foretells the length of the war. His transformation into a Trojan occurs in the later, pro-Trojan version of the legend that was the basis for the English accounts on which Shakespeare relied.

Cassandra Legendary figure and character in *Troilus and Cressida,* a princess of TROY, the daughter of King Priam and sister to the princes Hector, Troilus, and Paris. Cassandra, a seer, twice foretells the fall of Troy. First, she hysterically interrupts a council of war to warn, "Troy burns, or else let Helen go" (2.2.113), only to be dismissed as the victim of "brain-sick raptures" (2.2.123). In 5.3, in calmer tones, she joins Andromache and Priam in trying to persuade Hector not to enter battle on a day of ill omens. Rebuffed again, she bids her brother a sad farewell. Although the other characters do not believe her, Cassandra's prophecies contribute to the play's atmosphere of fateful destiny, for they are known by the audience to be correct.

In the *Iliad* of HOMER, Cassandra is a minor figure and not a seer. She first appears as a prophet in Greek literature of the fifth century B.C. According to the dramatist Aeschylus, her prophetic power was given to her by Apollo, but when she refused his love, he transformed it into a curse, causing her to be always disbelieved. This myth has been well known since ancient times, and Shakespeare could presume that his audience would recognize Apollo's curse as the cause of the Trojans' rejection of Cassandra's warnings.

Cressida Legendary figure and title character in *Troilus and Cressida,* lover of Troilus. Because Cressida's betrayal of her lover in favor of the Greek Diomedes is the focal event of the love plot, many commentators have seen her role as that of a villain, though in fact Shakespeare did not treat her unsympathetically. Her disloyalty is a necessary element of his story, and she is representative of human or perhaps (for Shakespeare) feminine weakness, but she is certainly not a vicious breaker of hearts; nor, despite Ulysses' mistaken assumption upon meeting her in 4.5, is she a prostitute, for she shows no hint of mercenary motives. Diomedes courts her in 5.2 with the same wiles she used on Troilus earlier—affecting disinterest and a readiness to ignore her—and she is susceptible, though she resists confusedly. She is a frankly sensual woman, as has been evident from her affair with Troilus, and now, alone in a new world, having just been removed from TROY to the Greek camp, she succumbs to her nature.

Cressida is frequently associated with Helen, the worthless prize of the TROJAN WAR, in order to underscore her similar deficiency as a motive for Troilus. She is a much more alert and interesting personality than Helen, however. She is a knowledgeable flirt, able to consider the tactics of courtship, and she is scornfully aware that Pandarus is "a bawd" (1.2.286). Once united with Troilus in 3.2, she frankly confesses her love, but in confusion she regrets abandoning her tactical game. Tellingly, she speaks of her "unkind self, that itself will leave / To be another's fool" (3.2.147–148). Swept up in the excitement of the moment, she deludes herself that a real romance is in the offing, but her profession of faith is couched in negative terms, allowing the prediction—recognized by the audience to be accurate, in a textbook instance of dramatic irony— that the future will call "false maids in love . . . 'as false as Cressid'" (3.2.188–194). Although she pledges her loyalty to Troilus in the enthusiasm of passion, she recognizes her need for Diomedes in Troilus's absence. She admits her guilt, attributing it to her gender: "Ah, poor our sex! . . . The error of our eye directs our mind" (5.2.108–109). Such simple awareness of guilt is unique in this play filled with hypocrisy and self-delusion.

Cressida's name stems from a character in the *Iliad* of HOMER. Briseis, a slave and concubine of first Achilles and then Agamemnon and a source of dispute between them; she had nothing to do with Troilus. The name evolved through Briseida, to Griseida, and then Criseyde—in the works of SAINTE-MAURE, BOCCACCIO, and CHAUCER, respectively—before Shakespeare used the variant that is now standard.

Deiphobus Legendary figure and minor character in *Troilus and Cressida,* a Trojan warrior. Deiphobus appears in five scenes but speaks only two lines, serving merely to flesh out the Trojan aristocracy. In the *Iliad* of HOMER, Deiphobus, a son of King Priam, is a prominent warrior.

Diomedes Legendary figure and character in *Troilus and Cressida,* a Greek warrior and seducer of Cressida. Diomedes plays a very minor role in the TROJAN WAR until he is assigned to oversee the

exchange of prisoners whereby Cressida is traded for Antenor. When he arrives among the Trojans, he expresses a sharply cynical view of Helen that makes plain his lack of the romantic idealism that has led Troilus to deceive himself about love. Thus, when he manipulates Cressida's emotions in 5.2, using an affected disinterest—the tactic with which she herself beguiled Troilus—we recognize him as a cold-blooded seducer. When she agrees to a sexual assignation, he demands from her the love token given her by Troilus, thus climaxing her betrayal. Diomedes is coolly amoral, contributing to our sense of the corruption that infects the play's world.

In the *Iliad* of HOMER, Diomedes is the king of Argos, a Greek state owing allegiance to Agamemnon, and he is second only to his overlord in prestige and power. He plays a prominent part in the Trojan War, as both a warrior and a strategist, and he is closely associated with Odysseus (the play's Ulysses). He has no love life in the *Iliad* (his connection to Cressida arose only with the development of her story in the Middle Ages), though a post-Homeric tradition gave him a wife whose infidelity while he was at Troy causes him to emigrate to Italy after his return; there he founded several cities and chivalrously refused to fight the Trojan refugees who also came there. He was an object of cult worship in Italy, especially on the shores of the Adriatic, where the sea birds were believed to be the souls of his followers.

Hector Legendary figure and character in *Troilus and Cressida,* the crown prince of TROY, son of King Priam and brother of Troilus and Paris. Hector, the leading Trojan warrior, holds to an ideal chivalric code centered on the notion of personal honor and the possibility of glory. Thus he is a principal element of the play's sardonic presentation of the false glamor of war.

Though he is to some extent a character type— the romantic warrior-hero—Hector is made more humanly interesting through his deviations from the chivalric norm. He recognizes the defects of his position when, at the Trojan council of war, he advocates returning Helen to the Greeks and ending the fighting, and he points out the evil consequences of permitting "the hot passion of distemper'd blood [to influence] a free determination / 'Twixt right and wrong" (2.2.170–172). However, he subordinates such wisdom to his enthusiasm for personal honor and glory and agrees with Troilus that they must carry on the conflict. Like his Greek counterpart as a spokesman for sanity, Ulysses, Hector presents an image of right behavior that he cannot live up to himself, reinforcing the play's bitter commentary.

Hector's humanly malleable ideals play a part in his death in 5.8, which results from an ironic combination of obsessive adherence to, and temporary abandonment of, his chivalric code. Citing "the faith of valour" (5.3.69), he ignores dire omens and refuses the pleas of his father, his wife, Andromache, and his sister, Cassandra, that he not fight. On the battlefield he chivalrously permits Achilles to recover from exhaustion in 5.6. Then, in an uncharacteristic moment of greed and vanity, Hector kills a Greek soldier (the One) in order to loot the corpse of its fine armor. While doing so, he removes his own armor, and in this vulnerable moment he is killed by the Myrmidons. Nevertheless, Hector remains one of the most positive figures in the play, self-deluded and weak at a critical moment but essentially honorable.

Hector's name is probably a variation of an ancient Greek word for "holder" or "stayer," and this leads scholars to surmise that he is an invention of HOMER or earlier Greek poets, rather than a rendering of a historical person. He has no importance in classical myth and literature outside Homer's *Iliad*, though he was the subject of cult worship in several places, notably at later settlements around Troy. Hector remained famous throughout medieval and RENAISSANCE times. He was one of the panoply of traditional heroes known as the Nine Worthies, and as such he is depicted in the comical pageant in *Love's Labour's Lost* (5.2.541–717).

Helen Legendary figure and character in *Troilus and Cressida*, the mistress of Prince Paris of TROY. Years before the play opens, Paris stole Helen from King Menelaus of Sparta, thereby sparking the TROJAN WAR. Helen appears only in 3.1, where she is portrayed as a simpering lady of fashion whose vapid coquetry induces Pandarus to sing a love song while she entirely misses her guest's transmission of a message to Paris. That the object of the conflict should be this inane society hostess illustrates the play's lessons on the false glamor of both sex and war, and these lessons are confirmed by the warriors' own opinions of Helen. She is repeatedly declared an inadequate cause of war by Hector, Priam, Diomedes (with particularly scathing remarks in 4.1.56–67), and even by Troilus in 1.1.90–93, although elsewhere Troilus, arguing for the continuance of the war calls Helen "a pearl / Whose price hath launched above a thousand ships" (2.2.82–83). (Shakespeare's alteration of this famous line by MARLOWE—even better known then than it is now—is significant; Helen's *price*, rather than her *face*, as in *Dr Faustus*, launches the ships.)

In classical mythology, Helen is one of the offspring resulting from the rape of Leda by Zeus, who was disguised as a swan. She was accordingly born from an egg, whose shell was reputedly preserved as a relic in Sparta into historical times. This cult, and the fact that her name is not Greek, may reflect Helen's status as a "faded" deity, a goddess in an earlier, now-lost religion who survived as a mortal in Greek mythology. Helen's abduction sparks the Trojan War in the *Iliad* of HOMER, as in the play, but in Homer she becomes Paris's wife rather than his mistress, and she is deeply disturbed by her bigamous status. A later tradition held that Paris, deceived by a friendly goddess, carried off a mere phantom of Helen to Troy. Helen thus preserved her honor, spending the war years in Egypt. After the war, she is reunited with Menelaus in all accounts.

Helenus Legendary figure and minor character in *Troilus and Cressida*, a son of King Priam. In 2.2.33–36 Helenus challenges Troilus's insistence on Trojan honor as a justification for retaining the kidnapped Helen and continuing the TROJAN WAR, but Troilus dismisses him with the remark, "You are for dreams and slumbers, brother priest" (2.2.37), and an accusation of cowardice, and Helenus is not mentioned again. Shakespeare took this incident—which appears in two of his sources. William CAXTON's *The Recuyell of the Historyes of Troye* and John LYDGATE's *Troy Book*—to help establish Troilus's hot-blooded chivalrousness. Helenus himself is of no consequence and has no personality.

Man Minor character in *Troilus and Cressida*, a servant of Troilus. In 3.2 the Man informs Pandarus that Troilus is waiting for him.

Margarelon (Margareton, Margariton) Legendary figure and minor character in *Troilus and Cressida*, an illegitimate son of King Priam. In 5.7 Margarelon challenges Thersites on the battlefield, identifying himself as "A bastard son of Priam's" (5.7.15). Thersites declares himself "a bastard, too . . . bastard begot, bastard instructed, bastard in mind, bastard in valour, in everything illegitimate" (5.7.16–18); he then flees. The episode serves only to display Thersites' coarse wit and cowardice. Margarelon speaks only three lines and has no personality.

In the earliest editions of the play, which reflect Shakespeare's manuscript, this character is identified merely as "Bastard." By a tradition dating from the 18th century, he is given the name of a son of Priam's, "bastard Margarelon," that appears in a list of Trojan warriors (5.5.7). Shakespeare took the name from either William CAXTON's *The Recuyell of the Historyes of Troye* or John LYDGATE's *Troy Book*, where it is variously spelled Margareton or Margariton. (The change from "t" to "l" was probably a typesetter's error.) Margareton, one of Priam's many illegitimate sons, had no other importance in classical mythology.

Menelaus Legendary figure and minor character in *Troilus and Cressida*, king of Sparta and a leader of the Greeks in the TROJAN WAR. Before the play opens, the theft of Menelaus's wife Helen by Prince Paris of Troy has sparked the war. However, although he is the ostensible beneficiary of the war and the younger brother of the Greek commander Agamemnon, he is an inconsequential figure. He speaks more than one line in only one scene, 4.5, where in brief exchanges he is wittily mortified by both Patroclus and Cressida. His insignificance makes the cause of the war seem all the more trivial, an important motif of the play. This theme is further supported by the frequent derisive references to Menelaus's status as a cuckold.

In the *Iliad* of HOMER, Menelaus is intermittently a major figure—defeating Paris in a duel but prevented from killing him by the goddess Aphrodite, for example—but he consciously subordinates himself to Agamemnon. In the *Odyssey* and later works, he resumes a comfortable domestic life with Helen after the war.

Myrmidons Several minor characters in *Troilus and Cressida*, followers of the Greek warrior Achilles. In 5.7 Achilles orders the Myrmidons to avoid combat in order to save themselves for a confrontation with Hector, and when the Trojan leader is encountered without his armor on, in 5.8, the Myrmidons kill him. The episode, presenting an extreme of unchivalrous behavior, caps the play's picture of the dishonor of war in general and of the TROJAN WAR in particular.

In the *Iliad* of HOMER, the Myrmidons were an ethnically distinct group of soldiers from Thessaly, in what is now northeastern Greece; they were named for a legendary ancestor, Myrmidon. Like Achilles, the Myrmidons came from beyond the world of ancient Hellenic civilization and were seen as somewhat barbaric and cruel by the more cosmopolitan Greeks. This attitude survives in Shakespeare's presentation.

Nestor Legendary figure and character in *Troilus and Cressida*, the oldest of the Greek leaders in the TROJAN WAR. Though respected for his great age, Shakespeare's Nestor is a faintly ludicrous old man who boasts about his longevity and is full of platitudes and long-winded speeches. For instance, agreeing with Ulysses that another character's purpose is plain, Nestor says, "True; the purpose is perspicuous as substance / Whose grossness little characters sum up" (1.3.324–325). He is chiefly a supporter of Ulysses' schemes to coax Achilles into battle and does very little otherwise.

Nestor was first presented in the *Iliad* of HOMER, where he is the same self-righteous and ineffectual old man we see in Shakespeare. In Homer he is somewhat more than 60, a very respectable age in the ancient world; in the Roman poet OVID's *Metamorphoses*, which Shakespeare read, he is an improbable 200 years old.

One Minor character in *Troilus and Cressida,* an anonymous Greek warrior killed by Hector. In 5.6 Hector spies the Greek fighter wearing a sumptuous suit of armor, and he declares he will take it from him. The Greek flees, but in 5.8 we see that Hector has killed him, and as the triumphant warrior takes off his own armor to put on his prize, he is treacherously killed by Achilles and the Myrmidons.

While stripping the dead Greek, Hector addresses the corpse as "Most putrefied core, so fair without" (5.8.1), contrasting the dead body with the pomp and splendor of his armor (in words reminiscent of Christ's condemnation of the Pharisees as "whited sepulchres" [Matthew 23:27]). The symbolic significance of the One is thus clear: he sums up the hypocrisy of the warriors' pretensions throughout the play. At the same time, the episode also reveals Hector's death to be the result of his abandonment of his code of honorable combat to pursue a rich prize.

Pandarus Legendary figure and character in *Troilus and Cressida,* uncle of Cressida who encourages her love affair with Troilus. Pandarus, though a comic character, is also a conventional representation of a procurer of prostitutes. As such he is a symbol of the moral corruption that permeates the world of the play. (Although Pandarus promotes only a single, nonmercenary affair in both Shakespeare's play and its sources, he was already well established in Shakespeare's day as a symbol of the profession.)

Pandarus uses a variety of humorously exaggerated dictions: the rather affected language of the court (as when he uses the word *fair* is several ways in one sentence, composing an elaborate compliment to Helen in 3.1.42–45); babytalk ("Come, come, what need you blush? Shame's a baby" [3.2.39]); and the bold language of braggadocio—e.g., in his deprecation of the Soldiers as "Asses, fools, dolts, chaff and bran, chaff and bran; porridge after meat . . . crows and daws, crows and daws" (1.2.245–248). In these passages Pandarus resembles such other Shakespearean comic characters as the Nurse of *Romeo and Juliet,* Falstaff in *1 Henry IV,* and Feste of *Twelfth Night.* Aeneas parodies him in 4.2.56–59, emphasizing both his comic aspect and his inferior social status.

Pandarus insinuates himself into other people's lives and is capable of outrageous interruptions, as in his interception of Cressida's despairing cry to Troilus, "Have the god's envy?" with the thoughtless "Ay, ay, ay, ay, 'tis too plain a case" (4.4.27–28), and even of physical intrusiveness ("Let me embrace, too" [4.4.13]). As we know from the eventual result of the liaison he arranges, Pandarus is ultimately malevolent. This is strikingly conveyed by his association with venereal disease in 5.4 and 5.10.

In the EPILOGUE, Pandarus steps somewhat out of character, speaking verse for the first time, as the formality of the device demands. However, he is still comically reprehensible. His recital on the humblebee, whose "Sweet honey and sweet notes together fail" (5.10.42–45) is a completely appropriate ending for this play of mistakes, misunderstandings, and failures. His flippant insults serve to distance the audience from the play as it closes. Because the audience is actually not composed of "traitors and bawds . . . traders in the flesh . . . Brethren and sisters of the hold-door trade" (5.10.37, 46, 52), it need not identify with the play's discouraging ending and can feel itself superior to its corrupt world. The satirical nature of the play is confirmed, implicitly allowing for the existence of human virtues in contrast to the vices depicted on stage. Thus Pandarus provides some sense of the high-spirited resolution typical in COMEDY.

Pandarus appears in the *Iliad* of HOMER, but although he is an unpleasant character in that epic, he has nothing to do with Troilus or any other lovers (Cressida does not appear in Homer). It was in the Middle Ages that Pandarus first acquired his role as the lovers' go-between. By Shakespeare's day his name had become a common noun (and later a verb), although the spelling had changed slightly to *pander,* in which form it is still in common use.

Paris Legendary figure and character in *Troilus and Cressida,* a prince of TROY, son of King Priam, and brother of Troilus and Hector. Before the play opens, Paris's theft of Helen, wife of the Greek leader Menelaus, has caused the TROJAN WAR. Thus his story is one of the examples of human folly that comprise a leading theme of the play. Paris is a decadent figure; his father calls him "besotted on your sweet delights" (2.2.144), referring to Helen, and Paris confirms this judgment when he avoids the battlefield, claiming, "I would fain have armed today, but my Nell would not have it so" (3.1.132–133). In his other appearances, he is merely one among the Trojan warriors, remarking on the events of the war; he also aids Troilus's courtship of Cressida, covering for his absence from a state dinner and sending a warning to the lovers that a diplomatic delegation is approaching in 4.1. In Act 5 Paris fights with Menelaus, provoking sardonic remarks from Thersites on "the cuckold and the cuckold-maker" (5.7.9).

In classical mythology, Paris was bribed by Aphrodite to select her as the most beautiful of three quarreling goddesses. She rewarded him by helping him to kidnap Helen. Though this well-known legend was pre-Homeric, HOMER does not mention it, saying only that Paris abducted Helen because of her beauty. In the *Iliad*, Paris is an effective warrior, specializing in archery, though he flees Menelaus in a moment of cowardice. Recovering, he challenges Menelaus to a duel but is defeated and must be rescued by Aphrodite. According to a later legend, Paris was the eventual killer of Achilles, placing an arrow precisely in his only vulnerable spot, his heel.

Patroclus Legendary figure and character in *Troilus and Cressida*, a Greek warrior in the TROJAN WAR and friend and follower of Achilles. While he himself is not an important figure, Patroclus's death is a key event in the plot, for it sparks Achilles to abandon his withdrawal from the combat and resume fighting, with the result that TROY loses the climactic battle. Patroclus represents Achilles in his dispute with the Greek leader, relaying his friend's statements of noncooperation and carrying messages back to him. In an incidental episode that heightens the aura of decadence that surrounds the warriors, Achilles' jester, Thersites, taunts Patroclus with a piece of malicious gossip, saying, "Thou art said to be Achilles' male varlet . . . his masculine whore" (5.1.14, 16), though the imputation is carried no further and has no dramatic significance.

In the *Iliad* of HOMER, which contains the original version of Patroclus's story, Patroclus was somewhat older than Achilles. He was an attendant of the warrior because, as a boy, he had been taken under the protection of Achilles' father after accidentally killing someone. In Homer, Achilles' devoted friendship for Patroclus is one of the warrior's fine attributes, and there is no hint of a homosexual relationship. However, the tradition that the two were lovers was established by the sixth century B.C.

Priam, King of Troy Legendary figure and character in *Troilus and Cressida*, the ruler of the city besieged by the Greeks in the TROJAN WAR. Despite his regal position, Priam plays an insignificant role, calling the war council to order in 2.2—but participating very little—and unsuccessfully attempting, along with Andromache and Cassandra, to persuade Hector not to fight on a day of disastrous omens in 5.3.

Priam was a well-known figure in classical mythology and is referred to in a number of Shakespeare's plays and in *The Rape of Lucrece*. His name was proverbial for someone who has experienced extremes of good and bad fortune. In the *Iliad* of HOMER, Priam is an old man, the father of 50 sons by various wives and concubines. His harem, along with his non-Greek name, suggests to scholars that he represents a folk-memory of some real Asiatic monarch of the second millennium B.C. His death at the hands of Neoptolemus (see Pyrrhus in *Hamlet*) is the most important incident of his life, both in Homer and in later literature. It is described in the dramatic monologue recited by the First Player in 2.2.464–493 of *Hamlet*.

Prologue Allegorical figure in *Troilus and Cressida* who speaks the PROLOGUE that opens the play. The Prologue tells how the TROJAN WAR stemmed from the abduction of Menelaus's wife, Helen, by Paris. He commences in the heroic style of traditional chroniclers of war, only to sum up, "Ravished Helen, Menelaus' queen / With wanton Paris sleeps—and that's the quarrel" (Pro. 9–10). This stylistic jolt, both rhythmic and rhetorical, serves notice that this account of the ancient epic will not be conventional. He goes on to caution the audience that it may not like what the play depicts, for its contents vary with "the chance of war" (Pro.

31). In belittling his warlike costume, the Prologue further hints at the satire of soldiery that is to come. Some scholars believe that the provision for an "arm'd" Prologue was inspired by, and perhaps intended as an allusion to, the armored Prologue in Ben JONSON's play *Poetaster* (1601).

Servant (1) Minor character in *Troilus and Cressida*, an employee of Prince Paris. In 3.1.1–40 Pandarus asks the Servant about Paris; the Servant replies with saucy witticisms that go over Pandarus's head. The episode exposes Pandarus's foolish and supercilious manner.

Servant (2) Minor character in *Troilus and Cressida*, follower of Diomedes. In 5.5 the Servant is instructed to take Troilus's captured horse to Cressida as Diomedes' testament of his superiority over her ex-lover.

Soldiers Several minor characters in *Troilus and Cressida*, Trojan troops. In 1.2 the Soldiers, who do not speak, march in front of Pandarus and Cressida, provoking Pandarus to sneer, "Asses, fools, dolts, chaff and bran, chaff and bran; porridge after meat . . . crows and daws, crows and daws" (1.2.245–248). This is one of the comically insulting remarks that pepper the play.

Thersites Legendary figure and character in *Troilus and Cressida*, the jester, or FOOL, to Ajax and Achilles. Thersites rails against everyone he encounters, and his diatribes are vicious and hateful. He is also a coward who avoids combat by unashamedly declaring himself too roguish a person to be fought by a chivalrous knight. The unhealthy aura of disgust that distinguishes this play and contributes greatly to its satire owes much to Thersites' outbursts. Thersites is not likable, but his language is inventive and funny, and he is capable of amusing imitations of his targets, especially when he enacts the prideful Ajax in 3.3.279–302. Further, his perception of the follies of the warriors of the TROJAN WAR is refreshingly acute, and we respect his capacity to see through the combatants' pretensions to reason and honor when they persist in fighting a sordid, irrational war.

Thersites is a composite of two ancient character types: the boastful MILES GLORIOSUS, a braggart soldier; and the scathing critic, a sort of CHORUS, whose usually comic commentary provides telling asides on the main action. As a court jester, he is licensed to insult his superiors, and he thus resembles, in a perverse way, other Shakespearean fools such as Feste and the Fool in *King Lear*. However, unlike them, Thersites is "lost in the labyrinth of [his] fury" (2.3.1–2), and his obscene jests often tell us more about his own disturbed nature than about the warriors he mocks. He displays a morbid excitement when other characters are suffering most, as when he cries out, "Now the pledge: now, now, now!" (5.2.65), when Troilus witnesses Cressida surrendering to Diomedes the token he had given her. Moreover, he often directs his venom at himself, declaring, for example, "I am a rascal . . . a very filthy rogue" (5.4.28–29), and "I am a bastard . . . I am bastard begot, bastard instructed, bastard in mind, bastard in valour, in everything illegitimate" (5.7.16–18). Thersites' pathology has dramatic value, heightening the sense of disease that the play's world conveys.

Thersites plays a similar, though much less prominent, role in the *Iliad* of HOMER, the ultimate source of the drama. In one episode he rails at Agamemnon until Odysseus (Shakespeare's Ulysses) beats him into silence. In a later tradition, Achilles kills him for insulting him while he is in mourning for an Amazon queen he has slain in combat.

Troilus One of the title characters of *Troilus and Cressida*, a prince of TROY, a Trojan leader in the TROJAN WAR, and the lover of Cressida. As the only character to have a major part in both of the play's plot lines—a fighter for the honor of Troy in the warriors' plot and the victim of Cressida's betrayal in the ill-fated love story—Troilus contributes greatly to the play's central theme: the inadequacy of good intentions in a corrupt world. Self-deluded both as a lover and a warrior, Troilus is a principal component of, and a sufferer from, the play's atmosphere of error and misdirection.

He is a typical romantic hero, but his complex and credible responses make him interesting as well. Most important, he is mistaken in his attitude toward Cressida. Although Pandarus's lewd jests and salacious attitude make perfectly plain what sort of game is afoot, Troilus persists in pretending to himself that Cressida is "stubborn-chaste" (1.1.97). In fact, their relationship is never more than a sexual affair that cannot be expected to last long. Subconsciously he is aware of the truth; from the outset he is suspicious that Cressida will prove unfaithful. His language is also revealing. With romantic rhetoric, he describes Cressida as a "pearl" (1.1.100), Pandarus as a ship, and himself as a merchant; unconsciously, he devalues his lover to the status of an object and the consummation of their love to that of a commercial transaction. When he approaches his long-sought rendezvous with Cressida, his thrill is distinctly sensual rather than emotional (as compared to, say, Romeo). He hopes to "wallow in the lily beds" (3.2.11) when his "wat'ry [i.e., salivating] palate tastes . . . Love's . . . nectar" (3.2.19–20). But he does not acknowledge this, preferring to see himself as a romantic figure, "a strange soul upon the Stygian banks" (3.2.8).

His capacity for self-deception is also important in the warriors' plot. Just as he deludes himself about Cressida, he also deludes himself about the pointless war for Helen. He feels that she too is a "pearl" (2.2.82) and the Trojans doers of "valiant and magnanimous deeds" (2.2.201) in their defense of her. In both cases he confuses the real world with a grander, more ideal situation—like that of traditional literature and legend.

As a self-deluded warrior arguing for the continuation of the war, Troilus unconsciously presents an important theme: the unreliable nature of value judgments that are likely to change with time. In the Trojan council of 2.2 he argues that circumstances determine worth: Helen is valuable enough to fight over simply because she has been fought over already. "What's aught but as 'tis valued?" (2.2.53), he says, but he is unaware that this argument applies to himself. Cressida will eventually value him differently, compared to the more available man, Diomedes.

When Troilus witnesses Cressida's betrayal while eavesdropping on her conversation with Diomedes in 5.2, his self-delusion becomes strikingly evident. He will not acknowledge Cressida's flighty nature, or that he was wrong about their romance. Instead, he hysterically insists that to do so would indict all womanhood, and further, that all "beauty," all "sanctimony . . . the gods' delight," and "unity itself" (5.2.137, 139, 140) would be flawed. His grief and confusion are real, but his expressions of it are shallow and rhetorical. His focus is on literary images of betrayal, rather than on the particular betrayal that has just taken place. He avoids admitting that his romance was merely a sexual affair by translating it into high-flown abstractions.

His final response is just as displaced: He translates his love for Cressida into hatred for Diomedes. Significantly, when the berserk Troilus encounters Diomedes on the battlefield, he has completely forgotten why he was so enraged and demands that his foe "pay the life thou ow'st me for my horse" (5.6.7), a line that is both funny and ironically revealing.

At the close of the play, Troilus has forgotten Cressida and is instead caught up in the death of Hector and Troy's loss of the climactic battle. Convinced that all is lost, he proposes to fight to the death. His despair is even more pitiful because, ironically, Troy will actually survive this immediate crisis. Just as when he refuses to fight, in 1.1, because his love seems so much more valuable than the war, Troilus attributes unwarranted grandeur to events concerning himself. In this way he demonstrates in his own person the central theme of the play.

In the *Iliad* of HOMER, Troilus was merely one of the many sons of Priam; he dies well before Hector does, and his role in the tale is insignificant. His connection with Cressida arose only in legends from the Middle Ages.

Ulysses Legendary figure and character in *Troilus and Cressida*, a Greek leader in the TROJAN WAR. Ulysses is a voice of sanity among the Greeks, who are fighting a dishonorable war for a pointless cause. Yet such is the corruption of the world of the play that Ulysses fails to influence his fellows and, indeed, gives up his own ideals. In both his idealism and his failure he corresponds to Hector among the Trojans.

However, the common sense and political wisdom of Ulysses provide a background against which to view the corrupt world of the play. He diagnoses the Greek failure in the war as due to their departure from strict adherence to a system of social hierarchy, like that of the "heavens themselves" (1.3.85). However, in his effort to convince Achilles that he should return to the battle, he abandons this idea and instead encourages the reluctant warrior to consider the loss of status he risks by permitting Ajax to receive the laurels he could receive himself. In giving up his ideals to promote this rivalry, Ulysses reveals himself to be a pragmatist, but the event contributes to our sense of disorder in the play's world. Moreover, his compromise fails in its purpose, for Achilles again withdraws from the battle, and only Patroclus's death finally brings his sword into play. Ulysses, though wise, is no less subject to the chances of war than anyone else.

Ulysses' judgments of the other characters, though firmly stated, are distinctly, if slightly, mistaken, adding to the play's network of self-deception and error. In 4.5, on the strength of his first impression, he declares Cressida to be a prostitute; while he has perceived her sexuality, he has misread it, for she is merely a frankly sensual woman whom circumstance has placed in temptation's way. Ulysses praises Diomedes for a spirit that "In aspiration lifts him from the earth" (4.5.16); he recognizes an intensity of purpose, but he fails to see that Diomedes' energies are to be expended on an extremely earthly aspiration: the seduction of Cressida. Similarly, Ulysses says of Troilus that he "gives not till judgement guide his bounty" (4.5.102), yet we know that Troilus has committed himself to Cressida without judgment. However, Troilus is an idealist in love, and Ulysses' opinion is not wrong, merely uninformed. We are made aware that wisdom and objectivity are no guarantee of knowledge in the world of the play.

Ulysses (better known by his Greek name, Odysseus) is a principal character in the *Iliad* of HOMER. He is noted for his wisdom and good sense as a strategist, and he is also a valiant warrior. He is the central figure in the *Iliad*'s successor, the *Odyssey*, which recounts his long series of adventures after the war. In Homer, Odysseus was famous for craftiness—reflected in the play in Thersites' reference to him as "that . . . dog-fox Ulysses" (5.4.11). Although he lies fluently when he needs to, he is essentially honorable. In later tradition, however, especially in the ancient Greek drama-

tists, he appears as a cowardly rascal. He was worshipped as a demigod in the cults of later antiquity.

True Tragedy, The

Abbreviated title of the BAD QUARTO version of *3 Henry VI*, originally titled *The true Tragedy of Richard Duke of Yorke, and the death of good King Henrie the Sixt, with the whole contention betweene the two Houses Lancaster and Yorke, as it was sundrie times acted by the Right Honourable the Earle of Pembrooke his servants*. It was published twice by Thomas MILLINGTON, in 1595 and 1600; these are known as the Q1 and Q2 editions, respectively, of *3 Henry VI*. (Although the 1595 edition, of which only one copy has survived, was actually published in octavo format, the term *quarto* is retained for convenience.)

It was once believed that *The True Tragedy* was the text of an earlier play, by Shakespeare or someone else, that Shakespeare revised. However, it is now generally agreed that it is a "reported" copy of *3 Henry VI*, probably recorded mostly by the actors who played Warwick, Clifford, and York. *The True Tragedy* is a good deal shorter than *3 Henry VI*, probably to reduce the playing time; the omitted sections are chiefly passages of rhetoric and poetic description that do not affect the progress of the plot. It is also possible that some passages, dealing with treason or usurpation of the crown, may have been subject to CENSORSHIP.

Q3 of *3 Henry VI*, a slightly edited version of *The True Tragedy*, was published in 1619 by Thomas PAVIER, in a volume with a bad quarto version of *2 Henry VI*. This edition is known by its abbreviated title as *The Whole Contention*.

Twelfth Night
SYNOPSIS
Act 1, Scene 1
Orsino, duke of ILLYRIA, speaks of his consuming passion for Olivia. His messenger, Valentine, reports that Olivia has turned him away, saying

that she proposes to enter seclusion for seven years in memory of her late brother. Orsino marvels at her dedication, hoping it will someday be directed toward himself.

Act 1, Scene 2

Viola, shipwrecked but safe, is assured by the Captain that her brother may have been saved also. The Captain informs her that they have landed in his home, Illyria, where the duke, Orsino, is courting a lady who has entered seclusion. Viola decides to become a follower of Orsino and pays the Captain to help disguise her as a man and introduce her to the duke.

Act 1, Scene 3

Sir Toby Belch complains of the asceticism of Olivia, his niece, with whom he is living. Olivia's chambermaid, Maria, suggests that he and his visiting friend Sir Andrew Aguecheek, who hopes to woo Olivia, lead less riotous lives, for her mistress dislikes their drunken behavior. Sir Andrew appears and announces that he will depart, given Orsino's rivalry for Olivia's hand, but Sir Toby assures him that Olivia disdains the duke, and he decides to stay.

Act 1, Scene 4

Valentine assures Viola, who is disguised as a boy named Cesario, that Orsino likes "him." The Duke appears and sends Cesario to try to persuade Olivia to marry him. Once alone, Viola muses on her distress: She has fallen in love with the man on whose behalf she must woo.

Act 1, Scene 5

Maria chastises Olivia's jester, Feste, for his absence from court. Olivia appears with her steward, Malvolio. She is angry with the truant Feste, but his witticisms cajole her into a friendly mood. Malvolio berates Feste, but Olivia accuses the steward of an egotistical dislike of anything contrary to his own grumpiness. Maria announces that a messenger from Orsino has arrived; she and Malvolio are sent to keep him away. Sir Toby has encountered the messenger, but he is too drunk to report on him. Malvolio returns and says that the emissary has refused to depart, describing him as more a boy than

Viola, a character in *Twelfth Night,* in a 19th-century illustration. Viola is put at the center of the play's conflict when she poses as a young man, Cesario. *(Courtesy of Culver Pictures, Inc.)*

a man. Olivia decides to greet this youth, who is the disguised Viola and who, as Cesario, speaks for Orsino in poetic terms that charm Olivia. She sends Cesario back to the duke with another refusal, but after the former leaves, Olivia confesses to herself that she has fallen in love with Cesario. She sends Malvolio after Cesario with a ring, which she asserts the duke's messenger had forced on her.

Act 2, Scene 1

Sebastian tells Antonio, who has saved him from a shipwreck, that his sister died in the same disaster. Now fully recovered, he proposes to visit Duke Orsino. He insists that Antonio not accompany him; he already owes his savior too much, he says, and his own bad luck might prove contagious. Sebastian then leaves alone, but Antonio decides that, although he has enemies at Orsino's court, he will follow his new friend.

Act 2, Scene 2

Malvolio gives Olivia's ring to the disguised Viola and departs. Viola realizes that Olivia has fallen in love with Cesario. She reflects on the complexity of the situation—she loves Orsino, Orsino loves Olivia, and Olivia loves her—and she observes that time will have to undo the tangle because she certainly cannot.

Act 2, Scene 3

Sir Toby, Sir Andrew, and Feste carouse drunkenly in Olivia's courtyard, when first Maria and then Malvolio appear to chastise them. Sir Toby mocks the steward, who departs, including Maria in his threats of reprisal as he goes. Maria proposes revenge upon Malvolio: she will write him love letters in Olivia's handwriting, and he will make a fool of himself when he responds to the supposed love of his mistress.

Act 2, Scene 4

Orsino talks of love with the disguised Viola; Cesario speaks of his affection for someone who resembles the duke. At Orsino's request, Feste sings a sad love song. Orsino sends Cesario on another mission to Olivia.

Act 2, Scene 5

Maria leaves a spurious love letter to be found by Malvolio. She, Sir Toby, Sir Andrew, and Fabian, a fellow conspirator, spy on the steward, who preens himself on Olivia's love. He pictures himself married to Olivia, and he envisions a future when, as her husband, he will chastise Sir Toby. Sir Toby is furious, and his friends must restrain him. Malvolio finds the planted letter and responds as predicted; he will follow the letter's instructions, behaving oddly and wearing peculiar clothes, to signify that he has received the message. Malvolio leaves, and the conspirators rejoice in the success of their scheme.

Act 3, Scene 1

Viola, as Cesario, bandies wit with Feste; Sir Toby and Sir Andrew take her to Olivia, whom she is vis-

iting on behalf of Orsino. Olivia confesses her love to Cesario, who rejects her suit, and she accepts rejection as her melancholy lot.

Act 3, Scene 2

Sir Andrew, seeing that Olivia favors Cesario, prepares to abandon his suit, but Sir Toby and Fabian reassure him, asserting that Olivia's behavior toward the young man is intended to make Sir Andrew jealous. Sir Toby suggests that Sir Andrew challenge Cesario to a duel; Sir Andrew leaves to write a challenge to the youth. Fabian and Sir Toby chortle over the prospect of watching two cowards—Sir Andrew and Cesario—try to get out of the duel. Maria appears with word that Malvolio is ridiculously dressed, in response to the spurious love letter, and about to meet Olivia. They all run to watch.

Act 3, Scene 3

Sebastian thanks Antonio for rejoining him; Antonio observes that, because he had once been an enemy of Duke Orsino's, he cannot afford to be seen in Illyria. He decides to seclude himself at an inn and meet Sebastian there later.

Act 3, Scene 4

Malvolio, garishly costumed, leers and flirts with Olivia, who is mystified. When word arrives that Cesario has arrived, Olivia leaves but insists that Malvolio, obviously demented, be treated with care. Malvolio interprets her concern as evidence of her love. Sir Toby and Fabian enter, suggesting that Malvolio may be possessed by the devil; he sneers at them and leaves. The exultant plotters plan to have their victim locked up as a lunatic. Sir Andrew appears with a comical letter challenging Cesario to a duel. Sir Toby sends him to find the youth, then declares that the letter is too foolish to scare anyone, so he will deliver his own version of it directly to Cesario. The plotters withdraw as Olivia and Viola enter. Olivia repeatedly offers her love, and Cesario insists that she should grant it to Orsino. Olivia leaves, and Sir Toby ferociously challenges Cesario, allegedly on behalf of a famous swordsman; the disguised Viola, alarmed, attempts to find an excuse to leave. Sir Toby fetches Sir Andrew and tells him that Cesario has responded fiercely; he and Fabian encourage the reluctant duelists to fight. Antonio appears and draws his sword in defense of Viola, believing her to be Sebastian, but two Officers appear and arrest him. He asks Viola to repay an earlier loan, which he now will need, but Viola naturally denies that she knows him. As he is taken away, Antonio accuses Viola of ingratitude and calls her Sebastian. Viola realizes that her brother must be alive, and she departs, ecstatic with hope. Sir Toby and Fabian point out that Cesario is a coward; Sir Andrew takes heart and sets out to resume the duel.

Act 4, Scene 1

Feste mistakes Sebastian for Cesario and is astonished to be treated as a stranger. Sir Andrew enters, and, making the same mistake, he strikes Sebastian, who responds by beating him. Sir Toby intervenes, and he and Sebastian draw their swords, as Olivia appears. Ordering everyone else to leave, she speaks to Sebastian, whom she also believes to be Cesario. She apologizes for the assault and invites him inside; mystified but delighted, he goes with her.

Act 4, Scene 2

Feste disguises himself as Sir Topas, a Puritan clergyman, and visits Malvolio in prison. He insists that Malvolio is indeed mad and denies the steward's complaint that his cell is dark. Sir Toby congratulates the jester on his performance but says that it is time to end the joke, for he is in enough trouble with Olivia already. Feste again visits Malvolio, this time undisguised. Malvolio asks him for pen and paper so that he can write to Olivia about his predicament. Feste teases him before agreeing to help.

Act 4, Scene 3

Sebastian muses happily on the bewildering fact that he is apparently loved by a beautiful noblewoman. Olivia appears with a Priest and suggests that she and Sebastian marry. He agrees.

Act 5, Scene 1

Orsino calls on Olivia with Viola and other followers. Antonio appears in the custody of the Officers and is identified as the duke's enemy. He tells of

Sebastian's disloyalty, referring to Viola's behavior in 3.3. Orsino does not believe him because he knows that Cesario has been with him during the time Antonio claims to have spent with Sebastian. Olivia arrives and again rejects Orsino, who responds hysterically that he will kill Cesario, not only because he knows of Olivia's fondness for him but also because he loves the youth himself, and he seeks the pain of sacrifice. Viola declares herself willing to die for the duke, and Olivia cries out to her husband, as she believes Cesario to be. Viola denies this, and Olivia summons the Priest, who testifies to their marriage two hours earlier. As the duke berates Cesario, Sir Andrew and Sir Toby appear, wounded, claiming to have been assaulted by him. They are followed by Sebastian, whose appearance confounds everyone. Sebastian and Viola identify each other and rejoice in their reunion. The duke declares that he will marry Viola. Malvolio is summoned and shows Olivia the letter that he believes she sent him. Olivia realizes that Maria has written it; Fabian defends Maria, saying that the plot was Sir Toby's idea and that Toby has married Maria. Feste teases Malvolio, who storms out vowing revenge. The duke declares that a double wedding shall soon occur, and all go indoors to celebrate, except Feste, who is left alone to sing a song of worldly resignation.

COMMENTARY

Twelfth Night was the last of Shakespeare's three "mature" COMEDIES, as it, *Much Ado About Nothing*, and *As You Like It* are called, and it was followed shortly by the first of the major TRAGEDIES, *Hamlet*. This crucial position in Shakespeare's oeuvre is reflected in the play's subtle complexity. It sustains the celebration of triumphant love that characterizes its predecessors, yet it is distinguished by a troubling undertone that suggests the playwright's need to deal with deeper realms of the human psyche.

Twelfth Night may be read or seen with pleasure on the level of traditional romantic comedy alone. Shakespeare assembles some stock features—separated twins, disguises, impediments to love—and freshly arranges them in a sequence that resembles a stately dance, all accompanied by a lusty SUBPLOT with a comic villain, Malvolio. The characters are exaggerated examples of human nature, placed in comically preposterous situations whose improbability we willingly accept as necessary for the retelling of a familiar tale. The world of the play is an undemanding one; there is always time for leisurely courtship, for SONGS, and for practical jokes; Malvolio deserves his lot, because he arrogantly and egotistically refuses to enter the fun.

However, Malvolio is merely a nuisance and not a threat; the triumph of love depends on opposition—such as that offered by the villainous Don John in *Much Ado*—and at first glance that opposition is not present in *Twelfth Night*. It turns out to be Orsino and Olivia, two of the lovers themselves, who inhibit the fulfillment of love, assuming wholly literary self-images as romantic lover and mourning lady, respectively. Their self-defeating posture suggests that something is amiss in the idyllic world of romantic comedy. The other important characters inspire a certain disquiet as well. Viola, the most clear-sighted and honest figure, is nevertheless tangled in the lie of her disguise, which prevents her from expressing her love. Sir Toby, for all his humor, is a parasite and, worse, a victimizer of the hapless Sir Andrew, as well as of Malvolio. Even the apparently frivolous Feste betrays a weary cynicism at times, as in his final song. Most significant, Malvolio's humiliation and imprisonment seem so out of proportion to his offense that they lend the comic subplot a vicious air that adds to our uneasy sense that the play's comedy is darker than it seems at first.

This disturbing quality is subtly reinforced by the repeated motif of madness. Olivia asserts that Sir Toby "speaks nothing but madman" (1.5.107), and Feste, pretending to excuse Toby's drunkenness, allows that "he is but mad yet . . . and the fool shall look to the madman" (1.5.138–139). When Sebastian arrives in Illyria, only to be pointlessly assaulted, he cries out, "Are all the people mad?" (4.1.126), and when Olivia mysteriously treats him as her lover, he exclaims, "[Either] I am mad, or else this is a dream" (4.1.60). Malvolio is especially associated with lunacy. His ludicrous behavior toward Olivia—induced by Maria's letter—is received as "midsummer madness" (3.4.55) by his mistress, and he is later imprisoned as a lunatic (the

commonest treatment for mental disorder in Shakespeare's day).

These elements have led some critics to regard the play as a social commentary resembling in spirit *Troilus and Cressida* or the satirical comedies of Ben JONSON. Olivia and Orsino may be taken as comic portraits of egotists, Olivia in her extravagant withdrawal from life and the duke in his absurd pose as a romantic lover. Most of the other Illyrians can be seen as socially ambitious and thus fit subjects for satire: In this view, Feste curries favor with Orsino because he may marry Olivia; Toby is a vulgar glutton who seeks a continued life of ease in Olivia's household; Malvolio, Sir Andrew, and Maria each seek a profitable marriage. Viola alone offers honest love in a society where affectation dominates.

Such propositions seem excessive, however, for the play lacks the acid taste of satire—although they accurately set off Viola, the drama's central figure, from the other characters. Viola is not invulnerable to love's irrationality, but unlike the others, she recognizes and acknowledges her blindness. She admits that the situation is beyond her control as soon as the three loves—hers for Orsino, Orsino's for Olivia, Olivia's for her—have become evident, saying, "O time, thou must entangle this, not I, / It is too hard a knot for me t'untie" (2.2.39–40). She knows what she wants, however—Orsino's love—and she maintains her disguise as the duke's page and waits for a miracle. In doing so, she is a splendid example of the Shakespearean comic heroine, resourceful and aggressive in pursuit of her man.

Her effect on her fellow lovers is positive also. As the spirited Cesario, her youthful good looks and imaginative compliments to Olivia bring out the would-be recluse's capacity to love. Similarly, the irrepressible femininity beneath her disguise offers Orsino the devotion and loyalty that he subconsciously desires and to which he unwittingly responds. Thus she rescues the two leading figures of Illyria from their own illusions and paves the way for the denouement. Moreover, Viola is the only character—aside from Feste, who is essentially an observer of the plot's intrigues—whose point of view includes a perspective on the whole action. She enters into the dramatic possibilities of her disguised state with enthusiasm, missing no opportunity for telling remarks on Orsino and Olivia or for double entendres about her ambiguous gender.

The sexual confusion implicit in Olivia's response to Cesario was of course magnified on the Elizabethan stage, where Viola and Olivia were played by boys. The humor in seeing a woman (played by a boy) respond sexually to another woman (also played by a boy) depends chiefly on the absurdity of the confusion, but it also has overtones of both male and female homosexuality. Homosexuality was rarely referred to in ELIZA-BETHAN DRAMA, but here it is certainly suggested implicitly. The modern use of actresses dampens our perception of this situation, but even so more complicated patterns of desire lurk beneath the surface of the conventional love comedy.

Thus, both socially and sexually, tremors of unease accompany the development of a classical comic complication that reaches its breaking point only in the final scene. Then, equally disquietingly, it generates potential violence on several fronts. Antonio is threatened with death, and Orsino hysterically threatens to "sacrifice the lamb that I do love" (5.1.128) by killing Cesario. The crisis is heightened by the appearance of Sir Andrew and Sir Toby, both of whom have been wounded in actual violence.

The giver of these wounds follows, and he brings the play's resolution with him. Sebastian's entrance provides not only Viola's missing brother, the return of Olivia's new husband, and the correct identification of Cesario; it also makes possible the final alignment of the lovers; his first encounter with Olivia in 4.1 had begun the process, and he unhesitatingly married Olivia when she suggested it in 4.3. His sudden reappearance in 5.1 confirms his power to dissolve the network of ambiguity that has entrapped the other lovers.

Shakespeare emphasizes Sebastian's sound sexual identity, a feature whose absence has heavily influenced the action thus far. In both 4.1 and 5.1 Sebastian displays the ancient warrior mystique of the wholly masculine man, overwhelming weaker males who affront his honor. More subtly, and more significantly, Sebastian represents fulfillment in the incomplete lives of the other characters. He is the figure

Viola has masqueraded as and the lover Olivia subconsciously desired before "Cesario" awakened her. He is the dominant male whom Malvolio sought to impersonate and whom Orsino, in his romantic role-playing, has forgotten he can be. Thus Sebastian—a rather wooden traditional leading man himself—embodies the positive capacity for love that has been needed to crystallize the swirling vapors of romance that have disturbed Illyria.

Yet our earlier uneasiness is not totally dispelled. Aside from the uncanny ease with which Olivia settles for a look-alike and Orsino translates his affection for a boy into love for a wife—these are part of the improbabilities to be expected in romantic comedy, even if they have here a slight taste of the perverse—there remains the difficult resolution of the subplot. The "problem of Malvolio," as it has long been termed, has attracted attention for centuries; in the 17th century the play was sometimes known as "Malvolio," and in the 19th century Charles LAMB found "tragic interest" in "the catastrophe of this character." This is an overstatement, for Malvolio lacks the grandeur of a tragic hero, but it reflects the potency of the part and of the moral question the steward's unjust imprisonment raises: How is his undeniably shabby treatment—or his unrepentant final response—to be reconciled with the happy ending?

It is true that Malvolio is a comic character, the villain of a rollicking subplot powered by the wit of Maria and the lusty excesses of Sir Toby. He has deserved his comeuppance, and it has been delivered in a comical fashion. Nevertheless, his anger at his humiliation makes him humanly sympathetic, and his raging departure seems justified, if ugly, leaving us with an ongoing sense of disturbance. Shakespeare's purpose here is subtle but effective: Our appreciation of the loving aura that closes the play is strengthened by our simultaneous sense of sadness that happiness is never pure.

Feste provides a final statement of the play's antiromantic undertone in his bitter song (5.1.388–407), which outlines the sorry life of a drunkard. For him, the loving resolution of the main plot seems to count for nothing: "the rain it raineth every day." Feste's song expresses the jester's loneliness, for he remains outside the lovers' world, but it also reminds us of the limitations of comedy, which has been part of Shakespeare's message in other ways, as we have seen. Tellingly, another stanza of the same song is sung by the tragic Fool of *King Lear* (3.2.74–77).

However, the form of Feste's summation—a song—eases the burden of its message; the song is never as painful in performance as its unpleasant lyrics suggest it might be. Music's charms leave us with an echo of the happy ending's harmony. The final stanza of Feste's song also has another function: to end the play formally and send the audience on its way. Like an EPILOGUE, it makes a bid for applause and promises that the actors will "strive to please you every day" (5.1.407).

This denouement suggests that although the play has unsettling aspects, the triumph of love is *Twelfth Night*'s major theme. Its subtitle, *What You Will*, obviously points to the possibility of different interpretations of the work, but its promise of that which "you will" also hints at the dominance of a positive view. The main title itself remains mysterious. To playgoers of Shakespeare's day, the term *Twelfth Night* designated January 6, or Epiphany, the last day in the traditional Christmas season, celebrated as the anniversary of the Magi's visit to the birthplace of Christ. In 16th-century writings, the polarity of earthly setting and heavenly signal—the manger in Bethlehem and the magical star that led the Magi—was seen as a powerful symbol of Christ's dual nature, part human and part divine. The twins Sebastian and Viola may be symbolic of this duality as well. Viola, through her patient offering of love to Orsino—expressed most vividly in her declaration "I . . . to do you rest a thousand deaths would die" (5.1.130–131), a remark that has distinctly Christian overtones—may illustrate Christ's suffering human aspect, while Sebastian, who brings redemption within the play's scheme of things, can be taken to represent Christ's divine dimension. This interpretation may seem somewhat strained, however, given the lack of explicit religious references in the play and the fact that there is little, if any, unambiguously religious content elsewhere in the plays. *Twelfth Night*'s title, as has often been observed, may simply advertise

the festive, comic quality of the work by naming a great holiday, as another title, *A Midsummer Night's Dream*, did. Also, the play was probably first performed in the autumn or early winter, as the Christmas holidays were approaching.

We have seen that the romantic comedy in *Twelfth Night* is the play's most powerful component, but the work's disturbing reverberations cannot be overlooked. In this respect the comedy points to the PROBLEM PLAYS, soon to be written. In the meantime, the play tells us that while comedy cannot dispel the pains of life, this knowledge only makes the genre a more necessary solace.

SOURCES OF THE PLAY

Shakespeare's chief source for *Twelfth Night* was a romantic tale, "Apolonius and Silla," in *Farewell to Militarie Profession* (1581), by Barnabe RICH. Shakespeare simplified this rambling narrative considerably, but it provided the essence of the relationships among Orsino, Olivia, Viola, and Sebastian (though the playwright took none of these names from his source). Rich himself took his tale from a French romance, a story in François BELLEFOREST's *Histoires Tragiques* (1570); Belleforest in turn took it from an Italian version in Matteo BANDELLO's collection of romances, *Novelle* (1554), and Bandello drew on the original source, an anonymous Italian play of the 1530s, *Gl'Ingannati* (The deceived ones). Shakespeare probably did not know the original play, and, although he did know both Bandello's and Belleforest's collections—he used them in writing other plays (notably *Hamlet* [Belleforest] and *Much Ado About Nothing* [Bandello])—they were not important for *Twelfth Night*. Only one passage—Viola's ironic evocation of a frustrated lover of Orsino (2.4.90–119)—may have been influenced by Bandello.

Gl'Ingannati spawned other works, including two plays by an Italian playwright, Nicolo Secchi (active ca. 1550), *Gl'Inganni* and *L'Interesse*, which both contain passages resembling Viola's description of a woman whom she claims to love in her male persona (2.4.25–28). Shakespeare may have consulted these works, though some scholars believe the similarity derives simply from their exploitation of the same source.

TEXT OF THE PLAY

Twelfth Night was written between 1599—the publication date of the "new map with the augmentation of the Indies" referred to in 3.2.76–77—and late 1601, in time for the earliest recorded performance in February 1602. The play may have been written for a performance on January 6, 1601, when Queen Elizabeth paid the CHAMBERLAIN'S MEN to entertain a visiting Italian nobleman named Orsino. If so, then the play must have been written in late 1600, but most scholars believe that this theory is inaccurate, although the much-talked-about visitor may have inspired Shakespeare's choice of a name for his duke, suggesting 1601 as the date of composition.

Two pieces of evidence point to the latter half of that year. First, the play's subtitle, *What You Will,* may have been Shakespeare's original title, altered when another *What You Will,* by John MARSTON, appeared in the spring of 1601. Second, Feste's remark that the word *element* is "overworn" (3.1.60) refers to a controversy of 1601. As part of the so-called WAR OF THE THEATERS, Thomas DEKKER's play *Satiromastix* made much fun of Ben JONSON's alleged overuse of the term. *Satiromastix* was performed by the Chamberlain's Men in the summer or fall of 1601 in answer to a Jonson play of the spring season; this suggests that Shakespeare was writing *Twelfth Night* no earlier than mid-1601.

Twelfth Night was first published in the FIRST FOLIO edition of 1623. The text was printed from a transcription of Shakespeare's FOUL PAPERS, made by a scribe employed by either the acting company that performed it (the Chamberlain's Men until May 1603, the KING'S MEN thereafter) or the publishers of the Folio. As the only early text of the play, it has been the basis of all subsequent editions.

THEATRICAL HISTORY OF THE PLAY

Twelfth Night was performed at one of the INNS OF COURT on February 2, 1602, according to the diary of John MANNINGHAM. This is the only record of a performance in Shakespeare's lifetime, though the King's Men presented the play at the court of King JAMES I in 1618 and 1623, suggesting its popularity. Robert ARMIN is believed to have created the role of Feste and Richard BURBAGE that of Malvolio. During the Restoration, William DAVENANT staged the play in 1661, 1663, and 1669, though he may have altered Shakespeare's text considerably, as was his practice; Thomas BETTERTON played Sir Toby.

In 1703 William BURNABY's *Love Betray'd* incorporated several scenes from *Twelfth Night,* but the play itself was not again performed until 1741, when Charles MACKLIN staged it and played Malvolio. Somewhat later in the 18th century Richard YATES was a popular Feste as a youth and played Malvolio later in his career. John HENDERSON also appeared as the steward with notable success. Dorothy JORDAN played Viola in 1790, opposite her brother as Sebastian, providing a natural similarity of looks.

In the 1810 production by J. P. KEMBLE, 1.1 and 1.2 were reversed, a practice that has continued intermittently to the present. Charlotte CUSHMAN was a popular Viola in 1846, Samuel PHELPS played Malvolio in his own productions of 1848 and 1857, and Henry IRVING's production of 1884 starred himself as Malvolio and Ellen TERRY as Viola. Ada REHAN played Viola in Augustin DALY's production (New York, 1893; London, 1894). Nineteenth-century stagings of *Twelfth Night* tended to have elaborate sets and costumes, often based on images of aristocratic English country life, a practice that reached an extreme with Beerbohm TREE's 1901 set, featuring a terraced garden with real grass and fountains.

In 1820 Frederick REYNOLDS produced a musical version incorporating, in the words of the producer, "Songs, Glees, and Choruses . . . from the Plays, Poems, and Sonnets of Shakespeare." Other 19th-century productions also introduced extra songs to the text; notable among these was Daly's usurpation of "Who Is Silvia?" from *The Two Gentlemen of Verona* (4.2.38–52), which had earlier (1827) been set to music by Franz SCHUBERT.

Among the most famous 20th-century productions of *Twelfth Night* was Harley GRANVILLE-BARKER's revolutionary rendering of 1912, which attempted to evoke the Elizabethan stage. Tyrone GUTHRIE's 1937 production featured Laurence OLIVIER as Sir Toby, and, in an experiment that was generally decried, Jessica Tandy (1909–94) played both Sebastian and Viola, a nonspeaking actor taking the former part in the reunion scene (5.1). Peggy ASHCROFT was acclaimed as Viola in 1950.

Other notable productions included John GIEL-GUD's (1955), starring Olivier as Malvolio and Vivien LEIGH as Viola, and that of John BARTON (1969), with Judi DENCH as Viola. In 2002 the Shakespeare's Globe Theatre (see WANAMAKER, SAM) presented *Twelfth Night* at its GLOBE THEATRE replica after opening the production on a stage at Middle Temple Hall, one of the Inns of Court, honoring the presumed location of its premiere exactly 400 years earlier. Staged with an all-male cast, as it had been historically, the production featured director Mark RYLANCE as Olivia.

A silent FILM of *Twelfth Night* was made in 1910, and Russian and German films were made in 1955 and 1963, respectively. In 1996 Trevor NUNN made his first Shakespearean film with *Twelfth Night*. The play has been broadcast six times on TELEVISION, beginning in 1939 with a BBC production featuring Michael REDGRAVE and Peggy Ashcroft. Another British production of 1969—with Alec Guinness (1914–2000) as Malvolio, Ralph RICHARDSON as Sir Toby and Joan PLOWRIGHT as both Viola and Sebastian (a feat more plausible on television than on the stage)—was also notable.

CHARACTERS

Aguecheek, Sir Andrew See Sir Andrew Aguecheek.

Antonio Character in *Twelfth Night*, friend of Sebastian. After rescuing Sebastian from a shipwreck, Antonio admires the young man so much that he wishes to become his servant. Sebastian rejects this offer, but Antonio follows him to the court of Duke Orsino of ILLYRIA, although he has many enemies there. In 3.4 he mistakes Sebastian's twin sister, Viola, who is disguised as a man, for Sebastian; the episode adds to the play's comic complexities. Antonio's increasing distress—he believes that Sebastian has betrayed him when Viola doesn't acknowledge him, and he is arrested and threatened with death as an old foe of Orsino—contributes to the play's undertone of disquiet and potential violence.

Antonio has had a career at sea, either as a privateer or a naval officer (described in 3.3.26–35 and 5.1.50–61), but otherwise he has little distinc-

tive personality. In addition to participating in minor twists of the plot, he is intended primarily to establish, through his attitude toward Sebastian, the young nobleman's attractive qualities. Indeed, Antonio's references to Sebastian—"I do adore thee so . . ." (2.1.46) and "how vile an idol proves this god" (3.4.374)—are cited by theorists who believe that Shakespeare intended a religious statement in his portrayal of the young man.

Belch, Sir Toby See Sir Toby Belch.

Captain Minor character in *Twelfth Night*, the rescuer of Viola. After saving Viola from a shipwreck, the Captain offers her hope that her brother may also have been saved, thereby establishing that Sebastian will eventually appear. The Captain goes on to direct Viola's attention to the court of Duke Orsino, which she determines to visit, disguised as a man. Unlike Antonio, who saves Sebastian, the Captain is not a salty mariner; oddly, he is something of a gentleman, speaking familiarly of the duke's affairs and drawing on images from classical myth (as in 2.1.15). Otherwise the Captain has no real personality; he simply introduces developments and indicates by his attitude that Viola is an attractive heroine.

Cesario In *Twelfth Night*, the name taken by Viola in her disguise as a young man.

Curio Minor character in *Twelfth Night*, a follower of Duke Orsino of ILLYRIA. Curio has no personality and very few lines, serving to fill out the Duke's retinue. In 1.1.16–18 Curio achieves his greatest prominence when he provides the occasion for a pun by his master.

Fabian Character in *Twelfth Night*, member of Olivia's household and friend of Sir Toby Belch and Maria. Fabian joins Sir Toby, Sir Andrew, and Maria in their plot to embarrass Malvolio, Olivia's steward. He shares their zest for good times and, like them, represents the spirit of fun that triumphs over Malvolio's stiff ill humor. In his final speech (5.1.354–367) he distinguishes himself as a peacemaker and diplomat, elevating the tone of the comic SUBPLOT.

As their scheme unfolds and the conspirators observe Malvolio envisioning himself as Olivia's husband, Fabian restrains an outraged Sir Toby from assaulting their victim, saying, "Nay, patience, or we break the sinews of our plot" (2.5.75–76). He later assists Sir Toby in his practical joke against Sir Andrew, who is maneuvered into a duel with Cesario (the disguised Viola) and shows himself a coward. Fabian's wit and common sense give him an ironic detachment, and in 5.1 he comes into his own, first reading Malvolio's letter (5.1.301–310) and then, more significantly, quick-wittedly protecting Maria when her forging of Olivia's handwriting becomes evident; he blames himself and Sir Toby, whose marriage to Maria he reveals. He goes on to hope that their plotting "may rather pluck on laughter than revenge" (5.1.365), forestalling Malvolio's aggrieved cry for vengeance and pointing to the reconciliation that follows.

Fabian's social position is unclear. He seems to be a servant when Olivia addresses him as "sirrah" (5.1.300), yet he can refer casually to Olivia's kinsman, Sir Toby, as "Toby" (5.1.358). Shakespeare may have pictured him as a flippant servant or as an impoverished gentleman, dependent on the charity of a wealthy relative or other connection, such as commonly lived in aristocratic households of the 16th and 17th centuries. The name Fabian, originally a Roman clan name (perhaps deriving from *faba*, meaning "bean"), became associated with licentiousness in ancient times, because members of that clan were hereditary priests of the god Pan and were therefore licensed—indeed, expected—to indulge in alcoholic and sexual excesses during the annual feast of Lupercalia. Thus, by Shakespeare's time, "fabian" was also a common noun, meaning a flamboyant roisterer or wastrel.

Feste Character in *Twelfth Night*, jester, or professional FOOL, in the household of Olivia. Feste represents the play's spirit of festivity, which eventually triumphs over the steward Malvolio's chilly ill humor. Outside the coils of the lovers' confusions, Feste can take an ironic view of them and their world. He appears in a number of settings, the better to apply his vision to all. He frequents the courts of both Olivia and Duke Orsino, encounters both Viola and Sebastian, challenges the first appearance of Malvolio, and takes part in the revelry of Sir Toby Belch and Sir Andrew Aguecheek. He also carries the comic SUBPLOT to its furthest extreme, disguising himself as a curate, Sir Topas, and pretending to exorcise the imprisoned Malvolio. As he himself observes, "Foolery, sir, doth walk about the orb like the sun, it shines everywhere" (3.1.39–40).

As an officially designated fool, it is Feste's duty to point out with jests and barbs the folly of those who are supposed to be wise. As Viola remarks when she meets Feste, "This fellow is wise enough to play the fool, / . . . For folly that he wisely shows is fit; / But wise men, folly-fall'n, quite taint their wit" (3.1.61, 68–69), and Olivia tells Malvolio, "There is no slander in an allowed fool, though he do nothing but rail" (1.5.93–94). Feste wittily demonstrates that Olivia is foolish to mourn her brother's ascent to heaven, and her good humor is immediately restored. Although his jests are less effective against Orsino's foolish self-image as a romantic melancholic, they make the duke's mental disorder plain. Feste compares himself to Sir Andrew, saying, "Better a witty fool than a foolish wit" (1.5.34), pointing out both Sir Andrew's limitations and his own role. He also cares for the drunken Sir Toby, observing bitingly, "the fool shall look to the madman" (1.5.138–139).

Finally, Feste's pretended exorcism of Malvolio casts light on the steward's character. Malvolio's humorless ambition and incapacity to love are metaphorically alluded to in Feste's diagnosis: "I say there is no darkness but ignorance, in which thou are more puzzled than the Egyptians in their fog" (4.2.43–45). The subsequent comic dialogue deals obliquely with Malvolio's underlying deficiency—his lack of concern for anyone but himself. Feste declares that Malvolio will "remain . . . in darkness [until] thou shalt . . . fear to kill a woodcock lest thou dispossess the soul of thy grandam" (4.2.58–61).

In *Twelfth Night* Shakespeare deliberately undercut the conventions of romantic comedy; one of his techniques was to establish what has long been called "the problem of Malvolio"; the steward's discomfiture seems out of proportion to his offense, giving rise to an uncertain response in the audience, which responds with both delight at Malvolio's comeuppance and sympathy for his victimization. Feste's final encounter with Malvolio, upon the steward's release, contributes to this ambiguity. Here, the fool cruelly uses Malvolio's own words against him and then observes that "the whirligig of time brings in his revenges" (5.1.375–376); while "whirligig" is funny, "revenges" is not.

Feste's songs are an important part of his role, illuminating different aspects of the play. In 2.3 he sings a love song for boisterous Sir Toby and Sir Andrew, and the audience shares the delight of the two knights, but the lyrics have a somewhat depressing tinge, for they advocate seizing love while one is young because "what's to come is still unsure" and "Youth's a stuff will not endure" (2.3.50, 53). This observation is part of the play's disturbing undertone, as is Feste's next song, "Come away death" (2.4.51–66), which is humorously suited to Orsino's affected sadness but is also strikingly melancholy in itself.

Feste's last song, which closes the play, offers a poignant moment. Left outside the happy ending the lovers enjoy, the fool sings a bitter ditty that sums up the play's antiromantic secondary theme. He sings of the sorry, loveless life of a drunkard for whom, as the chorus insists, "the rain it raineth every day" (5.1.391 et al.). These lyrics emphasize Shakespeare's ironic view of the limitations of comedy. However, this message is greatly offset by the music, and the gross exaggeration in the words makes them somewhat comical; also, the song's final stanza presents a standard EPILOGUE, asking for applause and promising that the actors will "strive to please you every day" (5.1.407). Feste remains a generally sunny character whose darker moments serve to make him, and the play, more complex and humanly interesting.

Malvolio Character in *Twelfth Night*, mean-spirited steward to Olivia. Malvolio is the focus of the comic SUBPLOT, in which a group of characters led by Maria and Sir Toby Belch conspire to embarrass him, with the result that he is incarcerated as a lunatic. This plot is clearly secondary to the main story of the lovers—Viola, Orsino, Sebastian, and Olivia—but Malvolio is such a strongly drawn character that the play sometimes seems to center

on him. In fact, several documents of the 17th century identify the play as "Malvolio," and leading actors have always been pleased to take the role. In addition to embodying an ordinary comic villain—an obvious misfit who mistreats others and in the end is humiliated by a crude stratagem—Malvolio is also a humanly interesting victim, and he inspires sympathy as well as derision, thus contributing to Shakespeare's ironic undercutting of the conventional romantic comedy.

Malvolio rejects humor and love in favor of a stern coldness and a consuming personal ambition. His dislike of merriment and his rigorously sober dress and behavior justify his name, an approximation of the Italian for "ill will." (These features also resemble the typical 16th-century—and later—stereotype of the Puritan, but Shakespeare certainly did not consider Malvolio a Puritan, as is clear in 2.3.146–147.) Malvolio opposes the frivolity of Sir Toby, Sir Andrew, and Feste in 2.3, inspiring Sir Toby's famous riposte, "Dost thou think because thou art virtuous, there shall be no more cakes and ale?" (2.3.114–115). Driven away by this assault on his dignity, the angry Malvolio gratuitously threatens Maria, thereby triggering the plot that brings him down.

The steward behaves badly to Viola, who is disguised as a young man, when he brusquely delivers Olivia's ring to her in 2.2, and he is unnecessarily nasty to Feste in 1.5. His churlish behavior quite plainly foreshadows the comeuppance that he later receives. Even more repellent is the cold ambition of his entirely loveless courtship of Olivia, undertaken in accordance with the comical instructions of Maria's letter but contemplated by him in 2.5, before he finds this missive. His musings on the power and position he hopes to gain strongly illuminate his personality, as he solemnly and pompously contemplates punishing Sir Toby. These boldly unattractive features have inspired scholarly speculations that Shakespeare intended Malvolio as a satire on a particular living person (see FFARINGTON, WILLIAM; HOBY, THOMAS POSTHUMOUS; KNOLLYS, WILLIAM; WILLOUGHBY, AMBROSE), but these hypotheses have never been convincingly established, and they do not alter the character's function in the play.

For all his noxious characteristics, Malvolio is not a serious threat in the manner of, say, Shylock in *The Merchant of Venice*; ultimately, he is simply laughed off the stage. Nor does he grow or change in the course of the play; instead, he is exposed for what he is by the actions of other characters. There is no question about his destiny; in a comedy such a hypocrite and would-be villain deserves his downfall, and this comes about in an entertaining manner.

Nevertheless, Malvolio's imprisonment and humiliation seem excessive relative to his offense. The "problem of Malvolio," as this imbalance has long been called, lends the subplot a viciousness that contributes to Shakespeare presentation of comedy's limitations. Feste's teasing of the imprisoned Malvolio in 4.2 is undeniably humorous, but even Sir Toby concedes that this continuing torment of their victim may be going too far, remarking, "I would we were well rid of this knavery" (4.2.69–70). Then, provoking the steward's angry final departure, Feste mocks the steward even more mercilessly (5.1.369–376). We sympathize with Malvolio's anger, which seems justifiable, and with his ugly departure and its cry for revenge "on the whole pack of you!" (5.1.377). Despite the play's happy ending, an aftertaste of bitter feeling remains. A 19th-century critic, Charles LAMB, went so far as to find "tragic interest" in "the catastrophe of this character." Although Malvolio lacks the grandeur of a tragic hero, Lamb's comment raises an interesting moral question: How is Malvolio's shabby treatment—or his unrepentant final response—to be reconciled with the happy ending?

While poetic justice requires that Malvolio be brought down, for his rejection of love is insane in the play's scheme of things, Shakespeare softens his actual defeat in several ways. The victim's final cry for vengeance is neutralized by Fabian's wish that the conspirators' "sportful malice . . . may rather pluck on laughter than revenge" (5.1.364–365). Moreover, the two leading figures of ILLYRIA offer the promise of reconciliation: Olivia, though amused at the plot against her humiliated steward, is sympathetic toward him, saying, "Alas, poor fool, how have they baffled thee!" (5.1.368), and Orsino orders that someone follow him and "entreat him to a peace" (5.1.379).

After Malvolio's exit, the play moves to its happy conclusion; the steward is simply too out of harmony with the joyful spirit of the ending to remain among the celebrants. Though his downfall gives an edge to the romantic comedy—we see that Illyria has its share of the sins of the real world— this point is easily abandoned in the enthusiasm of the lovers. Nevertheless, the "problem of Malvolio" makes both the character and the play more complex and humanly interesting.

Maria Character in *Twelfth Night*, chambermaid to Olivia. With Sir Toby Belch, Sir Andrew Aguecheek, and Fabian, Maria represents the spirit of fun that opposes the humorless severity of Olivia's steward, Malvolio, in the play's comic SUBPLOT. Of the group, Maria is much the smartest. She devises the plot to embarrass the steward, and she composes the remarkably clever forged letter to Malvolio— read aloud by the victim himself in 2.5.92–159— playing on his ambitions and his vanity to impel him to bring about his own downfall. Then, in 4.2, she devises a capstone to the joke, disguising the jester Feste as a curate, Sir Topas, to visit and torment Malvolio, who has been locked up as a lunatic.

In witty speeches like those in 3.2.65–80, Maria provides a commentary on Malvolio's actions that establish strongly our favorable, indeed indulgent, attitude toward a "knavery," as Sir Toby calls it (4.2.70), that might easily turn vicious. When, at the conclusion of the play, we learn that Sir Toby has married Maria out of delight with her wit, we realize that she will be able to control her new husband successfully without repressing his high spirits. Moreover, this marriage provides a parallel to the pairings of the characters in the main plot, Orsino with Viola and Sebastian with Olivia.

Officers Two minor characters in *Twelfth Night* who arrest and later act as custodians of Antonio. In 3.4 the Officers seize Antonio, who was an enemy of Duke Orsino of ILLYRIA in a recent war. 5.1.58–63 one of them describes Antonio's achievements as a naval warrior.

Olivia Character in *Twelfth Night*, wealthy mistress of an estate in ILLYRIA, the lover of Cesario—

who, although she does not know it, is Viola in disguise—and later the bride of Sebastian. Olivia is the object of Duke Orsino's unrequited romantic fantasies. Like Orsino, she impedes the drama's triumph of love; she, too, has a false view of herself that she must overcome. Olivia moves from one illusion to another, beginning with a willfull withdrawal into seclusion and denial of life and then falling headlong into a passion that is based on a mistake. Only the course of events, beginning with the appearance of Sebastian, can correct matters, for Olivia is never aware of her errors.

Mourning her late brother, Olivia adopts an exaggerated, irrational stance that is acutely described by Valentine: ". . . like a cloistress she will veiled walk, / And water once a day her chamber round / With eye-offending brine" (1.1.28–30). Ironically, her withdrawal gives her something in common with her steward, Malvolio, who scorns pleasure and love.

However, grief is counter to Olivia's true nature. In 1.5 the glee with which she responds to the jester Feste's comical teasing reveals that she is unsuited to the ascetic pose she has adopted, and she has the common sense to see Malvolio for what he is, saying, "O, you are sick of self-love, Malvolio, and taste with a distempered appetite" (1.5.89–90). She forgets her brother once she has been smitten with the charms of Cesario, and her pent-up instinct for love plunges her into a "most extracting frenzy" (5.1.279). However, her passion is misplaced, not only because a disguised woman is its object but also because she is excessively self-involved, using what she knows to be "shameful cunning" (3.1.118) to win her beloved. She admits, "There's something in me that reproves my fault: / But such a headstrong potent fault it is, / That it but mocks reproof" (3.4.205–207). Olivia has gone from scorning love in the name of propriety to being possessed by love beyond the reach of conscience.

Once Sebastian has replaced Cesario, Olivia remains impetuous, though she still recognizes the irrationality of her course. "Blame not this haste of mine" (4.3.22), she pleads as she leads Sebastian to the altar (thinking he is Cesario). At the play's near-hysterical climax in 5.1, Olivia struggles to keep Cesario, though he denies their marriage, until

Sebastian reappears to claim her and identify Viola. Olivia is almost silent as this occurs, for her role in the tale of tangled romances is over. She comes to herself only when she realizes that she has lost track of Malvolio, now incarcerated as a lunatic. She sees to his release and elicits the truth of the comic SUBPLOT that has been going on beyond her distracted attention. When the steward flees in rage, she is sympathetic but amused; she has become the humane lady of her establishment that the frenzy of misplaced love had prevented her from being.

Orsino Character in *Twelfth Night*, the Duke of ILLYRIA, lover first of Olivia and then of Viola. Orsino, like Olivia, presents a false view of love that must be corrected in the course of the play. Orsino is infatuated with Olivia, who has repeatedly rejected him, while Viola, who is disguised as Cesario, Orsino's page, loves the duke but cannot tell him so. Utterly involved in his self-image as a brooding, rejected lover, Orsino cannot accept the fact that his passion for Olivia is misplaced. Though he is a humorous figure, a parody of the melancholy lovers of conventional 16th-century romances, he also displays aspects of psychological disorder—as Feste observes, he is irrationally changeable, his "mind is a very opal" (2.4.75)—and his wrongheadedness contributes to a sense that all is not well in Illyria.

When we first see the duke, he demonstrates his amusingly distorted slant on reality. In his absurdly romantic pose, he demands music to satiate his lovesick soul, insists that a particular phrase be repeated, then immediately orders that the music be stopped, saying, "'Tis not so sweet now as it was before" (1.1.8). He tellingly reverses the image of Olivia as the object of a hunt, making himself the hunted (1.1.18–23). By the end of the scene, Olivia has almost no importance herself; Orsino is totally absorbed in his own fantasies. But Orsino is not in love with himself; he is in love with love. In 1.4 Viola, as Cesario, vainly tries to induce a sensible attitude in the duke. He boasts of his "unstaid and skittish" (2.4.18) behavior, which he associates with love. Feste amusingly sings him a dirge of a love song, "Come away death" (2.4.51–66), but Orsino does not recognize the implicit critique of his exaggerated melancholy.

The duke resembles such earlier Shakespearean lovers as Silvius in *As You Like It* and Valentine in *The Two Gentlemen of Verona*. As those figures are mocked by Rosalind and Speed, respectively, so Orsino is taken to task, comically by Feste and ironically by Viola, but like his predecessors, Orsino is hardheaded and resistant. Only the course of events can make things right for him, for he does not even recognize that they are amiss.

At the play's climax, the disquieting side of Orsino's misplaced emotions erupts in threatened violence, as Olivia's continuing rejection precipitates a menacing demonstration of frustrated masculine dominance as he decides to kill Cesario in a romantic gesture combining love and death. Proposing to "sacrifice the lamb that I do love, / To spite a raven's heart within a dove" (5.1.128–129), he inadvertently acknowledges his affection for the "boy." His blindness has kept him from recognizing this, but his instincts have nonetheless directed him truly, and once Viola's identity is revealed, Orsino is immediately ready to love her.

At the close of the play, when he orders that someone "pursue [Malvolio], and entreat him to a peace" (5.1.379), Orsino achieves something of the quality of Theseus in *A Midsummer Night's Dream*, or Prospero in *The Tempest* (though in a lesser key), wise rulers who understand the uses of power and mercy. He becomes the man his position requires once he is brought to a state of loving grace.

Priest Minor character in *Twelfth Night*, a clergyman. The Priest speaks only once, in 5.1.154–161, to confirm that he has married Olivia and Sebastian—whom he and the bride have both mistaken for Cesario, the disguised Viola—thereby adding to the confusion of the scene. At the same time, he provides comic relief from the intensifying crisis, for he is preposterously high-flown, using the most elaborate possible language to say a very simple thing; for instance, he observes, "Since [the marriage], my watch hath told me, towards my grave / I have travell'd but two hours" (5.1.160–161).

Sebastian Character in *Twelfth Night*, lover of Olivia and twin brother of Viola. Sebastian and

Viola's virtually perfect resemblance to each other—a convention of romantic COMEDY—permits the traditional comic confusion of mistaken identities, but it also provides for two different presentations of love's restorative power. Sebastian resolves issues that his sister has raised, and his entrance stimulates the play's climax and helps both Olivia and Orsino to fulfill their potential.

Much of Sebastian's tale is similar to his sister's: Both are shipwrecked and saved by helpful seamen—Antonio, in Sebastian's case—who direct them to the court of ILLYRIA; both are pursued by Olivia; both are threatened with combat by Sir Andrew Aguecheek; and both are betrothed in the play's happy ending. These parallels heighten the effect of the comic confusions that ensue when Sebastian is mistaken for the disguised Viola, and it also emphasizes the function Sebastian serves when the mistakes are cleared up in 5.1. While Viola's pose as Cesario has inspired love—hers for Orsino and Olivia's for Cesario—Sebastian's arrival is necessary for these passions to be properly directed.

The correct relationship among the play's lovers—skewed at first by Viola's disguise and Orsino's misplaced passion for Olivia—begins to take shape when Sebastian meets Olivia, who believes him to be Cesario, in 4.1. He is naturally mystified by this ardent woman, but he recognizes the value of her love, even knowing that it is based on some mistake, and he boldly plays along. In the same spirit, Sebastian immediately accepts Olivia's proposal of marriage in 4.3.

Sebastian's situation in Illyria differs from Viola's in one highly significant way: While Viola is disguised as a man, Sebastian's gender is unconfused and permits him a forthrightness not available to his sister. When Sir Andrew Aguecheek and Sir Toby Belch oppose him, his response is squarely in the tradition of masculine assertiveness: He fights and drives them away, in both 4.1 and 5.1. His clear-cut sexual identity allows Sebastian to provide the missing elements in the lives of the other characters. He is the manly youth of Viola's disguise, and he is the lover whom Olivia thought she had found in the disguised Viola. He is the dominant male that Orsino should be but has lost sight of through his romantic affectations. He is also to become the aristocratic husband that Malvolio has inappropriately aspired to be.

Sebastian thus helps to redeem other characters, and this fact, combined with Viola's capacity for devotion and sacrifice, has suggested to some scholars a religious interpretation of the play. In any case, his role in the resolution of the play's entanglements makes him the central figure of Acts 4–5, although he says relatively little and lacks a vibrant personality. He is not one of Shakespeare's more endearing heroes, but he is certainly a powerful one.

Servant Minor character in *Twelfth Night*, an employee of Olivia. In 3.4, just as Malvolio appears to have turned lunatic, the Servant announces Viola's arrival, contributing to a sense of the busyness of Olivia's household at a moment of comic crisis.

Sir Andrew Aguecheek Character in *Twelfth Night*, friend of Sir Toby Belch. Sir Andrew carouses with his friend while they visit the home of Olivia, Sir Toby's rich young niece, whom Sir Andrew is courting. Sir Toby takes merciless advantage of Sir Andrew, but it is impossible to pity such a ridiculous figure. He fancies himself a wit, though he is a dolt; a ladies' man, though he is gaunt and repulsive, as his name suggests; and a fighter, though he proves a coward.

Sir Andrew's inanity is well demonstrated when he tries to imitate Viola's rhetoric, though he clearly has no idea of its meaning. He proudly recites, "'Odours', 'pregnant', and 'vouchsafed': I'll get 'em all three all ready" (3.1.92–93). He is foolishly ignorant of ordinary references, as when he calls Jezebel a man in 2.5.41, and he mistakes Feste's drinking SONG—"a song of good life" (2.3.36–37)—for a hymn to virtue and rejects it, saying, "I care not for good life" (2.3.39). When Sir Toby offers to marry Maria out of delight with her plan against Malvolio, Sir Andrew duplicates the offer, forgetting his alleged love for Olivia, and then he seconds the next several remarks made (2.5.183–208) in a delicious example of comic slavishness.

Sir Andrew's combination of quarrelsomeness and cowardice—referred to by Maria in 1.3.30–33—typified the braggart, a character type dating to ancient ROMAN DRAMA. Traditional, too, is the comeuppance Sir Andrew receives when he assaults Sebastian and is pummeled in 4.1 and 5.1. When Sir Toby receives the same treatment, he lashes out at Sir Andrew, calling him, accurately if not charitably, "an ass-head, and a coxcomb, and a knave, a thin-faced knave, a gull!" (5.1.204–205).

However, Sir Andrew is sufficiently developed to have a few poignant and sympathetic moments. Rejected by Maria, he despondently (though comically) despairs, "Methinks sometimes I have no more wit than a Christian . . . I am a great eater of beef, and I believe that does harm to my wit" (1.3.82–85). When he wistfully remarks, "I was adored once" (2.3.181), we suddenly see that he has a past, a remembered youth. We may not need to know more, but we recognize his humanity.

Like many Shakespearean buffoons, Sir Andrew is a foil for other characters. Sir Toby's underlying selfishness manifests itself in his exploitation of Sir Andrew. As a ridiculous suitor, Sir Andrew magnifies by contrast the somewhat slender virtues of Orsino, who also pursues Olivia. And his self-image as a grand fellow is subtly similar to Malvolio's fantasies of aristocratic stature.

Sir Toby Belch Character in *Twelfth Night*, uncle of Olivia. The self-indulgent Sir Toby drinks and roars through life, and, with Maria, Sir Andrew Aguecheek, and Fabian, he represents a jocular, festive spirit that triumphs over the cold and humorless rigidity of Olivia's steward, Malvolio, in the play's comic SUBPLOT. His position is boldly presented in his first speech, when he complains of Olivia's mourning for her deceased brother, saying, "What a plague means my niece to take the death of her brother thus? I am sure care's an enemy to life" (1.3.1–3). Sir Toby laughs and carouses mightily and counters Malvolio's insistence on order with the famous rebuke, "Dost thou think because thou art virtuous, there shall be no more cakes and ale?" (2.3.114–115). Like another, greater drunken knight, Sir John Falstaff (of *1 Henry IV*), Sir Toby enacts a variety of comic roles: He is Sir Andrew's mentor in debauchery and joins the jester, Feste, in mockery and jokes. He is a singer of songs and a fierce master of the dueling code.

He makes numerous references to dancing, especially in 1.3.113–131.

However, Sir Toby has a darker side as well. His selfishness is very apparent. He exploits both his friend and his niece. He spends the foolish Sir Andrew's money while pretending to promote his mercenary marriage to Olivia, boasting that he has taken his dupe for "some two thousand strong, or so" (3.2.52–53). His drunkenness turns belligerent and incoherent in 1.5.129–130. His practical joking has a vicious edge: He forces two unwilling combatants to a duel in 3.4, and he also pushes Maria's plot against Malvolio to a new extreme, gloating, "we'll have him in a dark room and bound . . . we may carry it thus for our pleasure" (3.4.136–138). This course is implicitly criticized in his own fear of reprimand in 4.2.70–74 and by the efforts of Olivia and Orsino to mitigate Malvolio's humiliation in 5.1. Moreover, Sir Toby's final departure is ugly: he curses Sir Andrew after his own scheme to humiliate his friend has resulted in both of them being beaten by Sebastian.

Sir Toby's somewhat unpleasant traits offer a parallel in the subplot to the problematic elements of the main plot. As a result, some critics who view *Twelfth Night* as an ironic social satire regard Sir Toby as a vulgar parasite, a hanger-on in the household of his niece, concerned only with his debauched existence. Sir Toby's attitudes toward Sir Andrew and Olivia corroborate this theory somewhat, but it is surely too extreme. The knight is made to submit to his niece's anger at his ways—"Ungracious wretch . . . Out of my sight! Rudesby, be gone!" she shouts in 4.1.46–50—but on the other hand, the playwright permits him satisfaction at the defeat of Malvolio. While he is not present at the final scene of recognition and reconciliation, he marries the delightful Maria, as is reported in 5.1.363, again paralleling developments in the main plot. Sir Toby, though he has his faults, is basically a symbol of the values of humor and joyous living and is therefore a representative of the triumphant spirit of comedy.

Toby Belch See Sir Toby Belch.

Topas In *Twelfth Night*, name taken by Feste in 4.2, when he disguises himself as a Puritan clergyman and visits Malvolio, who has been imprisoned as a madman. The name refers to the topaz, a semiprecious gem believed in Shakespeare's day to be capable of curing lunacy.

Valentine Minor character in *Twelfth Night*, a follower of Duke Orsino of ILLYRIA. Valentine serves as Orsino's emissary to Olivia before Viola, disguised as Cesario, takes over the job. His name is appropriate to this task, and his flowery language in 1.1.24–32 matches his master's. In this speech he introduces the audience to the play's first development, Orsino's unrequited love for Olivia, and at the opening of 1.4 he informs Cesario that Orsino is fond of him, thus introducing a major complication of the plot.

Viola Character in *Twelfth Night*, lover of Duke Orsino of ILLYRIA and twin sister of Sebastian. Viola is at the center of the play's confusions. Separated from Sebastian in a shipwreck, Viola finds herself in Illyria. Disguised as a young man named Cesario, she meets and falls in love with Orsino, but her adopted persona prevents her from expressing her love for him except through service as his page. Orsino wishes her to court Olivia for him, placing her in a strange and difficult position that becomes worse when Olivia falls in love with Cesario. Viola, alone among the characters, knows the truth of this situation. While she is like the other Illyrians in her susceptibility to passion, she alone can honestly assess it, saying simply, "O time, thou must untangle this, not I, / It is too hard a knot for me t'untie" (2.2.39–40).

Viola's capacity for love is extreme: When Orsino, hysterical over Olivia's continued rejection, proposes to kill Cesario in a grand gesture, she calmly acquiesces, saying to him, "I . . . to do you rest, a thousand deaths would die" (5.1.130–131). Such self-sacrificing devotion strikes some readers as Christlike, and along with the powers of restoration displayed by Sebastian at the play's climax, it has influenced a religious interpretation of the play by some scholars, although an entirely secular reading is probably more appropriate to the comedy and Viola's personality.

Though extravagant, Viola's attitude toward love is much more wholesome than the posturings of Orsino and Olivia, and her effect on these characters is positive. Her spirit and candor arouse love in Olivia, who has been withdrawing into grief-filled seclusion. Similarly, although Orsino is wrapped up in his self-image as a melancholy rejected lover, he responds unconsciously to Viola's devotion, conceiving a fondness for Cesario that he eventually transforms into husbandly affection for the sort of loving wife he truly needs. Viola is the heroine of the play, performing the monumental task of liberating Olivia and Orsino from their misconceived selves and thus making the play's climax possible.

In the meantime, her frank good humor keeps the audience aware of the potential realignment of the lovers. She is not afraid to make telling remarks to Olivia on her unmarried state, arguing that ". . . you do usurp yourself: for what is yours to bestow is not yours to reserve" (1.5.188–190), and she is unafraid to counter Orsino's dramatic and boastful insistence that male love is grander than female, observing (while speaking as a man herself), "We men may say more, swear more, but indeed / Our shows are more than will: for still we prove / Much in our vows, but little in our love" (2.4.117–119). She entertains herself and the audience with ironic remarks on her own disguised state, asserting to Olivia that "what I am, and what I would, are as secret as maidenhead" (1.5.219) and, flatly, that "I am not what I am" (3.1.143). Speaking as Cesario, she ironically tells Orsino that she loves someone "of your complexion" and "about your years, my lord" (2.4.26, 28), hiding the fact, which the audience knows, that the object of her love is Orsino himself.

However, there is also an aspect of Viola's position that contributes to *Twelfth Night*'s disturbing undertone. She cannot openly express her love, for her disguise inhibits her, and she thus embodies a disorder in the world of romantic comedy, just as Orsino and Olivia do in their self-delusion, though less blatantly. She herself laments, "Disguise, I see thou art a wickedness" (2.2.26). Also, her disguise raises questions of sexual ambiguity that can be psychologically unnerving. In Shakespeare's time,

Viola would of course have been played by a boy (see ELIZABETHAN THEATER), making her situation both funnier and more troubling. The spectacle of one woman, played by a boy, mistakenly responding sexually to another one, also played by a boy, makes implicit reference to both male and female homosexuality, as well as to heterosexual love, in a way that is comical but also suggestive of hidden depths of human sexuality. While the modern use of actresses tends to obscure this point, the complexity of the situation retains some of its powerful and upsetting strength.

Nevertheless, these dark aspects do not interfere with Viola's essentially positive role. Until Sebastian arrives and resolves the play's intrigues, she alone has found an appropriate passion, and her strength and determination assure us that love will surely triumph. Whether recovering from disaster at sea, plunging into love and intrigue as Cesario, or turning to her betrothal at the play's close, Viola is one of Shakespeare's most attractive heroines—plucky, adventurous, and committed to the pursuit of love.

Two Gentlemen of Verona, The
SYNOPSIS
Act 1, Scene 1
A young gentleman, Valentine, preparing to travel to the court of the Duke of Milan, teases his lovesick friend Proteus about the infatuation that keeps him home. Valentine departs, and Proteus, in a brief soliloquy, expresses his love for Julia. Valentine's young page, Speed, enters. Speed has carried a letter from Proteus to Julia, and he reports that she made no response to it.

Act 1, Scene 2
Julia asks her waiting-woman, Lucetta, her opinion of the suitors who are wooing her. Lucetta favors Proteus, but Julia affects to disdain him. Lucetta gives her a letter from Proteus, delivered by Speed, but Julia pretends to take offense, eventually tearing the letter to pieces and sending Lucetta away. Alone, Julia berates herself and confesses that she loves Proteus.

Act 1, Scene 3

Proteus's father Antonio, decides that Proteus shall join Valentine at court, as befits a gentleman's son. Proteus enters, mooning over a love letter from Julia. Antonio reveals his plan to Proteus, leaving the young man to bemoan his misfortune.

Act 2, Scene 1

Speed gives Valentine a glove that has been dropped by the Duke's daughter Silvia, with whom Valentine appears to be in love. The witty Speed tauntingly diagnoses his master's condition. Valentine reports that Silvia has asked him to write a love letter to an unknown person for her. Silvia arrives, and Valentine gives his composition to her. She promptly returns it to him; Valentine is disturbed, but Speed, in an aside, immediately sees that she loves Valentine himself. When Silvia leaves, Speed attempts to explain this, but Valentine cannot understand.

Act 2, Scene 2

Proteus and Julia say farewell and exchange rings. Proteus vows to be faithful while he is away.

Act 2, Scene 3

Launce, a CLOWN who is Proteus's servant, appears with his dog Crab, whose hard-heartedness he complains about in a comic monologue. Launce is upset because he must leave his family and go to court with his master, but Crab shows no distress.

Act 2, Scene 4

The Duke reports that Proteus has arrived at his court, and Valentine praises his friend warmly. Valentine tells Silvia of the love between Proteus and Julia. Proteus enters and meets Silvia, who is then called away. Valentine reveals that he and Silvia are planning to elope. Proteus confesses in a soliloquy that he has fallen madly in love with Silvia, so much so that he is willing to betray both Valentine and Julia.

Act 2, Scene 5

Speed welcomes Launce to court. With clownish wit, the two servants gossip about their masters' love affairs.

Act 2, Scene 6

In a soliloquy, Proteus plots to steal Silvia from Valentine, finding justifications for his disloyalty to his friend and Julia. He proposes to reveal the intended elopement of Valentine and Silvia, scheduled for that night, to the Duke.

Act 2, Scene 7

Julia plans to journey to court to see Proteus. She will travel disguised as a page. Lucetta warns that Proteus's love may have diminished, but Julia is confident he will remain faithful.

Act 3, Scene 1

Proteus tells the Duke of the intended elopement, exiting as Valentine approaches. The Duke "discovers" the rope ladder hidden under Valentine's cloak and angrily banishes Valentine from his domain. Proteus arrives with Launce and offers to help Valentine flee. The two friends depart, leaving Launce, who speaks of his own love for a milkmaid. He has a written list of her good qualities. Speed appears, and the two comic figures review this document.

Act 3, Scene 2

The Duke speaks with Thurio, whom he has chosen to marry his daughter. Thurio complains that Silvia loves him even less than she did before Valentine's banishment. Proteus recommends maligning Valentine to her, and he volunteers for the job, observing that such slander will only be credible coming from someone believed to be Valentine's friend.

Act 4, Scene 1

Valentine and Speed are captured by Outlaws. Learning that Valentine is an educated gentleman, as they claim to be themselves, these desperadoes elect him their captain.

Act 4, Scene 2

Proteus soliloquizes that his ongoing career of betrayal, now directed at Thurio, has only brought him Silvia's scorn. Thurio arrives with Musicians. Also present, unknown to the others, is Julia, disguised as a page. The SONG "Who Is Silvia?" is performed, and Julia sees that Proteus loves its subject. Thurio and the Musicians depart, and Proteus converses with Silvia, who has appeared on her balcony. He takes credit for the serenade and speaks of his love, but Silvia rebukes him, referring to his former love, Julia. He claims that Julia has died, not knowing that she is listening, and adds that he has heard that Valentine is dead as well. He asks Silvia for a picture, and she agrees to give him one in the morning.

Act 4, Scene 3
Sir Eglamour agrees to accompany Silvia on a journey to find Valentine.

Act 4, Scene 4
In a monologue, Launce complains of Crab's doggy behavior, for he has urinated at the Duke's dinner. Proteus agrees to employ the disguised Julia as a page, ordering "Sebastian" to deliver a ring to Silvia, in exchange for the promised picture. Julia makes the exchange and learns that Silvia knows of and feels pity for Proteus's abandoned lover.

Act 5, Scene 1
Eglamour and Silvia flee.

Act 5, Scene 2
The Duke reports Silvia's flight. Thurio, Proteus, and Julia all join him in pursuit.

Act 5, Scene 3
The Outlaws have captured Silvia and are taking her to their captain.

Act 5, Scene 4
Valentine, alone, muses that his lonely exile is appropriate to his grief over his lost Silvia. Hearing a commotion, he hides himself, and Silvia, Proteus, and Julia enter. Proteus demands Silvia's love as a reward for having rescued her from the Outlaws; when she refuses, he attempts to rape her. Valentine comes forth and prevents him, cursing his supposed friend's disloyalty. Proteus, stricken with remorse, begs forgiveness. Valentine is so moved that he offers to yield Silvia to him; hearing this, Julia faints. Revived, she reveals her identity, and Proteus falls in love with her again. The Outlaws arrive with the Duke and Thurio as captives, whom Valentine releases. Thurio claims Silvia, but when Valentine offers to fight him, he fearfully declines. The Duke pardons Valentine and awards him Silvia's hand.

COMMENTARY

The Two Gentlemen of Verona is certainly among the most poorly received of Shakespeare's comedies. Some parts, especially the comic monologues of

Launce, are accomplished, but the play as a whole is unconvincing. It is perhaps best viewed as the work of a young and inexperienced playwright who was only beginning to experiment with comedy, a genre he was to master at a later date.

In the past, some scholars have claimed that the play was simply too bad to have been written by Shakespeare, that at most he may have touched up someone else's feeble effort. Modern criticism holds that the play, while an unsuccessful early effort, is nonetheless genuinely Shakespearean. Supporters of this opinion have focused on the young playwright's intelligent application of the literary conventions current in his day as he developed his own approach to comedy, or they have seen the play as at least in part a deliberate parody of these conventions. These two propositions are not mutually exclusive; a parodist may make use of a style for its entertainment value at the same time that he or she subverts it.

The play draws on two literary traditions: the "friendship literature" of the Middle Ages and romantic narrative. "Friendship literature" told tales of manly companionship, sometimes disrupted by romance but generally restored. The account of the relationship between Valentine and Proteus is an instance of this long-popular plot line. For instance, Valentine's renunciation of Silvia (5.4.82–83), though comically abrupt in context, represents a conventional demonstration of magnanimity that was standard in this tradition.

Romantic narrative derived ultimately from classical roots and was popular throughout the Middle Ages in the form of poetry and prose dealing with courtly love and adventure. Such narratives continued to be written and widely read during the Renaissance; Sir Philip SIDNEY's *Arcadia* was the best-known English example. This tradition was already familiar in the early Elizabethan theater. A number of plays written in the 1570s and 1580s share several of its characteristic devices: accounts of travels in several different settings; girls or women, abandoned by lovers, who assume disguises; a cynical villain; a mocking servant who comments on the romantic action; eventual reunion at the close. The audience finds in these exotic settings and stylized characters a life that seems both bolder and finer than its own, governed by values that are impossible in the real world. It is this body of conventions that Shakespeare uses in this play.

In *The Two Gentlemen of Verona*, lovers are separated through a flagrantly evil act of betrayal. After trials and rigors have been undergone, a happy ending reunites them and villainy is overcome. The promised escape has been provided. However, Shakespeare holds up the stereotype of romantic narrative to good-humored ridicule, especially in the treatment of his hero, Valentine, who is presented throughout as a gullible and foolish young man, a comic and ridiculous hero. When we first see him, he is ridiculing love, and we know, if only from his suggestive name, that his comeuppance surely lies ahead. Valentine's ineptness as a lover is demonstrated, for instance, when he fails to comprehend Silvia's flirtatious letter-writing ploy; when Speed attempts to explain it, he proves too slow-witted to appreciate it.

Valentine's high-flown rhetoric of love, as he recounts his infatuation to Proteus in 2.4, is the voice of exuberant enthusiasm, and he presents a pleasant picture of a young man in the first blush of romance. However, his bubbling account of his planned elopement seems indiscreet at best. Later in the scene, when Proteus reveals his plan to betray his friend, we pity Valentine for the blunder he has unknowingly committed in confiding in this villain, but at the same time we may chuckle that his effervescent "braggardism" (2.4.159) was so untimely.

We are not surprised when Valentine steps so neatly into the Duke's trap in 3.1, for his combination of naiveté and feigned sophistication seems entirely in character. So does his helplessness once the Duke rages off; he can only bemoan his fate until Proteus bundles him out of town.

We next see Valentine in the wholly comic scene (4.1) of his capture by the Outlaws, who immediately make him the leader of their gang, in what is clearly a broad parody of romantic adventure stories. He rescues Silvia from attempted rape by Proteus, but he is so silly a hero that it does not occur to him to claim his heroine at this obvious climax. In fact, he does not even speak to her for the remainder of the play. Instead, he responds only to his former friend, who is begging forgiveness, and he goes so far as to turn Silvia over to the would-be rapist. This absurd conclusion is prevented only by the quick-witted Julia, who wants Proteus for herself, and Valentine is united with his beloved only by default.

Only two of the characters in *The Two Gentlemen of Verona* anticipate the magical figures of later works. Launce, an early Shakespearean clown, voices the best writing in the play in his monologues concerning his dog Crab. The general artificiality of the play is countered to a considerable degree by the presence of this commonsensical man. However, Launce has literally nothing whatsoever to do with the plot; he simply provides intermissions, as it were, in the main action. Later, Shakespeare was to integrate his comic characters more fully. Julia, whose best material is in prose, is also something of a foil to Valentine and Proteus. Her pragmatic assumption of control over events begins with her intention to overcome her enforced separation from Proteus by following him to court, and it triumphs when she abandons her disguise and reconquers his love. She clearly foreshadows such later enterprising heroines as Rosalind in *As You Like It* and Viola in *Twelfth Night*.

SOURCES OF THE PLAY

The two strands that make up the plot of *The Two Gentlemen of Verona* came to the playwright from specific sources, although one derivation is not altogether clear, for Shakespeare made the material his own to a great extent. The relationships among Proteus, Valentine, and Silvia seem to be based on the story of Titus and Gisippus, a "friendship" tale originally found in Boccaccio's *Decameron* and very famous in Shakespeare's day. Gisippus bestows his fiancée on his friend Titus, who has fallen in love with her. This tale lacks the betrayal theme, but as his love develops, Titus contemplates such a course, in terms remarkably similar to those Proteus uses in his soliloquy in 2.6. Also, there are English variants of this tale, and several passages that resemble lines in the play appear in one of them, published in Sir Thomas ELYOT's *The Boke named the Governour* (1531). One such passage seems to have inspired Valentine's notorious couplet of renunciation. Just how Shakespeare knew the tale, and just what he took from which source, cannot be determined.

However, the story of the betrayed love of Proteus and Julia clearly came from *Diana Enamorada,* a prose romance written in Spanish by the Portuguese author Jorge de MONTEMAYOR and first printed in 1542. Although the first English translation, by Bartholomew YONG, was not published until 1598, Shakespeare probably knew the manuscript, which had been completed 16 years earlier, for there are many echoes of it in the play.

A third source was a long poem by Arthur BROOKE, *the Tragical History of Romeus and Juliet,* which was also the chief source for *Romeo and Juliet.* Here, Shakespeare's only important adoption was Valentine's rope-ladder, but there are suggestions of the later play in Silvia's conspiratorial visit to a friar's cell (4.3.43–44) and in the mention of a Friar Laurence (5.2.36).

Launce was apparently a Shakespearean invention, although his character type, the rustic clown, was already well established. The early plays of John LYLY offered models for Speed: also, some details of Speed's role derive from *Damon and Pithias,* a play of 1571 by Richard EDWARDS. The comical "catalogue" scene (3.1.270–371) seems to have been suggested by a scene in Lyly's *Midas* (1588–89). Lyly's immensely popular novel *Euphues* (1578) offered a famous instance of male friendship disturbed by sexual jealousy, and as the sensation of the age, it doubtless helped form the young Shakespeare's sense of romantic atmosphere.

TEXT OF THE PLAY

The Two Gentlemen of Verona is known to have been written by 1598, when it was mentioned by MERES, but features of its style suggest that it was written earlier. It has been nominated as possibly the first play Shakespeare wrote, but this cannot be proved. Proposed dates for its composition have ranged from 1590 to 1595, not counting a sometimes hypothesized rewrite of 1598. The only early publication of the play was in the FIRST FOLIO of 1623, and this text has therefore been the basis for all subsequent editions.

THEATRICAL HISTORY OF THE PLAY

No performance of *The Two Gentlemen of Verona* is recorded before 1762, although it is assumed to have been acted in the 16th century—at least on the strength of its inclusion in the list of plays compiled by Meres in 1598. The production of 1762, by David GARRICK, was of an altered text, as have been most of the scattered subsequent attempts. The play's many discrepancies have been amended to a greater or lesser extent, and additional material has often been added for Launce and Speed. The only version to achieve even a modest success with 19th-century audiences was a highly altered operatic version produced by Frederick REYNOLDS in the 1820s. There were successful 20th-century stagings—such as Joseph PAPP's musical adaptation of 1971, and a New York production of 1988 that featured a troupe of jugglers—but it remains one of the least performed of Shakespeare's plays. *Two Gentlemen of Verona* has not been made as a FILM, though it has been made for TELEVISION twice: in Germany in 1963 and by the BBC in 1983, as part of their complete cycle of Shakespeare's plays.

CHARACTERS

Antonio Minor character in *The Two Gentlemen of Verona,* the father of Proteus. Antonio appears only once, in 1.3, to make the decision that he will send his son to join Valentine at court, which results in Proteus's encounter with Silvia and its subsequent complications.

Crab Dog in *The Two Gentlemen of Verona.* Launce's pet is the subject of his two memorable comic monologues, in 2.3 and 4.4. The name refers to the crab apple, and it suggests an animal small in size and sour in expression.

Duke of Milan Minor character in *The Two Gentlemen of Verona,* the father of Silvia and the ruler of the court where the main action of the play takes place. Informed by Proteus that Silvia plans to elope with Valentine, the Duke banishes Valentine from the realm. In the final scene, the Duke appears, as ruler and as father of the future bride, to approve the final happy outcome.

Eglamour Minor character in *The Two Gentlemen of Verona,* the gentleman who helps Silvia flee her father's court in search of Valentine in 5.1. In selecting Eglamour as her confidant and guide, Silvia acclaims him "valiant, wise, . . . well-accomplished" (4.3.13) and is certain she can rely on his honor and courage. Yet when Silvia is captured by the Outlaws, he is reported to have fled ignominiously, "being nimble-footed" (5.3.6). This unlikely inconsistency, along with the fact that one of Julia's suitors is also named Eglamour (1.2.9), has sparked some debate. This may simply be one of the many instances of Shakespeare's carelessness in matters of detail, or it may reflect the former existence of two versions of the play. Also, it may be that a jocularly presented instance of cowardice is intended to undercut the seriousness of the romantic ideals that the play simultaneously depends on and laughs at.

Host   Minor character in *The Two Gentlemen of Verona*. Julia, disguised as a boy, converses with the Host in 4.2, having arrived at court to see her lover, Proteus. While she observes the infidelity of Proteus, the Host falls asleep, subtly isolating the heroine at this crucial moment.

Julia   Character in *The Two Gentlemen of Verona*, the betrayed lover of Proteus. Julia disguises herself as a boy and follows Proteus to court, where he has fallen in love with Silvia. Learning of his infidelity, Julia nonetheless remains true to Proteus, serving, in her disguise, as his messenger to her rival. She is present in the final scene, when Valentine offers Silvia to Proteus, and her quick wit tells her to swoon, interrupting the transaction. She reveals herself, her presence restores Proteus to his original loyalty, and he vows his love for her anew.

Julia is an early instance of a type of young woman Shakespeare clearly admired—independent, active, and capable of pursuing a man, even if he is unworthy of her. Other instances include Helena in *All's Well That Ends Well*, Rosalind in *As You Like It*, and Viola in *Twelfth Night*.

Launce (Lance)   Character in *The Two Gentlemen of Verona*, a CLOWN, the servant of Proteus. Launce is not involved with the plot of the play. However, the comparison of his jocular common sense with the absurdly rhetorical fancies of the protagonists helps to parody them, thus contributing to the play's tone. Launce's great speeches are his two prose monologues (opening 2.3 and 4.4) about his dog, Crab. In the first he bemoans the dog's lack of sympathy with his misfortune in having to leave his family to travel with Proteus. In the second, he recounts various canine offenses that Crab has committed, such as urinating under the Duke's table and on Silvia's dress. Launce himself has taken punishment for them to spare the dog. He also engages in two humorous dialogues with Speed, one of which is preceded by Launce's soliloquy on his love life (3.1.261–276).

Launce prefigures later, more consequential Shakespearean clowns, such as Dogberry in *Much Ado About Nothing* and Bottom in *A Midsummer Night's Dream*.

Lucetta   Minor character in *The Two Gentlemen of Verona*, the waiting-woman to Julia. Like the other servants in the play, Speed and Launce, Lucetta seems at least as alert and intelligent as her employer. She is aware of her mistress's love for Proteus before Julia is willing to admit it to herself, and she suspects Proteus of disloyalty when Julia is all too trusting.

Musicians   Minor characters in *The Two Gentlemen of Verona*, players hired by Thurio to assist him in wooing Silvia by performing a SONG in her honor.

Outlaws   Minor characters in *The Two Gentlemen of Verona*. The three Outlaws capture Valentine and Speed in 4.1. They are recognizable romantic types, gentlemen whose youthful hot-bloodedness has resulted in their exile. They are also comic figures to some extent, as is shown by their prompt election of Valentine as their chieftain because he is a handsome gentleman who is versed in foreign languages.

Panthino   Minor character in *The Two Gentlemen of Verona*, the servant of Antonio. Panthino helps his master arrive at his fateful decision to send his son Proteus to court. Later, at the close of two successive scenes (2.2, 2.3), he furthers the action, appearing in order to hasten the departures of Proteus and Launce, respectively.

Proteus One of the title characters in *The Two Gentlemen of Verona*, the villain who simultaneously betrays his lover Julia and his friend Valentine by pursuing Valentine's lover Silvia. Proteus initially presents himself as wholly in love with Julia. His father, Antonio, forces him to attend the court, for such a sojourn is proper for a young gentleman, and he bids farewell to his beloved, pledging to be faithful. Once at court, however, he falls in love with Silvia, who is already secretly betrothed to Valentine. Proteus knows his love is disloyal, but he is prepared to forsake both Valentine and Julia. Proteus plots against Valentine and even attempts to rape Silvia, but Valentine thwarts and forgives him. Reunited with Julia, who has followed him, Proteus vows renewed fidelity, and the play ends with the planning of a double wedding.

Shakespeare took this character's name from HOMER's *Odyssey*, in which Proteus is a sea god who can change his shape at will. The Proteus of *The Two Gentlemen of Verona*, whose attitudes toward others change with his appetites, is thus fittingly named.

Sebastian In *The Two Gentlemen of Verona*, the name Julia takes while disguised as a boy.

Silvia Character in *The Two Gentlemen of Verona*, the lover of Valentine, also loved by Proteus. Proteus betrays both Valentine and his own lover, Julia, for Silvia's sake. She has the good sense to recognize the rogue in Proteus and reject him, and Julia, disguised as a page, is pleased with the sympathy Silvia expresses for Proteus's abandoned lover. After Valentine's banishment, Silvia bravely resolves to follow him. Captured by the Outlaws whom Valentine now leads, she is rescued first by Proteus, who attempts to rape her, and then by Valentine. However, her lover, in a rapturous gesture of forgiveness to his friend, presents her to Proteus as a gift. Julia's intervention forestalls this development, and at the play's end, Silvia is betrothed to Valentine. Silvia is chiefly a conventional figure, intended only as the focus of the actions of the two men. Nevertheless, she anticipates such later, more humanly interesting Shakespearean women as Beatrice and Rosalind (of *Much Ado About Nothing* and *As You Like It*, respectively) in her forthrightness and pluck.

Speed Character in *The Two Gentlemen of Verona*. Speed, the servant of Valentine, is saucy and impertinent, teasing his master about his infatuation with Silvia and engaging in witty exchanges with Launce. He is an example of a character type frequently used by early Elizabethan dramatists, especially by John LYLY, whose comedies influenced the young Shakespeare.

Thurio Minor character in *The Two Gentlemen of Verona*, a suitor of Silvia. Thurio is inveigled by Proteus into hiring a group of Musicians to serenade Silvia, but Proteus takes credit with the lady. At the close of the play, Thurio claims Silvia's hand, but beats a cowardly retreat when challenged by Valentine.

Valentine One of the title characters in *The Two Gentlemen of Verona*, the lover of Silvia, whom his disloyal friend Proteus attempts to steal. Valentine is both a romantic leading man and an object of fun. At first resistant to love, he then becomes an inept suitor. Once Silvia has given him her affection, he naively brags of it to Proteus, whose plotting quickly sends Valentine into exile. Later, after he rescues Silvia from an attempted rape by Proteus, only Julia's intervention prevents him from inanely giving away his beloved to the man from whom he has just saved her.

Two Noble Kinsmen, The
SYNOPSIS

A Prologue declares that the play has a noble predecessor, in a work by CHAUCER, that it cannot hope to live up to.

Act 1, Scene 1

As Theseus, Duke of ATHENS, prepares to marry Queen Hippolyta of the Amazons, the ceremony is interrupted by a Queen who falls on her knees before Theseus, followed by two more who address

Hippolyta and her sister Emilia. The Queens tell of their husbands' deaths fighting King Creon of THEBES, who has refused to bury the kings' bodies, thereby exposing their souls to torment. They ask Theseus to conquer Creon, insisting that any delay is dishonorable. The wedding is then postponed as Theseus prepares for war.

Act 1, Scene 2
Two noblemen of Thebes, the cousins Arcite and Palamon, decide to leave the court of the villainous King Creon. Valerius brings word that Duke Theseus has declared war. The cousins realize that their honor requires them to stay and fight for Thebes.

Act 1, Scene 3
Hippolyta and Emilia bid farewell to Pirithous, who is about to join Theseus in Thebes. Hippolyta remarks on the long-standing friendship of Pirithous and Theseus. Emilia recalls her own, similar affection for a childhood girlfriend and declares that she will never love a man so well.

Act 1, Scene 4
The Queens thank Theseus for his victory over Creon, and he sends them to bury their husbands. A Herald informs Theseus that Palamon and Arcite, both badly wounded, are among his prisoners of war.

Act 1, Scene 5
The Queens lead funeral processions for their husbands.

Act 2, Scene 1
The Gaoler negotiates a marriage settlement with the Wooer of his Daughter. The Daughter appears on her way to see the new prisoners, Palamon and Arcite, whom she admires for the spirit with which they bear their imprisonment. The three commoners leave as the two prisoners appear, reflecting on the comfort they can take in each other's company; they believe that their honorable friendship will sustain them throughout their lives. Below their windows, in a courtyard, they see Emilia conversing with a Woman. First Palamon and then Arcite fall in love with Emilia on sight. After she leaves, they quarrel over who has the right to claim her as his beloved. Each feels that his honor is offended by the other, and they vow to fight a duel if they ever have the opportunity. The Gaoler appears and takes Arcite to the duke. Palamon muses on his love for Emilia until the Gaoler returns to report that Arcite has been freed but banished from Theseus's realm, on pain of death.

Act 2, Scene 2
Arcite, free, decides to stay in Theseus's realm and attempt to meet and woo Emilia. He encounters a group of Countrymen, who tell him of the wrestling and running competitions to be witnessed by Theseus and his court at a nearby country fair. Arcite decides to enter the competitions in order to come to the attention of the court and thus meet Emilia.

Act 2, Scene 3
The Gaoler's Daughter reflects on her hopeless love for Palamon. She realizes that he will never love a commoner, but she decides to help him escape from prison.

Act 2, Scene 4
The disguised Arcite, having won the competitions, is interviewed by Theseus, who accepts him as a courtier. He is assigned to serve as an attendant to Emilia.

Act 2, Scene 5
The Daughter reveals in a soliloquy that she has freed Palamon, who waits in a nearby wood until she can bring him food and a file to remove his shackles. She hopes he will come to love her.

Act 3, Scene 1
Alone in the wood, Arcite reflects on his good fortune in having become Emilia's attendant. Overhearing this, the fugitive Palamon emerges from the trees, and they resume their argument. Though their affection for each other still stands, they agree that they must duel to uphold their respective honors. Arcite declares he will bring Palamon food and a file to remove his shackles, and then they will fight.

Act 3, Scene 2
The Daughter cannot find Palamon and concludes that he has been eaten by wild animals. Hysterical, she reflects that her father will be hanged for her

treachery in letting Palamon escape, and she will be reduced to beggary if she does not commit suicide. She wishes she were already dead.

Act 3, Scene 3
Arcite returns to Palamon with food and a file. They agree not to mention Emilia but cannot refrain and fall to quarreling again. Arcite leaves, saying he will return when Palamon has removed his shackles, and they will fight.

Act 3, Scene 4
Raving wildly about Palamon, her father, and other things, the Daughter sings scraps of SONG.

Act 3, Scene 5
A Schoolmaster instructs a group of peasants, one of them costumed as a Bavian, or baboon, on the dance they are to perform before the duke. One of the women of their group is missing, however, so they despair about being able to perform. The Daughter appears, and although they see that she is mad, the dancers recruit her for their performance. Theseus and his court appear and, after a lengthy PROLOGUE from the Schoolmaster, the dance is presented.

Act 3, Scene 6
Palamon and Arcite meet to duel. As they put on their armor, they reminisce fondly, but they continually renew their quarrel. They begin to fight, but Theseus and his court arrive. The cousins identify themselves, and Theseus condemns them to death: Arcite for having violated his banishment and Palamon as an escaped prisoner of war. They plead to be permitted to finish their duel, with the survivor then being executed, and Theseus agrees. However, when Hippolyta and Emilia beg for mercy for them, Theseus compromises. He decrees that the cousins shall return to Thebes and recruit seconds, come back within a month, and then duel for Emilia's hand. The duel shall not be to the death, but rather consist of a contest to force the opponent to touch a pillar erected for the purpose. The winner will marry Emilia; only the loser and his seconds will be executed. The cousins agree and depart.

Act 4, Scene 1
The Gaoler hears of the duel from a Friend and worries that he will be blamed for Palamon's

escape. A Second Friend arrives and assures him that the duke, encouraged by Palamon, has pardoned the Gaoler and his Daughter. The Wooer then arrives with the news that the Daughter is mad. She appears, ranting about marrying Palamon and taking a sea voyage to meet him.

Act 4, Scene 2
Regretting the upcoming duel, Emilia reviews the virtues of each cousin in turn and admits that she loves them both. She is joined by Theseus and the court. Pirithous and a Messenger have witnessed the arrival of the cousins and their seconds, and they describe the gallantly arrayed Knights in detail.

Act 4, Scene 3
The Doctor witnesses the Daughter's ravings and prescribes that the Wooer should dress as Palamon and court her, in the hope that the apparent fulfillment of her fantasy will shock her out of it.

Act 5, Scene 1
In a temple Arcite and Palamon prepare to duel. They bid each other an affectionate farewell. When Arcite and his seconds make a sacrifice to Mars, the altar resounds with thunder. Palamon and his followers make one to Venus, and the altar gives forth doves. After the knights leave for the duel, Emilia appears and makes a sacrifice to Diana. A rose tree bearing a single rose emerges, but the rose falls from it. Emilia is confused by this omen.

Act 5, Scene 2
The Wooer, in the guise of Palamon, reports that he has kissed the Daughter. The Doctor directs that he go on to sleep with her, and he readily agrees. The Daughter emerges from the Gaoler's house and talks of a dancing horse Palamon has given her and how another horse loves it in vain. Still pretending to be Palamon, the Wooer proposes to her, and she accepts, adding that they should go to the end of the world for the wedding. She returns indoors, and the men go to witness the duel.

Act 5, Scene 3
Emilia, resisting all arguments, refuses to witness the duel, so a Servant is left with her to report. Going to and fro, he periodically recounts the action: first one cousin seems to be winning, then the other. Finally, he reports Arcite the victor. The

court returns, and Arcite and Emilia are formally declared engaged. Emilia declares that only her duty to comfort Arcite, who has lost his noble kinsman, keeps her from killing herself with grief.

Act 5, Scene 4

Palamon and his seconds prepare to be executed. Palamon asks the Gaoler about his Daughter; he reports that she has recovered and is to be married. As Palamon is about to be beheaded by the Executioner, Pirithous arrives with a pardon, reporting that Arcite is dying after being crushed by a runaway horse. Theseus, Hippolyta, and Emilia appear, with Arcite in a litter. Arcite accepts Palamon's grieving farewell, bequeaths Emilia to him, receives a final kiss from her, and dies. Theseus declares a period of mourning, to be followed by the marriage of Emilia and Palamon.

Epilogue

An anonymous actor, pretending to have stage fright, jests about the audience's hisses and laughter. He asks for their pardon, promises a better play some other night, and bids farewell.

COMMENTARY

The Two Noble Kinsmen is probably the least known of Shakespeare's plays, in good part because (in the opinion of all but a few scholars) much of it was written by someone else, probably John FLETCHER. It has rarely been performed or even published over the centuries, though modern commentators' growing interest in Shakespeare's ROMANCES encompasses this work.

Considered separately, the parts of *The Two Noble Kinsmen* written by Shakespeare present the germ of a better and more interesting work than the play as a whole turned out to be. Shakespeare wrote Acts 1 and 5—with some exceptions—plus 3.1 and perhaps some other minor passages. With the beginning and the end of the play, he could introduce characters and themes and bring them to the climax of the action. Scenes 1.1 and 5.1 are especially strong, containing much good poetry and several spectacular theatrical effects. Shakespeare's only substantial contribution to the development between these phases is the encounter between Arcite and Palamon, when they prepare to duel

even as they recognize their profound affection for each other. A number of fine passages of verse in 3.1—especially Arcite's lyrical praise of Emilia—sharpen the audience's appreciation that the developing story is more than an assemblage of clichés about knighthood and courtly love enlivened by a comic SUBPLOT.

In Shakespeare's portions of the play, *The Two Noble Kinsmen* displays many of the characteristics of his other late works, and it is properly grouped with the romances. The playwright was clearly employing the techniques of spectacle, exotic characters and settings, and bizarre plotting with much the same intention as in other romances—to demonstrate humanity's dependence on providence in the face of inscrutable destiny and to evoke the nobility of the human spirit in the face of this knowledge.

The spectacular is less dramatic and effective in *The Two Noble Kinsmen* than in, say, *The Tempest*, but it is nonetheless present. Theseus and Hippolyta's elaborate wedding opens the play on a ceremonious note, only to be interrupted by the extraordinary sight of the three Queens, all in black and thus contrasting strikingly with the wedding party's festive finery. The Queens' manner is sternly formal, as they first address Theseus and receive his response, then do the same in turn with Hippolyta and Emilia. This ritualistic exchange makes the gravity of their plea unmistakable. The effect is augmented as the plea is repeated with variations: when they receive a promise of support, they demand instant action; when Artesius is assigned to the task, they demand Theseus. The importance of this presentation becomes clear when we consider how Shakespeare has altered his source. In Chaucer's tale (see "Sources"), Theseus is already married, only a single Queen pleads—and only with him—and he consents immediately. In contrast, Shakespeare delayed the process, for action is less important in *The Two Noble Kinsmen* than emotion, here manifested in an almost religious atmosphere of courtliness and mystery. It is appropriate that the first character on stage should be Hymen, a god.

This religious atmosphere recurs in the funeral procession of 1.5. Throughout the play, references to rituals of various sorts, along with manifold allusions to the pagan gods, both singly and collectively, maintain our awareness of the need for harmony with the divine, a consideration that underlies the action. In 5.1 the play's evocation of religion and mystery is at its most intense. The three petitions to pagan gods and the divine responses are in themselves meaningful, as we shall see, but they are also important for the atmosphere they create. Highly elaborate, with startling sound and physical effects—doubtless devised with an eye to the increased technical capacities of the BLACK-FRIARS THEATRE—they evoke awe and wonder appropriate to the extraordinary twists of fate in the coming climax. The supplicants' prayers comprise the best poetry of the play, and the divine responses are gratifyingly spectacular. They are mysterious and yet, as the baffled Emilia observes, "gracious" (5.1.173). The exotic beauty of this scene is generally considered the high point of *The Two Noble Kinsmen.*

Such spectacle is effective simply for its own sake—Shakespeare was certainly inspired in part by the increasing popularity of the MASQUE—but it also helps further the themes of the play. As in the other late plays, the central proposition of *The Two Noble Kinsmen* is that humanity is dependent on providence. In the face of a destiny we cannot understand, we can only accept our fate and hope the gods will refrain from destroying us. This point of view is less pessimistic than it sounds when reduced to its essentials, for the nobility of humanity's continuing survival in the face of such knowledge is impressive. At least, we see the potential for such nobility in each individual.

We are repeatedly reminded of fate's importance. Even the celebratory, flower-filled opening hymn finishes with a sinister hint of fatality in its allusions to birds of ill omen. Theseus recalls the wedding day of the grieving Queen and rhetorically addresses destiny, "O grief and time, / Fearful consumers, you will all devour!" (1.1.69–70). In 1.2 Palamon declares that Creon is corrupting Thebes by making "heaven unfeared" (1.2.64); nevertheless, the young men seem powerless to avoid entanglement in Creon's corruption. Admitting that helplessness, Arcite entrusts their future to "th' event, / that never-erring arbitrator" (1.2.113–114). Hippolyta hopes that

Theseus, in combat, will be able "To dure ill-dealing fortune" (1.3.5), and a defeated knight, facing execution, declares that the winners have "Fortune, whose title is . . . momentary" (5.4.17). Even after victory Theseus speaks of "Th'impartial gods, who from the mounted heavens / View us their mortal herd" (1.4.4–5). Using a different metaphor for human helplessness before fate, Pirithous describes Arcite's flagging life as "a vessel . . . that floats but for / The surge that next approaches" (5.4.83–84). At the end, reviewing the final twist of fate, Theseus declares, "Never fortune / Did play a subtler game" (5.4.112–113). Fortune is omnipresent in the play's world, yet it is entirely beyond human control or understanding.

Tellingly, the gods answer the eloquent prayers of 5.1, but not in a way that could have been anticipated; fortune is certain but unpredictable. Arcite prays that he may "Be styled the lord o'th'day" (5.1.60), and he is indeed declared the winner of the duel, but he loses Emilia and his life, as the horse she gives him proves deadly. Palamon asks Venus for victory as "true love's merit" (5.1.128), but he only gains Emilia through Arcite's accidental death. Emilia prays that the cousin who loves her best should win. This would appear to be Palamon, for he is associated with Venus rather than Mars; moreover, since he saw her first and is more rightly her lover—as Arcite finally admits—he is more truly fighting in the cause of love, with Arcite more intent on defending his personal honor. Yet it is Arcite who wins, even though Emilia does in the end have her wish granted. As expectations are upset and then fulfilled, but fulfilled only tragically, our sense of the incomprehensibility of providence is compounded.

The play, however, counters any implicit fatalism by repeatedly stressing the importance of human nobility. The emphasis begins in the Prologue with the assertion that the story being told has in itself a "nobleness" (Prologue.15) that the creators of the drama are striving to uphold, and that Chaucer was its "noble breeder" (10). The nobility of Palamon and Arcite—explicit in the play's title—is repeatedly confirmed by the other characters. Their friendship is bound up in their appreciation of each other's noble qualities, and it is itself conventionally noble in a medieval literary tradition that was still very much alive in Shakespeare's day. Intense friendship between noble young warriors, especially when disrupted by heterosexual love, was the subject of many novels, poems, and plays—including *Two Gentlemen of Verona* and some of the *Sonnets*. The theme of these works was the essential nobility—the spiritual superiority—of such a relationship. Arcite and Palamon had been celebrated in this light before—even before Chaucer—and Shakespeare obviously intended to do so again. The theme is paralleled in Hippolyta's description of the friendship of Theseus and Pirithous in 1.3.26–47, and in Emilia's touching account of her own childhood relationship with the deceased Lavinia in 1.3.49–82.

Emilia herself is another instance of nobility. In Act 1 she and Hippolyta demonstrate their inherent magnanimity in their response to the Queens, and in Act 5 Emilia displays a noble combination of heightened emotion and disinterested concern for honorable propriety, which is pointedly isolated by the playwright in 5.3, when the duel is held offstage and reflected in her responses.

It is Theseus, however, who is the central figure at the play's opening and again at its end (although he is a less significant figure in Fletcher's portions of the play). His nobility is strongly emphasized. At least in Acts 1 and 5, his actions are strikingly courtly and generous at every turn: toward the Queens, toward his wounded prisoners of war, in his arrangements for the religious petitions of the duelists, and in his responses to them after the duel and its tragic aftermath. Most important, at the play's close, he adopts a pointedly serene and courageous attitude toward the buffetings of fate to which the play's world has been subjected. This stance has great moral weight, not simply because Theseus closes the play—as its highest-ranking figure, he would do that anyway in the theatrical protocol of Shakespeare's day—but because he has been established as a highly noble man.

The play's emphasis on nobility, while part of an old tradition of chivalric heroes in romance literature, also has a more immediate point: in the face of destiny, human beings are helpless, and it is necessary to accept this. In *The Two Noble Kinsmen* the nobility of the title characters lies in their unhesitating acceptance of their situation. Forced by circumstances to fight for Creon, they "follow / the becking of our chance" (1.2.115–116). Seized by an obsession, Arcite strives only to "maintain [his] proceedings" and "clear [his] own way with the mind and sword / Of a true gentleman" (3.1.53, 56–57). Palamon also accepts his fateful love, with its corollary of enmity to Arcite, "As 'twere a wreath of roses, [though it] is heavier / Than lead itself, stings more than nettles" (5.1.96–97). The kinsmen's seemingly senseless system of honor provides them with a recourse: In the face of an inexorable destiny, nobility consists in accepting our losses and maintaining our dignity. Although Emilia can cry, "Is this winning? / O all you heavenly powers, where is your mercy?" (5.3.138–139), she immediately concedes that if the gods' "wills have said it must be so" (5.3.140), then she must accept it. In the play's last lines, Theseus addresses the divinities, "O you heavenly charmers, / What things you make of us! . . . Let us be thankful / For that which is, and with you leave dispute[s] / That are above our question" (5.4.131–136). The characters in the play accept their circumstances, and therein lies their significance.

Had Shakespeare written the middle of the play as well as its introduction and close, *The Two Noble Kinsmen* might convey more of the mystery and beauty of human existence, with the power of *The Winter's Tale* or *The Tempest*. As it is, the play is greatly weakened by Fletcher's contribution. Shakespeare's resonant themes are diminished by a series of subplots, and his emphasis on ceremony and ritual is abandoned in favor of melodrama, and pathos. The story of the Gaoler's Daughter is weakened by the omission of any contact between her and Palamon, and her madness is an unconvincingly pastiche of conventional symptoms. The Doctor's lewd prescription is at best vulgar humor; it has no function but comic relief and bears no relation to lunacy, even to the unrealistic madness depicted. The second subplot, the presentation of the Schoolmaster's rustic entertainment, barely deserves to be called a subplot, for it is merely an excuse to present a popular dance number. Pleasant but irrelevant, it lacks the vigor of the real personalities that fill Shakespeare's equivalent scenes, most notably in *The Winter's Tale*.

More important, Palamon and Arcite are much less impressive figures. In 2.1, when they fall in love with Emilia and begin to quarrel, furthering the plot and observing the chivalric conventions, they are different men from the pair met in 1.2. Their revulsion at Thebes's corruption—their most prominent characteristic in 1.2—has been replaced by a nostalgia for "our noble country" (2.1.61). The reliance on personal honor that permitted them to entrust themselves to the "never-erring arbitrator" (1.2.114) is superseded by thoughts that "fair-eyed maids shall weep our banishments" (2.1.91). Sentiment takes precedence over character. Shakespeare's maintenance of the cousins' nobility in 3.1 is utterly wasted in 3.3, a scene filled with stale jests about "the wenches / We have known in our days!" (3.3.28–29). Only in 3.6, where they assist each other before beginning the duel and then face Theseus, do the kinsmen approach their earlier nobility. However, this scene is somewhat redundant thematically—combining the fondness and enmity already presented in 3.1—and Fletcher's poetry is distinctly more pedestrian than Shakespeare's.

The Two Noble Kinsmen has its virtues. It contains scattered passages of good poetry in Shakespeare's complex late style, especially in 1.1 and 5.1. The spectacles in 1.1 and 5.1, as well as the funeral procession of 1.5 and dance of 3.5, are theatrically impressive in a good production. Most important, enough of Shakespeare's premise comes through in Acts 1 and 5 that a fine performance permits an audience to experience some sense of awe at the inexorability of the human condition. However, one has only to compare this work with Shakespeare's undiluted efforts to realize how inadequate it is. It may be best seen as a business venture: Shakespeare, about to retire—possibly already living in STRATFORD—was called upon by his company, the KING'S MEN, to collaborate with its rising creative star, Fletcher, and the two produced a workmanlike job, which seems to have had at least a modicum of success. As such, it is an interesting demonstration of early-17th-century tastes, and since it incorporates what is quite possibly Shakespeare's last dramatic writing, it merits more attention than it would otherwise get.

SOURCES OF THE PLAY

The source for the main plot of *The Two Noble Kinsmen*—the conflict between Arcite and Palamon—was taken by Shakespeare and Fletcher from Geoffrey Chaucer's "The Knight's Tale," one of the most popular of *The Canterbury Tales* (ca. 1482). Chaucer had taken the story from an epic poem by Giovanni BOCCACCIO, *Teseide* (ca. 1340). The playwrights altered their source considerably, adding the interrupted wedding in 1.1 (perhaps deriving it from the similar disruption in A *Midsummer Night's Dream*, which was also altered from "The Knight's Tale"). More significantly, they added the stipulation that the loser of the duel over Emilia must be executed. Another *Dream* source, the "Life of Theseus" in PLUTARCH's *Lives* (1579; translated by Thomas NORTH), provided hints for Theseus's depiction, especially in 1.1.

The tragicomic subplot of the Gaoler's Daughter was apparently invented for the play, probably by Fletcher, who (according to most scholarly opinion) wrote most of the scenes in which it figures. The lesser subplot, the Schoolmaster's presentation of a rustic entertainment, is a restaging of a scene from a popular contemporary masque by Francis BEAUMONT, the *Masque of the Inner Temple and Gray's Inn* (1613).

TEXT OF THE PLAY

Modern scholars usually believe that *The Two Noble Kinsmen* was written jointly by Shakespeare and John Fletcher, though a few hold that Shakespeare wrote none of it and a few that he wrote it all. While precise agreement is lacking on the authors' distribution of labors, it is generally thought that Shakespeare was responsible for Act 1, 3.1, and all of Act 5 except 5.2. Many variations of this arrangement are proposed, most commonly the addition of 2.1 or the Daughter's soliloquy at the beginning of 3.2, or the deletion of 1.4 and 1.5. Also, some ascribe the remaining portions not to Fletcher but to Beaumont or Philip MASSINGER, or to some combination of the three.

The Two Noble Kinsmen was almost certainly written in 1613. The rustic entertainment in 3.5 was taken from a masque by Beaumont that was staged on February 20, 1613; the same troupe of dancers probably performed in both productions. A theatrical character named Palamon—presumably the hero of *The Two Noble Kinsmen*—is mentioned in Ben JONSON's 1614 play, *Bartholomew Fair*, suggesting that Fletcher and Shakespeare's play had already been staged by that date.

The Two Noble Kinsmen was the latest to be published of all Shakespeare's plays. It was omitted from the FIRST FOLIO (1623), probably because the editors knew that more than half of it was written by another playwright. The play was first published in a QUARTO edition of 1634 (known as Q1) by John WATERSON. Q1 was ascribed to Shakespeare and Fletcher on its title page and in its registration with the STATIONERS' COMPANY. Beginning in 1679, however, *The Two Noble Kinsmen* was often published as the work of Beaumont and Fletcher, and it did not appear in a collection of Shakespeare's plays until 1841. It is frequently omitted from modern collections.

Q1 is an excellent edition, with little garbling of text and relatively few misprints. It was based on a PROMPTBOOK, as is evident from some of the stage directions, which include instructions for the preparation of props. Two actors—"Curtis" and "T. Tucke"—are named in place of their characters; they are probably Curtis GREVILLE and Thomas TUCKFEILD, which suggests that the promptbook was prepared for a production of the 1620s. It may derive from the coauthors' FOUL PAPERS. Q1, as the only early text, has been the basis for all subsequent editions.

THEATRICAL HISTORY OF THE PLAY

Jonson's 1614 reference (see "Text of the Play") implies a performance of *The Two Noble Kinsmen* before that date, and the play was considered for performance at the royal court in 1619 (the choice made is unknown). Further, it was still in the King's Men's repertoire in the 1620s, when Q1 was printed from a promptbook. The Q1 title page asserts that the play had been staged at the BLACK-FRIARS THEATRE, but no specific record of an early performance is known.

In 1664 William DAVENANT produced his own version of the play, entitled *The Rivals*. He altered it immensely, changing all the names and locations and supplying a new beginning and a new conclu-

sion. He replaced much of the text—including most of what is attributed to Shakespeare—with his own (which was influenced in part by passages from *Macbeth*). The only known performance is that reported by Samuel PEPYS in 1664, but since *The Rivals* was published four years later, it was probably at least somewhat popular.

The Two Noble Kinsmen was not seen again until 1928, when it was produced at the OLD VIC THEATRE. It has only been staged occasionally since then, most recently at the Shakespeare's Globe Theatre (see WANAMAKER, SAM) in 2000, and it remains among the least performed of Shakespeare's works.

CHARACTERS

Arcite One of the title characters of *The Two Noble Kinsmen*, cousin of Palamon. In 1.2 Arcite and Palamon are affectionate friends, both nobly concerned with maintaining their honor as chivalrous knights. However, while prisoners of war in ATHENS in 2.1, both fall in love with the beauty of Emilia, sister-in-law of Duke Theseus, and their friendship crumbles as they dispute who may claim her as their loved one. They eventually fight a duel over Emilia, with the stipulation by Theseus that the loser be not killed in the fight but instead executed. Arcite wins the duel, but then he dies, crushed by a runaway horse, and Palamon gets Emilia.

As the protagonists of a stylized chivalric romance, the two cousins are very similar, and their characterizations tend to blur even more given the unevenness of the play, a collaboration between Shakespeare and John FLETCHER. Nevertheless, some distinctions can be drawn. In 1.1 Arcite is the leader of the two, introducing the idea of fleeing the corrupt court of THEBES and attempting to broaden Palamon's military orientation. When they are obliged to fight for Thebes, Arcite draws the deepest conclusion from their situation. Declaring that they will have to trust "th'event, / That never-erring arbitrator" (1.2.113–114), he presents an important theme of the play, humanity's helplessness to direct destiny. When their quarrel over Emilia arises, he is the more reasonable of the two, attempting to smooth things over in 2.1, when they meet again in 3.1, and as they prepare to duel in

3.3. He is also more sensible about the approach of Theseus, proposing that Palamon hide and they fight later. Nevertheless, he is perfectly willing to fight it out when Palamon insists, and when the combatants offer petitions to the gods in 5.1, Arcite speaks to Mars, the god of war. At his death, Arcite is simply a pawn of the plot, asking forgiveness with his last breath.

Arcite's personality is still further obscured by the fact that in Acts 2 to 4, Shakespeare probably wrote only one scene (3.1), and Fletcher's Arcite is a somewhat different character from Shakespeare's. A sentimentalist, he laments in 2.1 the fact that imprisonment means the cousins will not find "The sweet embraces of a loving wife" (2.1.84) or produce children, and he thinks achingly that "fair-eyed maids shall weep our banishments" (2.1.91). When, in 2.2, he decides to enter the wrestling and running competition to gain the attention of the duke's court, he is nothing more than a stereotypical hero-in-disguise. Perhaps in light of this, Shakespeare gives him a beautiful meditation on Emilia at the opening of 3.1. However, Arcite's inconsistencies merely reflect the failings of the play as a whole.

Artesius Minor character in *The Two Noble Kinsmen*, an officer under Theseus, Duke of ATHENS. When Theseus's wedding is interrupted by the demands of the Three Queens for vengeance against King Creon of THEBES, the Duke instructs Artesius to prepare the army for war in 1.1.159–165. He then disappears from the play. His only function is to lend a military air to the preparations.

Bavian Minor character in *The Two Noble Kinsmen*, a performer dressed as a baboon, or bavian. The Bavian is part of an entertainment performed before Theseus, Duke of ATHENS in 3.5. He speaks only two words, "Yes, sir" (3.5.37), in response to his director, the Schoolmaster, who tells him, "My friend, carry your tail without offence / Or scandal to the ladies; and be sure / You tumble with audacity and manhood, / And when you bark do it with judgement" (3.5.34–37). This directive casts an amusing light on English rustic entertainments of the 17th century. However, most scholars agree that Shakespeare did not write this scene; the

Bavian and his instructions are probably the work of John FLETCHER.

Boy Minor character in *The Two Noble Kinsmen*, a singer at the wedding of Theseus and Hippolyta. In 1.1.1–24 the Boy sings the SONG "Roses, their sharp spines being gone" and strews flowers. He provides a note of decorous festivity before the ceremony is interrupted by the arrival of the three Queens.

Brother Minor character in *The Two Noble Kinsmen*, brother of the Gaoler. In 4.1 the Brother accompanies the Gaoler's deranged Daughter, who is returning home. He is a mere pawn who speaks only a few lines. He was probably created by Shakespeare's collaborator, John FLETCHER, who wrote this scene, in the opinion of most scholars.

Countrymen Group of peasants, minor characters in *The Two Noble Kinsmen*. In 2.2 four Countrymen tell Arcite of wrestling and running competitions at a country fair. The outcast nobleman subsequently distinguishes himself at the fair, coming to the attention of the court of Duke Theseus and thus meeting his beloved, Emilia. Six Countrymen appear in 3.5, one of them dressed as a Bavian, or baboon, as part of the duke's entertainment; five of them, with Nell and her friends, perform a dance under the direction of the Schoolmaster. Most scholars agree that neither 2.2 nor 3.5 was written by Shakespeare; thus, the Countrymen are probably the creation of John FLETCHER.

Daughter Character in *The Two Noble Kinsmen*, deranged lover of Palamon and child of the Gaoler. Although she has already agreed to marry the Wooer, in 2.1 the Daughter falls in love with Palamon, a prisoner of war in her father's prison. After remarking to her father on the nobility of Palamon and his fellow prisoner, Arcite, in 2.1, the Daughter appears alone for her next four scenes, all soliloquies. In 2.3 she declares that she will help Palamon escape, and in 2.5 she reports that she has done so. In 3.2 she is alone in the woods, unable to find Palamon and clearly going mad. She decides that Palamon has been eaten by wild animals and contemplates suicide. Her fourth soliloquy in 3.4 is frankly insane, as she gabbles of shipwrecks and a magic frog and sings scraps of SONG. In 3.5, wandering insanely through the countryside, she is recruited for the rustic entertainment directed by the Schoolmaster. Finally, in Act 4 she returns home, where the Doctor prescribes that the Wooer, disguised as Palamon, take her to bed. The treatment apparently works, for her father later reports that she is is "well restored, / And to be married shortly" (5.4.27–28).

Though she resembles Shakespeare's Ophelia (in *Hamlet*)—both are unlucky in love, both gather flowers by a lakeside (see 4.1.54, 78), and both sing bits of song (in 4.1.108 the Daughter names a song Ophelia sings in *Hamlet* 4.5.184)—the Daughter is a very un-Shakespearean character. Her chief function is clearly as an object of humor, for in Shakespeare's day insanity was regarded as highly amusing (see, e.g., Pinch in *The Comedy of Errors*). Her diatribes are conventional indications of madness, artificial and unconvincing, and her cure is laughable, as it was doubtless intended to be. She was almost certainly not created by Shakespeare but by his collaborator, John FLETCHER, who probably wrote all the scenes she appears in (though some scholars attribute 2.1 and the best of her soliloquies, 3.2, to Shakespeare).

Doctor   Minor character in *The Two Noble Kinsmen*, a physician who treats the deranged Daughter of the Gaoler. The Daughter is obsessed with the nobleman Palamon, whom she helps escape from jail but does not see again. In 4.3 the Doctor prescribes that her Wooer humor her by pretending to be Palamon. In 5.2 he adds that the disguised Wooer should sleep with her, to which the young man readily agrees. In 5.4 the Gaoler reports that his Daughter is "well restored, / And to be married shortly" (5.4.27–28). The comic Doctor was probably created by Shakespeare's collaborator, John FLETCHER, to whom scholars usually assign both 4.3 and 5.2.

Emilia   Character in *The Two Noble Kinsmen*, sister of Hippolyta and the beloved of both Palamon and Arcite, the title characters. The subject of the obsession that destroys the friendship of the kinsmen, Emilia is merely a pawn of the plot. At first

unconscious of the situation, she is inconsequential; later, as the cousins prepare to duel for the right to marry her, she is emotionally distressed, but the focus remains on the men.

Shakespeare introduces Emilia as an attractive, serious young woman. In 1.1 her pity and magnanimity as she responds to the pleas of the three widows establish her as a noble person. In 1.3 she tenderly recalls a close childhood friendship with a girl who has died, and she is quietly confident that she will never love a man as much.

However, as a character, Emilia suffers from the defects of the play, which was written collaboratively by Shakespeare and John FLETCHER. Shakespeare's Emilia is a promising figure, but Fletcher, who wrote all of her scenes in Acts 2–4, did not develop her. At first she is simply another young woman of the court; then, Fletcher alters her radically, but the change is entirely artificial. She agonizes over her choice of lovers in a highly rhetorical passage (4.2.1–54) that introduces the arrival of the duelists in a melodramatic manner, but reduces her to a mere illustration of hysteria. Nevertheless, the speech furthers the course of the play, for it demonstrates that she, like the kinsmen, is trapped by destiny.

In Act 5, where she is again Shakespeare's creation, Emilia is a more dignified and credible character. In 5.1, before the duel, she addresses the goddess Diana, seeking assistance in her quandary. In 5.3 she is too distracted to watch the duel, which is reported to her by a Servant, and we cannot help but sympathize. When she is awarded to Arcite, and Palamon is sent to be executed, according to the rules for the duel, Emilia cries out, "Is this winning? / O all you heavenly powers, where is your mercy?" (5.3.138–139). This despairing cry is the nadir of the play. But Emilia immediately accepts her fate, rejecting suicide in the next line, because the gods' "wills have said it must be so" (5.3.140). By the play's end Emilia can accept the final twist of fate—Arcite dies accidentally and Palamon wins her by default—with equanimity. Her helplessness is an important illustration of the play's central theme: that human beings are unable to control their destiny but must strive to maintain dignity as they confront their fate.

Executioner   Minor character in *The Two Noble Kinsmen*, the ax man prepared to behead Palamon. The executioner does not speak as he stands ready in 5.4; his presence merely serves to heighten the tension with a visible reminder of Palamon's apparent end, before a pardon arrives.

Friend   Either of two minor characters in *The Two Noble Kinsmen*, acquaintances of the Gaoler. In 4.1 the Friends assure the Gaoler that Theseus, Duke of ATHENS, has forgiven him for the fact that Palamon has escaped from his jail with the assistance of his Daughter, and they sympathize with him when the Wooer brings evidence that the Daughter is deranged. The Friends, mere pawns of the plot, were probably not Shakespeare's creations, for most scholars agree that 4.1 was written by his collaborator, John FLETCHER.

Gaoler   Character in *The Two Noble Kinsmen*, the prison warden whose Daughter goes mad with unrequited love for Palamon, a prisoner of war and one of the title characters. The Daughter helps Palamon escape, but when he returns to the aristocratic world, she loses her mind. The Gaoler first appears in 2.1, where he agrees to the Wooer's suit for the Daughter's hand, and where he is a conventional warden to his prisoners. He is unaware of his daughter's state when he reappears in 4.1, worrying that he will be blamed for Palamon's escape. Once informed of the Daughter's madness, he is helpless to ease her plight. In 5.2 he objects mildly to the prescription offered by the Doctor—that the Wooer disguise himself as Palamon and sleep with her—but he goes along and reports her cure in 5.4. A simple pawn of the plot, he is believed to have been the creation of Shakespeare's collaborator, John FLETCHER.

Gentleman   Minor character in *The Two Noble Kinsmen*, a messenger from Duke Theseus of ATHENS to Emilia. In 4.2 the Gentleman informs the sorrowing Emilia that Arcite and Palamon are prepared to duel for her love. He serves merely to translate the scene from Emilia's soliloquy to the preparations for the duel. Most scholars agree that 4.1 and the Gentleman were the work of Shakespeare's collaborator John FLETCHER.

Herald   Minor character in *The Two Noble Kinsmen*, an attendant to Duke Theseus of ATHENS. In 1.4, following the defeat of King Creon of THEBES, the Herald informs Theseus of the identity of two of his noble prisoners of war, Arcite and Palamon, the title characters of the play. The main plot is thereby begun. The Herald is an extra whose splendid official uniform provides color, if not authenticity, to a scene of ancient warfare.

Hippolyta   Character in *The Two Noble Kinsmen*, Queen of the Amazons, fiancée and later wife of Theseus, Duke of ATHENS. Hippolyta helps establish the tone of magnanimous nobility and pity that dominates Act 1, but she is unimportant thereafter. In 1.1, when her wedding to Theseus is interrupted by the pleas of the royal widows, who seek the duke's aid, Hippolyta speaks in their support, insisting that her anticipated marital joy must be postponed in their cause. In 1.3 she describes the friendship between Theseus and Pirithous, which offers a parallel to the relationship between the title characters, Palamon and Arcite, and which also signifies nobility of spirit. She herself displays a serene spirit in observing without jealousy, in fact approvingly, that Theseus might be unable to choose between Pirithous and herself. In Acts 2–4, where her part is written by John FLETCHER, she is an ordinary aristocratic figure, graciously attending the duke at court. She is presumably married to Theseus by this time, although the rescheduled wedding is never mentioned. In Act 5 Hippolyta hardly speaks, but she makes a significant point after the duel fought by Palamon and Arcite for Emilia, when she offers a tender acknowledgment that the play's developments provoke "Infinite pity" (5.3.144).

Hymen   Minor character in *The Two Noble Kinsmen*, the Roman god of marriage, as portrayed by a celebrant in the interrupted wedding of Theseus and Hippolyta. Hymen does not speak; he is described in the opening stage direction as entering "with a torch burning" (1.1.1). He provides a note of formal dignity to the occasion.

Knight   Any of three minor characters in *The Two Noble Kinsmen*, companions of Palamon. The

Knights have agreed to serve as seconds to Palamon in his duel with Arcite over the love of Emilia. The rules of the combat, established by Duke Theseus, require that the loser and his escorts be executed, while the winner gets Emilia. In 5.4 Palamon has lost, and his Knights prepare gallantly to die with him, uttering brave mottos such as, "Let us bid farewell, / And with our patience anger tottering fortune" (5.4.19–20). They typify the chivalric ethos that the play depicts.

Messenger   Any of three minor characters in *The Two Noble Kinsmen,* bearers of news. In 4.2 a Messenger reports on the arrival of Arcite and Palamon for their duel, describing the combatants and their supporters in elaborately courtly terms. In 5.2 another Messenger (probably played by the same actor, however) tells the Gaoler, the Doctor, and the Wooer about the duel in a few brief lines. Scholars generally agree that Shakespeare's collaborator John FLETCHER wrote both 4.2 and 5.2, but that Shakespeare created the Messenger in 5.4, who dramatically races onstage to halt the execution of Palamon, crying "Hold, hold, O hold, hold, hold!" (5.4.40), as Pirithous arrives with a pardon. This bold coup de théâtre advances the play to its final episode. In some 17th-century productions, the Messenger was probably played by Curtis GREVILLE.

Nell   Minor character in *The Two Noble Kinsmen,* a country lass who performs in a dance before Duke Theseus. In 3.5 five young women assemble for the dance; Nell is the only one who speaks, assuring her director, the Schoolmaster, that they will do well. Her half-line—a scoffing "Let us alone, sir" (3.5.31)—contributes to the scene's sense of rustic festivity. However, most scholars agree that Shakespeare did not write 3.5, so Nell is probably the creation of John FLETCHER.

Palamon   One of the title characters of *The Two Noble Kinsmen,* cousin of Arcite. As introduced in 1.2, Palamon and Arcite are young noblemen whose chief concern is with their knightly honor and whose lives revolve around their friendship with each other. However, while prisoners of war in ATHENS, they both fall in love with Emilia, the

beautiful sister-in-law of Duke Theseus, and they argue over who saw her first. Eventually they fight a duel for Emilia, in which, following Theseus's rules, the loser is not to be killed but rather executed afterward. Palamon loses, but just before he is to be beheaded, Arcite is killed by a runaway horse, and Palamon prepares to marry Emilia at the play's close. As stylized knightly protagonists, Palamon and Arcite resemble each other fairly closely, but Palamon can be distinguished as the generally more belligerent of the two. On the other hand, he also seems somewhat disillusioned at the close of their story, making him the more interesting character finally.

In 1.2 Palamon is a shallow fellow whom Arcite criticizes for his narrow military outlook. In 2.1 he insists that their enthusiasm for the same, seemingly unapproachable woman is grounds for unsparing enmity, despite Arcite's efforts to find some other approach. Palamon escapes from prison with the help of the warden's Daughter—whom he immediately abandons—and in Act 3 he persistently pushes Arcite to duel, until Theseus intervenes and establishes the rules under which they finally fight.

Palamon's long prayer to Venus in 5.1 marks a turning point, for instead of the enraptured plea for Emilia's heart that we might expect, he vents a satirical recital of the ridiculous behavior love inspires. He mocks the tyrant who weeps to a girl and the old man who is confident his young wife is faithful, and he recites all the ugly betrayals and offenses a lover might commit, though he disclaims them. The pleasant aspects of love are not mentioned. He closes his prayer by apostrophizing the goddess as one "whose chase is this world / And we in herds thy game" (5.1.131–132). Such cynicism reflects the weight that the conflict has had—he wears Venus's "yoke, . . . [that is] heavier / Than lead itself [and] stings more than nettles" (5.1.95–97), for in the end he loses his friend. At the close, engaged to Emilia, he addresses his dead cousin with a plaint that typifies the confusion and helplessness of humanity in the hands of unpredictable fate, the play's most important theme: "O cousin, / That we should things desire which do cost us / The loss of our desire! That naught could buy / Dear love but loss of dear love!" (5.4.109–112).

Pirithous Minor character in *The Two Noble Kinsmen,* friend of Theseus, Duke of ATHENS. Pirithous attends Theseus in every scene in which the duke appears; he also provides commentary on Arcite in 2.4 and, as a messenger, dramatically halts the execution of Palamon in 5.4. However, he is significant only as the subject of a conversation in his absence. In 1.3 Hippolyta reflects on the long friendship of Theseus and Pirithous, saying, "Their knot of love, / Tied, weaved, entangled . . . May be outworn, never undone" (1.3.41–44). This striking parallel to the tie between Palamon and Arcite helps establish the theme of male friendship that is woven through the play. Hippolyta's remarks also spark a variant on the theme, the account by Emilia of her similar childhood friendship with a girl.

Prologue Allegorical figure in *The Two Noble Kinsmen,* the speaker of the PROLOGUE that opens the play. The Prologue tells us that the play derives from a famous poet, CHAUCER, and that it cannot compare with the original. He hopes, in the name of the acting company, that their production will be good enough to avoid disgrace. Scholars generally believe that the Prologue was written by Shakespeare's collaborator, probably John FLETCHER.

Queen Any of three minor characters in *The Two Noble Kinsmen,* deposed monarchs who seek the aid of Theseus, Duke of ATHENS. The Queens interrupt Theseus's wedding to tell him that their husbands have been defeated and killed by King Creon of THEBES, who has refused to bury the kings' bodies, thereby exposing their souls to torment. They ask Theseus to avenge this deed by conquering Creon. The First Queen, as she is designated, implores Theseus; the Second Queen addresses his intended bride, the Amazon Hippolyta; and the Third speaks to Hippolyta's sister, Emilia. All three respond favorably, but the Queens are not satisfied with anything but instant action, and their petitions are restated. Finally the wedding is postponed, and Theseus sets out. In 1.4, the conquest completed, the Queens thank Theseus, and in 1.5 they proceed with their husbands' funerals.

The Queens are part of the ritualistic aspect of the play that links it to Shakespeare's other ROMANCES. They are highly significant figures in 1.1, Shakespeare's spectacular opening scene. Their sudden appearance, all in black at a festive ceremony, is a coup de théâtre, with a grand effect on stage. Their repeated approaches, first to one character and then another, form a dancelike, stylized sequence, a kind of liturgy that reinforces the high seriousness of their purpose. In 1.5 they again offer an impressive tableau, as Act 1 closes in tragic triumph.

Schoolmaster Minor character in *The Two Noble Kinsmen,* the director of a country dance performance. In 3.5 the Schoolmaster directs a group of Countrymen and -women, including Nell, in an entertainment presented to the court of Duke Theseus. He is comically pedantic, both in instructing his charges and in his PROLOGUE to the performance. Since most scholars believe that Shakespeare did not write 3.5, the Schoolmaster is probably the creation of John FLETCHER.

Servant Minor character in *The Two Noble Kinsmen,* a member of the household of Emilia. In 5.3 the Servant reports to his mistress periodically on the progress of the duel between Arcite and Palamon, who are fighting over her. In this way the audience is able to experience the duel while the actual combat is kept offstage.

Taborer Minor character in *The Two Noble Kinsmen,* a drummer. The Taborer accompanies the Countrymen and the lasses led by Nell in their dance performed before Duke Theseus in 3.5. The Taborer speaks only one line, a boisterous greeting in 3.5.24. Since most scholars agree that Shakespeare did not write 3.5, the Taborer is probably the creation of John FLETCHER.

Theseus Character in *The Two Noble Kinsmen,* Duke of ATHENS. Theseus presides over the events of the main plot. He sets an example of noble action when he aids the royal widows who petition him in 1.1; in doing so, he undertakes a war against Creon of THEBES, in the course of which he captures the title characters, Arcite and Palamon, creating the basic situation of the plot. In 3.6 he intervenes in the quarrel between them, overseeing their duel for

Emilia; and at the play's close, he sounds the note of dignified acceptance of fate that is the play's central lesson. Recognizing that the fortunes of humanity are incomprehensible, and that we have no choice but to live with them, he rhetorically addresses the gods: "O you heavenly charmers, / What things you make of us! . . . Let us be thankful / For that which is, and with you leave dispute[s] / That are above our question" (5.4.131–136). He adds, in the play's final words, "Let's go off, / And bear us like the time" (5.4. 136–137)—that is, accept our circumstances.

Theseus is particularly dominant in Acts 1 and 5, written by Shakespeare, while in Acts 2 to 4, written by John FLETCHER, he is a less significant figure and his speeches are far less powerful as poetry. Theseus's importance as a model of nobility is particularly notable in Act 1, where he establishes a tone of magnanimity that would perhaps have dominated the play, had Shakespeare written it in its entirety. Throughout Shakespeare's portions of the play, Theseus's actions are quintessentially chivalrous: he aids the widowed Queens at their request; having triumphed in their cause, he offers to cover the expenses of their husbands' funerals; he demands the finest treatment for his noble prisoners of war; he orders the most opulent temple preparations for the "noble work in hand" (5.1.6), the duel; he will "adopt [as] friends" (5.4.124) Palamon's seconds at the play's close; and his concluding remarks offer an example of serene courage. On the other hand, the somewhat ignoble provision that the loser be executed was devised by Fletcher's Theseus.

With respect to aristocratic birth—a necessary component of nobility in chivalric romance—Theseus is literally of supernatural stature and can casually refer to "Hercules our kinsman" (1.1.66). He is pointedly contrasted with the vicious Creon, to his considerable advantage, and the Second Queen says that he was "Born to uphold creation in that honor / First Nature styled it in" (1.1.82–83). As the highest-ranking figure in the play's world, and especially since he is presented as a strikingly noble leader, Theseus carries great moral weight; his closing remarks are thereby clearly signaled as the play's essential position.

Valerius Minor character in *The Two Noble Kinsmen*, a gentleman of THEBES and friend of Arcite and Palamon. In 1.2 Valerius informs his friends of the challenge to King Creon of Thebes issued by Duke Theseus of ATHENS, who intends to conquer Thebes and avenge the king's evil behavior in refusing burial to his defeated foes. Valerius thereby provides the link between the two title characters and Athens, where, as prisoners of war, they will enact the main plot of the drama. Having fulfilled this function, Valerius disappears from the play.

Woman Minor character in *The Two Noble Kinsmen*, an attendant of Emilia. In 2.1 the Woman converses with her mistress, who speaks of the maidenly virtues. They are overheard by Palamon and Arcite, who both fall in love with Emilia. The Woman's decorous conversation simply offers openings for Emilia in an incident that furthers the plot. Since most scholars believe that 2.1 was not written by Shakespeare, the Woman is probably a creation of John FLETCHER.

Wooer Minor character in *The Two Noble Kinsmen*, the suitor of the Daughter of the Gaoler. In 2.1 the Wooer agrees with the Gaoler on a marriage contract, saying that he has the Daughter's consent to marry him. He is not seen again until Act 4, after the Daughter has gone mad with unrequited love for the nobleman Palamon. Though unafflicted with jealousy and sympathetic to her plight, the Wooer is helpless to ease it, until in 4.3 the Doctor prescribes that he disguise himself as Palamon and woo her, adding in 5.2 the instruction that he sleep with her, to which he readily assents. He proposes to her and is accepted, but she suggests bed before he can. The Doctor's ploy works, for the Daughter is later reported to be "well restored, / And to be married shortly" (5.4.27–28). Slightly buffoonish, the Wooer is a gentle but undistinguished fellow, merely a necessary part of the SUBPLOT. He is probably the creation of Shakespeare's collaborator John FLETCHER, to whom the scenes he appears in are ascribed.

Venus and Adonis

Narrative poem by Shakespeare that tells of the goddess Venus's infatuation for a mortal human, the young hunter Adonis. In erotic and humorous passages, Venus courts the youth, attempting to persuade him to make love. Adonis resists her advances, being unmoved by what he sees as simple lust; he prefers to go hunting. The next day, at dawn, Venus discovers the body of the dead Adonis, who has been killed by a wild boar. The poem closes with her lament.

Venus and Adonis has less relevance for most modern readers than do Shakespeare's dramas. Conventions that largely lack meaning today contribute to the overall tone and texture of the poem, and the work is now often perceived as frigidly artificial and remote from real human experience. But although its characterization and plotting are feeble by comparison with the plays, *Venus* boasts many charming passages. Moreover, and much more important, the poem does in fact deal with a humanly significant theme: sexual love.

Shakespeare dedicated *Venus and Adonis* to Henry Wriothesley, Earl of SOUTHAMPTON—a classically educated and highly sophisticated patron of the arts—thus indicating his intention that the poem be received as a fashionable exercise in delicate eroticism, deftly constructed in an artificial and elaborately rhetorical classical manner. From the literature available to Elizabethan readers, the poet turned to the best source for such a poem, the works of the Latin master of erotic poetry, OVID, which he probably knew both in Latin and in the English translation by Arthur GOLDING (1567). In Ovid's *Metamorphoses*, Adonis reciprocates Venus's love, but Shakespeare followed a variant of the tale that was also well known in England, incorporating elements from other Ovidian stories and portraying the mortal's rejection of the goddess. The epigraph to the dedication—promising a work meant for a select audience—comes from another work by Ovid, *Amores*. Classical literature was entirely familiar to 16th-century readers, and, in associating his work with Ovid's, Shakespeare was plainly declaring his intention to be similarly witty, charming, and delicately sensual. Some details, especially the episode of the stallion and the mare, were probably inspired by passages in the *Georgics* of VIRGIL, the greatest of Latin poets.

Shakespeare was probably also influenced by *Hero and Leander*, by Christopher MARLOWE. The date of composition of this poem is unknown—it was unfinished when the poet died in early 1593—and it was not published until 1598, but Shakespeare had probably read it in manuscript; certainly *Hero and Leander*'s unprecedented combination of wit and luxuriant sensuousness was unique before Shakespeare wrote his poem. Like *Hero and Leander*, *Venus and Adonis* was scandalously popular, to judge by the many references to it, both delighted and disapproving. It has often been speculated that the ferocity of the controversy impelled Shakespeare to follow *Venus* with a much primmer narrative poem, *The Rape of Lucrece*.

Venus and Adonis may be seen as simply a trivial entertainment, intended to attract the patronage of a cultured aristocrat. Or the poem may be given more weight and viewed as a scintillating example of RENAISSANCE art, an evocation of ancient ideals equivalent to, say, the paintings of Botticelli. Still, the thematic richness of the plays, which even at their weakest are intent on exploring ideas and human relations, suggest that a work by Shakespeare must have more point than simple entertainment or beauty. However, the moral to be found in *Venus and Adonis* has proven elusive, and the poem has been assessed in many different ways. Some critics feel that *Venus* is a failure, an immature effort that is confused and uncertain because the author was himself unclear about the nature of love and lust and therefore resorted to humor to patch up his undeveloped work. Others see the poem as a delightfully erotic comedy, a celebration of sexual passion. Although Adonis dies, his story is couched in humor, and his death is not a tragic one—his corpse vanishes into air and his blood becomes the goddess's nosegay. Still other readers find one of two tragic lessons in *Venus*. Accepting the erotic passages as indicative of the poet's attitude, one may see Adonis's death as the pathetic outcome of his cold and foolish aversion to love and sex. On the other hand, the horror of his death and Venus's condemnation of love at the end of the poem may be thought to condemn lust as a primal force of destruction.

All of these viewpoints offer salient truths about the poem; as is so often the case when considering Shakespeare, the most productive response combines various theories. Like *Romeo and Juliet* and *Antony and Cleopatra* in particular, *Venus* deals with perhaps the most difficult emotion to understand—love—and all three works present an essential paradox: Love, an obvious manifestation of an elemental life force, is often tied to a self-destructive inclination toward death. Thus two irreconcilable attitudes about love are established, and the poem, like the plays, attempts to resolve the opposition between them.

One must start with a pervasive and obviously positive aspect of *Venus and Adonis*: the poem is unquestionably funny. Venus's overbearing seizure of Adonis, beginning in line 25, is a virtual parody of male aggressiveness; the description of the stolid Adonis as a tiny, terrified waterbird (lines 86–87) provides a droll juxtaposition; Venus's erotic characterization of her own body as landscape (lines 229–240) is sufficiently amusing to extract a smile even from Adonis. Even at a moment of revulsion, as Venus first sees Adonis's corpse, the famous simile of the shrinking snail (lines 1033–1036) offers an irresistibly whimsical image that softens the blow; the situation is not permitted to inspire horror.

In a similar spirit, the poem boasts frequent vivid and sensual representations of country life—from such minor images as the comparison of the captive Adonis to a trapped bird (lines 67–68) or that of Venus to a "milch doe, whose swelling dugs do ache" (line 875), to the more elaborate descriptions of the boar (lines 619–630), the boar hounds (lines 913–924), and the hunted hare (lines 679–708). Particularly impressive is the fully developed anecdote of Adonis's stallion in pursuit of a mare (lines 258–324), the last couplet of which is itself a handsome miniature landscape. Venus's repeated enthusiasm for physical love (e.g., in lines 19–24) is part of the same charming presentation of the sensual life. The poem offers an idyllic world populated by delightful plants and animals, needing only the consummated love of man and goddess—or so Venus asserts—to complete the picture.

However, a distinctly darker strain complicates matters. Venus's attraction to Adonis is not simply a delightful infatuation, but rather a fever of the soul; she tears at her beloved like a bird of prey (lines 55–58), and when she refuses to stop kissing him, he is compared to a forcibly tamed hawk and a deer pursued to exhaustion (lines 560–561). Conversely, Adonis rejects not only Venus herself but also her idea of love, which he equates with lust, in a passage (lines 787–798) strikingly reminiscent of Sonnet 129, which decries lust as "Th' expense of spirit in a waste of shame" (see *Sonnets*). For Venus, love is entirely involved with physical life, but it is only in death that Adonis can find love, as he conceives it; he says, "I know not love . . . unless it be a boar, and then I chase it" (lines 409–410). Thus Venus and Adonis represent opposing points of view: the goddess finds fulfillment in the delights of sensuality, while the mortal man conceives of an ideal spiritual state.

We can see that the poem often supports Adonis's position by subtly undercutting that of Venus, and vice versa. The comical sight of Venus plucking Adonis from his horse (line 30) reflects the more serious point that her powers of seduction are so inadequate that she is reduced to this undignified action. When Venus argues—as Shakespeare himself does in several of the *Sonnets*—that love is the most appropriate human activity because it leads to reproduction (lines 163–174), she seems to represent the life force, but in the very next line all such high purpose is lost, as "the love-sick queen began to sweat." Even one of Venus's most delightful tactics—her somewhat lewd yet humorous description of herself in terms of landscape (lines 229–240)—results only in her further humiliation; Adonis smiles in disdain, she is reduced to helplessness by his dimples, and the poet remarks, "being mad before, how doth she now for wits?" (line 249). However, Adonis's ideal is similarly weakened. Although he rejects the animal nature of love that Venus extols, he is himself associated with animals throughout the poem, from the early parallels between him and birds, mentioned above, through the symbolism of his runaway horse as a male lover, to his almost sexual union with the boar in mutual death. The attitude of each protagonist is therefore compromised by the manner in which it is presented.

Thus the apparently hopeless dichotomy between Venus and Adonis is resolved even as it is presented, for Shakespeare's ultimate purpose here is to present opposing views as intertwined principles. The poem opens with a paradoxical introduction of the two protagonists: in the first stanza "rose-cheek'd Adonis" is contrasted with "sick-thoughted Venus" (lines 3, 5). A standard romantic convention—lovesick male pursues uninterested woman—is here reversed, and this switch is at the heart of Shakespeare's strategy. Venus is a parody of a typical male suitor, while Adonis is presented in a traditionally feminine role, a sex object, especially in lines 541–564, where he is virtually raped. He is also associated with imagery suggestive of women's physical charms, as in lines 9, 50, 247–248, and, most strikingly, 1114–16, where the boar's death blow is described in sexual terms. (Adonis's femininity is sometimes taken as evidence of a homosexual inclination in Shakespeare, but the image seems to function quite well in the poem without such a conclusion. However, it does certainly suppose the acceptability of homoerotic ideas to both the poet and his audience.) The confusion of gender anticipates the conjunction of the two points of view that is reached in the closing stanzas.

The poem simultaneously views love in contradictory ways. Though love is the noblest of imaginable states of mind, as Adonis insists, it also utterly prosaic, even ridiculous, grounded as it is in the physical desires embodied by Venus's lust. Although Adonis's death is brought about by his rejection of Venus's idea of love, it does not discredit her essentially comic approach; instead, it adds to it a tragic element, that of humanity's unachievable aspiration. Love's complicated blend of opposing qualities is asserted in the description of love in Venus's closing lament: "Sorrow on love hereafter shall attend, [and it] shall be raging mad, and silly mild, make the young old, the old become a child. . . . It shall be merciful and too severe, and most deceiving when it seems most just" (lines 1136–56). While Venus is "weary of the world" (line 1189) at the tale's end, yet she also has been able to realize that, for all its pain, love may "enrich the poor with treasures" (line 1150). This is the theme that the poem offers its readers, in as fine and showy a setting as the young Shakespeare could devise.

Venus and Adonis is a flawed, youthful work. The two protagonists display little credible personality, and differences in tone within the poem seem to reflect indecisiveness on Shakespeare's part. In particular, Venus's final position, in which she seems to reject love in light of Adonis's death, is uncomfortably at odds with her earlier, much lighter attitude. Therefore, many readers simply accept the pleasures of the poem's numerous delightful passages and disregard an otherwise seemingly unrewarding text. However, the poem is much richer than this. Like Shakespeare's greater works, it is concerned with the human predicament, and it illuminates the young playwright's attitude toward one of his most important concerns, sexual love.

In the poem's dedication Shakespeare calls his work "the first heir of my invention," and this is sometimes taken as evidence that *Venus and Adonis* was written before any of the plays. However, most scholars agree that it is much more likely to have been written between June 1592, when the London theaters were closed because of a plague epidemic, and April 1593, when the poem was registered with the STATIONERS' COMPANY. During this enforced break in his promising career, the young playwright turned to a mode of literature that was far more prestigious at the time. Thus the reference in the dedication is taken to allude to the poet's first effort at "serious" writing. Not only was poetry regarded as the only important branch of literature, while the stage was still somewhat disreputable (see ELIZABETHAN DRAMA), but, under the patronage system that prevailed until long after Shakespeare's death, it was potentially much more profitable than a career in the theater.

Venus and Adonis was first published in 1593 by the printer Richard FIELD in a QUARTO edition (known today as Q1), of which only one copy—in Oxford's BODLEIAN LIBRARY—has survived. Field, who also printed *The Rape of Lucrece*, was probably a friend of Shakespeare's, and this fact, plus the great care with which both texts were printed, suggests that the narrative poems were the only works whose publication was supervised by Shakespeare himself. *Venus* was very popular, and eight more editions were published during Shakespeare's lifetime. These are known as Q2–Q9 (plus one that is unnumbered, since only a title-page has survived), though all but Q2 were actually published in an octavo format. A 10th edition, Q10, appeared shortly after Shakespeare's death. Each of these editions was simply a reprint of one of its predecessors, incorporating such minor alterations as the printers saw fit to make, and while they all contain variant readings, none is thought to reflect any changes that Shakespeare made. Q1 is therefore regarded as the only authoritative text, and it is the basis for all modern editions.

Whole Contention, The

Abbreviated title of a publication of 1619 containing BAD QUARTO texts of *2* and *3 Henry VI*. The full title of the volume is *The Whole Contention between the two Famous Houses, Lancaster and Yorke. With the Tragicall ends of the good Duke Humfrey, Richard Duke of Yorke, and King Henrie the sixt. The Whole Contention* was printed by William JAGGARD and published by Thomas PAVIER as part of the FALSE FOLIO. It consists of slightly edited earlier versions of the plays; *The Contention* (Q1 of *2 Henry VI*) is combined in one volume with *The True Tragedy* (Q1 of *3 Henry VI*). *The True Tragedy* was altered only slightly by Pavier, but *The Contention* underwent many minor changes, along with the substantial addition of elaborated genealogical material, taken from the 1615 edition of John STOW's *Chronicle*.

Each of the texts in *The Whole Contention* is known as the Q3 edition of its play. For both plays, the FIRST FOLIO text is basic to all modern editions. The *Whole Contention* texts evidently had only minor influence on the composition of the Folio, except for the introduction of the new genealogical material into 2.2 of *3 Henry VI*.

Winter's Tale, The
SYNOPSIS
Act 1, Scene 1
The courtiers Camillo and Archidamus speak of their respective kings, Leontes of SICILIA and Polixenes of BOHEMIA, who have been friends since childhood. Polixenes has been visiting Sicilia and is about to leave. The courtiers also speak of the good qualities of Leontes' young son, Mamillius, who will certainly make a fine ruler.

Act 1, Scene 2
Leontes tries to persuade Polixenes to extend his visit, but he insists he must return to Bohemia. Leontes then asks Queen Hermione to convince Polixenes. When she does, Leontes suspects that they are lovers. He sends them away and talks with Camillo, who forcefully rejects his suspicions. Insisting that he is correct, Leontes orders Camillo to poison Polixenes. Camillo reluctantly agrees, but instead he informs Polixenes, and they leave together for Bohemia.

Act 2, Scene 1
When a Lord tells Leontes of the flight of Polixenes and Camillo, the king rages about treachery. He formally accuses Hermione of adultery and treason, declaring that she is currently pregnant with Polixenes' child. She defends herself, but he sends her to prison. Although Antigonus and the other lords try to dissuade the king, he insists that she is an adulteress and adds that he has sent messengers to the oracle of Apollo for confirmation of this.

Act 2, Scene 2
Antigonus's wife, Paulina, tries to visit Hermione in prison but is only permitted to see her attendant, Emilia, who reports that the queen has given birth to a daughter. Paulina resolves to take the infant to Leontes and convince him that the child is his.

Act 2, Scene 3
When Paulina brings the baby to Leontes, he is enraged. He sends her away and orders the baby killed. Antigonus pleads for the infant's life, and Leontes tells him to take the child—but only to abandon it in some wilderness, where it may or may not survive. Antigonus then leaves with the baby.

Act 3, Scene 1
Cleomenes and Dion return from the oracle and describe its awe-inspiring appearance. They bear a proclamation answering the king's inquiry.

Act 3, Scene 2
Hermione, accompanied by Paulina, is brought to trial for adultery; she again defends herself and

appeals to the oracle. Cleomenes and Dion read the oracle's judgment, which proclaims the innocence of Hermione, Polixenes, and Camillo, but Leontes refuses to believe it. Word then arrives of Mamillius's sudden death from fright at his mother's fate. Leontes interprets this event as a supernatural confirmation of the oracle and repents, but Hermione faints and must be taken away by Paulina. Just as Leontes resolves to welcome Camillo back and apologize to Polixenes, Paulina returns and reports Hermione's death. She excoriates Leontes, and he accepts her criticisms as entirely just.

Act 3, Scene 3

In stormy weather, on a remote part of the Bohemian coast, Antigonus reports a vision in which the ghost of Hermione instructed him to take the baby there and to name her Perdita. He is attacked and driven away by a Bear, but a Shepherd finds the infant. He is joined by his son, the Clown, who has seen Antigonus being eaten by the bear and his ship sinking in the storm. They discover that Perdita is wrapped in rich fabrics, which contain a supply of gold.

Act 4, Scene 1

Time appears and announces that 16 years have passed, that Leontes has shut himself off from the world in grief, and that the story continues in Bohemia. There, he tells us, we shall see Polixenes' son, Florizel, and the 16-year-old Perdita, who lives as the Shepherd's daughter.

Act 4, Scene 2

Camillo wishes to return to Sicilia, but Polixenes declares that he is now too important to the government to be permitted to leave. Moreover, he wants Camillo's help in preventing Prince Florizel from embarrassing the monarchy by marrying a shepherd girl.

Act 4, Scene 3

A vagabond, Autolycus, sings merrily and brags that he is now a petty thief, although he was once a servant to Florizel. The Clown appears on his way to market to buy supplies for the upcoming shepherds' feast, and Autolycus scents prey. He lies on the ground and pretends to have been robbed; then, as the Clown helps him rise, he picks his pocket. The Clown leaves, and Autolycus decides to attend the festival, which is likely to produce further loot.

Act 4, Scene 4

Perdita reveals her uneasiness at being courted by Florizel, for she knows that his father, the king, will oppose the match. Florizel insists he will marry her even if he has to abandon his royal status. The Shepherd and the Clown arrive for the festival, along with a group including the shepherd girls Mopsa and Dorcas, and the disguised King Polixenes and Camillo. Perdita, as hostess, distributes flowers among the guests. Mopsa and Dorcas lead a country dance, and Autolycus appears as a wandering peddler. Mopsa and Dorcas flirt with the Clown, who buys them presents, while Autolycus entertains them with SONGs; they all leave together, to continue singing and trading. At this point Polixenes reveals himself and demands that Florizel renounce Perdita. Threatening her and the Shepherd with death if she sees the prince again, he departs in a rage. The frightened Shepherd flees, and Perdita is in despair, but Florizel declares that he will not leave her. Camillo proposes that the couple should go to Sicilia, where they will be welcomed as emissaries of King Polixenes. Once there, they may eventually gain Polixenes' forgiveness. Autolycus returns, gloating over the purses he has stolen while selling his goods. Camillo makes him change clothes with Florizel, providing the prince with a disguise, and Perdita dresses as a young man. In an aside Camillo reveals that he intends to inform the king of the couple's flight and, in pursuit of them, get to Sicilia himself. When they leave, Autolycus, who has realized what is going on, plots how to profit from it. He then overhears the Shepherd and Clown planning to explain to the king that Perdita is not actually their relative, but a foundling. They have proof in the rich fabrics Perdita was found in, years before. Autolycus emerges and promises to take them to the king, for money. Privately, he plans to take them to Florizel and accept the prince's reward for keeping them from the king.

Act 5, Scene 1

In Sicilia, Paulina insists that King Leontes should never remarry until he encounters Hermione's equal, and he agrees not to marry without Paulina's approval. Florizel and Perdita arrive, asserting they are married. Leontes is delighted to renew relations with the son of his onetime victim, but then word arrives that Polixenes himself has come to Sicilia to arrest his son for eloping with a shepherd's daughter. Florizel confesses that he and Perdita are not married, but he pleads with Leontes to defend their love to Polixenes, and Leontes agrees, being greatly attracted by Perdita.

Act 5, Scene 2

Autolycus hears from a Gentleman and his friends that the king's missing daughter has been found, as the papers among the Shepherd's bundle of fabrics attest. The Third Gentleman describes the joy and reconciliation among the kings and their children, who are now considered engaged. He adds that the royal party has gone to Paulina's home to view a statue of Hermione. They go off to see it also, leaving Autolycus to bemoan his bad luck: He had brought the Shepherd and Clown to Florizel's ship, whereby they had come to Sicilia with their extraordinary evidence, and yet he cannot profit from it. When the Shepherd and Clown appear, dressed in new clothes and full of comical pretensions to gentlemanly status, Autolycus flatters them abjectly.

Act 5, Scene 3

Leontes, Polixenes, Florizel, Perdita, and Camillo all accompany Paulina to see her sculpture of Hermione. They marvel at its lifelike qualities, and Leontes regrets again his injustice to Hermione herself. Paulina asserts that she can make them marvel further; she tells the statue to move, and it walks down off its pedestal and takes Leontes by the hand. She then explains that the statue is Hermione herself, alive all these years but awaiting the proper moment for her return. Hermione confirms this account, identifying herself to Perdita. The king, ecstatic at being reunited with his wife and conscious that Florizel and Perdita are soon to marry, insists that Paulina and Camillo should also wed. The three couples withdraw to savour their happiness.

COMMENTARY

With *The Winter's Tale*, Shakespeare achieved his first great success in a new genre, the ROMANCES.

After flawed endeavors in *Pericles* and *Cymbeline*, the playwright found a way to integrate the various elements of romance literature—the exotic and magical mingled with stereotypical characters and situations—with his own strengths as a realistic playwright. *The Winter's Tale* combines the grim psychopathology of Shakespearean TRAGEDY with the visionary optimism of his earlier COMEDY. It is a play with its own distinctive moral tone, balancing the divine and the human.

The most obvious way in which this conjunction is effected is structural: The play falls neatly into two halves, with the hinge at 3.3, the first scene set in Bohemia. The first half is a tragedy centered on the madness of King Leontes, whose jealousy resembles Othello's and appears to have the same result, the death of his wife. The second half, however, is a traditional romantic comedy of young love triumphant and old love restored, complete with a PROLOGUE—the address by Time in 4.1—and a conventional happy ending in multiple marriages. The two halves of the play present a striking opposition between the sins of the powerful and elderly and the natural goodness of youth, but the two halves also offer another, more significant contrast. The tragic first half depends for its resolution on a supernatural phenomenon, the message from the oracle, while the second relies chiefly on the fine qualities of its young lovers to carry things through to the happy conclusion. While humanity is ultimately dependent on providence—a theme that pervades the romances—here divine intervention serves chiefly to enable human virtue to exercise itself and triumph over vice.

Although only Apollo can cure Leontes' madness, Camillo, Paulina, Hermione, and Antigonus all oppose it, and Hermione's forthright dignity is never sullied by the abuse she undergoes. Moreover, the human opposition is much more prominent than the brief intercession of the god. Similarly, the healing process that follows remains in the characters' hands; it is accomplished through Paulina's delaying tactics, the Shepherd's kindness, Camillo's craftiness, and Florizel and Perdita's exemplary courage and devotion. In Act 4 love, charm, and humor—abetted by luck and the plotting of the wily Camillo—triumph over the injustice of Polixenes (who here re-creates Leontes' tyranny in a milder key). The human component in the triumph of good—almost entirely absent in *Pericles* and but fitfully brought to bear in *Cymbeline*—is here given an importance that permits us to identify much more fully with the process.

Providence, however, is by no means ignored. The play is studded with overt references to the gods. Hermione's embattled confidence that "powers divine / Behold our human actions" (3.2.28–29) is particularly striking, but it is supported by many other instances. Leontes vows daily chapel visits in 3.2.238–243, Florizel cites the love stories of the gods in 4.4.25–31, and Perdita refers to the Proserpina myth and mythological flower lore in 4.4.116–127. Paulina's mystifications as she reveals Hermione's survival create an atmosphere of spirituality and magic in an entirely secular scene. Although theophany, or the actual appearance of a god, is avoided—in contrast to the two earlier romances—the descriptions of the "ceremonious, solemn and unearthly" rituals of Apollo (3.1.7) and "the eardeaf'ning voice o' th' Oracle, / Kin to Jove's thunder" (3.1.9–10) have a similar effect. The dramatic intensity of religious experience is evoked, and we are forcefully reminded of humanity's impotence before the divine.

Moreover, although the play's world is pre-Christian, some distinctly Christian ideas are alluded to, notably grace and redemption through suffering. Perdita and Hermione are associated with the words *grace* and *gracious* (e.g., in 1.2.233, 2.3.29, 4.1.24, and 4.4.8), as is the oracle itself (in 3.1.22). As the play ends, Hermione invokes a consummate blessing: "You gods, look down, / And from your sacred vials pour your graces" (5.3.121–122). Leontes' story is a virtual parable of sin redeemed. He blasphemes his saintly wife and the divine oracle, and he is punished by the death of his son and (he believes) his wife. After Leontes spends years in "saint-like sorrow" (5.1.2), Paulina (whose name is suggestive of Christianity's great preacher) effects the seemingly miraculous return of Hermione, which takes place in a "chapel" (5.3.86). Not for nothing does Paulina assert, "It is requir'd / You do awake your faith" (5.3.94–95). Of course, Hermione's apparent resurrection has obvi-

ous Christian overtones, and it becomes the central focus of the play's final scene, taking precedence over the more traditional conclusion of a comedy in marriage rites (though these are referred to).

Accompanying these expressly religious motifs is an implicitly sacred theme, a subtle emphasis on the cycles of nature. At the broadest level, the play is about the basic pattern of life and growth. Polixenes remembers when he and Leontes "as twinn'd lambs did frisk i' th' sun / And bleat the one at th' other" (1.2.67–68). Later, when their dire adult drama of hatred and death is replaced by the pastoral comedy of the shepherds' festival, a cycle has been completed. The festival itself, celebrating the annual wool harvest, is an ancient marking of the passage of the seasons. (Such rustic festivals were still common in preindustrial England, and Shakespeare could be sure that his audience would be familiar with them and at least aware of the pre-Christian religious sentiment behind them.) Perdita's enumeration of the different seasonal flowers is another potent evocation of nature's cycles. Most compelling of all is her reenactment of the passage from winter to spring—the original resurrection—when she wishes she had spring flowers for Florizel, "to strew him o'er and o'er!" He exclaims, "What, like a corpse?" and she replies, "No, like a bank, for love to lie and play on: / Not like a corpse; or if—not to be buried, / But quick, and in mine arms" (4.4.129–132). Such references point to our primitive awareness of nature as the source of religious awe.

However, the cycle of the seasons is a natural, not a supernatural phenomenon, and its celebration is a human one. In line with this the play's religious allusions and motifs are never permitted to overshadow the central theme: the power of human virtue. The role of the oracle is critical, but it is the main characters who complete the task and achieve happiness through their virtue. It is not Paulina's magic but her foresight that leads to the "revival" of Hermione; human intervention, not divine, produces the outcome. That Paulina's scheme seems singularly harebrained to the rational observer is irrelevant; romances are supposed to be illogical. It is only important that a happy ending of reconciliation and love has been reached, without the need for a deus ex machina. Given a single assist from Apollo's oracle, the essential good in humanity defeats life's potential for disorder and unhappiness. Leontes hopes Paulina's magic will prove as "lawful as eating" (5.3.111) and—because it is not magic after all, let alone black magic—it does. The moral drive of ordinary people is what powers *The Winter's Tale.*

Though Leontes certainly lacks such drive, he is nonetheless the central figure in the play's scheme. His sin sparks the action, and his consciousness of sin is necessary to its conclusion. That the king comes to recognize his susceptibility to error reflects Shakespeare's abiding concern for the responsibilities of rulers. Like such differing characters as Richard II, Henry IV, Cymbeline, and *The Tempest*'s Prospero, Leontes learns about himself through the exercise of power. Especially in the romances, the lesson is that the most valuable human capacity is the capacity for mercy since, more than justice, mercy acknowledges human equality before the divine. Like the medieval MORALITY PLAY, centered on God's mercy to humankind, Shakespeare's late works insist that the relationship between a secular ruler and subject must follow the same pattern.

Leontes moves from sin to remorse and finally finds forgiveness in the pastoral world of love represented by Perdita and Florizel. The most important moral lesson of the play is the power of love. Love is elaborately glorified and briefly threatened in 4.4—the longest scene in Shakespeare—where the pleasures of country life, a traditional romantic motif, are associated with the deep affection shared by Florizel and Perdita. As we have seen, connections are drawn to the divine, and Perdita is strongly linked to ancient emblems of fertility. The lovers acknowledge their sexuality but recognize the spiritual side as more important. Perdita notes that love can take a "false way" (4.4.151), and Florizel insists that his desire does not "Burn hotter than my faith" (4.4.35). In the crisis of Polixenes' wrath against Perdita, Florizel declares that if his faithful love fails, "let nature crush the sides o' th' earth together, / And mar the seeds within!" (4.4.479–480). The tragedy of the first half of the play results from jealousy, a gross distortion of sexual affection; the love of the second half contrasts in its purity.

The world of the lovers is a blessed one, as the play's transition from Sicilia to Bohemia makes clear, even before the powerful charm of 4.4 is exercised. In a passage that several commentators have pointed to as the pivotal moment of the play, the Shepherd, having just found Perdita and heard from the Clown of the death of Antigonus, says to his son, "Now bless thyself: thou met'st with things dying, I with things new-born" (3.3.112–113). The old world of Leontes' despotic madness is passing away, and a new dispensation has begun. The Shepherd appreciatively declares, "'Tis a lucky day, boy, and we'll do good deeds on 't" (3.3.135–136). The contrast with Leontes' despairing plea, "Come, and lead me / To these sorrows" (3.2.242–243)—spoken just moments before—could hardly be greater. A new world has been introduced, and the shepherds' festival is to be at its center.

Autolycus, his victim the Clown, and the shepherdesses Mopsa and Dorcas, all contribute to a delightful slice of English rustic life, viewed idealistically but not entirely unrealistically. Like the Forest of ARDEN and the GLOUCESTERSHIRE of *2 Henry IV*, Shakespeare's Bohemia evokes nostalgia for the solid virtues of country life, and the sense of community of that world is part of the moral regeneration of the second half.

It is interesting to note the care Shakespeare took to emphasize the importance of the human element in his play by altering the story that he found in his source, *Pandosto*. In the fashion typical of 16th-century romances, *Pandosto* is full of events and schemes that are not just improbable but absolutely impossible; credibility is not an issue, any more than in a fairy tale. Shakespeare, however, changed such features enough to create a plausible tale (if only just barely to our modern sceptical minds), a tale shot through with the fabric of real life. For example, we are prepared for Mamillius's death with reports of his illness, whereas in *Pandosto* the son of the unjustly accused queen simply drops dead of dismay. In the book the infant is abandoned in an open boat at sea; her survival—let alone her arrival in the homeland of the Polixenes figure—is entirely a whim of fate. Similarly, when the aggrieved lovers—the equivalents of Perdita and Florizel—flee the king, they simply wander about, ending up in the woman's homeland purely by chance. In Shakespeare, chance is eliminated in favor of human plans; it is Antigonus who brings the infant to Bohemia and Camillo who directs the couple to Sicilia. Another telling difference is in the fate of the Leontes figure. In *Pandosto* an angry Apollo strikes him dead, but, as we have seen, Shakespeare keeps the god at a distance and permits Leontes to survive to regret his deed.

The triumph of good in *The Winter's Tale* is accomplished only with grave difficulty, and the world of the play is shrouded with losses. The "things dying" encountered by the Clown in 3.3 are human beings, the Mariner and Antigonus, both faultless except for their association with Leontes' sin. Their deaths seem gratuitous, but as agents of the king's wrath they embody the evils of the play's first half, and those evils must be done away with. Even more shocking is the death of the utterly innocent Mamillius—surely the greatest cost of Leontes' madness. Shakespeare here insists on the seriousness of sin. Other serious consequences include Paulina's widowhood and Camillo's exile (both presumably eased by their marriage at the conclusion) and the irretrievable loss of 16 potentially happy years for Leontes and Hermione. For all its joy, the final scene does not restore the unsullied world of the play's opening. The observation of wrinkles on the Hermione statue acknowledges that. The possibility of happiness is limited by evil and its consequences.

Shakespeare's picture of a moral world in *The Winter's Tale* is not, of course, a dry dissertation on faith and good works but rather an entertainment. The very title insists on the play's intention to entertain. Although the article *the* suggests a tale as harsh as the season, in Shakespeare's day the title also conjured up the festive Christmas season, for the connection of tale-telling to celebration was much stronger then than now. Both connotations are supported when the title is alluded to in the play: Mamillius announces, "A sad tale's best for winter" (2.1.25), but he does so in play with his loving mother, and the telling of his tale is plainly fun. The play as a whole also fulfills both interpretations of its title: The cold and dark of winter dominate the tragedy of the first half, and the

warmth and light of holiday festivities suffuse the comedy that follows.

Referring to the play's title in the dialogue is one of several ways in which Shakespeare insists on the artificiality of his romance. Allusions to the artfulness of the story are scattered throughout the play: Hermione, for example, compares her plight to a drama, "devis'd / And play'd to take spectators" (3.2.36–37); dressed for the festival, Perdita muses, "Methinks I play as I have seen them do / In Whitsun pastorals" (4.4.133–134); and the Third Gentleman speaks of news that "is so like an old tale that the verity of it is in strong suspicion" (5.2.28–29). The naiveté of Mopsa, who declares, "I love a ballad in print . . . for then we are sure they are true" (4.4.261–262), is a playful jab at the willing self-deception of romantic literature's audience. Moreover, there are several highly theatrical episodes set within the play: Hermione's trial, Time's prologue, the shepherd's festival, and Paulina's dramatic unveiling of the supposed statue, at which Leontes declares, rightly, "We are mock'd with art" (5.3.68). The very structure of the play reinforces the point, as tragedy changes abruptly to comedy. In stressing the obvious, that *The Winter's Tale* is an artifact and not real life, Shakespeare adds another layer to the basic theme of the play. The very play that points out the need for goodness in human endeavors is itself a human endeavor. Art joins with virtue in challenging the threat to happiness presented by social and psychological disarray. Art, and *The Winter's Tale* in particular, orders human affairs so that we can see how they resist destruction, even the natural decay that comes with time.

SOURCES OF THE PLAY

Shakespeare's main source for *The Winter's Tale* was a prose romance, *Pandosto* (1588) by Robert GREENE. The play follows *Pandosto*'s plot fairly closely and Greene's language is reproduced almost verbatim in some passages, but there is much that Shakespeare invented. Autolycus, for instance, was derived from a colorless character, and the shepherds' festival in 4.4 was sparked by a mere hint in *Pandosto*. Most significant, Shakespeare deviated from Greene's plot in two important respects. In

Pandosto Hermione's counterpart dies and Pandosto (Leontes) commits suicide. Shakespeare's spirit of reconciliation at the end is not paralleled in Greene's work.

Two passages probably owe their genesis to specific models. Polixenes' argument justifying art in 4.4.89–96 resembles a similar passage in PUTTENHAM's *Arte of English Poesie* (1589). Autolycus's descriptions of torture in 4.4.773–793 were adapted from a tale in Giovanni BOCCACIO's *Decameron* (1353), which Shakespeare may have read in the original Italian or in a French translation, perhaps that of Antoine LE MAÇON (1545). The same tale was the source for *Cymbeline,* written shortly before.

Other minor sources, reflected in various references and word choices, include OVID's *The Metamorphoses* (an old favorite of the playwright); other stories by Greene; passages from *The Knight of the Burning Pestle* by Francis BEAUMONT; and possibly two stories, themselves based on *Pandosto,* by a very minor writer, Francis Sabie (active 1595). Most of the names in the play were taken from PLUTARCH's *Lives,* another favorite source.

TEXT OF THE PLAY

The Winter's Tale was probably written in 1610 or early 1611. It must have been written by May 1611, when a performance is recorded, but how much earlier it was composed cannot be precisely determined. Stylistically, it is unquestionably among the late plays, and its greater mastery of the romance genre suggests that it followed *Cymbeline* (1608–10). Some scholars believe that Shakespeare's mention of a royal performance by the play's dancing satyrs in 4.4.337–338 is a sly reference to the presentation of Ben JONSON's *Masque of Oberon*—which has a similar scene—at the court of King JAMES I on January 1, 1611. If so, then the play may have been begun in late 1610 and completed early in 1611, in time to be staged in May. Alternatively, the play could have been completed in 1610, with the reference to *Oberon* added in the course of early performances.

The play was not published in Shakespeare's lifetime but appeared in the FIRST FOLIO (1623). It was apparently printed from a transcript of Shakespeare's FOUL PAPERS (or possibly of a PROMPTBOOK) by Ralph CRANE, a professional copyist whose peculiar punctuation and other idiosyncrasies can be recognized in the printed text.

THEATRICAL HISTORY OF THE PLAY

The earliest known performance of *The Winter's Tale* was at the GLOBE THEATRE on May 15, 1611, as recorded by Simon FORMAN. The play apparently was popular, for it was performed at the courts of Kings James I and Charles I at least seven times; in 1613 it was one of the plays put on by the KING's MEN for the wedding festivities of the princess ELIZABETH STUART. However, there is no record of a 17th-century performance after 1640 (though the play inspired a popular ballad, published in 1664). The next recorded production, in 1741, was advertised as the first in a century.

The 18th century saw a number of adaptations of the play that excluded or diminished Leontes and Hermione and focused on the love story of Act 4. Among the best known was *The Sheep-Shearing: or, Florizel and Perdita* (1754) by McNamara MORGAN. In 1761 this was produced as an operetta with music by Thomas ARNE. Also well known was David GARRICK's *The Winter's Tale* (1756), with Garrick as Leontes and Hannah PRITCHARD as Hermione (though these parts were reduced to a few lines each). Susannah CIBBER played Perdita, the central role, and Richard YATES played Autolycus, whose part was greatly expanded in this and other adaptations. Garrick's version remained popular throughout the century, though Shakespeare's original text (except for some minor alterations by Thomas HULL) was staged in 1771.

In the 19th century *The Winter's Tale* was staged with spectacular sets and lavish costumes. John Philip KEMBLE produced the play in 1811. His sister Sarah SIDDONS, who had played Hermione in a staging of Garrick's version, finally took on Shakespeare's much greater part in her final season. William Charles MACREADY produced the play in 1837, and Samuel PHELPS followed in 1845, using a text very close to the original. Perhaps the most memorable *Winter's Tale* of the century was that of Charles KEAN in 1856. His elaborate sets and costumes, intended to reproduce ancient Sicily and BITHYNIA (for Bohemia) with archaeological exactitude, were accompanied by a lengthy set of program notes. This production was both immensely popular and widely ridiculed, and a satirical burlesque, *Florizel and Perdita* by William Brough (1826–70), enjoyed a successful run in a rival theater. In Kean's play, Ellen TERRY, aged eight, spoke her first lines from a stage, as Mamillius. In another noteworthy production, in 1887, Mary ANDERSON played both Hermione and Perdita, with Johnston FORBES-ROBERTSON as Leontes.

The Winter's Tale was less popular in the 20th century, though there were a number of notable stagings, beginning with Beerbohm TREE's 1906 effort. Still in the 19th-century vein, it starred Ellen Terry as Hermione, 50 years after her Mamillius. Harley GRANVILLE-BARKER's 1912 production featured a formally stylized, almost bare stage that scandalized traditionalists. Robert ATKINS produced the play twice, in 1937 and 1950. The most important 20th-century production was probably that of Peter BROOK in 1951, starring John GIELGUD as Leontes. More recently, Trevor NUNN's 1969 production starred Judi DENCH as both Perdita and Hermione, and Adrian NOBLE's 1992 staging was very highly regarded in London and traveled to New York in 1994. In 1995 the Swedish giant of cinema, Ingmar Bergman (b. 1918), directed a theatrical presentation of *The Winter's Tale* that toured internationally. The ROYAL SHAKESPEARE COMPANY chose *The Winter's Tale*—in a controversial version set in modern America—for the inaugural production of its new London theater in 2001.

The play was produced as a FILM three times (all silent) before 1915, but only once since, a 1968 filming of a stage performance starring Laurence Harvey (1928–73). It has been made for TELEVISION three times, twice in Great Britain (1962; 1981) and the United States (1980). In 1908 the composer Karl Goldmark (1830–1915) composed an OPERA, his last, based on *The Winter's Tale*.

CHARACTERS

Antigonus Character in *The Winter's Tale*, nobleman at the court of King Leontes of SICILIA. Antigonus, like his wife Paulina, defends Queen Hermione against the king's unjust accusation of adultery, and he protests against the cruelty of killing the infant Perdita, whom the king believes is illegitimate. Leontes threatens him with death for failing to control Paulina's bitter criticism and orders the old man to take the baby and abandon it in the wilderness. Antigonus accepts the king's order and leaves the child on the coast of BOHEMIA and is killed and eaten by a Bear.

Shakespeare has Antigonus die partly so that his knowledge of Perdita's whereabouts will not be available to the repentant Leontes of Act 3. But, more important, the old man's death has a moral point. The bear provides a particularly appalling end for Antigonus, an emblem of the sin of cooperating with evil. Though he is a generally sympathetic figure, humorous when admittedly overwhelmed by Paulina and courageous in his initial protests to Leontes, he must be compared with his wife, who resists the king's tyranny. Antigonus, though reluctant, is weak; he permits duty to the king to overrule his sense of justice and becomes the agent of Leontes' evil madness. He even comes to believe in Hermione's guilt, as he declares in his soliloquy before abandoning Perdita.

Antigonus's death is part of the workings of providence that underlies the play. At the same time, since he is himself a victim of the king's madness, his death—like that of Mamillius and the Mariner—is an example of the human cost of evil. Antigonus comes to embody the tragic developments of the first half of the play, and his death signals their end, as the drama moves from tragedy to redemption.

Antigonus undergoes a modest redemption himself. The hearty old gentleman who invokes "the whole dungy earth" (2.1.157) and acknowledges his overwhelming wife with a "La you now" (2.3.50) is altered by the experiences fate ordains for him. He dares to criticize the king, even if he cannot persist, and he assumes responsibility for Perdita. In his dream of Hermione, he also seems to have a supernatural visitation from the dead. As he leaves Perdita, he recognizes his involvement with evil, despairing, "Weep I cannot, / But my heart bleeds; and most accurs'd am I / To be by oath enjoin'd to this" (3.3.51–53). About to die, he speaks in a poetic diction that elevates him to a nobler level.

Archidamus Minor character in *The Winter's Tale*, a follower of King Polixenes of BOHEMIA. In

1.1 Archidamus exchanges diplomatic courtesies with Camillo, an adviser of King Leontes of SICILIA. Their conversation informs the audience of the play's opening situation. Archidamus has no real personality, but his fluent command of courtly language lends the episode a distancing formality, appropriately introducing an extravagant and romantic story. Nevertheless, his last line, "If the king had no son, they would desire to live on crutches till he had one" (1.1.44–45), closes the scene with a harshness that intimates the misery to come in the play's tragic first half.

Autolycus Character in *The Winter's Tale*, a vagabond thief who wanders through BOHEMIA. Autolycus appears, singing and bragging about his career as a petty thief, in 4.3. He picks the pocket of the Clown and proposes to find further victims at the sheep-shearing festival, making "the shearers prove sheep" (4.3.117). In 4.4 he attends the festival disguised as a peddler, singing SONGs, selling trinkets, and picking pockets. His songs and patter, his cheerful irresponsibility, and his insouciant delight in life add greatly to our enjoyment of the rustic scene. When King Polixenes rages against the love of his son Florizel and the shepherdess Perdita, Autolycus exploits the situation to rob Perdita's foster father, the Shepherd, who fears punishment and wants the king to know that Perdita was a foundling. Autolycus terrifies the old man and his son, the Clown, with accounts of the tortures they can expect and then offers, for money, to help them reach the king. However, he actually turns them over to the fleeing Florizel, in the hope of reward. In this way evidence of Perdita's identity gets to SICILIA—she is the long-lost daughter of the Sicilian King Leontes—resulting in reunions for the play's major characters and the incidental enrichment of the Shepherd and Clown with vast rewards. In 5.2 Autolycus admits that his life has earned no success, and he turns to flattering his former victims, now newly made gentlemen, in the hope of employment.

Autolycus is for the most part a charming rogue. He contributes greatly to the atmosphere of gaiety that surrounds the shepherds' world and thus to the comic tone of the play's second half. His crimes

are petty compared with those of Leontes in the tragic first half of the play, but in any case it is part of the virtue of the pastoral world that it has room for this comical villain. The importance of mercy as a moral virtue is emphasized by the fact that Autolycus's depredations are accepted as a part of life. He even has a place in the play's final forgiveness and reconciliation, though the playwright could easily have left him in Bohemia. Autolycus represents the irrepressible mischievousness of human nature; that he selfishly views the world entirely in terms of his own convenience is deplorable, but he compensates through his contagious pleasure in simple things and the delightful songs in which he expresses this pleasure.

Autolycus resembles traditional comic characters, but he is not quite classifiable. He is too sophisticated for a rustic CLOWN, nor is he a FOOL, for he is not a professional jester. He does, however, resemble a Fool in his mockery, his songs, and his disinterested position relative to the main developments. He resembles Falstaff in his anomalous social position, his predatory nature, and his pretensions to an anti-ethic (he boasts of a piece of "knavery," "therein am I constant to my profession" [4.4.682–683]). Both characters, though amoral, are admirably independent, and the conflict of our judgments on the two traits yields subtle humor, as our own pretensions and secret predilections are exposed.

Autolycus's nature (like Falstaff's) gradually changes. At first he charms us, and we are inclined to forgive his crimes. However, as the shepherds' festival closes, he seems less pleasant, crying, "Ha, ha! what a fool Honesty is!" (4.4.596) and gloating over his victims, who are sympathetic characters. When he plots how to profit from the desperate young lovers' situation, he is still funny, but we can no longer ignore his amorality, for it threatens the hero and heroine. His terrorizing of the Shepherd with truly horrible descriptions of torture adds to our unease, and Autolycus acquires a darkly satirical cast as he replicates Polixenes' wrath while himself disguised as a courtier. He has changed sides in Shakespeare's opposition of pastoral innocence and sophisticated machinations. It is the Clown who is the comic character in 5.2, while Autolycus is merely another practitioner of the courtier's bowing and scraping to which he at first seemed antithetical.

Autolycus's only real connection to the plot, his role in preventing the Shepherd from revealing Perdita's origins too early, comes from the play's main source, the novella *Pandosto* by Robert GREENE, in which a servant of the prince—and Autolycus was once Florizel's servant—performs this function. However, making this figure a vagabond and thief was Shakespeare's invention. The playwright probably took the idea, as well as the name Autolycus, from OVID's description of the god Mercury's son in *The Metamorphoses*. Shakespeare's Autolycus brags of the connection, "My father named me Autolycus; who, being as I am, littered under Mercury, was likewise a snapper-up of unconsidered trifles" (4.3.24–26).

Bear   Minor figure in *The Winter's Tale*, wild beast that kills Antigonus as he abandons the infant Perdita on the coast of BOHEMIA. Antigonus is warned by the Mariner that wild animals are present, and as he completes his task, he is attacked. At 3.3.58 one of Shakespeare's most famous stage directions instructs Antigonus, "Exit, pursued by a bear." Later in the scene, the Clown reports that the bear has "half dined upon the gentleman" (3.3.105). The startling appearance of a bear makes Antigonus's death a vivid event, forcefully elevating it as a symbol of the consequences of tragedy. At the same time Antigonus's appalling end suggests humanity's helplessness in the face of nature and thus reinforces a major theme of the play, our ultimate dependence on providence.

Although Antigonus's death is unquestionably horrific, it also has a slightly comic note. The bear's sudden appearance is as unexpected as a punch line and charged with the awkward unreality of an actor costumed as a bear. The Clown's later description is frankly humorous. The bear's brief appearance thus offers an emotional transition from the tragic first half of the play to the pastoral comedy of Act 4.

Carnivores of all sorts figure prominently in Shakespeare's imagery, and bears in particular consistently represent fearsome savagery. Sometimes the image is comical, as in the remark of a stubborn

bachelor, "As from a bear a man would run for life, / So fly I from her that would be my wife" (*Comedy of Errors*, 3.2.153–154); sometimes in earnest, as when Prospero describes the tormented Ariel: "thy groans / Did make wolves howl, and penetrate the breasts / Of ever-angry bears" (*Tempest* 1.2.287–289). In *The Winter's Tale* Antigonus himself uses such imagery, unconsciously and ironically anticipating his own end, when he hopes that wild animals, including "wolves and bears" (2.3.186), will be merciful to the abandoned Perdita. This desire is pointedly hopeless, given the nature of wolves and bears.

Scholars and theatrical directors have speculated on whether Shakespeare intended the use of a live bear on stage. Some scholars have suggested that he did, as live bears attracted crowds to the bear-baiting arena a few doors from the GLOBE THEATRE, where the audience paid to see dogs attack the bears. There is evidence to support the suggestion. In 1610, the year Shakespeare was probably writing *The Winter's Tale*, both Ben JONSON's courtly MASQUE, *Oberon*, and a new production of the anonymous play MUCEDORUS presented scenes involving bears (in the latter case, the scene was added to the play's earlier script). A year earlier, King JAMES I had been presented with a pair of young polar bears that had been captured by English explorers and were housed at the bear-baiting facility. In 1611, when *The Winter's Tale* was first performed, these bears were approaching two years old; they will have been the size of a man but—ideally, at least—not yet inclined to aggressive behavior. It may be that these bears were available for use in the theater at this time (though they were apparently in the charge of Philip HENSLOWE, a rival of Shakespeare's KING'S MEN). The details cannot be known unless further evidence surfaces, but it seems at least possible that Shakespeare knew of and wrote for these polar bears. However, there are also objections to this idea, beginning with the notoriously temperamental nature of bears (tame bears were known in 17th-century England, but they were always leashed—an inappropriate condition for the savage killer of the play). While King James's white bears may have been trained, there remains the dubious likelihood of their availability to the King's Men. Most scholars conclude, therefore, that an actor costumed as a bear was most probably what Shakespeare had in mind; a bear is much the easiest wild animal for a human being to imitate, and bear costumes are known to have been used fairly frequently in Shakespeare's day.

Camillo   Character in *The Winter's Tale*, an adviser of King Leontes of SICILIA. The mad Leontes suspects his best friend, King Polixenes of BOHEMIA, of committing adultery with his wife, and in 1.2 he orders Camillo to poison Polixenes. Instead, Camillo informs Polixenes and flees with him to Bohemia. Camillo reappears there in the second half of the play, set 16 years later. He has been a faithful adviser to Polixenes, and in 4.4 he helps the king thwart the romance between Prince Florizel and a shepherd girl, Perdita. However, he then helps the couple flee to Sicilia, where it is discovered that Perdita is the lost daughter of Leontes, and the play ends in an atmosphere of general reconciliation and love.

Camillo represents a familiar character type in the romantic literature on which *The Winter's Tale* is based: the servant who aids his master by disobeying him. As such, he is one of the good people who fight the evil that infects the play's world. Only providence, supported by the power of love, can bring the play's characters through to the happy ending, but human agency, chiefly that of Camillo and Paulina, is an important auxiliary. Thus, Camillo supports a major theme of the play, that humanity must energetically use its capacity for good. Fittingly, he becomes engaged to Paulina by royal command at the play's close.

Cleomenes (Cleomines) and Dion   Minor characters in *The Winter's Tale*, followers of King Leontes of SICILIA. Cleomenes and Dion are virtually indistinguishable, and they share their only significant function, so they are treated together here. Seeking support for his accusation that Queen Hermione is guilty of adultery, King Leontes sends them to consult the oracle of Apollo. They describe the oracle in awestruck tones, with Dion ecstatically reminiscing, "O, the sacrifice! / How ceremonious, solemn and unearthly" (3.1.6–7), and Cleomenes declaring that "the ear-deaf'ning voice o' th' Oracle, / Kin to Jove's

thunder, so surpris'd my sense, / That I was nothing" (3.1.9–11). Their remarks stand in for the actual appearance of a god—a feature of the other ROMANCES—and introduce the climactic moment of the play's first half, the checking of Leontes' madness through the apparent intervention of Apollo. However, when the oracle's pronouncement is delivered in 3.2, Cleomenes and Dion speak only half a line, in unison, swearing that they have not read the message. They reappear briefly in 5.1, but they are merely pawns of the plot.

Clown   Character in *The Winter's Tale*, foster brother of Perdita. The Clown is present in 3.3 when the abandoned infant Perdita is discovered in BOHEMIA by his father, the Shepherd. In Act 4, 16 years later, the Clown is part of Perdita's pastoral world, though he has no direct contact with her. As his designation implies (see CLOWN), he is an oafish rustic, a likable and well-meaning fellow who is somewhat stupid and unconsciously comical. In 3.3 he is unwittingly funny when describing the horrible deaths of Antigonus and the Mariner, helping to establish the comic tone of the play's second half. A gullible victim, he is robbed by Autolycus in 4.3, and in 4.4, at the shepherds' festival, his foolish pleasure in buying gifts for his girlfriend, Mopsa, adds to our enjoyment of the scene. He declares to the peddler (Autolycus in disguise), "If I were not in love with Mopsa, thou shouldst take no money of me; but being enthralled as I am, it will also be the bondage of certain ribbons and gloves" (4.4.233–236).

Later in 4.4, when King Polixenes, angry at Perdita's love for his son Florizel, threatens the Shepherd with death, the Clown encourages his father to disclaim his adopted daughter. Autolycus offers to take them to the king for a fee, but he tricks them onto the ship carrying Perdita and Florizel to SICILIA, where Perdita's identity as King Leontes' daughter is discovered. The Shepherd and the Clown are rewarded with a raise in status, and in 5.2 the Clown comically brags of being "a gentleman born . . . and [having] been so any time these four hours" (5.2.134–136). Despite his foolishness and his single act of cowardice—understandable in a shepherd facing a king's wrath—the Clown is clearly a good person. As such he contributes to the atmosphere of human virtue that characterizes the second half of the play, countering the evil of the first.

Dorcas Character in *The Winter's Tale,* a shepherdess. Dorcas appears only in the shepherds' festival in 4.4. She speaks briefly, chiefly to tease her friend Mopsa about her engagement to the Clown, and she sings a SONG with Mopsa and Autolycus. She has no personality to speak of, but she contributes to the festive atmosphere of the occasion. Dorcas's name is from the Bible (see Acts 9:36–42).

Doricles In *The Winter's Tale,* name taken by Prince Florizel of BOHEMIA when he disguises himself to court Perdita, a seeming shepherdess.

Emilia Minor character in *The Winter's Tale,* a lady-in-waiting to Queen Hermione. In 2.2, when Paulina attempts to visit the unjustly imprisoned Hermione, the Gaoler only lets her see Emilia. She tells Paulina that the queen has given birth and returns to her mistress with Paulina's suggestion that the infant be brought to the king in a bid for mercy. Emilia's role is small, and she is an uncomplicated messenger, a simple tool of the plot without any real personality.

Florizel Character in *The Winter's Tale,* son of King Polixenes of BOHEMIA and suitor of Perdita. Florizel defies his father's anger at his intention to marry Perdita, a shepherd girl deemed unsuitable for the heir to the kingdom, and the couple flees to SICILIA. There her identity as the daughter of King Leontes is discovered, leading to the couple's formal engagement and the reconciliation of their fathers. Florizel is present in only three scenes— 4.4, 5.1, and 5.3—and he does not speak in 5.3. Moreover, he is something of a cardboard hero, a stereotype of the chivalric young knight of traditional romantic literature—brave, handsome, and passionately loyal to his lover but with little further in the way of personality. Nevertheless, though his emotional range is restricted, Florizel is important to the play, for his cheerful adoration of Perdita is a charming and forceful manifestation of young love, and his courageous persistence in the face of Polixenes' wrath permits the pair to remain together

long enough for the solution to emerge. He is thus an emblem of the power of love to withstand tyrannous opposition. His name probably comes from that of a similar hero, Florizel de Niquea, the protagonist of a chivalric romance by the 16th-century Spanish author Feliciano de Silva (ca. 1492–1558).

Gaoler Minor character in *The Winter's Tale,* the custodian of the imprisoned Queen Hermione. When Lady Paulina visits the unjustly incarcerated queen, the Gaoler is sympathetic—calling her "a worthy lady / And one who much I honour" (2.2.5–6)—but he sticks to his duty, only allowing her to see Hermione's lady-in-waiting, Emilia, and only in his presence. When Paulina proposes to take Hermione's daughter—born in the prison— to the king, the Gaoler is reluctant, saying, "I know not what I shall incur to pass it, / Having no warrant" (2.2.57–58), but in the face of Paulina's insistence he accedes. This weak figure provides a foil for Paulina, establishing her as the powerful presence that will dominate several later scenes; at the same time, by reminding us of the authority he represents, he contributes to our growing sense of tragedy.

Gentleman Any of three minor characters in *The Winter's Tale,* courtiers at the court of King Leontes of SICILIA. They report to Autolycus on the offstage encounter of Leontes and his old friend King Polixenes, whom he had earlier wronged, and of the discovery by Leontes of his long-lost daughter, Perdita. The First Gentleman knows only that something extraordinary has happened, the Second knows the result, but only the Third Gentleman can describe the events as they happened, which he does at length, in 5.2.31–103. The language of all three Gentlemen is flowery and ornate, typical of the courtly idiom of the 17th century. Although they display little individual personality, they are nevertheless interesting as miniature portraits of Jacobean courtiers. (Some editors presume that the Servant [1] of 5.1 is another such courtier and designate him a Gentleman.) Shakespeare's presentation of crucial events through the reporting of minor characters is sometimes criticized, but here he avoids a scene that would repeat much that the audience already knows. He also provides a contrast with the play's true climax, still to come in 5.3.

Hermione   Character in *The Winter's Tale*, wife of King Leontes of SICILIA and mother of Perdita. Unjustly accused of adultery by her mad husband, Hermione gives birth in prison to Perdita, whom Leontes condemns to be abandoned in the wilderness; then her son Mamillius dies just as Leontes sentences her to death. The shock of this loss kills her, according to her ally Lady Paulina. However, Paulina keeps Hermione alive in secret, awaiting the time when Leontes shall have sufficiently repented. In 5.3, after Perdita has miraculously reappeared, Paulina offers to display a statue of Hermione, which is actually the still-living queen herself. As the others watch in awe, Hermione comes to life, and the play closes with reunion and reconciliation.

Hermione is a passive but highly important figure in the play. Her fate in the tragic first half makes her an emblem of a major theme of the play—indeed, of all Shakespeare's ROMANCES—the critical role of providence in securing human happiness in an unreliable world. Even more, she helps illustrate that the efficacy of providence depends on the moral strength of good people in the face of evil. Her dignity in the face of her undeserved fate is highly impressive. Even the steady strength of the poetry she speaks contrasts favorably with the hysterical ranting of Leontes. She puts her faith in providence, saying, "if powers divine / Behold our human actions (as they do), / I doubt not then but innocence shall make / False accusation blush" (3.2. 28–31). Upon her reappearance she restates this attitude when she invokes a blessing on Perdita—"You gods, look down, / And from your sacred vial pour your graces / Upon my daughter's head" (5.3.121–123).

Hermione displays a loving nature that anticipates the role of Perdita in the second half of the play. Her charm is evident in 1.2, when, at Leontes' request, she persuades King Polixenes of BOHEMIA to extend his visit. This arouses Leontes' jealous suspicions, but it also demonstrates Hermione's fine qualities: a readiness for friendship and an intelligent appreciation of the previous affection between her husband and Polixenes. Her capacity for love is delightfully demonstrated in 2.1, where we see her playing with Mamillius. Her evident goodness makes her apparent death all the more tragic and her apparent resurrection all the more Christlike. Although Hermione's significance diminishes in the second half, in the first—and at the conclusion—she is key to *The Winter's Tale's* presentation of humanity's capacity for good.

Lady   Any of several minor characters in *The Winter's Tale*, ladies-in-waiting to Queen Hermione. Two ladies, designated First Lady and Second Lady, join Hermione and her young son, Mamillius, in the playful exchange that opens 2.1. Mamillius teases the ladies about their cosmetics, and they in turn tease the prince about his prospective younger sibling, pointing out that Hermione is quite pregnant. The episode provides a striking contrast with the mad brutality of King Leontes, whose arrival interrupts these domestic pleasures. When the king appears, one of the ladies escorts Mamillius away, and the others leave with the queen when she is sent to prison. (Emilia, who appears by name in the prison scene [2.2], is presumably one of these ladies, but here she is anonymous.) Ladies, again nameless, mutely attend Hermione at the hearing in 3.2. The courtly ladies lend a charming atmosphere to Hermione's household, contrasting with the tragic developments that surround them; at the same time they help maintain the regal atmosphere appropriate to TRAGEDY in Shakespeare's literary world.

Leontes   Character in *The Winter's Tale*, the King of SICILIA, husband of Hermione and father of Perdita. Leontes' insane jealousy is the disorder at the center of the TRAGEDY that comprises the first half of the play. In 1.2. convinced that Hermione has committed adultery with King Polixenes of BOHEMIA, Leontes orders her tried for treason. In 2.3, believing the newborn Perdita to be Polixenes' child, he condemns her to abandonment in the wilderness. Even when the oracle of Apollo declares Hermione innocent in 3.2, Leontes refuses to believe it. Finally, the death from grief of his son Mamillius, taken as an act of vengeance by Apollo, convinces him, and he repents. However, Hermione is apparently dead of grief also, and the mournful Leontes "shuts himself up" (4.1.19), emerging only in Act 5, after 16 years of "saint-like sorrow" (5.1.2), to learn that both Perdita and Hermione have survived.

Shakespeare gives Leontes some weight as a particular person: He is about 30 in Act 1; he has inspired love in Hermione and Mamillius and demonstrates his own love for his son; he is conscious of public opinion when he sends messengers to the oracle to "Give rest to th' minds of others" (2.1.191) and holds a trial that he may "be clear'd / Of being tyrannous" (3.2.5). Nevertheless, his personality is not well developed, for it is not as a person that Leontes has importance. He functions as a symbol of disorder and chaos; he is not intended to be a realistic human being so much as an obstacle to happiness. He is villainous because the story calls for villainy, not from any well-established motive. His madness is as much a surprise to the other characters as it is to the audience or reader. Leontes is thus also a victim, a man rendered suddenly insane, subject to the whims of fate. It is highly significant that it takes an act of divine intervention to effect his cure. One of the lessons of the play—and of the ROMANCES in general—is that humankind depends on providence for happiness in an insecure world.

At the close of 3.2, Leontes subsides into grief, and there is a sense of calm acceptance of evil's consequences that resembles a tragedy's close. However, Leontes' repentance occurs as abruptly as the sin that made it necessary; it fails to produce any spiritual growth or any profound expressions of torment such as those offered by Othello and Lear. His repentance, like his jealousy, is archetypal. Still, though Leontes' psychology is not explored, his repentance nevertheless serves as a symbol of the gentler world in which the climactic reconciliations can occur.

Lord Any of several minor characters in *The Winter's Tale*, followers of King Leontes of SICILIA. A Lord, one of several present, objects to Leontes' brutal imprisonment of his Queen Hermione for her supposed adultery with King Polixenes of BOHEMIA. When another Lord, Antigonus, supports the first in his certainty that Hermione is innocent, the king goes so far as to admit that he has submitted the question to the oracle of Apollo. The Lords are present in 2.3 when the raging king sentences his infant daughter, Perdita, to death. Again, they and Antigonus temper the king's course somewhat, although Leontes still orders the baby abandoned in the wilderness. The Lords are present at Hermione's trial in 3.2, and a Lord announces the return of King Polixenes in 5.1, but their chief function has already been filled. They help maintain a background of outraged virtue against which the madness of Leontes stands out in the first, tragic half of the play.

Mamillius Character in *The Winter's Tale*, the son of King Leontes of SICILIA and Queen Hermione, who dies of grief when his father persecutes his mother unjustly. In 1.1 Mamillius is presented as the pride of his parents and the entire kingdom; his future as a man and ruler looks brilliant. These sentiments, however, will soon seem ironic. In 1.2 and 2.1 he appears a likable boy, especially in 2.1, when he jests with his mother's ladies-in-waiting and tells his mother a story "of sprites and goblins" because "a sad tale's best for winter" (2.1.26, 25). The remark confirms our sense of coming tragedy. Mamillius dies of grief, offstage, during his mother's trial. The shock of his death, reported in 3.2.144–145, stirs his father, too late, to recognize his own injustice. The death of Mamillius, a completely innocent victim, demonstrates the appalling cost of Leontes' madness; it is the low point of the play's tragic development.

Shakespeare created Mamillius from the mere mention of the analogous figure in his source, the prose romance *Pandosto* by Robert GREENE. His name may have been derived from the title of two earlier romances by Greene, *Mamillia* (1583, 1593).

Mariner Minor character in *The Winter's Tale*, a seaman who sets Antigonus ashore in BOHEMIA in 3.3 for the purpose of abandoning the infant Perdita. The Mariner dislikes their task, which has been ordered by the mad King Leontes, and he fears that the gods will dislike it as well. He warns

Antigonus to hurry because bad weather is approaching and because the coast is famous for its wild animals. He is borne out on both points as a storm arises—he perishes in it, as is reported in 3.3.90–94—and Antigonus is eaten by a Bear. The Mariner offers a point of view outside the story, that of the common man who pities the infant and fears the gods. Like a CHORUS, he provides a brief commentary on developments.

The Mariner's death has a dual significance in the play's scheme. A good man, repelled by Perdita's fate, he is himself a victim of Leontes' madness. As such he represents the human cost exacted by evil. On the other hand, as Antigonus's guide, he is Leontes' agent, albeit an unwilling one. His death is part of the necessary workings of providence, for the evil of Leontes' deeds must be thoroughly extirpated as a condition of redemption, and the Mariner, like Antigonus, embodies that evil to some degree.

Mopsa Character in *The Winter's Tale*, a shepherdess. Mopsa appears only at the shepherds' festival in 4.4, where she is a charming representative of rustic youth. She is engaged to the Clown, for which she is teased by her companion, Dorcas. She and Dorcas sing a ballad with Autolycus, and their enthusiasm is infectious, contributing to the pleasure of the occasion, which contrasts sharply with the pathos and stress of the first part of the play. Mopsa is pleasingly comical as well. When she declares that she wants the Clown to buy her some sheet music, she adds naively, "I love a ballad in print . . . for then we are sure they are true" (4.4.261–262). She then supposes there is truth in a ballad about a usurer's wife who gives birth to bags of money.

The name Mopsa was conventionally rustic, used for peasant women in several 16th-century romantic works, including the greatest of them, Sir Philip SIDNEY's *Arcadia*. It may have been a feminine version of Mopsus, a name given to several mythological Greek prophets. However, Shakespeare clearly took the name directly from the play's chief source, *Pandosto* by Robert GREENE, where Mopsa is the foster mother of Perdita's equivalent. Oddly, Mopsa is the only name taken from Greene, though Greene's Mopsa is the only character in *Pandosto* that does not reappear, under a different name, in Shakespeare's play.

Officer Any of several minor characters in *The Winter's Tale*, officials of the law court assembled by King Leontes to try Queen Hermione for adultery. In 3.2.12–21 an Officer reads the formal indictment of Hermione, and in 3.2.124–130 he (or another) swears in Cleomenes and Dion, who bring a message from the oracle of Apollo. He then reads the oracle's proclamation that Hermione is innocent. As extras, merely providing an official presence to a trial scene, the Officers have no personality.

Old Shepherd See Shepherd.

Paulina Character in *The Winter's Tale*, defender of Queen Hermione against the injustice of her husband, King Leontes, and later the instrument of their reconciliation. Paulina boldly criticizes the king for accusing Hermione of adultery, and her courage and common sense contrast tellingly with the king's jealous madness. After failing to prevent the king from exiling Perdita, the infant daughter he believes illegitimate, Paulina enters into an amazing scheme: She stages Hermione's death and isolates her for 16 years, against the time when Leontes will have thoroughly repented. Perdita's return signals the ripeness of this plan, and Paulina reveals Hermione's existence in 5.3—in a stage-managed presentation of the long-lost queen as a statue. This revelation brings about the play's final reunion. Thus Paulina, despite her bluff worldliness and overpowering manner, is an agent of redemption.

Paulina thinks clearly and acts decisively; she courageously takes it on herself to defend the queen as soon as she hears of her plight, and she handles the Gaoler with the powerful courtesy of the grande dame that she is. Her criticism of the king is excoriating; he is reduced to insult—calling her a "witch" (2.3.67), a "callat [prostitute]" (2.3.90), and a "gross hag" (2.3.107). When he threatens to burn her as a witch, she boldly replies, "I care not" (2.3.113). Her boldness, however, does not always produce the envisioned results; her tactic of presenting the infant Perdita to the king merely aggravates his anger and results in the child's abandonment. Paulina alone cannot remedy the defect in the play's world—providence must see to that—but her efforts are important evidence that good has not died and may be restored.

Paulina has often been compared to King Lear's faithful Kent. Like him, she offers a cure for the king's madness, declaring, "I / Do come with words as medicinal as true" (2.3.36–37). Her therapy is a raw and intrusive one. In Act 5 she continues her powerful ministrations. She reinforces Leontes' repentance by continually reminding him of the supposedly dead Hermione and demands that he vow never to take a wife without her approval. She reveals Hermione's survival with a fine theatrical sense, raising dramatic expectations of sorcery by disclaiming "wicked powers" (5.3.91), and she prevents Hermione from disclosing too much with a hasty "There's time enough for that" (5.3.128). At the close, within the atmosphere of love and reconciliation, Paulina finally permits herself to lament the loss of her own husband, Antigonus, which stirs the king to ordain her remarriage to Camillo. Her value in the world of the play is acknowledged when the king calls her one "whose worth and honesty / Is richly noted" (5.3.144–145). The central theme of *The Winter's Tale* is that human moral energy must support divine providence, and Paulina's valiant efforts are a prime source of this ingredient.

Perdita   Character in *The Winter's Tale*, long-lost daughter of King Leontes and Queen Hermione of SICILIA. The love of Perdita and Prince Florizel of BOHEMIA is the central element in the romantic COMEDY that constitutes the second half of the play, balancing the TRAGEDY of Leontes' mad jealousy in the first. Though she is prominent only in 4.4, her virtue, beauty, and charming personality make Perdita a powerful symbolic force in the remainder of the play.

At the turning point of the play, in 3.3, the infant Perdita is abandoned in the wilderness because Leontes believes she is the offspring of Hermione's alleged adultery with King Polixenes of Bohemia. A Shepherd adopts Perdita, and by Act 4, 16 years later, she has become a charming young woman, the "Mistress o' th' Feast" (4.4.68) at the

shepherds' festival. Florizel's father, King Polixenes, disapproves of the love between his royal son and a peasant girl. When he attends the feast in disguise, he is charmed by Perdita, finding her "Too noble for this place" (4.4.159), but he will not accept her as a daughter-in-law. He threatens her with death, and the couple flees to Sicilia, where Perdita's identity is discovered. This leads to their formal engagement, the reconciliation of Leontes and Polixenes, and the restoration of Queen Hermione, who has been kept in hiding. The prophecy of the oracle of Apollo—that only Perdita can restore the happiness Leontes has destroyed—is thus fulfilled. Perdita's love is essential to the workings of providence in the play's outcome, thereby supporting the play's major theme, that the moral virtue of good people is necessary for providence to function as a savior in human affairs.

Raised as a shepherdess, Perdita is an honest, open young woman with no trace of pretension or sentimentality. She is embarrassed to be "most goddess-like prank'd up" (4.4.10) in a fancy costume for the festival, and she is frankly worried about Polixenes' opposition to her, though more for Florizel's sake than her own. A clever lass, she briskly counters Camillo's flattery in 4.4.110–112 and more than holds her own in the debate with Polixenes in 4.4.79–103, in which she defends the simple ways of nature against the sophistication of art. She values a maidenly decorum in sexual matters while acknowledging the physical side of love. She mentions, for example, a "false way" of love (4.4.151) and speaks against "scurrilous words" (4.4.215) in ballads, yet when Florizel jests that strewn with flowers he would be like a corpse, she replies, "No, like a bank, for love to lie and play on: / Not like a corpse; or if—not to be buried, / But quick, and in mine arms" (4.4.130–133).

This lovely passage is suggestive of primordial rituals of death and rebirth. Along with her remarks on the Proserpina myth and mythological flower lore in 4.4.116–126, it links her with the ancient veneration of natural fertility, of which the shepherds' festival is a survival. As Florizel puts it, "This your sheep-shearing / Is as a meeting of the petty gods, / And you the queen on 't" (4.4.3–5). All this reinforces Perdita's association with providence.

It was the protection of providence that brought the tragic first half of the play to an end, and it is the love Perdita represents that proves instrumental in effecting the final reconciliations of the second.

Polixenes Character in *The Winter's Tale*, the King of BOHEMIA. In 1.2 Polixenes, visiting his old friend King Leontes of SICILIA, is persuaded by Leontes' wife, Queen Hermione, to extend his stay. However, Leontes goes mad and imagines adultery between Polixenes and Hermione. Warned by Camillo that Leontes intends to poison him, Polixenes flees to Bohemia and is not seen again until late in the play. Leontes believes his infant daughter, Perdita, is the illegitimate child of Polixenes, and orders her abandoned in the wilderness. In Act 4, 16 years later, Polixenes' son, Prince Florizel, falls in love with Perdita, who has been raised by shepherds in Bohemia. Polixenes opposes the match of a prince and a shepherdess, and the couple, pursued by the king, flees to Sicilia. There Perdita's identity is revealed, the couple becomes engaged, and Polixenes is reconciled with his old friend in 5.3, the play's final scene.

Polixenes is a rather colorless victim in 1.2—though his perspicacity in reading the situation contrasts sharply with Leontes' obtuseness—and he is mostly an observer in 5.3. In Act 4 he is more prominent, even though his role is a stereotype of the status-conscious adult who opposes young love. He is charmed by Perdita at the shepherds' festival, but after he removes his disguise, he threatens her with "a death as cruel for thee / As thou art tender to 't" (4.4.441–442). Thus, in the romantic COMEDY of the play's second half, Polixenes takes the role of villain that Leontes had in the TRAGEDY of the first half.

Servant (1) Any of several minor characters in *The Winter's Tale*, workers in the household of King Leontes of SICILIA. In 2.3 a Servant informs the king of the progress of his son, Mamillius, who is ill, thereby preparing the ground for the announcement by another Servant (or perhaps the same one) of the boy's death in 3.2. In 5.1 a Servant announces the approach of Florizel and Perdita, describing Perdita's charms rapturously. This last Servant seems to be a Gentleman of the court; the king speaks with him of his poems about Queen Hermione. He is probably one of the Gentlemen who appear in 5.2, and many editions designate him as such. He is often referred to by commentators as the Gentleman-poet.

Servant (2) Minor character in *The Winter's Tale*, the employee of the Shepherd. The Servant appears twice in 4.4, to announce the arrival of Autolycus and the presentation of a MASQUE at the shepherds' festival. His comical enthusiasm heightens our pleasure in the festivities. He comments, for instance, on Autolycus's singing: "O master! if you did but hear the pedlar at the door, you would never dance again after a tabor and pipe; no, the bagpipe could not move you" (4.4.183–185). He is a rustic CLOWN whose naiveté contributes to the fun; for example, he foolishly construes Autolycus's songs as "without bawdry," but adds that they contain "delicate burdens [choruses] of dildoes and fadings, jump her and thump her" (4.4.195–196).

Shepherd (Old Shepherd) Character in *The Winter's Tale*, the foster father of Perdita. The mad King Leontes of SICILIA, believing his infant daughter, Perdita, to be illegitimate, orders her abandoned in the wilderness of BOHEMIA. In 3.3 the Shepherd discovers her, wrapped in rich fabrics and supplied with identifying documents. He raises her as his daughter. In 4.4, 16 years later, the Shepherd hosts a country festival, at which King Polixenes threatens him with death, for Prince Florizel has fallen in love with Perdita, offending the royal dignity. The Shepherd and his son, the Clown, try to show Perdita's documents to the king, to prove that they are not related to her and should not be punished, but they are tricked by Autolycus into joining the fleeing couple and sailing to Sicilia. There, Perdita's identity is discovered, and the Shepherd is amply rewarded; in 5.2 he and the Clown display their new finery, having been created gentlemen by King Leontes.

The Shepherd is one of Shakespeare's most charming minor creations, a true English rustic. He speaks in an upcountry dialect, remarking, "Mercy on 's, a barne!" on discovering Perdita

(3.3.69). In his touching reminiscence of his late wife (4.4.55–62), he conveys a strong and pleasant sense of rural domesticity. He is carefully distinguished from his buffoonish son by his gravity and sense of responsibility. Barring his understandable cowardice when threatened by a king, the Shepherd is a fine, upstanding man. As such he helps maintain the play's insistence on the essential goodness of humanity in the face of evil. (In some editions, the Shepherd is designated the Old Shepherd.)

Time Allegorical figure who appears as a CHORUS in *The Winter's Tale*. Time appears only in the 32 lines of 4.1, where, alone on the stage, he informs us that 16 years will have passed before the play resumes, in BOHEMIA. He briefly sums up the intervening years for King Leontes and Perdita and tells us we shall meet Florizel, the son of King Polixenes. After wishing the audience a good time, he withdraws. This isolated speech, which is virtually a PROLOGUE, makes it clear that we are about to witness a new drama altogether. From Time's pleasant, mildly humorous manner, we sense that the TRAGEDY of the first half of the play will be replaced by a COMEDY. Time's stilted language, which sounded somewhat old-fashioned even in Shakespeare's day, is arranged in rhyming couplets, unlike the speech of any other character. This is appropriate to his singular role, for as a chorus, Time is outside the world of the play and should not sound like anyone in it. Time says, "remember well / I mentioned a son o' th' king's" (4.1.21–22), referring to earlier passages (1.2.34, 163–171) where Florizel was spoken of but not named; the use of the first person singular here has suggested to some commentators that Time represents the author of the play—Shakespeare himself. However, this is unlikely, for as a virtually abstract figure, Time is distinctly not human. He is expressly immune from the change he brings to others—"The same I am, ere ancient'st order was, / Or what is now receiv'd" (4.1.10–11)—and as he is winged, he is visually nonhuman as well. The reference to his having "mentioned" simply means—with the mild humor that characterizes this figure—that the mentioning occurred in the past, which is a function of time.

PART III

Related Entries

academic drama Sixteenth-century literary and theatrical movement, the predecessor of ELIZABETHAN DRAMA. Beginning ca. 1540, a body of plays was written and performed, mostly in Latin, by faculty and students of England's two 16th-century universities, Oxford and Cambridge; of its chief graduate school, the INNS OF COURT in LONDON; and of several of England's private secondary schools. The best-known creators of academic drama were Nicholas UDALL and William Gager (ca. 1560–1622). Academic plays were secular, but they shared the moralizing, allegorical qualities of their medieval religious predecessors (see MORALITY PLAY). They were often intended to improve the Latin and public speech of the students, and compared to the popular theater of the 1580s they were often quite dull. Nevertheless, they created a generation of theatergoers and the first important group of English playwrights, the so-called UNIVERSITY WITS.

Actium Peninsula on the west coast of Greece, and thus the name given to the naval battle fought near it, which is enacted in 3.7–10 of *Antony and Cleopatra*. The battle of Actium marks the downfall of Mark Antony, whose fleet, allied with that of Queen Cleopatra, is defeated by the forces of Octavius Caesar. In 3.7 Cleopatra insists on participating in the battle despite the objections of Enobarbus, and Antony supports her by deciding to fight at sea—for the queen has only naval forces—despite the advice of his followers that Caesar is much weaker on land. In 3.8–9 the leaders deploy their

men, and in 3.10 Enobarbus, Scarus, and Canidius witness the climax of the battle as Cleopatra's ships flee and Antony orders his to follow hers. Canidius declares that he will desert Antony and joins Caesar, and though Enobarbus and Scarus remain loyal, they are severely downcast. We are convinced that Antony's fate has been determined by this battle, and this soon proves to be the case.

Shakespeare followed his source, PLUTARCH's *Lives*, fairly closely, though both he and Plutarch—who used an anti-Antony source—laid more emphasis on Antony's misjudgment than do modern scholars. In the summer of 31 B.C. Antony actually had a larger and better-equipped fleet than Caesar, while his land forces were somewhat undermanned. However, his men had not had much recent experience of naval warfare—conducted largely by ramming and boarding the enemy's ships in what amounted to infantry fighting on seaborne platforms—and Caesar's men had just completed a successful campaign against Pompey. Treachery was to be the most important factor, however; in the weeks before the battle, Antony's followers, including Enobarbus, began to desert. When the fleets met on September 2, it appears that most of Antony's men refused to fight, though scholars are in disagreement over the few details that have survived. In any case, Cleopatra's navy fled to Egypt, and Antony followed with a fraction of his own ships. The actual fighting was therefore confined to minor skirmishes, though the outcome was decisive, resulting in Caesar's assumption of complete power over the Roman world.

Adams, Joseph Quincy (1881–1946)   American scholar. A longtime professor at Cornell University and director of the FOLGER SHAKESPEARE LIBRARY from 1931 to 1946, Adams wrote a respected biography, *The Life of William Shakespeare* (1923), a volume on Elizabethan theaters, and other works. He was one of the successors to H. H. FURNESS as editor of the *New Variorum* edition of Shakespeare's works (see VARIORUM EDITION).

Addenbrooke, John (active 1608)   Debtor to Shakespeare. In December 1608 the STRATFORD court ordered Addenbrooke to pay a debt of £6 that he owed to Shakespeare. This was a sizeable amount of money, perhaps equal to a tenth of the playwright's annual income. In March 1609 the court reported that the debtor had moved from Stratford, and Shakespeare was forced to sue Addenbrooke's guarantor, the town blacksmith, Thomas Horneby, from whom he received the debt plus damages and court costs. Nothing more is known of Addenbrooke.

Adlington, William (active 1566)   English writer, translator of *The Golden Ass* by APULEIUS, a probable inspiration for *A Midsummer Night's Dream* and a possible minor source for *Cymbeline*. Adlington published his translation—from a French translation of Apuleius's second-century Latin—in 1566, and his book was popular, being reprinted in 1571, 1582, and 1596. Little is known about Adlington's life beyond an apparent association with Oxford University.

Admiral's Men   Acting company of the ELIZABETHAN THEATER, possible employer of the young Shakespeare, and later the chief rivals of his CHAMBERLAIN'S MEN. The company was originally organised in 1576 as Lord Howard's Men, under the patronage of Charles HOWARD, later Lord High Admiral of England. After touring the provinces for several years, they are first recorded in LONDON—as the Admiral's Men—in 1585, when the great actor Edward ALLEYN joined the troupe and became its leader. The company quickly established itself as a rival to the QUEEN'S MEN in the London theater world. They were especially famed for their presentations of the grandiose tragedies of Christopher MARLOWE.

By 1590 the Admiral's Men had a new rival, STRANGE'S MEN, but in that year the two companies joined forces at the THEATRE, owned by James BURBAGE. In May 1591 a dispute between Alleyn and Burbage disrupted the link, and Alleyn, along with many players of the combined group, moved to the ROSE THEATRE, owned by Philip HENSLOWE. However, when the theaters of London were closed by plague for much of 1593–94, Alleyn led a combined Admiral's-Strange's company on tour. When the theaters reopened in 1594, the two troupes separated again, with the Admiral's Men settling at the Rose for the next six years. From then on, the Admiral's and the Chamberlain's Men (as Strange's was now known) were the two leading London theater companies.

The Admiral's Men continued to revive Marlowe, but they also produced many new plays. Among the playwrights employed by the company were George CHAPMAN, Thomas DEKKER, Michael DRAYTON, Thomas HEYWOOD, and Anthony MUNDAY. Besides Alleyn, the principal actors included Thomas DOWNTON, Richard JONES, Martin SLATER, and Gabriel SPENCER. The company's name was formally changed to the Earl of Nottingham's Men when Howard was awarded the title in 1597, but they are invariably referred to as the Admiral's Men.

In 1598 the Admiral's Men were somewhat weakened when Spencer was killed (by Ben JONSON) and Alleyn retired from acting, though he continued as a partner in the company. He returned to the stage in 1600—at the personal request of Queen Elizabeth, according to rumor. The troupe moved to the new FORTUNE THEATRE, which they and their successors occupied for a quarter of a century. After the accession of King JAMES I in 1603, Howard was succeeded as patron by the new king's son, Prince Henry, after which the Admiral's Men were known as PRINCE HENRY'S MEN. They later became the PALSGRAVE'S MEN, finally closing in 1625.

Scholars believe that Shakespeare was probably a member of the combined troupe of the Admiral's Men and Strange's Men in 1590 and early 1591. This speculation is supported by the texts of *2* and *3 Henry VI*, which were apparently printed from the author's manuscript and included the names of the actors John HOLLAND and John SINCKLO, known to have been part of the combined company. Thus, it is thought that the young playwright wrote these works for production by the Admiral's-Strange's combine at the theater in 1590 or 1591. If this was indeed so, then he was doubtless an actor in the company as well.

Age of Kings, An   British Broadcasting Company production (1960) of Shakespeare's two tetralogies (see TETRALOGY) of HISTORY PLAYS. These eight works, which depict a continuous period from 1399 to 1485, were presented in 15 parts. This extraordinary production, which has been called "the first miniseries," offered a fresh point of view on several stories and characters. For instance, such episodes as the fall of Humphrey, Duke of Gloucester, are lent greater coherence by being isolated from their surroundings, and certain characters—notably Queen Margaret; the Duke of York; and Prince Hal, who becomes Henry V—demonstrate their growth as individuals over the several plays in which they appear.

Agincourt   Town in northern FRANCE, battle site in the HUNDRED YEARS' WAR and location for Act 4 of *Henry V.* The battle of Agincourt provides the climax of *Henry V* and of the second TETRALOGY of Shakespeare's HISTORY PLAYS. The English army, led by King Henry V, wins an impressive victory over a much larger French force. Henry attributes the triumph to divine intervention in favor of the English. Soundly defeated, FRANCE signs, in 5.2, a treaty granting Henry the inheritance of the French crown, as well as marriage to the King of France's daughter, Katharine. England thus achieves a glorious ascendancy over its traditional enemy.

Shakespeare's presentation of the battle focuses on King Henry. Henry may be seen as a chivalric hero, whose courage and high spirits—reflected particularly in his famous "St. Crispin's Day" speech (4.3.20–67)—and democratic identification with his soldiers, shown in 4.1, give his army the morale necessary to defeat the foe. On the other hand, Henry's assertion in the St. Crispin's Day

oration that he prefers to be outnumbered in order to garner greater honor smacks of the irrational bravado condemned in Hotspur in *1 Henry IV.* Similarly, his order to kill the French prisoners (4.6.37) may indicate a praiseworthy decisiveness at a critical moment, but it can also be interpreted as an act of militaristic savagery.

Historians place much more emphasis on the common soldiers than on Henry. A landmark battle in English and military history, Agincourt—fought on October 25, 1415—was indeed an extraordinary event: a crushing defeat was administered by a weary, sick, and badly damaged English force to a French army three times its size. The English victory was chiefly due to the shrewd use of batteries of longbowmen, who cut down the French cavalrymen before they could approach; it was the first victory of massed infantry over the mounted knights who had dominated medieval battlefields. Shakespeare omits this key feature of the battle in order to direct attention toward his protagonist more effectively. Moreover, despite the impressive English victory, Agincourt did not win France for Henry; it merely staved off defeat. He took his army back to England and reinvaded in 1417. Only three years later, after the conquest of Normandy, were the French prepared to negotiate the treaty of TROYES, presented in 5.2 of the play.

Aldridge, Ira   (ca. 1807–1867)   American actor. The first highly successful black actor, Aldridge was generally acknowledged to be the most accomplished American on the London stage in the 19th century. Particularly noted for his performances as Othello and Aaron (*Titus Andronicus*), Shakespeare's most prominent black characters, Aldridge was also acclaimed as Lear, Hamlet, Richard III, Shylock (*The Merchant of Venice*), Macbeth, and others. He performed in most of the major capitals of Europe and was universally regarded as among the great actors of his generation.

Born to a New York City minister, Aldridge was intended for the ministry himself, but he was attracted to the stage very early, appearing with a black acting company at the age of 14. Befriended by an English actor, Henry Wallack (1790–1870), Aldridge went to England in 1824 when he

Ira Aldridge as Othello. Denied opportunity in the United States because of his race, the actor found great success on the stages of Europe in the 19th century. *(Courtesy of Picture Collection, New York Public Library)*

recognized that racial prejudice would not permit him an acting career in America. He was immediately popular, and his evident talent and sophistication helped promote the growing movement for the abolition of slavery throughout the British Empire. Aldridge underwent a period of apprenticeship in provincial touring companies before he achieved success in London. He remained at the top of his profession for almost 40 years. He died on tour in Poland while preparing for a homecoming to America.

Alexander, Peter (1894–1969) British Shakespearean scholar, editor of an edition of Shakespeare's works and author of many works on the playwright and his times. A longtime professor at Glasgow University, Alexander is best known for his *Shakespeare's Life and Art* (1964) and his one-volume edition of the complete works (1951). He also convincingly established Shakespeare's authorship of the *Henry VI* plays in his *Shakespeare's Henry VI and Richard III* (1929).

Alexandria City in Egypt located on the Mediterranean coast at the western edge of the Nile River delta, the setting for many scenes in *Antony and Cleopatra*. Alexandria was the capital of the Ptolemaic Empire inherited by Cleopatra and was the site of her palace, where she conducted her affair with Mark Antony. It is to this sanctuary that the lovers retreat after being defeated by Caesar in the battle of ACTIUM, and it is where they die.

The magnificence of the Ptolemaic capital is implicit in the luxurious decadence of Antony and Cleopatra's life, with its servants and banquets—the reputation of "fine Egyptian cookery" (2.6.63) is several times admired—and in the pomp of their enthronement in "the market place" of Alexandria (3.6.3). The richness of Cleopatra's personal adornment, detailed in Enobarbus's famed description in 2.2.190–218 (though she was not in Alexandria at the time), confirms the impression. The city's huge and cosmopolitan population is hinted at in Antony's description of when he and the queen would "wander through the streets, and note / The qualities of people" (1.1.53–54). Cleopatra's recollections of delightful fishing expeditions, in 2.5.10–18, suggest the pleasures of a great city's riverfront.

Alexandria was the chief city of the eastern Mediterranean from its founding by Alexander the Great in 332 B.C. until its conquest by Arab invaders in the seventh century A.D. Until around the time of the play when its population—probably about 1 million—was surpassed by that of Rome, Alexandria was the largest city of the entire Western world. It remained the major cultural center of the Roman Empire and, later, the Byzantine Empire. The library at Alexandria was one of the great treasures of the ancient world, containing at one point around 750,000 volumes. Although the library's final destruction when it was torched by the Arabs ca. A.D. 640 is regarded as one of the greatest single acts of vandalism known, the Arab conquest merely completed a process that had begun much earlier; in fact, an early installment occurred when Antony's men, burning their vessels as Caesar approached after the battle of Actium, accidentally set fire to the library and destroyed an unknown quantity of its contents.

Allde, Edward (ca. 1583–1624)   London printer, producer of editions of several of Shakespeare's works. In 1597 Allde printed part of the first, pirated, QUARTO edition of *Romeo and Juliet* when the original printer, John DANTER, was suspended by the STATIONERS' COMPANY for another such piracy. Allde himself underwent suspensions later in the same year, and again in 1599, for printing illicit Catholic materials. However, he was generally successful, printing mostly poetry and plays. In 1611 he printed the third quarto of *Titus Andronicus* for publisher Edward WHITE, and the second quarto of "The Phoenix and Turtle."

Alleyn, Edward (1566–1626)   English actor, the leader of the ADMIRAL'S MEN and the foremost actor of Shakespeare's day. The son of a LONDON innkeeper, Alleyn was a teenage actor in WORCESTER'S MEN, then a provincial company, before joining the Admiral's Men around 1585 and soon becoming its leader. In 1592 he married the daughter of the theatrical entrepreneur Philip HENSLOWE and formed a partnership with him that lasted until Henslowe's death in 1616. From 1590 to 1594 Alleyn led the combined Admiral's and STRANGE'S MEN companies, which toured the provinces during an outbreak of plague in London. Alleyn's letters from this tour to his wife and father-in-law have survived, and they reveal an amiable and conscientious young man. In the 1590s Alleyn was famous as a great tragedian, especially in the plays of Christopher MARLOWE; Thomas NASHE declared him the best actor "since before Christ was borne" and Ben JONSON was later to declare to him, "others speak, but only thou dost act." When he retired briefly, around 1598, it was said that Queen Elizabeth personally asked him to return to the stage. He did so in 1600 but retired for good in 1604.

He retained a financial interest in PRINCE HENRY'S MEN, as the Admiral's Men were known after the accession of King JAMES I, along with other investments, theatrical and otherwise. By this time Alleyn was quite a wealthy man. With Henslowe, he was a part-owner of the FORTUNE THEATRE, which they had built, and of the licence to operate the London bear-baiting arena. He also had profitable real-estate holdings in and around London, and he later inherited Henslowe's interest in the HOPE THEATRE and the Fortune. In 1605 he bought a manor in Dulwich (now a south London suburb, then a rural hamlet), where he moved in 1613. He founded Dulwich College there, a hospital and school for poor families; it is now the site of a small museum, housing a collection of European paintings along with Alleyn and Henslowe's papers, which provide a rich assemblage of 16th-century theater lore. Alleyn's wife died in 1623; he remarried in the same year, to the daughter of the poet John Donne (1573–1631).

Amyot, Jacques (1513–1593)   French writer and translator of PLUTARCH's *Lives*. Amyot's Plutarch, published in 1559 and now regarded as one of the greatest works of 16th-century French prose, was in turn translated into English by Sir Thomas NORTH and became Shakespeare's primary source for *Antony and Cleopatra, Coriolanus, Julius Caesar,* and *Timon of Athens* and a minor source for other plays. Amyot, born in great poverty, became a leading humanistic churchman and scholar, serving as Bishop of Auxerre and tutor to two French kings-to-be.

Anderson, Judith (1898–1992)   Australian-born American actress. Anderson came to America in 1918 and began a long and successful career on the New York stage. Perhaps best known for her Medea, she is particularly associated with passionate and ruthless characters. Her Shakespearean roles included Lady Macbeth—in the 1941 production of Margaret WEBSTER and in a 1960 FILM, both times opposite Maurice Evans—and Queen Gertrude, opposite John GIELGUD's Hamlet, in 1936. Anderson also played Hamlet herself, carrying on a tradition of female Hamlets extending back to the 18th century; she took the part in 1971, at the age of 73.

Anderson, Mary (1859–1940)   American actress. Anderson, a California native, made her debut as Juliet in Louisville, Kentucky, at 16. She then toured American cities for several years and established herself in New York at 18, in 1877. In 1882 she went to London, where she was successful in a variety of roles, including Juliet and Rosalind. She returned to New York in 1885 and was regarded as one of the leading lights of the American theater. In 1887 she was the first actress to play both Perdita and Hermione in *The Winter's Tale*. Two years later she married and retired from the stage. She settled in England, near STRATFORD, where she lived the rest of her life.

Andrew Ship mentioned in *The Merchant of Venice*, a reference that helps scholars to date the play. Salerio alludes to a shipwreck as an "Andrew dock'd in sand" (1.1.27); in the original published edition of the play, the name *Andrew* was printed in italics, evidently denoting a ship. Shakespeare was referring to an event of 1596 in which an English naval force, commanded by Robert Devereux, Earl of ESSEX, and Charles HOWARD, captured or sank most of the ships in Cadiz, Spain's greatest Atlantic port, and sacked the town. One of the principal prizes of this expedition was the ship *St. Andrew,* which was seized after having run aground during the battle; this vessel became an important British warship over the next few years. The news of the battle at Cadiz reached London on July 30, 1596; therefore Shakespeare could not have completed *The Merchant of Venice* before then. Shakespeare's audiences doubtless recognized the reference, but its sense was lost to later generations until 20th-century scholarship rediscovered its meaning.

Angiers City in northwestern FRANCE, present-day Angers, location for Acts 2 and 3 of *King John* and one scene in *1 Henry VI*. Angiers, capital of ANJOU, the ancient homeland of the PLANTAGENET kings, is presented as a focus of the conflict between France and England. In 2.1 of *King John* two armies face each other at the gates of the city, which is acknowledged to be loyal to England. King John of England is opposed by the French ruler, King Philip, who is backing Arthur, whose crown John is said to have usurped. Each side attempts to persuade the town to admit its forces and honor its choice of king. The representative of Angiers—a Citizen or Hubert in various editions—devises a diplomatic solution: John's niece Blanche can marry Philip's son Lewis.

However, this alliance is quickly dissolved when the papal legate Pandulph persuades Philip to declare war on John, and Angiers is the scene of a battle in 3.2. England's Queen Eleanor is almost captured, but John defeats the French and seizes Arthur.

The events of 2.1 are fictitious, devised by Shakespeare to dramatize the disputed succession. He sets the scene in Angiers, the traditional Plantagenet seat, to provide a recognizable symbol of the English holdings in France. Similarly, the events of 3.1 are transferred to Angiers from their historical site at Mirabeau, a castle elsewhere in Anjou. In 5.3 of *1 Henry VI*, another invented scene, Joan La Pucelle, or Joan of Arc, attempts to summon supernatural Fiends while at Angiers.

Anjou Region in northwestern FRANCE, a theater of operations in the HUNDRED YEARS' WAR and the location for several scenes in *1 Henry VI*. Three scenes, 5.2–4, are set in Anjou and concern the capture and trial of Joan La Pucelle, or Joan of Arc. In 5.3 Joan attempts to enlist the aid of Fiends at ANGIERS, present-day Angers, the capital of Anjou. Angiers is also the location of several scenes in *King John*.

Annesley, Brian (d. 1603) Contemporary of Shakespeare, a possible model for King Lear. In 1603 Annesley, a onetime gentleman of the court of Queen Elizabeth, had become insane and was the object of a court case; two of his three daughters sought to have him committed and his estates turned over to them. The third daughter, Cordell (a variant form of Cordelia), opposed them and wrote to King JAMES I's minister, Robert CECIL, asserting that her father's service to the late monarch deserved a better reward than the madhouse. Cecil intervened and Annesley lived his final months in the care of a family friend. He bequeathed his estates to Cordell, and the other sisters went to court again but failed to break the will. This family was known to Shakespeare's patron and friend Henry Wriothesley, Earl of SOUTHAMPTON; in fact, Cordell Annesley married Southampton's stepfather, William HERVEY, not long after her father's death. It is thus quite likely that the playwright—who was writing *King Lear* at the time of or shortly after Brian Annesley's death—knew of this case of madness and filial loyalty and may have incorporated something of it in his play.

Antioch   Capital city of the ancient Seleucid Kingdom, located in what is now Turkey, the setting for the first scene of *Pericles*. Pericles discovers the secret of the incestuous love between King Antiochus the Great and his Daughter, and he must flee the king's anger. Thus, the decadence of Antioch, a famously opulent center of luxury and power in the ancient world, is seen to harbor the root of the evil that propels Pericles into a wandering exile.

Antium   Ancient Italian city on the Mediterranean coast south of ROME, the setting for three scenes of *Coriolanus*. Antium is the home of Aufidius, the leader of the Volscians. When the Roman general Coriolanus is expelled from Rome, he seeks revenge and goes to Antium, in 4.4 and 4.5, and offers his services to his country's enemies. Coriolanus's mother dissuades him from sacking Rome with his victorious Volscian troops, and he makes a treaty instead. After this, in 5.6 he reports to the Volscian leaders in Antium, where Aufidius accuses him of treason and kills him. There is no hint, in dialogue or stage directions, as to the character of the city; Shakespeare merely followed his source, PLUTARCH's *Lives*, when he placed the action there. (There is some confusion as to the location of 5.6, which seems to be Antium in 5.6.50, 73, and 80, and CORIOLES in 5.6.90. However, the latter reference is probably rhetorical, though Shakespeare may have carelessly incorporated two settings. This is the sort of error that recurs throughout the plays, and most editors omit a location in the introductory stage directions or place the scene in Antium.)

The historical Antium—the modern Anzio—was an important Volscian stronghold, but it became a Roman colony several centuries after the time of the play's action. Later, as part of the Roman Empire, Antium was an aristocratic resort town. It has provided several artistically significant archaeological sites, including the famed villa of the emperor Nero.

apocrypha   Works of dubious authenticity, a term usually associated with certain biblical texts but also useful in literary scholarship. Numerous plays and poems have been attributed to Shakespeare at various times, but it is generally thought that they were written by others and are thus outside the CANON; these comprise the Shakespeare apocrypha. While nearly 50 works, in whole or in part, have been assigned to Shakespeare at some time, only a few have ever been seriously enough proposed to be regarded as (even) apocryphal. Six of these were attributed to the playwright in the Third FOLIO. They are LOCRINE, THE LONDON PRODIGAL, THE PURITAN, SIR JOHN OLDCASTLE, THOMAS LORD CROMWELL, and A YORKSHIRE TRAGEDY. Others include ARDEN OF FEVERSHAM, THE BIRTH OF MERLIN, EDMUND IRONSIDE, FAIR EM, THE MERRY DEVIL OF EDMONTON, and MUCEDORUS. *Edward III*, long numbered among the apocrypha (as in the first edition of this book), has received a critical reappraisal in the last decade and is now considered by many commentators to be at least in part by Shakespeare and thus part of the canon. In addition, the authorship of *Pericles* and *The Two Noble Kinsmen* remains in sufficient dispute that these two plays, though commonly included in the canon (as they are in this book), are sometimes placed among the apocrypha, as is *Sir Thomas More*, which contains only a few pages by Shakespeare.

Apuleius, Lucius   (b. ca. A.D. 123)   Roman writer, author of a rare surviving Latin novel, a probable inspiration for *A Midsummer Night's Dream* and a possible minor source for *Cymbeline*. Apuleius's *Metamorphoses*, better known as *The Golden Ass*, is a delightful account of a young traveler who dabbles in magic and is accidentally transformed into an ass; in this form he undergoes many adventures before he is restored by the goddess Isis. The transformation of Bottom in *A Midsummer Night's Dream* probably comes from this famous tale, still widely read today, and the substitution of a sleeping potion for a poison in *Cymbeline* may reflect Apuleius's use of the same device.

Apuleius specifically identifies his hero—named Lucius—with himself, and his account of an initiation into the sacred mysteries of Isis and Osiris—of great interest to scholars—is presumed to be autobiographical. Apuleius was born in Carthage and in his youth he traveled throughout the Roman Empire. While in Egypt he married and was charged with witchcraft by his bride's disappointed suitor. His defense, which survives as his *Apologia*, offers a tantalizing glimpse of provincial life in the ancient world. He returned to his home, where he became a noted poet, philosopher, and religious leader. A number of works survive besides *The Golden Ass* and the *Apologia*, mostly miscellaneous philosophical and literary essays, while a great deal more, including his famed poetry, is lost.

Arden, Forest of   Anglicization of the Ardennes, a wooded region on the borders of France, Belgium, and Luxembourg, the setting for most of *As You Like It*. Shakespeare's Forest of Arden, like BELMONT in *The Merchant of Venice* and the island in *The Tempest*, is an artificial world, explicitly removed from society. Here, relatively free from pressure and stress, the characters can find themselves and settle conflicts that escape solution in the real world. Arden is equivalent to Arcadia, the land where amorous shepherds and shepherdesses lead an ideal existence in the PASTORAL literary tradition that *As You Like It* both draws on and lovingly parodies.

We first hear of Arden as the place where the exiled Duke Senior "and a many merry men with him . . . live like the old Robin Hood of England . . . and fleet the time carelessly as they did in the golden world" (1.1.114–119), referring to the classical myth of a golden age when an idyllic life was led in the countryside. However, Arden is not a paradise. The duke's praise of his bucolic exile is tempered by his awareness of nature's implacable strength, the "churlish chiding of the winter's wind" (2.1.7), and his dislike of the need to kill the forest's deer for food. The duke acknowledges that he has "seen better days" (2.7.120). Moreover, Shakespeare's shepherds are not at all idealized: Silvius is a parody of the sentimental Arcadian shepherd, and Corin is a down-to-earth representative of real rural life. Arden may provide a refuge, but it does not offer a perfect existence. Further, when the duke is restored to power at the close of the play, all of the exiles—except the pessimistic and melancholy Jaques—are instantly ready to return from Arden to the real world. In the mean-time, love has culminated in four marriages, the traditional happy ending in a COMEDY; the artificial world has produced the expected resolutions.

Shakespeare followed his source, Thomas LODGE's *Rosalynde*, in placing his Arcadia in the Ardennes. This forest seemed especially significant in the 16th century because it was a romantic setting in Ludovico ARIOSTO's *Orlando Furioso*, one of the most popular books of its day (from which Shakespeare probably took the name Orlando). The name Arden will also have been familiar to the playwright and his audience as that of an ancient wooded area in WARWICKSHIRE—Shakespeare's mother's family may have taken their name from it (see ARDEN, ROBERT)—though no forest remained there in Elizabethan times.

Arden, Robert (d. 1556)   Shakespeare's maternal grandfather. A gentleman farmer, Arden was a minor member of the gentry. He owned land in both Wilmcote and Snitterfield, villages near STRATFORD, most of which he leased to other farmers. One of these was Richard SHAKESPEARE, whose son was to marry Arden's youngest daughter, Mary Arden SHAKESPEARE, around 1558.

Arden was one of the most prosperous farmers of the Stratford region. He had eight daughters, six of whom married (and were supplied with dowries), and when he died he left Mary several substantial parcels of land. He is traditionally associated with the Ardens of Park Hall, a lordly WARWICKSHIRE family that was among the very few English families whose ancestry could be traced to before the Norman Conquest. In the Domesday Book (A.D. 1085), an Arden held more land than any other Englishman, and the family took its name from a vast forest that it owned (not to be confused with the Forest of ARDEN in *As You Like It*). However, no records substantiate this connection, and while Robert Arden may have had an ancestor who was a younger son of the Park Hall Ardens, his own circumstances were quite modest by comparison.

Arden of Feversham   Anonymous play formerly attributed to Shakespeare, part of the Shakespeare APOCRYPHA. *Arden of Feversham* was published in

1592, 1599, and 1633. It was not until 1770 that a printer and amateur scholar from Faversham—the modern spelling of the play's setting—published a fourth edition of the play in which he attributed it to Shakespeare and sparked a century of debate. Among many notable commentators, only Algernon SWINBURNE favored the attribution. Modern scholars generally ascribe the play to Thomas KYD, but in any case it is unlike any of Shakespeare's known works and thus is an unlikely candidate for inclusion in the CANON.

Arden of Feversham is the story of a famous murder that took place in the English town of Faversham in 1551: One Thomas Arden was killed by men hired by his wife, Susan, and her lover, a family servant. The play records Mistress Arden's obsessive intent, through several failures and the withdrawal of several conspirators. She finally succeeds, only to be discovered and sentenced to death with her lover, who romantically declares, "Faith, I care not, seeing I die with Susan."

argument Literary device, a plot summary preceding or concluding a long work. Shakespeare used a prose argument as a preface to his narrative poem *The Rape of Lucrece.* The argument was a conventional attribute of long poems in the 16th century; RENAISSANCE writers adopted it from classical tradition and used it to present the reasons why a work was written and to state the points that the author intended to make. Readers were thus provided with a prior awareness of the contents of the work, freeing them to focus on its purely literary values.

In the argument to *Lucrece,* Shakespeare briefly rendered the story of Tarquin's lust for Lucrece and its consequences. This account is somewhat fuller than it is in the poem itself. It describes the despotic and warlike ways of the Roman king and relates how his son, Tarquin, was seized with an uncontrollable desire for Lucrece, the wife of Collatine, a Roman general. (It is at this point that the poem begins.) The argument goes on to summarize the poem, and its last sentence makes clear what the poem only implies—that the revenge later taken upon Tarquin resulted in the downfall of the monarchy and the establishment of the Roman Republic. The argument thus offers a larger view of the personal tragedy that the poem details, demonstrating the breadth of political and social concern that also informs many of Shakespeare's plays.

Ariosto, Ludovico (1474–1533) Italian poet whose work became source material for several of Shakespeare's plays. Ariosto's epic poem *Orlando Furioso* (1516, and a longer version in 1532) was one of the most popular literary works of the 16th and 17th centuries. One of the many stories in it contributed an important element to the plot of *Much Ado About Nothing*: the disguising of Margaret as Hero in order to deceive Claudio. Also, Shakespeare gave the name of Ariosto's title character to the romantic lead in *As You Like It,* knowing that his audience would associate it with the lush enchantment of *Orlando Furioso.* The playwright may have known the work in both an Italian edition (probably that of 1532) and the English translation by Sir John HARINGTON (1591).

Another work by Ariosto contributed to two other Shakespeare plays. His play *I Suppositi* (1509), translated into English as *Supposes* by George GASCOIGNE (performed 1566, published 1575), provided the subplot concerning Bianca in *The Taming of the Shrew.* Further, *Supposes* provided the device used to fool the Pedant in the same play, an invented hostility between cities said to endanger the traveling citizen of one of them. A ruse in Ariosto and *The Shrew,* the same situation is real in *A Comedy of Errors,* where Egeon faces the death penalty in consequence.

Italian literature—and the work of Ariosto in particular—was extremely fashionable in Elizabethan England, but behind Ariosto were ancient roots that Shakespeare will also have appreciated. In the original Italian text of *I Suppositi,* a PROLOGUE, thought to have been spoken by Ariosto himself at the first performance, expressly refers to *his* sources—the ancient Roman dramatists PLAUTUS and TERENCE—and also mentions *their* sources in Greek New Comedy. Thus, in deriving his tale of romantic intrigue from Ariosto's work, Shakespeare was adding to a theatrical tradition already almost 2,000 years old.

Aristotle (384–322 B.C.) Ancient Greek philosopher, author of a source for *Troilus and Cressida* and possibly *The Tempest*. Aristotle is one of the few Shakespearean sources to be mentioned in a play using his work. Hector, in *Troilus*, cites the philosopher's opinion that young men are "Unfit to hear moral philosophy" (2.2.168) because in their immaturity they form opinions based on their emotions rather than reason. Shakespeare knew this dictum from the *Nicomachean Ethics*, translated into English by John Wilkinson in 1547. Not only does Shakespeare have Hector employ Aristotle's arguments, scholars surmise that the personalities of Hector and Troilus, and perhaps other characters, were influenced by the psychological types Aristotle proposed in the *Ethics* to illustrate points of morality.

A related aspect of the *Nicomachean Ethics* may have influenced Shakespeare's creation of Caliban in *The Tempest*. Aristotle believed in the necessity of civilization, seeing humanity as naturally incapable of moral behavior. He saw "natural man"—as morally defective, unable to distinguish good from bad, and thus "bestial." He cited "canibals," reported among the remote barbarians outside the Greek world, as an instance of such people. The animal-like nature of "the beast Caliban" (4.1.140), as Prospero matter-of-factly calls him, is repeatedly referred to, and he is pointedly incapable of understanding wrong, as when he casually acknowledges having attempted to rape Miranda. His name, moreover, is an anagram of "canibal," an accepted 17th-century spelling.

Aristotle was the first thinker to analyze the way drama works; his *Poetics* is regarded as the fountainhead of European dramatic criticism. This book on TRAGEDY (a companion work on COMEDY has not survived) assesses the Greek drama of Aristotle's day and concludes that the best tragedies have certain characteristics in common. They focus on characters who are essentially good people but who commit a gross moral error through no fault of their own; these plays also deal with family relationships, thereby intensifying the conflict. A well-written work inspires both pity and fear in the audience, so intensely as to elevate our awareness of these emotions. The release from this highly charged response is called *catharsis*—an idea, in various interpretations, that has influenced most critical thought since Aristotle.

However, although Aristotle and his followers were widely studied in universities throughout the Middle Ages, and his ideas were the common coin of literate society (he is mentioned as an object of study in *The Taming of the Shrew* [1.1.32]), his influence on ELIZABETHAN DRAMA was largely indirect, for the *Poetics* was not translated into English until after Shakespeare's day. The *Nicomachean Ethics* was the only translation of Aristotle available in the playwright's lifetime. Though Sir Philip SIDNEY and others wrote about Aristotle's critical theory, it had a greater effect on poetry than the theater. Shakespeare and his fellow dramatists knew classical drama chiefly through the works of SENECA, which are very different from those Aristotle analyzed. Nevertheless, the similarity between the Aristotelian ideal of tragedy and Shakespearean practice indicates that the ancient thinker's opinions had been effectively transmitted.

Aristotle was, with the slightly earlier Plato (ca. 429–347 B.C.), one of the Western world's seminal thinkers. Between the two, they formulated most of the categories and concepts—from theology to aesthetic criticism—that have since governed philosophy. The son of a Macedonian physician, Aristotle began to study in ATHENS under Plato at the age of 17. After Plato's death he headed schools of his own in various locations, and for several years he tutored Alexander the Great (356–323 B.C.). He taught again in Athens after 335, establishing a scholarly community that conducted research on a large scale, on subjects ranging from politics to botany. After Alexander's death, anti-Macedonian sentiment led to Aristotle's flight from Athens, and he died in exile. Much of his writing has been lost, but the remainder constitutes a major component of the Western intellectual heritage, and his work is still studied intensively by students in a variety of disciplines.

Armin, Robert (d. 1615) Famed English comic actor, probably the original portrayer of Touchstone (*As You Like It*), Feste (*Twelfth Night*), and other comic roles in Shakespeare. Listed in the FIRST FOLIO as among the 26 "Principall Actors" of Shakespeare's plays, Armin joined the CHAMBERLAIN'S MEN in 1599, apparently replacing Will

KEMPE as the company's chief comic actor. Shakespeare's comic characters changed significantly at that time to exploit Armin's particular talents. Armin was a small man whose skills were verbal and musical, in contrast to the physical humor of Kempe, and he was accordingly better cast as a clever FOOL than a bumbling CLOWN. The dialogue Shakespeare provided for him is filled with wordplay and ingenious arguments, and his characters often sing. Among the Shakespearean parts he is believed to have originated, besides Feste and Touchstone, are Thersites, in *Troilus and Cressida,* and the Fool of *King Lear.* Shakespeare may have intended Viola's remark upon meeting Feste—"This fellow is wise enough to play the fool" (*Twelfth Night,* 3.1.61)—as a compliment to Armin.

By all reports a highly competent actor, Armin was capable of playing different sorts of comic parts; he is known to have played Dogberry, in *Much Ado About Nothing,* reviving a part originated by Kempe, and he probably played *Cymbeline's* Cloten as well. Moreover, outside his Shakespearean roles, Armin specialized in a character type that he devised himself, a doltish simpleton called John of the Hospital. Armin wrote at least one play, *The Two Maids of Moreclacke* (ca. 1598), and two books of comedy routines and jokes, *Foole upon Foole* (1600, reissued as *A Nest of Ninnies* in 1608) and *Quips upon Questions* (1600).

Arne, Thomas Augustine (1710–1787) English composer, creator of music for several Shakespearean SONGS. The leading theatrical composer of the mid-18th century, Arne wrote for OPERAS, MASQUEs, and plays. He composed incidental music for seven of Shakespeare's plays and set a number of the songs to music, including "Under the greenwood tree" and "Blow, blow, thou winter wind" from *As You Like It* (2.5.1–8, 35–42; 2.7.174–193). "When daisies pied" from *Love's Labour's Lost* (5.2.886–921), and "Where the bee sucks" from *The Tempest* (5.1.88–94). However, Arne is probably best known today for having written "Rule Britannia."

Asche, Oscar (1871–1936) English actor, playwright, and producer. Asche is probably best known as the author and director of *Chu-Chin-Chow* (1916), a musical that ran for five years, setting a record that was astonishing for its day. However, he was also a notable Shakespearean director and actor, famous for his portrayals of Othello, King Claudius, Falstaff, and Shylock. In 1906–07 he staged a season of acclaimed Shakespearean productions: *Measure for Measure, As You Like It, The Taming of the Shrew,* and *Othello.* Another famous presentation was his modern-dress *Merry Wives of Windsor,* notorious for Falstaff's repeated exit line: "Taxi!"

Ashbourne portrait (Kingston portrait) Oil painting once thought to portray Shakespeare. Upon its discovery by art historians in 1847, when it was owned by a Clement Kingston of Ashbourne in Derby, the Ashbourne portrait, also known as the Kingston portrait, was acclaimed as a likely depiction of the playwright, and it was so considered for over a century. However, when it was cleaned in 1979, the coat of arms of the true sitter, one Hugh Hammersley, was revealed. (See also PORTRAITS OF SHAKESPEARE.)

Ashcroft, Peggy (1907–1991) English actress. After achieving stardom at 23 playing Desdemona opposite Paul ROBESON, Ashcroft, who was created a Dame Commander of the Order of the British Empire in 1956, played most of Shakespeare's major roles for women. In her youth she was acclaimed as virtually all of Shakespeare's romantic heroines. In 1932 alone, she played Imogen, Juliet, Miranda, Perdita, Portia, and Rosalind; remarkably, she could still triumph in these roles many years later—for instance, as Beatrice in 1950 (opposite John GIELGUD) and as Imogen in 1957. She played the great tragic heroines as well: Desdemona, Ophelia, Cordelia, Cleopatra. Perhaps her most remarkable role—often cited as one of the great performances of all time—was as Queen Margaret in the BBC's "The Wars of the Roses" (1964). She portrayed Margaret as she appears in all four plays of the minor TETRALOGY, growing from the naive young woman of *1 Henry VI* to a courageous military leader to the shrieking and cursing, half-insane ex-queen of *Richard III.*

Aspinall, Alexander (ca. 1546–1624)   Resident of STRATFORD and probable friend of Shakespeare. Aspinall was master of the Stratford grammar school for 42 years, beginning in 1582; however, Shakespeare had probably left the school a few years earlier (records for the period have not survived). Aspinall and Shakespeare both became prominent figures in Stratford—Aspinall was an alderman and a clerk of the town council—and were neighbors when the playwright lived at NEW PLACE. They were certainly among the most literate and cultured citizens of Stratford, and thus they must have been closely acquainted, at least after Shakespeare retired from London in about 1610.

In 1594 Aspinall was married. In courting his wife, he sent her a pair of gloves, accompanied by the following three-line poem that—according to an account written half a century later—Shakespeare composed: "The gift is small / The will is all / Alexander Aspinall." The tradition is highly questionable but it has not been disproved, and, if true, it provides a charming glimpse of the newly successful poet and playwright playfully assisting the romance of an older friend.

Aspley, William (d. 1640)   Publisher and bookseller in LONDON. In 1600 Aspley, in partnership with Andrew WISE, published QUARTO editions of both *Much Ado About Nothing* and *2 Henry IV*. He was also a member of the syndicates that published the FIRST FOLIO (1623) and the Second FOLIO (1632), apparently by virtue of his rights in these two plays. He also published and sold plays by several other playwrights, including George CHAPMAN and Thomas DEKKER.

Astor Place riot   See FORREST, EDWIN.

Athens   City in Greece, the setting for *A Midsummer Night's Dream, Timon of Athens, The Two Noble Kinsmen*, and two scenes of *Antony and Cleopatra*. Although references in the dialogue and stage directions of the three full plays set in Athens make it clear where the action is occurring, there is nothing distinctively Athenian in any of them. Shakespeare simply followed his sources in placing his stories in the ancient cultural capital of the

Mediterranean world, without troubling to depict the city itself. Only in *Timon* is there any hint of the historical Athens, for the controversial career of Alcibiades is sketchily presented.

In *Antony and Cleopatra*, Mark Antony establishes his headquarters in Athens between the reestablishment of his alliance with Octavius Caesar and its crumbling into the warfare that results in his final defeat in 3.4 and 3.5. Here Shakespeare simply followed history (as presented in PLUTARCH's *Lives*) in establishing Antony in Athens, and again he makes no effort to delineate the city itself.

Atkins, Robert (1886–1972)   English actor and producer. Atkins joined the company at the OLD VIC THEATRE in 1915, and between 1919 and 1925 he directed the Old Vic's complete cycle of Shakespeare's plays. His was the first modern production of *Pericles* (1921), and he startled London with an *Antony and Cleopatra* presented on a bare stage (1922). In 1927–28 he led a Shakespeare company in Egypt. During World War II he ran the Shakespeare Memorial Theatre in STRATFORD, and after the war he produced plays in an outdoor theater in London. Among his notable later productions was *All's Well That Ends Well* (1949), in which he played Lafew.

Atkinson, William (active 1613)   London clerk, a witness to the sale of the BLACKFRIARS GATEHOUSE to Shakespeare in 1613. Atkinson, who was employed by the brewers' guild, may have been recruited as a witness to the signing of this complex business deal by Shakespeare's cotrustee William JOHNSON. Johnson was the proprietor of the MERMAID TAVERN and was probably acquainted with Atkinson through his business.

Auden, Wystan Hugh (1907–1973)   English-American poet and essayist, commentator on Shakespeare in essays and lectures, and author of a long poem, *The Sea and the Mirror*, based on *The Tempest*, and of the libretto for an OPERA version of *Love's Labor's Lost*. Having established himself as both the leading English poet of the 1930s and one of the major British intellectual presences of the day, Auden moved to America just before World

War II. He became an American citizen and lived in New York for many years, writing some of his best and most significant work there before returning to England late in life.

In 1946–47 Auden taught a course on Shakespeare at the New School for Social Research in New York City. His lectures, reconstructed from the notes of students, were published posthumously as *Lectures on Shakespeare* (2000) and have been regarded since as an important resource for readers of both Shakespeare and Auden. A recent convert to Anglicanism, Auden stressed what he called the "Christian psychology" of Shakespeare's plays (without regarding them as explicitly religious), arguing that "Shakespeare's understanding of psychology is based on Christian assumptions . . . [including that] everyone has a will capable of choice. Man is a tempted being, living with what he does and suffers in time, the medium in which he realizes his potential character. . . . The good may fall, the bad may repent, and suffering can be, not a simple retribution, but a triumph."

Auden's book-length poem, *The Sea and the Mirror*, subtitled *A Commentary on Shakespeare's Work*, was written between 1942 and 1944 and is often considered the masterpiece of his career. The poem is formally in dialogue, as if it were a drama, though each character speaks a monologue, each in a different verse style. The poem begins as though set in a theater after a performance of *The Tempest*. After a "Preface" consisting of remarks by the Stage Manager, each of *The Tempest*'s characters speaks: First Prospero, seemingly about to leave his island, as at the close of Shakespeare's play, makes a farewell speech to Ariel that, though loving, stresses a need for independence of the magic the sprite represents, saying, "I am glad I have freed you . . . / for under your influence death is inconceivable" and true human fulfillment not possible. He regrets having only stirred hatred in Caliban but is otherwise content to be leaving, though he is wearily conscious of his mortality. Then, aboard ship en route to Milan, the other characters (excepting Caliban and Ariel) converse, talking about the world of the play and their possible futures, each of them seeming to represent some human tendency or characteristic, and each speaking in a different verse form. Next, Caliban addresses the audience, in a long prose reflection on the relationship between art and life. He seems, he knows, to be a crude interloper in Ariel's magical world, but he proposes himself as a necessary repository, as it were, for Ariel's magic, as the crude realities of life are necessary if art's refinement is to have an audience. He goes on to warn artists, however, that they must beware of Ariel's disinclination to accept this conjunction; art claims a high calling. He insists, nevertheless, that the Caliban in the artist must be given his due. In a "Postscript," Ariel responds to Caliban in a brief poem that is a lyrical profession of love—he is, he says, "helplessly in love with you, / Elegance, art, fascination, / Fascinated by / Drab mortality"—and confirms the necessary blending of art and life. Ever since its publication, *The Sea and the Mirror* has generated comment about both itself and *The Tempest*.

Acclaimed as one of the greatest poets of the 20th century, Auden wrote some of the best-known poems of his time, including "September 1st, 1939," "Law Like Love," "O Tell Me the Truth About Love," "Musée des Beaux Arts," and "In Praise of Limestone." He was also a prolific essayist, writing mostly on literary topics, including Shakespeare, but also a wealth of other material, notably including reportage on two wars, in Spain and China. He also wrote several opera libretti, set to the music of Igor Stravinsky (1882–1971) and others, including Nicholas NABOKOV, for whom he and Chester Kallman (1921–75) wrote the words to the opera *Love's Labor's Lost* (written 1969; premiered 1973).

authorship controversy Dispute surrounding the identity of Shakespeare. Despite a wealth of evidence, a modern cult supports the proposition that someone other than Shakespeare—the identification varies—wrote the plays that are attributed to him. Shakespeare, it is contended, was an ignorant, perhaps illiterate, minor actor who was surely incapable of producing such literature. It is further contended that only an aristocratic, learned person could have done so, and that such a person would not have wished to be associated with the theater. Therefore, it is concluded, the learned man assumed the actor's name as a disguise. A wide range of people have been nominated as the genuine author. Francis

Bacon (1561–1626) was the favorite when the craze first developed in the mid-19th century, though there have been many others since, including Christopher MARLOWE; Robert Devereux, Earl of ESSEX; William Stanley, Earl of DERBY; Francis Manners, Earl of RUTLAND; Edward de Vere, Earl of OXFORD; and Queen Elizabeth (see Elizabeth I in *Henry VIII*)—to name only some who actually lived during Shakespeare's lifetime. The current trend is toward Oxford, although he was a playwright without benefit of disguise and died midway through Shakespeare's career. Scholars of the period know beyond doubt that Shakespeare wrote Shakespeare, but the authorship controversy remains a minor sideshow of the literary world, and it will doubtless continue to get publicity. S. SCHOENBAUM summed up scholarly opinion of the controversy when he wrote, "One thought perhaps offers a crumb of redeeming comfort . . . the energy absorbed by the mania might otherwise have gone into politics."

Auvergne   Region   in   south-central   FRANCE, where 2.3 of *1 Henry VI* is set. The Countess of Auvergne attempts to capture the English lord Talbot there.

Ayscough, Samuel (1745–1804)   English scholar, the compiler of the first concordance of Shakespeare's works. Ayscough, a librarian at the British Museum, published his *Index, or Concordance of the Works of Shakespeare* in 1790.

B

bad quarto An early edition of a Shakespeare play, usually in QUARTO format, whose text was reconstructed from memory by actors who had performed the play, rather than coming from an authoritative source that accurately reflected what Shakespeare had written, such as his FOUL PAPERS. These texts, which the editors of the FIRST FOLIO described as "stolen, and surreptitious copies, maimed, and deformed by the frauds and stealthes of iniurious impostors," were presumably made for purposes of piracy. Publishers—or, in some cases, a rival acting company—could profit from a play's popularity even though the script was jealously kept secret by the acting company that had produced the play.

The eight undoubted bad quarto editions of Shakespeare's plays are: Q1 of *2 Henry VI* (1594); Q1 of *3 Henry VI* (1595); Q1 of *Romeo and Juliet* (1597); Q1 of *Henry V* (1600); Q1 of *The Merry Wives of Windsor* (1602); Q1 of *Hamlet* (1603); Q1 of *King Lear* (1607); and Q of *Pericles* (1609). Q is the only surviving early text of *Pericles*; the other seven bad quartos may be compared with the First Folio, and *Romeo and Juliet* and *Hamlet* also appeared as GOOD QUARTOS. In addition, two other plays are often classed as bad quartos: *The Taming of a Shrew* (1594), considered a bad quarto of *The Taming of the Shrew*; and THE TROUBLESOME RAIGNE OF KING JOHN (1591), probably a reconstruction of *King John*.

Bad quartos exhibit certain characteristics that result from errors of memory, including repetitions and omissions of words, phrases that recollect earlier lines or anticipate later ones, many metrically flawed lines (see METER), paraphrases and summaries of speeches, stage directions that summarize missing dialogue, and snippets from other plays in which the rememberer had also performed. Also, some passages are less flawed than others. This reflects an actor's firmer recollection of the lines he spoke than of the rest of the play. For instance, the bad quarto of *Hamlet* was probably recorded by a man who had played Marcellus, since that role is the only one whose dialogue is very accurately rendered.

A bad quarto's flaws can be disastrous, as in the notorious misrendering of Hamlet's most famous soliloquy, which in Q1 begins (with modernized spelling): "To be, or not to be. Aye there's the point, / To die, to sleep, is that all? Aye all: / No, to sleep, to dream, aye marry there it goes . . ." (compare *Hamlet* 3.1.56–65). Although a corrupt text can be replaced by a sound one—except in the case of *Pericles*—a bad quarto is nonetheless useful to scholars in establishing a true text, as in another notable instance from *Hamlet* (in 2.2.415). Q1 records "godly Ballet" (i.e., ballad) for Q2's "pious chanson" and the First Folio's "Pons Chanson"; we see that the actors of the day recognized—even if they did not precisely recall—a wry reference to a popular song on a religious subject. The Folio's reading, with its suggestion of the bridges of Paris, is therefore rejected.

Bandello, Matteo (1485–1561) Italian writer, author of tales that served as sources for several of Shakespeare's works. Bandello's collection of tales, *Novelle* (1554), based loosely on the example of BOCCACCIO's *Decameron* (1353), was adapted in French by François BELLEFOREST and in English by

Arthur BROOKE, Geoffrey FENTON, and William PAINTER. Various of these versions and, probably, the Italian original were used by Shakespeare. Much of the playwright's account of King Edward's immoral infatuation in *Edward III* came from Painter's adaptation of Bandello. The creation of Aaron in *Titus Andronicus* may have been influenced by a Bandello tale in Belleforest; for *Romeo and Juliet*, the playwright adapted a love story taken from Bandello in versions by Brooke and Painter. The tale of Hero and Claudio in *Much Ado About Nothing* was taken from Bandello's Italian original and *his* source, a tale by ARIOSTO. A single passage in *Twelfth Night* may also have been inspired by Bandello.

Bandello led a highly dramatic life. An aristocrat, he joined the Dominican order as a youth and traveled widely with his uncle, a noted theologian who visited monasteries throughout Europe. However, he soon withdrew from the church to pursue a career as a courtier and man of letters—for instance, for eight years he was court poet to the Duchess of Mantua. Here he began to write the tales that were eventually to make him famous. A political intriguer, Bandello was forced in 1525 to flee hastily from Milan, abandoning all he owned including the manuscripts of many tales. He became an adviser to a pro-French Venetian general, but in 1542 the general was exiled to France, and Bandello followed him.

The French king granted Bandello the income from a bishopric, and he was finally free to assemble the novellas he had been writing for almost half a century. The first edition of *Novelle*, containing some 200 tales, was instantly popular throughout Europe. It consists for the most part of romantic legends retold in a racy, briskly journalistic style. Some stories were virtually pornographic by the standards of the day. Today Bandello's tales are considered to have very little literary merit, but at the time their influence was widespread in Italy, France, Spain, and England. Besides Shakespeare, other English writers who drew upon Bandello include the English dramatists John WEBSTER, Francis BEAUMONT and John FLETCHER, and Philip MASSINGER.

Bangor Town in WALES, possibly the setting for 3.1. of *1 Henry IV.* Some editors of the play, beginning with THEOBALD in the 18th century, have followed Shakespeare's chief source, HOLINSHED, and placed this scene, in which the conspirators against Henry IV plan to divide the realm among themselves, in the home of the Archdeacon of Bangor. However, Shakespeare made no designation of location, and the host of the meeting appears to be Glendower.

Barber, Samuel (1910–1981) American composer, creator of an OPERA based on *Antony and Cleopatra* and musical settings for various Shakespearean passages. Barber, one of the most highly regarded and frequently performed of 20th-century composers, wrote a great deal of music for voices, including *Antony and Cleopatra*, whose first production (by Franco ZEFFERELLI in 1966) was a failure, but which, revised by Barber and restaged by Gian Carlo Menotti (b. 1911) in 1975, has found a place in the modern operatic repertoire. Barber also wrote choral music for passages from *Antony and Cleopatra* ("Two Choruses: On the Death of Antony; On the Death of Cleopatra") and from *Twelfth Night* ("To be Sung on the Water"), both from 1968.

Barents, Willem (Willem Barentz) (ca. 1550–1597) Dutch explorer. Between 1594 and 1597, Barents led several naval expeditions to the Arctic in search of a northeast passage to the Orient; the Barents Sea, north of Scandinavia, is named for him. An account of Barents's voyage of 1596–97 was published in London in 1598 and was very popular, being reprinted for years. Fabian is believed to allude to Barents when, in *Twelfth Night*, he tells Sir Andrew, who has earned Olivia's disdain, that he has "sailed into the north of my lady's opinion, where you will hang like an icicle on a Dutchman's beard" (3.2.25–26).

Barker, Harley Granville See GRANVILLE-BARKER, HARLEY.

Barkloughly Castle Welsh castle seen in 3.2 of *Richard II.* Shakespeare's source, HOLINSHED's history, incorrectly identified Hertlowli, an ancient name for Harlech Castle, as Barclowlie and thus led the playwright into error. Nevertheless, this name indicates that the scene is in WALES and that Richard has returned to Britain from Ireland.

Barkstead, William (active 1606–1629)   English poet and dramatist. A very minor figure in English literature, Barkstead is best known for a long poem, *Myrrha, the Mother of Adonis* (1607), in which he modestly (and correctly) referred to Shakespeare as a much greater poet who had dealt with the Adonis story (see *Venus and Adonis*). He was employed by several minor acting companies, though his only surviving drama is *The Insatiate Countess* (ca. 1610), written in collaboration with John MARSTON.

Barnes, Barnabe (ca. 1569–1609)   English poet and dramatist, author of a play that served as an influence on *Pericles*, and possibly the "rival poet" of the *Sonnets*. Barnes's play *The Devil's Charter* (1607) derived from a work by the Italian historian Francesco Guicciardini (1483–1540), and it featured Guicciardini as a CHORUS. Shakespeare used this idea in *Pericles*, where the source, the poet John GOWER, serves the same function; in fact, some of Gower's speeches echo the words of Barnes's Guicciardini. Because Barnes was a noted SONNET writer who eulogized Henry Wriothesley, Earl of SOUTHAMPTON—Shakespeare's patron—some commentators, following scholar Sidney LEE, consider him a likely nominee for the "rival poet" of Shakespeare's sonnets.

Barnet   Location in *3 Henry VI*, a town near London and a battle site of the WARS OF THE ROSES. King Edward IV, having taken London and captured Henry VI, marches north to meet the army of Warwick. In 5.2–3 their forces meet in a conflict that is depicted as a simple rout of Warwick's troops, in which Warwick dies and the other Lancastrian leaders flee to join the army of Queen Margaret. The historical battle of Barnet, which occurred on Easter Sunday, 1471, was very closely fought; it was won for Edward only when one element of Warwick's army mistakenly attacked another in the heavy fog that shrouded the field. However, Shakespeare chose to emphasize the strength of the Yorkist forces, for the dynamic of his play at this point is directed toward their final victory at the battle of TEWKESBURY, which occurs over the next two scenes.

Barnfield, Richard (1574–1627)   Landed gentleman and amateur poet, an early admirer of Shakespeare. Barnfield published his first work, an imitation of *Venus and Adonis* titled *The Affectionate Shepherd*, at the age of 20; he published three more collections of poems over the next four years, but he then retired to his country estate and apparently stopped writing. He wrote the first published verse in praise of Shakespeare, a stanza in a poem called "A Remembrance of Some English Poets" (1598). Barnfield was a prominent member of the London literary scene in the 1590s, and Shakespeare was probably acquainted with him. Two of Barnfield's poems were published as Shakespeare's in William JAGGARD's spurious anthology THE PASSIONATE PILGRIM (1599), and it is chiefly for this reason that his work is remembered today.

Barrett, Lawrence (1838–1891)   American actor. An actor from the age of 14, Barrett established himself in New York in 1857 and became a friend and partner of Edwin BOOTH, playing Iago opposite Booth's Othello and Cassius in *Julius Caesar*—the part for which he was best known—opposite Booth's Caesar. He also played Richard III, Lear, and Shylock (*The Merchant of Venice*). Barrett served in the Union army in the Civil War; he then managed a theater in San Francisco, from 1867 to 1871, before returning to New York to run the Booth's Theatre. In 1884 he took over Henry IRVING's Lyceum Theatre in London, while Irving toured America. Barrett was unusual among actors of his day in taking an intellectual interest in the American theater; he introduced revivals of several plays and was a theater historian, the author of *Edwin Forrest* (1881) (see FORREST, EDWIN) and *Edwin Booth and his Contemporaries* (1886).

Barry, Ann (1734–1801)   English actress. Ann Barry's earliest recorded performances were at the Dublin theater of Spranger BARRY, opposite whose Lear and Othello she was acclaimed as Cordelia and Desdemona. She went with Barry to London and later married him. Though particularly successful in COMEDY, she played all sorts of parts, both new and classical. She was much admired as Juliet, Rosalind, Isabella, Imogen, and Perdita. Highly popular, she was regarded as one of the few rivals of Sarah SIDDONS. She died shortly after retiring and was buried in WESTMINSTER ABBEY.

Barry, Elizabeth (1658–1713) English actress. The leading actress of the late 17th century, Barry is sometimes called the first great English actress. Often playing opposite Thomas BETTERTON, she was especially acclaimed as Lady Macbeth, Queen Katherine in *Henry VIII*, and Cordelia in Nahum TATE's version of *King Lear*. She was said to have garnered her first training as an actress while the mistress of the notorious rake, poet, and aesthete, the Earl of Rochester (1640–80), by whom she bore a child. Throughout her life she was named in similar scandals, though at least one man, the playwright Thomas OTWAY, is said to have suffered from her rejection.

Barry, Spranger (1719–1777) Irish actor. Barry was among the leading Shakespearean actors of the 1750s, especially noted for his portrayal of Othello. His rivalry with David GARRICK was much publicized; the so-called *Romeo and Juliet* war—their simultaneous performances as Romeo (Barry in the adaptation by Colley CIBBER)—was followed by similar matchups as Lear and Richard III. In 1758 Barry attempted to establish a theater in Dublin but quickly went bankrupt. He did, however, meet and bring back to London a new leading lady, soon his wife, Ann Barry. Upon his return to London, he joined Garrick's company for the remainder of his career.

Barrymore, John (1882–1942) American actor. After establishing himself as a glamorous leading man—a "matinee idol"—Barrymore stunned the New York theatrical world in 1922 with an

John Barrymore as Mercutio (left) in his swordfight with Tybalt (*Romeo and Juliet* 3.1). George Cukor's 1936 film also starred Leslie Howard (center) as Romeo and Basil Rathbone (right) as Tybalt. *(Courtesy of Movie Star News)*

electrifying portrayal of Hamlet, repeating the accomplishment in London in 1925. His Hamlet was regarded as one of the great performances of the day, but Barrymore largely abandoned the stage for film in the remainder of his career. He appeared as Mercutio in George Cukor's 1936 film of *Romeo and Juliet.*

John and his siblings, Lionel and Ethel, were regarded as leaders of the American theater—*The Royal Family,* as the title of a 1927 play about them had it. Both his mother and his father were from long-established theatrical families, and John DREW was his uncle.

Bartley, George (ca. 1782–1858) Nineteenth-century English actor who specialized in playing Falstaff. Bartley's success as the fat knight began in 1815 and carried him through to his retirement in 1852. In 1818–19 he made a triumphal tour of America, although in Hartford, Connecticut, he was arrested by a puritanical official who objected to dramatic readings and enforced a colonial-era "blue law."

Barton, John (b. 1928) Twentieth-century English theatrical producer. Barton, a longtime director with the Royal Shakespeare Company, has staged many of Shakespeare's plays. Among his most notable productions have been *The Taming of the Shrew* (1960), *Twelfth Night* (1969), *Measure for Measure* (1970), and *Much Ado About Nothing* (1976). With Peter HALL, Barton codirected "The Wars of the Roses" (1964), the TELEVISION productions that combined the *Henry VI* plays and *Richard III.* He has also written a respected book, *Playing Shakespeare: An Actor's Guide* (1984).

Barton, Richard (active 1584–1601) Vicar at STRATFORD. In 1585 Barton baptized Hamnet and Judith SHAKESPEARE, the playwright's twin children. Barton, originally from COVENTRY, was vicar in Stratford from 1584 to 1589. He was apparently a man of Puritan leanings, for he was recorded in a Puritan critique of WARWICKSHIRE ministers as a superior cleric. He was much appreciated by the town, which offered him pay raises and miscellaneous gifts in the hope that he would remain, but

he accepted a better-paying post elsewhere after five years.

Basse, William (ca. 1583–ca. 1653) English poet. A minor figure in English literature, Basse is best known today for a 20-line EPITAPH on Shakespeare, written ca. 1621. This poem was originally published as John DONNE's in 1633; it was credited to "W. B." when it appeared in the 1640 edition of Shakespeare's *Poems* (see BENSON, JOHN). The only other Basse work that is read today is *Angler's Song,* an appreciation of fishing.

Baylis, Lilian (1874–1937) English theatrical entrepreneur, director of the OLD VIC and SADLER'S WELLS THEATREs. In 1898 Lilian Baylis, the daughter of professional singers, joined her aunt in the management of the Royal Victoria Coffee Music Hall—a temperance organization dedicated to liquor-free entertainment—in the theater building already known as the Old Vic. Baylis added opera performances, and the Old Vic soon became a leading operatic theater. In 1914, joined by Ben GREET, she added Shakespearean performances to the schedule, and the Old Vic was soon established as a national center of Shakespearean production. At her instigation and with her support—though she made a point of leaving all artistic decisions to others—the entire CANON of Shakespeare's plays had been staged by 1923. In 1931 Baylis acquired the Sadler's Wells Theatre as a companion theater in north London for the Old Vic in south London and put on Shakespeare there as well, although since 1934 it has been chiefly associated with opera. As a leading light of the Shakespearean theater, Lilian Baylis was regarded as a British national treasure, and she received many honors, including one of the first Oxford honorary degrees given to a woman outside academia.

Baynard Castle London fortress, a setting in *Richard III.* In 3.7 Richard III receives the Mayor of London, accompanied by a number of citizens, in Baynard Castle. Manipulated by the Duke of Buckingham, this group offers Richard the crown, insisting that he take it when he cynically feigns reluctance.

Shakespeare took this historical incident and its setting from his sources. Richard's use of Baynard

Castle signaled the strength of his drive for the crown, for it was an important bastion of royalty in London, second in strength and importance only to the TOWER OF LONDON. Like the Tower, it was built by England's Norman conquerors to control the city. Looming across the river from SOUTHWARK, Baynard Castle was a familiar landmark in Shakespeare's day; it was later destroyed in the Great Fire of London in 1666.

Beaumont, Francis (ca. 1584–1616)   English dramatist best known as a collaborator with John FLETCHER. As a young man, Beaumont studied at the INNS OF COURT, where he began writing poetry, possibly with the encouragement of Michael DRAYTON, a family friend. He began writing plays under the influence of Ben JONSON, whose friend and protégé he became. His earliest play, a COMEDY OF HUMOURS entitled *The Woman Hater* (1606), was staged by the Children of Paul's (see CHILDREN'S COMPANIES). In 1608 his *The Knight of the Burning Pestle*, a satire on the conventions of drama and literature, flopped dismally, though modern commentators regard it as one of the most endearing Jacobean comedies. In the same year he began his brief but highly successful collaboration with Fletcher. They wrote 15 plays together—one of them, *Philaster* (1610), was among the most important works of the age (see JACOBEAN DRAMA)—and in the 1630s their plays were more popular than Shakespeare's. Their partnership ended in 1613, when Beaumont married a wealthy heiress and retired from the theater. Beaumont's last dramatic work, written by himself, was *The Masque of the Inner Temple and Gray's Inn* (1613), a courtly MASQUE written to celebrate the marriage of the princess ELIZABETH STUART. A scene from it was restaged by Fletcher in *The Two Noble Kinsmen*.

Bedford, Lucy, Countess of (1581–1627)   English literary patron. Lucy Harington was married at the age of 13 to Edward Russell, Earl of Bedford; their marriage is one of several suggested as the occasion of the first performance of *A Midsummer Night's Dream*. Lucy Bedford was the patron of many of the most important English writers of her day, including John Donne (1573–1631), Samuel DANIEL, Michael DRAYTON, John FLORIO, and Ben JONSON. She was also a person of affairs, serving on the council of the Virginia Company and, when her husband was disabled by illness, as a leader of an important political faction in the turbulent 1620s.

Beeston, Christopher (d. 1638)   English actor and theatrical entrepreneur. Beeston began his career as an apprentice to Augustine PHILLIPS of the CHAMBERLAIN'S MEN. He may have appeared with STRANGE'S MEN in 1590, though his earliest certain role was with the Chamberlain's Men in 1598. In 1602 he joined the WORCESTER'S MEN, remaining with the company when it became the QUEEN'S MEN. He managed the company—ineptly and perhaps dishonestly—from 1612 until it dissolved upon the queen's death in 1619. He then joined PRINCE CHARLES' MEN as its manager and went on to run LADY ELIZABETH'S MEN (1622–25) and Queen Henrietta's Men (1625–37). He had already expanded his operations: In 1617 he had built a theater, the Phoenix, where these and other companies performed. Shortly before his death, he formed his own troupe of boy actors, the King and Queen's Young Company, popularly known as "Beeston's Boys" (see CHILDREN'S COMPANIES).

His son, William Beeston (d. 1682), also an actor, later provided the antiquarian James Aubrey (1626–97) with anecdotes about Shakespeare, reporting that his father had found the playwright "a handsome, well-shaped man; very good company, and of a very ready and pleasant smooth wit . . . [who] wouldn't be debauched." He also is the source of the report that Shakespeare had briefly been a schoolteacher as a young man.

Beethoven, Ludwig van (1770–1827)   German composer, several of whose works were inspired in part by Shakespeare. Like many artists of the Romantic movement of the late 18th and early 19th centuries, Beethoven was deeply moved by Shakespeare and his broad presentation of life that dealt with grand themes and was written in stirring poetry. One movement of a string quartet (opus 18, no. 1; ca. 1798) is thought to be based on Beethoven's response to *Romeo and Juliet,* and while his "Overture to *Coriolanus*" (1807) was composed to accompany a contemporary Viennese imitation of Shakespeare's play, he surely considered the original as well. Beethoven's Piano Sonata no. 17 (1802) is known as *The Tempest* because he once declared that a clue to its meaning could be found by reading Shakespeare's play.

Belleforest, François de (1530–1583) French author and translator who possibly influenced Shakespeare. An aristocratic courtier, Belleforest wrote poetry and compiled a collection of tales entitled *Histoires Tragiques* (1572), largely translations from the work of the Italian author Matteo BANDELLO. As a young man, Belleforest was a court favorite of Queen Margaret of Navarre (1492–1549), who wrote a famous book of tales, *The Heptameron* (published 1559), that doubtless inspired his own work.

Shakespeare may have taken ideas or details for several of his works—for example, *Hamlet*, *Titus Andronicus*, and *Twelfth Night*—from the *Histoires Tragiques*, but other sources were available to him in each instance, so we cannot be sure he knew Belleforest's tales. Nevertheless, the fact of several such coincidences suggests that he did, possibly from editions of 1576 or 1582. He may also have known the partial translation by Geoffrey FENTON, which was published in English in 1566, before the complete French version had appeared.

Bellini, Vincenzo (1801–1835) Italian composer, creator of an OPERA based on *Romeo and Juliet*. Bellini was one of the originators of bel canto–style opera in the early 19th century. His *I Capuleti e I Montecchi* was popular for a number of years following its premiere in 1830, but after 1847 it was not performed for almost a century. It now holds a place in modern operatic repertory, though Bellini is much better known for *La Sonnambula*, *Norma* (both of 1831), and *I Puritani* (1835).

Belmont Location in *The Merchant of Venice*, the estate of Portia. Bassanio comes to Belmont to court Portia and succeeds in the lottery of caskets, in 3.2, before being called away by news of Shylock's intended villainy. The estate is also a refuge for Lorenzo and Jessica. At the close of the play,

Lorenzo and Jessica rhapsodize romantically about love and the beauties of the night while ensconced at Belmont, where the episode of the betrothal rings is played out and the comedy is concluded, as was proper to a 16th-century comedy, with the union of lovers.

Belmont, a fictitious place, is apparently located on the mainland near VENICE; its name means "beautiful hill." Shakespeare simply took the estate and its name from his source, FIORENTINO's *Il Pecorone*, but he made the place his own. Belmont, like the Forest of ARDEN in *As You Like It*, is an artificial world, removed from the dreary acquisitiveness and commercialism represented by Shylock, where the conflicts that burden human affairs in the "real" world can be resolved.

Belott, Stephen (active 1602–1613) Wigmaker of LONDON, plaintiff in a lawsuit in which Shakespeare testified. Belott, the son of French Huguenot immigrants, was apprenticed to Christopher MOUNTJOY, a "tire-maker"—creator of the elaborate, ornamented headresses worn by aristocratic women. After serving his term and becoming Mountjoy's hired employee, he married his master's daughter. Shakespeare, who was a lodger in Mountjoy's house, participated in the negotiations about the marriage settlement, carrying messages between the father and the prospective bridegroom. After their marriage the Belotts established a rival business, initiating a feud with Mountjoy. After Mountjoy's wife died in 1606, the couple moved back in with him, but arguments over money soon resulted in their departure. Eventually Belott sued Mountjoy for refusing to relinquish money agreed upon in the marriage settlement. Shakespeare testified in the case. Belott was eventually awarded a token settlement, though the arbitrators criticized him for debauchery. No more is known of his life.

Benfield, Robert (d. ca. 1650) English actor. Benfield was one of the 26 men listed in the FIRST FOLIO as the "Principall Actors" in Shakespeare's plays. He specialized in dignified figures such as kings and old men. He was with LADY ELIZABETH'S MEN in 1613 and may have joined the KING'S MEN upon the death of William OSTLER in 1614, for he took at least one of Ostler's parts. In any case he was a member of the company by 1619 and remained with the company until its dissolution in 1642, with the opening of the Civil Wars.

Bensley, Robert (1742–1817)   English actor. Best known for his portrayal of Malvolio in *Twelfth Night*, Bensley was a highly mannered actor who frequently played in the productions of David GARRICK. He was a major figure on the London stage of the last decades of the 18th century.

Benson, Frank Robert (1858–1939)   English actor and producer. F. R. Benson formed a touring company in 1883 that pointedly de-emphasized spectacle in staging Shakespeare, in contrast to the prevailing fashion for lush productions, such as those of Henry IRVING and Herbert Beerbohm TREE. From 1888 to 1919, with few exceptions, Benson directed the annual Shakespeare Festival at STRATFORD. His own performances in leading roles were acclaimed. More important, he presented almost all the plays—only *Titus Andronicus* and *Troilus and Cressida* were omitted—in texts with few cuts or interpolations and on plain stages that focused attention on Shakespeare's words. In 1900 he staged the complete four-to five-hour-long text of *Hamlet* in London, and at Stratford in 1908 he produced the complete HISTORY PLAYS as a single unit for the first time. In 1916, on the occasion of the tercentenary of Shakespeare's death, Benson was knighted by King George V for his services to the British Shakespearean tradition.

Benson, John (d. 1667)   London publisher and bookseller, producer of the first collection of Shakespeare's poems. Benson's *Poems* contains most of the *Sonnets*, *A Lover's Complaint*, "The Phoenix and Turtle," excerpts from *Measure for Measure* and *As You Like It*, THE PASSIONATE PILGRIM (much of which is not Shakespeare's), a few other misattributed works, and a number of poems about Shakespeare by other poets, including John MILTON, Ben JONSON, Francis BEAUMONT, Leonard DIGGES, and William BASSE. Only six of the Sonnets (numbers 18, 19, 43, 56, 75, and 76) are missing, though the remainder are altered to make them appear to be addressed only to a woman. Although the text of Thomas THORPE's 1609 edition was employed, the Sonnets are arranged in a different order, with titles occasionally assigned to a group of two or three.

Bentley, John (1553–1585)   English actor, a member of the QUEEN'S MEN. Bentley, one of the original members of the Queen's Men, is best known as the central figure in a brawl of 1583 in which a would-be gate-crasher of a Queen's Men's performance was killed. Though Richard TARLTON attempted to restrain him, Bentley pursued the fleeing miscreant, who hit him with a rock. Bentley and a companion drew their swords, and in the ensuing fight one of them killed the man. There is no record of a criminal prosecution for the killing, which occurred in 1583 during the Queen's Men's first season. As an actor, Bentley was well regarded by his contemporaries, being compared with Tarlton and William ALLEYN, acknowledged leaders of the profession.

Berlioz, Hector (1803–1869)   French composer, creator of an OPERA and several other works inspired by Shakespeare's plays. Berlioz, the leading French composer of the Romantic school, wrote the "King Lear Overture" (1831) and a "dramatic symphony," as he called it, based on *Romeo and Juliet* (1838). A symphonic fantasy on *The Tempest* (1830) was absorbed into a later work. Two choral works, "Death March for the Last Scene of *Hamlet*" (with sung but wordless cries of grief) and "La Mort d'Ophelia" (with a French text after Shakespeare by Ernest Legouvé [1807–1903]), were published in 1848 but may have been written much earlier. Later in his career Berlioz wrote an opera based on *Much Ado About Nothing*, called *Béatrice et Bénédict* (1862), a work that is considered among his finest. Another opera, *Les Troyens* (1859), contains a lyrical episode inspired by the love scene in 5.1 of *The Merchant of Venice*.

Berlioz profoundly influenced 19th-century French culture with dramatic compositions that reflected the romantic spirit of the age. As a young man he abandoned medical studies for music. In 1828 he fell in love with a leading actress, Harriet SMITHSON—famous in France for her Ophelia—and he may have written his works inspired by *Hamlet* at this time. His *Symphonie Fantastique* (1830)—

intended as an expression of his passion for Smithson—established him as a leading composer. He married her in 1833 but then abandoned her for another woman, though he did return to her much later and nursed her through her final illness. His own last days were solitary and unhappy; he proposed for his epitaph Macbeth's despairing cry that life is "a tale / Told by an idiot, full of sound and fury, / Signifying nothing" (*Macbeth*, 5.5.26–28).

Berners, John Bourchier, Lord (1467–1533) English translator. Lord Berners's translation (1523–25) of the 14th-century *Chroniques* of FROISSART may have influenced the composition of *Richard II*, and his English version of a 13th-century French adventure tale, *The Boke of Duke Huon of Bordeaux* (1534), may have inspired something of Shakespeare's Oberon in *A Midsummer Night's Dream*.

Lord Berners was an important political figure; as a young nobleman he supported the Earl of Richmond (who appears in *Richard III*) when he seized the throne as King Henry VII in 1485. He was appointed Lord Chancellor by King Henry VIII in 1516 (though he is not the Chancellor of the play *Henry VIII*), and in his later years he served as Deputy of Calais, the English outpost on the coast of FRANCE.

Bernhardt, Sarah (1845–1923) French actress. Though not chiefly a Shakespearean actress, Bernhardt scored one of her first great successes as Cordelia in a French translation of *King Lear*. She also made an important contribution to the role of Lady Macbeth, as the first to display an overt sensuality that was heavily stressed by most of her 20th-century successors. In addition, she is strongly associated with Hamlet, a part she played in Paris, London, and New York in 1899–1901, as well as in the first FILM of *Hamlet*, a silent movie of 1900.

Bestrafte Brudermord, Der (**Fratricide Punished**) Eighteenth-century German version of *Hamlet* thought to derive in part from the UR-HAMLET. This work, fully titled *Tragoedia der Bestrafte Brudermord oder Prinz Hamlet aus Dän-*

Sarah Bernhardt was one of several women to play the title role in major late 19th-century productions of *Hamlet*. *(Courtesy of Culver Pictures, Inc.)*

nemark but conventionally referred to as *BB*, is known only from the 1789 publication of a manuscript said to have been dated 1710. *BB* is essentially a BAD QUARTO of *Hamlet* with additional scenes, including an allegorical PROLOGUE and several episodes of slapstick comedy. English actors frequently performed in Germany in the 16th and 17th centuries (see, e.g., BROWNE, ROBERT; GREEN, JOHN; KEMPE, WILLIAM), and the actors who provided the dialogue translated into German as *BB* knew *Hamlet* in both of its early forms, published as the Q1 (1603) and Q2 (1604) editions; the additional material stems largely from medieval German traditions. However, some details in *BB* do not come from *Hamlet* yet correspond to a source for the play, François BELLEFOREST's version of the story. For instance, Queen

Gertrude blames her remarriage for Hamlet's madness, and Hamlet accuses his mother of hypocritically pretending to cry during their confrontation in her bedroom. These may have been introduced by actors who had performed in the *Ur-Hamlet*.

Betterton, Thomas (1635–1710)   English actor, the dominant figure in Restoration theater. Betterton was apprenticed to a bookseller in 1660, when English theaters reopened with the restoration of the monarchy after 18 years of Puritan government. His employer opened a theater, and Betterton was among the actors absorbed into William DAVENANT's troupe when two companies were licensed. Betterton quickly became the leading actor in London. Best known as Hamlet, his versatility was such that his other most appreciated role was as Sir Toby Belch in *Twelfth Night*. He was also especially acclaimed as Macbeth, Mercutio *(Romeo and Juliet)*, Othello, and Henry VIII. After Davenant's death in 1671, Betterton led the company until it merged with the other London company in 1682. In 1695 he established a rival company, with which he was successful until he retired shortly before his death.

Betterton wrote a number of dramas of his own, including a libretto derived from *A Midsummer Night's Dream* for Henry PURCELL's OPERA, *The Fairy Queen* (1692), a text that contains none of Shakespeare's lines. He also adapted Shakespeare's *Henry IV* plays to the tastes of the period. When his version was first staged in 1682, he played Hotspur; it was so popular that it was revived repeatedly for 18 years, by which time he played Falstaff. Betterton and his wife, Mary SAUNDERSON, were much loved in the London theater world for their ready assistance to young players, most notably Anne BRACEGIRDLE.

Betterton's talent was viewed as more than extraordinary by his contemporaries. Samuel PEPYS reported that his Hamlet was "beyond imagination" in 1661; when the actor took the part again in 1668, Pepys described the performance as "the best . . . that ever man acted." At the other end of his career, Betterton inspired Colley CIBBER to write that he "was an actor as Shakespeare was an author, both without competitors, formed for the mutual assistance and illustration of each other's genius."

Betty, William Henry West (1791–1874)   English actor. A famous child prodigy, Master Betty, as he was known, was the greatest sensation of the London theatrical season of 1804–05, having previously achieved success in Ireland and Scotland. He played several of the great classical roles of English drama that winter, including Romeo and Hamlet (he was said to have memorized the latter role in a few hours). He also was notable as Arthur in *King John*. For a year he was the most popular English actor by far, overshadowing such established figures as John Philip KEMBLE. However, his star faded rapidly. In 1808, playing Richard III, he was booed off the stage, and he retired long enough to graduate from Cambridge; his subsequent attempt to resume his career was unsuccessful. His father squandered the fortune his earlier success had brought him, and he lived the remainder of his long life in poverty and obscurity.

Bible   The Christian sacred scripture. The Bible was basic reading for Shakespeare and his age, and this is evident throughout the plays. Although the Bible is mentioned by name only once (*Merry Wives*, 2.3.7; it is also referred to as "Holy Writ" several times) and explicit references to biblical characters or tales are few, Shakespeare, like many other authors, was influenced by biblical idioms and linguistic rhythms.

Several versions of the Bible were available in England in the 16th century. The version Shakespeare knew best was the Geneva Bible, named for the Swiss city, the center of European Calvinism, where it was translated into English by Protestant exiles during the reign of the Catholic queen Mary I (1553–58) and published in England in 1560. He also knew the Bishop's Bible (1568), a revision of an earlier English text that was undertaken in part to counter the influence of radical Calvinism on the Geneva version. However, the Geneva Bible was so powerful a literary text that the Bishop's Bible actually relied on it to some extent, as, later, did the creators of the King James Version (1611), which was prescribed in the Anglican Church until late in the 19th century and is still commonly used and read. Shakespeare doubtless knew it, but only after his career was nearly over. As a reader of Latin, Shakespeare could also refer to the Vulgate of St. Jerome, the basic Bible for western Europe from the fifth century to the 16th, when the Reformation stimulated the use of translations.

Birmingham Shakespeare Memorial Library Major collection of Shakespeareana in Birmingham, England. Founded in 1864 on the occasion of the playwright's 300th birthday, the library, despite its destruction by fire in 1879, now houses one of the most important collections of early texts and records of later productions of Shakespeare's plays, with a particular strength in 18th-century materials.

Birnam Wood   See DUNSINANE.

Birth of Merlin, The   Play formerly attributed to Shakespeare, part of the Shakespeare APOCRYPHA. The earliest known text of *The Birth of Merlin* is a QUARTO published in 1662 by Francis KIRKMAN, who ascribed the play to Shakespeare and William ROWLEY. *Merlin,* a lively entertainment that features dragons, visions, a comet, and a devil, is usually dated to the 1620s based on the evidence of its style and vocabulary. Thus it is too late to be Shakespeare's play. Also, the writing is inferior and it is generally dissimilar to the playwright's known work. However, most scholars believe that Rowley wrote at least part of the play, perhaps in collaboration with Thomas MIDDLETON.

birthplace, Shakespeare's   House in STRATFORD where the playwright was probably born. The birthplace consists of two buildings on Henley Street that were bought on separate occasions by Shakespeare's father, John SHAKESPEARE, and joined together. Tradition assigns Shakespeare's birth to the western half, but no actual evidence exists. John Shakespeare lived in an unspecified building on Henley Street in 1552, and in 1556 he bought the eastern half of what was to be the birthplace, but at the same time he bought another house, and it is unclear where he lived. An unrecorded purchase could have been made before the playwright's birth, but John's only other known real-estate acquisitions are two houses bought in 1575, one of which may have been the western

half. In any case the family was living in the western half by 1597, and the eastern half was used for business.

In 1601 Shakespeare inherited the house upon his father's death. The eastern half was leased to the keepers of an inn called the Maidenhead, and the western half continued to be inhabited by the family; the playwright's sister Joan SHAKESPEARE Hart and her family were living there when Shakespeare died. He left Joan a lifetime lease on it, while leaving the building to his daughter Susanna SHAKESPEARE Hall, who in turn left it to her daughter Elizabeth HALL. In the meantime Joan's son and grandsons continued to live there. In 1670 Elizabeth Hall bequeathed it to Joan's grandson George Hart (1636–1702), whose descendants continued to occupy it for another century.

In 1806 the Harts sold the property to one Thomas Court, under whose ownership it became a butcher shop; his widow auctioned it off in 1846, advertising it as "the house in which the immortal Poet of Nature was born." The house was purchased by a nonprofit organization formed for the purpose and 10 years later was restored, using the public's contributions (among the fundraisers was Charles DICKENS). In 1891 the Birthplace Trust was incorporated to care for the building and such other properties as NEW PLACE (acquired in 1862), Anne HATHAWAY's cottage (1891), the supposed ARDEN home (1930), and Hall's Croft, the Stratford residence of Dr. John HALL (1949).

Bishop, Henry Rowley (1786–1855)   English composer and conductor. Best known for writing the song "Home, Sweet Home," Bishop also composed the music for many of the operatic adaptations of Shakespeare's plays by Frederick REYNOLDS. In 1842 Bishop became the first musician to be knighted by a British monarch.

Bithynia   An ancient region on the Black Sea coast of what is now Turkey. Bithynia's name appears in place of BOHEMIA in some editions of *The Winter's Tale.* The 18th-century scholar Thomas HANMER, disturbed by Shakespeare's casualness in ascribing a seacoast to Bohemia, a landlocked country, first made this ingenious substitution in his 1744 edition of the plays. Many subsequent editors followed his lead, but modern practice generally ignores it.

Blackfriars Gatehouse   House in LONDON owned by Shakespeare. In 1613 Shakespeare bought a residence that had once served as the gatehouse on the estate of the BLACKFRIARS PRIORY. This was his last investment that we know of and his only nontheatrical one in London. He bought the building for £140 from Henry WALKER, paying £80 in cash and immediately mortgaging the house to Walker for the remaining £60. He had three trustees who were technically co-owners with him: William JOHNSON, John JACKSON, and John HEMINGE. They put up no money and had no ownership rights; this arrangement had the effect of eliminating the rights in the property of Shakespeare's wife, Anne HATHAWAY Shakespeare—perhaps because Shakespeare intended to leave the property to his daughter Susanna SHAKESPEARE Hall, which he did in fact do. The trustees surrendered their shares to her in 1618, "in performance of the confidence and trust in them reposed by William Shakespeare," as the legal document had it.

The gatehouse was very close to the BLACKFRIARS THEATRE, the principal venue for the KING'S MEN, but Shakespeare clearly did not intend to use it. He already lived in STRATFORD full time, and the purchase was simply an investment. The location, however, suggests how the property could have come to his attention. He leased the gatehouse, soon after buying it, to one John ROBINSON, who was still living there in 1616. The later history of the building is obscure. It was probably destroyed in the Great Fire of London (1666).

Blackfriars Priory   Former Dominican priory building in LONDON, a setting for a scene in *Henry VIII*. In 2.4 the Blackfriars priory houses the proceedings that lead to King Henry VIII's divorce from Queen Katherine, the king having declared it "The most convenient place [he could] think of / for such receipt of learning" (2.2.137–138). Shakespeare followed his source, HOLINSHED's *Chronicles,* in placing this meeting at the Blackfriars. After

England adopted Protestantism, the priory's property was seized by the Crown and sold to various private interests. By Shakespeare's time, different buildings of the old priory had become the BLACKFRIARS THEATRE and BLACKFRIARS GATEHOUSE.

Blackfriars Theatre   Playhouse in LONDON established by Richard BURBAGE, the home from 1600 to 1608 of the Children of the Chapel (see CHILDREN'S COMPANIES), and later of Shakespeare's company, the KING'S MEN. Burbage inherited the Blackfriars from his father, James BURBAGE, who died before it was ready for use. The theater was part of the medieval BLACKFRIARS PRIORY, which had been broken up and sold to private investors at the Reformation. The theater was rented to Henry EVANS of the Children of the Chapel, but after Evans's failure, Burbage bought back the lease, in partnership with his brother Cuthbert BURBAGE, four King's Men—Shakespeare, Henry CONDELL, John HEMINGE, and William SLY—and a relative of Evans. The King's Men used the theater in the winter from 1609 on. (Before the Burbages' enterprise, between 1576 and 1584 there had been a smaller theater in part of the same building, which is known as the original, or first, Blackfriars Theatre.)

The Blackfriars was called a "private" theater, for it had a roof, unlike the King's Men's summer venue, the GLOBE THEATRE, and other public playhouses. Because admission prices were as much as five times greater than in the public theaters, the audiences were socially higher ranking, and generally better educated. Their tastes were correspondingly different—more influenced by literature and by the courtly MASQUE whose popularity was on the rise in the first decades of the 17th century. All this, combined with the greater intimacy of the theater itself and its novel and striking candlelit stage, produced important changes in JACOBEAN DRAMA. Shakespeare's ROMANCES and the plays of Francis BEAUMONT and John FLETCHER, the King's Men's other main playwrights, were directly influenced by the Blackfriars Theatre.

The physical appearance of the Blackfriars Theatre is unknown, but in the early 17th century King JAMES I commissioned a theater design from the great architect Inigo Jones (1573–1652) that is thought to have been intended as a close imitation of the Blackfriars. Jones's theater was never built, but the new Shakespeare's Globe Theatre in London (see WANAMAKER, SAM), a multibuilding complex, includes a building constructed from Jones's plans, though its interior contains several small theaters, rather than one. The exterior, however, offers modern theatergoers some idea of what the Blackfriars looked like.

Blackheath   Open land on the south bank of the Thames east of LONDON, a traditional fairground and public meeting place and the location of several scenes in *2 Henry VI*. Blackheath was famous in Shakespeare's time, as in the period of the play's action, as an assembly point for rebellious bands marching on London, and it figures as such in 4.2–3 of the play. The army of Jack Cade, arriving from KENT, gathers here to be harangued by its leader and to fight its first skirmish before proceeding to the capital. Ironically, when the Duke of York returns from Ireland with his army in 5.1—ostensibly to oppose Cade but also, secretly, to foster insurrection—he also appears at Blackheath.

blank verse   Metrical pattern (see METER) composed of lines of unrhymed iambic pentameter. The typical pattern in English poetry—though neither exclusively nor originally English—blank verse is the medium of many long poems and nearly all verse dramas, including Shakespeare's, though the plays also contain prose and, more rarely, other forms of verse. Iambic pentameter is especially appropriate for drama and narrative poetry, for it more closely resembles the normal patterns of English speech than does any other sort of poetic pattern. Its stresses imitate the natural flow of clauses and phrases, while the line endings fall at intervals that are easily followed without counting. Unlike rhymed patterns such as, say, the couplet or the limerick, which subtly suggest a point of view by the way they sound, blank verse is neutral in tone and allows the content of the poetry to determine its emotional shading. This is both an advantage and a challenge: Blank verse does not easily lend itself to the lively and varied tone that a work of any length requires.

Blank verse was first used in English poetry in the early 16th century in translations of VIRGIL by Henry Howard, Earl of SURREY. Surrey was inspired by similar Italian verse and, probably, the example of unrhymed verse in traditional Middle English poetry. The form became popular in England after Christopher MARLOWE established the pattern, in *Tamburlaine* (ca. 1587), as the standard for dramatic works. Shakespeare's poetic genius led him to vary the pattern much more freely than his predecessors had, permitting the expression of a wider range of effects, from broad comedy to lyrical ecstasy to raging anger. For the first time, the musical patterns of poetry could approximate the range and specificity of prose.

In Shakespeare's day, blank verse was a very familiar medium; he could expect at least part of his audience to recognize it when spoken, as Jaques does in *As You Like It*, upon hearing only a single line (4.1.28). Except during the late 17th and early 18th centuries, blank verse remained prominent in English poetry until recent times. It was the favored medium of such masters of the long poem as John MILTON, William Wordsworth (1770–1850), Robert Browning (1812–89), and T. S. ELIOT. In the 20th century the use of blank verse has declined, due largely to the disappearance of an audience for verse drama and the long poem. To some extent, it has come to be seen as conservative poetry, compared to free verse.

Bloch, Ernst (1880–1959)   Swiss-born American composer, creator of an OPERA based on *Macbeth*. Bloch, an eclectic modern composer who drew on a wide range of influences both musical and literary, established himself as a composer for voice with his *Macbeth*, a "lyrical drama" first performed in Paris in 1910, before he moved to America (in 1916) and became a major figure on the American musical scene. Bloch is probably best known for a number of settings of texts from the Old Testament and for symphonic works incorporating quotations from various sorts of American popular music.

Blount,   Edward (1564–1632)   English bookseller and publisher, a partner in the production of the FIRST FOLIO (1623). In 1601 Blount published LOVE'S MARTYR, including Shakespeare's "The Phoenix and Turtle." In 1608 he registered two of Shakespeare's plays for publication—*Antony and Cleopatra* and *Pericles*—but did not produce either of them; scholars believe this reflects a "blocking action" undertaken on behalf of the KING'S MEN to protect their plays from pirated publication. This degree of cooperation with the acting company suggests that Shakespeare may have known him personally. Blount and Isaac JAGGARD jointly held the rights to 16 plays in the First Folio—all but two of those that had not been previously published—making them leading members of the syndicate that financed its printing (the others were John SMETHWICK and William ASPLEY). Jaggard and Blount are designated copublishers of the book on its title page.

Blount became a member of the STATIONERS' COMPANY in 1588 after 10 years of apprenticeship, and he prospered, eventually owning two book-shops and remaining active until at least 1630. He was evidently a sincere appreciator of literature, publishing prefaces praising his authors and apologizing for printer's errors. He published works by Christopher MARLOWE and John LYLY in addition to Shakespeare.

Boar's Head Tavern   Inn in EASTCHEAP, in LONDON, setting for several scenes in *1* and *2 Henry IV* and possibly one in *Henry V.* The Boar's Head, run by the Hostess and frequented by Falstaff, Prince Hal, and their friends, is a haven for petty criminals whose riotous drinking and wenching is depicted with a colorful vigor unmatched until Charles Dickens in the 19th century. In addition to Falstaff's principal followers—Bardolph, Pistol, Peto, and Doll Tearsheet—numerous minor characters, such as Gadshill, Francis, the Vintner, the Musicians, and the Drawers, add verisimilitude to this world.

In *1 Henry IV* the Boar's Head is the scene of several typical episodes in the delinquent career of Prince Hal. In 2.4 he baits Falstaff about his bungled highway robbery, and he joins the fat knight in a mirthful mockery of King Henry IV. In 3.3 a comical dispute erupts between Falstaff and the Hostess, and the Prince deflects an attempt by a Sheriff

to arrest Falstaff. In 2.1 of *2 Henry IV*, the Hostess attempts to have Falstaff arrested for debt, and a potential brawl is averted only by the timely arrival of the Chief Justice. In 2.4 Falstaff hosts an uproarious dinner party at the tavern. Mournful meditations on Falstaff's death are offered by his companions in 2.3 of *Henry V.* This scene is traditionally located in front of the tavern, and, although the original texts provide no site designation, it seems appropriate that the Boar's Head should witness the remembrances for its most famous patron.

The Boar's Head was a famous establishment in Elizabethan London, and, although Shakespeare does not actually name it explicitly (a broad hint is made in *2 Henry IV*, 2.2.138–140), his audiences clearly recognized it, as surviving contemporary references reveal. However, the Boar's Head Tavern is not to be confused with the Boar's Head Theatre, the suburban venue of the QUEEN'S MEN, an early-17th-century acting company.

Boas, Frederick S. (1862–1957)   British scholar. Boas wrote several important books on Shakespeare, including *Shakspere and his Predecessors* (1896)—in which he introduced the term PROBLEM PLAY to Shakespeare studies—and *An Introduction to the Reading of Shakespeare* (1927). He also wrote about other figures of the age, including Thomas HEYWOOD, Christopher MARLOWE, and Sir Philip SIDNEY. He was the longtime editor of *The Year's Work in English Studies*, an annual collection of essays that summarized significant scholarly work.

Boccaccio, Giovanni (1313–1375)   Italian story writer and poet, a frequent source for Shakespeare. The main plots of *All's Well That Ends Well* and *Cymbeline*, as well as details in *The Winter's Tale*, all derive from Boccaccio's *Decameron* (1353), a collection of tales that Shakespeare probably knew in the translation of William PAINTER. The *Decameron* may also have provided the main plot of *The Two Gentlemen of Verona*, though this material was heavily modified by other sources. The playwright's other uses of Boccaccio's works were indirect: Geoffrey CHAUCER's *Troilus and Criseyde*, the source for *Troilus and Cressida*, was itself based on Boccaccio's poem the *Filostrato* (1338); Boccaccio's epic poem the *Teseide* (1339–40) was the source for Chaucer's "The Knight's Tale," which was in turn the source for both *The Two Noble Kinsmen* and parts of *A Midsummer Night's Dream;* lastly, the stories of Giovanni FIORENTINO, probably sources for *The Merchant of Venice* and *The Merry Wives of Windsor*, were modeled on tales in the *Decameron.*

Boccaccio is considered a founder of Italian REN-AISSANCE literature. Among his works are the *Filostrato*, a romance in verse; the *Teseide*, the first epic poem in Italian; the *Fiammetta* (ca. 1343), sometimes seen as the earliest European novel; the *Ninfale Fieselano (The Nymph of Fiesole*, ca. 1345), a PASTORAL romance in verse that is considered Boccaccio's second greatest work; and the greatest, the *Decameron.* All of these works were written in Italian, but following a religious crisis, Boccaccio decided that writing in the vernacular was sinful and rejected all his works. His later writings in Latin, scholarly works on classical culture, were important to the development of European humanism.

Bodleian Library Major collection of Shakespeareana, at Oxford University, England. The library was founded by the diplomat and scholar Thomas Bodley (1545–1613) in 1597 when an earlier university library, dating to 1445, was reorganized. The Bodleian Library was originally composed largely of theological materials, but in 1821, with the acquisition of the library of Edmond MALONE, it became a great Shakespearean library. It has maintained that status to the present day, with a collection that is especially noted for its early texts of Shakespeare's nondramatic poetry.

Boece, Hector (Hector Boyce) (ca. 1465–1536) Scottish historian, author of a source for *Macbeth.* Boece's *Scotorum Historiae*, a history of Scotland in Latin, was the source for Raphael HOLINSHED's Scottish history in his *Chronicles of England, Scotland, and Ireland* (1577), which was Shakespeare's source for the tale of *Macbeth*, as well as for other materials used in the play.

Boece, a native of Dundee, was a famous professor at the University of Paris when, in 1498, he was invited back to Scotland to participate in the founding of King's College in Aberdeen. His *Scotorum Historiae* was the first work to cover all of Scotland's history (to 1488). It is heavily infused with legendary material—including much of Macbeth's story—but it was for generations regarded as the best text on its subject. Translated into French, it became well known throughout Europe. In 1536 the King of Scotland commissioned a translation into Scots; this work, by the poet John Bellenden (ca. 1500–ca. 1548) is the oldest surviving work of Scots prose. In the academic fashion of the times, Boece took a Latin surname and is sometimes still referred to as Hector Boëthius, after the Roman philosopher (ca. 480–ca. 524).

Bohemia Central European region, part of the modern Czech Republic, the setting for part of *The Winter's Tale.* In 3.3 Antigonus abandons the infant Perdita—banished from SICILIA by her father, King Leontes, who believes her illegitimate—on the Bohemian seacoast. She is found by the Shepherd and his son, who raise her as a shepherdess. In Act 4, 16 years later, Prince Florizel, son of the King of Bohemia, falls in love with Perdita, and she with him. The king, however, opposes their marriage, and they flee to Sicilia, where Act 5 takes place.

Bohemia is specified as the setting for the rugged seacoast of 3.3 and the pastoral world of the shepherds in Act 4, but there is nothing nationally distinctive in the text of the play. Shakespeare merely took the name from his source, *Pandosto* by Robert GREENE (though there the princess was exiled from Bohemia and raised in Sicilia). In many ways Shakespeare's Bohemia is a lovingly idealized portrait of English rural life, although the rugged coast and man-eating Bear of 3.3 add overtones of nature's harshness.

Shakespeare's attribution of a seacoast to Bohemia has inspired much comment, for that land does not in fact have one. It has been argued that the discrepancy points to the playwright's ignorance and provinciality, or to his carelessness in simply accepting the notion from *Pandosto.* The 18th-century scholar Thomas HANMER substituted BITHYNIA, a region of Asia Minor, for Bohemia, and many later editions of the play followed his lead. Other commentators hold that Shakespeare may legitimately have thought Bohemia bordered the Adriatic Sea, since after 1526 it was part of the Hapsburg Empire, which did so. Also, medieval Bohemia (a powerful nation) had briefly controlled a stretch of the same coast. However, the actuality of Bohemia's coast is irrelevant; *The Winter's Tale*, as one of the ROMANCES, was expected to dazzle its viewers with exotic locales. Bohemia was very little known in England during Shakespeare's lifetime, for it was small and deep within continental Europe, in an age of difficult travel and communication (but see ELIZABETH STUART). Most of *The Winter's Tale*'s original audience doubtless accepted a Bohemian coastline without thinking about it; it was a satisfying image, providing a dramatic approach to a fabulous land. For those who knew the truth, probably including Shakespeare himself, the anomaly may have been mildly amusing, like modern jokes about the Swiss navy.

Boito, Arrigo (1842–1918)   Italian operatic composer and librettist. Boito, who composed several OPERAS of his own, is best known for two librettos—both adaptations of Shakespeare—that he wrote for Giuseppe VERDI: *Otello* (1887; based on *Othello*) and *Falstaff* (1893; based on *The Merry Wives of Windsor*). In a letter to Verdi, Boito charmingly described his intention "to extract all the juice from that great Shakespearean orange." He is generally thought to have succeeded: These are widely regarded as among the best opera librettos ever written. Boito's first libretto, written at age 23, was also Shakespearean; it was for the opera *Amleto (Hamlet)* (performed only once, in 1865) by the little-known composer Franco Faccio (1840–91).

Bonian, Richard (active 1598–1611)   London publisher and bookseller. Bonian began as a printer's apprentice and flourished, becoming a member of the STATIONERS' COMPANY and owning three London bookshops. In 1609 he copublished, with Henry WALLEY, the QUARTO edition of *Troilus and Cressida*. By the time of the publication of the FIRST FOLIO in 1623, Bonian had died. Little more is known of him.

Booth, Barton (1681–1733)   English actor. Booth was Thomas BETTERTON's successor as the leading

tragic actor on the London stage. He was particularly noted for his portrayal of Othello, but he also played many other Shakespearean roles, including Lear, Hotspur, Brutus, Timon, and Hamlet. A reformed alcoholic, he became a comanager of the Drury Lane Theatre with Colley CIBBER and was one of the most influential figures in the London theater world of the early 18th century.

Booth, Edwin (1833–1893)   American actor. Booth, son of Junius Brutus BOOTH, was the leading American actor of his day. He first achieved acclaim when he stood in for his ailing father as Richard III in 1851. Among Shakespearean roles, he was best

Edwin Booth in the role of Hamlet. Booth's famous 100-night run in this role in 1864 was a record that stood until 1922. In 1865 Booth was forced into temporary retirement by the scandal of Lincoln's assassination at the hand of his brother John Wilkes Booth. *(Courtesy of Culver Pictures, Inc.)*

known for his portrayal of Hamlet, but he also played most of the other tragic heroes. In 1862 he became manager of a New York theater, where he staged a number of Shakespeare's plays. In the winter of 1864–65 he presented a production of *Hamlet* that ran for 100 performances, then a record for the play. Almost immediately thereafter, his brother John Wilkes BOOTH assassinated Abraham Lincoln, and Booth retired temporarily. He returned to the stage in 1866. The theater he ran burned down, and he built his own, which opened in 1869, but in four years he was bankrupt. He then toured for several years in America and abroad. In London in 1882, he and Henry IRVING alternated the parts of Othello and Iago. Returning to America, he became partners with Lawrence BARRETT and performed a variety of roles with him, Helena MODJESKA (in *Macbeth*), and Tommaso SALVINI (who played Othello to Booth's Iago). His last performance was as Hamlet in 1891.

Booth, John Wilkes (1839–1865)   American actor best known for assassinating Abraham Lincoln. Booth, son of Junius Brutus BOOTH and brother of Edwin BOOTH and Junius Brutus BOOTH, Jr., was a well-known actor in 1865—the year of Lincoln's murder. He had played a variety of classical and modern roles, and was particularly noted for his portrayal of Richard III. Contemporary opinion varied as to his sanity when he assassinated Lincoln; he himself claimed patriotic motives in support of the Confederacy, which had just lost the Civil War, and for which he may have once been a secret agent. In any case he was at least a competent professional actor, though in the shadow of his great brother Edwin. He is said to have adopted his father's grandiloquent style in conscious opposition to Edwin's more restrained manner. He was killed while fleeing after the assassination.

Booth, Junius Brutus (1796–1852)   English actor, father of three notable American stars, Edwin BOOTH, John Wilkes BOOTH, and Junius Brutus BOOTH, Jr. The elder Booth, born to a London lawyer whose republican political sentiments were reflected in his son's name, became a major rival of Edmund KEAN after making his debut as Richard III in 1815. He was noted for his portrayals of Hamlet

and Shylock. Joining Kean's company in 1820, he played Iago to Kean's Othello and Edgar to his Lear. In 1821 he deserted his wife and son and emigrated to the United States with his lover, a London flower seller who was to be the mother of the actors and seven other children. Booth helped popularize Shakespeare in America, playing a variety of roles in New York and on extensive tours. He made his last appearance in New Orleans, before dying on a Mississippi River steamboat.

Booth, Junius Brutus, Jr. (1821–1883)   American actor. Booth, son of Junius Brutus BOOTH, was regarded as a lesser actor than either his father or his younger brother Edwin BOOTH, though he had a long and successful career in a variety of parts, mostly non-Shakespearean. He played Iago opposite his father's Othello on several occasions and once played Cassius opposite his two brothers, Edwin and John Wilkes BOOTH, who played Brutus and Antony, respectively. He was respected as a highly competent producer and stage manager.

Bordeaux   City in southwest FRANCE, the site of a battle in *1 Henry VI*. In 4.2 Talbot approaches the walls of Bordeaux and demands its surrender. He is spurned by a French General, who declares his confidence in the approaching French army. In 4.6 and 4.7, the battle takes place, and Talbot and his son, John, are killed.

In reality, Talbot and his forces occupied Bordeaux, which welcomed the English, months before the fatal battle, and the fight took place 50 miles away at Castillon, where Talbot had marched to relieve a siege. The historical battle took place in 1453 and was the last major conflict of the HUNDRED YEARS' WAR. Shakespeare placed it earlier in the war in order to suggest that Talbot's death was a direct consequence of the rivalry between York and Somerset. The playwright thereby emphasized the aristocratic discord that led, in the play's sequels, *2* and *3 Henry VI* and *Richard III*, to the WARS OF THE ROSES.

Boswell, James the younger (1778–1822)   British scholar, editor of the Third VARIORUM EDITION of Shakespeare's works. Boswell's father (1740–95), the famed biographer of Samuel JOHNSON, was a close friend and colleague of the Shakespearean scholar Edmond MALONE. When Malone died in 1812 while assembling his second edition of Shakespeare's works, the younger Boswell completed the task. The 21-volume result (1821) added to Malone's many notes and essays much of George STEEVENS's and Isaac REED's 1803 Second Variorum edition. It remained the most comprehensive work of its kind for over a century, until the New Variorum of H. H. FURNESS was completed. The Third Variorum, also known as "Boswell's Malone," is regarded as one of the most important editions of Shakespeare ever published. Its wide range of scholarship has been basic to virtually all later research on the playwright and his work.

Bosworth Field   Battle site in central England, the setting of the final three scenes of *Richard III*. Arguably the most famous battle in English history, Bosworth, fought in August 1485, provides the finale for Shakespeare's first TETRALOGY of HISTORY PLAYS. The army led by the Earl of Richmond defeats the forces of King Richard III, killing Richard. The WARS OF THE ROSES end, and the TUDOR DYNASTY is established, as Richmond claims the throne to rule as Henry VII.

Shakespeare's presentation of this event is highly elaborate and symbolic. The prelude to the battle, in 5.3, features councils of war and opposing statements of purpose, climaxed by the appearance of the spirits of Richard's victims. This is far more significant to the narrative than the minor vignettes of combat in 5.4 and the opening action of 5.5, although these scenes encompass the death of Richard. The play is then closed by Richmond's coronation, as he proclaims an end to the wars. Historically, this prediction could not have been certain, of course, and in fact skirmishes and minor risings were to continue for years. However, the playwright's purpose was not reportorial but dramatic, almost sacramental: the treachery and violence enacted in *Richard III* and the *Henry VI* plays are expiated in a ritual letting of blood followed by a formal reconciliation.

Bowdler, Thomas (1754–1825)   English editor. Bowdler published a censored version of Shakespeare's plays, his 10-volume *Family Shakespeare* (1818), in which "those words and expressions are omitted which cannot with propriety be read aloud in a family" or "by a gentleman to a company of ladies." A professed admirer of the playwright, he nonetheless felt that without "profaneness or obscenity . . . the transcendent genius of the poet would undoubtedly shine with more unclouded lustre." He accordingly changed all expletive uses of "God" to "Heaven" and cut extensive passages that he deemed obscene. Some plays involved more drastic action—Doll Tearsheet is simply eliminated from *2 Henry IV* and *Henry V*, for instance—and sometimes he had to confess himself defeated, publishing *Measure for Measure* and *Othello* with warnings.

Bowdler's *Shakespeare* was immensely popular and was reprinted many times. It became so well known—or notorious—that it sparked a new word that is still in use: bowdlerize, meaning to censor a text by omitting vulgarities. Bowdler also produced a bowdlerized version of Gibbons's *The Decline and Fall of the Roman Empire*, published posthumously in 1826.

Boyd, Michael (b. 1955)   English theatrical director. Born in Northern Ireland and trained in Moscow and Belgrade, Michael Boyd has been the artistic director of the ROYAL SHAKESPEARE COMPANY (RSC) since March 2003. Boyd was the founding director of the Tron Theatre in Glasgow before directing numerous plays by Shakespeare and others for the RSC, including a highly controversial *Measure for Measure* in 1998 and award-winning productions in *1–3 Henry VI*, *Richard III* (2000), and *The Tempest* (2001).

Boydell, John (1719–1804)   British engraver and publisher. Boydell founded an art gallery devoted to depictions of scenes from Shakespeare's plays, engravings of which were published for profit. He was supported in this endeavor by Britain's leading artist, Joshua Reynolds (1723–92), who hoped to promote an indigenous school of English history painting. The gallery was opened in 1789 with a collection of 34 paintings commissioned from a number of notable artists, including Reynolds, Joseph Wright of Derby (1734–97), and

Henry Fuseli (1741–1825). The collection eventually grew to almost 200 pieces, and many engravings were sold. Despite their popularity, however, the venture foundered economically, and Boydell's heirs were forced to sell the collection in 1805.

Bracegirdle, Anne (ca. 1673–1748) English actress. Bracegirdle began her career as a child actress and a student of Thomas BETTERTON and Mary SAUNDERSON. She was best known for her roles in the comedies of William Congreve (1670–1729), whose wife or mistress she was (the record is unclear), but she also played many Shakespearean roles, especially Cordelia, Desdemona, Ophelia, and Portia (in *King Lear, Othello, Hamlet,* and *The Merchant of Venice,* respectively).

Bradley, Andrew Cecil (1851–1935) British critic and scholar. Bradley was a professor of literature at several English universities. He is best known for his book *Shakespearean Tragedy* (1904), which centers on comprehensive analyses of the characters in *Hamlet, King Lear, Macbeth,* and *Othello.* Though criticized by modern commentators as overly dependent on the idea that the characters—who are, after all, fictions—can have genuinely human psychologies, it was nonetheless a dominant work among students of Shakespeare for almost 30 years.

Bradock, Richard (Richard Bradocke) (active 1581–1615) London printer. Bradock, about whom little is known, printed several editions of *Venus and Adonis* for William LEAKE between 1599 and 1603. In 1608 Thomas PAVIER hired him to print the first edition of A YORKSHIRE TRAGEDY, a play that was falsely attributed to Shakespeare.

Branagh, Kenneth (b. 1960) English actor and director. Kenneth Branagh's career has encompassed a wide range of acting and directing for both stage and screen, but he is best known for his FILM adaptations of Shakespeare's plays. In the 1980s Branagh was a leading member of the ROYAL SHAKESPEARE COMPANY, noted especially for his portrayals of Henry V and Hamlet. In 1987 he began directing Shakespeare's plays (and others), leading to his well-known movies of *Henry V* (1989), *Much Ado About Nothing* (1993), *Hamlet* (1996), and *Love's Labour's Lost* (2000), in each of which he also played the lead role.

Bretchgirdle, John (d. 1565) Vicar at STRATFORD. Bretchgirdle probably christened Shakespeare on April 26, 1564. The record does not include the name of the officiating clergyman, but it was probably Bretchgirdle, who was vicar at Stratford from 1561 until his death. A graduate of Oxford, Bretchgirdle had been a vicar and schoolmaster in Cheshire before coming to Stratford. He was a literate man who bequeathed a large library, much of it to the Stratford Grammar School, where Shakespeare was educated.

Bright, Timothy (1550–1615) English author of a probable source for *Hamlet.* Bright, a science writer and the inventor of shorthand notation, was a physician and clergyman. His *A Treatise of Melancholy* (1586) analyzed depression and mental illness in general; numerous similarities in ideas and wording suggest that this book influenced Shakespeare's portrait of his melancholy prince Hamlet. However, Bright's *Treatise* was one of many contemporary books on mental depression, a subject that fascinated Elizabethan England, and it need not have been the only inspiration for the creation of a melancholy protagonist, as was once commonly asserted.

A successful physician as a young man, Bright became so obsessed with developing his shorthand system—a rather cumbersome one that was soon superseded—that he neglected his medical practice until he was dismissed from his post in a London hospital. He moved to the country to live as a rural clergyman, but he was dismissed from two positions there for similar reasons, and he retired.

Bristol (Bristow) City in western England, a location in *Richard II.* King Richard II's cowardly friends Bushy and Greene flee to Bristol when Henry Bolingbroke appears with an army to challenge the king. Bristol was the principal port for trade with Ireland and thus a logical place for them to meet Richard upon his return. However, Bolingbroke arrives ahead of Richard, and he captures

Bushy and Greene. In 3.1 he condemns them to death before the walls of Bristol Castle.

Britten, Benjamin (1913–1976) British composer, creator of an OPERA of *A Midsummer Night's Dream*. Britten began composing orchestral music as a child, and by the 1930s he was an influential modern composer. He created many operas and choral works, including *The Rape of Lucretia* (1946), a "chamber opera" based on Ottorino RESPIGHI's *Lucrezia*; and *A Midsummer Night's Dream* (1960), which has been called "the most successful Shakespearean opera since VERDI." Britten's *Dream* is also the only major opera deriving from Shakespeare that employs only Shakespeare's words (but for a single line, needed to establish facts lost when a scene was cut), a libretto devised by Britten himself and the tenor Peter Pears (1910–86), who also played flute in the original production. In a particularly delightful element, Shakespeare's parodic send-up of Elizabethan theatrical conventions in the rustics' performance of PYRAMUS AND THISBE is paralleled by Britten's simultaneous takeoff on the routines of grand opera.

Brook, Peter (b. 1925) British theatrical and FILM director. Brook, an innovative director who has consciously attempted to incorporate influences from many times and cultures into his work, is one of the most important figures in contemporary world theater, as well as in the more restricted context of Shakespearean production. His many stagings of Shakespeare have varied in style from the Watteauesque romanticism of a 1947 *Love's Labour's Lost* to a brutal 1962 *King Lear*—with Paul SCOFIELD in what is acclaimed as one of the greatest Shakespearean performances of modern times—to the dramatically avant-garde 1970 presentation of *A Midsummer Night's Dream*, which incorporated circus routines, played within a set that was a huge white box. Other famous Brook productions include *Measure for Measure* and *The Winter's Tale* in 1951, both with John GIELGUD; and *Titus Andronicus*, starring Laurence OLIVIER, in 1955.

Brook was an adviser on a 1953 TELEVISION version of *King Lear* starring Orson WELLES, and he made his own film of *Lear* in 1969 with Scofield.

While filming *Lear* in Denmark, Brook corresponded about the project with Grigori KOZINTSEV, who was also filming the play in Russia. Brook's result is a bleak depiction characterized by the purposefully disconcerting use of such cinematic techniques as montage, hand-held camerawork, and silent-screen titles. It attracted both great praise and disgusted criticism.

Brook has written several books that have greatly influenced the contemporary theater, most notably *The Empty Space* (1968) and *The Shifting Point* (1987). Also, a lecture on Shakespeare was published as *Evoking Shakespeare* (1998).

Since the 1970s, Brook has been living in Paris and has been largely concerned with non-Shakespearean projects, the most notable of which was probably his 1987 staging of the ancient Indian epic *The Mahabharato* (filmed 1989). Critics sometimes find Brook's experiments pretentious or criticize a disparity between style and content, but all agree that his successes are major ones, and that his energy and daring have contributed greatly to late-20th-century theater.

Brooke, Arthur (d. 1563) English poet, author of the principal source for *Romeo and Juliet*. Brooke's poem *The Tragicall Historye of Romeus and Juliet* (1562)—a loose translation of a French prose tale that was in turn derived from an Italian story by Matteo BANDELLO—served Shakespeare as his chief source for his version of the tale of tragic lovers. The poem also contributed details to *The Two Gentlemen of Verona* and *3 Henry VI*.

Little is known of Brooke's life, except that he drowned while still a young man on a military expedition to aid the Huguenots in the Wars of Religion of FRANCE. He may well have entered the military out of religious conviction, for his introductory remarks to *Romeus and Juliet* are moralistic in a Protestant vein.

Brooke, C. F. Tucker (1883–1946) American scholar. A longtime professor at Yale University, Tucker Brooke wrote several significant books on Shakespeare, including *The Shakespeare Apocrypha* (1908), *The Tudor Drama* (1911), and *Shakespeare's Sonnets* (1936). He was also a general editor of the

Yale edition of Shakespeare's works, published in 40 volumes between 1917 and 1927.

Brooke, William, Lord Cobham   See COBHAM, WILLIAM BROOKE, LORD.

Browne, Robert (active 1583–1620) English actor and theatrical entrepreneur. Browne was a member of WORCESTER'S MEN in 1583–84, Derby's Men (see DERBY, WILLIAM STANLEY, EARL OF) in 1599–1601, and a partner in the Children of the Queen's Revels (see CHILDREN'S COMPANIES) in 1610, but he is best known for his career in Europe, especially in Germany. Between 1590 and 1620 he toured Germany and the Low Countries with a series of his own acting companies. He performed chiefly English plays, at first entirely in English but increasingly in German. His was the most important of a group of English acting companies whose tours were extremely popular and are generally thought to have contributed greatly to the German theater of the time. Another prominent figure was Browne's follower, John GREEN. Browne's company is known to have performed plays by Christopher MARLOWE, and he probably staged Shakespeare's plays as well, for Green is known to have done so. In 1593, while Browne was on tour, his wife and children died in a London epidemic. Two years later he remarried, possibly to a sister of William SLY, who in 1608 bequeathed his share in the GLOBE THEATRE to a Robert Browne who is thought to be this man.

Bryan, George (active 1586–1613) English actor. Bryan appears in the list of 26 "Principall Actors" who performed in Shakespeare's plays recorded in the FIRST FOLIO (1623), though he is not known to have played any specific role. He was among the English actors who visited Denmark in 1586 and was a player in STRANGE'S MEN at least from 1590 to 1593. He was probably still among them when they became the CHAMBERLAIN'S MEN in 1594, for he is recorded as a coreceiver of a payment to that company in 1596, implying that he was an important member of the group. However, he is not listed among the casts of particular Chamberlain's Men plays; the earliest such list dates from 1598, and scholars speculate that Bryan had retired

by then. Apparently successful as a minor courtier, Bryan was recorded as a member of the Queen's household, in an unspecified capacity, in 1603 and in 1611–13.

Buchanan, George (1506–1582) Scottish poet and historian, Scotland's leading Protestant humanist of the 16th century and the author of a minor source for *Macbeth*. Buchanan's history of Scotland in Latin, *Rerum Scotiarum Historia* (1582), may have influenced Shakespeare in the development of Macbeth's character, as well as providing several political details.

The history, considered one of the great works of late Latin literature, was the crowning achievement of a long and varied career. As a student at the University of Paris, Buchanan wrote notorious satires aimed at the clerical corruption that was stimulating the Protestant Reformation. Back in Scotland ca. 1528, Buchanan was imprisoned for his writings, but he escaped and established himself as a professor at a college in Bordeaux, where one of his pupils was MONTAIGNE. He wrote a number of notable Latin plays at this time. In 1548 he was appointed the head of a university in Portugal, but while there he was imprisoned by the Inquisition. In prison he wrote an acclaimed Latin rendition of the Book of Psalms.

Buchanan returned to Scotland in 1560 and converted to Calvinism. Tutor to Mary, Queen of Scots, he later became her enemy, assisting in her prosecution for treason in England. Upon her imprisonment he was made tutor to her son, later King JAMES I of England. During James's childhood as ruler of Scotland, Buchanan was an important figure in the government. In his last years he wrote his major works: a treatise on government that was condemned for its democratic tendencies and the history of Scotland that Shakespeare read.

Bullough, Geoffrey (1901–1982) British scholar. Bullough, longtime professor of English literature at London University, is best known for his eight-volume *Narrative and Dramatic Sources of Shakespeare* (1957–75). This definitive work is commonly known as "Bullough" and is considered a necessary reference for any Shakespearean scholarship. Bullough also edited a collection of the poems and plays of Fulke GREVILLE.

Burbage, Cuthbert (ca. 1566–1636) English theatrical entrepreneur, son of James BURBAGE and brother of Richard BURBAGE. Cuthbert, unlike his brother and father, was never an actor, but he was nevertheless an important figure in ELIZABETHAN THEATER. Cuthbert managed the first LONDON playhouse, the THEATRE, which he inherited when his father died in early 1597, just before the expiration of the lease for the land on which the building was constructed. After fruitless negotiations over its renewal, Cuthbert simply had the building torn down and reassembled as the GLOBE THEATRE, which was owned half by himself and Richard, and half by a group of actors from the KING'S MEN, including Shakespeare. Cuthbert was also a partner in a similar arrangement for the BLACKFRIARS THEATRE.

Burbage, James (ca. 1530–1597) English theatrical entrepreneur, builder of the first LONDON theater and father of Cuthbert and Richard BURBAGE. A poor carpenter who turned actor, Burbage was a leading member of LEICESTER'S MEN when he decided, in 1575, to construct a building devoted only to the performance of plays, in the hope of profiting from the admissions fees. His wealthy brother-in-law John Brayne provided the capital for the venture, and Burbage took a 21-year lease on a plot of land just north of the city. On it he built the THEATRE, which was opened sometime in late 1576 or early 1577. Burbage was evidently a fiery and argumentative man, and he and Brayne, and later Brayne's widow, disputed vigorously about the distribution of the profits in court and, on one occasion, in a physical brawl in front of an arriving audience. Burbage prospered at the Theatre, and in 1596 he bought a building that he converted into the BLACKFRIARS THEATRE. At his death he left the Theatre and its ground lease to Cuthbert, and the Blackfriars Theatre to Richard.

Burbage, Richard (ca. 1568–1619) English actor, son of James BURBAGE and brother of Cuthbert BURBAGE, the leading actor of the CHAMBERLAIN'S MEN and the original portrayer of many of Shake-

Richard Burbage, one of the greatest English actors of Shakespeare's time, originated the roles of Richard III, Hamlet, Othello, and Lear. He was the leading tragedian of the Chamberlain's Men. *(Courtesy of Billy Rose Theatre Collection; New York Public Library at Lincoln Center; Astor, Lenox and Tilden Foundations)*

speare's protagonists. With William ALLEYN, Burbage is said to have been the greatest actor of the ELIZABETHAN THEATER. Contemporary allusions establish that Burbage played Hamlet, Lear, Malvolio (*Twelfth Night*), Othello, and Richard III, and he probably played many more major Shakespearean roles.

Burbage's early career is obscure. He probably appeared with the company composed of the ADMIRAL'S MEN and STRANGE'S MEN, who played at his father's playhouse, the THEATRE, in 1590–91. He first achieved widespread recognition in *Richard III*, the play that also established Shakespeare as a playwright, around 1591. (In connection with this role, Burbage figures in the only surviving contemporary anecdote about Shakespeare; see MANNINGHAM,

JOHN.) He apparently did not tour with this troupe during the plague years, 1593–94, but he was an early member of the Chamberlain's Men, as Strange's was known after 1594. He may have been with PEMBROKE'S MEN in the interim. He remained with the Chamberlain's Men, later the KING'S MEN, until his death, though the last record of a performance dates from 1610.

When James Burbage died in 1597, he left Cuthbert the theater (which he tore down and reassembled as the GLOBE THEATRE) and Richard the BLACKFRIARS THEATRE; the brothers shared them through partnerships with each other. Burbage was also a painter. A well-known likeness of him is thought to be a self-portrait, and the CHANDOS PORTRAIT, once thought to be of Shakespeare, was traditionally attributed to him. As a painter, he collaborated with Shakespeare on an allegorical shield for Francis Manners, Earl of RUTLAND.

Burby, Cuthbert (d. 1607) London publisher and bookseller. In 1594 Burby published *The Taming of a Shrew*, probably a BAD QUARTO of Shakespeare's *The Taming of the Shrew*. He also published the first edition of *Love's Labour's Lost* (1598) and the second (Q2) of *Romeo and Juliet* (1599). In 1607, just before his death, he sold the rights to all three works to Nicholas LING. He also published the first two editions of *Edward III* (1594, 1599), though no record survives of their transfer after the publisher's death. Burby was a brother-in-law of the printer Thomas SNODHAM.

Burghley, Lord (William Cecil, Lord Burleigh) (1520–1598) The leading statesman of Elizabethan England, chief minister to Queen Elizabeth I; sometimes said to have been a model for Polonius in *Hamlet*. An aristocratic courtier, Burghley was the most important member of Elizabeth's government from her accession in 1558 until his death. After the pope excommunicated the Protestant Elizabeth and encouraged her assassination (and that of her chief minister) in 1570, Burghley set up an early variety of secret police, using espionage and torture in a ruthless and largely successful campaign to cripple the Counter-Reformation in England. Though he privately declared his dislike of

these methods, he remains a symbol of unscrupulous state power. He is also remembered for his *Ten Precepts*, a pamphlet of sententious advice on gentlemanly conduct addressed to his son Robert CECIL, who succeeded him as the most powerful man in England.

Hamlet's Polonius is associated with the statesman because this character bears an obviously satirical name, Corambis, in the BAD QUARTO (Q1) of *Hamlet*, and he resembles Burghley in being a high government official and in delivering "precepts" (1.3.58) to his son. Also, in 2.1 Polonius sends his servant Reynaldo to spy on his son Laertes, who is at school in Paris, and a connection has been drawn to Burghley's espionage network and to the fact that his eldest son, Thomas CECIL, led a notoriously dissolute life on the Continent for several years in his youth. The name Corambis is thought to allude to a well-known Latin proverb on triteness: *Crambe bis posita mors est* ("Cabbage served twice is deadly"); this seems appropriate to the long-winded Polonius.

However, Q1 is probably a version compiled from the memories of actors who played in it, and scholars believe that Corambis was the name of the equivalent character in an earlier play, now lost, the UR-HAMLET, and that the name was inserted in Q1 by an actor who also knew the earlier version. If so, then any satirical point was intended not by Shakespeare but by the author of the *Ur-Hamlet*, probably Thomas KYD. In fact, Shakespeare may well have changed the name in order to defuse any such reference.

Even if Kyd's Corambis might be linked to Burghley, Shakespeare's Polonius seems almost certainly not. Burghley had been most powerful in the 1570s and 1580s—and had been dead for several years by the time *Hamlet* was written—making a satire on him by Shakespeare almost pointless. Also, Shakespeare was not given to personal satire—he had been willing to change the names of characters in *1* and *2 Henry IV* (such as Harvey, Oldcastle, Sir John Rossill) to avoid offense—and the likelihood that he would have attempted to mock the father of a powerful member of the court is slim.

Other factors also weigh against the association of Burghley with Polonius. *Ten Precepts* was not published until 1637, and, although the sophisticated literary world may have known of it in 1601, most of the satire's hypothetical audience would not have. In any case, such collections of paternal wisdom were widely popular, and Polonius's version does not particularly resemble Burghley's. A father spying on his high-living son was likewise not unusual in literature, and the episode in *Hamlet* has legitimate dramatic purposes and need not be associated with anything outside the play.

Burleigh, William Cecil, Lord   See BURGHLEY, LORD.

Burnaby, William (ca. 1672–1706)   Minor English playwright. Burnaby is remembered primarily because he incorporated adaptations of scenes from *Twelfth Night* into his 1703 comedy *Love Betray'd, or The Agreeable Disappointment.*

Bury St. Edmunds   Town in the English county of Suffolk, site of a famed medieval abbey and the setting for Act 3 of *2 Henry VI*. Here, in the ancient abbey, the Duke of Gloucester is prosecuted and then murdered by the clique surrounding Queen Margaret and the Duke of Suffolk. Consequently, the king exiles Suffolk for life at the insistence of an outraged mob, and Cardinal Beaufort, one of the conspirators, dies with a bad conscience.

Bury St. Edmunds was an unusually isolated location for a meeting of Parliament. Although Shakespeare does not mention it, much of his audience will have realized that this town was deep in the home territory of the Duke of Suffolk, far from Gloucester's power base in London. The mob appearing in the play to demand Suffolk's punishment is fictitious; precisely because of its location, Gloucester's arrest went unprotested. Suffolk was not in fact banished until much later, and for different reasons.

As ST. EDMUNDSBURY, the town is a location in *King John.*

Busby, John (active 1576–1619)   London bookseller and publisher. Busby was associated with apparently pirated publications of three of Shakespeare's plays. In 1600 Busby and John MILLINGTON published the first QUARTO edition of *Henry V.* In 1602 he registered a forthcoming publication of *The Merry Wives of Windsor* with the STATIONERS' COMPANY but immediately sold his "rights" to his longtime business partner, Arthur JOHNSON, whose name appeared alone on the title page of the play. In 1607 he registered *King Lear* jointly with Nathaniel BUTTER, though again, when the play was published the next year, Busby's name was dropped. Each of these editions was a BAD QUARTO, that is, it was transcribed from the recollections of actors who had performed in the play. This method was used by publishers who had no access to the proper text of a play—carefully withheld by acting companies in the hope of foiling pirates such as Busby.

Butter, Nathaniel (d. 1664)   London bookseller and publisher who issued the first edition of *King Lear.* In 1607, jointly with John BUSBY, who several times pirated Shakespeare's plays, Butter registered a forthcoming edition of the play with the STATIONERS' COMPANY. However, when the QUARTO edition of the play appeared the next year, it was attributed solely to Butter. It was a BAD QUARTO, an inaccurate text assembled from the recollections of actors, a frequent recourse of unauthorized publishers. Butter also published THE LONDON PRODIGAL (1605), a play that was falsely attributed to Shakespeare, and he is known to have pirated a play by Thomas HEYWOOD.

Butter, the son of a printer and bookseller, published his first book in 1604, opened a bookshop (at the sign of the "Pied Bull") the next year, and sold books at various locations until his death. After 1622 he specialized in publishing news sheets, early predecessors of newspapers (one of which was satirized by Ben JONSON), but he did not flourish and is said to have died a pauper.

C

Calais Location in *Edward III*, a city in FRANCE that is besieged by King Edward during the HUNDRED YEARS' WAR. In 4.2, having demanded Calais's surrender and been met with defiance, King Edward receives a deputation of refugees from the city. The First Poor Man reports that they have been expelled by the town's leaders, who have declared them not worth feeding. The King grants them food, alms, and passage through his army's lines, in an episode that magnifies his virtue. A French Captain appears with an offer of surrender, on condition that the townsmen be permitted "benefit of life and goods" (4.2.66). The King declares that, having refused his clemency at first, they may not have it now. He says he will destroy the town unless six of its richest citizens appear before him within two days, with nooses around their necks, prepared "To be afflicted, hanged, or what I please" (4.2.78). After delivering this grisly ultimatum, the King departs, and the Captain is left to rue the city's dependence on the unreliable French army.

In 5.1, again outside the gates of Calais, the six "burghers of Calais" (as they are known) appear, prepared to sacrifice themselves in exchange for mercy on their fellow citizens. Edward orders a painful death for them, but his wife, Queen Phillipa, intercedes for them, and the King grants them mercy.

The remainder of the scene (and of the play) occurs in this location, but it is not mentioned again. The triumphs of the English are detailed, as King David of Scotland is presented to King Edward as a prisoner, and the Prince of Wales arrives triumphant from the battle of POITIERS, which has been enacted in 4.4–4.7, between the two scenes at Calais.

Historically, the siege of Calais lasted about a year, though in the play it seems just a few days. Moreover, this brief period is broken into two parts (4.2 and 5.1), framing the battle of Poitiers, which actually occurred almost 10 years later (see *Edward III*, "Commentary"). Many other details are inaccurate as well. However, setting the play's climax at this coastal city was quite appropriate to an account of King Edward's campaigns in France, for the acquisition of Calais was the major strategic gain for England during Edward's reign, and, indeed, in the entire 116-year span of the war; this fortress town was to provide the English with an invaluable base of operations on the Continent and in the English Channel. It remained in English hands for more than two centuries, until 1558.

Caldwell, Zoë (b. 1933) Australian-born British actress. Caldwell was a prominent actress in Australia in her early 20s when she went to England and played a variety of roles at STRATFORD. Her first major role was as Helena in Tyrone GUTHRIE's 1959 production of *All's Well That Ends Well*. She has been acclaimed in many other Shakespearean parts, including Cordelia—opposite Charles Laughton's Lear—Ophelia, Lady Macbeth, and, perhaps most notably, Cleopatra.

Calvert, Charles (1828–1879) British theatrical producer. Calvert was a follower of Samuel PHELPS in restoring Shakespeare's texts and simplifying productions. After a career as an actor, he became the manager of a theater in Manchester, England, where he established his reputation as a producer. From 1864 to 1875 he staged many revivals of Shakespeare plays in London, focusing on works that were traditionally less frequently performed, such as *2 Henry IV* and *Henry VIII*, but also presenting popular pieces like *Richard III* and *The Merchant of Venice* (the latter in 1871 with music by Arthur SULLIVAN). However, his theater was not financially successful, and he returned to touring at the close of his career.

Camden, William (1551–1623) English historian, author of a minor source for *Coriolanus*. Camden, a noted educator, scholar, and antiquarian, wrote a massive Latin work on ancient and medieval England, *Britannia* (1586). An English translation by Philemon HOLLAND came out in 1610, but English excerpts had already been published in *Remaines of a greater Worke concerning Britaine* in 1605. From the *Remaines*, Shakespeare took some details for MENENIUS's famous "belly speech" (*Coriolanus*, 1.1.95–159). The *Remaines* also contains an appreciation of Shakespeare as one of England's greatest writers.

Camden was a longtime secondary school teacher and headmaster who taught poetry composition to Ben JONSON, among others. He remained a lifelong friend of Jonson and through him may have known Shakespeare personally. He was also a noted authority on heraldry and the chief founder of the Society of Antiquaries, an important intellectual institution of the day. In addition to *Britannia*, Camden wrote a Latin history of the reign of Queen Elizabeth I and an English account of the Gunpowder Plot (see GARNET, HENRY).

canon An authoritative list of the works of an author. The canon of Shakespeare's plays varies slightly according to the opinions of various scholars, but until recent times it has usually included 38 titles: the 36 plays of the FIRST FOLIO, plus *Pericles*, and *The Two Noble Kinsmen*. However, some scholars have doubted the Folio's reliability, especially with regard to *Henry VIII*—probably written in part by John FLETCHER—while others often relegate *Peri-*

cles or *The Two Noble Kinsmen*—especially the latter—to the APOCRYPHA, a list of dubious titles. Recently, a considerable shift in scholarly opinion has introduced a "new" play to the canon: *Edward III* has been widely recognized as having been written, at least in part, by Shakespeare, and it is accordingly treated as his in this edition of this book.

Thus, this book assumes that the canon consists of the 39 plays specified above, i.e., in alphabetical order: *All's Well That Ends Well*; *Antony and Cleopatra*; *As You Like It*; *The Comedy of Errors*; *Coriolanus*; *Cymbeline*; *Edward III*; *Hamlet*; *1 & 2 Henry IV*; *Henry V*; *1, 2, & 3 Henry VI*; *Henry VIII*; *Julius Caesar*; *King John*; *King Lear*; *Love's Labour's Lost*; *Macbeth*; *Measure for Measure*; *The Merchant of Venice*; *The Merry Wives of Windsor*; *A Midsummer Night's Dream*; *Much Ado About Nothing*; *Othello*; *Pericles*; *Richard II*; *Richard III*; *Romeo and Juliet*; *The Taming of the Shrew*; *The Tempest*; *Timon of Athens*; *Titus Andronicus*; *Troilus and Cressida*; *Twelfth Night*; *The Two Gentlemen of Verona*; *The Two Noble Kinsmen*; and *The Winter's Tale*.

In Shakespeare studies, the term *canon* often applies only to the plays. However, a broader usage, equally correct, would also include the 154 *Sonnets* (though a few of them are disputed); the long poems *Venus and Adonis* and *The Rape of Lucrece*; and various shorter poems, including "The Phoenix and Turtle," some of the works in THE PASSIONATE PILGRIM, and some EPITAPHS (though other epitaphs are clearly apocryphal). Other poems are sometimes suggested for the canon, e.g., "SHALL I DIE?" and *A FUNERAL ELEGY*; scholars periodically nominate new discoveries for inclusion, and disputes over the correct list can last for decades without resolution.

Capell, Edward (1713–1781) Shakespearean scholar. Capell was the first scholar to collate the old editions of Shakespeare's plays to arrive at the most accurately rendered texts possible, and he also introduced the first serious scholarly consideration of Shakespeare's sources. After 24 years of labor, his edition of the collected plays was published in 1768. His *Commentary, Notes and Various Readings to Shakespeare*, begun in 1774, was published posthumously in 1783. He also published the first modern edition of *Edward III*, though he did not include it in his edition of Shakespeare's plays. Though his judgments are still acclaimed today, he is very little read except by specialists, in part because of his tedious prose. As Samuel JOHNSON put it, "he doth gabble monstrously."

Carew, Richard (1555–1620) English scholar and contemporary admirer of Shakespeare. Carew, a country gentleman and self-taught student of languages and early English history, translated poetry from Italian and Spanish and also published his own verse. His major work was a history of Cornwall (1602), but he is remembered today chiefly for a remark in a letter (1603) to William CAMDEN, in which he offered an early assessment of "Shakespeare," declaring him the equal of Catullus as a poet. The letter was published in the second edition (1614) of Camden's *Remaines*.

Casson, Lewis (1875–1969) British actor and producer. After a successful career as an actor, Casson turned to production and was especially known for staging ancient Greek drama and Shakespeare, usually in collaboration with his wife, the actress Sybil THORNDIKE. Particularly noteworthy was his 1938 production of *Coriolanus*, starring Thorndike and Laurence OLIVIER, which is widely credited for establishing the play's place in the British theatrical repertory.

Castelnuovo-Tedesco, Mario (1895–1968) Italian composer of numerous works based on various Shakespearean texts. A refugee from Fascism, Castelnuovo-Tedesco, who had seen his work suppressed in Italy because he was a Jew, lived in America from 1939. He wrote music for several hundred Hollywood movies, but he is best known for symphonic and choral works, including an OPERA based on *All's Well That Ends Well* (written in the mid-1920s but not performed until 1958) and his popular *Merchant of Venice* (1956). He also wrote overtures to 11 of Shakespeare's plays, as well as settings for numerous SONGS from the plays and for many of the *Sonnets*.

Castiglione, Baldassare (1478–1529) Italian writer and diplomat, author of *Il Libro del Corte-*

giano (*The Book of the Courtier*, 1528), a possible influence on *Much Ado About Nothing*. Castiglione, a nobleman of MANTUA, was a highly successful diplomat, serving the Montefeltro family, dukes of Urbino. When they were dispossessed of their dukedom by the pope in 1516, Castiglione returned to Mantua and served as the city's envoy to Rome. His famous book, on which he worked for 20 years, is one of the most important documents of the Italian RENAISSANCE. In it he describes an ideal courtly society, set in the ducal court of Urbino, renowned in his day as one of the most artistic and intellectually accomplished courts of Europe. Castiglione's vision of excellence included the idea—revolutionary at the time—that women have much to contribute to society. To illustrate this point, he composed a series of sprightly debates between a man and a woman that may well have inspired the battles of wit between Beatrice and Benedick in *Much Ado*. *Il Libro del Cortegiano* was translated into English by Sir Thomas HOBY, appearing in 1561 as *The Courtyer*. Shakespeare may have read Castiglione in Italian, however.

Caxton, William (ca. 1422–1491) English translator and printer. In 1475 Caxton produced the first book printed in English, *The Recuyell of the Historyes of Troye*, his own translation (from a French version) of Guido delle COLONNE's Latin history of the TROJAN WAR. This work, probably in its fifth edition (1596), provided Shakespeare with much of the detail for his account of the war in *Troilus and Cressida*. Caxton also translated and published, in 1484, a French tale that may have inspired the husbands' wager on their wives' obedience in 5.2 of *The Taming of the Shrew*.

Caxton, who is known as the father of English printing, began as an apprentice to a cloth merchant. A capable businessman, he became the representative of the Merchants' Guild in the busy European commercial center at Bruges, eventually being appointed governor of the English commercial and diplomatic colony. In 1469 Caxton became an adviser to the Duchess of Burgundy; as such he had the leisure to devote to literature, and he began his translating career. He also learned printing while in the duchess's employ, and the *Recuyell* was printed in Bruges. He returned to England in 1476 and continued publishing until his death. His publications (more than 100 titles, including many of CHAUCER's works) were extremely influential on English literature for more than a century.

Cecil, Robert, Earl of Salisbury (1563–1612) Elizabethan and Jacobean statesman, one of the most powerful men in Shakespeare's England. The son of Lord BURGHLEY, Cecil was intended for statesmanship from his youth. He was an enemy of Robert Devereux, Earl of ESSEX, in the 1590s, but after Essex's attempted rebellion, Cecil intervened to save Henry Wriothesley, Earl of SOUTHAMPTON, Essex's follower and Shakespeare's patron, from the death penalty. Cecil was acting secretary of state before he turned 30, and he held the office officially from 1596 until just before his death, thus controlling English foreign policy for almost 20 years. He helped prepare for the peaceful accession of King JAMES I in 1603, for which he was rewarded with great wealth and high rank, becoming the first Earl of Salisbury in 1605. After 1608 he effectively ran the government.

Cecil spent much of his money on the patronage of art, including the creation of one of the finest Jacobean mansions, Hatfield House. He was responsible for the downfall of Sir Walter RALEIGH in 1606, but eventually his political rivals brought him down the same way, by poisoning the king's opinion of him. He fell from favor in 1611, dying not long thereafter.

Cecil, Thomas (1542–1623) Soldier, opponent of Robert Devereux, Earl of ESSEX. The eldest son of Lord BURGHLEY, Cecil led a notoriously dissolute life in Paris and Germany before taking up a military career. His father is sometimes thought to have been a model for *Hamlet*'s Polonius, in part because of the letters of moralistic advice he sent to the young Cecil. He served with distinction in Scotland and the Netherlands and at sea against the Spanish Armada. In 1599 he was appointed military governor of northern England; visiting London while on leave from this post in February 1601, Cecil improvised the military opposition to Essex's abortive uprising, crushing it immediately.

Cecil, William See BURGHLEY, LORD.

censorship Imposed regulation of the content of plays and other literary works. In Shakespeare's England, plays had to be submitted to the MASTER OF REVELS, who often required revisions both large and small before granting the required license for performance. After 1606 his powers were extended to the publication of plays as well. As early as 1559, Queen Elizabeth (see Elizabeth I in *Henry VIII*) prohibited the dramatic treatment of religious or political issues. It is believed that the absence of the "deposition scene" of *Richard II* (4.1) from the first three editions of the play is a result of this law. (As late as 1680, Nahum TATE's adaptation of *Richard II* was suppressed by the government, despite his attempt to disguise the work as *The Sicilian Usurper.*) A 1606 statute—called an Act to Restrain Abuses of Players—outlawed the slightest profanity, and this feature is reflected in many of Shakespeare's plays, where such expletives as "God," which appear in the earliest published versions, are replaced with "Jove" or "heavens" in the FIRST FOLIO (1623).

Sometimes the texts reveal self-censorship practiced by the playwright or the acting companies. While not strictly censorship, in not being imposed, the excisions might not have been made but for the possibility of trouble with the authorities. For instance, some scholars believe that a passage deleted from Q2 of *Hamlet*—2.2.335–358, mocking the CHILDREN'S COMPANIES—was removed for fear that it might offend the new king, JAMES I, who had just taken a children's company under royal protection. Another passage, on the drunkenness of Danes (1.4.17–38), does not appear in the FOLIO edition of the play, perhaps to avoid giving offense to King JAMES I's queen, Anne of Denmark.

An informal, quasi-governmental censorship sometimes operated alongside the official system, as when pressure from an offended aristocrat apparently brought about the change of a notable character's name from Oldcastle to Falstaff (see COBHAM, WILLIAM BROOKE, LORD). Such efforts were unusual, but their effectiveness was ensured by the threat of official censorship, for the government frequently used a heavy censorial hand. For instance, when a play by Thomas NASHE, *Isle of Dogs* (1597; now lost), was declared seditious, all the LONDON theaters were closed for the summer and three of the actors were given jail sentences. In 1605 George CHAPMAN and Ben JONSON were jailed because their play *Eastward Ho!* contained passages that offended King James. (Jonson had been one of the three *Isle of Dogs* actors.) The ultimate form of state censorship came from the STUART DYNASTY's opposition, however, when the revolutionary Puritan government outlawed the theater altogether at the outset of the Civil Wars in 1642. Drama of any sort (excepting "opera"; see DAVENANT, WILLIAM) was illegal until the restoration of the monarchy in 1660. (See also BOWDLER, THOMAS.)

Cervantes Saavedra, Miguel de (1547–1616) Spanish novelist, author of *Don Quixote* (1605–15), a probable influence on the lost play *Cardenio*, possibly by Shakespeare and John FLETCHER. The first part of *Don Quixote* was translated into English by Thomas Shelton (active 1612–20) and published in 1612. A story within it is presumed to be the source for *Cardenio*, and Fletcher used Cervantes's work as inspiration for several of his own plays.

Cervantes had an adventurous military career: he lost a hand at the battle of Lepanto (1571), was later captured, and spent five years as a slave in Algiers before returning to Spain in 1580. He was disappointed not to receive a lucrative appointment as a reward and was reduced to extreme poverty. He struggled through his later life as a petty government employee—he was once jailed for irregularities in handling funds—but he nevertheless managed to write a number of plays, poems, and novels, including the only one that was successful in his own time, the masterpiece for which he is still famous. He died on the same day as Shakespeare.

Chamberlain's Men Acting company of the ELIZABETHAN THEATER, the troupe in which Shakespeare was a partner. Though Shakespeare may have been involved with various other acting companies (see ADMIRAL'S MEN, DERBY'S MEN, LEICESTER'S MEN, PEMBROKE'S MEN, QUEEN'S MEN, STRANGE'S MEN, and SUSSEX'S MEN), he is most closely associated with the Chamberlain's Men (known as the KING'S MEN after the accession of King JAMES I in 1603). He was a partner in this troupe from at least December of 1594 until his retirement almost 20 years later.

The Chamberlain's Men was created in the spring of 1594 as a reorganization of Derby's Men—originally Strange's Men—following the death of Lord Ferdinando STRANGE, the patron of the company. A patron was legally necessary for an acting company, so Henry Carey, Baron HUNSDON, agreed to place the actors under his protection. Since Lord Hunsdon was the Lord Chamberlain to Queen Elizabeth I (see Elizabeth I in *Henry VIII*), the company was known thereafter as the Chamberlain's Men. In July 1596, when the Lord Chamberlain died, his son, George Carey, Baron HUNSDON, became patron of the company, which was briefly known as HUNSDON'S MEN. However, Lord Hunsdon became Chamberlain himself, in March 1597, and the troupe resumed its old name.

The earliest surviving mention of the Chamberlain's Men records an appearance at NEWINGTON BUTTS in June 1594, though it soon moved to the THEATRE, whose owner, James BURBAGE, had earlier been part of a provincial company patronized by Hunsdon. The original partners in the Chamberlain's Men were probably George BRYAN, Richard COWLEY, John HEMINGE (who functioned as the group's business manager), William KEMPE, Augustin PHILLIPS, Thomas POPE, Richard BURBAGE, and Shakespeare, though the last two may have joined the others later in 1594. Bryan retired sometime before 1598, and Pope did likewise around 1600. They were replaced by William SLY and Henry CONDELL, both of whom had performed earlier with the company; Kempe left in 1599 (though he may have returned briefly in 1601 or 1602) and was replaced by Robert ARMIN. The makeup of the partnership did not otherwise change until after the creation of the King's Men in 1603.

The Chamberlain's Men originally played at the Theatre in summer and the CROSS KEYS INN in winter, but in 1596 the latter venue was closed by the city, and the company is thought to have moved to the SWAN THEATRE. A year later it played the CURTAIN THEATRE, and a group of the partners built their own house, the GLOBE THEATRE, in 1599; there they remained for the duration of their existence. Each year over the Christmas holidays, the troupe also performed at the court of the queen, whose invitations were a mark of success and prestige. At first their rivals, the Admiral's Men, vied closely with them for this honor, but gradually the Chamberlain's Men dominated the competition; over their nine-year lifetime, the Chamberlain's Men performed at court 32 times and the Admiral's Men only 20. The Chamberlain's Men specialized in plays by their own Shakespeare, though they also performed a number of Ben JONSON's dramas as well as occasional works by others, including Thomas DEKKER and John MARSTON. (For the history of the troupe after 1603, see KING'S MEN.)

Chambers, Edmund Kerchever (1866–1954) English scholar, author of several standard works on Shakespeare and the ELIZABETHAN THEATER. Chambers was a civil servant who also wrote dramatic criticism. In the 1890s he began writing a small book on Shakespeare that eventually grew to become *The Medieval Stage* (2 vol., 1903), *The Elizabethan Stage* (4 vol., 1923), and *William Shakespeare: A Study of the Facts and Problems* (2 vol., 1930). He also produced critical editions of Francis BEAUMONT, John Donne (1572–1631), John FLETCHER, John MILTON, and others. He wrote biographies of Matthew Arnold (1822–88) and Samuel Taylor COLERIDGE, and he edited the *Shakespeare Allusion Book* (1932) (see INGLEBY, CLEMENT MANSFIELD).

Chandos portrait Possible portrait of Shakespeare. The Chandos portrait—named for its longtime owners, the Dukes of Chandos—was traditionally said to have been painted by Richard BURBAGE, but modern scholars find this tradition improbable. A connoisseur's notebook of 1719 contains the earliest trace of the Chandos portrait, recording that the painting's then-current owner had bought it from the estate of Thomas BETTERTON, who in turn had bought it from the estate of William DAVENANT, who had inherited it from its painter, one "John Taylor, a Player," that is, a professional actor. A John Taylor is known to have been a member of the cathedral choir affiliated with the Children of Paul's acting company (see CHILDREN'S COMPANIES) in the 1590s. Thus he could have been an actor around 1605, when, if the sitter was Shakespeare, this portrait of a 30ish man will have been painted. Further, a John Taylor is recorded in the London painter's guild from 1623 (earlier records are lost). However, whether these two are the same John Taylor and whether either of them had any connection to Shakespeare is unknown. The identity of the painter therefore remains questionable.

The Chandos portrait is quite competent, almost certainly painted from life—unlike either of the two portraits regarded as authoritative (see DROESHOUT, MARTIN; JANSSEN, GHEERART). However, since it only vaguely resembles the authoritative likenesses, the identity of the sitter is questionable. The Chandos portrait was widely considered to be a picture of Shakespeare until well into the 19th century, and some commentators still argue that it is possibly genuine. In 1856 it became the first possession of the fledgling British National Portrait Gallery. It was the basis for Peter SCHEEMAKER's statue of Shakespeare in WESTMINSTER ABBEY, and a copy of it, painted for John DRYDEN by the renowned portraitist Sir Godfrey Kneller (1646–1723), now hangs in the FOLGER SHAKESPEARE LIBRARY. (See also PORTRAITS OF SHAKESPEARE.)

Chapel Lane Cottage Property in STRATFORD owned by Shakespeare. In 1602 Shakespeare bought the Chapel Lane Cottage and its garden of about one-quarter of an acre, as a supplement to his residence, NEW PLACE, which was directly across the lane. The cottage may have been intended for a hired gardener. The purchase indicates to us the playwright's continuing success, and for him it further consolidated his position as a member of Stratford's elite. Shakespeare left the Chapel Lane Cottage, with New Place, to his daughter Susanna SHAKESPEARE Hall.

Chapman, George (ca. 1559–1634) English poet and playwright, a major figure in both ELIZABETHAN and JACOBEAN DRAMA, a noted translator of HOMER, and the author of minor sources for *The Merry Wives of Windsor* and *Troilus and Cressida.* Chapman may have been the model for the character HOLOFERNES in *Love's Labour's Lost,* and he is sometimes identified with the "rival poet" of the *Sonnets.* Scholars who believe that many of Shakespeare's works were written in part by other playwrights (see, e.g., FLEAY, FREDERICK GARD; ROBERTSON, JOHN MACKINNON) have attributed to Chapman passages or whole scenes in a number of the plays, especially *All's Well That Ends Well*, *Measure for Measure*, and *Troilus and Cressida*; however, modern scholars dispute most such attributions.

Chapman was a melancholy and disputatious man who made many enemies, possibly including Shakespeare, for some scholars believe that the playwright satirized him as the pedantic Holofernes. In any case Chapman's book-length philosophical poem *The Shadow of Night* (1594) is probably alluded to several times in the obscure jests that stud *Love's Labour's Lost*, and the drama may have been conceived as an answer to *The Shadow of Night*'s denigration of pleasure and practicality in favor of a contemplative life. Shakespeare exploited Chapman in other works. Nym's comical use of the word *humour* in *The Merry Wives of Windsor* is borrowed from Chapman's highly successful COMEDY OF HUMOURS, *The Blind Beggar of Alexandria* (1596), and several passages in *Troilus and Cressida* echo Chapman's initial partial translation of Homer's *Iliad* (1598). Some scholars believe that the latter play was also intended to counter Chapman, who rejected the usual English view that favored the Trojans in the TROJAN WAR.

Chapman's only literary friends appear to have been the equally acerbic Ben JONSON and Thomas MARSTON. His embittered bellicosity emerged in his writing, sometimes with disastrous effects. In 1605 he and Jonson were briefly jailed when King JAMES I took offense at remarks about SCOTLAND in their play *Eastward Ho!* (1605, written with Marston). He encountered government CENSORSHIP again in 1608 over another play, and he retired from the theater to concentrate on his translation of Homer, which was only completed in 1615. This was his masterpiece and remained the standard English version for generations, though it is full of inaccuracies and has long been superseded.

Although Chapman was more a poet than a playwright, Francis MERES classed him as a leading writer of both COMEDY and TRAGEDY. *The Blind Beggar of Alexandria* (his first play) was a great success, and his tragedy *Bussy D'Ambois* (1607) is still performed occasionally today. However, despite the appreciative opinions of his contemporaries, Chapman's works are largely ignored by modern readers. He is now probably best known through John KEATS's great SONNET, "On First Looking into Chapman's Homer."

Chatterton, Frederick Balsir (1831–1886) English theatrical producer. Between 1863 and 1879, F. B. Chatterton was manager of the Drury Lane Theatre in London, and he was a notable promoter of Shakespeare's plays, especially as presented by Samuel PHELPS. Unfortunately, these productions were not generally profitable, and Chatterton is remembered for a famous witticism, inspired by a production of an ephemeral play by the poet Byron: "Shakespeare spells ruin and Byron bankruptcy."

Chaucer, Geoffrey (ca. 1340–1400) English poet, Shakespeare's greatest predecessor and the author of sources for several of the plays. Chaucer's *Troilus and Criseyde* was the main source for the Trojan scenes in *Troilus and Cressida*. The same work taught Shakespeare about leitmotifs—recurring images that provide a sense of aesthetic continuity in a work whose tone changes considerably—a technique that he used in *Romeo and Juliet* and elsewhere. Moreover, *Troilus and Criseyde* had influenced the *Romeus* of Arthur BROOKE, the chief source for *Romeo and Juliet*, and Chaucer's *Parliament of Fowles* provided material for Mercutio's "Queen Mab" speech in the same play. Chaucer's "The Knight's Tale" in *The Canterbury Tales* was the main source for *The Two Noble Kinsmen* and for parts of *A Midsummer Night's Dream*. "The Merchant's Tale" and "Sir Tophas" from *The Canterbury Tales* contributed further details to the *Dream*. The personality of the Host in *The Merry Wives of Windsor* was probably influenced by Chaucer's innkeeper in *The Canterbury Tales*. Lastly, various works of Chaucer provided minor details in other plays (e.g., *2 Henry VI* 3.2.115–116).

Chaucer was the son of a vintner with connections to the court of King Edward III (ruled 1327–77), and he is first recorded as a teenaged page to the Duke of Clarence, the king's son, with whom he went to war in FRANCE at the outset of the HUNDRED YEARS' WAR. For the rest of his life he was an employee of the royal courts in one way or another, mostly as an official of the customs service. His greatest patron was John of Gaunt (who appears in *Richard II*), probably because he married a sister of Katherine Swynford, Gaunt's longtime mistress and eventual wife (although the identity of Chaucer's wife remains obscure). Little is known of Chaucer's private life, though passages in his works suggest that he was improvident and a bad administrator, that he had an unhappy marriage but a loving mistress (by whom he probably had a son), and that he possessed a sunny disposition. He had many friends—among them the poet John GOWER—who attested to his virtues.

Chaucer, who wrote in Middle English (an early dialect), was the first great poet in English and is still considered among the finest English poets of all time. His works cannot be dated precisely as they were not published until after his death (printing did not exist in his lifetime). Nevertheless, his career can be divided into periods. Among his best-known early works is *The Book of the Duchess*; his middle period—following two trips to Italy in the 1370s, when he encountered the works of Dante and BOCCACCIO—produced *The Legend of Good Women*, *The Parliament of Fowles*, and *Troilus and Criseyde*. Chaucer's final period encompasses the composition of one of the masterworks of the English language, the unfinished *Canterbury Tales*. These lively, often bawdy stories are supposedly told by various pilgrims on their way to the shrine at Canterbury. Though difficult to read without practice, the *Tales* are immensely gratifying, filled with sharp character studies, sly asides on human behavior, and inimitable descriptions. After his death, Chaucer was the first poet to be buried in what became the famous "poet's corner" in WESTMINSTER ABBEY.

Chester, Robert   See *LOVE'S MARTYR*.

Chettle, Henry (ca. 1560–ca. 1607) English printer and dramatist. As a printer, Chettle (briefly a partner of John DANTER) is best known for having published *Groatsworth of Wit* (1592) by Robert GREENE, which contains a denunciation of Shakespeare as an arrogant young plagiarist, the first published reference to the playwright. Chettle, who

had apparently edited Greene's work, subsequently apologized for it in a pamphlet of his own and wrote that he knew Shakespeare to be an honest man and a good writer. Chettle had turned to writing plays by 1598, when he was mentioned by Francis MERES as a fine writer of comedies, and he is known to have written or collaborated on at least 48 dramas—one of them being *Sir Thomas More*—for the ADMIRAL'S MEN and Philip HENSLOWE.

children's companies   English acting companies in the 16th and 17th centuries composed of boys. Before the ELIZABETHAN THEATER became well established in the 1570s, professional companies tended to be troupes of acrobats and mimes, more appropriate to a country fair than to the court of Queen Elizabeth I (see Elizabeth I in *Henry VIII*). There, entertainment was often provided by schoolboys from Eton and Westminster, and by the Chapel Royal, a boys' choir that provided schooling for the boys it recruited from church choirs around the country. These groups traditionally staged plays in Latin (the language of their education). The Chapel Royal even had its own dramatic company, known as the Children of the Chapel, as early as the 1520s. In the 1550s two more such groups were created: the Children of Paul's at the school attached to St. Paul's Cathedral and the Children of Windsor at the church grammar school in WINDSOR. These groups were very popular at the queen's court: In the first 20 years of Elizabeth's reign, boys performed at court half again as often as did men. Though composed of children, these companies performed plays written for adults and featuring adult characters.

However, by the late 1570s, the adult troupes had become legitimate theater companies. LEICESTER'S MEN became favorites at court, and one member, James BURBAGE, built the first LONDON playhouse, the THEATRE, in 1576. The children's companies appeared to be falling from favor, but their course also changed in 1576. The Children of Windsor and of the Chapel merged under the direction of Richard FARRANT, who leased rooms at a former priory and created the first BLACKFRIARS THEATRE, where his boys played to the public as well as continuing to perform at court. After Farrant's death, the company was directed by William HUNNIS, but its popularity waned and play production ceased after 1584, when the landlord took back the Blackfriars building. In the final season, another children's company, patronized by Edward de Vere, Earl of OXFORD, joined the troupe at Blackfriars.

From 1584 to 1600 the children's companies ceased performing plays, as the QUEEN'S MEN and other professional troupes took over, though the choirs were maintained. In 1600, however, Nathaniel GILES and Henry EVANS revived the Children of the Chapel as a theater company, leasing the second Blackfriars Theatre from Richard BURBAGE. They were immediately popular, due in good part to the involvement of Ben JONSON, as both actor and playwright. The Children of Paul's also reentered the theatrical arena at this time, performing at court and at the school, which had a theater. They staged plays by George CHAPMAN, Thomas DEKKER, Thomas MIDDLETON, and John WEBSTER, and they too completed with the adult companies. The children's companies were fierce rivals, and their competition spilled over into the contents of the plays they staged, in the so-called WAR OF THE THEATERS—a development alluded to in *Hamlet* 2.2.330–358.

In 1602 Giles and Evans were accused of graft and the misuse of the Chapel Royal's recruiting privileges to enroll nonsingers; Evans fled the country, and Giles retired from play production. Under King JAMES I, who was crowned in 1603, Evans returned to the theater, but his connection with the Chapel Royal was severed. Instead, he and Edward KIRKHAM formed the Children of the Queen's Revels under the patronage of the queen. However, they lost the royal favor by staging controversial plays—especially the allegedly seditious *Eastward Ho!*, by Jonson, Chapman, and Thomas MARSTON (see CENSORSHIP)—and in 1605 they changed their name to Children of the Revels, and then, at the insistence of the Crown, to Children of Blackfriars.

In 1606 a new children's company entered the field, the Children of the King's Revels, owned by a group including Michael DRAYTON and managed by Martin SLATER. (This troupe may have been the Children of Paul's, reorganized, for that company

disappears from the records at this time.) They performed at a new playhouse founded for the purpose, the WHITEFRIARS THEATRE. The King's Revels company was unsuccessful, however, and died in 1609 amid rancorous litigation among the partners.

In 1608 Evans's old company, now under new direction, moved to the new theater as the Children of Whitefriars. In 1610—under yet another management group including Robert BROWNE, Richard JONES, and others—they were restored to royal favor and once again were known as Children of the Queen's Revels. Their chief actor and playwright was Nathan FIELD. This company was absorbed into LADY ELIZABETH'S MEN in 1613. Though troupes of boys were occasionally organized as late as the 1630s, the great era of the children's companies was over.

chorus Dramatic device, originally from ancient Greek drama, employed by Shakespeare in various forms. A chorus is a character or allegorical figure who usually does not participate in the action of the play, but rather provides a commentary on it. He does this either by offering a critique of the actions and attitudes of the other characters or by supplying missing facts or filling in the narrative where it is not actually enacted. Two such figures in Shakespeare are frankly designated as choruses—the Chorus of *Romeo and Juliet* and the Chorus of *Henry V*—while one allegorical figure and one named character are in fact choruses: Time in *The Winter's Tale* and Gower in *Pericles*. Also, a number of plays have a figure designated the PROLOGUE, whose choric function is limited to the introduction of the action. Rumour (*2 Henry IV*) is also a prologue figure. In addition, some regular characters occasionally step aside from the action and speak about it in a choric manner—a good example is the Bastard of *King John*—and other characters are obviously commentators on the action without stepping back from it, as exemplified by *King Lear*'s Fool, who is often figuratively referred to as a chorus.

The use of a chorus, whether frankly or subtly employed, lets the playwright establish a point of view that the characters themselves, by and large, do not share, thus bringing the audience into the play without making it identify with some characters to the exclusion of others. The chorus also invites the audience to help ensure the success of the drama by willingly engaging its own imagination and sympathies. This is especially important if the play is an allegorical spectacle like *Pericles,* whose story Gower concedes he could not "convey / Unless your thoughts went on my way" (4.Chorus.49–50). Or, as the Chorus of *Henry V* demands, in an appropriately military tone, we must "Follow, follow! / Grapple [our] minds to sternage of this navy" (3.Chorus.17–18).

In the Greek theater, the chorus was a group of actors—originally 50, later as few as 12—who sang lyrical passages of commentary and explanation while dancing; their passages are also referred to as choruses. In RENAISSANCE and later plays, a chorus is usually a single character or small group who speaks similar lyrical explanatory passages. (In a more literally accurate use of the term, a chorus is also the group of singing and dancing background figures in opera or musical theater.) The ancient Greek use of the chorus probably evolved from singing in religious ceremonies. However, the practice was not transmitted to Roman drama, where choruses appear only in SENECA's works, which were not intended for performance. For Seneca, the chorus was a conscious archaism intended to invoke the spirit of Greece as the fountainhead of Roman culture. However, in Shakespeare's day, ancient drama was known only from Seneca's work; thus, the Renaissance delight in classicism encouraged the use of choruses in English plays, although such a ritualistic device is actually quite inappropriate to the distinctly secular ELIZABETHAN DRAMA. It was never employed in the strict sense of group recitation, let alone singing and dancing; rather, various approximations, like those of Shakespeare, came into use.

Cibber, Colley (1671–1757)   English actor, playwright, and producer. Cibber, the son of a Danish sculptor who had moved to England, began his career in 1690 as an actor in Thomas BETTERTON's company, and by 1696 he had his first play staged. He was a successful actor, portraying mostly comical fops, often in his own plays, which were fashionable

comedies of sentiment set in high society. His tragedies were generally unsuccessful, except for his adaptation of *Richard III* (1700)—more than half of which he wrote himself—which was immensely popular and became the standard version of Shakespeare's play for more than a century. As a longtime manager of the Drury Lane Theatre, Cibber staged a number of Shakespeare's plays—or rather adaptations of them—including his own *Romeo and Juliet* and *Papal Tyranny in the Reign of King John.* He played a number of Shakespearean characters, including Cardinal Wolsey, Iago, and Jaques (the last in LOVE IN A FOREST by Charles JOHNSON). His autobiography, *Apology for the Life of Colley Cibber, Comedian* (1740), provides many interesting glimpses of 18th-century theater life. Cibber was named Poet Laureate in 1730, and he was the principal butt of Alexander POPE in the second version of his satirical epic poem *The Dunciad* (1742). Theophilus CIBBER was his son.

Cibber, Susannah Maria (1714–1766)   English actress. Susannah Cibber, a sister of Thomas ARNE, married Theophilus CIBBER in 1734, though they only lived together briefly. Originally an opera singer, she was coached as an actress by her father-in-law, the actor and producer Colley CIBBER. Her husband's flight from England, to avoid creditors, exposed the scandalous ménage à trois they had maintained with another man, and Susannah retired from the stage for several years. She later returned to a successful career in the productions of David GARRICK. She was especially acclaimed as Constance in *King John.*

Cibber, Theophilus (1703–1758)   English actor. The son of Colley CIBBER, Theophilus Cibber was best known for comic roles, especially Pistol and Parolles. After the scandalous dissolution of his marriage to Susannah Maria CIBBER, Theophilus Cibber's stage career collapsed, and he supported himself as a hack writer. He wrote a brief biography of Shakespeare in his *The Lives of the Poets* (1753)—probably ghostwritten—that is the only source for the almost certainly spurious anecdote that Shakespeare began his career as a "horse boy," holding horses for members of the audience as they dismounted outside the theater.

Cinthio (Giovanni Battista Giraldi) (1504–1573) Italian poet, novelist, and playwright, author of sources for *Measure for Measure* and *Othello*. The story of Othello and Desdemona and the main plot of *Measure for Measure* came from two different tales in Cinthio's *Hecatommithi* (1565), a cycle of novellas modeled on BOCCACCIO's *Decamaron*. The tales in Cinthio's collection were only translated into English piecemeal, and the *Othello* source tale did not appear until the 18th century, so Shakespeare must have known Cinthio's work elsewhere. He may have read it in the original Italian or in an anonymous French translation of 1584, or there may have been an English translation that is now lost.

The tale behind *Measure for Measure* had earlier inspired an English play by George WHETSTONE, who introduced the comic SUBPLOT, and Shakespeare used this work as his primary source. However, Cinthio also wrote a play, *Epitia*, based on the same story, to which he added a new character, the original of Mariana, and the device of substituting a dead man's head for that of Claudio. Shakespeare clearly knew this work as well, for though Whetstone also translated *Epitia*, Shakespeare does not appear to have used this version.

Giraldi (known as Cinthio in England from the name *Cinzio*, which he called himself in his poetry) was a famed professor of philosophy and rhetoric. As a playwright he was noted for his efforts to reform tragic drama, based in his time on ancient models, so that it reflected tenets of Christian humanism. In his eight published plays, including *Epitia*, a CHORUS comments on the action, which consists in good part of debates on such subjects as the proper relationship between love and justice. This aspect of his work is reflected particularly in the highly moral character of Isabella and the political musings of the Duke in *Measure for Measure*. On the other hand, Cinthio was also the first RENAISSANCE playwright to present atrocities on stage, which perhaps indirectly influenced Shakespeare to write such noteworthy scenes of violence and gore as those in *Titus Andronicus*, *King Lear*, and *Othello*.

Clarke, Mary Cowden (1809–1898), and **Clarke, Charles Cowden** (1787–1877) British Shakespearean commentators. The Clarkes, who married in 1828, studied and wrote about Shakespeare throughout their married life. Mary Cowden Clarke prepared a concordance to Shakespeare's work (1844–45), and wrote a best-selling three-volume collection of short fictions entitled *The Girlhood of Shakespeare's Heroines* (1851–52). Charles Cowden Clarke published his lectures on *Shakespeare's Characters* (1863). The couple produced jointly an edition of the complete plays (1868), a popular guide to Shakespeare's language entitled *Shakespeare Key* (1879), and editions of the works of George Herbert (1593–1633) and others. Their *Recollections of Writers* (1878) is a memoir of their friendships with such 19th-century luminaries as John KEATS, Charles LAMB and Mary Lamb, and Charles DICKENS.

Clive, Kitty (1711–1785) English actress. A great comic actress, Clive spent most of her career playing opposite David GARRICK. She was especially acclaimed as Celia in *As You Like It*, and she also played Olivia in *Twelfth Night*. She was perhaps best known for her performances in the title role of Garrick's *Catherine and Petruchio*, an adaptation of *The Taming of the Shrew*. Though she played Portia (to the Shylock of Charles MACKLIN), Ophelia, and Hamlet (in accordance with the 18th-century vogue for female Hamlets), her strength was in broad COMEDY, and she is said to have fought with Garrick over his reluctance to cast her in TRAGEDY. She was especially popular in the London literary world and was a good friend of Samuel JOHNSON and the writer Horace Walpole (1717–97).

clown Character type often used by Shakespeare, a humorously ignorant and unsophisticated figure, usually male and often associated with rustic ways. The clown is to some extent a comic caricature of a peasant; his humor is earthy and simple, often featuring awkwardness and confusion, such as the unintentionally comic misuse of language, but there is an underlying element of shrewdness as well. Shakespeare's clowns include some of his most delightful characters, from such early creations as Launce in *Two Gentlemen of Verona* and Costard in *Love's Labour's Lost*, through Dogberry in *Much Ado About Nothing* and Bottom in *A Midsummer Night's Dream*, to the Clown in *The Winter's*

Tale. Most common in COMEDY, the clown is usually minor in the HISTORY PLAYS—though Mistress Quickly, the Hostess of the BOAR'S HEAD TAVERN in *1* and *2 Henry IV* and *Henry V,* has something of the clown and was probably played by an actor who specialized in the type. The clown, however, often appears in TRAGEDY, where he provides comic relief. The Clown of *Titus Andronicus* foreshadows such more developed figures as the Clown who is the incongruous bearer of Cleopatra's deadly asps in *Antony and Cleopatra,* the Porter in *Macbeth,* and, perhaps most famous of Shakespeare's clowns, the Grave-digger in *Hamlet.*

The clown is usually distinguished from another Shakespearean character type, the FOOL, although the Elizabethans used the terms synonymously. (For example, *Twelfth Night*'s Feste, who is unquestionably a fool, being a professional jester, and who is called a "fool" by the other characters, is identified as "Clown" in speech headings and stage directions throughout the play.) Nevertheless, the difference between the two comic roles is unmistakable. Where the clown's comic effects are accidental results of his bumbling nature, the fool is intentionally witty. Clowns, moreover, tend to operate outside the main plots and often—especially in such early figures as Launce and Launcelot Gobbo (of *The Merchant of Venice*)—address the audience in somewhat elaborate asides, usually narratives. In contrast, the fool is more involved with the main characters and speaks more analytically.

Although, to some extent, these different comic figures may reflect changes in the actors Shakespeare wrote for (see ARMIN, ROBERT; KEMPE, WILLIAM), the distinction is significant in itself. The fool's subtle and intellectual comedy provides a satirical edge, whereas the clown serves a different symbolic function. He is to some extent a parody of the sublimely simple rustic of PASTORAL tradition, but the mockery is not cruel. The clown is ridiculous but worthy; he retains the virtues of nature and is fundamentally sensible, as is demonstrated when Dogberry accidentally discovers the villains, or when Bottom is the only mortal to experience fairyland. To some extent this is a reflection of his social position—because he has nothing to lose, he can speak the truth as he sees it—but the clown is also closer to nature and thus closer to the unconscious. He manifests our simplest, often "vulgar" impulses, with the solid strength of one who is relatively uncorrupted by society. With a natural good grace, he accepts his clumsiness, like his inferior social position, as part of his destined lot. Because he is more obviously long-suffering than profound, the clown parallels on a more accessible plane the stoicism of the tragic hero.

coat of arms, Shakespeare's   Heraldic escutcheon signifying the social status of the family as members of the gentry, awarded in 1596 to Shakespeare's father, John SHAKESPEARE, by the Garter King of Arms (a government official charged with authorizing such honors [see DETHICK, SIR WILLIAM]). This honor was said to reflect the services of an unnamed ancestor to King Henry VII, founder of the TUDOR DYNASTY, but it was in fact purchased and thus depended on the growing success of John's son as a playwright. John Shakespeare had applied for a grant of arms 20 years earlier, but his financial reversals derailed the effort. In a class-conscious society such as 16th-century England, such an award was an important symbol of a family's honorable place in society and was commonly acquired by men who had attained social prominence and wealth. As a visual emblem, the coat of arms could be displayed on one's door, on personal items, and the like. Specifically, the Shakespeare coat of arms consists of a gold shield with a diagonal black band bearing the image of a gold spear—a visual pun on the name "Shakespeare"—with a silver head. Above the shield is a falcon holding another spear. Below it is a motto—*Non Sanz Droict* (medieval French for "Not Without Right")—which is often said to have inspired Ben JONSON's mocking allusion "Not Without Mustard" in a play of 1598 (though Jonson may well have taken the line from an unrelated joke published years earlier by Thomas NASHE). The coat of arms appears on Shakespeare's tomb in the parish church in STRATFORD.

Cobham, William Brooke, Lord (d. 1597)   Contemporary of Shakespeare, powerful aristocrat whose pressure probably resulted in the change of the name Oldcastle to Falstaff (see *1 Henry IV*). Cobham was descended from the historical Oldcastle and was offended by the use of the name for a gluttonous lecher and coward in *1* and *2 Henry IV.* His position as Lord Chamberlain, the official responsible for the royal entertainment budget, made him important to the acting companies, and therefore the character's name was altered.

Cobham held his office only from August 1596 until his death in March 1597. His predecessor, Henry Carey, Baron HUNSDON, had used the position to protect the theatrical profession from the London government, which was dominated by Puritans and thus opposed to public drama. However, under Cobham the London authorities achieved a long-sought goal and banished the players from the city limits.

The power of his office and his antipathy to the theater suggest that it was Cobham who instigated the change in Oldcastle's name, but the complainant may have been his son, Henry Brooke. In either case, the family may well have regretted the attempt to protect their ancestor's name, for their protest became a public joke, as various references in surviving letters of the time make clear. Moreover, the substitution of the name Falstaff was in itself another joke, for, in addition to its punning suggestion of sexual impotence, it referred to a notorious coward, Sir John Fastolfe, or Falstaffe, who appears in *1 Henry VI.* Oldcastle's descendants were now associated not only with the offensive character in the *Henry IV* plays but also with a second unpleasant character from another very popular work. In addition, in *The Merry Wives of Windsor,* when Frank Ford foolishly worries that he is being cuckolded by Falstaff, he disguises himself and adopts the name Brook, a probable reference to the Cobhams' family name. (Ford's pseudonym was later changed, possibly after further protest by Henry Brooke.) A number of subtle references to Oldcastle are made in *The Merry Wives* (e.g., in 4.5.5), further ensuring that the audience would not forget the increasingly comical conflict. Worst of all, from the Cobhams' point of view, the *Henry IV* plays were frequently performed using the name Oldcastle until well into the 17th century, despite Shakespeare's changes. Further, in other writings of the period

the name Oldcastle is linked to the gluttonous, lascivious behavior we call Falstaffian.

Coburn, Charles Douville (1877–1961)   American actor and producer. With his actress wife, Ivah Wills Coburn, Coburn founded the Coburn Shakespearian Players in 1906, and they produced many of Shakespeare's plays, as well as others, with great success. In 1934 they founded one of the first summer theater festivals at Union College in Schenectady, New York. Coburn retired upon his wife's death in 1937, returning to the stage only once more, in 1946, to play Falstaff, the role for which he had been best known.

Coleridge, Samuel Taylor (1772–1834)   English poet and literary critic. Best known as a poet, Coleridge also lectured and wrote on literature. His lectures on Shakespeare, delivered between 1802 and 1818, were not published until 1849, but they were nevertheless influential in their own time. While regarded as highly uneven in quality, they offer telling insights into the process of creating characters and letting the play evolve through that process. On certain plays—*Richard II,* for instance—Coleridge's opinions are still regarded as among the most stimulating available. He was among the first English critics to acclaim Shakespeare's poetry—as opposed to the theatrical virtues of the plays—since the 17th century, for the intervening generations had tended to ignore this aspect of the playwright's work. Inspired in part by the work of A. W. SCHLEGEL, which he had studied in Germany, Coleridge's lectures were an important stimulus to the literary criticism of the English Romantic movement.

Collier, Constance (1878–1955)   English actress. Constance Collier began her long career playing Peaseblossom at the age of three. She subsequently became one of the famous Gaiety Girls but left to play in more serious dramas. A member of Beerbohm TREE's company from 1901 to 1908, she played numerous Shakespearean parts. Beginning in 1908 she divided her career between New York and London and was very popular in both cities. She played Queen Gertrude to John BARRYMORE's Hamlet in his London production of 1925.

Collier, John Payne (1789–1883)   English scholar and forger. A onetime journalist and lawyer, Collier established himself as a Shakespeare scholar with a series of books published between 1835 and 1850. He is best known, however, for having forged a number of documents in support of his literary theories: annotations in 17th-century books, contemporary references to Shakespeare, theatrical business records, a source for *The Tempest*, etc. Collier claimed to own an annotated copy of the second FOLIO and published the notations as *Notes and Emendations to the Text of Shakespeare's Plays* (1852). The authenticity of this material was questioned by a number of scholars, and further investigation revealed both its falseness and the existence of other forgeries. Collier's forgeries still have an impact on Shakespearean scholarship, for the extent of his handiwork cannot be precisely established, and any documents to which he is known to have had access must be viewed with scepticism.

Collins, Francis (d. 1617)   Lawyer in STRATFORD, the drafter of Shakespeare's will. Collins, who served Shakespeare as a lawyer on a business deal in 1605, was probably also a friend, for he received a sizable bequest in the playwright's will, though it probably included his fee for drawing it up. He also witnessed the will. Collins held various public offices in Stratford, beginning in 1600, though by 1613 he lived in Warwick. He was a close friend of John COMBE and drew up his will (which contained a bequest to Shakespeare). He moved back to Stratford in 1617, when offered the post of town clerk on the condition that he do so, but he died a few months later.

Colman, George (1732–1794)   English playwright and theatrical entrepreneur. Colman was a close associate of David GARRICK, who produced his plays, including *The Jealous Wife* (1761), one of the most popular comedies of its time. After a dispute with Garrick over the casting of a play, however, Colman leased the Covent Garden Theatre, where, from 1767 to 1774, he produced many plays, including those of Oliver Goldsmith (1730–74). He staged *Cymbeline*, but his most important Shakespearean production was *King Lear*, from which he dropped many of the alterations made by Nahum TATE, though he added some of his own. He later managed another theater before retiring in 1789. Among the plays Colman produced were the early works of his son, also George Colman (1762–1836), later a notable comic dramatist.

Colonne, Guido delle (active late 13th century)   Sicilian writer, author of a source of *Troilus and Cressida*. Colonne translated the *Roman de Troie* by Benoit de SAINTE-MAURE, a 12th-century poem on the TROJAN WAR, into Latin prose. His version, the *Historia destructionis Troiae* (published 1270–87) became the standard work on the subject until the rediscovery of HOMER during the RENAISSANCE. Colonne's book influenced Shakespeare through two English works. A French translation was retranslated into English by William CAXTON as *The Recuyell of the Historyes of Troye* (1471), and John LYDGATE was inspired by the *Historia* to compose a long poem entitled *Troy Book* (1420, publ. 1512, 1555). These two works provide much of the detail in the account of the war reported in *Troilus and Cressida*.

Combe, John (before 1561–1614)   Landowner and moneylender in STRATFORD, a friend of Shakespeare. Said to have been the richest citizen of Stratford in his day, Combe was noted for his charities. Though he often sued for repayment of the loans he made, several of these creditors later named him in their wills as their good friend. He died a bachelor, and in his will he left the large sum of £30 to be distributed among the poor of the town. He and his uncle William COMBE sold Shakespeare 127 acres of land near WELCOMBE in 1602. His brother Thomas and his nephews Thomas and William COMBE were also associates of Shakespeare. Combe and the playwright appear to have been close friends. He left Shakespeare £5 in his will—a quite sizable token. His tomb in Stratford's Holy Trinity Church, like Shakespeare's memorial nearby, was designed by Gheerart JANSSEN. Later in the 17th century, two EPITAPHS on Combe were attributed to Shakespeare. One is simply a variant on a traditional rhyme about usurers, and the other seems un-Shakespearean stylistically, so modern scholars tend to doubt the ascriptions.

Combe, Thomas (d. 1609)   Landowner in STRAT-FORD, a business associate of Shakespeare and the brother of his friend John COMBE. Thomas Combe was partner with Shakespeare in a lease to collect the tithes—or church taxes—on some agricultural land near WELCOMBE (the rights to such taxes were transferable, like commodities shares). When he died, his share in the lease was passed on to his elder son, William COMBE, who proved a difficult business partner. His second son, another Thomas COMBE, was a friend of Shakespeare. According to an 18th-century tradition, Shakespeare wrote an insulting poem about this Thomas Combe, by way of a humorous EPITAPH; it was published in 1740. Modern scholars generally reject the attribution.

Combe, Thomas (1589–1657)   Lawyer in STRAT-FORD and friend of Shakespeare, son of Thomas COMBE. In his will Shakespeare left Thomas Combe his sword, as a mark of esteem and friendship, but nothing more is known of their relationship. Thomas supported his brother William COMBE in the controversy over the enclosure of lands at WEL-COMBE, and like William, he seems to have been a violent man; Thomas GREENE recorded an account of Combe "kicking and beating" a shepherd who demanded his pay.

Combe, William (1551–1610)   Landowner in WARWICKSHIRE. Combe, the uncle of Shakespeare's friend John COMBE, lived in the city of Warwick but owned land in and around STRATFORD and served as a lawyer for that town. In 1602 he and his nephew sold Shakespeare some land near WEL-COMBE. Combe was frequently a member of parliament for Warwickshire.

Combe, William (1586–1667)   Lawyer, money-lender, and landowner in STRATFORD, a business associate of Shakespeare. Combe was a son of Thomas COMBE and brother of Thomas COMBE the younger. From his father he inherited a share with Shakespeare in a tithe lease—the leased right to collect the taxes on a piece of land. In 1611 Shakespeare sued him for tardiness in paying his share of the rent, leaving the lease open to seizure. This was part of a complicated series of legal actions involv-ing a number of others, and it was settled equally between Shakespeare and Combe. Combe supported an attempt to enclose large tracts of culti-vated land at WELCOMBE for sheep grazing, an episode in which he played a brutal part. At one point Julian SHAW, the bailiff, or mayor, of Strat-ford, wrote to Combes that it seemed his con-science was "blinded . . . with a desire to make yourself rich with other men's loss." In the 1620s he was said to be richer than his uncle John COMBE had been, suggesting a considerable fortune. Dur-ing the Civil Wars he fought for the Parliamentar-ian side, and Royalist troops sacked his house in Stratford. His fortunes declined during the decade of the wars, and in 1650 he was reported to be in considerable debt, with all his land up for sale.

comedy   Drama that provokes laughter at human behavior, usually involves romantic love, and usu-ally has a happy ending. In Shakespeare's day the conventional comedy enacted the struggle of young lovers to surmount some difficulty, usually presented by their elders, and the play ended hap-pily in marriage or the prospect of marriage. Some-times the struggle was to bring separated lovers or family members together, and their reunion was the happy culmination (this often involved mar-riage also). Shakespeare generally observed these conventions, though his inventiveness within them yielded many variations.

Eighteen plays are generally included among Shakespeare's comedies. In approximate order of composition, they are *The Comedy of Errors, The Taming of the Shrew, The Two Gentlemen of Verona, Love's Labour's Lost, A Midsummer Night's Dream, The Merchant of Venice, The Merry Wives of Windsor, Much Ado About Nothing, As You Like It, Twelfth Night, Troilus and Cressida, Measure for Measure, All's Well That Ends Well, Pericles, Cymbeline, The Winter's Tale, The Tempest,* and *The Two Noble Kins-men.* These works are often divided into distinct subclasses reflecting the playwright's development. The first seven, all written before about 1598, are loosely classed as the "early comedies," though they vary considerably in both quality and character. The last four of these—*Love's Labour's Lost,* the *Dream,* the *Merchant,* and the *Merry Wives*—are sometimes separated as a transitional group, or linked with the next three in a large "middle comedies" classification. The *Merry Wives* is somewhat anomalous in any case; it represents a type of comedy—the "city play," a speciality of such writers as Ben JONSON and Thomas DEKKER—that Shakespeare did not otherwise write. The next three plays, *Much Ado, As You Like It,* and *Twelfth Night,* are often thought to constitute Shakespeare's greatest achievement in comedy; all written around 1599–1600, they are called the romantic, or mature, comedies. The next group of three plays, called the PROBLEM PLAYS, were written in the first years of the 17th century, as Shakespeare was simultaneously creating his greatest tragedies. The final cluster, all written between about 1607 and 1613, make up the bulk of the playwright's final period. They are known as the ROMANCES. (The problem plays and romances were intended to merge TRAGEDY and comedy in TRAGICOMEDY, and they are treated separately in this book.) Many minor variations in this classification scheme are possible; indeed, the boundaries of the whole genre are not fixed, for *Timon of Athens* is often included among the comedies, and *Troilus and Cressida* is sometimes considered a tragedy.

Shakespeare's earliest comedies are similar to existing plays, reflecting his inexperience. *The Comedy of Errors*—thought by many scholars to be his first drama, though the dating of Shakespeare's early works is extremely difficult—is built on a play by the ancient Roman dramatist PLAUTUS. Characteristically, Shakespeare enriched his source, but with material from another play by Plautus. The SUBPLOT of *The Taming of the Shrew* was taken from a popular play of a generation earlier, and the main plot was well known in folklore, though the combination was ingeniously devised. *The Two Gentlemen of Verona* likewise deals with familiar literary material, treating it in the manner of John LYLY, the most successful comedy writer when Shakespeare began his career.

However, the young playwright soon found the confidence to experiment, and in *Love's Labour's Lost,* the *Dream,* and the *Merchant,* he created a group of unusual works that surely startled Elizabethan playgoers, though pleasurably, we may presume. In the first he created his own main plot and used a distinctively English variation on COMMEDIA DELL'ARTE traditions for a subplot. He thus produced a splendid array of comic situations. The play's abundant topical humor was certainly appreciated by the original audiences, although today we don't always know what it is about. In any case, the major characters are charming young lovers, the minor ones are droll eccentrics, and the closing coup de théâtre, with which a darkening mood brings the work to a close, is a stunning innovation. Already the eventual turn toward tragicomedy is foreshadowed. *A Midsummer Night's Dream* mingles motifs from many sources, but the story is again the playwright's own; moreover, the play's extraordinary combination of oddity and beauty was entirely unprecedented and has rarely been approximated since. *The Merchant of Venice* mixes a social theme, usury, into a conventional comedy plot to deepen the resonance of the final outcome as well as to vary the formula. Here, the threat that is finally averted is so dire as to generate an almost tragic mood, again anticipating developments later in the playwright's career.

The mastery that Shakespeare had achieved by the late 1590s is reflected in the insouciance of the titles he gave his mature comedies (*Twelfth Night's* subtitle—"What You Will"—matches the others). That mastery is accompanied by a serious intent that is lacking in the earliest comedies. Shakespeare could not ignore the inherent poignancy in the contrast between life as it is lived and the escape from life represented by comedy. In *Much Ado,* as in *The Merchant of Venice,* a serious threat to life and happiness counters the froth of a romantic farce. Even in *As You Like It,* one of the most purely entertaining of Shakespeare's plays, the melancholy Jaques interposes his conviction that life is irredeemably corrupt. Feste's song at the close of *Twelfth Night* gives touching expression to such sentiments, as he sends us from the theater with the melancholy refrain, "the rain it raineth every day" (5.1.391–403). We are not expected to take him too seriously, but we cannot avoid the realization that even the life of a jester may be a sad one. The mature comedies thus further a blending of comedy and tragedy.

In the end, however, all of Shakespeare's comedies, including the later problem plays and romances, are driven by love. Love in Shakespearean comedy is stronger than the inertia of custom, the power of evil, or the fortunes of chance and time. In all of these plays but one (*Troilus and Cressida*), the obstacles presented to love are triumphantly overcome, as conflicts are resolved and errors forgiven in a general aura of reconciliation and marital bliss at the play's close. Such intransigent characters as Shylock, Malvolio, and Don John, who choose not to act out of love, cannot be accommodated in this scheme, and they are carefully isolated from the action before the climax.

In their resolutions Shakespeare's comedies resemble the medieval MORALITY PLAY, which centers on a sinful human who receives God's mercy. In Shakespeare's secular works, a human authority figure—Don Pedro or Duke Senior, for instance—is symbolically divine, the opponents of love are the representatives of sin, and all of the participants in the closing vignette partake of the play's love and forgiveness. Moreover, the context of marriage—at least alluded to at the close of all but *Troilus and Cressida*—is the capstone of the comedic solution, for these plays not only delight and entertain, they affirm, guaranteeing the future. Marriage, with its promise of offspring, reinvigorates society and transcends the purely personal element in sexual attraction and romantic love. Tragedy's focus on the individual makes death the central fact of life, but comedy, with its insistence on the ongoing process of love and sex and birth, confirms our awareness that life transcends the individual.

comedy of humours Genre of ELIZABETHAN DRAMA, plays in which each character possesses some strong, clearly identifiable personality trait or quirk that determines his or her behavior in any circumstances. For instance, a lecher will find all occasions appropriate for chasing women; a glutton will continually be concerned with food; a jealous husband will always look for evidence of his wife's infidelity. Among Shakespeare's plays, *The Merry Wives of Windsor* and *Twelfth Night* most nearly exemplify the genre, although he tended to combine features of several types of play. The most important practitioner of the comedy of humours was Ben JONSON.

In the late 1580s and early 1590s the term *humour*, referring to striking aspects of personality or patterns of behavior, became prominent in Elizabethan London. It stemmed from a medieval medical theory—in its last decades of respectability and increasingly recognized as problematical—holding that human health depends on a proper balance among four "humours," or bodily fluids: black bile, yellow bile, blood, and phlegm. When the balance was upset and one "humour" dominated, a person was likely to become ill and/or act strangely. The word became associated with all striking behavior, and it began to take on the association with comedy that it has today.

In the 1590s the attribution of prominent humours to dramatic characters arose as a plausible way to use the elaborate system of character types that occur in ancient Roman drama, especially in the plays of PLAUTUS. Comedies of humours were generally intended to ridicule the "humorous" behavior they presented. Elaborate complications involving intrigue and deceit typified their plots. Characters often bore tag names indicating their qualities, as do Shakespeare's Shallow (*2 Henry IV*) and Malvolio (*Twelfth Night*).

The vogue for comedy of humours—and for using the word *humour* (or *humor*)—was itself a subject for comedy. For example, Nym, who appears in *The Merry Wives of Windsor* and *Henry V,* uses the word *humour* in almost every speech he makes. He took this trait from a character in a successful play by George CHAPMAN, *The Blind Beggar of Alexandria* (1596). The comedy of humours reached its peak with Jonson's works of the early 17th century, but it remained popular for about another 100 years.

commedia dell'arte Genre of 16th- and 17th-century Italian COMEDY, a probable influence on several of Shakespeare's plays. In commedia dell'arte—which was frequently performed in England by traveling Italian companies, especially in the 1570s and 1580s—dialogue was largely improvised, as the action followed prescribed general lines familiar to both players and spectators; the plays were in any case so obvious that the troupes could find success with non-Italian-speaking audiences. The melodramatic and/or sentimental plots usually featured farcical intrigues involving love and money, though several involved a shipwreck on a magician's island, perhaps suggesting to Shakespeare the basic situation of *The Tempest*. The principal characters wore masks and were thus immediately recognizable; their personalities were understood before they said a word. They represented stock character types, some of which are thought to have influenced Shakespeare's characters.

Among the most important of these types was the pantaloon, an avaricious and lecherous old man, often a miser offering windy and moralistic advice to the young lovers. He may have contributed something to *Hamlet*'s Polonius. At any rate, Shakespeare presumed his audiences were at least familiar with this figure, for in *As You Like It* he has Jaques cite "the lean and slipper'd pantaloon . . . His youthful hose well sav'd" (2.7.158–160) as a symbol of old age. Another commedia figure was a lawyer, Dr Graziano, or the *dottore*, also amorous but distinguished by his pretentious pedantry. Holofernes, of *Love's Labour's Lost*, is quite similar to the *dottore*, and his fellow comical rustic in that play, Armado, resembles a third commedia figure, the *capitano*, a braggart soldier, the descendant of the ancient Roman MILES GLORIOSUS. Several other Shakespearean characters resemble the *capitano*, including most notably Parolles (*All's Well That Ends Well*) and Falstaff (*1 Henry IV*).

An important feature of the commedia dell'arte was a group of ostensibly minor comic characters called *zanni*—the root of our word *zany*—who were servants to the major figures but often dominated the action. In fact, another name for the genre is *commedia dei zanni*. They shared the characteristics of greed and shrewdness but evolved into a number of distinctive figures. Chief among them were Arlequino, a clever rascal (who survived the passing of the genre as Harlequin), and Pulcinella (Punch), a violent egotist. The *zanni* were descendants of the stock clever slaves and servants of Roman drama, which Shakespeare knew from PLAUTUS. So, although the Dromios of *The Comedy of Errors* and Tranio of *The Taming of the Shrew* resemble *zanni*, Shakespeare need not have taken them from the commedia. However, the playwright's demonstrable awareness of the Italian players strongly suggests that the commedia dell'arte exercised at least some influence on Shakespeare's characters.

complaint   Poem intended to express unhappiness. A popular genre from the 14th through the 17th centuries, the complaint could take many forms, from meditations on the general sorrows of life to the bewailing of a particular event or situation—especially unrequited love—to humorous laments over trivial subjects, though these last were less common. Shakespeare's *The Rape of Lucrece* is often classed as a complaint—although the form was usually written in the first person—and it was written in RHYME ROYAL, the pattern that theorists prescribed for the genre. After Shakespeare's time the complaint was gradually replaced by the less expressly plaintive lament or elegy.

Compton, Fay (1895–1978)   English actress. Fay Compton played numerous Shakespearean parts in her long and distinguished career, most notably appearing as Ophelia opposite the Hamlets of both John BARRYMORE and John GIELGUD. She was the sister of the noted novelist Compton Mackenzie (1883–1972), and her own memoirs (*Rosemary: Some Remembrances*, 1927) were very popular.

Condell, Henry (d. 1627)   English actor and coeditor, with John HEMINGE, of the FIRST FOLIO edition of Shakespeare's plays. Listed in the Folio as one of the 26 "Principall Actors" in the plays, Condell became a partner in the CHAMBERLAIN'S MEN in 1598 and had probably acted with the company from its inception in 1594. He remained with its successor, the KING'S MEN, until his death. He acted in both tragedies and comedies, but he is not known for any particular Shakespearean role. His friendship with Shakespeare is evidenced by the playwright's small legacy to him in his will. Condell was one of the original partners in the BLACKFRIARS THEATRE, and he later acquired shares in the GLOBE THEATRE as well. He apparently invested well, for he died a wealthy man.

Cooke, Alexander (d. 1614)   English actor, one of the 26 men listed in the FIRST FOLIO as the "Principall Actors" of Shakespeare's plays. Cooke apparently became a member of the KING'S MEN in 1604—having served as a hired actor earlier—and he remained with them at least into 1613. He was probably apprenticed to John HEMINGE, whom he refers to as "my master" in his will.

Cooke may have appeared with PEMBROKE'S MEN in *The Taming of a Shrew,* sometime between 1592 and 1594. In that BAD QUARTO of *The Taming of the Shrew* (where the text was assembled from actors' memories), one of the Players is designated "San" or "Sander," and Sander—a common Elizabethan nickname for Alexander—is the name of the equivalent of Shakespeare's Grumio. Their speeches are fairly accurately reproduced in *A Shrew,* so if Cooke did play these parts, he was one of the actors who compiled the text.

Cooke, George Frederick (1756–1811)   English actor. Cooke was a rival of John Philip KEMBLE in the early years of the 19th century. He was especially noted for his Othello, with which he established himself as a respected actor. He played many Shakespearean roles, including Richard III, Henry VIII, and Falstaff. He eventually moved to America and died in New York. Remarkably, Cooke played a Shakespearean role nearly 170 years after his death, when his skull—preserved by his physician upon his death and eventually given to a Philadelphia university—was employed as that of Yorick in a 1980 TELEVISION production of *Hamlet.*

Corioles (Corioli)   Ancient Italian city of the Volscians, located about 25 miles southeast of ROME, setting for four scenes of Act 1 of *Coriolanus.* In 1.2 the Volscians make their plans to defend against the expected siege by the Romans. In 1.4–6 the Romans Martius displays great bravery after an initial success by the Volscians when he charges single-handed through the city gates and turns the tide of battle. In 1.7 the Roman general Lartius leaves a Lieutenant in charge of the city. In 1.9 Martius is honored for his bravery at Corioles with a new name, Coriolanus, by which he is known for the rest of the play.

There is nothing to distinguish Corioles from the many other besieged towns in Shakespeare—the gates and walls of a medieval city are called for in the stage directions, and nothing more is shown. Shakespeare presented the town because it was called for in his story. The ancient Volscian city, which was besieged and taken by the Romans in 493 B.C., has been lost, but it is believed to have been located near the modern Velletri.

Cornell, Katharine (1898–1974)   American actress. Though best known as a leading lady in contemporary romantic dramas, Cornell also played in classic works by Chekhov, G. B. SHAW, and Shakespeare. She was closely associated with the role of Juliet, which she played several times, perhaps most notably on a 77-city tour of the depression-era United States beginning in 1932.

Cottom, John (John Cottam) (active 1566–1581)   STRATFORD schoolmaster, one of Shakespeare's teachers. Cottom taught at Stratford from 1579 to 1581 and probably supervised the last years of Shakespeare's formal education (though the records of Shakespeare's attendance have not survived). He was recruited for the job by his predecessor, to whom he paid £6 (about a third of a year's pay) for the opportunity. Cottom's younger brother, a Jesuit priest, was tried for treason in November 1581 for his active opposition to the Protestant state religion; he was executed the next spring. In December 1581 John Cottom resigned his position at Stratford, probably under pressure because of his brother's situation. He eventually inherited a country estate where he lived in retirement and practiced Catholicism. His religion may have influenced Shakespeare, who seems to have been at least tolerant of Catholicism in an intolerant age, and who some scholars believe may have been a secret Catholic himself.

Covell, William (d. 1614)   English author of an early allusion to Shakespeare. Covell, a minor poet and anti-Catholic propagandist, praised *Venus and Adonis* and *The Rape of Lucrece* in brief printed marginal notes appended to an account of the poetry of Edmund SPENSER and Samuel DANIEL. Published in 1595, this assessment is among the first acknowledgments of Shakespeare's place in English literature.

Coventry City in WARWICKSHIRE in central England, the setting for a scene each in *3 Henry VI* and *Richard II*. In *3 Henry VI*, Coventry is the site of an encounter (5.1) between the Earl of Warwick and the Yorkist leaders at which George is brought to abandon Warwick's cause, prior to a battle in the following scenes. In *Richard II*, Coventry is the scene (1.3) of the scheduled trial by combat between Henry Bolingbroke and Mowbray that Richard II cancels, sending the two disputants into exile instead.

Cowley, Richard (d. 1619) English actor, one of the 26 men listed in the FIRST FOLIO as the "Principall Actors" in Shakespeare's plays. Cowley is known to have performed with STRANGE'S MEN as early as 1590, and he was probably with the CHAMBERLAIN'S MEN from their formation in 1594, though the earliest surviving documentation dates from 1600. He was a member of the KING'S MEN—as the Chamberlain's Men became—at least through 1605 and probably much later, for several associates of the King's Men witnessed his will in 1618. Speech prefixes in early texts reveal that Cowley played VERGES in *Much Ado About Nothing* and QUINCE in *A Midsummer Night's Dream*; he is thus presumed to have worked well as a straight man to the great comic actor Will KEMPE, who played Dogberry and Bottom, the respective counterparts to Cowley's roles.

Cox, Robert (d. 1655) English actor, famed for his performances of DROLLS, which were brief playlets at fairs and in taverns from 1642 to 1660, when English theaters were closed by the revolutionary government. Cox performed his drolls illegally until he was arrested and imprisoned in 1653. A collection of his scripts—some of which he wrote, though most were adaptations of scenes from well-known plays including some of Shakespeare's—was published by Henry MARSH and Francis KIRKMAN in 1662.

Craig, Gordon (1872–1966) English actor, producer, and theatrical designer. The son of Ellen TERRY and the famed architect and designer Edward Godwin (1833–86), Craig was a successful child actor and in his late teens and early 20s was a member of Henry IRVING's company. He played many leading Shakespearean roles, but his fame rests on his later career as a producer, designer, and theoretician. He advocated simple productions and aspired to approximate the Elizabethan stage; he was an important influence on Harley GRANVILLE-BARKER. Among Craig's most important books are *The Art of the Theatre* (1905), *Towards a New Theatre* (1911), and *The Theatre Advancing* (1921). He also wrote books on both Terry and Irving.

Craig, Hardin (1875–1968) American scholar, author of several important works on Shakespeare. A longtime professor at the University of Missouri, Craig believed that an understanding of the cultural and intellectual world in which Shakespeare lived was crucial to the comprehension of his poetry and plays. Craig's best-known works were *The Enchanted Glass: The Elizabethan Mind in Literature* (1935) and *New Lamps for Old: A Sequel to the Enchanted Glass* (1960).

Crane, Ralph (active 1620s) Professional copyist, or scribe, whose copies of some of Shakespeare's plays were probably published in the FIRST FOLIO. Crane, a legal clerk who chiefly copied documents for lawyers, also did freelance work copying plays—either from the playwrights' FOUL PAPERS or from a PROMPTBOOK—for private libraries (a common practice of the day). He also worked for the KING'S MEN in the early 1620s. Several signed Crane transcripts survive (though none of a Shakespeare play), so his idiosyncratic style can be identified. On the basis of this style, scholars believe that he provided the copy used in printing five of the plays in the First Folio (1623)—*Measure for Measure, The Merry Wives of Windsor, The Tempest, The Two Gentlemen of Verona,* and *The Winter's Tale.*

Scholars distinguish Crane's work by his peculiar habits of punctuation—especially his use of hyphens to join adjectives and their nouns, as in "palsied-Eld" (*Measure for Measure* 3.1.36), and his frequent use of parentheses to set off words or phrases, as in "that same knave (Ford her husband) hath" (*Merry Wives of Windsor* 5.1.18). Scholars also point to Crane's idiosyncratic spellings, like "sirha" for "sirrah," and his provision of "massed entrances," in which all of the characters in a scene are listed in a group at its opening, without regard for when they actually come on stage.

Crécy   Location in *Edward III*, town in FRANCE, site of a famous battle of the HUNDRED YEARS' WAR. Two brief scenes lead up to the battle: French refugees flee the English army in 3.2, and in 3.3 the French and English leaders encounter each other and exchange claims, insults, and challenges. In 3.4 the battle itself is presented in a series of brief sketches. First, the French leaders despair of their losses and leave to organize a last resistance; then the English commanders arrive, pleased with an apparent victory. Then word arrives that the Prince of Wales is surrounded and in danger. King Edward coolly decides not to send assistance, asserting that he is confident his son will survive and triumph. Finally, the Prince appears, victorious and bearing the corpse of his opponent, the King of Bohemia. King Edward then orders part of the army, under the Prince, to pursue the retreating French to POITIERS, while he takes the remainder to besiege CALAIS.

Shakespeare and his collaborators (see *Edward III*, "Commentary") took major liberties with the chronology of the war as they found it in their sources (see *Edward III*, "Sources of the Play"), in the interests of dramatic flow. The action at Crécy thus seems to follow directly from the naval victory at SLUYS in 3.1 and to lead directly to the battle of Poitiers. In reality, these three battles—Sluys, Crécy, and Poitiers—occurred in the years 1340, 1346, and 1356, respectively. Otherwise, however, the battle is accurately, if very sketchily, presented. Various details are altered (the most striking of which, perhaps, is the anachronistic status of King John of France, who was not yet crowned). Also, the Prince's initiation before the battle (in 3.3.172–218) and his knighting after it (3.4.101–106) are fictions, introduced to heighten the spectacle of the English triumph and to aggrandize the role of the Prince.

The historical battle of Crécy is regarded as one of the crucial encounters in European military his-

tory. After its defeat of the French at Crécy, England was regarded as a major European power for the first time, a status it had not had earlier and which it has never relinquished. Moreover, the battle marked the first important demonstration of the superiority of missile power over cavalry—the missiles being arrows, capable of inflicting their damage on an enemy that was not within range to counter with its handheld weapons. This democratization of warfare—archers were yeomen and cavalry were aristocrats—was more fully exhibited at the battle of AGINCOURT, enacted in Shakespeare's *Henry V*. Neither play emphasizes these matters, being more concerned with the activities of their regal protagonists.

Creede, Thomas (active 1578–1617)   London printer, producer of editions of several of Shakespeare's plays. Creede printed the first editions of *2 Henry VI* (Q1, 1594, for Thomas MILLINGTON); *Henry V* (Q1, 1600, for Millington and John BUSBY); and *The Merry Wives of Windsor* (Q1, 1602, for Arthur JOHNSON). He also printed second editions of *Henry V* (Q2, 1602, for Thomas PAVIER) and *Romeo and Juliet* (Q2, 1599, for Cuthbert BURBY). Creede also produced four editions of *Richard III* (Q2–Q5, 1598, 1602, 1605, 1612; the first two for Andrew WISE and the others for Matthew LAW). In 1595 he produced, on his own behalf, an edition of LOCRINE credited to "W. S.," perhaps in order to pass it off as Shakespeare's work. Creede is regarded as among the most skillful printers of the period, and he had a long and successful career. He became a member of the STATIONERS' COMPANY in 1578 and operated his own press from at least 1593. His partner became sole owner of his company in 1617, which provides us with Creede's probable date of death.

Créton, Jean (ca. 1340–after 1400)   French writer whose poem *Histoire du Roy d'Angleterre Richard* may have influenced the writing of *Richard II*. Créton, a French nobleman, was a visitor to Richard II's court beginning in 1398. He accompanied Richard to Ireland and was with the King when he was captured by Henry Bolingbroke. His account is highly favorable to Richard.

Crosse, Samuel (active ca. 1604)   English actor, a member of the CHAMBERLAIN'S MEN or KING'S MEN. Cross is listed in the FIRST FOLIO among the "Principall Actors" in Shakespeare's plays, but he is unknown elsewhere. He may have been with the company only before it became the King's Men in 1603, for he was not among the nine members listed in the patent granted at that time. On the other hand, he may have joined soon thereafter, since the group numbered 12 in the summer of 1604. However, he was apparently not with the company in May 1605, when Augustine PHILLIPS bequeathed small legacies to 12 named members of the company; some scholars believe he died in the interim.

Cross Keys Inn   Inn in LONDON whose courtyard was used for play performances in the 16th century, and at which Shakespeare performed early in his career. From its foundation in 1594, the CHAMBERLAIN'S MEN, of which Shakespeare was a member, performed in the winter at the Cross Keys and in the summer at the THEATRE—the first true playhouse in England. Plays had been performed at the inn—in summer and winter—since at least as early as 1579. Other entertainments were also conducted there; a performing horse, for example, is recorded sometime before 1588. In 1596 the London government outlawed play performances within the city limits, and the Cross Keys Inn ceased to function as a playhouse.

Crowne, John (ca. 1640–1703)   English dramatist who adapted 2 and 3 Henry VI. In 1680 Crowne combined the last two Acts of 2 Henry VI with 3 Henry VI in a play entitled *The Misery of Civil War*. This was a topical work, intended as propaganda for the early Whig political party in the disputes of the day, as was its successor, which was based on the earlier parts of 2 Henry VI, though titled *Henry VI, the First Part* (1681).

Cumberland, Richard (1732–1811)   British playwright, creator of an adaptation of *Timon of Athens*. A minor politician, Cumberland also wrote a number of sentimental plays, most of which are now forgotten. His adaptation of *Timon* was unsuccessfully staged in 1771. He was caricatured as Sir Fretful

Plagiary in Richard Brinsley Sheridan's play *The Critic* (1779).

Curtain Theatre   Second LONDON playhouse, probably built by Henry LANEMAN in 1577. It was apparently a round or multisided three-story building, located near the first playhouse, the THEATRE, in Shoreditch, a northern suburb of London. Its name refers to its neighborhood, the Curtain Close, and not to theater curtains, which were not in use at that time. Between 1590 and 1592 STRANGE'S MEN—perhaps including the young Shakespeare—often played at the Curtain, and in 1597–98, the CHAMBERLAIN'S MEN, definitely Shakespeare's company, played there before moving to the new GLOBE THEATRE in the following year. It was during this period that Shakespeare wrote *Henry V*, with its mention of a circular theater as "this wooden O" (Prologue, 13). This is often taken as an allusion to the Globe but more probably refers to the Curtain. From 1603 until at least 1609, the QUEEN'S MEN was a usual tenant of the Curtain, and PRINCE CHARLES' COMPANY played there after 1621. The theater is last mentioned in 1627.

Cushman, Charlotte (1816–1876)   American actress, generally considered the first great American-born actress. Cushman, who began her career as an opera singer, was particularly noted for her fierce portrayals of Lady Macbeth, whom she played opposite William MACREADY, Edwin FORREST, Edwin BOOTH, and others. She was also highly praised as *Othello*'s Desdemona and *Henry VIII*'s Queen Katherine of Aragon. In addition, she was noted for her successes in male parts, especially Romeo (opposite the Juliet of her sister, Susan), Cardinal Wolsey (*Henry VIII*), and Hamlet.

Cyprus   Large island in the eastern Mediterranean, now a country, the setting for much of *Othello*. Although there is nothing especially exotic—let alone specifically Cypriot—about Acts 2–5 of *Othello*, Shakespeare's placement of the action on this remote outpost of the Venetian Empire is significant. After leaving VENICE, the characters are removed from the buffering effects of society. In the isolation of Cyprus, Iago's influence over Othello works its poison in the absence of any social or political distractions that might direct the general's attention elsewhere, or suggest different responses. Similarly, Desdemona has no peers to turn to for advice or intervention.

To effect this isolation, Shakespeare invented the "Cyprus wars" (1.1.150) of the play, which do not appear in his source, CINTHIO's tale. Moreover, although conflict between Venice and the Ottoman Turks was constant in the 15th and 16th centuries, the situation described in *Othello*—with the Turks threatening both Cyprus and Rhodes (see 1.3.14)—never arose. The Turks did not attack Cyprus until 1570, long after they controlled Rhodes. However, Shakespeare may have had this attack in mind, mistaking the details while intending to associate his hero with it, for its direct result was the naval battle of Lepanto (1571), in which an alliance led by Venice and Spain defeated the Turkish fleet. This was united Christendom's last great victory over Islam, and in Shakespeare's day and for generations thereafter it was regarded as one of the key events of European history. Its aura of epic victory doubtless influenced early audiences' sense of Othello as a grand figure. Nevertheless, Lepanto was an expensive victory, and Venice, retrenching in its aftermath, ceded Cyprus to the Turks in 1573. Thus, for Shakespeare, Cyprus was associated with vulnerability as well as strength, a combination reflected in Othello's personality.

Czinner, Paul (1890–1972) Hungarian-born British movie director, creator of a FILM of *As You Like It*. Czinner's 1936 presentation of Shakespeare's play starred Laurence OLIVIER as Orlando and had a score by William WALTON. Based on a treatment of the play by J. M. Barrie (1860–1937), the creator of *Peter Pan*, the film has been criticized as a shadow-free rendering, with most of the melancholy of Jaques and the cynical amusement of Touchstone edited out.

D

Daly, Augustin (1838–1899) American theatrical entrepreneur. Daly operated theaters in both London and New York. With Ada REHAN as the centerpiece of his company, he specialized in classical COMEDY (along with modern drama) and produced most of Shakespeare's comedies, usually with greatly abridged texts and spectacular scenic effects. He was also a playwright with about 100 plays to his credit (though scholars believe his brother may have written most of them, and they are virtually all adapted from earlier plays, mostly French or German). These works were all highly colorful melodramas: His first great success in the theater was with a famous and often imitated scene of a man tied on railroad tracks in front of an oncoming train.

Dance, James (1722–1774) English actor and playwright, author of an adaptation of *Timon of Athens*. Dance, son of a famous architect, took the name James Love for his acting career. He was best known for his portrayals of Falstaff. His version of *Timon* (1768) combined Shakespeare's text with Thomas SHADWELL's earlier adaptation. It was only moderately successful. Dance also wrote a popular long poem on cricket.

Daniel, Samuel (ca. 1562–1619) English poet and dramatist, author of sources for several of Shakespeare's plays. Daniel's epic poem *The Civil Wars between the two Houses of York and Lancaster* (1595) influenced Act 5 of *Richard II* and the minor TETRALOGY of HISTORY PLAYS in general. His *The Complaint of Rosamund* (1592), a love story in verse, inspired

several passages in *Romeo and Juliet*; moreover, Shakespeare's use of it helps date the play. Daniel's TRAGEDY *Cleopatra* (1594) influenced Shakespeare's treatment of his Egyptian queen, and another Daniel play, *The Queen's Arcadia* (1605), provided minor details for *Macbeth*. Also, Daniel's immensely popular SONNET sequence *Delia* (1592) may have helped inspire Shakespeare to write his *Sonnets*.

A minor diplomat early in his career, Daniel was later a tutor to William Herbert, Earl of PEMBROKE. His connection with Pembroke has inspired speculation that he may be the "rival poet" of Shakespeare's *Sonnets*. By 1595 Daniel was well established as a major literary figure of the day, and after 1603 he often composed MASQUES for the court of King JAMES I. A play produced by the Children of the Revels (see CHILDREN'S COMPANIES) in 1604 got him in trouble with state CENSORSHIP, for it seemed to express sympathy for the rebellious Robert Devereux, Earl of ESSEX, but Daniel nevertheless continued to write for the court. He also wrote a prose *History of England* (1612) that was very influential during the political turmoil of the 1620s and 1630s, as England approached civil war. In the last years of his life he became reclusive; Shakespeare is said to have been among the few people he would accept as visitors.

Danter, John (d. 1599) London printer, producer of editions of two of Shakespeare's plays. In 1594 Danter printed the first QUARTO edition of *Titus Andronicus* for publishers Thomas MILLINGTON and Edward WHITE, and in 1597 he undertook a pirated edition, the first, of *Romeo and Juliet*, only

to have his press seized by the STATIONERS' COM-
PANY for other such piracies before the job was finished. It was completed by Edward ALLDE. Danter
was in trouble for piracy throughout his career, but
he always reestablished himself. However, all of his
surviving work is sloppily done. He was also suspended in 1596 for printing illegal Catholic materials. He was a business partner of Henry CHETTLE
from 1589 to 1591.

Dark Lady See *Sonnets*.

Davenant, William (William D'Avenant) (1606–
1668) English poet, playwright, and theatrical
entrepreneur. Davenant, along with Thomas KILLI-
GREW, dominated the London theatrical world during the 1660s. When the monarchy was restored
in 1660, the theaters of England were reopened
after their long closure by the Puritan revolutionary government, and Davenant received one of
the two licenses to put on plays in London. His
Duke of York's Company—named for its patron,
the future King James II—staged many plays by
Shakespeare and others. Davenant's license
assigned him the rights to 10—later amended to
13—of Shakespeare's plays: *Hamlet*, the *Henry VI*
plays (considered as one work), *Henry VIII*, *King
Lear*, *Macbeth*, *Measure for Measure*, *Much Ado
About Nothing*, *Pericles*, *Romeo and Juliet*, *The Tempest*, *Timon of Athens*, *Troilus and Cressida*, and
Twelfth Night.

Davenant is notorious for his adaptations of the
plays. He combined *Measure for Measure* and *Much
Ado About Nothing* in THE LAW AGAINST LOVERS
(1662), and he greatly abridged and altered the
texts of the others, changing names, rewriting passages, inserting his own words—or sometimes
merely inserting Shakespeare's words into his own
play—and taking care to "refine" (his word) Shakespeare's language. This process was particularly
egregious in his *Macbeth*. With John DRYDEN, he
adapted *The Tempest* as *The Tempest, or The
Enchanted Island* (1667, published 1670), adding
many characters and situations from the work of
the Spanish playwright Pedro Calderón (1600–81)
and retaining little of Shakespeare's text. This
adaptation was hugely popular, especially in

Thomas SHADWELL's operatic version (1674; Henry
PURCELL provided a new score in 1690; see OPERA).
Modern commentators condemn it, but the Dav-
enant/Dryden *Tempest* influenced all other versions
of the play for almost 200 years.

As a young man, Davenant was a playwright,
composing several tragedies in the style of
JACOBEAN DRAMA and a popular comedy of manners, *The Wits* (1633). He collaborated on several
MASQUEs with Inigo Jones, the royal architect, and
when Ben JONSON died in 1637, Davenant was
awarded his masque-writing duties and his pension
(the equivalent of being named Poet Laureate). He
fought for the royalists in the Civil Wars and was
knighted for valor by King Charles I. Captured in
1650, he was imprisoned for more than a year
before being freed by the poet John MILTON, who
was a member of the revolutionary government.
(Davenant was to repay the service upon the
restoration of the monarchy in 1660, when Milton
was sentenced to death.) Upon his release, Davenant wrote plays that he managed to stage despite
the ban on theaters, by adding music and calling
them operas. His *The Siege of Rhodes* (1656) is considered the first opera performed in England. Thus,
when the restored monarchy legalized the theater
again, Davenant was already in business.

Davenant claimed to be Shakespeare's illegitimate son. His parents had run an inn on the road
between STRATFORD and London, and Davenant
declared that he had been conceived during a
stopover. In a variation of this claim—the version
reportedly varied with alcohol consumption—he
took the status of godson. Neither claim is supported by any evidence.

Davies, John, of Hereford (ca. 1565–1618)
English poet, author of early references to Shakespeare. Davies published several volumes of poetry
between 1603 and 1617. One of these, *The Scourge
of Folly* (ca. 1610), contained a poem entitled "To
our English Terence, Mr. Will. Shake-speare" [sic]
(see TERENCE), which in praising the playwright
also suggests that he had played "Kingly parts" as
an actor. Davies's *Microcosmos* (1603) and *Civil
Wars of Death and Fortune* (1605) contain praises of
the actors "W. S." and "R. B.," presumed to be

Shakespeare and Richard BURBAGE. Davies taught writing to the ill-fated Prince of Wales, Henry (1594–1612), son of King JAMES I.

Davies, Sir John (1569–1626)   English poet and lawyer, author of a minor source for *Julius Caesar*. Davies published several volumes of poetry, including *Epigrams* (1590); *Orchestra, or a Poeme of Dauncing* (1596)—a long poem justifying the pleasures of dancing; and *Hymnes of Astraea* (1599), a collection of acrostics based on the name of Queen Elizabeth. Also published in 1599 was his *Nosce Teipsum* ("Know Thyself"), a long philosophical poem on the nature of the human soul. Several minor echoes of this text in *Julius Caesar* establish that Shakespeare was familiar with the work.

Davies was by profession a lawyer. He was disbarred from 1598 to 1601 after he assaulted a fellow attorney, but he was reinstated and was highly successful under King JAMES I. He was first solicitor general and then attorney general of Ireland from 1603 to 1619. He supported King Charles I in his early disputes with Parliament and in return was appointed Lord Chief Justice, the highest-ranking judicial post in England, but he died before taking office.

Davies, Richard (d. 1708)   English clergyman and antiquarian, transmitter of noteworthy lore about Shakespeare. Davies annotated the personal notes of a fellow antiquarian with an early reference to the legend that the young Shakespeare had poached deer from the estate of Sir Thomas LUCY, and with the assertion that the playwright had been a Catholic when he died. Neither remark is supported by any evidence at all, however, and Davies is not regarded as a reliable source by modern scholars. His reports are regarded more as examples of a flourishing body of 18th-century gossip about Shakespeare than as information about his life.

Day, John (ca. 1574–ca. 1640)   English playwright, possible collaborator with Shakespeare. Day, a minor figure in the ELIZABETHAN THEATER, collaborated with many playwrights, including Thomas DEKKER, Samuel ROWLEY, George WILKINS, and possibly Christopher MARLOWE. He may also have had a hand in *Timon of Athens* and/or *Pericles*, though in both cases the identity—or even existence—of collaborators is uncertain.

Day became a hack writer in LONDON after being expelled from Cambridge University for theft in 1593. Little is known of his life except that he was chronically in debt, and that in 1599 he stabbed and killed the playwright Henry PORTER, apparently in self-defense. Day wrote plays for the ADMIRAL'S MEN from 1599 to 1603, usually in collaboration, though after this period he mostly wrote alone. The later plays, of which six have survived, were generally staged by the Children of the Revels (see CHILDREN'S COMPANIES). One of them, *Isle of Gulls* (1606), a satire on Anglo-Scottish relations, offended the government and resulted in the imprisonment of several of its producers. He also wrote a series of nondramatic dialogues, *The Parliament of Bees* (1608), which is considered his masterpiece, though it is a minor work.

Dekker, Thomas (ca. 1572–ca. 1632)   English dramatist. Between 1598 and 1605, Dekker wrote about 44 plays (many of them in collaboration) for the ADMIRAL'S MEN and WORCESTER'S MEN, but only six have survived. He is best known for two comedies, *The Shoemaker's Holiday* (1599) and *The Honest Whore* (1604, with Thomas MIDDLETON). Writing for the Children of Paul's (see CHILDREN'S COMPANIES), he participated in the WAR OF THE THEATERS, an exchange of satirical plays among rival playwrights. His *Satiromastix* (1601, with John MARSTON) was a reply to Ben JONSON's satire of him in an earlier work. Jonson struck again in *The Poetaster* (1601), calling Dekker a "playdresser and plagiary."

Dekker went on to write many pamphlets, including a vivid group describing a plague epidemic. In the 1620s he returned to writing plays, mostly for PRINCE CHARLES' MEN and mostly in collaboration with such dramatists as John DAY, John FORD, and Philip MASSINGER. Little is known of Dekker's life, though his works reveal him to have been a pleasant, cheerful man, with an admiration for the strengths of London's poor, of whom he was one. He was perennially in debt; he spent almost eight years in debtors' prison between 1612 and 1619 and may have returned just before his death.

Deloney, Thomas (ca. 1550–1600) English writer, possibly the author of a poem sometimes ascribed to Shakespeare. The poem, "Crabbed age and youth cannot live together," published as number XII in THE PASSIONATE PILGRIM (1599) where it was attributed to Shakespeare, appeared as Deloney's work in a posthumously published anthology, *Garland of Goodwill* (1631). Most modern scholars do not believe the poem was written by Shakespeare, though a minority opinion holds that it might be an early work of the playwright. If Deloney's, it is one of his best poems.

Best known for three long ballads on the Spanish Armada, Deloney was a minor poet of the 1580s and 1590s who turned to prose and wrote several so-called craft novels. These were prose narratives which celebrated various urban occupations. One of them, *The Gentle Craft* (1598), about shoemakers, was the chief source for Thomas DEKKER's well-known play *The Shoemaker's Holiday* (1599). Deloney's novels are notable for their descriptions of LONDON life, and although they were popular, Elizabethan novelists were ill-rewarded, and Deloney died in poverty.

Dench, Judi (b. 1934) English actress. Dench began her Shakespearean career in 1957 as Ophelia, in *Hamlet*, and went on to a much-acclaimed Juliet in Franco ZEFFERELLI's 1960 staging of *Romeo and Juliet*. She has played many of Shakespeare's best female roles since, including a remarkable performance as both Hermione and Perdita in *The Winter's Tale* (1969). She played Lady Macbeth both in Trevor NUNN's 1976 production at STRATFORD and in his 1979 TELEVISION version. She appeared in two of Kenneth BRANAGH's Shakespearean FILMS: as the Hostess, Mistress Quickly, in *Henry V* (1989); and, in a cameo role, as a mute Hecuba in *Hamlet* (1996). In 1999 she won an Oscar as best supporting actress for her portrayal of Queen Elizabeth I in the film *Shakespeare in Love*. In 2003 she played the Countess of Rossillion in a ROYAL SHAKESPEARE COMPANY production of *All's Well That Ends Well* in STRATFORD.

Denmark Country in northern Europe, the setting for *Hamlet*. The entire play takes place in and around the royal castle in ELSINORE, a seaport in northern Denmark. Denmark was familiar to English audiences as a rival in the Baltic Sea trade, and Shakespeare offers several glimpses of Danish ways, focusing chiefly on the Danes' reputation for excessive drinking, which Hamlet remarks on disparagingly in 1.4.13–38. Sixteenth-century accounts confirm bits of information provided in the play, such as the popularity of Rhine wines (1.4.10) and the habit of accompanying a toast with kettledrums (1.4.11) or, more extravagantly, with cannon fire (1.2.126). Further, it is thought that the description of Danish preparations for war in 1.1.74–81 reflects news of contemporary conflicts between Denmark and Sweden.

Scholars have occasionally proposed that Shakespeare's knowledge of Denmark reflects a visit he made to that country with an English acting company in 1585 or 1586, when such trips are known to have occurred (see, e.g., KEMPE, WILLIAM), but many contemporary sources provided sufficient information on the country and its customs to account for the play's descriptions. In fact, Shakespeare's extremely faulty knowledge of the geography of Denmark—a flat country with no "cliff / That beetles o'er his base into the sea" (1.4.70–71) and that is not connected by land to Norway or Poland, as the route of Fortinbras's army would imply (see 2.2.75–78; 4.4.10–12)—suggests strongly that he had not been there.

Dennis, John (1657–1734) English playwright. Dennis, a minor poet and dramatist, wrote and produced two unsuccessful adaptations of Shakespeare plays. His *The Comical Gallant* (1702) is a crude version of *The Merry Wives of Windsor*. It was unpopular and disappeared quickly; it is now remembered only for its preface, where Dennis recorded the belief that Shakespeare had written *The Merry Wives* in 14 days at the command of Queen Elizabeth. Dennis's *The Invader of His Country* (1719) employed excerpts from *Coriolanus* in its political statement against FRANCE for having aided the exiled STUART DYNASTY's attempted invasion of England in 1715. It was booed off the stage and closed after three performances. Dennis wrote other anti-French plays, and he amused the literary world by being egotistical enough to ask

Kronborg Castle in Elsinore, Denmark, is thought to be the place Shakespeare had in mind as the setting for *Hamlet*. Here a crew sets up to film a 1964 joint BBC-Danish Television Service production of the play. *(Courtesy of Culver Pictures, Inc.)*

that a special clause be inserted in the Treaty of Utrecht (1713), specifically protecting him from French reprisals.

De Quincey, Thomas (1785–1859) English essayist. Best known for his memoir *Confessions of an English Opium Eater* (1822), De Quincey also wrote many miscellaneous essays in an impressionistic style reflective of the tumultuous Romantic period. These include a remarkable piece that is still widely read, "On the Knocking on the Gate in *Macbeth*" (1823), interpreting the role of the Porter in the play. De Quincey also wrote a long article on Shakespeare for the seventh edition of the *Encyclopaedia Brittanica* (1838).

Derby, Ferdinando Stanley, Earl of   See STRANGE, FERDINANDO STANLEY, LORD.

Derby, William Stanley, Earl of (1561–1642) English theatrical patron and writer, younger brother and successor of Ferdinando, Lord STRANGE. In 1594 William Stanley succeeded Strange as Earl of Derby, and in January 1595 he married; the wedding may have been the occasion for the first performance of *A Midsummer Night's Dream*. From 1594 to 1618 Derby maintained a troupe of actors known as Derby's Men. This group is not to be confused with his brother's STRANGE'S MEN, who also briefly used that name (see DERBY'S MEN) and with whom Shakespeare may have been associated. The Derby's Men of William Stanley appeared at court in 1599–1601 under the leadership of Robert BROWNE, but they usually toured the provinces. In 1599 it was said that Derby's Men performed comedies written by Stanley; his plays have not survived, but this report has led to Derby's occasional nomination as the "real" Shakespeare (see AUTHORSHIP CONTROVERSY).

Derby's Men Name used between September 25, 1593, and spring 1594 by the theatrical company better known as STRANGE'S MEN or the CHAMBERLAIN'S MEN. Shakespeare may have been a member of the company during this time. The LONDON theaters were closed by a plague epidemic and Strange's Men were on tour when the father of their patron, Ferdinando Stanley, Lord STRANGE, died. Lord Strange assumed his father's title, Earl of Derby, so the company changed its name accordingly. On the following April 16, the new Earl of Derby also died, and the actors, still on tour as Derby's Men, sought a new patron. When they returned to London, where the theaters had reopened, they found one in Henry Carey, Baron HUNSDON, the Lord Chamberlain, and they were known thereafter as the Chamberlain's Men. The exact date of the transition is not known, but they performed under the new name on June 5, 1594, at the theater in NEWINGTON BUTTS. The earliest professional record of Shakespeare as an actor places him in the Chamberlain's Men in December 1594, but he may have been with the company earlier, when it was still Derby's Men.

Earlier, in the 1560s and 1570s, Lord Strange's father had maintained a company of players, which became known as Derby's Men after 1572, when the father had become Earl of Derby. This troupe played the provinces exclusively and is not to be confused with the later company, basically a London organization.

Dering manuscript Early-17th-century document, the handwritten text of a play combining and abridging *1* and *2 Henry IV*. Possibly prepared for a private performance, perhaps at the court of King JAMES I, the Dering manuscript contains various revisions made by Sir Edward Dering (1598–1644), a gentleman from Kent. The manuscript is based on the Q5 edition (1613) of *1 Henry IV* and Q (1600) of *2 Henry IV*; most of the former play is represented, but much of the latter is not. The primary emphasis of Dering's version is the relationship between Henry IV and Prince Hal, especially at the expense of Falstaff. For instance, the scenes of *2 Henry IV* set in GLOUCESTERSHIRE are entirely omitted. Dering's alterations seem to incorporate some minor features from the FIRST FOLIO versions of the plays and are thus dated to 1623 or 1624.

Dethick, Sir William (1543–1612) Government official who granted Shakespeare's father a COAT OF ARMS. Dethick, as Garter King of Arms (his esoteric title derived from medieval regulations), approved the application of John SHAKESPEARE for a much sought-after emblem of gentlemanly status, a registered coat of arms, in 1596. Six years later Dethick was charged with abusing his authority by granting arms to unqualified applicants, and John Shakespeare's grant was among those cited as illegitimate (though it was mistakenly said to have been granted to William himself, who was dismissively denoted "Shakespear [sic] ye player"). The complaint was itself dismissed, and modern scholars believe it had more to do with Dethick's character than with any real failings in his work as King of Arms. Dethick was a temperamental and violent man—he is known to have assaulted at different times his father, his brother, and an officiating minister during a funeral—and he often made enemies, one of whom was doubtless behind these charges.

De Witt, Johannes Contemporary of Shakespeare, a Dutch traveler to England. See SWAN THEATRE.

Dickens, Charles (1812–1870) English novelist. Dickens lent his prestige as a world-famous novelist to help raise funds to preserve Shakespeare's birthplace in STRATFORD, and he took a prominent part in the project. He also wrote numerous articles on the playwright. Dickens maintained a small theater in his house where he performed in amateur productions; he was particularly noted for his portrayal of Shallow in a production of *The Merry Wives of*

Windsor that toured northern England and Scotland to raise money for the birthplace project.

Digges, Dudley (1583–1639) English politician, entrepreneur of colonial expeditions, and possible source of inspiration for *The Tempest*. Digges, brother of Leonard DIGGES and stepson of Shakespeare's friend, Thomas RUSSELL, was probably acquainted with Shakespeare. He was closely involved in the exploration of the New World and could have been the playwright's source for the 1610 letter by William STRACHEY describing a shipwreck in Bermuda. Scholars speculate that Digges edited a pamphlet that was another possible source of inspiration for the play, *A True Declaration of the state of the Colonie in Virginia* (1610), which was published by a group of investors defending the colonial enterprise.

Digges was financially and intellectually involved in numerous other foreign expeditions. He was active in the East India and Muscovy companies, as well as the proposed colony in Virginia, and he also promoted geographical exploration with only remote commercial applications. He helped finance Henry Hudson's search for the Northwest Passage and wrote tracts asserting the existence of that route to China; he even advocated a purely scientific expedition to the North Pole. In 1618 he traveled to Russia on a combined scientific and diplomatic mission. Politically, he served in Parliament intermittently from 1601 to 1628 and in the 1620s was a leader of the opposition to King Charles I that would eventually lead to the Civil Wars. He was twice briefly imprisoned for his opposition, but was reconciled with the king before his death.

Digges, Leonard (1588–1635) Poet, translator, and acquaintance of Shakespeare, author of two notable poems commending the playwright. Digges knew Shakespeare through his stepfather, Thomas RUSSELL, and probably wrote the poems about the playwright in 1616 on the occasion of his death. The first was published as part of the preface to the FIRST FOLIO edition of the plays (1623); the other appeared posthumously in the 1640 edition of Shakespeare's *Poems*, published by John BENSON. Digges, brother of Dudley DIGGES, was a respected poet and a translator of several languages, especially noted for his renderings from Spanish.

Dover City in southeastern England, near which much of *King Lear* is set. The invasion of England by an army under Cordelia and France draws the play's action to this seaport on the English Channel, famous for the white chalk cliffs overlooking the sea that are vividly described by Edgar in 4.6.11–24. Some scholars think this description may reflect Shakespeare's personal response to the natural phenomenon, for he probably visited Dover as an actor; his company—the CHAMBERLAIN'S MEN, later the KING'S MEN—performed there in 1597 and 1605.

Dowden, Edward (1843–1913) Irish literary scholar. Dowden was a longtime professor of English literature at Dublin's Trinity College. He established himself as a significant Shakespearean scholar with his *Shakespeare: A Critical Study of his Mind and Art* (1875), the first book in English (but see GERVINUS) to consider the growth of the playwright through the course of his career. Though regarded by later critics as a sentimental work, too inclined to idealize its subject, Dowden's book influenced all later Shakespearean biography because of its developmental approach. Dowden also published other works on Shakespeare, editions of some of the plays, biographies of other literary figures, and editions of SPENSER and other English poets.

Downton, Thomas (active 1593–1622) English actor, a leading member of the ADMIRAL'S MEN for many years. Downton was probably one of the amalgamated troupe of Admiral's Men and STRANGE'S MEN that toured England in 1593–94 while the LONDON theaters were closed by the plague. He was a charter member of the reorganized Admiral's Men of 1594, and he was still with the company in 1615 when it was the PALSGRAVE'S MEN, though he had briefly performed for PEMBROKE'S MEN in 1597. He played a variety of roles and was involved in the business affairs of the troupe. In 1618 he married the widow of a wine merchant and took up that profession.

Drayton, Michael (1563–1631) English poet and dramatist. Though best known for his poetry,

Drayton also wrote for the stage. In the late 1590s and early 17th century, he wrote about 20 plays for the ADMIRAL'S MEN, all in collaboration with other playwrights, including Anthony MUNDAY and Richard HATHWAY. One of their plays was SIR JOHN OLDCASTLE, later published as Shakespeare's. In 1598 Francis MERES praised Drayton as among England's best writers of tragedies. Drayton helped found the WHITEFRIARS THEATRE in 1608 and joined Martin SLATER in forming a short-lived boy's troupe (see CHILDREN'S COMPANIES) that played there. Drayton was raised as a page in an aristocratic household near STRATFORD and visited there often later in life. He was treated by Shakespeare's son-in-law, Dr. John HALL, and so may have known the playwright. However, there seems to be no truth in the legend that Shakespeare died after a drinking bout with Drayton and Ben JONSON, for Drayton was well known for his strict sobriety.

Drew, John (1853–1927) American actor. One of the leading actors of his day, John Drew was especially noted for his Petruchio in *The Taming of the Shrew.* For many years he appeared in the productions of Augustin DALY, often opposite Ada REHAN. Through his sister he was the uncle of John BARRYMORE.

Droeshout, Martin (1601–ca. 1650) English engraver, creator of the portrait of Shakespeare that illustrates the FIRST FOLIO edition (1623) of the plays. This is one of the two PORTRAITS OF SHAKESPEARE considered by scholars to reflect his actual appearance (the other is a sculpture by Gheerart JANSSEN). Droeshout was a poor draftsman, and the portrait is badly flawed—for instance, the head is much too big relative to the torso, and one eye is larger and lower than the other. However, because it was acceptable to Shakespeare's friends, the Folio editors who published it and Ben JONSON who praised it, it is presumed to have provided a reasonable likeness. Scholars believe that Droeshout worked from a drawing or painting and probably never saw the playwright. For all its defects, the Droeshout portrait has been copied many times and is probably the basis for most people's sense of Shakespeare's appearance.

Droeshout was the grandson of a Protestant artist who fled from religious persecution in Brabant (in what is now Belgium) in 1566. His family were members of the same LONDON church as that of Gheerart Janssen, and it is thought that the sculptor may have helped secure the Folio commission for a fellow Netherlander. Droeshout later produced portraits of other notable figures.

droll Brief playlet, often an adaptation of scenes from full-length plays, performed in 1642–60, when theaters were closed by the English revolutionary government. Drolls were presented at fairs and in taverns in conjunction with such licensed forms of entertainment as rope dancing. One of the best-known performers of drolls was Robert COX, a collection of whose scripts was published by Henry MARSH and Francis KIRKMAN—after the restoration of the monarchy and the reopening of the theaters—as *The Wits, or Sport upon Sport* (1662). Among the most famous of drolls were "The Grave-diggers," from *Hamlet,* and "The Merry conceited Humours of Bottom the Weaver," from *A Midsummer Night's Dream.* The latter was published separately in 1661, when it was described on the title page as having been performed in legitimate, public performances and ". . . lately, privately, presented by several apprentices for their harmless recreation."

Dryden, John (1631–1700) English poet, playwright, and literary critic. One of the leading playwrights of the Restoration period (1660–88), Dryden also wrote extensive assessments of English writers and was an acute appreciator of Shakespeare. However, while admiring "the divine Shakespeare," he also felt that ELIZABETHAN DRAMA was in general crude, and that Shakespeare shared in its defects. Thus, like many others of his day, he did not hesitate to alter Shakespeare's works. He is notorious for his rewriting of *The Tempest,* in collaboration with William DAVENANT, as *The Tempest, or The Enchanted Island* (1667, published 1670). This adaptation adds whole SUBPLOTS—many of the additions taken from a Spanish playwright, Pedro Calderón (1600–81)—and retains little of Shakespeare's text. Dryden nonetheless claimed Shakespeare's inspiration, proclaiming unembarrassedly in his Prologue to the work:

> As when a Tree's cut down a secret root
> Lives underground and thence new
>   Branches shoot
> So, from old Shakespeare's honour'd
>   dust, this day
> Springs up and buds a new reviving Play.

Although this work was hugely popular, it is deplored by modern commentators. Dryden also adapted *Troilus and Cressida*, which he described in his preface as a "heap of rubbish," in an equally radical and unfortunate alteration known by its subtitle as *Truth Found Too Late* (1679). His own best play, *All for Love* (1677), was a version of *Antony and Cleopatra*; it has appealed to audiences ever since.

Du Bartas, Guillaume de Sallust   (1544–1590) French poet, author of a minor source for *Romeo and Juliet*. A poem by Du Bartas—featured in English translation in the *Ortho-epia Gallica* (1593) of John ELIOT—inspired the debate on bird song between Romeo and Juliet in 3.5 of *Romeo and Juliet*.

Most of Du Bartas's work was of a more serious nature. Born a nobleman in Gascony, Du Bartas was a friend of the King of Navarre—later Henri IV of France—the leader of the Protestant faction in the civil and religious conflict that tore France apart in the late 16th century. The poet composed monumental poems on religious themes and fought on the battlefield. In 1587 Henri sent Du Bartas on a diplomatic mission to Scotland, where he became a close friend of King James, later JAMES I of England. His works were highly regarded throughout Protestant Europe, were widely translated, and greatly influenced 17th-century religious poetry, including, most notably, John MILTON's *Paradise Lost*.

Ducis, Jean-François (1733–1816)   French dramatist and adaptor of Shakespeare. Ducis, an unsuccessful playwright, made a name for himself in middle age with a series of adaptations of Shakespeare. Basing his versions on the translations of Pierre-Antoine de LAPLACE, Ducis, who had no

English, produced *Hamlet*, *Romeo and Juliet*, *King Lear*, *Macbeth*, and *Othello*, between 1769 and 1792. Published, these versions of the plays had a wide influence. Altered and adulterated in many ways, they nevertheless introduced Shakespeare to French theatergoers and set the stage for the reception of the much better translations of Pierre LA TOURNEUR. (See also TRANSLATION OF SHAKESPEARE.)

Duffett, Thomas (active 1673–1678)   English dramatist, author of parodies of two adaptations of Shakespeare. Passages in Duffett's *The Empress of Morocco* (ca. 1673) mocked William DAVENANT's extravagant production of *Macbeth*, and his *The Mock-Tempest, or The Enchanted Castle* (1674) was a full-scale comic imitation of Thomas SHADWELL's operatic version of *The Tempest* (1674).

Duffett was a milliner who took up playwrighting with some success. Four of his plays were staged between 1673 and 1676. Three—including the two named above—were burlesques of other works, and the fourth was a MASQUE.

Duke Humphrey   Possible lost play by Shakespeare. In 1660 the publisher Humphrey MOSELEY claimed the copyrights to a number of old plays, including *Duke Humphrey*. The 18th-century antiquarian John WARBURTON reported owning a copy as well, but otherwise the play is unknown. However, since both Moseley and Warburton were mistaken in claiming other plays as Shakespeare's, scholars generally do not believe that *Duke Humphrey* was written by him, unless the title refers to *2 Henry VI*. This was originally published as "The First part of the Contention betwixt the two famous Houses of Yorke and Lancaster, with the death of the good Duke Humphrey" (a reference to the Duke of Gloucester [see *Henry VI, Part 1*]). (See also *The Contention*.)

Duke of York's Men   See PRINCE CHARLES' MEN.

Dumas, Alexandre (Dumas père) (1802–1870) French novelist and playwright, an adapter of Shakespeare's works. Dumas, the son of a brilliant Napoleonic general and grandson of a Dominican slave, was one of the leading figures in 19th-century French literature. Perhaps best known today for *The Three Musketeers* (1844; dramatized 1845) and *The Count of Monte-Cristo* (1845; 1848), Dumas was extravagantly prolific, producing many novels, travel books, memoirs, and other nonfiction, and about 90 plays, among them two adaptations of Shakespeare's works. Though based on the fairly accurate translations of Pierre LE TOURNEUR (see TRANSLATION OF SHAKESPEARE), they are nevertheless very free adaptations and are quite at variance with Shakespeare's plays in both tone and plot line. For instance, his *Une fille de régent* (1846) is a version of *Romeo and Juliet* set amid the French Revolution, and his *Hamlet* (1847), climaxes in a happy ending in which the hero lives and is crowned King of Denmark. (This work was to be the basis for the OPERA by Ambroise THOMAS.)

dumb show Scene performed in pantomime, especially as part of an Elizabethan TRAGEDY. Shakespeare employed dumb shows in several scenes of *Pericles*, a single scene in *Cymbeline*, and in *Hamlet*. A dumb show could function as a PROLOGUE or CHORUS; it sometimes illustrated an offstage event, presented plot elements that were not fully acted out, or enacted what was shortly to come in the main action, intimating a symbolic meaning.

In *Pericles* three dumb shows are employed in the choric narrations of Gower. At 2.Chorus.16 a dumb show enacts the reception of a letter by Pericles, followed by his hasty departure; Gower reveals that the message has warned the hero of danger and he has fled. At 3.Chorus.14 a more elaborate enactment depicts Pericles receiving another letter, read also by his new father-in-law, Simonides. The attending courtiers kneel to Pericles. He then departs with his new wife, who is pregnant. Gower explains that the letter has summoned Pericles to TYRE, where he is ruler, thus revealing his royalty and sparking another journey. Lastly, in 4.4 a dumb show presents Pericles weeping at the tomb of his supposedly dead daughter, Marina, though the audience knows that Marina is actually alive. Thus, in *Pericles* the dumb show is a simple device that compresses the plot by providing brief summaries of what would otherwise require complete scenes.

In *Cymbeline* a brief dumb show occurs at the close of 5.3. In it Posthumus, disguised as a Roman soldier, is brought as a prisoner to Cymbeline, who turns him over to a Gaoler. This may not be a dumb show proper, but rather a survival in the printed play of notes for a scene that was never actually written (see *Cymbeline*, "Text of the Play").

The Players in *Hamlet* stage a dumb show before their performance of THE MURDER OF GONZAGO, the playlet that Hamlet hopes will inspire an unconscious revelation of guilt in his uncle, the King, who has murdered his father. The dumb show is described in an elaborate stage direction at 3.2.133. After being affectionately embraced by his queen, a king sleeps and a man puts a poison in his ear. The queen returns and mourns the dead king, but she responds to the attentions of the poisoner, who takes her away with him as the king's body is removed. This enactment resembles the real king's crime—as Hamlet has been informed by the Ghost—but the king does not respond until the spoken dialogue of the playlet later in the scene.

This delay presents one of the many small problems that have puzzled commentators on *Hamlet* for generations: Have two different renderings of the playlet been accidentally preserved, when only one was intended for performance? Are we supposed to believe that the King was not paying attention or that he did not recognize his crime in the dumb show, only in the more elaborate rendering that followed? Or was he able to stand the sight of his guilty action once but not twice (the so-called second tooth theory)? In Shakespeare's text the King remains inscrutable during the dumb show, perhaps to heighten the buildup of tension, but many productions present him as engaged in conversation with the Queen and thus not seeing the dumb show, or as silently but visibly aghast, recovering himself only to collapse later.

The "second tooth" theory has been most widely accepted by scholars, but whatever theory is correct, the King's inscrutability works well on stage, and the dumb show serves a definite theatrical purpose: A formal device that is not itself a part of the plot, it outlines the coming playlet, permitting the audience to concern itself with the responses of Hamlet and the King. Moreover, the playlet is never completed after the King's guilty reaction disrupts it, so its closure with the queen's acceptance of the murderer—analogous to the behavior of Hamlet's mother, the real Queen—is known only through the dumb show.

It is likely that the dumb show originated in RENAISSANCE Italy. Probably always accompanied by music, it was intended as an elaborate and diverting spectacle, and Shakespeare assumed his audience would recognize it as having this function for the Danish court in *Hamlet,* just as it presumably did for the actual viewers of *Pericles.*

Dunsinane (Dunsinnan) Castle near Perth in central SCOTLAND, the setting for Act 5 of *Macbeth.* "Great Dunsinane" (5.2.12), whose "strength / Will laugh a siege to scorn" (5.5.2–3), is clearly an imposing structure—one appropriate to the grim events of the play's climax. Within its walls Macbeth resists the army of Prince Malcolm, Lord Macduff, and the English Lord Siward. A few miles away lies Birnam Wood, the royal forest featured in the Witches' prediction that Macbeth believes ensures his safety: ". . . until / Great Birnam wood to high Dunsinane hill / Shall come against him" (4.1.92–94). When the camouflage devised by Malcolm seems to bring the wood to the castle, in 5.5, Macbeth's fate becomes apparent. The castle proves to be no hindrance to the invaders, being "gently render'd" (5.7.24) by all its inhabitants but the doomed king.

Historically, Dunsinane was not the site of Macbeth's final defeat, though Siward did win a battle there in 1054. Malcolm was only finally victorious—and Macbeth slain—at a battle elsewhere in Scotland, three years later. Shakespeare took the error from his source, HOLINSHED's *Chronicles,* and doubtless believed it to be correct.

D'Urfey, Thomas (1653–1723) English dramatist, author of an adaptation of *Cymbeline.* D'Urfey's *The Injured Princess or the Fatal Wager* was staged and published in 1682 (though its EPILOGUE notes that it had been written nine years earlier). Shakespeare's language—including most of the names—was much altered by D'Urfey, but the plot remained fairly close to the original. It differs only in the addition of an elaborate subplot in which Cloten kidnaps a daughter of Pisanio, and the fact that Pisanio mistrusts Imogen as much as Posthumus does. *The Injured Princess* was quite popular and was revived periodically for almost 60 years.

Tom D'Urfey wrote plays and song lyrics; the latter were set to music by his composer friends, among them Henry PURCELL. His songs were published in six volumes entitled *Wit and Mirth, or Pills to Purge Melancholy* (1720). He also wrote 29 plays, many of which were very popular.

Dutton, Laurence (active 1571–1591) English actor. Dutton was a member of at least five different acting companies, including OXFORD'S MEN and the QUEEN'S MEN; his brother John worked with him in three of them. Their reputation for fickleness prompted an anonymous satirist of 1580 to refer to them as the "chameleon" Duttons.

Eastcheap Neighborhood in LONDON, location of the BOAR'S HEAD TAVERN and setting for several scenes in *1* and *2 Henry IV* and *Henry V.* Eastcheap, an ancient and impoverished commercial district—"cheap" comes from an Anglo-Saxon word for "bargain"—was noted for its butcher shops and meat markets. It was also known as a dangerous and disreputable area and was thus an appropriate locale for Falstaff's world of petty crime and dissipation, which Prince Hal samples and rejects. The neighborhood is specified as the scene of the Prince's delinquencies in Shakespeare's source, the FAMOUS VICTORIES.

Ecclestone, William (active 1610–1623) English actor, a member of the KING'S MEN. Ecclestone is one of the 26 men listed in the FIRST FOLIO as the "Principall Actors" in Shakespeare's plays. He was with the King's Men from 1610 until at least 1623, except for two years (1611–13) when he was with the newly formed LADY ELIZABETH'S MEN. He may have played a Lord in *All's Well That Ends Well*, designated as "E" in the Folio text of the play. He performed in many of the plays of Francis BEAUMONT and John FLETCHER, and is thought to have specialized in playing spirited young men given to sword fights.

Eden, Richard (ca. 1521–1576) English translator of a probable minor source for *The Tempest.* Eden's *History of Travaille* (1577) provided Shakespeare with several details for his play, including the name of Caliban's god, Setebos. The book, which was published posthumously, was composed of two translations; Shakespeare's material came from an account of the first circumnavigation of the globe, led by Ferdinand Magellan (ca. 1480–1521).

As a young man, Eden was secretary to the statesman Lord BURGHLEY. He then traveled for several years before taking up a career as a scientific translator from Latin, Italian, and Spanish. He helped advance the capabilities of English seamanship with his *Arte of Navigation* (1561), from the pioneering manual by the Spaniard Martin Cortes (active 1551), and his subsequent translations of various writings on navigation and exploration increased English awareness of the New World. Eden's other books, like the *History of Travaille*, focused on the exploration of the New World, and he is regarded as the most important predecessor of Richard HAKLUYT.

Edmund Ironside Anonymous play sometimes attributed to Shakespeare but generally regarded as part of the Shakespeare APOCRYPHA. Known in a single manuscript (owned by the British Museum), *Edmund Ironside* is thought to have been written some time between 1585 and 1600. It remained unpublished until the 20th century, when it was published several times as an anonymous work (though once accompanied by the hypothesis that it was Shakespearean) and once as Shakespeare's own work (by Eric SAMS in 1986). It is a play about the early medieval English resistance to Danish rule, led by the title character. The leader of the Danes is Canutus (i.e., King Canute, or Cnut [reigned 1017–35]). Ironside is valiant; Canutus is shrewdly opportunistic. The villainous Edricus (a Latinized peasant's name), clearly an example of a traditional medieval theatrical type, the VICE, attempts to flatter and then betray first one and then the other of the leaders. This slight plot culminates in an unconvincing reconciliation between the two kings. Though Sams perceives many verbal parallels between *Edmund Ironside* and Shakespeare's known work, few scholars or commentators agree with him that the play is Shakespearean.

Edward III, King of England   See Edward III, King of England, in *Edward III*.

Edward IV, King of England   See Edward IV, King of England, in *Henry VI, Part 3*.

Edwards, Richard (Richard Edwardes) (ca. 1523–1566)   English poet, musician, and playwright, author of a minor source for *The Two Gentlemen of Verona* and of a song quoted in *Romeo and Juliet*. Edwards was choral director of the Children of the Chapel (see CHILDREN'S COMPANIES). Under his direction the choirboys performed two of his plays, *Damon and Pythias* (1565) and *Palamon and Arcite* (1566), two of the earliest musical dramas. The former, published in 1571, was a tale of male friendship, an ancient genre, and it provided minor details for Shakespeare's similar effort, *The Two Gentlemen*, *Palamon and Arcite*, like *The Two Noble Kinsmen*, was based on CHAUCER's *The Knight's Tale*, but it is not believed to have influenced Shakespeare and his collaborator, John FLETCHER. In *Romeo and Juliet*, Peter sings a few lines of a well-known song, "In Commendation of Musique," written by Edwards and published posthumously in *The Paradise of Dainty Devises* (1575), an anthology of his and others' works. Long after his death, Edwards was celebrated by Frances MERES as one of England's best writers of COMEDY, along with Shakespeare.

Eld, George (George Elde) (d. 1624)   London printer and publisher, producer of first editions of *Troilus and Cressida* and the *Sonnets*. In 1609 Eld printed the QUARTO edition of Shakespeare's play for publishers Richard BONIAN and Henry WALLEY, and Thomas THORPE's edition of the *Sonnets*. Eld himself sometimes published the plays he printed, including THE PURITAN (1607), which was attributed to "W. S.," perhaps in an effort to falsely associate the work with Shakespeare. Eld, apprenticed to a printer from 1592 to 1600, acquired his business by marrying a woman twice the widow of earlier owners. He died in a plague epidemic, but little more is known of his life.

Elegy by W. S.   See FUNERAL ELEGY, A.

Eliot, John (b. 1562)   English author and translator, creator of a minor source for *Romeo and Juliet* and several other plays. Eliot's *Ortho-Epia Gallica* (1593) was a collection of lively colloquial essays—written in French and published with Eliot's English translation on facing pages—that dealt with LONDON life, European travel, and contemporary French poetry. It contained a translation of a poem by the French poet Guillaume DU BARTAS that influenced the lovers' debate on bird song in 3.5. Other material in *Ortho-Epia* inspired minor details in other plays as well, most notably elements of Pistol's roguish language.

Like Shakespeare, Eliot was from WARWICKSHIRE. After he attended Oxford he became a novice monk, but he withdrew before he took his vows. Instead, he wandered in Europe and supported himself as a schoolmaster, a hack journalist, and, possibly, a spy for one (or more) of the factions in the religious and civil wars of FRANCE. He returned to England in 1589—apparently fleeing the aftermath of King Henri III's assassination—and settled in London as a teacher and translator of French. His *Survey or Topographical Description of France* appeared in 1592, followed by the popular *Ortho-Epia*. After this Eliot disappeared from history. Scholars assume he returned to France, possibly when King Henri IV was crowned in 1594. Eliot was probably acquainted with Shakespeare, for they are known to have had mutual friends in the London literary and theatrical worlds.

Eliot, Thomas Stearns (T. S. Eliot) (1888–1965)   American-British poet and critic. T. S. Eliot is best known as one of the leading poets of the 20th century, but he also wrote a great deal of literary criticism. Much of this focused on the Elizabethan era and included critical essays on a number of Shakespeare's plays. As a Shakespearean critic he is notorious for his assessment of *Hamlet* as "an artistic failure." Less controversially, he observed, "About any one so great as Shakespeare, it is probable that we can never be right; and if we can never be right, it is better that we should from time to time change our way of being wrong."

References to Shakespearean characters occur in a number of Eliot's poems, and his "Coriolan" (a suite of two poems: "Triumphal March" and "Difficulties of a Statesman") probably helped spark the tremendous increase in critical and theatrical attention given Shakespeare's *Coriolanus* in the 20th century. Eliot's enthusiasm for, and perceptive studies of, Elizabethan literature certainly did much to generate a revival of interest in the subject as a whole. Eliot also wrote several modern plays in verse, the best known of which is *Murder in the Cathedral* (1935).

Elizabeth, Queen of England   See Elizabeth I, Queen of England, in *Henry VIII*.

Elizabethan drama   Art of writing for the theater as practiced in England during the reign of Queen Elizabeth I (1558–1603; see Elizabeth I in *Henry VIII*). Shakespeare was undeniably the major figure of Elizabethan drama, but many other playwrights were active, and the period constitutes a Golden Age in English drama, indeed in the drama of the world.

In 1558, when Elizabeth became queen, almost no English drama was being written; Elizabethan drama came of age in the late 1570s, growing out of the competition between the CHILDREN'S COMPANIES, composed of schoolboys, and the adult companies who had come to LONDON under the protection of noble patrons, both seeking the favor of the queen and her courtiers (see ELIZABETHAN THEATER). The children's companies performed Latin plays (both ancient Roman works and modern imitations) and English works modeled on them. These plays had greater appeal to the edu-

cated tastes of the court than did the often bawdy INTERLUDE—derived from native English roots in medieval festivals and the MORALITY PLAY—that was the stock-in-trade of the adult companies, just beginning to perform in public theaters. The adult companies, however, sought playwrights who could appeal to court tastes as well and found them in the literary world growing up in early modern London. A tremendous wellspring of talent was tapped, and thousands of plays were produced over the next several decades.

In the 1580s Elizabethan drama was dominated by a group of playwrights known as the UNIVERSITY WITS, who brought together various influences: classical literature and its contemporary imitation in ACADEMIC DRAMA, morality plays, and contemporary RENAISSANCE literature from Italy and France. In the 1590s a broader range of playwrights emerged, including Shakespeare.

Elizabethan TRAGEDY (which was strongly influenced by the ancient dramas of SENECA) consisted of two general varieties. The REVENGE PLAY was introduced by Thomas KYD in his very popular *Spanish Tragedy* (ca. 1588) and was most fully developed in *Hamlet*. John MARSTON was a later practitioner of the revenge play. Another sort of tragedy presented grandiose fantasies about the downfall of powerful rulers; this genre burst forth in the *Tamburlaine* of Christopher MARLOWE, in which BLANK VERSE was established as the medium for Elizabethan drama. Shakespeare brought the genre to complex new levels in such works as *Macbeth*, *King Lear*, and the ROMAN PLAYS.

Elizabethan COMEDY took several distinct forms. Romantic comedy, a popular genre centered on young love, reached its pinnacle in Shakespeare's comedies of the 1590s, such as *Much Ado About Nothing* and *As You Like It*. Lesser figures writing this sort of play included Robert GREENE and Thomas DEKKER. Toward the end of the 1590s, a variation arose, the COMEDY OF HUMOURS, in which bold character types were employed to ridicule contemporary behavior. Ben JONSON was the leading exponent of the comedy of humours. The so-called court comedy was written with an aristocratic audience in mind. These plays often used mythological or classical subjects and were distinguished by their emphasis on refined dialogue and prominent allusions to Renaissance learning. John LYLY was the most important writer of court comedy; his plays influenced Shakespeare's early work, especially *Love's Labour's Lost*. Another category, the chronicle or HISTORY PLAY, while it had roots in didactic, allegorical dramas akin to morality plays, was essentially developed by Shakespeare, in his enactments of the WARS OF THE ROSES.

Elizabethan drama is sometimes considered to include work from the next two reigns, those of Kings JAMES I and Charles I (1603–42), until the theaters of England were closed by revolution. However, the more restricted sense is used here, for the subsequent period, which includes Shakespeare's late work, saw pronounced changes in taste and in theatrical techniques, making for differences in tone and subject matter (see JACOBEAN DRAMA).

Elizabethan theater Professional presentation of dramas as practiced in Shakespeare's time, especially during the reign of Queen Elizabeth I (1558–1603; see Elizabeth I in *Henry VIII*). Elizabethan theater was very different from today's theater in its organization, methods, and even the nature of the buildings used. Before the 1570s English theater barely existed, but in the course of Shakespeare's lifetime, a thriving center of dramatic art evolved in LONDON.

At the outset of Elizabeth's reign, in 1558, English drama consisted largely of religious enactments such as the MORALITY PLAY presented at medieval festivals, and these were generally performed by members of the trade guilds of different towns. Professional entertainers were mostly wandering acrobats, musicians, and clowns, more like circus performers than actors. They were legally classed with vagabonds and could be jailed merely for pursuing their calling. Some troupes, however, were taken into the households of aristocrats and were therefore exempt from such laws. They provided entertainment for the lord and his guests, often performing an INTERLUDE at a meal, a much more drama-like feature than the "feats of activitie" commonly recorded. These troupes often traveled, performing for other nobles and gradually taking over the guilds' functions for the dramatic elements of seasonal festivals.

London naturally became a focus for such activities. London companies were still under the patronage of some great nobleman but were no longer closely affiliated with his household, though they might perform at his country home on special occasions. (The law required that actors be members of a noble household, and certain nobles cooperated with the actors, but the patrons generally had nothing else to do with the operations of a company.) Performances in London were usually held in large inns or taverns, most of which were within the walls of the city. However, the London government, largely controlled by Puritans, was particularly hostile to actors, so the companies began to arrange their performances in nearby areas. In 1576 the THEATRE, the first building in England intended solely for the performance of plays, was built by James BURBAGE, just north of the city line. Other playhouses soon followed.

In a different social world, Queen Elizabeth catered extensively to performers, and the royal court became a second center of the nascent theater world. In 1574 the queen proclaimed one of the acting companies, LEICESTER'S MEN, to be members of her household and thus exempt from even London's laws against performing. Also during this time, students at schools, universities, and the INNS OF COURT, affected by the RENAISSANCE revival of classical literature, began to read and perform the plays of ancient ROME and their modern imitations. These sophisticated entertainments were more to the taste of the queen and her courtiers than the interludes of the adult acting companies, so the CHILDREN'S COMPANIES were generally more featured at court. Entrepreneurs such as Burbage and Philip HENSLOWE then began to hire dramatists to produce work that would attract sophisticated patrons and gain them the prestige of association with the court. ELIZABETHAN DRAMA was born.

For almost a decade, Leicester's Men were the most important theater company in London, but the QUEEN'S MEN, created by Elizabeth in 1583, soon eclipsed them. In the early 1590s, two other companies arose that were to dominate Elizabethan theater thereafter: the ADMIRAL'S MEN and STRANGE'S MEN, later the CHAMBERLAIN'S MEN, Shakespeare's company. Other companies included OXFORD'S MEN, PEMBROKE'S MEN, and SUSSEX'S MEN. They played at court and at the Theatre and the other public playhouses: the CURTAIN THEATRE (built near the Theatre in 1577), the ROSE THEATRE (the first in SOUTHWARK, which became the most important theater district), the SWAN THEATRE, the GLOBE THEATRE, and the FORTUNE THEATRE. Plays were also staged at the CROSS KEYS INN, until London outlawed the theater in 1596, and in an outlying district, NEWINGTON BUTTS.

These theaters were generally roughly cylindrical, three-storied buildings surrounding a central, unroofed space containing the stage, built out from a section of the building that served as a backstage area. (Indoor theaters appeared somewhat later, in Shakespeare's lifetime but during the reign of King JAMES I; they are part of the story of JACOBEAN DRAMA.) The actual appearance of these theaters is obscure, since the only evidence is a single drawing—of unknown reliability—depicting the interior of the Swan Theatre and the contract for the building of the Fortune (but see GLOBE THEATRE and ROSE THEATRE for recent archaeological findings). Some spectators stood on the ground around the stage, within the "wooden O" (*Henry V*, Prologue, 13) of the building; the "groundlings," as they were called, paid a cheap admission price. Each floor of the building was divided into galleries, which offered a better view of the stage and were more expensive. In the most expensive galleries, seating was provided; seats were also available, at the highest price, on the stage itself. A canopy, called the "heavens" or the "shadow," extended over the stage from its rear wall. The stage itself probably contained one or more trapdoors, often used to represent graves or the mouth of hell. (Supernatural phenomena were popular on the Elizabethan stage, and Shakespeare often presented them—e.g., Apparition, Asnath, Ghost.) Behind the stage, the building contained dressing rooms—the "tiring [attiring] house"—and upper rooms for musicians and for the machinery used to hoist actors or props in spectacular ascents or descents through the "heavens." A balcony or upper stage was commonly provided and was used in such scenes as the famous balcony scene (2.2) of *Romeo and Juliet*. Atop the whole structure was a hut, or "penthouse," from which flags were flown and trumpets sounded to announce a performance.

Plays were held outdoors (very few seem to have been canceled by weather, suggesting a hardy audience). They usually began at two o'clock in the afternoon, and they had to be finished before nightfall, for the only illumination besides the sun were torches to provide partial relief on an overcast day or at the onset of dusk. (This limitation is often incorporated into the texture of the play. For instance, near the end of *Julius Caesar* a character witnesses the suicide of Cassius and observes, "O setting sun, / As in thy red rays thou dost sink to night, / So in his red blood Cassius' day is set / The sun of Rome is set. Our day is gone" [5.3.60–63], and the audience could confirm his remarks with their own eyes.) The average duration of a performance was about two hours—the Chorus of *Romeo and Juliet* speaks of "the two hours' traffic of our stage" (Prologue, 12)—though many plays must have taken longer. Often the play was followed by a jig—a brief, often bawdy, miniature comic opera, with wild dancing and simple lyrics set to the melodies of popular SONGs.

A performance in the Elizabethan theater was very different from one today. The stages were simply raised areas amid the audience, with very little if any scenery. No curtain opened on a prepared scene or closed on a finished one. The actors had to enter at the beginning and immediately command the audience's attention, with the consequence that scenes tended to begin with powerful material. They also had to exit at the end to make room for the next sequence, so scenes generally did not end on a note of crisis, as is common in modern plays.

Acting styles seem to have been very different as well, according to written evidence that values a very formal and artificial style. Rhetorical flourishes and conventional poses created a distance that was felt to enhance the effect of the lines. Realistic portrayals were simply not expected, though some of Shakespeare's characters begin the evolution toward modern dramatic realism. Costumes were contemporary for the most part, regardless of the setting of the play, except for special outfits that conventionally identified figures from the classical world (a toga or a plumed helmet and armor), from the exotic Middle East (billowing trousers, a turban, and a scimitar), or supernatural beings such as gods or ghosts.

The strangest feature of the Elizabethan stage, by comparison with our own, was the absence of women. In the children's companies all the roles were taken by boys, but among the adult companies the effect was even stranger, for the boys played the women (though old, comical women, such as Mistress Quickly in *The Merry Wives of Windsor* or the Nurse in *Romeo and Juliet*, could be played by men). Even then boys as the heroines of romance must have seemed somewhat comic, for playwrights often built on this peculiarity by having the heroine disguise herself as a boy. Thus, a boy played a girl who played a boy. A further complication was often invoked by having a woman (played by a boy) mistakenly fall in love with the disguised woman (also played by a boy). The situation was not only comical, but also suggestive of hidden depths of human sexuality. The use of boys as women was commonly attacked by Puritan critics as immoral, and many non-Puritans agreed. When the English theaters were reopened in 1660, after being closed by the Puritan revolution, only women were allowed to play women.

In Elizabethan times the boys also played the parts of boys, of course, and some of these roles, though brief, were demanding (e.g., Boy in *Henry V*, Son in *Macbeth*, Moth in *Love's Labour's Lost*). A boy was sometimes apprenticed to an adult actor, who trained, educated, and supported him until he was capable of playing men's roles. The adult recovered his expenses by "selling" the trained boy to an acting company, perhaps his own. Neither party was bound by strict contracts, as in other trades, for members of noble households—as actors formally were—were not covered by the laws on apprenticeship.

An actor's status as an aristocratic retainer was merely a legal fiction, for acting companies were actually commercial enterprises, with shareholding partners and paid employees. Some companies, including the Admiral's Men, used a performance space owned by an entrepreneur, such as Philip HENSLOWE or Francis LANGLEY, while others, typified by the Chamberlain's Men, controlled their own theater. Five of the Chamberlain's Men, including Shakespeare, owned half of the Globe, with Cuthbert BURBAGE and Richard BURBAGE—himself an actor in the company—owning the other half. As owners, or "housekeepers," these men profited from the owner's share of the theater's receipts and paid the owner's expenses; as partners in the acting company, or "sharers," they profited from the other side of the arrangement. The housekeepers received half the receipts from the galleries, with which they maintained the building and paid the ground rent for the land on which it stood. The sharers received the company's part of a performance's receipts: all of the income from the cheaper admissions paid by the groundlings and half of that from the more expensive galleries. They shared this as profit after meeting their own expenses. They hired their employees—extra actors, stagehands, musicians, and others—and paid for costumes and props. Most important and most expensive, they commissioned dramas.

Playwrights sold plays to acting companies, who then owned the script; unless he was a member of the company, the author received no further income from his efforts. Some playwrights worked under contract, especially with Henslowe, who employed dozens of writers. Others, most notably Shakespeare, wrote only for a company in which they were sharers. A few, like Ben JONSON, freelanced, writing for a variety of companies in succession.

Plays were performed in a repertoire that was rotated frequently; a given play was rarely staged more than once a week but might be staged frequently during a season, which might include a dozen or more plays. Popular plays, such as those of Shakespeare or Christopher MARLOWE, might be revived periodically over many years or rewritten to appeal to changing fashions.

New plays were in great demand and were produced at an extraordinary rate. It has been estimated that at least several thousand plays were written for London theater companies during the years of Shakespeare's career; he himself wrote 40 (including *Cardenio*), for an average of almost two a year (though at least three of these—and probably more—were collaborative). Thomas HEYWOOD declared that he had written or collaborated on 220 plays. Once a company bought a play, they submitted it, with the necessary fee, to the MASTER OF THE REVELS, who had to approve it for performance. He might refuse or demand changes for political or religious reasons (see CENSORSHIP). The company might sell a script to a publisher, who then profited exclusively from it, but they preferred not to, for as long as they owned it, they could anticipate further profits. Thus, the vast majority of the plays that were written in Shakespeare's time were never published and are lost.

Elizabeth Stuart, Queen of Bohemia (1596–1662)

Daughter of King JAMES I of England and Scotland, patron of the theater company LADY ELIZABETH'S MEN, and somewhat later an international figure by virtue of her ill-starred marriage to a powerful German prince, Frederick V, Elector Palatine and briefly king of BOHEMIA. Elizabeth's marriage was celebrated by a season-long series of festivities over the winter of 1612–13, in which Shakespeare's acting company, the KING'S MEN, had a notable part. They put on 20 different plays, eight of them Shakespeare's, probably including *1* and *2 Henry IV, Julius Caesar, Much Ado About Nothing, The Winter's Tale,* and *The Tempest.* (Some scholars believe that the MASQUE in 4.1 of *The Tempest* was inserted into the play for this occasion.) Her marriage stirred nationwide enthusiasm and was regarded as the consummation of an idyllic romance.

However, Elizabeth's destiny was tragic. After five years of comfort and pleasure at Frederick's capital in Heidelberg, the couple were swept up in the complex religious politics of the Holy Roman Empire. Frederick unwisely accepted the throne of Bohemia, a Protestant country that had rebelled against the Catholic Hapsburgs, rulers of the empire. After a brief reign—Frederick is known to history as "the Winter King"—he was deposed by the emperor, in the first phase of the Thirty Years' War. Elizabeth spent the rest of her life in exile, mostly in The Hague, attempting to recover her husband's position.

Frederick died in 1632, leaving Elizabeth unhappy and, by royal standards, poor, especially after the STUART DYNASTY was also dethroned by the English revolution. She had 13 children but quarreled with them all; when her eldest son recovered the Palatine Electorate, he refused to provide her with a home. Finally, with the restoration of the monarchy in England, she returned to London in 1661, only to die within months. Eventually her grandson ruled England as George I (1714–27).

Elsinore Danish seaport (Helsingør in Danish), setting for *Hamlet.* The royal castle of the King of Denmark, located in Elsinore, is the setting for every scene in the play except 5.1, which is set in a nearby graveyard; three dramatically striking early scenes (1.1, 1.4–5) are set on its fortified walls. The town is mentioned several times (e.g., in 1.2.174), but it is not described at all.

Elsinore was well known to Elizabethan England, being located on the narrow straits between DENMARK and Sweden, an important trade route for English ships. It was the site of a Danish fortress, Kronborg, doubtless the castle envisioned by Shakespeare, from which tolls were collected from all ships entering or leaving the Baltic Sea. The castle is now a maritime museum where Shakespeare's plays are regularly performed. English acting companies traveled to Elsinore in 1585 and 1586—and possibly on other, unrecorded tours—and it has been speculated that Shakespeare may have been among the players who performed there, although there is no clear evidence of this, and his faulty knowledge of the physical place—Elsinore has no "cliff / That beetles o'er his base into the sea" (1.4.70–71), for example—suggests that he never made the trip.

Ely Palace portrait Possible portrait of Shakespeare. The Ely Palace portrait, discovered in 1845, bears an inscription stating that the anonymous sitter was 39 years old in 1603—as was Shakespeare—when it was painted. It closely resembles the Martin DROESHOUT engraving, one of the two authoritative likenesses of the playwright, and it may be the original from which the engraver worked. However, it may also be a postdated copy of the engraving; scholars remain uncertain. The portrait at one time hung in the official residence of a 19th-century bishop of Ely and is now owned by the Shakespeare's BIRTHPLACE Trust and hangs in STRATFORD. (See also PORTRAITS OF SHAKESPEARE.)

Elyot, Sir Thomas (ca. 1490–1546) English author, an influence on several of Shakespeare's plays. Elyot's most famous work is *The Boke Called the Governour* (1531), an extended essay on political morality and the education of statesmen. Echoes of this work appear in a number of Shakespeare's early works, including *The Two Gentlemen of Verona* and *2 Henry IV.* Elyot covers the WARS OF THE ROSES at length, and observes that they represent a deterioration of the English nation's unity that the TUDOR DYNASTY had fortunately repaired. These ideas were highly important to Shakespeare when he wrote his HISTORY PLAYS. Though such doctrines were also widely available elsewhere, Shakespeare's evident familiarity with the *Governour* makes it clear that he was especially influenced by these ideas through Elyot.

Elyot was an important figure in RENAISSANCE English literature. He translated a number of Latin works, promoted the study of the classics, and compiled the first Latin-English dictionary (1538). He also published a popular health manual. He served King Henry VIII as a diplomat, and attempted fruitlessly to gain the support of the Holy Roman Emperor for Henry's divorce of Katherine of Aragon.

Emery, John (1777–1822) English actor. An actor from childhood, Emery was typically cast as an old man even in his teens, and he became a leading character actor and comedian. He was best known for his portrayal of *The Tempest*'s Caliban, and he was also acclaimed as Dogberry in *Twelfth Night*, the Grave-digger in *Hamlet*, and Sir Toby Belch in *Much Ado About Nothing*. Emery also had a career as a successful painter.

enclosure controversy   See WELCOMBE.

Epenow (active 1611) Historical figure probably alluded to in *Henry VIII*, a Native American who visited LONDON. In *Henry VIII* the Porter alludes to the enthusiasm of women for a "strange Indian with the great tool come to court" (5.3.33–34). Scholars believe this lewd reference is to Epenow, a large man of impressive courage and equanimity, whose appearance in London is recorded in several contemporary sources. He was one of a number of American natives brought to England in the first quarter of the 17th century, some under the auspices of Shakespeare's patron, Henry Wriothesley, Earl of SOUTHAMPTON. Their celebrity as mysterious visitors from the New World may have influenced Shakespeare's creation of Caliban, in *The Tempest*.

Brought to England in 1611, Epenow was lionized for a time, but his hosts soon turned to exhibiting him for a fee in a traveling show. Dissatisfied, Epenow devised an escape from England. He persuaded a group of investors that he knew of a gold mine on an island off New England. A vessel was outfitted, and Epenow sailed with it as a guide, but as soon as the ship reached familiar shores, the guide dove overboard, swam ashore, and disappeared.

Ephesus   Ancient city in Greek Asia Minor (now in Turkey), the setting for *The Comedy of Errors* and several scenes of *Pericles*. In Shakespeare's chief source for the play, *The Menaechmi* by PLAUTUS, the setting is in another city, Epidamnum. The playwright is presumed to have made the change for two reasons. First, Ephesus was certainly better known to his audience through St. Paul's Epistle to the Ephesians and other New Testament references. Second, Ephesus was notorious, through these allusions, as a center of witchcraft and sorcery. This made it an appropriate setting for Shakespeare's tale of strangeness and confusion. In 1.2.97–102 Antipholus of Syracuse refers to this characteristic of the city to which he has come.

One reason for this reputation was the importance of Ephesus as an ancient center of paganism, especially due to the presence of a famous temple to Diana that figures in *Pericles*. Pericles' wife, Thaisa, is mistakenly buried at sea, near Ephesus. She recovers, but, believing that she will never see her husband again, she decides to enter a convent dedicated to Diana. In Act 5, after the goddess has appeared in a vision to Pericles, he comes to the Temple of Diana where Thaisa has become a priestess and they are reunited. Shakespeare took this episode from his source, and, except for the references to the temple, the play does not evoke the actual city. However, the herbal lore with which Cerimon revives the unconscious Thaisa is appropriate to an ancient center of magical arts.

epilogue   A speech at the end of a play referring to the performance that has just been completed, often asking for applause. The actor who speaks the epilogue speaks directly to the audience and is often not in character (in which case, he may be designated as "Epilogue" himself, in stage directions and speech headings). The device provides a sense of closure to the work and acknowledges its artificiality, returning the spectator to the real world. Eleven of Shakespeare's plays conclude with an epilogue: *All's Well That Ends Well, As You Like It, 2 Henry IV, Henry V, Henry VIII, A Midsummer Night's Dream, Pericles, The Tempest, Troilus and Cressida, Twelfth Night,* and *The Two Noble Kinsmen.*

epitaph Brief literary work memorializing a deceased person. A number of epitaphs are attributed to Shakespeare, with varying degrees of probability (see COMBE, JOHN; JAMES, ELIAS; JONSON, BEN; STRANGE, FERDINANDO STANLEY, LORD), including one to himself. A number of other poets wrote epitaphs to Shakespeare shortly after the playwright's death (see BASSE, WILLIAM; DIGGES, LEONARD; HOLLAND, HUGH; JONSON, BEN; MILTON, JOHN).

Although an epitaph is by definition suitable for inscription on a grave marker, it need not be intended for that purpose and may simply be a brief expression of sentiment, ranging from elegiac to humorous, about the deceased. Shakespeare's reputed epitaph on Jonson (said to have been written jointly with Jonson himself) is a four-line jest; Milton's on Shakespeare, on the other hand, is a 16-line masterpiece on the capacity of art—Shakespeare's plays in particular—to negate mortality.

Eschenburg, Johann Joachim (1743–1820) German scholar. Eschenburg translated all of Shakespeare's plays into German prose. Based in part on the translations of C. M. WIELAND, Eschenburg's edition (1775–82) was the first complete rendering of the plays in German. It dominated German Shakespeare studies until it was superseded by the verse versions of A. W. von SCHLEGEL in the early 19th century.

Essex, Robert Devereux, Earl of (1566–1601) English aristocrat, a major political figure in Elizabethan England and a close friend of Shakespeare's patron, Henry Wriothesley, Earl of SOUTHAMPTON. Essex, long a favorite of Queen Elizabeth I (see Elizabeth I in *Henry VIII*), attempted to raise a rebel-

lion against the queen on February 8, 1601. It failed miserably, and Essex was executed in March. The day before the scheduled uprising, Essex's followers hired Shakespeare's acting company, the CHAMBERLAIN'S MEN, to stage a performance of *Richard II*, apparently with the hope that the depiction of a sovereign's deposition might inspire backing among the citizens of LONDON. After Essex's defeat, the company had to send a representative to explain themselves, but they were exonerated and in fact performed for the queen the day before Essex's execution.

Essex succeeded his stepfather, Robert Dudley, Earl of LEICESTER, as the queen's closest courtier, and he probably was her lover. He fought in the Netherlands in 1589–90 alongside Philip SIDNEY, whose widow he married on his return. The queen was

The Earl of Essex was one of the most compelling figures of Shakespeare's time. A daring military victory at Cadiz led to his becoming a national hero, and he was a favorite of Queen Elizabeth. But he attempted to seize the throne and was tried and executed for treason in 1601, with Elizabeth herself signing the death warrant. *(Courtesy of National Portrait Gallery, London)*

angry, but she eventually forgave Essex, and he was again in favor. He became involved in the factional politics of the court, emerging as the chief rival of Lord BURGHLEY. Among his enemies was Sir Walter RALEIGH, and it is thought that the many now-incomprehensible inside jokes that stud *Love's Labour's Lost* may have been intended as a satire on Raleigh's circle, on behalf of Essex and Southampton. In 1596 Essex achieved his greatest success, leading, with Charles HOWARD, a successful raid on the Spanish port of Cadiz. Nevertheless, his relations with the queen deteriorated to the point where his rudeness caused her to strike him, and he drew his sword in anger. Another reconciliation took place, and he was given command of a military expedition to put down a revolt in Ireland in 1599.

At this point, probably because Shakespeare's patron was Essex's close friend and political ally, the playwright alluded to Essex flatteringly in a play, one of the few times that contemporary political affairs are noticed at all in the plays. In *Henry V,* written just as Essex left for Ireland, the Chorus suggests that the audience envision Henry V's triumphant return to England as though it were that of "the general of our gracious empress, / . . . from Ireland coming, / Bringing rebellion broached on his sword" (5.Chorus.30–32). However, Essex failed in Ireland; apparently gripped by inertia, he was unable to conquer the rebels, and he made a treaty that England regarded as shameful. He returned before he was ordered, in September 1599, and the angry queen arrested him. Eventually a board of inquiry ordered him deprived of his titles. His rebellion was his last hope, so he attempted to raise the city of London against the government but found no support, and after one day of minor skirmishing, he surrendered. (Apparently, the relationship between Essex and Southampton has led conspiracy theorists to suppose that the former may have been the "real" Shakespeare [see AUTHORSHIP CONTROVERSY].)

Evans, Edith (1888–1976) British actress. One of the most acclaimed actresses of the 20th century, Dame Edith Evans played a great range of parts in plays of all sorts. She made her stage debut in 1912 as Cressida in the first known production of the complete text of *Troilus and Cressida.* She eventually portrayed most of Shakespeare's comedic heroines as well as the Nurse in *Romeo and Juliet.* She was also successful in tragic roles, playing such differing characters as Cleopatra, Volumnia, and Queen Katherine of Aragon in *Antony and Cleopatra, Coriolanus,* and *Henry VIII,* respectively.

Evans, Henry (active 1583–1612) Welsh-born LONDON theatrical entrepreneur. In 1583–84 Evans was a partner with William HUNNIS, master of the Children of the Chapel (see CHILDREN'S COMPANIES), in productions staged at the original BLACKFRIARS THEATRE. Beginning in 1584, Evans was also associated with a boys' company patronized by Edward de Vere, Earl of OXFORD. In 1600 he joined Nathaniel GILES, the new master of the Children of the Chapel, and they produced plays at the revived Blackfriars, which Evans leased from Richard BURBAGE. However, in 1602 Evans and Giles were accused of graft and other improprieties. Evans fled the country but returned in 1603 after the accession of King JAMES I. He then joined Edward KIRKHAM as director of the successor to the Children of the Chapel, the Children of the Queen's Revels. They again performed at Blackfriars, which Evans continued to lease from Burbage. However, the company lost its royal patronage when it performed allegedly seditious plays, and Evans surrendered the lease of the theater to Burbage and the KING'S MEN in 1608, though a Thomas Evans, believed to be Henry Evans's representative, retained a one-seventh interest in the proceeds of the theater. Events of Evans's later life are unknown, though in 1611–12 he was the subject of several lawsuits filed by his onetime partner Kirkham.

Evans, Maurice (1901–1989) Anglo-American actor, one of the leading Shakespearean performers of the 1930s and 1940s. Though born in England, Evans acted in America for much of his career and became a citizen of the United States in 1941. As a member of the armed forces, he organized entertainment for troops and toured the Pacific in an abridged version of *Hamlet* that he later staged in America as well. Having achieved great acclaim as Hamlet in 1938—in the play's first full-length staging in

America, produced by himself and directed by Margaret Webster—Evans was particularly associated with the part. Other notable roles included Romeo, opposite Katharine CORNELL, Richard II in the Margaret Webster production of 1937, and Falstaff in her 1939 *1 Henry IV.* In 1962 Evans performed with Helen Hayes in "Shakespeare Revisited," a program of excerpts from the plays that was staged in 69 American cities. He also starred in TELEVISION productions of *Hamlet, Richard II,* and *Macbeth.*

F

Fabyan, Robert (d. 1513) English historian, author of a source for Shakespeare's HISTORY PLAYS. Fabyan, a wealthy merchant, assembled a history book by combining miscellaneous works by earlier writers in his posthumously published *New Chronicle of England and of France* (1516). It has very little historical value, but it includes, at its close, an account of the LONDON of his own times that is of interest to scholars of Tudor England. His chronicle was consulted by Shakespeare, particularly when he wrote *1 Henry VI*.

fair copy In textual studies, an amended manuscript of a play prepared for a printer or a theatrical company, usually by a professional scribe. No original Shakespearean manuscript exists (except, probably, three pages of *Sir Thomas More*), but scholars can determine from what sort of copy the printers of an early edition set their type—whether from a manuscript or an earlier printing, and if from a manuscript, whether fair copy or FOUL PAPERS (the author's uncorrected manuscript). Modern editors can determine from such information how closely a given printed text represents what Shakespeare actually wrote.

If the printers used fair copy as their source, the published text is likely to contain many of the characteristic signs of a copyist's work: uniformity of proper names in speech headings and stage directions, consistent spelling, and edited colloquialisms or contractions. This last feature, editorial intervention, is often identified by a resulting metrical defect. For instance "Before the game's afoot thou still let'st slip" (*1 Henry IV*, 1.3.272) is a pentameter line (see METER) as it appears in the early QUARTO editions of the play; someone, however, changed "game's" to "game is" in the fair copy from which the FIRST FOLIO edition was printed, and the resulting line does not scan properly. This item alone would mean very little, but numerous such instances indicate that the Quarto edition of *1 Henry IV* presents Shakespeare's foul papers and the Folio the fair copy. Modern editors are therefore inclined to favor the Quarto version over the Folio text when they conflict, because it was probably printed from Shakespeare's actual manuscript, rather than a copy.

Fair Em Anonymous play formerly attributed to Shakespeare, part of the Shakespeare APOCRYPHA. *Fair Em* is a romantic comedy set in the time of William the Conqueror. It was published in 1593 by an unknown publisher who declared that the play had been acted by STRANGE'S MEN, who probably employed the young Shakespeare. Though the play was included with MUCEDORUS and THE MERRY DEVIL OF EDMONTON in King Charles II's specially assembled collection of Shakespeare's plays, the 19th-century scholar Richard SIMPSON was the chief supporter of the theory that *Fair Em* was written by Shakespeare. Simpson argued that the comedy was a retort to the 1592 attack upon the playwright by Robert GREENE. Modern scholars unanimously reject this idea, for aside from the convoluted quality of Simpson's argument, it fails to address the considerable difference between *Fair Em* and Shakespeare's known works. The anonymous comedy is an extremely feeble play that lacks wit or poetry of any quality and contains only the crudest of characters and two almost totally unrelated plots.

False Folio   Collection of 10 pirated or spurious plays published as Shakespeare's in 1619. William and Isaac JAGGARD and Thomas PAVIER produced a group of QUARTO editions of plays attributed to Shakespeare, though only a few were proper texts of Shakespeare's plays. (Though not in FOLIO format, they are named by analogy with the earliest legitimate collection of Shakespearean plays, the FIRST FOLIO.) Two of the False Folio's offerings, A YORKSHIRE TRAGEDY and *Part 1* of SIR JOHN OLDCASTLE, were not by Shakespeare at all, and six more were BAD QUARTOS of Shakespearean plays (*2 and 3 Henry VI* [see *The Whole Contention*], *Henry V, The Merry Wives of Windsor, King Lear,* and *Pericles*). The publishers held the rights to only one of the two respectable texts, that of *A Midsummer Night's Dream*, which had been brought by Jaggard as part of his purchase of James ROBERTS's company in 1608. The rights to the other, *The Merchant of Venice*, were held by Laurence HEYES, who protested to the STATIONERS' COMPANY, as did the Lord Chamberlain at the time, William Herbert, Earl of PEMBROKE, who spoke on behalf of the KING'S MEN. The publishers responded by backdating the unprinted titles (only three had been issued) so that they could pass for the original editions. However, they were printed in a distinctive format, slightly taller than a standard quarto, on paper with the same watermark, and bibliographical scholars have no difficulty identifying these pirated editions. While the publishers seem blatantly dishonest by modern standards, in the world of 17th-century publishing, their behavior was not particularly unscrupulous and it did not prevent the Jaggards from joining the syndicate that published the First Folio a few years later.

Famous Victories, The   Abbreviated title commonly used for *The Famous Victories of Henry the Fifth*, an anonymous, late-16th-century play that was an important source for *1 and 2 Henry IV* and a minor one for *Henry V* and possibly *Edward III. The Famous Victories* is a farce in two parts, the first of which concerns the adventures of Prince Hal before he accedes to the throne and the second of which covers his reign as Henry V.

There are numerous resemblances between the farce and Shakespeare's plays, including appearances by Gadshill, Poins, the Chief Justice, Princess Katharine of France, and Sir John Oldcastle, which was the original name of Falstaff in *1 and 2 Henry IV*. Many of the incidents in *1 and 2 Henry IV* also occur in *The Famous Victories*, though they are presented very crudely by comparison. Such similarities make it clear that Shakespeare used *The Famous Victories* as a source, but he made major alterations, quite aside from his integration of its farcical material with another, more serious plot line. The Prince in *The Famous Victories* is simply a hooligan, wishing his father dead and roaring drunkenly about the stage. Shakespeare's Hal is a reflective young man who states early in *1 Henry IV* his intention to reform, and his participation in Falstaff's highway robbery is limited to stealing from the thieves. He is generally intent on affairs of state in *2 Henry IV*, his mischief extending only to disguising himself as a Drawer in 2.4. Oldcastle is an insignificant character who bears little resemblance to his successor. And in *Henry V* several incidents, including the insulting presentation of tennis balls to the title character in 1.2, Pistol's exploit in 4.4, and King Henry's wooing of Princess Katharine in 5.2 were developed from similar but less elaborate scenes in *The Famous Victories*. The first of these may also have inspired a similar insult in 4.4 of *Edward III*.

The only surviving version of *The Famous Victories* was published in 1598; it is clearly a "memorial" version of the play, a BAD QUARTO assembled from the recollections of actors. It is a very poor text, commonly judged to be unactable, and it is generally presumed that Shakespeare knew a superior version, perhaps a publication recorded in 1594 that is now lost. However, some scholars hold that *The Famous*

Victories, along with Shakespeare's plays, derives from an earlier play on the same subject (perhaps the one published in 1594, perhaps one that Shakespeare himself wrote earlier in his career).

farce A play, usually short, that has no purpose but to generate laughter in the audience. A form of COMEDY, it uses artificial situations, unrealistic plots, and physical humor rather than wit to achieve its end. Common plot components include mistaken identity, overheard information, accidental encounters, reunions of long-separated people, and extraordinary coincidences. Characterization, meaningful plotting, or any intellectual elements are eschewed. Farce has been widely popular from ancient times to the present. None of Shakespeare's plays is properly called a farce, though *The Comedy of Errors* is very like one but contains additional elements.

Farrant, Richard (d. 1580) English composer and theatrical entrepreneur, founder of the first BLACKFRIARS THEATRE. In 1564 Farrant, a court musician, became director of the Children of Windsor, a boys' choir in the service of Queen Elizabeth I. The boys also performed plays (see CHILDREN'S COMPANIES), and in 1576, when Farrant became the deputy of William HUNNIS, director of the similar Children of the Chapel, he was assigned responsibility for the productions of the combined companies. He accordingly leased rooms in the defunct BLACKFRIARS PRIORY and staged plays there, in what became known as the original Blackfriars Theatre. Farrant, who was also the queen's organist, composed church music, some of which is still performed, and he may also have composed music for the boys' plays.

Faucit, Helen (1817–1898) British actress. Faucit played most of Shakespeare's major female roles, usually opposite W. C. MACREADY, but she was particularly associated with Beatrice (*Much Ado About Nothing*) and Hermione (*The Winter's Tale*). She recorded her interpretations in a book, *On Some of Shakespeare's Female Characters* (1885).

Fenton, Geoffrey (ca. 1540–1608) English translator, creator of a possible minor source for several

of Shakespeare's plays. As a young nobleman living in Paris, Fenton wrote English versions of 13 of Matteo BANDELLO's Italian tales, working from the French translations of Pierre Boaistuau (d. 1566) and François BELLEFOREST. The resulting book, *Certaine Tragicall Discources* (1566), was very popular, and Shakespeare almost certainly knew it. He may have been influenced by it when he wrote *Hamlet, Titus Andronicus,* and *Twelfth Night,* all of which were based on tales that appear in Bandello, though which of several possible versions was used by the playwright is in each case uncertain.

Fenton translated several other French works, mostly religious in nature, including an attack on drama that was popular among English Puritans who opposed ELIZABETHAN THEATER. He was best known in his day for his *History of the Wars of Italy* (1579), taken from French translations of the writings of the Italian political theorist Francesco Guicciardini (1483–1540). After 1580 Fenton deserted literature for a successful career as a member of the Irish colonial establishment and lived out his life in Dublin.

Fenton, Richard (1746–1821) English author. Fenton, a lawyer, wrote and published poetry and essays. In his *A Tour in Quest of Genealogy through several Parts of Wales* (1811), published anonymously, he claimed to have found a copy—in the handwriting of Anne HATHAWAY—of a journal kept by Shakespeare, from which he quotes a number of passages concerning the playwright's career. Though some contemporaries took this material seriously, most scholars, then and now, believe that Fenton's discovery was merely a mild hoax, intended humorously.

Ffarington, William (1537–1610) Steward to Ferdinando Stanley, Lord STRANGE, and possibly a model for Malvolio in *Twelfth Night* and Oswald in *King Lear.* Ffarington—whose personality and habits have been recorded in his own elaborate housekeeping accounts and elsewhere—resembled both characters to some degree. Like Malvolio in *Twelfth Night,* he was noted for his severe mode of dress but was also fond of fine fabric and precious stones (2.5.48, 61), and he disinherited his son for refusing a financially and socially advantageous marriage, betraying an attitude suggestive of Malvolio's own matrimonial ambition. Ffarington's style of dress also was reminiscent of Oswald, castigated by Kent as a vain and pretentious imitator of gentlemen in *King Lear*, 2.2.13–23. Kent also calls Oswald "action-taking" and "super-serviceable" (2.2.16), evoking Ffarington's noted readiness to begin a legal action and his undeniable devotion to his master.

Ffarington's employer was the patron of an acting company, STRANGE'S MEN, to which the young Shakespeare probably belonged. Strange's Men often visited their patron's home in Lancashire, as did other companies whose members were later Shakespeare's associates. Thus Shakespeare may have known Ffarington personally and almost certainly had at least heard of him. Ffarington was probably a singularly unpleasant figure to the traveling players, for he detested actors and the theater, as his own accounts make clear (he commented adversely on his employer's enthusiasm). In fact, Ffarington disliked all festivities; in 1580 he attempted to suppress the local May games, a long-standing tradition.

This gentleman certainly seems a plausible target for satire. Moreover, unlike Sir Ambrose WILLOUGHBY and Sir William KNOLLYS—the other chief candidates as models for Malvolio—he was not so high in the social hierarchy as to be too dangerous to satirize (both the others were valued servants of Queen Elizabeth I). However, most scholars regard the true identity of the model for Shakespeare's stewards—and for most other Shakespearean characters—as ultimately unknowable.

Field, Nathan (1587–1620) English actor and dramatist. Field was one of the 26 men listed in the FIRST FOLIO as the "Principall Actors" in Shakespeare's plays. He joined the KING'S MEN in 1615 or 1616—scholars speculate that he replaced Shakespeare just before or after the playwright's death—after a long association with one of the CHILDREN'S COMPANIES and with the LADY ELIZABETH'S MEN. He was particularly noted in the title role of George CHAPMAN's *Bussy d'Amboise*. As a playwright he collaborated with Philip MASSINGER, John FLETCHER, and perhaps others, and he wrote two comedies himself, along with a defense of the stage.

Field, whose Puritan father had written fiercely against the stage before his death in 1588, was recruited from the choir of a secondary school into the Children of the Chapel (later the Children of the Queen's Revels [see CHILDREN'S COMPANIES]) in 1600. As a boy actor in this company Field continued his education under the tutorship of Ben JONSON, who was later to name Field and Richard BURBAGE as the finest English actors. After the Children of the Revels were absorbed by the Lady Elizabeth's Men in 1613, Field became the leader of the combined company before he joined the King's Men.

Field, Richard (1561–1624) London printer, producer of the first several editions of *Venus and Adonis* and the first editions of *The Rape of Lucrece* and "The Phoenix and Turtle." A native of STRATFORD whose father knew Shakespeare's father, Field is presumed to have been a friend of the playwright's. Scholars speculate that Shakespeare may have playfully referred to Field in *Cymbeline* when the disguised Imogen claims employment with one "Richard du Champ" (4.2.377), i.e., "Richard Field" in French. In 1593 Field published the young playwright's first ambitious literary undertaking, *Venus and Adonis*, in a QUARTO edition known today as Q1. He then sold the rights to this work and *Lucrece* to John HARRISON, who hired him to print the second, third, and fourth editions (Q2–4, 1594–1596) of *Venus and Adonis* and the first quarto (Q1, 1594) of *Lucrece*. He later printed, for publisher Edward BLOUNT, the first edition of LOVE'S MARTYR (1601), which contained "The Phoenix and Turtle."

Field's early life in Stratford is unknown, apart from the fact that his father was a tanner. He was apprenticed to a London printer in 1579; on the death of his second master, in 1587, he took over that man's business and married his widow. He doubtless regretted the sale of the rights to *Venus and Adonis* and *Lucrece*, which became very popular, but he prospered nonetheless. Among other works, he produced the first edition of HARINGTON's translation of *Orlando Furioso*, a 1598 edition of SIDNEY's *Arcadia*, and several editions of NORTH's translation of PLUTARCH.

Fife Region in SCOTLAND, the setting for 4.2 of *Macbeth*. When Fife's ruler, Lord Macduff, betrays the usurper Macbeth and joins the rebels led by

Prince Malcolm, Macbeth sends murderers to Macduff's castle, where they kill his wife, Lady Macduff, and his son in an episode that marks the depths of Macbeth's evil. Shakespeare took the setting from his source, Raphael HOLINSHED's history, but there is nothing in the scene that particularly denotes Fife.

film Entertainment medium in film. Most of Shakespeare's plays have been produced. Many of the plays have been filmed more than once, in numerous languages. *Hamlet*, for example, has been filmed more than two dozen times. The earliest movie made from Shakespeare was of a single scene from Beerbohm TREE's stage production of *King John*, but the film has been lost. Oddly, many silent films of Shakespeare plays were made, perhaps because the medium sought respectability in its earliest days. Among the most notable directors and producers of Shakespearean films have been Grigori KOZINTSEV, Akira KUROSAWA, Laurence OLIVIER, Max REINHARDT, Orson WELLES, and Franco ZEFFIRELLI.

Fiorentino, Giovanni (active 14th century) Italian author, writer of a collection of tales that included sources for *The Merchant of Venice* and *The Merry Wives of Windsor*. Little is known of Fiorentino, whose collection of stories, *Il Pecorone (The Simpleton)*, was written in the 1370s but not published until 1558. He was a Florentine clerk, and his tales were closely modeled on the works of BOCCACCIO.

There is no known Elizabethan translation of *Il Pecorone* into English, yet Shakespeare's use of it seems extremely likely, especially in the case of *The Merchant of Venice*. The playwright may have read the work in Italian, although his ability to do so is not certain. There may have existed an English version that has not survived, or he may have been told the relevant details by someone who had read it. In any case, his knowledge of Latin would have permitted him to struggle through the Italian, once he knew there was material there that he was interested in.

First Folio Earliest published collection of Shakespeare's plays, appearing in 1623. Produced in the FOLIO format, the First Folio was edited by John HEMINGE and Henry CONDELL, who had been professional associates of Shakespeare in the CHAMBERLAIN'S MEN and its successor, the KING'S MEN. The First Folio contains 36 plays, 18 of which were not otherwise published and would probably have been lost without this edition. These plays are *All's Well That Ends Well*, *Antony and Cleopatra*, *As You Like It*, *The Comedy of Errors*, *Coriolanus*, *Cymbeline*, *3 Henry VI*, *Henry VIII*, *Julius Caesar*, *King John*, *Macbeth*, *Measure for Measure*, *The Taming of the Shrew*, *The Tempest*, *Timon of Athens*, *Twelfth Night*, *Two Gentlemen of Verona*, and *The Winter's Tale*.

The editors' intention in publishing Shakespeare's plays was also to counter the imperfect editions that did exist. Since they knew the works intimately, having worked with the playwright for most of his career, their corrections of other editions are significant to scholars, as is their selection of 36 plays. Heminge and Condell would have selected only plays they knew to have been written by Shakespeare—or at least mostly by him, in cases of collaboration. Thus, the First Folio constitutes a basic CANON of the plays. (However, the earliest part of Shakespeare's career may not have been known to them very well, and even in the case of the more mature works, while those included are almost certainly Shakespearean, the editors could have excluded plays for such reasons as defective texts, copyright problems, or CENSORSHIP.)

Besides the plays, the First Folio contains various minor elements: a title page decorated with a portrait by Martin DROESHOUT, facing a poem by Ben JONSON commending the likeness; a brief introduction by the editors, stating their purpose; a dedication to William Herbert, Earl of PEMBROKE, and Philip Herbert, Earl of MONTGOMERY; verses on Shakespeare by Jonson, Hugh HOLLAND, Leonard DIGGES, and "I. M." (probably James MABBE); a list of 26 "Principall Actors in all these Playes"; and a table of contents. It was printed in an edition of about 1200, of which about 230 have survived. Oddly, it appears that no two copies are identical (though they have not all been collated), for proofreading and correction went on simultaneously with printing. The process began in April 1621, but it was interrupted and not completed until December 1623.

The title page contains the information that the book was printed by Isaac JAGGARD and Edward BLOUNT. A colophon on the last page states that it was printed for William JAGGARD (Isaac's father, who died just before the book was issued), Blount, John SMETHWICK, and William ASPLEY. The members of this syndicate held copyrights to the previously published plays. Blount and Isaac Jaggard held most of them, which probably accounts for their joint listing on the title page, for Blount was not in fact a printer. Isaac Jaggard oversaw the publishing process, and Heminge and Condell may have done little more than supply Jaggard with the texts. The actual editing may have been done by Edward KNIGHT, the King's Men's bookkeeper, who was responsible for maintaining the PROMPTBOOK of each play.

Fisher, Thomas (active 1600–1602) London publisher and bookseller, publisher of the first edition of *A Midsummer Night's Dream*. Fisher hired an unknown printer (possibly Edward ALLDE or Richard BRADOCK) to produce Q1 of Shakespeare's play, which appeared in 1600. This was Fisher's only noteworthy publication. He was a draper who joined the STATIONERS' COMPANY in 1600 and operated a bookshop for the next two years, but little more is known of him.

Fitton, Mary (1578–1647) Maid of honor to Queen Elizabeth I, possibly the model for the "Dark Lady" of the *Sonnets*. Mary Fitton joined the queen's court in 1595 through the influence of Sir William KNOLLYS, a friend of her father. Knollys fell in love with her—generating gossip that may have helped inspire Shakespeare's creation of Malvolio's courtship of Olivia in *Twelfth Night*—but she became the mistress of William Herbert, the Earl of PEMBROKE, by whom she became pregnant in 1600. She was banished from the court in disgrace, Pembroke refused to marry her (preferring a prison term instead), and the infant died shortly after it was born. Fitton went on to marry and be widowed twice.

In his 1890 edition of the *Sonnets*, Thomas TYLER suggested that Mary Fitton was the Dark Lady—on the assumption that the poems were addressed to Pembroke—and the theory was made widely popular by Frank HARRIS. However, most scholars now find the hypothesis improbable, chiefly because two surviving portraits of Fitton show that she had a fair complexion, brown hair, and gray eyes.

Fleay, Frederick Gard (1831–1909) Shakespearean scholar. F. G. Fleay, who turned to the study of ancient Egypt and Assyria after publishing several works on Shakespeare and his world, was among the early advocates of close study of the plays. He helped develop the VERSE TEST as an analytic tool and was one of the first "disintegrators," a school of critics who believe that many of the plays attributed to Shakespeare were written by more than one person and who attempt to determine by literary analysis who wrote what. Fleay, like J. M. ROBERTSON, approached this question through a subjective comparison of styles, a procedure that is generally frowned on by more scientifically minded scholars.

Fletcher, Giles (1546–1611) English diplomat and writer, author of a possible influence on *Love's Labour's Lost*. Fletcher, after a journey to Russia to negotiate trading rights, wrote *On the Russe Common Wealth* (1591). He was highly critical of the Russians, who had treated him badly. English merchants, fearful of insult to their potential customers, attempted to have the book suppressed. However, parts of it were republished by Richard HAKLUYT and others, and the book went on to become quite popular. Scholars believe that Fletcher's book was the stimulus for the pageant of comic Russians performed at the INNS OF COURT in 1594; this performance influenced in turn Shakespeare's comical Russian masquerade in 5.2 of *Love's Labour's Lost*.

Fletcher was born into a clerical family—his brother (the father of the playwright John FLETCHER) became the bishop of London—and he was a prominent lay administrator in the Church of England before becoming a diplomat. He was also noted for a volume of sonnets in the style of SPENSER, published in 1593. In 1600 he served as executor for his brother, the bishop, who had died in debt, and he was almost imprisoned for that debt himself. He was saved through the influence of his friend Robert Devereux, Earl of ESSEX, and when the earl staged an unsuccessful rebellion against Queen Elizabeth I (see Elizabeth I in *Henry VIII*) the next year, Fletcher stood up for his savior to the extent that he was imprisoned for several years and his diplomatic career was ended.

Fletcher, John (1579–1625)   English playwright, collaborator with Shakespeare, and a leading figure of JACOBEAN DRAMA. Fletcher wrote parts of *The Two Noble Kinsmen* and possibly parts of both *Henry VIII* and a lost play, *Cardenio*. He succeeded Shakespeare as principal dramatist for the KING'S MEN theater company. Fletcher's earliest works, influenced by Ben JONSON's COMEDY OF HUMOURS and written for the CHILDREN'S COMPANIES, were not very successful. In 1608 he began to collaborate with Francis BEAUMONT, a similarly unsuccessful young writer of COMEDY. The two enjoyed tremendous success and became the closest of friends, sharing the same lodgings—and, reportedly, the same mistress—while writing about 15 plays in eight years. They were the most important English dramatists in the generation that followed Shakespeare's retirement. Beaumont retired in 1613, but Fletcher wrote many more plays, all of them for the King's Men, many in collaboration with other playwrights, especially Philip MASSINGER but also Jonson, George CHAPMAN, and Thomas MIDDLETON.

Beaumont and Fletcher first achieved success with *Philaster* (1610), a TRAGICOMEDY that was hugely popular and influenced English drama for decades. They followed their success with more of the same, as well as with tragedies and romantic comedies. Among their best-known works are *Cupid's Revenge* (1608), *The Maid's Tragedy* (1610), *A King and No King* (1611), and *The Scornful Lady* (1613). In the 1630s, and again in the 1660s, the popularity of Beaumont and Fletcher surpassed that of all other English dramatists, including Shakespeare.

Fletcher's own dramas are often difficult to identify, for so much of his work was collaborative. However, scholars believe that he wrote at least 16 works of his own. They included tragicomedies,

such as *The Island Princess* (ca. 1619–21), which confirmed the style set by *Philaster*; and comedies of manners, like *The Wild-Goose Chase* (1621), which were to be very influential on Restoration comedy. In all his works, Fletcher's goal is simply entertainment, whether provided in high-flown rhetoric of death and love, farcical romantic entanglements, or graceful songs. His work is part of an escapist and decadent period in English drama, but in its own terms it is undeniably successful.

Fletcher, Laurence (d. 1608)   English actor active in SCOTLAND. Fletcher was recorded as an "English player" employed by the king (later, King JAMES I of England). He was at the head of the list of members of Shakespeare's KING'S MEN when they received their license in 1603 upon the occasion of the accession of King James to the English throne. However, since there is no other mention of Fletcher in connection with the King's Men, scholars believe that he may have been included on the license simply because he had headed James's company in Scotland and was never actually an active member of the London company. He was a minor member of King James's household until his death. Some scholars believe that Shakespeare may have performed with Fletcher in Scotland in 1601, but no solid evidence exists to support this notion. Shakespeare may have left London in the wake of the seeming involvement of the CHAMBERLAIN'S MEN in the rebellion of Robert Devereux, Earl of ESSEX.

Flint Castle   Fortified castle in northern WALES, location in *Richard II*. In 3.3 Henry Bolingbroke takes custody of King Richard II at Flint while professing to be his humble subject. Historically Richard was already the prisoner of Bolingbroke's lieutenant, Northumberland, when he was taken to Flint, a notoriously impregnable castle. It was the first of the many castles that the English built in Wales when they occupied the country in the 13th century.

Florence   Italian city, a location in *All's Well That Ends Well*. Various French noblemen, including Bertram, join the army of the Duke of Florence in his war with Siena, and Helena, pursuing Bertram, follows them. Much of Acts 3 and 4 take place in

Florence and vicinity. However, nothing in the play is distinctively Florentine—or even Italian—and it is clear that Shakespeare merely followed BOCCAC-CIO, his ultimate source, in setting part of the action there.

Florio, John (Giovanni Florio) (ca. 1553–1625) English translator whose version of the French essays of Michel de MONTAIGNE supplied minor sources for *The Tempest, Hamlet,* and *King Lear.* Florio's *Essayes on Morall, Politike, and Millitarie Discourses* (1603), his most significant work, was an eccentric elaboration of Montaigne's writing rather than a literal translation. Florio indulged in extravagant alliteration and euphuistic imagery (see LYLY, JOHN), and he frequently included his own pedantic digressions and fantasies. Although a very inaccurate rendering of Montaigne's spare, crisp prose, Florio's book is a minor English masterpiece in its own right. Florio also wrote an Italian-English dictionary, *A Worlde of Wordes* (1598, 1611), and a series of textbooks for the study of Italian.

Florio taught Italian to Henry Wriothesley, Earl of SOUTHAMPTON, and was a friend of Ben JONSON; scholars accordingly assume that Shakespeare was at least acquainted with the translator. Less probably, it is sometimes supposed that Shakespeare's comic pedant of *Love's Labour's Lost,* Holofernes, was intended as a caricature of Florio. Holofernes does quote an Italian proverb found in Florio's *Second Fruits* (1591) in 4.2.93–94. Further, an anonymous SONNET in praise of Florio, published with *Second Fruits,* is sometimes attributed to Shakespeare.

Florio was born in LONDON to Italian Protestants who had fled from religious persecution. He attended Oxford, where he later taught French and Italian. He moved to London sometime before 1600 and became a tutor to the wife and children of King JAMES I. Florio was a notable member of the London literary world; besides his acquaintance with Jonson and (probably) Shakespeare, he was married to a sister of Samuel DANIEL.

Flower portrait Portrait of Shakespeare, probably a copy of the Martin DROESHOUT engraving. Some commentators hold that the Flower portrait—named for Sir Desmond Flower, who donated it to the Shakespeare Museum in STRATFORD in 1911—was the original from which Martin Droeshout did his engraving, which is considered an authoritative likeness. However, most scholars believe that it is a copy of the engraving, for it more closely resembles a corrected version of Droeshout's work rather than his initial effort. Moreover, the painting's inscription, "Willm. Shakespeare, 1609," is in a script that did not come into use until somewhat later, and the paint includes a pigment not used until the 18th century. Therefore the portrait was probably made in the 18th century, as a forgery. (See also PORTRAITS OF SHAKESPEARE.)

Folger Shakespeare Library Major collection of Shakespeareana in Washington, D.C. The Folger Library was founded in 1930 by Henry Clay Folger (1857–1930), an oil executive whose private collection provided the core of the library's holdings. The library houses 79 copies of the FIRST FOLIO, more than 200 QUARTO editions of the plays, and thousands of other volumes in one of the world's largest and finest collections. From 1970 to 1992 the library, which is administered by Amherst College, also offered Shakespearean and modern plays on an Elizabethan-style stage (see ELIZABETHAN THEATER), and it publishes books and pamphlets of general interest on Shakespeare and his world.

folio Format for a page or a book. A folio is a sheet of paper that is folded in half to make two leaves—four pages—or a book composed of such pages. (See also QUARTO.) Since printing paper is large to begin with, a folio volume is large in size, usually about 15 inches tall. In Shakespearean studies the term *Folio*—capitalized—usually refers to the FIRST FOLIO, the earliest collected edition of Shakespeare's plays (1623), which was published in the folio format. Three more folio-size editions appeared in the 17th century, the Second, Third, and Fourth Folios (1632, 1663, 1685). Each was printed from the preceding edition and added its own corrections and errors. Since they have no connection to an original manuscript or other pre-publication source, they are of little scholarly interest. However, the Third Folio (copies of which are relatively rare, probably because many were lost in the fire that destroyed much of London in 1666) incorporated *Pericles* for the first time and introduced a number of plays into the Shakespeare APOCRYPHA as well.

fool Character type often used by Shakespeare, a sharp-tongued comic, usually a professional jester, who wittily insults the other characters and comments on their actions. He often serves as a CHORUS, providing a position outside the plot with which we, the audience, can identify. Real jesters were well known in Shakespeare's day—Queen Elizabeth I employed fools, for instance—and the playwright found in this recognized social figure, with his well-defined traditional role, a useful embodiment of objectivity to balance the improbabilities of COMEDY.

Shakespeare did not use fools in his early work, though Speed in *Two Gentlemen of Verona* and the Bastard in *King John* foreshadow later figures. In *A Midsummer Night's Dream*, Puck serves as a jester to Oberon, and he demonstrates an important attribute of the fool, a cool detachment from the problems of the plot and a somewhat self-centered focus on his own notions of humor. The Falstaff of the *Henry IV* plays also has points in common with the jesters of later plays. Not only does he present some similar attributes—verbal dexterity, a facility for imitation, and an inventive sense of the absurd—but he also shares the fool's deeper significance as an emblem of freedom from convention. It is with the development of Shakespeare's mature comedy that we find his true jesters. Feste in *Twelfth Night* and Touchstone in *As You Like It*, are quintessential fools. Delighted by Touchstone, Jaques describes and defines the fool's profession and purposes at length, in a striking series of speeches (2.7.12–61). The fool's critique is seen as powerful enough to "cleanse the foul body of th'infected world" (2.7.60).

A fool can also prove useful in TRAGEDY, providing comic relief as well as his customary objectivity. The Fool who serves King Lear, for example, develops the character type to a new level of dramatic expression. He is virtually an alter ego of the king. His jests are a foil to Lear's frenzy, and his riddles, songs, and scraps of rhyme—combined with his ridicule of the king's folly—offer a sense that some-

where outside the terrifying universe of the play there remains a real world in which sanity still exists.

In Shakespeare's PROBLEM PLAYS, the fools are less attractive figures. In *All's Well That Ends Well*, the jester to the Countess of Rossillion—named Lavatch but designated Clown—is a melancholy and sometimes slightly obnoxious character; rather strikingly, when Parolles, the comic villain of the play, is defeated, he finds recourse in becoming a professional fool, with the hope that his reputation as a hapless knave will seem entertaining. Thersites in *Troilus and Cressida* is an abusive and rancorous bandier of insults; while funny, he is also somewhat dispiriting. In *Timon of Athens* (sometimes classed with the darker comedies), Apemantus, though technically not a fool—in that he is not a jester—is similar to Thersites. (The Fool who does appear in *Timon*, an unfinished play, is not a fully developed figure, though he demonstrates the type.) *Measure for Measure* has no fool, but the malicious defamation practiced by Lucio gives him something of Thersites' quality also. The fool's objectivity is not desirable in the unreal world of the ROMANCES, Shakespeare's last works, and the only fool to appear in them—Trinculo of *The Tempest*—is, although a jester, rather more a CLOWN than a fool.

The distinction between clown and fool is significant, although the Elizabethans tended to treat the terms as synonyms (Lavatch and Feste—both professional jesters—are designated "Clowns"). The clown tends to be outside the plot's main developments, while the fool is involved with the central characters. Whereas the clown's humor is unintentional, the fool's intellectual wit and trenchant observation are deliberate. With his blunt, earthy spontaneity, the clown lacks the fool's satirical edge. Shakespeare's fools may reflect the stage manner of Robert ARMIN, who joined the playwright's troupe just before the creation of Touchstone, but the type also carries meaning: the fool's sardonic attitude toward the defects of human society adds an underlying melancholy to the essentially positive stance of comedy.

Forbes-Robertson, Johnston (1853–1947) British actor. Forbes-Robertson studied acting under Samuel PHELPS. He was especially noted for his Hamlet,

Johnston Forbes-Robertson was renowned for the power of his voice. His portrayal of Hamlet (as seen here) was said to be the greatest of his time. *(Courtesy of Culver Pictures, Inc.)*

Romeo, Macbeth, and Othello and often starred in Henry IRVING's productions. He succeeded Irving as manager of the Lyceum Theatre in 1895 and produced several of Shakespeare's tragedies, including *Hamlet* (1897), to which he restored the closing episode following Hamlet's death, seldom enacted in the 19th century.

Ford, John (1586–ca. 1639) English dramatist, one of the last playwrights of JACOBEAN DRAMA. Ford has been in the limelight of Shakespearean scholarship early in the 21st century, as scholars increasingly credit him with a poem, A FUNERAL ELEGY, that was briefly ascribed to Shakespeare. However, Ford is best known as a playwright. He began to write plays around 1612, collaborating with Thomas DEKKER, John WEBSTER, and others. Of his own works, he is chiefly remembered for several tragedies marked by bitter resignation and despair, the best known of which is *'Tis Pity She's a Whore* (ca. 1632), a tale of incest between brother and sister. His historical drama *Perkin Warbeck* (1633) is also highly regarded. Ford lived much of his life in poverty and is thought to have spent his last years in seclusion.

Forman, Simon (1552–1611) English astrologer and diarist. Forman recorded several early performances of Shakespeare's plays. His written records—generally brief synopses—help scholars determine the dates, and in some cases the likelihood of variation from the published texts, of various plays, including three of Shakespeare's works: *Macbeth*, *Cymbeline*, and *The Winter's Tale*.

Astrology was a more reputable occupation then than now, but Forman may have been less than scrupulous. He was frequently jailed for practicing medicine without a license, and because of his reputation, when he drowned in the Thames after predicting the date of his death, it was suspected that he was a suicide.

Forrest, Edwin (1806–1872) American actor. The first great American Shakespearean actor, Forrest helped create popular enthusiasm for Shakespeare in the United States, especially with his performances as Othello and Lear. He appeared in London in 1836 and 1845, and a rivalry developed between him and W. C. MACREADY. Comparisons of the two took on a nationalistic color, especially in America, and led to the notorious Astor Place riot in New York in 1849, when a mob of Forrest fans—and opportunistic, anti-England political agitators—stormed a theater where Macready was playing; the commotion left 22 dead. In the opinion of contemporaries and most subsequent scholars, Forrest personally instigated the affair, and the actor's popularity slowly waned after this incident. He eventually fell from favor entirely, dying an embittered failure.

Fortune Theatre Playhouse built in a northern LONDON suburb by Philip HENSLOWE and William ALLEYN in 1600, long the home of the ADMIRAL'S MEN and its successors, PRINCE HENRY'S MEN and the PALSGRAVE'S MEN. The Fortune may have been built in response to the construction of the GLOBE THE-ATRE near Henslowe and Alleyn's ROSE THEATRE in SOUTHWARK, south of the city. Some scholars theo-rize that when Cuthbert BURBAGE and the CHAM-BERLAIN'S MEN moved to the Globe in 1599, Henslowe and Alleyn saw an opportunity to avoid direct competition while at the same time filling the vacuum created by the Chamberlain's departure from the CURTAIN THEATRE, to the north of London. Moreover, their lease on the ground the Rose was built on was about to expire. In any event, the For-tune was meant to rival the Globe; it was commis-sioned from the same builder, under a contract requiring that it be "finished and done according to the manner and fashion of the said house called the Globe." It took its name from a statue of the God-dess of Fortune over its entrance. When the For-tune burned down in 1621, it was described as "the fairest playhouse" in London. It was rebuilt in 1623 and was used for surreptitious play productions after the Puritans' revolutionary government made the-ater illegal in 1642, at the beginning of the Civil Wars. The building was pillaged by soldiers in 1649 and finally destroyed around 1656.

foul papers   In textual studies, a playwright's origi-nal, unpolished manuscript from which the printers of an early edition of a play might set the type. This version differs from FAIR COPY, which was used for the same purpose but was provided by a scribe, who might make various corrections to the original manuscript. A published text set from foul papers is therefore distinctively flawed by minor errors and inconsistencies taken from the source.

In the case of Shakespeare, the playwright's careless slips survived into the printed text: his spelling is often irregular, and inconsistent names occur in speech headings and stage directions. Lady Capulet, for instance, is designated in the Q2 edi-tion of *Romeo and Juliet* as *Capu. Wi, Ca. Wi, Wife, Old La., La., Mo.,* and *M.* Sometimes an actor's name will appear as a speech heading—e.g., Kempe for Dogberry in 4.2 of *Much Ado About Nothing*—which is evidence that Shakespeare created the part with a particular player in mind. GHOST CHAR-ACTERs may appear without again being mentioned, like Innogen in 1.1 and 2.1 of *Much Ado*. In fair

copy most of these problems were corrected. Also, when a text was printed from foul papers, new errors resulted from the use of a rapidly composed manuscript that was likely to be difficult to read and was further confused by handwritten amend-ments and marginal insertions.

Sometimes material was retained by the typeset-ter that the author intended to cut. For instance, Q2 of *Hamlet* preserves a line Shakespeare had rejected; two lines of similar meaning occur together, and the first one does not rhyme with any other although it is in the midst of a long passage of rhyming couplets. Clearly, the playwright rejected it in favor of the second (3.2.162) as he was writing, but the substitution was not evident to the printer, who simply reproduced everything he saw. The error was corrected in the FIRST FOLIO edition.

Stage directions in foul papers are sometimes casually imprecise, as in "Enter . . . others, as many as can be" (*Titus Andronicus*, 1.1.70). They may also reveal the playwright's thoughts on production in more elaborate and specific stage directions than usual, such as: "Enter Volumnia and Virgilia, mother and wife to Martius. They set them down on two low stools and sew" (*Coriolanus*, 1.3.1 S.D.). These parenthetical remarks were normally abbre-viated or eliminated by a copyist.

With the probable exception of three pages of *Sir Thomas More*, no original Shakespearean manu-script exists, but by observing such features as those mentioned above, scholars can determine what sort of copy was the basis for an early edition—whether a manuscript or an earlier printing; and if a manu-script, whether fair copy or foul papers. Modern editors can determine from such information how closely a given printed text represents what Shake-speare actually wrote.

Fourth Folio   See FOLIO.

Foxe, John (John Fox) (1516–1587)   English his-torian of religion, author of a source for *2 Henry VI*, *King John*, and especially *Henry VIII*. Foxe's *Actes and Monumentes*, better known as the *Book of Martyrs*, is a history of Protestantism focusing on the English Protestants who were persecuted during the reign of Queen Mary (ruled 1553–58), a zealous Catholic.

Passages from his account of Thomas Cranmer's life were Shakespeare's principal source for Cranmer's trial in 5.1–2 of *Henry VIII*. Other material provided details for *2 Henry VI* and *King John*.

Foxe's book was written in Latin during his exile from England during Mary's reign. He returned in 1559 and translated and published his work in 1563, enlarging it for a second edition in 1570. It immediately became immensely popular and influential—the 1570 edition was required by law to be available to worshippers in all English cathedrals, and for generations it was regarded by English Protestants as a virtual supplement to the Bible. Many houses contained only those two books. The *Book of Martyrs* was republished many times in the 16th and 17th centuries; Shakespeare probably used the fourth edition (1583).

France Country in Europe. France, England's most powerful neighbor and perennial rival, was its enemy in the HUNDRED YEARS' WAR and earlier conflicts. It thus provides settings in four of the HISTORY PLAYS and is prominent in several other plays as well.

In the early play *Edward III*, written by a young Shakespeare in collaboration with others, the beginnings of the Hundred Years' War are enacted; the battles of SLUYS, CRÉCY, and POITIERS, and the siege of CALAIS, all fought in France, are presented in Acts 3–5, though scholars believe that this part of the play was largely written by Shakespeare's collaborators. In *Henry V* and *Henry VI*, Shakespeare presented the later phases of the war, the major struggle between England and France in the 14th and 15th centuries. King Henry V's triumph at the battle of AGINCOURT (1415) is enacted in Act 4 of *Henry V* and followed by the negotiation of the treaty of TROYES in 5.2, completing the English conquest. King Henry V is betrothed on this occasion to Princess Katharine of France; their child is to be King Henry VI.

In *1 Henry VI*, English forces besiege ORLÉANS and ROUEN, and the young Henry is crowned king of France in PARIS. However, the English conquest of France is actually being undone under the leadership of Joan La Pucelle and Charles VII. The final battle of the war, the English loss at BORDEAUX,

occupies most of Act 4, though Shakespeare salvaged a seeming victory by staging Joan's trial at ANGIERS in 5.3.

France is unimportant in the other *Henry VI* plays, though one scene of *3 Henry VI* (3.3) is set at the court of King Lewis, who offers aid to English rebels. In *King John*, set much earlier in history, King John also fights in France, protecting PLANTAGENET lands against the French king Philip Augustus. This war centers on Angiers, where fighting occurs in 2.1 and 3.2.

Long after the Hundred Years' War, rivalry with France remained a prominent feature of English politics. Only in 1564, the year of Shakespeare's birth, did England finally renounce its last claims to French territory (see CALAIS), and during the playwright's lifetime, war between the two countries seemed likely on more than one occasion. Catholic France was seen by Protestant England as a potential religious enemy, for Europe was still plagued by sectarian wars. Thus, along with another rival, Spain, France loomed as large in the fears of Shakespeare's contemporaries as the Soviet Union did to many Westerners during the cold war. England and France remained hostile for centuries after Shakespeare's time; only from the 20th century on has warfare between them seemed improbable.

Because Shakespeare's audiences shared an interest in France and French affairs, he also used this country and its people outside the history plays. A king of France (called France) finds his way into ancient British myth in *King Lear*. In *Love's Labour's Lost*, the presentation of a King of Navarre reflects the importance in contemporary French politics of the then-current king of Navarre, soon to become King Henri IV of France. A comical Frenchman, Dr Caius, is mocked in *The Merry Wives of Windsor*.

All's Well That Ends Well is set partially in France, in the province of ROSSILLION (the French Roussillon), and Shakespeare elaborates on his sources in providing a realistic political relationship between France and Italy that reflects the French military involvement in Italy throughout the first half of the 16th century.

It has been speculated that Shakespeare traveled in France, although no evidence has survived to confirm this. It is clear, though, that he knew the French language. Not only did he sometimes use French sources that had not been translated into English, but his French dialogue—e.g., in *Henry V*, 3.4, 4.4, 5.2—is only slightly flawed.

French, George Russell (1803–1881) English architect and amateur scholar, publisher of a genealogy of Shakespeare. French's *Shakespeareana Genealogica* (1869) covered Shakespeare's ancestors, relatives, and descendants, along with genealogical notes on the characters in the HISTORY PLAYS, *Hamlet*, and *Macbeth*. His was the first work in this area, and it is still valuable to scholars. French also wrote genealogies of Admiral Horatio Nelson (1758–1805) and the Duke of Wellington (1769–1852), and he was a well-known campaigner against the drinking of alcohol.

Friday Street Club See MERMAID TAVERN.

Frith, John (active 1582) Clergyman who may have officiated at Shakespeare's wedding in November 1582. Confusion in the license for the marriage of Shakespeare and Anne HATHAWAY has led to scholarly speculation that the wedding took place in Frith's parish at TEMPLE GRAFTON. This village was five miles from STRATFORD, more remote than seems necessary, and was perhaps chosen expressly to have Frith preside over the ceremony. The future playwright's bride was pregnant, and the marriage had been hurriedly arranged (see RICHARDSON, JOHN; SANDELLS, FULK; WHITGIFT, JOHN), and Frith previously had been chastised by the authorities for marriages conducted without proper license. Also, he may have been a Catholic sympathizer, as were many people in Stratford, perhaps including the Shakespeare family (see SPIRITUAL TESTAMENT OF JOHN SHAKESPEARE) and may therefore have been an attractive choice. Whether he did in fact marry William and Anne cannot be determined with the surviving evidence, but the effort has led to the discovery of a 1586 report by the Puritan authorities on Frith that paints a charming if scant sketch of a rustic Englishman of the period: "an old priest and unsound in religion [this refers to suspected Catholic tendencies], he can neither preach nor read well, his chiefest trade is to cure hawks that are hurt or diseased, for which purpose many do usually repair to him."

Frogmore Village near WINDSOR, the setting for 3.1 of *The Merry Wives of Windsor*. In this scene the curate Evans, challenged to a duel by Dr. Caius, awaits his foe in a field near Frogmore. The duel is averted, and the enemies return to Windsor as allies. Shakespeare used the name Frogmore simply to evoke the neighborhood of Windsor, which was well known to his original audience, members of the court of Queen Elizabeth.

Froissart, Jean (1338–1410) French chronicler whose work provided a source for *Edward III* and may have influenced the writing of *Richard II*, particularly in presenting a highly favorable account of John of Gaunt. Further, it is speculated that Froissart's romantic presentation of the pomp and pageantry of medieval ceremonies may have helped form Shakespeare's sense of the courtly world of King Richard II. Froissart also provided Shakespeare with the basic material for Acts 1 and 2 of *Edward III*, the story of King Edward's infatuation with the Countess of Salisbury, which was probably the playwright's major contribution to a play that was written collaboratively, as well as having been the chief source for the history presented in the play as a whole. Shakespeare would have known Froissart's work in Lord BERNERS's translation (1523–25).

In his *Chroniques* Froissart wrote of the contemporary HUNDRED YEARS' WAR, interviewing many key participants and observing some events himself. His colorful history ends with the deposition of Richard II. Froissart is considered to have been the last great medieval writer; his vivid and exciting description of the traditions and practices of the chivalric aristocracy records a world that was fast vanishing in his own time. His chronicles are still regarded as classics of European literature.

Funeral Elegy, A Poem controversially attributed to Shakespeare. In 1983 Don Foster, now a professor of English at Vassar College, proposed in his doctoral thesis that *A Funeral Elegie* (now more often given its modern spelling), an obscure, 578-

line poem published in 1612 over the initials "W. S." might be by Shakespeare. In 1989 he published a book on the subject, *Elegy by W. S.—A Study in Attribution*, and in 1996 he presented a firmer statement of Shakespeare's authorship, based on a computer analysis of word choice. This assertion was widely publicized in the media throughout the world, for the poem in question is mildly homo-erotic and thus Foster seemed to be raising the question of Shakespeare's homosexuality, an issue that is perennially debated among enthusiasts (see William Shakespeare's Biography [Part 1]; *Sonnets*). However, in the absence of evidence that Shakespeare had known the subject of the elegy, an Oxford student who was killed in a drunken fight, and in view of the generally inferior quality of the poetry, the attribution was from the first received with reservations. In the wake of further studies, scholars have come for the most part to believe that the likeliest author of *A Funeral Elegy* was John FORD.

Furness, Horace Howard (1833–1912)   American scholar, first editor of the *New Variorum* edition of Shakespeare's plays (see VARIORUM EDITION). Furness began work on this annotated collection of the plays in 1871 with *Romeo and Juliet*. In this edition he provided textual notes and excerpts from pertinent critical writings from many eras and several languages. With the assistance of his wife, Helen Kate Furness (1837–83), and his son, H. H. Furness, Jr. (1865–1930), he had completed 18 volumes before he died. His son succeeded him as general editor of the series, which was not completed until 1953.

Furnivall, Frederick James (1825–1910)   English scholar. Furnivall encouraged the study of Shakespeare's works as a whole—still a new pursuit in his day—in his notable introductions written for each play, in his scholarly edition of the *Works* (1876), and with the English translation of G. G. GERVINUS's *Shakespeare Commentaries* (1875). He was particularly associated with the development of the VERSE TEST as a tool for determining the chronological order of the plays. He also edited a 43-volume collection of facsimiles of the QUARTO editions of the plays (1880–89).

Furnivall was a prolific scholar and educator with many interests besides Shakespearean studies. He founded many scholarly organizations, including the Early English Text, Chaucer, Ballad, New Shakespeare, Wyclif, Browning, and Shelley Societies. He was involved in the creation of the Oxford English Dictionary, and he produced a number of scholarly editions, most notably a collection of six texts of CHAUCER's *The Canterbury Tales* (1868).

G

Gad's Hill (Gadshill, Gads Hill) Geographical feature near the city of ROCHESTER, setting for the highway robbery in 2.2 of *1 Henry IV.* Gad's Hill, in KENT, on the road from Rochester to London, was a notorious site for highway robberies, both in the 16th century and in the period when the play is set. It is there that Gadshill, Falstaff, and others rob the Travellers, only to be robbed themselves by Prince Hal and Poins.

The name of this infamous setting provided a nickname for a robber who operated there in the playwright's source, THE FAMOUS VICTORIES, and Shakespeare simply adopted the name for the Gadshill of *1 Henry IV.* In old editions of the play, the site is spelled as one word, and some modern editors follow this style. Others adopt one of the two-word variants, also used in Elizabethan times, and thus ease the slight confusion that the duplication can produce. Shakespeare's double use of the name is one of many instances of the playwright's toleration for minor confusions and inconsistencies in his texts.

Gardiner, William (1531–1597) Contemporary of Shakespeare, a wealthy London real-estate investor and Justice of the Peace who figured in a dispute that also involved Shakespeare. Gardiner, who bought his judgeship, seems to have been a notorious swindler; he was also imprisoned several times for abusive and violent actions and even faced charges of murder by witchcraft. In 1596 he feuded for unknown reasons with Francis LANGLEY, the proprietor of the SWAN THEATRE, and Langley sought the protection of the courts against him and his stepson William Wayte. In response, apparently, Wayte sought the same protection against Langley, Shakespeare, and two women who are otherwise unknown. Shakespeare's connection with the quarrel cannot be determined, but some scholars have inferred (though others disagree) that either he lived in BANKSIDE, which was part of Gardiner's judicial jurisdiction, or that Shakespeare's acting company at the time, the CHAMBERLAIN'S MEN, played at the Swan, although there is no other evidence of this.

The noted scholar Leslie HOTSON has proposed that Shakespeare intended the comical Justice Shallow in *The Merry Wives of Windsor* as a satirical portrait of Gardiner, with his dim-witted relative Slender intended as Wayte. Shallow's coat of arms, described in *The Merry Wives,* 1.1.15–25, resembles Gardiner's, and, like Gardiner, Shallow threatens to use the law against an enemy. Moreover, Shallow intends to marry Slender to a rich young woman, a circumstance that might refer to Wayte's marriage to an heiress whom Gardiner subsequently swindled. Since *The Merry Wives* was written a few months after Wayte's complaint against Shakespeare, a literary retaliation, if one were attempted, might reasonably appear there.

However, this evidence is somewhat weak. The Elizabethan era was highly litigious, and the use of the law against one's enemies was quite ordinary. Though the coats of arms of Gardiner and Shallow both include luces, a kind of fish, the heraldic resemblance between them is not especially close (closer to Shallow's arms are those of Sir Thomas

LUCY). Moreover, Shallow is losing his memory and is based in rural GLOUCESTERSHIRE, whereas Gardiner was a wily London businessman. Further, no slightest resemblance to Gardiner can be found in Shallow's appearance in *2 Henry IV*, written at the same time. Most significantly, although Shallow is a comic figure, his personality seems inappropriate to a scoundrel such as Gardiner appears to have been. Shakespeare's pleasant portrait of a garrulous and gullible but warmhearted elderly country gentleman seems an unlikely weapon of vengeance.

Garnet, Henry (1555–1606)   English Jesuit priest whose execution for treason is cryptically referred to in *Macbeth*. As the play's horror mounts, the Porter, in a comical interlude, drunkenly pretends to serve as the doorkeeper to Hell. He welcomes "an equivocator, that could swear in both the scales against either scale; who committed treason enough for God's sake, yet could not equivocate to heaven" (2.3.8–11). The word *equivocate* was highly charged in the English political world at the time that this scene was written (ca. 1606), and it had particular pertinence to Garnet's treason trial, a notorious public event. Moreover, the Porter also welcomes to Hell "a farmer, that hang'd himself" (2.3.4–5), a reference to the name "Mr Farmer," used by Garnet as an underground alias. Shakespeare's original audiences will certainly have understood these lines as a political joke.

In 1605 England was shaken by the exposure of the Gunpowder Plot, an attempt by radical Catholics to blow up the Houses of Parliament and kill King JAMES I as part of an effort to install a Catholic monarch. Garnet, a Catholic convert, was the director of the clandestine Catholic Church in England. Though not one of the plotters, he was charged with complicity in the scheme for he had known of it ahead of time and had concealed his knowledge, itself a treasonable act under English law. He denied his foreknowledge at first, but when faced with an informer he confessed and justified his perjury with the doctrine of equivocation, a term he used repeatedly at his trial. *Equivocation* was a Catholic theological term describing morally acceptable perjury, condoned when undertaken in the name of Catholic opposition to Protestantism.

This defense was of course rejected, and Garnet was convicted of perjury as well as treason; he was sentenced to death and hanged.

Garrick, David (1717–1779)   British actor and producer. For 35 years, beginning in 1740, Garrick dominated the London stage. He led a revolution in acting, rejecting the tradition of formal declamation still employed by James QUIN and others in favor of naturalistic speech and actions. As the longtime manager of the Drury Lane Theatre (1747–66), he also altered the presentation of plays, introducing realistic scenery and hidden lighting and eliminating the presence of spectators on the stage. He did much to popularize Shakespeare, producing 24 of his plays. He often restored excised text and eliminated the additions of earlier producers such as Nahum TATE and William DAVENANT. Among the Shakespeare plays he resurrected in this way were *Macbeth*, *Coriolanus*, *Cymbeline*, *Antony and Cleopatra*, *The Tempest*, *Romeo and Juliet*, and *King Lear*—though he added his own passages to several of these and altered some of the other plays quite radically. He rewrote two plays as operas—*A Midsummer Night's Dream* (*The Fairies* [1755]) and *The Tempest* (1756)—and his *Catherine and Petruchio* (1754) and *Florizel and Perdita* (1756) were severely altered versions of *The Taming of the Shrew* and *The Winter's Tale*, respectively. His *Hamlet* (1772) was his most notorious adaptation, for he eliminated most of Act 5.

As an actor, Garrick played 17 different Shakespearean roles. He was best known as Benedick (*Much Ado About Nothing*), Richard III (the part that established him as a major actor), Hamlet, Macbeth, and Lear. In 1769 Garrick organized the Shakespeare Jubilee at STRATFORD, an elaborate celebration of the playwright that did much to make Stratford a mecca for Shakespearean enthusiasts. Garrick also wrote several successful plays, mostly farces, and several volumes of poetry. He was buried at WESTMINSTER ABBEY.

Gascoigne, George (ca. 1535–1577)   English poet, author, and playwright, creator of a source for several of Shakespeare's plays. Gascoigne's *Supposes* (performed 1566, published 1575), a translation of the Italian drama *I Suppositi* (1509) by Ludovico ARIOSTO, provided the SUBPLOT concerning Bianca in *The Taming of the Shrew,* along with many details in *The Comedy of Errors* and *The Two Gentlemen of Verona.*

Gascoigne, who wrote poetry, prose, and plays, was a literary innovator. His *Notes concerning the making of verse* (1575) is one of the earliest examples of literary criticism in English, and his TRAGEDY *Jocasta* (1566) was only the second English play to be written in BLANK VERSE. His adaptation of Ariosto helped introduce a taste for RENAISSANCE Italian literature into England.

Born into a wealthy family, Gascoigne led a dissolute life as a young man. He studied "such lattyn as I forgat" at Cambridge, and supposedly studied law at the INNS OF COURT. He was chronically in debt and occasionally in trouble for questionable financial dealings. In 1561 he married a wealthy widow—and thus became stepfather to the noted poet Nicholas Breton (ca. 1545–ca. 1626)—but in 1570 he again had money troubles and was jailed for debt. In 1572 he joined the English volunteer soldiers aiding the Dutch rebellion against the Spanish. He was intermittently in the Low Countries for the last years of his life, although he returned to England to write and publish several works, among them a final volume—*The Glass of Government* (1575)—that recorded his moral conversion.

Gascony Region in southwestern FRANCE, an English colony from 1204 to 1453 and the location for Act 4 of *1 Henry VI.* Much of the act focuses on the battle near BORDEAUX, in which the English hero Talbot is killed; 4.3–4 are set at English camps elsewhere in Gascony. The loss of the region following this battle, fought in 1453, effectively ended the HUNDRED YEARS' WAR.

Gaultree Forest Extensive woodland near YORK in northern England, setting for 4.1–3 of *2 Henry IV.* Following his sources, Shakespeare recorded an encounter between the army of King Henry IV and that of the rebels led by the Archbishop of York at the ancient royal hunting grounds of Gaultree, or Galtres. Prince John of Lancaster, Henry's son, offers the rebels a fair hearing of their grievances before the king if they will disband their forces. Once they do so, he has them arrested for treason and executed. He justifies this treachery by contending that all he had promised was that the king would hear their complaints, not that they would be safe from prosecution. The episode brings Lancaster to the fore—Falstaff delivers an amusing assessment of him in 4.3.84–123—and it offers a closer look at the rebels. The situation is discussed, especially by the Archbishop and Westmoreland in 4.1, in terms that offer a human understanding of the rebels' position but that also condemn rebellion as an unjustifiable disruption of society, particularly when linked to religious sentiments.

Shakespeare substituted Lancaster for Westmoreland, who actually conducted the negotiations and perpetrated the betrayal, in order to emphasize the importance of Henry's family in the web of treachery and conflict that followed his usurpation of the throne (enacted in *Richard II*). Otherwise, the historical event is accurately depicted. Lancaster is presented as a cold-blooded Machiavellian, although his ruse is not explicitly disparaged; many such ploys were used in late medieval warfare, and neither the historians whom Shakespeare read nor the playwright himself seem to treat this one as particularly heinous, particularly when compared to the much greater crime of rebellion against an anointed ruler.

Geoffrey of Monmouth (ca. 1100–1154) English medieval writer, creator of the Arthurian cycle of tales. Geoffrey's *Historia Regum Britanniae* (ca. 1140) provided much material for Raphael HOLINSHED's *Chronicles of England, Scotland, and Ireland* (1577, 1587), Shakespeare's principal source for his two plays dealing with premedieval Britain, *King Lear* and *Cymbeline.* Geoffrey's book was not actually a history so much as a collection intended to appeal to the fashion for courtly tales—for example, the French stories of Charlemagne—and it immediately became very popular. It claimed to be a Latin translation of a book in Cymric, the language of WALES, that told the history of Britain up to the reign of King Arthur. It was in fact a mixture of various old chronicles, traditional stories, and, probably, outright fictions. It established King Arthur as a British cultural hero, and it has been called the most important literary work of the 12th century.

Geoffrey was born into a family of clergymen and was educated at Monmouth's famed Benedictine abbey. He was probably a monk, though he was primarily a writer rather than a man of the cloth. In his old age he was made a bishop due to the influence of his aristocratic patrons—possibly including King Stephen of England—but he had to be ordained a priest for the occasion.

German, Edward (1862–1936) British composer, creator of incidental music for *Henry VIII*. German—whose name is pronounced with a hard "G"—established himself as a composer for the theater with three dances created for Henry IRVING's 1892 production of *Henry VIII*. These pieces were immediately popular and were staples of the music-hall repertoire for years, besides adorning subsequent productions of Shakespeare's play. German went on to a successful career as a composer of light opera—most notably *Merrie England* (1902)—and miscellaneous theatrical music.

Gervinus, Georg Gottfried (1805–1871) German scholar. A professor of literature at the University of Heidelberg, Gervinus published a four-volume collection of commentaries on Shakespeare's plays (1849, translated as *Shakespeare Commentaries* in 1863), which was highly influential on Shakespeare scholars in both Germany and England. He was an important advocate of the VERSE TEST, used to determine the chronology of the plays, and he is considered the first writer to study the development of the playwright's work over the course of his career.

ghost character Person mentioned in stage directions but not actually appearing in a play, having been excised or possibly simply forgotten about in the course of composition. The existence of such a character is often taken as evidence that the text in which it first appears was printed from the playwright's FOUL PAPERS, for such a superfluous figure would presumably have been deleted from any more evolved, text, such as a PROMPTBOOK. Ghost

characters in Shakespeare's plays include Violenta in *All's Well That Ends Well*; Lamprius, Rannius, and Lucillius in *Antony and Cleopatra*; Beaumont in *Henry V*; Innogen in *Much Ado About Nothing*; Petruchio in *Romeo and Juliet*; and the Mercer in *Timon of Athens*.

Gibborne, Thomas (active 1624) English actor. Though known as a member of the PALSGRAVE'S MEN according to a document of 1624, Gibborne is thought by some scholars to have been the actor who played Shakespeare's RAMBURES in *Henry V*, because the character is designated as "Gebon" in speech headings and stage directions of the BAD QUARTO edition of the play (1600). However, Samuel GILBURNE is generally thought a more likely nominee.

Gide, André (1869–1951) French author and translator of Shakespeare. Gide is best known for his novels (*The Immoralist* [1902], *The Plague* [1947], etc.) but he also translated *Hamlet* and *Antony and Cleopatra* into French and wrote prefaces to translations of several other of the plays. He was awarded the Nobel Prize in literature in 1947.

Gielgud, John (1904–2000) British actor and director. Gielgud's long and distinguished career began with an appearance as the Herald in *Henry V* at the OLD VIC THEATRE in 1921. His portrayals of Hamlet and Richard II were especially renowned, but he also played most of Shakespeare's other protagonists. He produced a number of Shakespeare's plays, including *Hamlet*, *Macbeth*, and *Romeo and Juliet*. His 1949 production of *Much Ado About Nothing*, with himself as Benedick, was revived several times in the 1950s. With Laurence OLIVIER and Ralph RICHARDSON, Gielgud was considered one of the greatest Shakespearean actors of the 20th century.

Gilbard, William (d. 1612) Stratford teacher and clerk, possible inspiration for Shakespeare's character Nathaniel of *Love's Labour's Lost*. Gilbard is recorded as the assistant schoolmaster in 1561–62 and as the acting schoolmaster on many occasions thereafter until 1574; thus, he probably taught the young Shakespeare. By 1576 Gilbard was a curate and assisted the parish priest. His literacy enabled him to supplement his income as a clerk—he drew up many wills, for instance, including that of Anne HATHAWAY's father—and from 1603 to 1611 he was the parish clerk. The records he kept in this capacity contain a much higher proportion of Latin words and phrases than other clerks of the time used, which suggests that he was proud of his education. Gilbard has been suggested as a model for Nathaniel, also a curate, though there is no actual evidence to support the idea.

Gilburne, Samuel (active 1605)   English actor. Gilburne is listed in the FIRST FOLIO as one of the 26 "Principall Actors" in Shakespeare's plays, but he is otherwise known only as a beneficiary of Augustine PHILLIPS's will (1605), where he is said to have been Phillips's apprentice, presumably as a boy. Gilburne may have played a Lord in *All's Well That Ends Well*—designated as "G" in the Folio text of the play—and *Henry V*'s Rambures, who is designated as "Gebon" in the BAD QUARTO edition (1600).

Gildon, Charles (1665–1724)   English playwright and critic. Trained as a Roman Catholic priest, Gildon abandoned his calling to become a hack writer. He published popular commentaries on English poetry and drama, including an anthology of biographical pieces (some written by him, though all unsigned) that included a brief and entirely unreliable life of Shakespeare. In 1699 he produced a play entitled *Measure for Measure, or Beauty the Best Advocate*, based loosely on Shakespeare's play—or rather on William DAVENANT's earlier adaptation, THE LAW AGAINST LOVERS. Gildon dropped much of Davenant's introduced material and replaced it, not with Shakespeare's text but with a play within a play, an operatic MASQUE on the ancient Roman legend of Dido and Aeneas. In 1710 Gildon published *Poems* by Shakespeare, which was bound as a seventh volume of Nicholas ROWE's six-volume collection of the plays though not published by the same publisher. This piece of near-piracy earned Gildon an insulting passage in the famous literary satire *The Dunciad* (1728), by Alexander POPE.

Giles, Nathaniel (ca. 1559–1634)   Choirmaster and sometime director of the Children of the Chapel (see CHILDREN'S COMPANIES). Giles, a Protestant minister and musician, was appointed director of the Chapel Royal, the court choir of Queen Elizabeth, which recruited boys from church choirs all over the country and placed them in a school at court, where they were educated while performing for the queen. In 1600 Giles joined Henry EVANS in producing plays performed by the Chapel school's acting company, the Children of the Chapel, at the WHITEFRIARS THEATRE. However, in 1602 Giles and Evans were accused of misusing the Chapel Royal's recruiting power to enroll nonsingers for the acting company. Evans fled the country and only returned after the queen's death. Giles continued to run the company, but in 1616 the choir's connection with Evans and the actors was severed by royal command. Giles remained as choirmaster until his death. He also was a noted composer of church music.

Giulio Romano (Giulio Pippi) (1492–1546)   Italian painter and architect, the only RENAISSANCE artist mentioned in Shakespeare. In *The Winter's Tale*, when Paulina announces that she has a statue representing Queen Hermione, believed long dead, the statue is said to be "performed"—meaning either made or painted—"by that rare Italian master, Julio Romano, who, had he himself eternity and could put breath into his work, would beguile Nature of her custom, so perfectly he is her ape" (5.2.95–99). Since the sculpture turns out not to be a sculpture at all, its ascription to Giulio proves irrelevant; the use of the name merely lends verisimilitude to the gossip surrounding Paulina's cover story.

That Shakespeare should use Giulio's name in such a context suggests that his audience knew the artist's work, but that he should mistakenly make him a sculptor—or a mere finisher of sculptures—suggests that the playwright and presumably his audience did not know his work very well. It is of course an anachronism to name a Renaissance artist in a tale set in ancient times, but Shakespeare was tolerant of such inconsistencies, which appear throughout his plays. In any case, in Shakespeare's ROMANCES, with their welter of languages and exotic settings, a degree of confusion is probably intentional, promoting a sense of timelessness that furthers the playwright's ends.

The historical Giulio Romano (born Pippi but later named for his birthplace, ROME) was the chief pupil and assistant of Raphael (1483–1520), one of the most important Italian painters. Giulio himself became one of the leading painters and architects of his day, an innovator with a boldly pioneering style. He completed a number of Raphael's great decorative programs at the Vatican on the master's death and then moved to MANTUA, where he was court painter and architect to Duke Federigo Gonzaga (1500–40). His masterpiece is a ducal palace, the Palazzo del Tè, begun in 1526; both its architecture and its elaborately painted decor broke the conventions of Renaissance art to create bizarre and startling effects—an early example of the Mannerist style that dominated the second half of the 16th century. Giulio's painting, which combined elements from Raphael and Michelangelo (1475–1564), was widely influential.

Globe Theatre   Theatre in SOUTHWARK built by Cuthbert BURBAGE in 1599, the principal home of Shakespeare's acting company and the site of the first performances of many of his plays. The Globe was built for the CHAMBERLAIN'S MEN when Burbage was unable to renew the ground lease for the land on which their old home, the THEATRE, stood. He therefore had the Theatre, a timber building, taken down and reassembled at a new site in Southwark, on the south side of the Thames River, beyond the jurisdiction of the LONDON government, which was opposed to theater. The lease for the land was jointly held, half by Burbage and his brother Richard BURBAGE, and half by a group of five actors—Shakespeare, John HEMINGE, Augustine PHILLIPS, Thomas POPE, and Will KEMPE—who put their shares in trust with William LEVESON and Thomas SAVAGE. The Globe opened in late 1599; *As You Like It* may have been written for the occasion, and when Shakespeare had Jaques say, "All the world's a stage . . ." (2.7.139), he may have been slyly alluding to the new theater.

The Globe was a roughly cylindrical—probably polygonal, with 20–24 sides—three-storey timber building, unroofed over the stage in the center.

Each floor contained open galleries with seats. The galleries extended around much of the circle, and the stage was built out into the center from the remaining part of the building. In the building behind the stage were dressing rooms—the "tiring house"—perhaps galleries for musicians, and apparatus for scenery and props. Above the thatched roof rose a tower, or "penthouse," from which flags were flown and trumpets sounded to announce a production. An 18th-century account asserted that on its facade the Globe sported a painted sign depicting Hercules supporting the planet Earth (one of his legendary tasks was to stand in for Atlas). If this was so—and scholars generally believe it was—this sign may be alluded to in *Hamlet*, where the CHILDREN'S COMPANIES, in a satirical passage on the WAR OF THE THEATERS, are said to have triumphed over both the Players and "Hercules and his load too" (2.2.358).

On June 29, 1613, the Globe's thatched roof was set on fire by a cannon fired during a performance of *Henry VIII*, as called for in the stage direction at 1.4.49, and the building burned to the ground. It was open again within a year, rebuilt to much the same plan, but this time the roof was tiled. In 1644, two years after the theaters of England were closed by the revolutionary government, the Globe was torn down and tenements built on the lot.

In 1989 the fortuitous discovery of the foundations of the ROSE THEATRE sparked a successful search for those of the Globe, which were uncovered later in the same year. The Globe's remains are much less extensive than those of the Rose and accordingly less informative, but enough has been revealed to excite scholars of ELIZABETHAN THEATER. That the second Globe, built after the fire of 1613, was constructed on the foundation of the first has always been supposed, in view of the speed with which the theater reopened. This is now less certain, for different methods of foundation construction can be detected in the excavations. A likely scenario, experts argue, is that the fire damaged the foundation as well as destroying the superstructure, and that an alternative mode of construction was used in patching it up before the new superstructure was built atop it.

The base of a stair turret has been uncovered. These structures, abutting the theater building proper, housed only a spiral staircase that provided access to the galleries. It appears from 16th-century images that the first Globe did not have this feature but that the second did, and the excavation apparently confirms this. Such a turret was a new device, designed to speed the flow of the crowds, and it was surely a sensible addition to the Globe, when necessity required rebuilding. Also, the angle between two of the polygonal building's walls has also been excavated, and it suggests that the Globe had 20 sides (though the Rose excavation has made it clear that the polygon could be irregular, so this matter remains a subject of debate) and was larger than anticipated, with a diameter of perhaps 100 feet. However, much remains unknown; only a small fraction of the Globe site can be excavated, for most of it is beneath a building—Anchor Terrace, a residential development of 1839 recently converted to modern apartments—that is a designated landmark. It is hoped that a means of excavating beneath this building can be devised; until then, most details of the Globe's construction and appearance remain unknown, outside of the evidence that was already available before the 1989 archaeological discoveries.

Before the Rose and Globe foundations were discovered, theorists relied on drawings of the theaters in several large-scale panoramic scenes of London; on the builder's contract for the FORTUNE THEATRE (which was expressly modeled on the Globe); and on the only known sketch of the interior of an Elizabethan theater, a drawing of the SWAN THEATRE. On the strength of this admittedly inconclusive evidence, two modern "replicas" of the Globe were begun during the 1980s. One opened in Tokyo in 1988 and has served chiefly as a venue for English-language productions of Shakespeare's plays. In 2003 it succumbed to economic troubles and ceased operations, and its future is uncertain. The other, built near the actual Globe's location in Southwark under the leadership of Sam WANAMAKER, opened in 1991 and has become a major London tourist attraction.

The new London playhouse, known as Shakespeare's Globe Theatre, is part of a complex of buildings, including a large underground museum devoted to Elizabethan theater; other exhibition

Artists' depictions such as this one, while not fully trustworthy, give us an idea of what the Globe Theatre might have looked like. *(Courtesy of Culver Pictures, Inc.)*

space; and several theatrical workshop areas within a replica of a 17th-century indoor theater, built to a design by Inigo Jones (1573–1652), the leading architect of Shakespeare's day (see BLACK-FRIARS THEATRE).

Gloucestershire County in southwestern England, setting for three scenes of *2 Henry IV* and one of *Richard II*.

In 3.2 of *2 Henry IV* Falstaff, marching to join the army at GAULTREE FOREST, drafts several recruits from among a number of villagers assembled by the local justice of the peace, Shallow. The scene is chiefly a satire of corrupt Elizabethan recruiting practices, but it also presents a collection of humorous provincial portraits, both of the gentry—bluff, silly Shallow and his taciturn cousin Silence—and of the villagers Mouldy, Shadow, Wart, Feeble, and Bullcalf. A reference to the Lincolnshire market town of Stamford (3.2.38) suggests that this scene may have been intended to be set in that county, which would make much more sense in terms of

Falstaff's march from London to Gaultree. However, Shallow's jurisdiction is specified as Gloucestershire in 4.3.80 and 126, as well as in the opening lines of *The Merry Wives of Windsor.* It is thought that Shakespeare changed his mind about the location while writing *2 Henry IV*—possibly while interrupting that task to write *The Merry Wives of Windsor*—and with his typical inattention to minor contradictions, he did not rewrite the earlier scene.

In 5.1 and 5.3 of *2 Henry IV* Shallow's home is the setting for another delightful sampling of rural England, where the daily tasks of a small country estate are attended to and a party honoring Falstaff is arranged and then held. Shallow reminisces windily about his hell-raising student days, while Silence turns mildly boisterous when drunk. Shallow's steward, Davy, is introduced; he sees to the running of his master's farm and demands a court ruling in favor of a friend, in an amusing vignette of small-time corruption. Place-names and family names—e.g., William Visor of Woncot and Clement Perkes "a'th'Hill" (5.1.35)—are used with a congenial familiarity. Although this rural ambience is somewhat comical and its inhabitants humorously limited, it is plain that Shakespeare was fond of these people, and the Gloucestershire scenes of the play contribute greatly to *2 Henry IV*'s depiction of English life.

In 2.3 of *Richard II,* Gloucestershire's location, near WALES and the Irish Sea, makes it strategically important. Henry Bolingbroke marches there to intercept King Richard II as he returns from Ireland. The Earl of Northumberland speaks of Gloucestershire's "high wild hills and rough uneven ways" (2.3.4), referring to the Cotswold Hills. Although this region seems tame today, it was heavily forested and difficult to cross in Shakespeare's day.

Glover, Julia (1781–1850)   English actress. One of the most respected performers of her time, Glover, who claimed descent from Thomas BETTERTON, made her debut as a child, playing the Duke of York, young nephew of Richard III. Although she became quite obese, she successfully portrayed Desdemona, Lady Macbeth, Hamlet, and other Shakespearean characters, and she was one of the few women ever to play Falstaff.

Glyn, Isabel (active 1849–1867)   English actress. Isabel Glyn was best known for her performances as Cleopatra. She played the role in several revivals of *Antony and Cleopatra,* most notably that of Samuel PHELPS in 1849, which reintroduced the play to the London stage. She also succeeded as Queen Gertrude in *Hamlet.*

Goethe, Johann Wolfgang von (1749–1832)   German poet, dramatist, novelist, and critic. Goethe was one of the leaders of the Romantic movement that swept Europe in the early 19th century, and he found some of his inspiration in the scale and power of Shakespeare's plays. As the foremost German writer of his day—or any other, in most opinions—his enthusiasm made Shakespeare's position in German literature permanent. His influence in this respect, as in many others, spread beyond Germany to the rest of Europe.

A lawyer, the young Goethe wrote poems and plays, including *Götz von Berlichingen* (1773), a historical drama modeled on Shakespeare's HISTORY PLAYS. His novel *The Sorrows of Young Werther* (1774), the story of an unrequited lover who commits suicide, was a sensation throughout Europe and established Goethe as a leading literary figure. In 1775 he became a government minister in Weimar, one of the many small countries of 18th-century Germany, and remained there for the rest of his life. In addition to serving as the chief aide to the ruling Duke, he also ran a small theater that was highly influential on subsequent German drama. Oddly, however, he did not find Shakespeare's plays successful on stage, and he focused instead on their literary qualities. The only one he produced was his own radical abridgement of *Romeo and Juliet* (1812), using the translation of August von SCHLEGEL.

Goethe is still regarded as one of the giants of European literature—one of the few writers of Shakespeare's stature—and one of the great men of German history. Among his many works are the play *Iphigenia in Tauris* (1788), the epic poem *Faust* (published at intervals from 1790 to 1832), and the novel *Wilhelm Meister* (1796). He was also a scientist, and he published respected works on optics, anatomy, and botany.

Goffe, Matthew (Matthew Gough) (d. 1450) Historical figure mentioned briefly in *2 Henry VI*. In 4.5, during the battle to drive Jack Cade's rebels from London, Lord Scales asserts that he will assign Goffe to a sector of the fighting, and in a stage direction at the beginning of 4.7, Goffe is said to be killed in a skirmish. The historical Gough, a renowned warrior in the French wars, had shared command of the TOWER OF LONDON with Scales, and he was indeed killed while fighting the rebels. His phantom presence in the play may reflect an actual appearance that was deleted in a revision.

Golding, Arthur (ca. 1536–ca. 1605) English writer and translator. In 1567 Golding published his famous translation of OVID's *Metamorphoses*, which appears to have been one of Shakespeare's favorite books; material derived from it, as well as direct quotations, pepper the plays and poems. The work was widely popular among other Elizabethan readers as well, at least in part because Ovid's poetry is somewhat racy, though Golding was himself a staunch conservative Protestant who allegorized and moralized the ancient poet's mythological tales. He also translated selections from the classical historians and from contemporary Protestant reformers, most notably John Calvin (1509–64).

good quarto An early edition of a Shakespeare play, printed in QUARTO format. A good quarto was derived from an authoritative source, such as Shakespeare's FOUL PAPERS, and reflects what the author actually wrote, as opposed to a BAD QUARTO, which was reconstructed from memory. Fourteen early editions of Shakespeare's plays are good quartos. They are: Q1 of *Titus Andronicus* (1594); Q1 of *Richard II* (1597); Q1 of *Richard III* (1597); Q of *Love's Labour's Lost* (1598); Q0 of *1 Henry IV* (1598); Q2 of *Romeo and Juliet* (1599); Q of *2 Henry IV* (1600); Q1 of *The Merchant of Venice* (1600); Q1 of *A Midsummer Night's Dream* (1600); Q of *Much Ado About Nothing* (1600); Q2 of *Hamlet* (1604); Q of *Troilus and Cressida* (1609); Q1 of *Othello* (1622); and Q of *The Two Noble Kinsmen* (1634). *Romeo and Juliet* and *Hamlet* also appeared as bad quartos, and Q1 of *Richard III* is sometimes classed as a bad quarto, for its generally sound text contains certain minor flaws that suggest that it was reconstructed from memory.

Goslicius, Laurentius Grimaldus (Wawrzyniec Goślicki) (d. 1604) Polish statesman and author whose chief work was possibly a minor source for *Hamlet* and *Measure for Measure*. Goslicius (sometimes known in English as Grimaldus) is considered the greatest statesman of 16th-century Poland. He wrote, in Latin, a manual of advice for government officials and diplomats, *De Optimo Senatore* (Venice, 1568), that was among the most admired books of its kind for several generations. An anonymous English translation, *The Counsellor*, appeared in 1598 (2nd ed., 1604), and it is echoed in several passages in *Hamlet*. Goslicius is thought to have inspired the name Polonius; the title page of *The Counsellor* declared the work "consecrated to the Polonian Empire," and it seems likely that Shakespeare whimsically appropriated the author's nationality as a name for his Danish minister. Further, Goslicius's work may have influenced the creation of both the Duke and Angelo—for it expounds on both good and bad magistrates—in *Measure for Measure*.

Gosson, Henry (active 1601–1640) LONDON publisher and bookseller, producer of the first two editions of *Pericles*. In 1609 Gosson capitalized on the great popularity of Shakespeare's ROMANCE and had William WHITE print a pirated edition of *Pericles*. Known as Q1, it is a BAD QUARTO, whose text was taken from the recollections of actors or viewers. The publication was a great success, and Gosson produced a second edition (Q2) in the same year. This made *Pericles* one of the few Shakespeare plays to appear in two Quartos in the same year.

Gosson, who inherited his business from his father, published mostly short-lived literature such as ballads, news sheets, and joke books. *Pericles* was the only play text he published. He prospered and owned several shops in London, but little else is known of his life.

Gosson, Stephen (1554–1624) English writer, a Puritan opponent of the professional theater. Gosson, a poet, dramatist, and—probably—actor, changed his life in his early 20s and became a clergyman. He wrote three books (published between 1579 and 1582) that declared poetry and drama unsavoury influences on society. The theater—which he called a "market of bawdry"—came in for particular abuse. He was willing to exclude only a few sober plays, including one of his own, from his general verdict that drama "was not to be suffered in a Christian common weale." Thomas LODGE began his literary career with a rejoinder, *Defence of Plays* (1581), and Sir Philip SIDNEY may have been inspired by him to write his great *Apology for Poetry* (1583). Several companies revived Gosson's plays, hoping to embarrass him and capitalize on the publicity the controversy had created. Despite his enmity toward his former profession, Gosson remained a lifelong friend of the great actor Edward ALLEYN.

Gosson was among the most prominent of Puritan opponents of the theater. Although in the 16th century such opinions were merely a nuisance to the profession (see, e.g., COBHAM, WILLIAM BROOKE, LORD), they triumphed later during the Civil Wars. Beginning in 1642 the Puritan revolutionary government closed the theaters of England for almost 20 years.

Gough, Robert (Robert Goughe) (d. 1624) English actor. Gough is one of the 26 men listed in the FIRST FOLIO as the "Principall Actors" in Shakespeare's plays, but he is not known to have performed in any particular role and was clearly a minor player. He may have played a Lord in *All's Well That Ends Well,* for the character is designated as "G" in speech headings in the Folio text of the play (but see GILBURNE, SAMUEL). Gough was probably a member of STRANGE'S MEN by 1590—"R. Go" appears in a Strange's Men's cast list. He was probably employed by the CHAMBERLAIN'S MEN or its successor, the KING'S MEN, sometime before 1603, when Thomas POPE willed him some of his costumes and stage weapons. He was married to Augustine PHILLIPS's sister in 1603, and he witnessed Phillips's will in 1605. He is recorded as a partner in the King's Men in 1619 and 1621, but no more is known of him. His son, Alexander Gough (1614–after 1655), was also an actor for the King's Men who specialized in female characters. He was with the company until the theaters were closed by the revolutionary government in 1642, after which he participated for some time in clandestine performances at private homes. He eventually became a publisher.

Gounod, Charles François (1818–1893)   French composer who wrote an OPERA based on *Romeo and Juliet.* A popular composer in his own day, Gounod is now considered a minor figure in French music history, best known for *Roméo et Juliette* (1867) and another opera, his masterpiece, *Faust* (1859). Few of his other compositions are still performed.

Grafton, Richard (d. 1572)   English chronicler and historian whose works, published between 1562 and 1571, were consulted by Shakespeare when writing his HISTORY PLAYS. They provided the playwright with a number of minor details.

Granada, Luis de (1504–1588)   Spanish mystic and writer, author of a minor source for *Hamlet.* Granada, a Dominican monk and theologian, wrote several works on prayer and mystical contemplation, including *Libro de la oración y consideración* (1554), usually translated as *Of Prayer and Meditation,* which probably influenced some of Hamlet's observations on graves and death in 5.1. This book was among the most popular religious treatises of the 16th century, and many English translations were published, beginning with the work of Richard HOPKINS in 1582. Granada emphasized the presence of God as manifested in nature in lyrical works that are still appreciated; an anthology in English, *The Summa of Christian Life,* was published as recently as 1954.

Granville, George (1667–1735)   English dramatist and politician, creator of an adaptation of *The Merchant of Venice.* After graduating from Cambridge University, Granville wrote *The Jew of Venice,* a farce based on Shakespeare's play that was produced in 1701 with Thomas BETTERTON playing Bassanio and the popular comic Thomas Doggett (ca. 1670–1721) as Shylock. Though it has little literary merit, this work was popular for 40 years before it was superseded by Charles MACKLIN's revival of Shakespeare's play.

Granville was elected to Parliament in 1702, which was the beginning of his meteoric political career. He became secretary of war in 1710 and a peer in 1711, but he was imprisoned in 1715 for supporting the Jacobite invasion (see STUART DYNASTY). From 1722 to 1782 he lived in exile in France.

Granville-Barker, Harley (1877–1946) English actor, director, and Shakespearean commentator. After a successful career in the theater, Granville-Barker wrote a series of *Prefaces to Shakespeare* (1927–46) that covered 12 of Shakespeare's plays. He addressed questions of interpretation and staging that arise in actual production in the theater, rather than taking a scholar's point of view. It is for these well-written and influential texts that he remains best known today.

As a director, Granville-Barker specialized in modern works, chiefly those of Ibsen and George Bernard SHAW. He only staged three of Shakespeare's plays—*The Winter's Tale* and *Twelfth Night* in 1912, and *A Midsummer Night's Dream* in 1914—but they were revolutionary and have greatly influenced the modern staging of ELIZABETHAN DRAMA. He used uncut texts and sped up the pace, and he also cut much traditional stage business to focus attention on the plays themselves. He extended the stage into the audience in an effort to simulate the theater of Elizabethan times. By applying William POEL's notions of simplified staging, though he didn't go so far as to eliminate scenery altogether, Granville-Barker succeeded in making a commercial success of an idealistic approach to Shakespearean production.

As a young man, Granville-Barker acted in the productions of Poel and Ben GREET; he was especially acclaimed as Richard II. He also wrote plays, and his *The Voysey Inheritance* (1905), a satirical comedy in the vein of his close friend Shaw, is regarded as one of the best dramas of its period.

Gravelot, Hubert (1699–1773) French painter and engraver, illustrator of Shakespeare's plays. Gravelot worked on two illustrated editions of Shakespeare, THEOBALD's second edition (1740)

and HANMER's deluxe volumes (1744), each of which contained 36 illustrations. For the first of these, Gravelot provided all of the 36 illustrations but engraved only eight of them himself; for the second, he provided only five illustrations but engraved all 36. The other images were provided by Francis HAYMAN.

During his residency in London (1732–45), Gravelot was for English artists the most important source of the French rococo style in painting and decoration. He was more important as an illustrator than as a painter, and few of his paintings survive, but he was an important influence on painters such as his close friend William Hogarth (1697–1764) and his students Hayman and Thomas Gainsborough (1727–88).

Green, John (active 1606–1627) English actor active in Germany. Green was a member of one of Robert BROWNE's touring companies as early as 1606, and he had his own company beginning in 1615 until at least 1627. He succeeded Browne as the most important English influence on the roots of German drama, which were influenced by English touring companies between the 1590s and the middle of the 17th century. A listing of Green's repertoire in 1626 has survived; it included plays titled *Romeo und Julia*, *Julius Caesar*, *Lear König von Engelandt*, and *Hamlet einem printzen in Dennemark*, almost certainly Shakespeare's plays or adaptations of them.

Greene, Robert (1558–1592) English writer, a possible collaborator with Shakespeare and author of the earliest literary reference to him, as well as of the chief source for *The Winter's Tale* and a minor source for *Troilus and Cressida*. Greene was one of the UNIVERSITY WITS who revolutionized ELIZABETHAN DRAMA in the 1580s. He wrote at least 10 plays, mostly romantic comedies, the best-known of which is *Friar Bacon and Friar Bungay* (1589), still occasionally staged. He also wrote romantic novels—including *Pandosto* (1588), from which Shakespeare took the plot of *The Winter's Tale*—and numerous essays, such as those collected in *Eupheus his Censure to Philautus* (1587), which provided minor ideas and incidents for *Troilus and Cressida*.

Greene's reference to the young Shakespeare was made in *Greene's Groatsworth of Wit* (1592), one of several brief repentant but embittered autobiographies written as he approached death (he had led a dissolute life among criminals and whores after abandoning his wife and child). In this angry tract Greene advised other playwrights not to trust actors, declaring them to be uneducated, dishonest poseurs and citing the example of "an upstart Crow . . . that with his *Tygers hart wrapt in a Players hyde* [Greene's emphasis], supposes he is as well able to bombast out a blanke verse as the best of you: and . . . is in his owne conceit the onely Shake-scene in a country."

After Greene's death, his editor, Henry CHETTLE, issued a public apology to Shakespeare, but the power of slander survives retraction: the parody of "O tiger's heart wrapp'd in a woman's hide" (*3 Henry VI* 1.4.137) has been offered as evidence that Greene wrote the play—or at least part of it, including that line—and that he was complaining of plagiarism, or at least usurped credit. But although 21st-century commentators have come to believe that at least several of Shakespeare's early plays were written collaboratively, and accept that Greene may have had a hand in several of them (most probably *Edward III*, *Titus Andronicus*, *The Comedy of Errors*, and *The Two Gentlemen of Verona*), most believe that the parody in *Groatsworth of Wit* was simply a mocking of Shakespeare's bold language.

Greene, Thomas (ca. 1578–1641)   Lawyer in STRATFORD, friend and possibly kinsman of Shakespeare. Greene, who was from nearby Warwick, became the town clerk of Stratford in 1602, shortly after becoming a lawyer. He may have known Shakespeare in LONDON when he studied at the INNS OF COURT, for he knew the playwright John MARSTON, but he was in any case close to the Shakespeare family for years in Stratford. His children were named after the playwright and his wife, Anne HATHAWAY Shakespeare, and he and his family lived at Shakespeare's NEW PLACE for a time, perhaps more than a year, while waiting on the renovation of another home. Some of his correspondence has survived, and in it he several times refers to Shakespeare as his "cousin." No family

connection is known, and the word was used loosely in those days, but Greene may have been a blood relation of the playwright. His brother John (ca. 1575–1640), was also a lawyer and close to the family. He represented Susanna SHAKESPEARE Hall as a trustee of BLACKFRIARS GATEHOUSE after she inherited that property from the playwright.

Thomas Greene was closely involved in the political crisis that gripped Stratford in the years just preceding Shakespeare's death (see WELCOMBE). He and Shakespeare jointly owned a contract to collect the taxes on agricultural lands that were proposed in 1614 for conversion to sheep farming—a politically unpopular process known as enclosure. Shakespeare negotiated an arrangement whereby if enclosure went through they were protected against loss but still might profit. However, the town of Stratford opposed enclosure, and as town clerk, Greene worked against it successfully. It has been suggested that disagreements over this political crisis, which gripped Stratford for two years, may have led to the odd fact that Greene is not mentioned in Shakespeare's will. A year after Shakespeare's death, Greene moved to Bristol.

Greet, Philip Barling Ben (1857–1936)   British actor and theatrical entrepreneur. As an actor, director, and producer, Ben Greet was dedicated to presenting Shakespeare's plays with fidelity to the playwright's text, after centuries of adaptation and traditional stage business had become attached to virtually all of the plays. He insisted on simple staging, in contrast to the late-19th-century fondness for extravagant spectacle, and he endeavored to bring Shakespeare's plays to a wide audience. Between 1886 and 1914 he toured Britain and America with a repertory company that he then took to the OLD VIC THEATRE, which he helped establish as Britain's most important center of Shakespearean production.

Greg, Walter Wilson (1875–1959)   British scholar. Widely regarded as among the greatest of Shakespearean scholars, Greg edited the diaries and papers of Philip HENSLOWE (published 1904–08), and assisted A. W. POLLARD in researching his groundbreaking *Shakespeare Folios and Quartos* (1909). He went on to produce many valuable studies, including *Dramatic Documents of the Elizabethan Playhouses* (1931), *The Editorial Problem in Shakespeare* (1942), *Shakespeare First Folio* (1955), and the monumental four-volume *A Bibliography of the English Printed Drama to the Restoration* (1939–59).

Greville, Curtis (active 1622–1631)   English actor who may have performed in early productions of *The Two Noble Kinsmen* and *The Taming of the Shrew*. In the first edition of *Kinsmen* (Q1, 1634), the stage direction at 4.2.70 designates the Messenger as "Curtis"; in the opening stage direction of 5.3, the Attendants called for—one of whom is presumably the Servant—are named, and one of them "Curtis." Scholars believe that these references are to Greville, indicating that he played the parts in an early production by the KING'S MEN. Greville was with the company from before 1626 until 1631, so this clue (with similar evidence concerning Thomas TUCKFIELD) suggests that Q1 was printed from a PROMPTBOOK of the 1620s. Some scholars believe that *The Shrew*'s CURTIS similarly takes his name from Greville's portrayal.

Little is known of Greville. In 1622 he moved from LADY ELIZABETH'S MEN to the PALSGRAVE'S MEN, presumably as part of the latter company's effort to reopen the FORTUNE THEATRE, closed by fire. By 1626 Greville was with the King's Men, with whom he is known to have played several minor roles.

Greville, Fulke (Lord Brooke) (1554–1628)   English poet and author, possibly a patron of Shakespeare. Greville is best known for his biography of Philip SIDNEY, whose close friend he had been since the age of 10. However, he also wrote a considerable body of poetry; two plays; and several treatises on politics, religion, and education. He was a significant figure in RENAISSANCE English literature in other ways, as well. As a member of the "Areopagus" group of poets—with Sidney, Edmund SPENSER, and others—he helped stimulate the use of classical METER in English poetry. As a wealthy man he was a patron of writers and assisted Samuel DANIEL, among others. He also served as a diplomat and economic adviser to both Queen Elizabeth I (see Elizabeth I in *Henry VIII*) and King JAMES I. The latter monarch made him a baron on his retirement

from government in 1621, and therefore he is sometimes known as Lord Brooke.

The young Shakespeare may have benefited from Greville's largesse. According to a 1665 account, Greville once described himself as worthy only because he had been "Shakespeare and Ben JONSON's master . . . and Sir Philip Sidney's friend." Most scholars regard this anecdote as apocryphal, but whether or not he did indeed act as an elder adviser and patron to the young playwright, the remark reflects Greville's famed modesty. His EPITAPH, composed by himself, reads "Servant to Queen Elizabeth, Counsellor to King James, Friend to Sir Philip Sydney."

Griffin, Bartholomew (d. 1602)   Author of at least one and probably four of the poems attributed to Shakespeare in THE PASSIONATE PILGRIM (1599). Little is known of Griffin, who is remembered primarily because one SONNET from his 62-sonnet sequence, *Fidessa* (1596)—a conventional and undistinguished work—was published as no. 11 in William JAGGARD's spurious anthology. Three other poems in the collection (nos. 4, 6, and 9) resemble no. 11 closely enough that they are often attributed to Griffin as well. His preface to *Fidessa* suggests that Griffin may have been a gentleman and a lawyer, and it also asserted that he was writing a long pastoral poem, but, if this was completed and published, it has not survived.

Guthrie, Tyrone (1900–1971)   British theatrical producer. Guthrie directed the OLD VIC THEATRE from 1933 to 1945, and he was chiefly responsible for the creation of the Shakespeare Festival in Stratford, Ontario, in 1953 and the Guthrie Theatre in Minneapolis in 1963. His daringly experimental productions sparked controversy in England and America. Particularly noted were his 1937 *Twelfth Night* and his renderings of *All's Well That Ends Well* as a farce (1953 and 1959, in Ontario and STRATFORD, England, respectively). He wrote several books, including *Theatre Prospect* (1932) and *A New Theatre* (1964).

Gwinne, Matthew (Matthew Gwinn) (ca. 1558–1627)   English physician and playwright, author of a possible inspiration for *Macbeth*. Gwinne's Latin MASQUE *Tres Sibyllae* was performed on the occasion of King JAMES I's visit to Oxford in 1605. It features prophecies addressed to Macbeth and Banquo, and alludes to the king's legendary descent from Banquo. Some scholars believe that its success with its royal auditor may have inspired Shakespeare to compose his own version of the Macbeth tale.

Gwinne was closely associated with Oxford, though he also had a medical practice in London. He was the supervisor of theatrical productions at the university in the 1590s, and he was highly respected as an academic dramatist, chiefly on the strength of two Latin plays, *Nero* (1603) and *Vertumnis* (1605). The latter work gained an unfortunate notoriety when it put the king to sleep.

H

Hacket, Marian See Hostess, in *The Taming of the Shrew*.

Hakluyt, Richard (ca. 1552–1616) English geographer. Hakluyt (pronounced "haklit") was a clergyman, but he devoted his career to the publication of materials concerning the exploration of the New World and the promotion of English efforts in this realm. He learned the major European languages in order to have access to all possible sources of information. In 1582 he published *Divers voyages touching the discoveries of America*. He was also employed as a diplomat and spy by the government, serving as chaplain to the British ambassador in FRANCE from 1583 to 1589. During this period he compiled his most important work, *The Principall Navigations, Voyages, and Discoveries of the English Nation* (1589). As revised in 1600, this work contained a well-known map, probably the "new map with the augmentation of the Indies" referred to in *Twelfth Night* (3.2.76–77). Some of Hakluyt's material was gathered by John PORY, and the collection was further enlarged by Hakluyt's friend Samuel Purchas (ca. 1575–1626), who published an account of a shipwreck by William STRACHEY that influenced Shakespeare's *The Tempest*. Hakluyt's *Voyages*, as his book is known, was very influential on the course of English exploration, besides being extremely popular among lay readers. It is still in print. In 1846 the Royal Geographic Society founded the Hakluyt Society, which continues to publish historical accounts of explorations and travels, including new editions of Hakluyt's works.

Hall, Arthur (ca. 1540–1604) English writer. Hall completed the first English translation of HOMER; his version of the first 10 books of the *Iliad* was published in 1581. Shakespeare surely knew this work, and it may have influenced his treatment of Homeric materials in *The Rape of Lucrece* and *Troilus and Cressida* (although it is clear that in the latter work he relied chiefly on the translation by George CHAPMAN).

Hall, an orphan, was raised in the household of the leading Elizabethan statesman Lord BURGHLEY. As an adult, he was notorious for riotous living and was imprisoned several times. Although he began his translation of the *Iliad* while in his 20s, he did not complete it for many years. Inaccurate and awkward, it was completely overshadowed by Chapman's *Iliad*, which appeared between 1598 and 1611, and has been little read ever since.

Hall, Edward (Edward Halle) (ca. 1498–1547) English historian, author of an important source for Shakespeare's HISTORY PLAYS. Hall's account of the 15th-century WARS OF THE ROSES, *The Union of the Two Noble and Illustre Families of Lancaster and York* (1548), was particularly influential on the *Henry VI* plays, though echoes of it occur throughout the eight plays (see TETRALOGY) that deal with the wars. Hall's central theme in the *Union* is that the weakness of King Henry VI and the resulting wars were God's punishment for the sin of Henry's grandfather, Henry IV, who altered God's intended line of kings when he usurped the throne. This notion is in turn based on the premise that history has a moral purpose, set by God. Both of these ideas are strongly evident in Shakespeare's plays. However, Hall's work was also employed by Shakespeare's most important source on British history, Raphael HOLINSHED, and it is often difficult to determine which source the playwright was using. Scholars generally feel that Hall was his major source for the history of the wars, while Holinshed was used chiefly for additional details, particularly in the *Henry VI* plays and *Richard III*.

Hall incorporated earlier histories into the *Union*, notably Sir Thomas MORE's *History of King Richard III* (published in Richard GRAFTON's chronicles), and Polydore VERGIL's *Historia Anglia* (1534). Hall was in turn incorporated by later writers, including Holinshed and John STOW. Thus, his work is a central element in the 16th century's picture of the 15th. Hall was a lawyer and politician who wrote his history with the specific intention of glorifying the TUDOR DYNASTY, whose foundation ended the Wars of the Roses. In this, he was part of a well-established tradition of Tudor history writing that was consciously instituted by King Henry VII as a type of propaganda. Shakespeare, though his own sensibility permeates his work and makes it more interesting and comprehensive, was also a part of this tradition.

Hall, Elizabeth (1608–1670) Shakespeare's granddaughter, child of Susanna SHAKESPEARE and John HALL. Elizabeth was eight when Shakespeare died, and the playwright left her most of his silver. After her mother's death in 1649 she also inherited most of the rest of the Shakespeare estate, including NEW PLACE and the BIRTHPLACE. She married Thomas NASH in 1626 and lived with him at New Place, though probably not until after her father's death in 1635. Nash died in 1647, and she remarried in 1649 to John Bernard (d. 1674), with whom she moved to Northamptonshire. She had no children by either husband and was Shakespeare's last descendant. She left the Shakespeare birthplace to her cousin George Hart, grandson of Joan SHAKESPEARE, and the remainder of her grandfather's estate, including New Place, to Bernard, whose heirs sold it.

Hall, John (1575–1635) Shakespeare's son-in-law, the husband of Susanna SHAKESPEARE and

father of Elizabeth HALL. Hall was a notable doctor who probably treated his father-in-law and was certainly well regarded by him, for with his wife he was executor of the playwright's will. Hall, the son of a physician from Bedfordshire, studied medicine at Cambridge University and possibly in France, though he never received a formal degree in the subject. He settled in STRATFORD around 1600 and was soon regarded as the region's leading doctor. He was reportedly a very devout Protestant, perhaps with Puritan leanings, and it has been speculated that he did not approve of his famous father-in-law's profession. During the Civil Wars his widow sold one of his Latin medical notebooks—apparently not realizing that he had written it—and it was later published as *Select Observations on English Bodies* (1657). It contains accounts of many of his patients—including his wife and Michael DRAYTON—but unfortunately begins only in 1617 and so does not include Shakespeare.

Hall, Peter (b. 1930) British theatrical director. Hall directed the ROYAL SHAKESPEARE COMPANY in STRATFORD from 1960 to 1968 and the National Theatre Company of Britain from 1972 to 1988. Among his most notable Shakespearean productions have been *Henry V* (1960), two stagings of *Coriolanus* (1959 and 1984, starring Laurence OLIVIER and Ian MCKELLEN, respectively), and a rare uncut *Hamlet* (1975).

Hall, Susanna Shakespeare See SHAKESPEARE, SUSANNA.

Hall, William (active 1577–1620) English printer, a possible "Mr. W. H." of the dedication to the first edition (1609) of the *Sonnets*. Hall was mostly a printer of business papers and had no known connection with Shakespeare or his works. However, he has been suggested by the scholar Sidney LEE as a possible "Mr. W. H." on the strength of the coincidence of initials and the fact that the next word in the dedication is "all." Lee speculated that Hall acquired for publisher Thomas THORPE the copies of the poems from which the book was published, and was thus called the "onlie begetter" of the *Sonnets*. Aside from this supposition there is no evidence to associate Hall with the work.

Halle, Edward See HALL, EDWARD.

Halliwell-Phillips, James Orchard (1820–1889) British scholar. A longtime librarian at Jesus College, Cambridge, Halliwell-Phillips was one of the most important 19th-century Shakespeare scholars. He published a *Life of Shakespeare* (1848), an edition of the *Works* (1853–61), and a collection of documentary materials on the playwright's life, *Outlines of the Life of Shakespeare* (1881). The *Outlines* is a trove of material that has been used by all later biographers. He was a founder of the original Shakespeare Society in 1840 and the first editor of the STRATFORD archives.

Hamlett, Katherine (d. 1579) Englishwoman whose death may be reflected in that of Ophelia in *Hamlet*. A resident of Tippington, a village near STRATFORD, Mistress Hamlett was drowned in the Avon River while fetching water, and a coroner's jury hesitated over the possibility of suicide before declaring, two months later, that she had died a natural death. It has been speculated that the coincidental similarity between a family name he once knew and the name of his protagonist might have recalled Katherine Hamlett's death to the playwright—who was 15 when it occurred—as he described Ophelia's death by drowning, declared "doubtful" (5.1.220) by the Priest, although the coroner "finds it Christian burial" (5.1.4–5).

Hands, Terry (b. 1941) British theatrical director. Hands was associated with the ROYAL SHAKESPEARE COMPANY in STRATFORD from 1966 to 1991, serving as artistic director and chief executive from 1986. He has directed many of Shakespeare's plays, at Stratford, in the United States, and on the Continent. Since 1997 he has headed a leading theater in Wales.

Hanmer, Thomas (1677–1746) Early editor of Shakespeare's plays. Hanmer, a former Speaker of the House of Commons, was the fourth editor of the collected plays. His edition was published in 1744 in an elaborately bound and expensive set of six volumes. It was illustrated by Hubert GRAVELOT and Francis HAYMAN and was intended for a wealthy market. Hanmer was a disrespectful editor who inserted alterations of his own, insisted that passages he did not approve of could not have been by Shakespeare, and failed to annotate adoptions of the readings of earlier editors. In addition, he did not go back to the early texts but simply worked from the collection published by Alexander POPE in 1725.

Harfleur City on the northern coast of FRANCE, location in *Henry V*. Harfleur is besieged by the army of Henry V. In 3.3 the king describes the bloody terror Harfleur can expect if it continues to resist, and the Governor surrenders the city. This episode is a good instance of the play's ambiguity. Henry may be seen as merciful and statesmanlike; he spares the town, and he explicitly orders Exeter, "Use mercy to them all" (3.3.54). On the other hand, his brilliant evocation of a sacked city, with vivid descriptions of rape and murder, stresses the horrors of an army gone amok, an emphasis that reinforces a reading of *Henry V* as a mordant antiwar work.

Harington, Sir John (1561–1612) First English translator of ARIOSTO's *Orlando Furioso*, a source for *Much Ado About Nothing*. Harington, a godson of Queen Elizabeth I (see Elizabeth I in *Henry VIII*), spent much of his life at court. It is thought that his translation of *Orlando Furioso* (1591) was made at the queen's command, as an ironic punishment for having independently translated one of its indecent passages.

Harris, Frank (James Thomas) (1856–1931) British author and editor. Best known today for his sexually explicit autobiography, *My Life and Loves* (1927), Harris also wrote short stories, two plays, a novel, essays, biographies, and other works. Among these were *The Man Shakespeare and His Tragic Life Story* (1909), a biography laced with elaborate interpretation of the *Sonnets* and various plays as detailed evidence of Shakespeare's life, especially his love life. For example, Harris advocated the theory, first suggested by Thomas TYLER, that Mary FITTON was the "Dark Lady" of the *Sonnets*, and he furthered this notion in his play *Shakespeare and His Love* (1910) and in another book, *The Women of Shakespeare* (1911). He saw Shakespeare's works as delivering a message to humanity, extolling forgiveness and love, and he equated it with Christ's. Being immensely egotistical, he identified himself with these two personages—and GOETHE—as "God's spies" (*King Lear*, 5.3.17).

Harris was an adventurer before he became a literary figure; he ran away from his home in Ireland at 14 and worked at various jobs, including as a cowboy, in America and Europe, before settling in London and establishing himself as a writer of fiction. He became the editor of two of Britain's most important magazines, the *Fortnightly Review* (1886–94) and the *Saturday Review* (1894–98), in which he published H. G. Wells, Oscar Wilde, and George Bernard SHAW, among others. He later wrote biographies of Wilde and Shaw. He cultivated a scandalous reputation, aided by his persistent campaign against Victorian prudery and his pro-German sentiments during World War I. He made many enemies, and by 1920 he was neglected and impoverished. While his reputation as a writer has improved since his death and his importance in literary history is acknowledged, his scholarship—including his work on Shakespeare—is generally derided; even his autobiography has been found to be grossly inaccurate and self-serving.

Harris, Henry (ca. 1630–1681)   English actor. A leading man in William DAVENANT's theater company, Harris acted many Shakespearean parts, including Cardinal Wolsey in *Henry VIII*, for which he was particularly noted. He also played Horatio opposite the Hamlet of the great Thomas BETTERTON, in the first staging of *Hamlet* (1661) after the reopening of the English theaters following the Puritan revolution. In 1662 he became the first Romeo to play opposite a female Juliet (Mary SAUNDERSON), as actresses were admitted to English stages. He was felt by some contemporaries, including Samuel PEPYS, to be as fine an actor as Betterton. He joined Betterton in 1671 in the management of London's Dorset Garden Theatre, serving as the artistic director.

Harrison, George Bagshawe (1894–1991)   English scholar, author of many works on Shakespeare. An authority on the Elizabethan background of Shakespeare's life, Harrison was also the general editor of the Penguin editions of Shakespeare's works, published between 1937 and 1959. His *England in Shakespeare's Day* (1928) and *Shakespeare at Work* (1933) are general studies, and he compiled a wealth of primary material from the period 1590 to 1610 in his *Elizabethan* and *Jacobean Journals* (1928, 1933, 1941), which remain essential references for the Shakespeare scholar.

Harrison, John (d. 1617)   Highly successful London publisher and bookseller, a founding member of the STATIONERS' COMPANY. In 1594 Harrison purchased the rights to Shakespeare's narrative poems *Venus and Adonis* and *The Rape of Lucrece* from Richard FIELD, who had already produced the first edition of the former. Between 1594 and 1596 Harrison published the second, third, and fourth editions (known as Q2–4, though only the first of them was a QUARTO; the others were published in an octavo format), employing Field as the printer. In 1596 he sold the rights to the poem to William LEAKE. Harrison published the first edition of *Lucrece*, printed by Field, in 1594 and the second, printed by Peter SHORT, in 1598. He passed on the rights to this work to his younger half-brother, also named John Harrison, who published Q3 and Q4 (both 1600), printed by Short, and Q5 (1607), printed by Nicholas OKES. The younger Harrison sold the rights to *Lucrece* to Roger JACKSON in 1614.

Harrison, William (1534–1593)   English historian, collaborator with Raphael HOLINSHED on Holinshed's *Chronicles of England, Scotland, and Ireland* (1577), which in its second edition (1587) was an important source for Shakespeare. Harrison, a clergyman who was personal chaplain to Lord COBHAM, served as Holinshed's assistant editor and contributed greatly to the *Chronicles*. He translated Hector BOECE's Latin history of SCOTLAND and wrote descriptions of the geography of England and Scotland. After his work with Holinshed, Harrison wrote extensively on his theory that Britain had once been inhabited by giants. He left a massive history of the world unfinished at his death.

Harsnett, Samuel (1561–1631) English clergyman and writer, author of a source for *King Lear*. An ambitious clerical politician, Harsnett wrote *A Declaration of Egregious Popish Impostures* (1603), a diatribe against Catholic priests who had claimed to exorcise demons from several lunatics in a famous case of 18 years earlier. Shakespeare took many details from this work to depict the pretended insanity of Edgar, who, in his disguise as a wandering lunatic, claims to be pursued by demons. Early in his career Harsnett was denounced as a Catholic, but he recovered and rose to be a leading figure at Cambridge University as well as bishop of several different sees. He was famous for his harsh manner and was forced to resign from his position at Cambridge when his fellow scholars launched a formal campaign against him. However, in 1628 he was named archbishop of York, the second-highest position in the Anglican Church.

Hart, Charles (d. 1693) Leading actor of the Restoration period, once thought to have been Shakespeare's grandnephew. Hart was apprenticed to Richard ROBINSON of the KING'S MEN and performed at the BLACKFRIARS THEATRE as a child, playing women's roles. During the Civil Wars, he achieved distinction in combat as an officer in the Royalist forces, and after the war he was a member of Thomas KILLIGREW's King's Company. He was particularly distinguished as Othello and Brutus (in *Julius Caesar*). Hart may have been the illegitimate son of William HART and thus mistakenly thought related to Shakespeare.

Hart, Joan Shakespeare See SHAKESPEARE, JOAN.

Hart, William (d. 1650) An actor once thought to have been Shakespeare's nephew. Hart was a member of the KING'S MEN in the mid-1630s and played Falstaff, among other roles. He apparently died unmarried, though Charles HART is believed to have been his illegitimate son. William Hart has sometimes been identified with Shakespeare's nephew, William Hart (1600–39), the son of Joan SHAKESPEARE Hart, but scholars are now confident that this idea was mistaken.

Harvey, Gabriel (ca. 1545–1630) English writer, a major literary figure of Shakespeare's day and possibly a model for the pedantic Holofernes of *Love's Labour's Lost*. Harvey was a lecturer at Cambridge University and an unpopular gadfly of the academic world. He published his generally critical opinions of the literature of the day and spent much energy futilely advocating the use of Latin prosody in English poetry. Extremely vain and critical of others, he made many enemies, and his disputatious nature hindered his aspirations to higher office in the educational establishment. In the 1590s Harvey quarreled with both Robert GREENE and Thomas NASHE in a battle of pamphlets that was much talked about in LONDON. This dispute may be the subject of the obscure topical jokes that fill *Love's Labour's Lost*, and some scholars propose that Harvey was satirized as Holofernes, though the point cannot be proven with the existing evidence. Harvey annotated the margins of his books densely, and his *Marginalia* (published 1913) record his opinions of what he read, along with much else, providing scholars with a detailed glimpse of the academic and literary world of the late 16th century. Among other things, Harvey observed that "the younger sort takes much delight in Shakespeare's *Venus and Adonis*, but his *Lucrece*, and [*Hamlet*] have it in them to please the wiser sort."

Harvey, William See HERVEY, WILLIAM.

Hathaway, Anne (Anne Hathaway Shakespeare) (ca. 1556–1623) Shakespeare's wife. Anne Hathaway was the daughter of a farmer in Shottery, a village a mile from STRATFORD. (The farmhouse in which she grew up was bought by the Shakespeare BIRTHPLACE Trust, which maintains it as a showplace.) She was eight years older than her husband, with whom she had three children: Susanna SHAKESPEARE, born in 1583, and twins, Hamnet and Judith SHAKESPEARE, born in 1585. Susanna was born only six months after the wedding, and it is obvious that Anne's pregnancy prompted the marriage, which was arranged in haste (see RICHARDSON, JOHN; SANDELLS, FULK; TEMPLE GRAFTON; WHITGIFT, JOHN). A number of commentators have presumed that the

Anne Hathaway's picturesque thatched-roof house has been restored and is now a popular tourist attraction. *(Courtesy of British Tourist Authority)*

playwright came to regret his marriage to Anne—at 21 he found himself "saddled" (as some see it) with three children and a wife nearing 30, and the plays contain a number of recommendations against both premarital sex and the taking of older wives by young men—but these are conventional remarks by fictional characters, and there exists no actual evidence of such discontent. While Shakespeare conducted his career in LONDON—as he had to—he maintained close contact with Stratford, and he eventually returned there and again lived with Anne. In his will he notoriously left Anne only the "second best bed," though this probably had no emotional significance, for she was by ancient custom

entitled to one-third of the estate, so he knew she was provided for. The special bequest of the bed was most likely made in response to some particular association with it, of which we cannot know.

Hathway, Richard (Richard Hathaway) (active 1598–1603)   English playwright. In 1598 Hathway was named by Francis MERES as a leading writer of comedies, along with Shakespeare. He wrote plays for the ADMIRAL'S MEN, usually in collaboration with other playwrights such as Michael DRAYTON and Anthony MUNDAY. Payment to Hathway for 18 such works is recorded, but the only play that has survived is *SIR JOHN OLDCASTLE*, a work that was later misattributed to Shakespeare. Hathway, whose name was often spelled "Hathaway," is sometimes confused with Shakespeare's brother-in-law, also Richard, but the playwright was no relation to Anne HATHAWAY,

Hayman, Francis (1708–1776) English painter, illustrator of the HANMER edition of Shakespeare's plays. Hayman was a onetime scene painter at the Drury Lane Theatre. He had become a well-known painter of portraits and "conversation pieces"—informal group portraits—when he was commissioned, along with Hubert GRAVELOT, to illustrate Shakespeare's plays. These he executed in a light rococo style. Hayman provided 31 of the 36 images for the illustrations, but Gravelot engraved all of them.

Under the influence of his master, Gravelot, Hayman was one of the artists who translated the French rococo style into an English idiom. He was an important influence on the young Thomas Gainsborough (1727–88) and, later, a founding member of the Royal Academy.

Hazlitt, William (1778–1830) English essayist and literary critic. Hazlitt, a journalist who published essays on the leading English political figures of the first decade of the 19th century, turned to literary and dramatic criticism around 1815. He wrote *Characters of Shakespeare's Plays* (1817), in which he expressed his delight in Shakespeare's poetry, an aspect of the playwright's accomplishment that was largely ignored in earlier periods. His *Lectures on the English Poets* (1818) and *Lectures on the English Comic Writers* (1819) covered English literature from the 16th century to his contemporaries. Like his close friend Charles LAMB, Hazlitt was an early admirer of the Romantic poets. He later turned again to political subjects in *The Spirit of the Age* (1825), with its studies of the great public figures of his times, and a massive *Life of Napoleon* (1830). Along with Samuel Taylor COLERIDGE, he contributed to the Romantic era's idea of Shakespeare as a consummate literary artist as well as simply a great dramatist, and he helped begin the systematic study of the history of English literature.

Heicroft, Henry (ca. 1549–1600) Vicar of STRATFORD, baptizer of Susanna SHAKESPEARE.

Heicroft was the vicar of Stratford from 1569 to 1584, when he left for a better paying position. In 1583 he baptized Shakespeare's first child. Heicroft was a graduate of Cambridge University. He married two years after his arrival in Stratford and had five children, three of whom died before he moved to his new post. Little more is known of his life.

Heminge, John (John Heminges) (d. 1650) English actor and a coeditor, with Henry CONDELL, of the FIRST FOLIO edition of Shakespeare's plays. One of the 26 "Principall Actors" listed in the First Folio, Heminge was a member of STRANGE'S MEN, of the CHAMBERLAIN'S MEN (probably from its inception in 1594), and of its successor, the KING'S MEN, until his death. Thus, most of his career was spent alongside Shakespeare. He was apparently the business manager of the company, probably beginning at least in 1596, and he seems to have stopped acting after 1611.

Heminge served as a trustee in Shakespeare's purchase of the BLACKFRIARS GATEHOUSE, and he was executor or overseer of the wills of several of the King's Men. Shakespeare and most of the other members of the troupe left him small legacies, tokens of their friendship. Heminge was a shrewd businessman and became quite wealthy. At his death, he owned about a quarter of the shares in the GLOBE THEATRE and the BLACKFRIARS THEATRE, including the shares originally owned by his late son-in-law William OSTLER, which he had claimed despite a lawsuit by his daughter.

Henderson, John (1747–1785) British actor. Henderson established himself as a fine classical actor in 1777 with a portrayal of Shylock (*The Merchant of Venice*). During his brief career, he was acclaimed as the leading Falstaff of his day, and he played a variety of other Shakespearean parts, including Malvolio and Iago.

Henry I* and *Henry II Lost plays attributed, probably wrongly, to Shakespeare and Robert Davenport (ca. 1590–1640). In 1653 the publisher Humphrey MOSELEY claimed the copyrights to a number of old plays, including "Henry ye first, & Hen: ye 2. by Shakespeare and Davenport." The 18th-century collector John WARBURTON reported owning a copy of *Henry I*, by "Will. Shakespeare & Rob. Davenport." However, none of these manuscripts have survived, and their attribution to Shakespeare, even as a collaborator, is extremely doubtful. *Henry I* was licensed for the KING'S MEN to perform in 1624—eight years after Shakespeare's death—but only in Davenport's name. Moreover, Davenport himself is first recorded only in 1620; a much younger and inferior playwright, he would have been an unlikely collaborator for Shakespeare.

Henry IV, King of England   See Henry IV, King of England, in *Henry IV, Part 1*.

Henry V, King of England   See Henry V, King of England, in *Henry V*; Prince of Wales, Henry, in *Henry IV, Part 1*.

Henry VI, King of England   See Henry VI, King of England, in *Henry VI, Part 1*.

Henry VII, King of England   See Richmond, Earl of, in *Richard III*.

Henry VIII, King of England   See Henry VIII, King of England, in *Henry VIII*.

Henry Frederick, Prince of Wales   (1594–1612) Son of King JAMES I, heir-apparent to the English throne until his early death, and patron of PRINCE HENRY'S MEN, formerly the ADMIRAL'S MEN. Though Prince Henry died young, he was already a significant supporter of the arts. He patronized George CHAPMAN and Ben JONSON, and he defended Walter RALEIGH. He was the first major supporter of Inigo Jones (1573–1652), later the royal architect and collaborator with Jonson (see MASQUE). Most significant for the theatrical world, he became the patron of the Admiral's Men. Unfortunately, the young prince died of typhoid fever just before the planned wedding of his sister, ELIZABETH STUART. Her husband-to-be, a German prince, took over the patronage of Henry's theater company, which became known as the PALSGRAVE'S MEN.

Henryson, Robert   (ca. 1430–before 1506) Scottish poet, author of a poem known to Shakespeare as part of Geoffrey CHAUCER's long poem *Troilus and Criseyde*, a chief source for *Troilus and Cressida*. Henryson's *Testament of Cresseid* continued Chaucer's story. Although it is written in a Scots dialect, Henryson's poem, like Chaucer's, is written in RHYME ROYAL, and for centuries it was regarded as Chaucer's work. In every edition of *Troilus and Criseyde* from 1532 to 1710, it was published as part of the poem. In Henryson's sequel to the story, Cressida is stricken with leprosy as a punishment for her faithlessness and Troilus gives her alms without recognizing her. This development is referred to in *Henry V* (2.1.76) and *Twelfth Night* (3.1.56), so we know that Shakespeare had read Henryson, but oddly it is not mentioned in *Troilus and Cressida*, unless Cressida's future status as a beggar is alluded to in Troilus's pained complaint that the "orts of her love, / The fragments, scraps, the bits, and greasy relics / Of her o'er-eaten faith are given to Diomed" (5.2.157–159).

Henslowe, Philip   (d. 1616) English theatrical entrepreneur, owner of the ROSE, FORTUNE, and HOPE THEATRES and the keeper of a record book that has survived to be a principal source on ELIZABETHAN THEATER. Henslowe, the son of a gamekeeper, was a servant to the bailiff of a nobleman in the 1570s. He married the bailiff's widow and thereby acquired the money to establish himself in business. He was first a dyer, then a pawnbroker and a dealer in real estate, mostly in SOUTHWARK, just across the Thames River from LONDON. In 1585 he leased a plot of land there, upon which he built the Rose Theatre, which opened in 1588. In 1592 his stepdaughter married the great actor William ALLEYN, who became Henslowe's partner. His company, the ADMIRAL'S MEN, played at the Rose for most of the rest of the century, making theatrical history while also making Henslowe and Alleyn rich. Henslowe also had other theatrical properties. By 1594 he either owned or leased the theater at NEWINGTON BUTTS, and he and Alleyn bought a license to put on bull- and bear-baiting entertainments, a profitable sideline. In 1600 he and Alleyn built the Fortune Theatre, to which the

Admiral's Men moved, while the Rose was abandoned when its ground lease expired. In 1613 Henslowe tore down the old animal-baiting arena and built the Hope Theatre, where various companies played, financed by Henslowe. These arrangements resulted in a lawsuit of 1615, in the records of which Henslowe is shown to have had a reputation as a tough businessman. However, his relations with theatrical companies seem otherwise to have been mostly good.

Henslowe's *Diary*, as the collection of his papers is called—though it is actually an account book—covers the years 1592 to 1603, recording the performances at the Rose through 1597 and the revenues each earned, as well as the loans and advances that Henslowe made to acting companies (mostly the Admiral's Men) and to individual players, for he was essentially a banker to them. Henslowe bought the plays the Admiral's Men performed, as well as their costumes and props, all of which are recorded in the *Diary*. He was repaid—with great interest—from the company's share of the playhouse revenues. His papers were inherited by Alleyn, who left them in the collections at Dulwich College, where they were forgotten until Edmond MALONE discovered them in 1790.

Herbert, Henry (1595–1673)   Longtime MASTER OF REVELS for King JAMES I and King Charles I. Herbert was a minor nobleman, a cousin of the Earls of PEMBROKE and brother of the famed poet George Herbert (1593–1633). Beginning in 1622, Herbert leased the office of Master of Revels—licenser of theatrical productions and publications—from its appointed holder, Sir John Ashley (d. 1641), a minor courtier. He paid £150 a year and collected for himself the many fees that were paid to the Master. Though Herbert was nominally the Deputy to the Master of Revels, he was formally recognized as the rightful exerciser of the Master's powers and was knighted by King JAMES I in 1623.

Upon Ashley's death, Herbert became Master in name as well as fact, but in the summer of 1642, when the civil war erupted and the Puritan government of London closed the theaters, the office ceased to pay. In 1660 when the monarchy was restored, Herbert attempted to reclaim the powers of the Master of Revels, but the new, unfettered licenses granted to producers William DAVENANT and Thomas KILLIGREW took precedence. After a series of unsuccessful lawsuits, Herbert retired.

A volume of Herbert's official records, known as his *Office Book,* survived into the 18th century, when it was used and recorded in part by such scholars as George CHALMERS and Edmond MALONE. It was subsequently lost, but extensive quotations from it remain and provide scholars with an important glimpse of the 17th-century English theater.

Hervey, William (William Harvey) (ca. 1565–1642)   English soldier, possible "Mr. W. H." of the dedication to the *Sonnets.* Hervey was the stepfather of Shakespeare's patron Henry Wriothesley, Earl of SOUTHAMPTON, and some scholars believe that he provided manuscripts of the *Sonnets* to the publisher Thomas THORPE, who therefore dedicated his 1609 edition to him as the "onlie begetter" of the poems, "begetter" being taken to mean "procurer."

As a young man, Hervey distinguished himself fighting against the Spanish Armada in 1588, and he was knighted for his service under Robert Devereux, Earl of ESSEX, at Cadiz in 1596. He married the Countess of Southampton in 1599, and after her death in 1607 he married Cordell Annesley, whose concern for her mad father, Brian ANNESLEY, may have helped inspire *King Lear.* Hervey continued soldiering, mostly in Ireland, and was rewarded with great estates by King JAMES I. He died a wealthy man.

Shakespeare probably had Hervey (also known as Harvey) in mind when he changed the name of his character Harvey, in *1 Henry IV,* to Peto. Several such name changes were made (such as Oldcastle to Falstaff and Sir John Rossill to Bardolph) to avoid giving offense to powerful aristocrats.

Heyes, Thomas (d. ca. 1604)   LONDON bookseller and publisher, producer of the first edition of *The Merchant of Venice.* In 1600 Heyes bought the copyright to *The Merchant* from the printer James ROBERTS. He published a QUARTO edition, known as Q1, and used Roberts as the printer. When he died, Heyes left the rights to the play to his son Laurence (d. 1637), whose protest at Thomas PAVIER's illicit publication in 1619 led to the exposure of Pavier's FALSE FOLIO.

Heywood, John (ca. 1497–ca. 1580) Early English dramatist. Heywood was a musician at the courts of King Henry VIII (see Henry VIII in *Henry VIII*), King Edward VI, and Queen Mary I, and he wrote dramatic dialogues for the intermissions in musical entertainments (see INTERLUDE). He contributed to the evolution from the medieval MORALITY PLAY toward the secular ELIZABETHAN DRAMA. He was also famous for his ballads. Heywood's four extant interludes—probably written between 1519 and 1528—are comedies in the form of moral debates. They are pious by later standards, but they are significantly different from their predecessors. The allegorical figures of the morality plays are replaced with real characters, drawn from contemporary society. They are inclined to a boisterous and obscene humor that was startling for the day. However, although Heywood's farcelike works stimulated a broader sense of theatrical possibility, Shakespearean COMEDY has different roots.

Heywood was probably the son of a provincial coroner. He began his career when he was recruited as a boy for the choir of St Paul's School (see CHILDREN'S COMPANIES). An ardent Catholic and a relative by marriage of Sir Thomas MORE, Heywood feared persecution early in the reign of Queen Elizabeth I (see Elizabeth I in *Henry VIII*). Protestantism was forcefully instituted as the state religion, and he fled England for the Spanish Netherlands in 1564. In 1578, when he was in his 80s, he again faced religious persecution when he was among the Catholics expelled from Antwerp by a Protestant mob. This was a minor episode of Protestant revolt against Spanish rule. He lived out his life in nearby Louvain, a more securely Catholic city.

Heywood, Thomas (1573–1641) English actor and playwright, possible collaborator with Shakespeare. Heywood acted and wrote for the ADMIRAL'S MEN from 1596 to 1602, and with WORCESTER'S MEN (later the QUEEN'S MEN) until their dissolution in 1619. He then retired from acting but continued to write plays, both by himself and collaboratively. Some scholars believe he may have written parts of *Timon of Athens* and/or *Pericles, Prince of Tyre*. Heywood was astoundingly prolific and claimed to have "had either an entire hand or at the least a main finger" in 220 plays. However many there may in fact have been, only about 20 have survived, though the names of a dozen more are known. The best-known survivors are *Four Prentices of London* (1600), which was satirized in *The Knight of the Burning Pestle* by Francis BEAUMONT, *A Woman Killed with Kindness* (1603), and *If You Know Not Me, You Know Nobody* (1605). Heywood also wrote a prose pamphlet countering Puritan objections to the theater, *Apology for Actors* (published 1612), which is important for the light it casts on the ELIZABETHAN THEATER. In a digression in it, he points out that two of his poems had been published in THE PASSIONATE PILGRIM as Shakespeare's, and he objects on Shakespeare's behalf; the publisher, William JAGGARD, withdrew the ascription.

Higgins, John (ca. 1545–1602) English poet, author of sources for both *Julius Caesar* and *King Lear*. Higgins was a classical scholar and a writer on early British history. He collaborated with Nicholas UDALL on translations from the Roman dramatist TERENCE, but he is best known for his contribution to A MIRROR FOR MAGISTRATES, a popular anthology of verse biography that Shakespeare knew well. Higgins edited the third and fourth editions of *A Mirror* (1574, 1578) and contributed to it 16 long poems dealing with "the first unfortunate Princes of this lande," the quasi-mythical kings and heroes of ancient Britain. His account of "Leire" provided Shakespeare with a number of significant details for his *King Lear*. For the fifth edition (1587) of *A Mirror*, probably the one Shakespeare used, Higgins provided another 24 poems, all but one on figures from the classical world. Among them was a life of Julius Caesar that Shakespeare used in composing his play on the Roman leader.

Hilliard, Nicholas (1547–1619) English painter, the foremost English artist of Shakespeare's times and the creator of a portrait formerly believed to be of Shakespeare. The "Hilliard miniature" was reproduced in James BOSWELL's 1821 edition of Shakespeare's works. It had been brought to the editor's attention by its owner, a descendant of a Mr. Somerville, and the painting is also known as the "Somerville miniature." Somerville allegedly was a STRATFORD friend of the retired Shakespeare and the commissioner of the portrait. However, the Hilliard miniature does not much resemble the most authoritative portraits (see DROESHOUT, MARTIN; JANSSEN, CORNELIUS), and modern scholars are confident that the portrait is not of Shakespeare.

Hilliard, chiefly a painter of miniature portraits, was inspired by the work of the great German painter Hans Holbein the younger (1497–1593). Holbein had been court portraitist to King Henry VIII (see Henry VIII in *Henry VIII*), and Hilliard worked for both Queen Elizabeth I (see Elizabeth I in *Henry VIII*) and King JAMES I. His elaborately detailed renderings of jewelry and rich costumes give his portraits an exquisite, gemlike presence that is still admired.

history plays Shakespeare's 11 plays dealing with events in English history. In the order in which they were written, the history plays are (a) *Edward III*, composed, probably in collaboration with others, around 1590; (b) the so-called minor TETRALOGY—consisting of *1, 2,* and *3 Henry VI* and *Richard III*—written in 1590–91; (c) *King John* (1591, possibly 1595); (d) the major tetralogy—*Richard II, 1* and *2 Henry IV,* and *Henry V*—written between 1595 and 1599; and (e) *Henry VIII*, perhaps written in collaboration with John FLETCHER in 1612, one of Shakespeare's last works.

Edward III, parts of which were almost certainly written by Shakespeare, while the authorship of other parts is disputed by scholars, concerns the early years of the HUNDRED YEARS' WAR against FRANCE, from its beginnings in 1337 through the battle of POITIERS in 1356 (though these events are severely compressed in time). King Edward and his son the Prince of Wales go from triumph to triumph, though only after an unhistorical prelude in which the King is distracted by an obsession with a woman, the Countess, in the first two acts (which are believed to have been Shakespeare's chief contribution to the play). The minor tetralogy deals with the English defeat by France in the last years of the Hundred Years' War (enacted in *1 Henry VI*), fol-

lowed by the disputes and battles of an English civil conflict, the WARS OF THE ROSES (in the other three plays). The tetralogy begins with the death of King Henry V in 1422 and ends with the foundation of the TUDOR DYNASTY in 1485. *King John* presents much earlier events, a series of incidents during the reign of King John (1199–1216). The major tetralogy covers the deposition and murder of King Richard II in 1398 (*Richard II*); two unsuccessful rebellions against his usurper, King Henry IV, and that ruler's death (*1* and *2 Henry IV*); and the invasion and defeat of France by Henry's son and successor, King Henry V, closing with the signing of the treaty of TROYES in 1420 (*Henry V*). *Henry VIII* consists of a series of tableaux that present various events in the reign of Henry VIII, ending with the christening of Queen Elizabeth I in 1533. It is very different from the other histories and is often regarded as more appropriately classified with the ROMANCES.

The two tetralogies are Shakespeare's major achievement in the histories. (*Edward III*, besides being largely the work of other hands, is by comparison a crude effort; *King John*, although a fine play, is nevertheless an isolated excursion into an earlier, almost mythic, period.) The tetralogies cover English history from 1398 to 1485. Shakespeare plunged into the disorder of a civil war in the first four plays and then, in the second, delved into the history that preceded this cataclysm, examining its causes and painting a portrait of the nation as it changed, traumatically, from medieval to modern.

The central theme of these plays is political—they deal with the gain and loss of power—but Shakespeare transcended this subject. As he wrote his histories, the playwright increasingly pursued the definition of the perfect king. After presenting two distinctly bad rulers, the ineffectual Henry VI and the villainous Richard III, he turned to a consideration of kingly virtues. He began to explore the psychology of political leaders, and these plays are, at their best, as much psychological as historical.

In *Richard II* a weak king jeopardizes the stability of the realm, but, although we recognize his opponent, Henry Bolingbroke, to be a superior ruler, we nonetheless sympathize with Richard, whose spiritual qualities make him more open and responsive to life. A conflict is established between human vulnerability and cold political calculation, and the question that dominates the next three plays is whether a successful ruler can combine humane sympathy and ruthless efficiency. Such a monarch would be able to hold the country together, as Richard cannot, while staying in touch with his subjects, a connection Bolingbroke never had and does not acquire as Henry IV.

The *Henry IV* plays focus on the development of the king's son, young Prince Hal. In *1 Henry IV* Hal is presented with two alternatives, represented by Hotspur and Falstaff, respectively, and he finds his way between them, seeing both their weaknesses and their virtues. However, in *2 Henry IV* the Prince is psychologically remote, and as he inherits the crown from his father, he seems to abandon his friends among the commoners in order to focus on his duty as a ruler. Hal's increasing coldness is evident, but the play's great question—is personal loyalty morally superior to public duty?—is left unanswered by the Prince's final rejection of Falstaff, as is shown by the debate that the episode has engendered ever since.

In *Henry V* this basic ambivalence toward Hal—now King Henry V—remains the major theme. On the one hand, he is plainly a successful king, uniting all Britain behind him in a conquest of France and displaying the combination of leadership and camaraderie typical of an epic hero. On the other, he seems a cynical manipulator of war and peace, a hypocrite who uses a religious sensibility to mask his political ends. Both points of view are legitimate in the context of the play; Shakespeare's recognition of political complexities compelled him to explore Henry's defects. His discovery of the psychological limitations of his ideal king was to influence the great tragedies (see TRAGEDY) in the next phase of his career.

Not content to deal with the nature of kingship solely from the point of view of the rulers, Shakespeare also focuses on the lives of the common people of England, especially in the major tetralogy. Sometimes fictitious minor figures, such as the Gardener in *Richard III* or Williams in *Henry V,* fulfill an important function simply by offering their own interpretation of political events and historical personalities and thus influencing our own responses. But many common people are developed as characters in their own right. Indeed, in the *Henry IV* plays, often considered the greatest of the histories, Falstaff and a number of fully sketched minor characters offer a sort of national group portrait that is contrasted with political history. The juxtaposition generates a richly stimulating set of relationships.

That secular accounts of the past, neither legendary nor religious, were presented on the stage—and were highly popular—reflects the Elizabethan era's intense interest in history. In the late 16th century, when these plays were written, England was undergoing a great crisis. As a leading Protestant state, it found itself at odds with the great Catholic powers of Counter-Reformation Europe, including its traditional enemy, France, and a new foe, Spain. The latter, at the height of its power, was a very dangerous adversary, and England felt seriously imperiled until the defeat of the Spanish Armada in 1588. This situation sparked a tremendous patriotism among all classes of English society, and with that came an increasing interest in the nation's history, an interest that the theater was of course delighted to serve.

Written not long after the peak of nationalistic fervor in 1588, the history plays, which were extremely popular, deal with great crises of English history. *King John* depicts an actual invasion of the country by France; *Edward III* depicts a successful English invasion of the continent (and it also adverts to the Armada). The tetralogies' central theme was the WARS OF THE ROSES, the great crisis that had formed the nation, as Shakespeare and his contemporaries knew it. Its resolution at BOSWORTH FIELD lay in the relatively recent past—closer to the author's own day than the American Civil War or the Crimean War is to ours. Thus, Elizabethans were very much aware of the significance of the events depicted in these plays. Moreover, although in hindsight the reign of Queen Elizabeth seems very different from those of the troubled 15th century, this was not so clear at the time. A number of threats to the government arose—including the failed rebellion of Robert Devereux, Earl of ESSEX, in 1599, when the rebels used a performance of *Richard II* as propaganda. The English of the late

16th century felt a strong fear of civil war and anarchy; for both moral and practical reasons, they valued an orderly society ruled by a strong monarch. The history plays addressed this attitude by presenting a lesson in the evils of national disunity.

This view of English history was held not only by both the playwright and most of his audience, but also by the historians whose works Shakespeare consulted. When the Tudor dynasty came to power, among the policies adopted by King Henry VII (the Richmond of *Richard III*) was the use of scholarly propaganda to justify his seizure of the throne. He encouraged and commissioned various works of history and biography to emphasize the faults of earlier rulers and present his own accession as the nation's salvation. Among them was an official history of England by the Italian humanist Polydore VERGIL, which was to have a strong influence on subsequent historians, including Raphael HOLINSHED and Edward HALL, whose chronicles were Shakespeare's chief sources. Holinshed's book, the most up-to-date and authoritative work of its kind in the 1590s, provided much of the historical detail, especially in the minor tetralogy. Hall's history of the Wars of the Roses foreshadowed Shakespeare by stressing the theme that England's happiness under its last great medieval king, Edward III, Richard II's predecessor, had been lost through Richard's weakness, which necessitated Henry IV's profoundly sinful act of deposition. This guilty deed brought down God's wrath on England, plunging the country into generations of civil conflict that was ended only by the triumph of Henry VII and the founding of the Tudor dynasty.

Such writings shaped the understanding of the past that was available to Shakespeare when he wrote the history plays. He saw—and passed on—a story of inevitable progress toward the benevolent reign of the Tudors. Shakespeare's account of historical events varies considerably from that developed by later scholarship, in part because the sources available to him were highly unreliable by modern historical standards. In any case, Shakespeare was not writing history; he was concerned with dramatic values more than with historical accuracy.

The history play, a theatrical work dealing realistically with great events of the past, was a novelty in Shakespeare's day. Shakespeare himself is often credited with inventing the genre, although its origins are somewhat obscure, since the texts of most Elizabethan plays are lost. Dramatic works dealing with historical events had been staged somewhat earlier, but these works had treated their materials allegorically, like the MORALITY PLAY from which they derived. Shakespeare was probably among the first playwrights to depict real events in works expressly intended to illuminate the past, although some lost plays may have anticipated them in some respects.

Other Elizabethan playwrights also wrote histories, whether influenced specifically by Shakespeare or simply by the age. However, most of these works are familiar only to scholars. Shakespeare' work has survived because he was not merely exploiting a current interest; nor was he a mere purveyor of Tudor propaganda. In writing history plays, he pursued his own concerns, exploring political values and social relations. Throughout his career he was preoccupied with the value of order in society; this theme is present in such very early and apparently unlikely works as *The Comedy of Errors*, and it recurs in most of the plays. But nowhere is it as explicitly dealt with as in the histories.

What, then, do the history plays say about this subject? As we have seen, the ideal king of the history plays, Henry V, is a highly ambiguous figure. While Shakespeare's belief in the need for authority is evident in his work, so also is a distrust of those who hold authority. This paradox reflects a fundamental irony: the only rational form of rule—power that is humane yet absolute—is also impossible to achieve. Thus the history plays point up an underlying characteristic of human societies: Political power inspires disturbing fears as well as profound ideals.

Hoby, Sir Thomas (1530–1566) First English translator of CASTIGLIONE's *Il Cortegiano*, thought to have influenced *Much Ado About Nothing*. As a young man, Hoby traveled widely on the Continent. In 1552–53, while living in Paris, he translated *Il Cortegiano*, though the resulting work, *The Courtyer*, was not published until 1561. It became immensely popular, being reissued several times before 1588. Hoby died in 1566, while serving as the English ambassador in Paris. Thomas Posthumous HOBY was his son.

Hoby, Sir Thomas Posthumous (1566–1640)

Contemporary of Shakespeare, Puritan landowner who may have been a model for Malvolio in *Twelfth Night*. Born after the death of his father, Sir Thomas HOBY, Hoby ran away from home as a young man to pursue a military career; then he settled down as the husband of a wealthy heiress from Yorkshire. He acted as an agent for the Protestant government in his wife's very Catholic district, and his enthusiasm for prosecuting Catholics made him highly unpopular. In 1600 he sued several of his neighbors for coming uninvited to his house, where they drank, played cards, mocked his religious practices, and threatened to rape his wife. The case was notorious (Hoby won), and some scholars believe that it may be reflected in the antagonism between Malvolio and SIR TOBY in the play. (For other possible Malvolios, see FFARINGTON, WILLIAM; KNOLLYS, SIR WILLIAM; WILLOUGHBY, SIR AMBROSE.)

Holinshed, Raphael (ca. 1528–ca. 1580)

English historian, compiler, and author of a source for several of Shakespeare's plays. Holinshed's *Chronicles of England, Scotland, and Ireland* (probably in its second edition, 1587) was a major source for the HISTORY PLAYS and *Macbeth* and a minor one for *Cymbeline* and *King Lear*. The *Chronicles*—along with the work of Edward HALL—provided much of Shakespeare's knowledge of the WARS OF THE ROSES, which is the subject of eight of the history plays (see TETRALOGY). Holinshed's work also provided details for Shakespeare's treatment of the HUNDRED YEARS' WAR in *Edward III* and *1 Henry VI*. With the work of John FOXE, it contributed the history covered in the two others, *King John* and *Henry VIII*. For *Macbeth*, Shakespeare used the *Chronicles'* account of the medieval King Macbeth of SCOTLAND. The ancient British kings Cymbeline and Lear were also treated by Holinshed, and details of his treatments are reflected in Shakespeare's plays about them.

Holinshed's *Chronicles* was the most authoritative history of Britain in Shakespeare's day, and other Elizabethan dramatists besides Shakespeare used it as a source. Its 3.5 million words were not all written by Holinshed, whose principal contribution was the section dealing with England's history. In writing it, he relied on a number of earlier works, most notably that of Hall. The history of Scotland was a translation by William HARRISON of the Latin chronicle of Hector BOECE, and the history of Ireland was written by Edmund Campion (1540–81). Prefatory geographical essays were provided by Harrison for England and Scotland, and Campion and Richard Stanyhurst (1545–1615) for Ireland.

The book was the remnant of a much larger project, led by Reginald Wolfe (d. 1573), a "cosmography of the whole world [including] the histories of every known nation," for which Holinshed was a translator. Holinshed succeeded Wolfe as editor-in-chief, though only one other volume, an atlas, was published. The *Chronicles* was published in 1578 and again, in a revised and enlarged version, in 1587. Holinshed wrote nothing else—even the second edition of the *Chronicles* was brought out by others (including John STOW)—and he became a steward on a country estate, where he died.

Holland, Hugh (ca. 1574–1633)

Poet and antiquarian, friend of Shakespeare's. Holland wrote an EPITAPH on Shakespeare, a SONNET that was one of the introductory poems in the FIRST FOLIO (1623). Like Shakespeare, he was a good friend of Ben JONSON and a member of the group that met regularly at the MERMAID TAVERN. Holland wrote in four languages—English, Greek, Italian, and Welsh—and he was a well-known poet in his own time, noted particularly for a long poem on Owen Tudor's courtship of Queen Katharine.

Holland, Philemon (1552–1637)

English translator of minor sources for *Othello*, *Coriolanus*, and possibly *The Rape of Lucrece*. Holland's version of PLINY the Elder's *Natural History* (1601) provided details for *Othello*, mostly in the hero's account of his adventures in 1.3. A passage in Holland's translation of LIVY's history of ROME, *Ab urbe condita*, published as *The Roman Historie* (1600), is echoed in certain details of MENENIUS's famous "belly speech" in *Coriolanus* (1.1.95–159). The same passage was also influenced by Holland's translation of

William CAMDEN's *Remaines* (1605), excerpts from a Latin history of Britain. Holland's Livy may also have inspired parts of *Lucrece*, whose story it tells. However, there are no literary echoes of Holland in Shakespeare's poem, so the playwright may have only used the original.

Holland, the son of a clergyman, practiced medicine in COVENTRY. He was famous for his translations from the Latin; in addition to those already mentioned, he produced English versions of three other ancient works of history, published in 1606, 1609, and 1632. After 1608 Holland gave up medicine and became the headmaster of a grammar school.

Holmedon (Humbleton)   Site of a battle between England and SCOTLAND (1402) that is reported in 1.1.62–74 of *1 Henry IV*. Holmedon, known today as Humbleton, is near the Scottish border. An invasion by the Scots was repelled by English forces under Hotspur, who captured many aristocratic prisoners—usually held for ransom under medieval practices of war—including the Scottish commander, Lord Douglas. Hotspur's refusal to turn these prisoners over to King Henry IV triggers enmity between the two, leading to the rebellion that the play depicts.

Shakespeare alters the chronology surrounding this battle in minor ways. He asserts that the battle occurred simultaneously with another, against the Welsh, in which Lord Mortimer was captured, but in fact they happened months apart. His alteration heightens the dramatic impact of their accounts. Both are placed closer to the beginning of Henry's reign than they actually were, thus stressing the connection of the rebellion against Henry to his usurpation of the crown (enacted in *Richard II*).

Homer   Ancient Greek poet, a source, through the translation of George CHAPMAN, of *Troilus and Cressida*. Two great epics—the *Iliad*, an account of the TROJAN WAR, and the *Odyssey*, which tells of the wanderings of Odysseus, known in Latin as Ulysses—are attributed to Homer, as they have been since remote antiquity. However, Homer may be an apocryphal figure, and his works may have been written by more than one unknown author. In the absence of persuasive evidence one way or the other, the works continue to be conventionally regarded as Homer's. In the ancient world, estimates of Homer's dates ranged over many centuries, but by comparing passages in the works with the archaeological evidence, scholars generally believe that the poems were composed in the eighth or seventh century B.C.—i.e., 400–600 years after the era depicted in them. Internal evidence further suggests that the poet(s) lived in Ionia, or Greek Asia Minor.

In the Middle Ages it was believed that other accounts of the Trojan War preceded Homer's, but they were actually written much later. Only in the RENAISSANCE were Homer's works restored to the position of eminence they had held in ancient Greece and Rome. Some of the information Shakespeare used in writing *Troilus and Cressida* came from the medieval tradition, which took a Trojan rather than a Greek point of view. However, Homer entered English literature in Shakespeare's time, and the playwright certainly knew two partial translations of the *Iliad*, that of Arthur HALL, taken from a French version (1581), and Chapman's from the Greek (published in part in 1598 and in full in 1612). Indeed, he could have read nine different translations—five Latin, two French, and two English. However, it is clear that he used Chapman's translation in composing the play (ca. 1602), for the incidents from Homer that he used were those covered in Chapman's first edition. Chapman's *Odyssey* was completed in 1615, and numerous translations of both works have been made since, some of them masterful works of English literature in their own right.

Hope Theatre   Theater near LONDON built by Philip HENSLOWE in 1613 on the site of a bear-baiting house—an arena for audiences to watch bears or bulls being attacked by dogs—which was torn down for the purpose. Henslowe held a license for animal baiting, a very popular entertainment, and he wished to expand this business while perhaps attracting the audiences of the GLOBE THEATRE, which had just burned down. The Hope thus had accommodations for the animals along with the usual attributes of a theater. The smell of the animals was apparently offensive, but LADY

ELIZABETH'S MEN and other companies played there in 1614–15. However, disputes between Henslowe and the players resulted in a series of lawsuits, which continued after Henslowe's death, and his heir, William ALLEYN, could not negotiate a settlement. During this period, few plays were produced at the Hope, and by 1619 it had reverted to animal baiting exclusively. This pastime was outlawed in 1642, and the Hope was eventually torn down to make way for tenements in 1656.

Hopkins, Richard (ca. 1545–ca. 1594)   English translator of the works of Luis de GRANADA. Hopkins, a Catholic, spent his life abroad in religious exile. A student in Catholic universities in the Netherlands, Spain, and France, he probably lived chiefly in Paris, although details of his life are obscure. His translation of Granada's *Of Prayer and Meditation* was published in London in 1582 and may have influenced Shakespeare's writing of *Hamlet*.

Hotson, Leslie (1897–1992)   Canadian literary scholar. Hotson specialized in scholarly detective work and distinguished himself with many striking discoveries, including the probable murder of Christopher MARLOWE, the likely first performance of *The Merry Wives of Windsor*, and Shakespeare's connections to William GARDINER and Francis LANGLEY. On the other hand, many of his proposals—such as the identification of *Troilus and Cressida* as *Love's Labour's Won*—have not been generally accepted.

Howard, Charles (1536–1624)   English admiral, a leading military figure of the late 16th century and the aristocratic patron of an acting company, the ADMIRAL'S MEN. Howard was a cousin of Queen Elizabeth I (see Elizabeth I in *Henry VIII*). He was trained for the admiralty from an early age, and after a successful career as a soldier in the Low Countries and as an English diplomat, he was appointed Lord Admiral of England in 1585. He commanded the country's resistance to the Spanish Armada in 1588, and in 1596 he was a co-commander of the successful English attack on Spain at Cadiz. The latter event is alluded to in *The Merchant of Venice*. Under King JAMES I, Howard continued to influence naval and foreign policy

until his retirement in 1619. He was renowned for his civility and honesty and has always been regarded as one of the finest public figures of the era. Beginning in 1576, Howard was the patron of an important LONDON theater company known first as Lord Howard's Men and later as the Admiral's Men. His role consisted of permitting them to use his name—necessary under restrictive Puritan laws (see ELIZABETHAN THEATER)—and he had nothing to do with the company's productions.

Howard's Men   See ADMIRAL'S MEN; HOWARD, CHARLES.

Hughes, Margaret (d. 1719)   The first recorded English actress. In 1660, when English theaters were reopened following the Puritan Revolution, actresses were for the first time permitted to take the female parts, previously played by boys (see ELIZABETHAN DRAMA). Margaret Hughes was the first woman to do so, playing DESDEMONA in Thomas KILLIGREW's production of *Othello*. She had a long and successful career, joining William DAVENANT's company in 1676. She was also the mistress of the king's famous cousin, the military hero Prince Rupert (1619–82), and mother of his illegitimate daughter.

Hugo, François-Victor (1828–1873)   French translator of Shakespeare's works. Son of the famous man of letters, Victor HUGO, F.-V. Hugo shared his father's exile to the English island of Guernsey, where he spent much of his time learning English. He then proceeded to study the works of Shakespeare, writing numerous essays on them, and, ultimately, translating the English playwright's complete works, which he published between 1859 and 1866. F.-V. Hugo's was the first important TRANSLATION OF SHAKESPEARE's plays into French since that of Pierre LE TOURNEUR, almost a century earlier. Moreover, Hugo's work encompassed the first translation of the *Sonnets* into French. His Shakespeare remained the standard French translation for generations and is still much read and greatly respected.

Hugo, Victor (1802–1883)   French poet, novelist, dramatist, and commentator on Shakespeare. Best known to English readers for such novels as *Les*

Misérables (1862) and *Notre-Dame de Paris* (1831; better known in English as *The Hunchback of Notre Dame*), Hugo is also regarded as one of the greatest French poets. As a leading light of French Romanticism, he meant to revolutionize literature, not least in drama, and in a preface to his first play, *Cromwell* (1827), he praised Shakespeare and presented him as a model for writers seeking freedom from the constraints of 18th-century French neoclassical conventions. This essay, still admired as a vibrant example of Romantic rhetoric, became a manifesto for French artists for decades. When his son, François-Victor HUGO, translated the complete works (published between 1859 and 1866), Hugo wrote a forward to the work that grew into a book-length essay, *William Shakespeare* (1864), a quasi-mystical invocation of the playwright as a universal prophet. Neither a biography nor a study of the works, it is, rather, a wandering meditation on literary greatness.

Hugo was one of the major figures of 19th-century France, taking a political role as well as a literary one. In his 20s and 30s, he produced floods of poetry, novels, and plays, becoming a giant of French literature. He turned to politics, and in the Revolution of 1848, he became a legislator. In his fury at the 1851 coup d'état that created the Second Empire, ruled by Napoléon III, Hugo exiled himself from France, settling on Guernsey, in the Channel Islands, English territory not far from French shores. There he stayed for almost 20 years, writing some of his best-known work. He refused to return under an amnesty, saying he would wait for France to repudiate the empire. When it did, in the Revolution of 1870, he returned to find himself a legend. His writing in the 1870s did not equal his earlier work, and though elected to the Senate, he had no political influence to speak of, but he was revered nationally. When he died, his body lay in state under the Arc de Triomphe before being taken (in a pauper's hearse, as he had requested) across Paris for a ceremonious burial in the Pantheon.

Hull, Thomas (1728–1808)   English actor and theatrical entrepreneur, producer of adaptations of two of Shakespeare's plays. Hull produced adaptations of *Timon of Athens* (1786) and *The Comedy of Errors* (1793). The first of these was an economic failure, but his *Comedy* was restaged for many years and only disappeared from the English stage when Shakespeare's original text was restored in the second half of the 19th century. Hull was well known in his own day as a successful actor of secondary parts who spent a nearly 50-year career in one establishment, London's Covent Garden Theatre.

Hundred Years' War (1337–1453)   Fourteenth- and 15th-century conflict between England and FRANCE, parts of which are enacted in *Edward III, 1 Henry VI*, and *Henry V*. The Hundred Years' War, which actually lasted 116 years, consisted of three distinct phases separated by periods of peace. Shakespeare dealt only with the early part of the war in *Edward III*, from 1337 to 1356, and the third stage, which began in 1415, in *Henry V* and *1 Henry VI*.

The war was basically a dynastic quarrel between the PLANTAGENET family and France's House of Valois. King Edward III of England claimed the French throne by inheritance through his mother. The French countered that the ancient Salic Law—disparaged by Artois in *Edward III*, 1.1.17–27, and Canterbury in *Henry V*, 1.2.33–95—excluded women from the succession. The French, having sided with King David of SCOTLAND in a dispute with England, precipitated the war, in 1337. After several years of petty skirmishing, Edward invaded France, fighting the successful naval battle of SLUYS, in 1340, described in *Edward III*, 3.1.62–184. Following a period of sporadic truce, the English won the pivotal battle of CRÉCY (enacted in 3.4) in 1346 and besieged CALAIS (4.2, 5.1). A subsequent truce lasted into the 1350s, when a campaign in central France resulted in the English victory at POITIERS in 1356, the climactic event of *Edward III* (4.4–4.7). In 1360 a peace treaty ended this first phase of the war. Nine years later a revolt broke out, and the French recovered most of their lost territory. Two decades of sporadic fighting ensued before Richard II negotiated a peace treaty in 1396. England conceded its losses, and the second phase of the conflict came to a close.

The third phase of the war began when Henry V invaded France in 1415, as presented in *Henry V*. In Shakespeare's play the English victory at AGINCOURT leads directly to the French surrender at TROYES, enacted in 5.2, but in fact five more years of fighting were necessary before Henry was granted the inheritance of the French crown. However, when Henry died in 1422, the French rebelled. Their subsequent success is presented in *1 Henry VI*: over the next 30 years, aided by a charismatic leader, Joan of Arc (Joan La Pucelle), they drove the English from France (except a tiny foothold at Calais, which England held for another century) in campaigns that culminated in the battle of BORDEAUX (1453). The English were soon engaged in the internal WARS OF THE ROSES, and they never attempted another conquest; the Hundred Years' War was over.

The Hundred Years' War was a watershed in the history of both countries. France, finally free of English colonization, began to unify the territories that constitute the modern French nation. England, defeated on the Continent, began to develop its naval power. In military history, the war was also decisive. Medieval warfare, which depended on the mounted knight, was now obsolete; the development of tactics involving many archers and foot soldiers—plus the first use of gunpowder in Europe—spelled the beginning of more modern armies, involving masses of common troops. Moreover, the long and bloody war almost wiped out the knights, the traditional feudal nobility of both countries, permitting the monarchs to begin to ally themselves with the rising middle class, a process that was to result in the modern nation-state. This is to some extent reflected in Shakespeare in the fall of the medieval ideal of kingship represented by Richard II, although in the playwright's day this effect was not clearly perceived.

Hunnis, William (d. 1597) English poet and musician, master of the Children of the Chapel (see CHILDREN'S COMPANIES). In 1566 Hunnis succeeded Richard EDWARDS as director of the choirboys. They performed numerous plays at the court of Queen Elizabeth I, some of which Hunnis may have written himself. In 1576 he delegated his theatrical responsibilities to his deputy, Richard FARRANT, who organized the first BLACKFRIARS THEATRE where the boys performed. Upon Farrant's death in 1580, Hunnis resumed direction of the troupe, which he led until his death, though their play production ceased almost entirely after 1584.

An accomplished composer, Hunnis was a court musician for King Edward VI as early as 1550. Under Queen Mary, his ardent Protestantism led him to join a plot against the queen. For this he was imprisoned, being freed upon Elizabeth's accession in 1558, when he resumed his career. His poetry was largely religious, though he also wrote secular works, including parts of the elaborate festivities held at KENILWORTH in 1575, which may have been witnessed by the 11-year-old Shakespeare.

Hunsdon, George Carey, Baron (1547–1603) English diplomat and theatrical patron. George Carey, the second Lord Hunsdon, was the son of Henry Carey, Baron HUNSDON, Lord Chamberlain to Queen Elizabeth I (see Elizabeth I in *Henry VIII*). Upon his father's death in 1596, Hunsdon assumed the patronage of his theatrical company, the CHAMBERLAIN'S MEN, of which Shakespeare was a member. Because Hunsdon did not immediately succeed his father as Chamberlain (see COBHAM, WILLIAM BROOKE, LORD), the company was known for nine months as HUNSDON'S MEN. When he was appointed Chamberlain in 1597, the company resumed its old name, which it retained until the patronage was assumed by King JAMES I in 1603, shortly before Hunsdon's death.

George Carey had a successful career as a soldier and diplomat before he succeeded to his father's title. As Lord Chamberlain, he continued his father's policy of protecting the budding ELIZABETHAN THEATER from the persecution of the puritanical London government. He provided many occasions for performances by the Chamberlain's Men, either at court or in his own home, Hunsdon House.

Hunsdon, Henry Carey, Baron (1524–1596) English statesman and theatrical patron. Lord Hunsdon, as he was known, was Lord Chamberlain of England. In 1594 he assumed the patronage of Shakespeare's theatrical company, DERBY'S MEN, after the death of their previous patron. In recognition of Hunsdon's high office, the company was renamed the CHAMBERLAIN'S MEN. As Lord Chamberlain, Hunsdon protected the theatrical profession (see ELIZABETHAN THEATER) from persecution by the London government, which was controlled by Puritans, an increasingly powerful religious sect that opposed public drama.

In February 1596 Hunsdon's granddaughter was married, and scholars speculate that her wedding may have been the occasion of the first performance of *A Midsummer Night's Dream*, staged by his company. Upon his death, the company's patronage was assumed by his son George Carey, Baron HUNSDON. The elder Lord Hunsdon was one of the most valued advisers of Queen Elizabeth I (see Elizabeth I in *Henry VIII*), and he held a series of high offices in her government. His mistress, Emilia LANIER, is among the women identified by commentators as the possible Dark Lady of Shakespeare's *Sonnets*.

Hunsdon's Men Name used by Shakespeare's theatrical company, better known as the CHAMBERLAIN'S MEN, between July 22, 1596, and the following March 17. On the first date, the patron of the Chamberlain's Men—Henry Carey, Baron HUNSDON, Lord Chamberlain for Queen Elizabeth I—died. He left his baronial title and the patronage of the company to his son, George Carey, Baron HUNSDON, but since the younger Lord Hunsdon did not immediately succeed his father as chamberlain, the company's name was changed to Hunsdon's Men. Nine months later the new baron was appointed to his father's old office, after the death of the intervening holder, William Brooke, Lord COBHAM, and the company resumed their old name. As Hunsdon's Men, the company continued to be the leading London troupe; during this time they introduced *Romeo and Juliet*—as is known from the title page of the play's first edition—and they rehearsed *The Merry Wives of Windsor*, which was first staged just after the second Lord Hunsdon became chamberlain.

The elder Lord Hunsdon had maintained another company as early as 1564, also known as Hunsdon's Men. They had been associated with the ADMIRAL'S MEN in the 1580s but had chiefly toured in the provinces and are not to be confused with the brief incarnation of the Chamberlain's Men. The provincial Hunsdon's Men were disbanded around 1590.

Hunt, Simon (active 1571–1575) STRATFORD schoolmaster, Shakespeare's teacher. Hunt was master of the Stratford Grammar School from 1571 to 1575. Sometime during this period, Shakespeare probably advanced in school to the point where he was taught by the master. Younger pupils were taught by an assistant, called an usher, but since no usher's names have survived from the period, Hunt probably is the earliest known teacher of Shakespeare. However, it is uncertain who Hunt was. A Simon Hunt who began a career as a Catholic clergyman in 1578 and died in 1585 is recorded. If he was Shakespeare's teacher, he may conceivably have influenced the religious sensibilities of his pupil and promoted a tolerance for Catholicism. Many scholars see this tolerance in the adult Shakespeare's work, some going so far as to believe that the playwright was a secret Catholic (see SPIRITUAL TESTAMENT OF JOHN SHAKESPEARE). However, another Simon Hunt is known to have died in Stratford in 1598, and whoever the Simon Hunt of Stratford Grammar School was, he did not teach Shakespeare long before being succeeded by Thomas JENKINS.

Huntington Library Major collection of Shakespeareana in San Marino, California. The Huntington Library was created by Henry E. Huntington (1850–1927), the heir to a railroad fortune. Huntington spent much of his wealth on the art museum and library that bear his name. The library contains the largest American collection of early printed books, including many QUARTO and FOLIO editions of Shakespeare's plays. It also contains other Shakespeareana and a large collection of 16th-century music.

Hyman, Earle (b. 1926) African-American actor. Best known today for having portrayed Grandpa Huxtable on television's popular *The Cosby Show* (1984–92), Earle Hyman has played many parts in both classical and modern plays since beginning his career in 1942 at the American Negro Theatre of Harlem. Among his noted Shakespearean portrayals have been Othello and *The Tempest's* Caliban. In 1955 he was part of the founding company of the American Shakespeare Festival at Stratford, Connecticut. He is also noted for his performances in the plays of Henrik Ibsen (1828–1906), and though few of his American fans know it, he is a highly respected actor in Norway, Ibsen's home country, where he has performed many roles in Norwegian, in Ibsen's plays and other work.

I

Illyria Region on the Adriatic coast of present-day Croatia, Serbia, and northern Albania, setting for *Twelfth Night*. As in most of Shakespeare's plays set overseas, there is nothing specifically Illyrian about the surroundings in which the action occurs; Illyria was simply remote and exotic and therefore suitable to a tale of disguise, intrigue, and romance. Like such idealized locales as the Forest of ARDEN in *As You Like It*, Illyria is pervaded with music and song and its inhabitants are concerned chiefly with love and revelry. However, Antonio observes that "these parts . . . often prove rough and unhospitable" (3.3.9–11), reflecting the unsavory reputation of the Illyrian coast, which was a notorious den of piracy until the 17th century. There are references to Illyrian pirates elsewhere in Shakespeare (*2 Henry VI*, 4.1.107; *Measure for Measure*, 4.3.70) and in other Elizabethan literature.

induction Dramatic device of the 16th and 17th centuries—an introductory scene or set of scenes that frankly announces the presentation of a play—that Shakespeare used at the outset of *The Taming of the Shrew*. In two successive scenes, the drunken tinker Christopher Sly is persuaded by the Lord that he is a nobleman, by way of a practical joke, and a group of players performs a play for him; that play is *The Taming of the Shrew*.

Strictly speaking, an induction, though similar in purpose to a PROLOGUE, consists of dialogue instead of a single speech. However, the FOLIO edition of *2 Henry IV* labels the introductory speech by Rumour as "Induction," and it is traditionally separated from 1.1.

An induction was generally found most appropriate in a COMEDY, for it emphasizes the artificiality of the presentation to follow and prepares the audience to accept the ridiculous confusions that characterize the genre. It places the audience at a distance from the main action, which effectively becomes a play within a play.

Ingleby, Clement Mansfield (1823–1886) English scholar. In 1859 Ingleby helped expose the forgeries of J. P. COLLIER in his *The Shakespeare Fabrications*. He followed it with *A Complete View of the Shakespeare Controversy* (1861), which is still regarded as a definitive book on Collier. He wrote a number of other books on Shakespeare and assembled *Shakespeare's Centurie of Prayse* (1875), an anthology of references to the playwright in surviving documents from the period 1591–1693. It was the first of its kind, and later editors have expanded and revised Ingleby's collection, which remains at the core of *The Shakespeare Allusion Book* (1932) edited by Sir Edmund CHAMBERS.

Inns of Court Four law schools in LONDON, in whose buildings at least two of Shakespeare's plays were staged, and which served as a location for a scene in *1 Henry VI*. The Inns of Court—Gray's Inn, Lincoln's Inn, the Middle Temple, and the Inner Temple—were so called because part of their function was to prepare young men to be gentlemen of the royal court. In addition to academic and legal studies, students learned dancing and music, and the Inns were famous for their elaborate MASQUES and other entertainments. The masque presented in 5.2 of *Love's Labour's Lost* is believed to be based on a noteworthy pageant presented at the annual Gray's Inn Christmas Revels in 1594. Shakespeare presumably saw this event, for *The Comedy of Errors* was performed by his acting company as part of the same festival (the earliest recorded performance of the play). It is thought that the "houses" (see PHOENIX; PORCUPINE; PRIORY) described in the *Comedy*'s stage directions reflect the classically influenced stage of the Inn. Also, *Twelfth Night* was performed at the Middle Temple in 1602.

In 2.4 of *1 Henry VI*, the antagonists of what will be the WARS OF THE ROSES engage in a dispute in the Temple Garden, a precinct of the Inns of Court. They bait each other by pointedly selecting emblems from two rose bushes, one red and one white. The incident, which is fictitious, is well placed, for the Inns were legally sanctuaries, where violence of any kind was strictly forbidden. Therefore, the dispute could not come to blows but rather had to be fully explicated in words and symbols.

interlude Sixteenth-century term for a play—especially a short one with few characters—used more specifically to refer to elements in two of Shakespeare's plays. In *The Taming of the Shrew*, the passage 1.1.248–253 is spoken of as an interlude because it is a return to the story of Christopher Sly, begun in the INDUCTION. It is believed that there were originally several other interludes and an EPILOGUE, completing the tale, and that these are presented, although in altered form, in the anonymous play *The Taming of a Shrew* (published 1594), thought to be a BAD QUARTO of Shakespeare's play. These passages are sometimes included in modern editions of the play, although they are missing from the original publication of *The Taming of the Shrew*; they were probably cut from an early production because of a shortage of available actors.

The term *interlude* is also used in *A Midsummer Night's Dream*—and by writers about the play—to refer to the performance of PYRAMUS AND THISBE

staged by the artisans of ATHENS. The term was probably old-fashioned in Shakespeare's day and may have carried a connotation of rustic quaintness.

Inverness City in northern SCOTLAND, the site of Macbeth's castle and the location of several scenes in *Macbeth*. Beginning in 1.5 when Lady Macbeth learns of the WITCHES' prediction that Macbeth will be king, through 2.4, when Macbeth's upcoming coronation is abruptly announced, Inverness is associated with the planning, execution, and aftermath of the assassination of King Duncan. In 1.6 Duncan and Banquo describe the castle at Inverness as a lovely building, thronged with birds and characterized by a pleasant atmosphere, but its nature quickly changes as our sense of it is influenced by the evil done there. It is associated with hell in 2.3.1–21, where the Porter comically portrays a gatekeeper of hell, an ancient dramatic tradition of medieval religious drama. The description of terrible omens in 2.4 leaves us with an impression of Inverness as a castle of horrors. Productions of *Macbeth* have commonly emphasized this idea, with sets that stress darkness and Gothic detail.

Historically, the inclusion of Inverness in the play is an anachronism. Macbeth did not murder Duncan at Inverness—he didn't murder him at all—and there was no castle at Inverness until at least a century later. However, Shakespeare took this error from his source, HOLINSHED's history, and doubtless believed it was correct.

Ireland, William Henry (1777–1835) English forger. In 1794 the 17-year-old Ireland, a lawyer's clerk, forged a number of documents relating to Shakespeare. These included business papers, letters (one to Anne HATHAWAY, with a lock of hair), and the playwright's profession of religious faith. He claimed they had been given by Shakespeare to a friend, a descendant of whom had disclosed them anonymously. Ireland's father, an amateur scholar, exhibited these materials in good faith and published them as *Miscellaneous Papers and Legal Instruments under the Hand and Seal of William Shakespeare* (1796). They caused a sensation, and Ireland responded by creating two Shakespearean plays. One of them, a tragedy entitled *Vortigern and*

Rowena, was produced by J. P. Kemble in April 1796, although scholars, led by Edmond MALONE, were already suspicious. The play was laughed off the stage, and the second work (*Henry II*) was never performed. Under pressure after the publication of Malone's *Inquiry into the Authenticity of Certain Miscellaneous Papers and Legal Instruments* (1796), Ireland confessed, and wrote *An Authentic Account of the Shakespearian Manuscripts* (1796), in which he described his procedures and cleared his father. He became a hack writer and produced a number of poor novels and a memoir (*Confessions of William Henry Ireland* [1805]), before he died in poverty.

Irving, Henry (1838–1905) British actor and producer. Irving was London's leading Shakespearean actor and producer for the last quarter of the 19th century. Though he played few Shakespearean parts during the first 15 years of his acting career, Irving was highly acclaimed as Hamlet in 1874, and over the next few years he portrayed Macbeth, Othello, and Richard III, establishing himself as one of the best classical actors of the day. From 1878 to 1902 he managed his own company at London's Lyceum Theatre, with himself and Ellen TERRY as the featured performers. They staged many of Shakespeare's plays, including *Hamlet* (1879), *The Merchant of Venice* (1879), *Othello* (1881), *Romeo and Juliet* (1882), *Much Ado About Nothing* (1882), *Twelfth Night* (1884), *Macbeth* (1888), *Henry VIII* (1892), *King Lear* (1892), *Cymbeline* (1896), and *Coriolanus* (1901). He was famous for his extravagant productions, with many extras, elaborate sets and costumes, and special scenic effects. Irving was a tyrannical director by all accounts, "incapable of caring for anything outside his work," in Terry's words. His business manager at the Lyceum was Bram Stoker, the author of *Dracula,* and it has been thought that Stoker's famous protagonist reflects the actor-producer's domineering personality. Irving's acting and production were not without detractors, but he was generally praised, and in 1895 he became the first actor to be knighted. In 1902 his lease on the Lyceum was not renewed, and he turned to touring. He died a few hours after a performance on the road.

Italy European country, the setting for many of Shakespeare's plays. Though not yet a single nation in Shakespeare's day, Italy was the fountainhead of the RENAISSANCE and the cultural leader of Europe. Many of Shakespeare's sources were Italian, with the consequence that Italian cities were the locations of many of his plays, especially the comedies. Also, Italy had been the center of the ancient Roman Empire, so Shakespeare's ROMAN PLAYS tended to feature Italian locations, especially ROME. However, there is nothing especially Italian about Shakespeare's settings, and the Italian cities ostensibly shown—such as MANTUA, MESSINA, PADUA, VENICE, and VERONA—tend to resemble Shakespeare's LONDON. The plays in which some or all of the action is set in Italy include *All's Well That Ends Well, Antony and Cleopatra, Coriolanus, Cymbeline, Julius Caesar, The Merchant of Venice, Much Ado About Nothing, Othello, Romeo and Juliet, The Taming of the Shrew, Titus Andronicus, The Two Gentlemen of Verona,* and *The Winter's Tale.*

J

Jackson, Barry (1879–1961) British theatrical producer. Jackson was extremely influential on 20th-century Shakespearean production, especially with his modern-dress productions of *Cymbeline* (1923), *Hamlet* (1925), and *Macbeth* (1928), staged at the Birmingham Repertory Theatre, which he founded in 1913. He was director of the Shakespeare Memorial Theatre in STRATFORD from 1945 to 1948.

Jackson, John (ca. 1574–ca. 1625) Friend of Shakespeare in LONDON. Jackson was a partner with Shakespeare and others in the purchase of the BLACKFRIAR'S GATEHOUSE in 1613. He was probably the John Jackson, a shipping magnate from northern England, who was a regular patron of the MERMAID TAVERN and a close friend of Thomas SAVAGE.

Jackson, Roger (1601–1625) London publisher and bookseller. Jackson bought the rights to *The Rape of Lucrece* from the younger John HARRISON in 1614, and he published Q6 of the poem, the first edition to bear the full title, in 1616.

Jacobean drama Art of writing for the theater as practiced in England during the reign of King JAMES I (1603–25). The drama of this period clearly evolves from ELIZABETHAN DRAMA, and that term is often taken to cover the Jacobean period as well. However, by about 1610, Jacobean drama was quite different. It is usually characterized as decadent, by comparison, in that substantive themes and fine poetry were increasingly subordinated to the titillating effects of the spectacular and bizarre. There are certainly exceptions to this indictment, most notably the late work of Shakespeare, but commentators over the centuries have generally agreed that the period is markedly inferior to its predecessor.

Early in the Jacobean period, Shakespeare manifested the continuing vitality of English TRAGEDY with *Othello, King Lear, Macbeth, Antony and Cleopatra,* and *Coriolanus.* Another major Jacobean tragedy was written early in the period, George CHAPMAN's *Bussy D'Ambois* (1604), but besides Shakespeare, the only great Jacobean writer of tragedies, in most opinions, was John WEBSTER, whose *The White Devil* (1612) and *The Duchess of Malfi* (1614) are still frequently performed. He may also have written most of *The Revenger's Tragedy* (1606), though it is frequently attributed to Cyril Tourneur (ca. 1575–1626), a much lesser talent. Webster's tragedies are all REVENGE PLAYs (as is *Bussy*), a genre that continued to be popular. Thomas MIDDLETON also wrote tragedies, and late in the period another figure arose, John FORD.

In line with the decadence of the period, Jacobean tragedies often rely on false starts, sudden changes of motivation, and gratuitous accidents. The artificiality of these devices reflects a different emotional tone: These works largely ignore the implications of human disaster for society or for humanity as a whole, and focus instead on the pathos of the individual. Even that tends to be diminished by a predilection for cheap sensationalism and unsavory sexual themes, as the open bawdiness of the Elizabethans yields to a furtive indecency.

Perhaps the best-known Jacobean dramatists are Francis BEAUMONT and John FLETCHER, who collaborated on a number of plays that typify the spirit of the era, so much so that in the 1630s they were rated well above Shakespeare by most playgoers. Their *Philaster* (1610) sparked a vogue for a characteristic TRAGICOMEDY that was widely imitated for decades. Its unrealistic protagonist, who changes his motivation repeatedly, rejects his lover on ludicrous suspicions of infidelity. By a series of absurd coincidences, lives and nations are placed at stake while he splits hairs at great length over perverse notions of honor. Only further improbable accidents bring about a final reunion of the lovers. Mysterious in their way, grand in their pretensions, and entirely escapist, *Philaster* and its successors appealed immensely to the decadent court society that made up its audience.

In COMEDY, Shakespeare's ROMANCES, written early in the period, evidence the emerging taste for spectacle, exotic locales, romantic characters, and improbable plots. However, these works are singular for their interest in the virtues of innocence and the role of providence in human affairs. The romance literature at their roots is uproariously satirized in Beaumont's *The Knight of the Burning Pestle* (ca. 1608), but Jacobean comedy in general is not so genial as this work. Ben JONSON's "city comedies," which evolved from the earlier COMEDY OF HUMOURS, satirized 17th-century LONDON with sharp and biting acerbity. These works—most notably *Volpone* (1606), *Epicoene* (ca. 1609), *The Alchemist* (1610), and *Bartholomew Fair* (1614)—are among the greatest English comedies. They represent the positive aspect of Jacobean comedy, which otherwise tended toward coarser works chiefly concerned with the pursuit of money through bald sexual intrigue. Among the other Jacobean dramatists who wrote notable comedies are Middleton, Fletcher, and Philip MASSINGER.

Jacobean drama (the term is taken from *Jacobus*, Latin for James) is often considered to cover Caroline or Carolean drama (1625–42), that is, during the reign of Charles I until the closure of the theaters by the Civil Wars. The only important playwrights of this period were Ford and James Shirley (1596–1666). The Jacobean tendencies to deca-

dence continued to grow, and Puritan opposition to the theater grew with it; the result was the 18-year demise of the theaters. The Caroline period is considered the end of the RENAISSANCE in England.

Jacobi, Derek (b. 1938) British actor. As a young actor, Derek Jacobi was recruited by Laurence OLIVIER to become a founding member of the new National Theatre of Great Britain in 1963. His first role was as Laertes opposite Olivier's Hamlet. He has played a wide range of parts in Shakespeare, including Aaron (*Titus Andronicus*), Touchstone (*As You Like It*), Richard II, Richard III, Benedick (*Much Ado About Nothing*), Prospero (*The Tempest*), Macbeth, and Hamlet. He has appeared in two of Kenneth BRANAGH's Shakespeare FILMS, as the Prologue in *Henry V* and as King Claudius in *Hamlet*. While Jacobi has for many years been regarded as one of Britain's finest theatrical actors, in both classic and contemporary drama, he is perhaps best known to a wider audience for his portrayal of the title character in the BBC's 1977 presentation of Robert Graves's *I, Claudius*.

Jaggard, William (ca. 1568–1623), and **Jaggard Isaac** (1597–1627) London printers and publishers, father and son, producers of the FIRST FOLIO and other editions of Shakespeare's works. In 1599 William Jaggard published THE PASSIONATE PILGRIM, an anthology of poems said to be by Shakespeare, though only about a quarter of them actually were. In 1612 he reissued this work, adding to it two poems by Thomas HEYWOOD. When Heywood publicly protested, on his own behalf and Shakespeare's, Jaggard replaced the title page with one that named no author.

Beginning in about 1613, Isaac Jaggard increasingly controlled the firm, due to his father's failing eyesight. In 1619 the Jaggards, with Thomas PAVIER, produced a group of QUARTO editions of 10 plays attributed to Shakespeare, though only a few were proper texts of Shakespeare's plays. These are known collectively as the FALSE FOLIO. Protests prompted the publishers to backdate most of these titles so that they could pass for the original editions.

Such practices were more acceptable then than now and did not prevent the Jaggards from joining the syndicate that published the FIRST FOLIO edition of Shakespeare's works in 1623. William Jaggard was blind by this time, and Isaac headed the project; William died before it was completed.

James, Elias (ca. 1578–1610) London brewer whose EPITAPH is attributed to Shakespeare. The six-line memorial to James first appeared in a manuscript collection of poems dating from the 1630s, some years after Shakespeare's death. The poem is ascribed to Shakespeare in an unknown hand, but modern scholars are inclined to accept the attribution, for James may well have been a friend or acquaintance of the playwright. James's brewery was located near the BLACKFRIARS THEATRE, and Shakespeare's friend John JACKSON married the widow of James's brother and partner Jacob James.

James I, King of England (1566–1625) Ruler of England during the last years of Shakespeare's life and the patron of his acting company. James and his court were enthusiastic playgoers, and their tastes were highly influential on JACOBEAN DRAMA. James had been interested in the theater before he came to England; as James VI of SCOTLAND, he had employed English actors led by Laurence FLETCHER. As king of England, he took over Shakespeare's CHAMBERLAIN'S MEN, and they performed at his court—as the KING'S MEN—more than twice as often as they had for his predecessor, Queen Elizabeth I (see Elizabeth I in *Henry VIII*). Moreover, the other two leading LONDON companies came under royal patronage, as the QUEEN'S MEN and PRINCE HENRY'S MEN. The family added two more troupes around 1610, PRINCE CHARLES' MEN and LADY ELIZABETH'S MEN. On the other hand, state CENSORSHIP increased under King James, whose strong religious sentiments combined with his worries as the first ruler of the STUART DYNASTY—especially after the Gunpowder Plot (see GARNET, HENRY)—to demand strict controls on the public's exposure to ideas.

Twice Shakespeare alluded to James in his plays, both times in the words of characters making auspicious prophecies of Britain's future. In *Macbeth*, James's purported ancestor Banquo is a very positive figure, and eight spectral Kings appear to Macbeth, who realizes they represent Banquo's progeny

and notes that some of them carry "two-fold balls and treble sceptres" (4.1.121). To Shakespeare's original audiences, this was an easily recognized reference to James's royal regalia as the ruler of both England and Scotland. In *Henry VIII* the play reaches its climax with Archbishop Cranmer's eulogy to the infant Elizabeth, and he adds a postscript praising her heir, declaring that he "Shall star-like rise, as great in fame as she was, / And so stand fix'd" (5.4.46–47). James was presumably flattered by these references; that he enjoyed Shakespeare's works is attested to in Ben JONSON's poem on Shakespeare (published in the FIRST FOLIO [1623]), where he speaks of the playwright's "flights . . . that did so take . . . our James!"

James I was an enthusiastic patron of the theater, and he particularly enjoyed Shakespeare's works. Ben Jonson, speaking also of James's predecessor Queen Elizabeth, wrote of Shakespeare's "flights . . . That so did take Eliza, and our James!" *(Courtesy of National Maritime Museum, Greenwich)*

James was the son of Mary, Queen of Scots (1542–87), and in 1567, as an infant, he was made King James VI of Scotland, on his mother's forced abdication. He never saw his mother again; after losing a civil war, she fled to England and was eventually executed by her enemy, Queen Elizabeth. He was raised a Protestant by a series of regents. The cornerstone of his policy as king was to secure his succession to the childless Elizabeth, who was his cousin. In 1589 he married Princess Anne of Denmark (1574–1619), and though he was homosexual by preference, they had seven children, three of whom survived infancy: Prince HENRY FREDERICK, Prince Charles—later King Charles I (ruled 1625–49)—and Princess ELIZABETH STUART. Though James was at first well liked in England—not least because his accession had been bloodless, despite fears of civil war—soon his popularity waned. His increasingly blatant homosexuality offended many, his sale of monopolies to his favorites angered Parliament, and his policy of alliance with Spain enraged the country.

Further, his tendency to preach to his subjects eventually aroused resentment. James was undeniably a pedant; John HARINGTON, meaning no compliment, called him "schoolmaster of the realm." He published a number of works on theology, two books asserting the divine right of kings, and a pamphlet denouncing the evils of smoking (*A Counterblaste to Tobacco* [1604]). He also wrote and translated poetry in English, Latin, and Scots, and published a manual of Scots prosody. Though James was an intelligent king who sincerely desired to be a good ruler, he was a failure. Out of touch with the English people and by nature disinclined to compromise, he was a bad politician, and his reign widened the gap between Crown and Parliament that led to the Civil Wars.

Janssen, Cornelius (Cornelius Johnson, Cornelius Jonson) (1593–1661) English painter to whom a possible portrait of Shakespeare is attributed. The "Janssen portrait," or "Somerset portrait," as it is known (it was owned by a Duke of Somerset in the late 18th century), somewhat resembles the most authoritative portraits of Shakespeare (see DROESHOUT, MARTIN; JANSSEN, GHEERART; PORTRAITS OF SHAKESPEARE). However,

it is chiefly associated with the playwright for its inscription, which indicates that the anonymous sitter was 46 years old in 1610, the date the portrait was painted, as was Shakespeare. Even so, this could easily be coincidence, and that the painting depicts Shakespeare is regarded as highly questionable by most scholars. The work is apparently a copy of another portrait from the period, also possibly by Janssen—the clothes, elaborately detailed, are exactly identical in the two paintings—with the facial features altered to resemble the known images of Shakespeare. The creation of a portrait of a well-known figure was often done this way in both the 17th and 18th centuries, so the altered copy could have been made then.

Janssen, whose name is often Anglicized, was born in England of Dutch parents, but, probably returned to Holland for his training. He was painting in London at least as early as 1617, and he maintained a thriving practice as a portraitist until he returned to Holland for good in 1643, when he fled from the English Civil Wars. He is regarded as among the leading English painters of his day.

Janssen, Gheerart (Gerard Johnson) (active 1600–1623) English sculptor, creator of the memorial bust of Shakespeare in Holy Trinity Church at STRATFORD, one of the two PORTRAITS OF SHAKESPEARE considered by scholars to reflect his actual appearance (the other is an engraving by Martin DROESHOUT). Because the Janssen bust was presumably commissioned and approved by Shakespeare's family, it probably provides a satisfactory likeness, although it is a conventionally stylized image rather than a psychologically revealing portrait. Presumably it was made from an earlier portrait, probably a drawing or painting that is now lost. Made of painted limestone, the bust depicts a well-dressed gentleman with auburn hair and a quill pen in his right hand. The bust and its elaborate frame were installed sometime between 1616 and 1622; in the late 18th century it was whitewashed and repainted in its present colors—though they may not be those originally provided by Janssen—in 1861. In 1790 the original pen, made of lead, was replaced with a real goosefeather quill, and a new quill is provided every year on Shakespeare's birthday.

Gheerart Janssen, whose name is sometimes Anglicized to Gerard Johnson, was the son of a Dutch stone carver who arrived in England in the 1560s and established a flourishing business in SOUTHWARK, near the GLOBE THEATRE. This location suggests that Janssen may have known Shakespeare, at least by sight. Janssen inherited the family business in 1611. Another of his clients was Shakespeare's friend John COMBE, whose memorial is also in the Stratford church.

Jeffes, Humphrey (d. 1618)   English actor. Jeffes may have played a minor role in an early production of *3 Henry VI*, for in the FIRST FOLIO text of the play a Keeper is designated "Humfrey" in a stage direction. If this is Jeffes, he was probably a member of PEMBROKE'S MEN in 1592–93, when they are believed to have staged the play. Jeffes is first recorded, however, as a member of the ADMIRAL'S MEN in 1597, after the Pembroke's Men collapsed in the wake of the *Isle of Dogs* scandal. He remained with his new company for almost 20 years and finally left its successor, the PALSGRAVE'S MEN, in 1616 to take a company on tour in the provinces, though his company soon had its permit revoked for unknown reasons.

Jenkins, Thomas (active 1566–1579)   STRATFORD schoolmaster, Shakespeare's grammar school teacher. Jenkins was master of the Stratford Grammar School from 1575–79, the period when Shakespeare learned much of the Latin literature that was at the core of the Elizabethan grammar school curriculum. Jenkins was a well-qualified teacher of the material, as he was an Oxford-educated clergyman and an experienced teacher. The Stratford burgesses recruited him from a similar position in Warwick. His Welsh name has suggested to scholars that he may be the inspiration for Shakespeare's creation Sir Hugh EVANS, the Welsh schoolteacher of *The Merry Wives of Windsor*. However, Jenkins was born in London, the son of a servant. His education was presumably provided by his father's master, who was a founder of the college at Oxford where he studied. In 1579 he resigned his position at Stratford and recruited his own successor,

John COTTOM. Jenkins was married—a daughter died and a son was born during his tenure at Stratford—but little more is known of his life.

Jerusalem Chamber   Room in WESTMINSTER ABBEY, the setting for 4.4 of *2 Henry IV*. The dying King Henry IV talks there with his younger sons and other noblemen about Prince Hal, who the king fears is dissolute and will make a bad heir to the throne. News arrives that the rebels against the king have been defeated, but the excitement causes the king to swoon and he is taken to another room. The encounter between Hal and his father in 4.5 takes place in the second chamber; the king asks the name of the first room. Told that it is the Jerusalem Chamber, he asks to be returned there, thus fulfilling a prophecy that he would die in Jerusalem.

King Henry did in fact die in the Jerusalem Chamber, but the prophecy, which Shakespeare took from HOLINSHED, is not recorded elsewhere. The same story—a prophecy to death in Jerusalem followed by death in a church or room of that name—is told of several medieval figures and is probably apocryphal in most cases, including this one. The name of the room, which was originally part of the Abbot's residence, comes from an inscription surrounding the fireplace.

Johnson, Arthur (d. 1631)   LONDON bookseller and publisher, producer of the first edition of *The Merry Wives of Windsor*. Johnson published a wide range of literature, including several plays. In 1602 he brought out the BAD QUARTO (Q1) of *The Merry Wives* and in 1608 the first edition of THE MERRY DEVIL OF EDMONTON, a play that was later wrongly attributed to Shakespeare. Sometime after 1624 Johnson moved to Dublin, where he became a stationer.

Johnson, Charles (1679–1748)   English playwright. Johnson wrote 18 plays, several of them quite successful, but he is best known today for two works derived from Shakespeare. *The Cobbler of Preston* (1716), a political play that commented on the Jacobite rebellion of 1715, was embedded in a version of the Christopher Sly episode of *The Taming of the Shrew*. His LOVE IN A FOREST (1723) was a loose adaptation of *As You Like It*. A prominent figure in the London literary world of his day, Johnson was among the targets of the satirical *Dunciad* (1728, 1743), by Alexander POPE.

Johnson, Cornelius See JANSSEN, CORNELIUS.

Johnson, Gerard See JANSSEN, GHEERART.

Johnson, Robert (d. 1611) Vintner and innkeeper of STRATFORD and Shakespeare's tenant. Johnson owned a tavern, known at different times as the White Lion and the Swan Inn, that abutted the property on which Shakespeare's BIRTHPLACE stood. He rented a barn on that property from Shakespeare and presumably used it in connection with the inn. This rental is known only because the lease is mentioned in the inventory of possessions accompanying Johnson's will, recorded in October 1611 by Thomas ASPINALL. In 1670 Johnson's son still rented the barn, when it was mentioned in the will of Elizabeth HALL, Shakespeare's granddaughter.

Johnson, Robert (ca. 1585–ca. 1634) English musician and composer, probable writer of music for several of Shakespeare's plays. In the *Cheerful Ayres* (ca. 1660) of John WILSON, Johnson is credited with music for "Where the bee sucks" and "Full fadom five" from *The Tempest,* possibly written for the performance of the play given as part of the wedding festivities of the princess ELIZABETH STUART in 1613. Scholars believe that Johnson also composed SONG music for *Cymbeline* and *The Winter's Tale,* although the surviving sheet music is anonymous. Music he wrote for a MASQUE by Francis BEAUMONT, also performed at Princess Elizabeth's wedding, was probably also used in performances of *The Two Noble Kinsmen.* Johnson also composed songs for *The Duchess of Malfi* (1614) by John WEBSTER, *The Witch* (1615) by Thomas MIDDLETON (this music may have been used in early productions of *Macbeth,* as well), and five plays by Beaumont and John FLETCHER.

As a boy, Johnson was a servant in the household of George Carey, Baron HUNSDON; his abilities were already recognized, for he was employed as a music teacher. It was doubtless through Hunsdon, who was the patron of the CHAMBERLAIN'S MEN,

Shakespeare's acting company, that Johnson became a theatrical composer. After 1604 he was also the royal lutenist for King JAMES I and King Charles I, composing and performing music for royal masques and other entertainments.

Johnson, Samuel (1709–1784) English poet, scholar, literary critic, and lexicographer, the leading figure in English literature in the mid-18th century. Dr. Johnson, as he is universally known, wrote poems, biographies, and essays on a wide range of subjects, and he compiled the first great English dictionary (1755). In 1765 he published an edition of Shakespeare's plays. While it is not regarded as significant in terms of scholarship—it was based on an inferior text and added little in the way of notes and commentary—it was nevertheless the basis for the greater edition of George STEEVENS, and it includes a preface that is regarded as one of Johnson's finest works. Johnson's intellectual and social life as a leader of his age are still accessible to us through the *Life of Samuel Johnson* (1791) by James Boswell (1740–95), a masterpiece of English literature.

Johnson, William (active 1591–1616) Landlord of the MERMAID TAVERN in London and a friend of Shakespeare. Johnson, with John HEMINGE and John JACKSON, assisted Shakespeare by serving as a trustee in his purchase of the BLACKFRIARS GATEHOUSE in 1613. While no other connection is known, this one assumes a fairly close acquaintance. Shakespeare may have been a member of the Friday Street Club, a literary gathering that met informally at the Mermaid, or he may have stayed there while visiting London after he moved back to STRATFORD.

Johnson had served an apprenticeship with the previous landlord of the Mermaid, taking over the management himself in 1603. Shortly after his involvement in Shakespeare's purchase, Johnson found himself in legal difficulties, charged with serving meat at the tavern during Lent, though the case may not have gone to court.

Jones, James Earl (b. 1931) African-American actor. Jones, one of the leading black actors of the New York stage, made his Broadway debut in 1958

and soon established a reputation as a classical actor. He was especially acclaimed as the title character in a 1973 production of *King Lear* by Joseph PAPP. He was also noteworthy as Othello, opposite Christopher PLUMMER's Iago, in Nicol WILLIAMSON's 1982 staging.

Jones, Richard (active 1583–1624)   English actor. Jones was a member of WORCESTER'S MEN in 1583–84 with the young Edward ALLEYN, and he was probably a member of Alleyn's ADMIRAL'S MEN by 1585. He traveled in Germany with a company headed by Robert BROWNE in 1592–93, but he rejoined the Admiral's Men again in 1594. Except for a brief period in 1597, he was with them until 1602. He is known to have played Priam in *Troilus and Cressida*. In 1610 he was a partner, with Browne and others, in a CHILDREN'S COMPANY that performed at the WHITE-FRIARS THEATRE, but by 1615 he was again in Germany, this time with John GREEN. By 1622 he was employed as a musician in a minor German court, but he returned to England the next year. He is last known from a letter of 1624 to his German employer, asking to return, since he had not found work in England.

Jones, Robert (active 1590–1615)   Composer and theatrical entrepreneur. Jones was a famed lute player and composer of settings for SONGs. Shakespeare apparently adapted the song "Farewell, dear heart" (*Twelfth Night*, 2.3.102–112) from a work in Jones's *The First Book of Songes and Ayres* (1600), though the playwright may have known the song elsewhere.

Jones, William (d. 1618)   LONDON bookseller and publisher, producer of first editions of two plays of the Shakespeare APOCRYPHA. Between 1598 and 1615 Jones published the first six editions of MUCE-DORUS, one of the most popular plays of the day; none of these editions attributed the play to Shakespeare. In 1602 Jones published the first edition of *THOMAS LORD CROMWELL*, which was credited to "W. S.," though it is unclear whether this attribution was intended to associate the work with Shakespeare. Jones was apprenticed to a printer in 1578, was a member of the STATIONERS' COMPANY by 1587, and when he died in 1618, he left an impoverished widow who was forced to sell his copyrights. Little more is known of his life.

Jonson, Ben (1572–1637)   English poet and playwright, a great satirist and a leading light of JACOBEAN DRAMA. Jonson's greatest achievements were works of satiric COMEDY—especially *Volpone* (1606), *Epicoene* (ca. 1609), *The Alchemist* (1610), and *Bartholomew Fair* (1614)—and MASQUEs written for the court of King JAMES I. Jonson's satire influenced Shakespeare's own most satirical works, such as *Troilus and Cressida* and *Timon of Athens*, and the popularity of Jonson's masques helped create the theatrical world in which Shakespeare wrote his ROMANCES. Jonson is regarded as second only to Shakespeare among the playwrights of the period. Jonson also wrote on literary theory, and his stress on clarity over personal style, on classical forms of aesthetic organization, and on relevance to one's own times influenced English poets and dramatists for a century.

Jonson received a good secondary education at the Westminster School, where he was taught by William CAMDEN, but as the stepson of a bricklayer, he was apprenticed to that trade. Instead, he enlisted in the army and went to the Low Countries, where he reportedly killed an enemy soldier in a man-to-man combat staged between the opposing armies. By 1592 he was back in LONDON and married, though his life for the next five years is otherwise unknown. In 1597 he was a member of PEMBROKE'S MEN and was jailed as a player in the "seditious" play *Isle of Dogs* (see CENSORSHIP), which he may have helped write. A year later he was again imprisoned, this time for killing his fellow actor Gabriel SPENCER in a duel. He escaped the death penalty only through an archaic technicality: clergymen were exempt from punishment, and clergymen were defined as all those capable of reading Latin.

Jonson's first successful play, *Every Man in His Humour*, was staged by the CHAMBERLAIN'S MEN in 1598; Shakespeare may have been responsible for its acceptance by the company, and he was in the cast. One of the finest examples of the COMEDY OF HUMOURS, this work was extremely popular. Unfortunately, its sequel the next year, *Every Man out of*

His Humour, was equally unsuccessful. It was one of the first shots in the WAR OF THE THEATERS, an exchange of satirical plays by Jonson on one side and John MARSTON and Thomas DEKKER on the other. Jonson's other efforts in this fray were produced by the Children of the Chapel (see CHILDREN'S COMPANIES). Jonson next worked for Philip HENSLOWE and the ADMIRAL'S MEN, writing additional material for *The Spanish Tragedy* (ca. 1588) by Thomas KYD before creating his own major work, *Sejanus* (1603). This TRAGEDY, modeled on SENECA, was staged by the KING'S MEN, again with Shakespeare in the cast (this is the last record of Shakespeare as an actor).

Beginning in 1605, Jonson began his collaboration with Inigo Jones (1573–1652), the royal architect, who designed the settings and machinery for the masques that Jonson composed. Over the next quarter century, this partnership produced brilliant spectacles that influenced both drama and theater design for generations. However, near the beginning of this period, Jonson once again courted royal disfavor, this time as coauthor with Marston and George CHAPMAN of *Eastward Ho!* (1605), a play containing political remarks that the king declared seditious. Jonson was briefly jailed again, before the affair blew over. In the next few years Jonson reached his peak of achievement with *Volpone, Epicoene,* and *The Alchemist.* The first and last of these was produced by the King's Men. *Bartholomew Fair* was staged by LADY ELIZABETH'S MEN in 1614, after Jonson returned from a year's travel in Europe as the tutor to Sir Walter RALEIGH's son.

In 1616 Jonson issued a collection of his works—poetry, prose, and drama—a deed that was widely ridiculed because plays were not generally considered to have literary value at the time. In the same year the king gave Jonson a pension for life, making him effectively the first Poet Laureate, though the honor was not so named until later. He traveled in SCOTLAND, where William Drummond of Hawthornden noted his conversational remarks on himself and his contemporaries—a record that has served modern historians of the theater. After his return, his career deteriorated. Only one further play was a success: *The Staple of News* (1625), a satire on the newsletter of Nathaniel BUTTER. A

bitter fight with Inigo Jones ended his creation of masques. (Characteristically, Jonson recorded the quarrel in *A Tale of a Tub* [1633], a play that flopped in London.) He also suffered from illness and lost his extraordinary library to a disastrous fire. He died with a play half-written and was buried in WESTMINSTER ABBEY.

Shakespeare and Jonson were very different men, with different sensibilities and different attitudes toward life and art, yet they seem to have been friends, beginning with the production of *Every Man in His Humour.* The tradition that Shakespeare died after a drinking bout with Jonson and Michael DRAYTON is almost certainly not true, but it reflects a reality. They probably met often at the MERMAID TAVERN, and they seem to have enjoyed criticizing each other. Another story, possibly apocryphal, demonstrates the tone of their friendly rivalry: Jonson and Shakespeare, "being merry at a tavern," composed an EPITAPH for Jonson. Jonson composed the first two lines, "Here lies Ben Jonson / that was once one," and Shakespeare devised the final two: "Who while he lived was a slow thing, / And now, being dead, is nothing." (Jonson's agonizing slowness in writing was often jested about.)

An amateur play about the theater world, performed at Cambridge University in 1601 (see PARNASSUS PLAYS), refers to Shakespeare's having given Jonson "a purge" in response to criticism. This may merely express the author's preference for Shakespeare, but it may also echo some otherwise lost piece of gossip. At least once Shakespeare alluded to Jonson in his work. In *Twelfth Night* Feste remarks that the word *element* is "overworn" (3.1.60), a casual reference to Dekker's satire of Jonson's alleged overuse of the term. Further, Shakespeare's Ajax, Jaques, and Nym (in *Troilus and Cressida, As You Like It,* and *Henry V,* respectively) have all been suggested as possible parodies of Jonson.

For his part, Jonson frequently remarked on Shakespeare, often acknowledging his friend's greatness. For instance, after Shakespeare's death, Jonson wrote, "I lov'd the man, and do honour his memory (this side idolatry) as much as any." However, this remark followed a criticism of Shakespeare's carelessness as a writer, and most of

Jonson's recorded comments on his friend are like-wise combinations of praise and censure. Jonson was an arrogant man, by all accounts, including his own, and he was a fierce critic; he once declared that John Donne (1573–1631) "deserved hanging" for writing poetry in an irregular METER. While he could not but admire Shakespeare's virtues, he could not refrain from finding things to criticize, particularly when such "defects" contrasted with his own traits. For instance, Jonson's famous con-tention (quite untrue) that Shakespeare "never blotted" a line, implicitly praised his own laborious technique. Similarly, his notorious remark that Shakespeare had "small Latin and less Greek" was true only by comparison to his own great erudition. Nevertheless, each derogation was coupled with praise—"There was ever more in him to be praised, than to be pardoned," he wrote—and it was Jonson who penned one of the most famous tributes to Shakespeare, in his prefatory verses to the FIRST FOLIO (1623): "He was not of an age, but for all time!"

Jordan, Dorothy (1761–1816)   Irish actress. Mrs. Jordan—the adopted name by which Dorothea Bland was known—made her stage debut in Dublin in 1777, playing Phebe in *As You Like It*. After 1775 she established herself in London, where she mostly played comedic heroines. Her best-known Shake-spearean roles were Rosalind, Imogen, and Viola (in *As You Like It*, *Cymbeline*, and *Twelfth Night*, respec-tively). She also played in William Henry IRELAND's forged Shakespearean play, *Vortigern* (1796). She was the longtime mistress of the Duke of Clarence, later King William IV (ruled 1830–37), by whom she had 10 children.

Jourdain,   Sylvester (Sylvester   Jourdan) (ca. 1580–1650)   English colonial entrepreneur and writer, author of a probable source for *The Tempest*. Jourdain was a member of an expedition to Virginia that was shipwrecked in Bermuda in 1609. He was marooned for 10 months, and his recounting of his experiences in *The Discovery of the Barmudas* [sic] (1610) provided Shakespeare with such details for *The Tempest* as the mysterious "supernatural" noises that Caliban describes in 3.2.133–138. Jourdain's account also confirmed Shakespeare's principal source, a letter by William STRACHEY, which stressed the miraculous nature of their survival. Shakespeare follows these accounts in emphasizing the role of providence in *The Tempest*. Jourdain was a Puritan merchant from Dorsetshire who settled in LONDON after his adventures.

K

Kean, Charles (1811–1868) British actor and producer. Charles Kean, the son of Edmund KEAN, was acclaimed as Hamlet, but his greatest importance was not as an actor but as the producer of Shakespeare's plays (and others) in a lavish style, incorporating elaborate spectacles that laid claim to historical accuracy. Costumes and sets were designed with scrupulous attention to archaeological detail, and immense casts of extras were used. Among his most notable productions were *Henry VIII* (1855), *The Winter's Tale* (1856), *Richard II* (1857), and *Henry V* (1859). He established a style of production that was to last into the early 20th century in the work of his followers, including Henry IRVING and Beerbohm TREE.

Kean, Edmund (1787–1833) British actor. The abandoned son of an actress, Kean was raised in provincial touring companies, by various people—including his guardian, Moses Kean, a comic and ventriloquist who may have been his uncle, though his paternity was never clearly established. He already had many years of acting experience when he achieved a London triumph in *The Merchant of Venice* as Shylock in 1814. His acting style was frenzied and active, in marked contrast to the reigning Shakespearean actor, the dignified J. P. KEMBLE. A contemporary, using a political metaphor, declared that Kean was "one of the people . . . a *radical* performer," and Samuel Taylor COLERIDGE remarked of his "rapid descents from the hyper-tragic to the infra-colloquial" that "to see him act, is like reading Shakespeare by flashes of lightning." His greatest successes were as villains—especially Shylock, Richard III, Othello, and Barabas in *The Jew of Malta* by Christopher MARLOWE—while his Hamlet and Lear were sometimes criticized as unthoughtful. He was a temperamental and undisciplined man who often missed performances, and he figured in a notable sex scandal with the wife of a popular politician. Nevertheless, only Kemble and W. C. MACREADY rivaled him in popularity. His success was so great that he has been called the theater's first star, to whom all other features of a production were subordinated. He collapsed onstage while playing Othello—opposite the Iago of his son Charles KEAN—and died a few weeks later.

Keats, John (1795–1821) English poet much influenced by Shakespeare. Generally regarded as among the greatest of all poets, Keats kept a bust of Shakespeare in his study and believed, at least sometimes, that the spirit of Shakespeare presided over his work in a supernatural way, dictating choices as he wrote his poems. In any case Shakespeare's influence on Keats's poetry—in a conventional literary sense—is very evident; his poems are steeped in Shakespearean imagery, and his letters, a literary masterpiece in themselves, abound in allusions to the playwright.

Keats had a set of small volumes of the plays (an 1814 reissue of the 1765 edition of Samuel JOHNSON), which he annotated heavily. His notes have been published by Caroline SPURGEON as *Keats' Shakespeare* (1928). Some of the plays were plainly of greater interest than others; the HISTORY PLAYS, for

In the early 19th century, Edmund Kean (seen here as Richard III) helped replace the classical ideal of acting that had prevailed through the 18th century with a new, romantic style marked by violent emotion. The poet and critic Samuel Taylor Coleridge remarked that Kean could reveal Shakespeare through "flashes of lightning." *(Courtesy of Culver Pictures, Inc.)*

example, were virtually ignored, while *A Midsummer Night's Dream* and *The Tempest* sparked frequent and enthusiastic commentary. Keats's remarks on Shakespeare in his letters have offered much grist for subsequent writers. In one such comment, still often cited, Keats observed that Shakespeare had the "quality [that] went to form a Man of Achievement, especially in Literature . . . I mean *Negative Capability*, that is, when a man is capable of being in uncertainties, mysteries, doubts, without any irritable reaching after fact and reason."

Kemble, Charles (1775–1854)   British actor and producer, brother of John Philip KEMBLE, Stephen KEMBLE, and Sarah SIDDONS, and father of Fanny KEMBLE. As an actor, Charles Kemble was best known as a player of secondary parts—such as *Macbeth's* Malcolm and Macduff, *Romeo and Juliet's* Mercutio, and *Hamlet's* Laertes—opposite his brother, though he was also acclaimed as Benedick *(Much Ado About Nothing)* and Orlando *(As You Like It)*. He succeeded his brother as manager of the Covent Garden Theatre, where he presented Shakespeare's works in productions that aimed at historical accuracy in sets and costumes. Beginning with the *King John* staged by him and J. R. PLANCHÉ in 1823, his ideas influenced Shakespearean productions for the rest of the 19th century. Kemble was an unsuccessful manager and was only saved from bankruptcy by the success of his daughter Fanny.

Kemble, Fanny (1809–1893) British actress, daughter of Charles KEMBLE. Fanny Kemble's stunning performances as Juliet saved her father's Covent Garden Theatre from bankruptcy in 1829, and she went on to triumphs as Beatrice (in *Much Ado About Nothing*) and Portia (in *The Merchant of Venice*). Unlike the other members of the family, she was not committed to a theatrical career, and she retired in 1834 when she married a Philadelphian. After her divorce in 1845, she returned to Britain and in the 1850s and 1860s toured both there and in America with a highly popular series of readings from Shakespeare. She finally retired in 1868 and settled in London.

Kemble, John Philip (1757–1823) British actor and producer, brother of Charles KEMBLE, Stephen KEMBLE, and Sarah SIDDONS. J. P. Kemble played most of Shakespeare's protagonists, often opposite his sister, and was especially acclaimed for his portrayals of Hamlet, Coriolanus, and Henry V. He initially established himself as Hamlet in 1783 at the Drury Lane Theatre in London, which he managed from 1788 until 1802. After that he ran the Covent Garden Theatre, finally retiring in 1817. As a producer, he continued the trend toward more realistic costumes and sets, which was begun by David GARRICK and eventually resulted in the elaborately "historical" productions of Charles Kemble, Charles KEAN, and Henry IRVING. A stately and dignified actor, Kemble dominated the English stage until the rise of his only great rival, Edmund KEAN. The son of an actor and actress, Kemble was a child performer before training for the priesthood. He abandoned his studies and returned to the theater in 1776, though the experience is thought to have influenced his deliberate and ascetic acting style.

Kemble, Stephen (1758–1822) British actor, brother of Charles KEMBLE, John Philip KEMBLE, and Sarah SIDDONS. A child actor like his siblings, Stephen became a chemist before returning to the stage in his late 20s. Being very heavy, he often played Falstaff (see *1 Henry IV*). His girth and the fact that he was quite overshadowed by John Philip led to the contemporary witticism that they were "the big Kemble and the great Kemble."

Kempe, William (William Kemp) (d. ca. 1608) English actor, a member of the CHAMBERLAIN'S MEN and one of the 26 men listed in the FIRST FOLIO as the "Principall Actors" in Shakespeare's plays. Kempe's name appears in early texts of *Romeo and Juliet* (stage direction at 4.5.99) and *Much Ado About Nothing* (speech headings in 4.2), proving that he was the original portrayer of Peter and Dogberry, respectively. As a CLOWN, he is also believed to have originated such other Shakespearean comic parts as Bottom, Costard, Launce, Launcelot, and possibly Falstaff, before leaving the company in 1599, when he was replaced by Robert ARMIN.

Based on the differences in such comic parts written before and after 1599, it is clear that Shakespeare wrote the earlier ones with Kempe in mind. From analysis of these characters, combined with other surviving references to Kempe, we know something of his style. He was a big man who specialized in plebeian clowns who spoke in earthy language, with seemingly ingenuous spontaneity, often addressing the audience in frank asides. Kempe's characters have a tendency to confuse and mispronounce their words, and contemporary references to his dancing and his ability to "make a scurvy face" suggest a physical brand of humor. He

Will Kempe created many of the great Shakespearean comic roles. He was also famous for his stunt of dancing a morris, as shown in this contemporary illustration, along the road from London to Norwich—a distance of almost 100 miles. *(Courtesy of Bodleian Library, Oxford)*

was especially famous for an extraordinary publicity stunt, as it would now be called, of 1600, when he performed a morris dance along the road from LONDON to Norwich—a distance of almost 100 miles, which he covered in nine days. He then wrote a book about it, *Kemps nine daies wonder* (1600).

Kempe is first known as the jester, or FOOL, to Robert Devereux, Earl of LEICESTER, with whom he traveled to the war in the Netherlands in 1585–86. He may even have been a member of LEICESTER'S MEN at this time. During the summer of 1586 he performed with an English company in DENMARK. He was a member of STRANGE'S MEN by 1593, when he was already a noted comedian, hailed by Thomas NASHE as the successor to Richard TARLTON, another famous Elizabethan comic. Kempe is assumed to have been an original member of the Chamberlain's Men in 1594, for he was a principal partner in it the next year. In 1599 he was one of the original partners in the GLOBE THEATRE, but for reasons unknown, he left the troupe in the same year and sold his share in the theater to Shakespeare, John HEMINGES, Augustine PHILLIPS, and Thomas POPE. He toured in Germany and Italy before returning to England in 1601. He may have rejoined the Chamberlain's Men briefly, but by 1602 he was with WORCESTER'S MEN. Nothing is known of his life after 1603; he was mentioned as dead in 1608.

Kenilworth   Castle in WARWICKSHIRE, a location in *2 Henry VI* and the scene of an extraordinarily lavish entertainment held for Queen Elizabeth I in 1575, when Shakespeare, who lived nearby, was 11 years old. It is thought that he was probably among the multitudes of commoners from the neighborhood who were permitted to gather and view parts of the spectacle. This fabulous occasion, which lasted for three weeks, featured many MASQUEs and other theatrical entertainments. Contemporary accounts of these have survived, and it is often supposed that one of them may have provided the germ of a passage in *A Midsummer Night's Dream* (2.1.148–154). In 4.9 of *2 Henry VI* King Henry VI and Queen Margaret retreat to Kenilworth, in the remote countryside, as Jake Cade's rebellion sweeps London. Kenilworth Castle is now a ruin.

Kent   County in southeasternmost England, the setting of a number of scenes in *2 Henry VI*. The play reflects the position of William de la Pole, Duke of Suffolk, as the most powerful aristocrat in Kent. Historically, although Shakespeare does not point out the connection, Suffolk's death on a beach in Kent in 4.1 was a trigger for the rebellion led by Jack Cade, depicted in the following scenes, for Suffolk was a grasping and extortionate landlord and his power was a source of popular discontent. In the play, Cade retreats to Kent when his uprising fails, to be killed by Alexander Iden in 4.10.

Cade's rebellion was a typically Kentish phenomenon, one of several major revolts to arise in the county between the 14th and 16th centuries. Kent, located on the coast at England's nearest point to FRANCE, had since prehistory been a relatively prosperous and cosmopolitan region by virtue of its trade with the Continent. In the late Middle Ages it was thus a center of political and social discontent, as the growing merchant class combined with artisans and rising small landholders to protest against the inequities and restrictions of feudalism.

Two settings in *1 Henry IV*, ROCHESTER and GAD'S HILL, are also located in Kent.

Kesselstadt death mask   Death mask formerly thought to be Shakespeare's. Discovered in 1847 at the estate sale of a Count Kesselstadt, this death mask—a cast made of the face of a dead person—was once widely believed to be Shakespeare's, chiefly because it is inscribed "WS/1616." However, it does not resemble either of the most authoritative PORTRAITS OF SHAKESPEARE (see DROESHOUT, MARTIN; JANSSEN, GHEERART), and the date is almost certainly false, for no other nonroyal death masks are known from that period. Scholars are therefore in agreement that the Kesselstadt death mask is a forgery, but it provides a good demonstration of the appeal of dramatic Shakespeareana.

Killigrew, Thomas (1612–1683)   English playwright and theatrical producer. Killigrew, along with William DAVENANT, dominated the London theater world in the 1660s. Killigrew wrote several moderately successful tragicomedies (see TRAGICOMEDY) before the London theaters were closed by the Puritans in 1642, when the Civil Wars began. A royalist, he went into exile with the future king Charles II, and when the monarchy was restored in 1660, he was granted one of the two licenses to produce plays in London. His King's Company was granted the rights to 20 of Shakespeare's plays, but he staged only four of them: *The Merry Wives of Windsor* (one of the first plays staged after the restoration), *1 Henry IV* (at least four times), *Julius Caesar,* and *Othello.* In Killigrew's *Othello,* on December 8, 1660, Margaret HUGHES played Desdemona and became the first woman to act on an English stage.

Kimbolton Castle   Manor house near Cambridge, England, a setting for a scene in *Henry VIII.* In 4.2 Henry VIII's divorced and deposed queen, Katherine of Aragon, lives in exile at Kimbolton, accompanied by only a few attendants. When she sees a vision of herself receiving garlands from spiritlike creatures, she knows she is near death.

Kimbolton was one of several residences where the historical Katherine lived out her exile. At the time it was a fortified manor built over an ancient castle. Today a grand neoclassical country house of the early 18th century overlays the older establishment and is open to the public as a museum.

King, Tom   (1730–1804)   English actor, famous as Touchstone (*As You Like It*) and Malvolio (*Twelfth Night*). King, one of the most popular members of the acting company run by David GARRICK, played comic roles exclusively, both in Shakespeare and 18th-century works. In the 1770s he managed the SADLER'S WELLS THEATRE. King was very successful and made a great deal of money in the theater, but he was addicted to gambling and died in poverty.

King Leir   Anonymous play of ca. 1588 (publ. 1605) that influenced Shakespeare's version of the same tale, *King Lear.* The earlier play presents the general lines of the king's misjudgment of his daughters and characters who are equivalent to Kent, Albany, and Oswald. Also, many minor

details from it are echoed in Shakespeare's play. However, at the play's close Cordelia lives and King Leir is restored to his throne. The authorship of *King Leir* has been attributed to various playwrights, including Thomas LODGE, George PEELE, Robert GREENE, and Thomas KYD, but scholars remain divided on the question.

King Leir—fully titled *The True Chronicle History of King Leir and his three daughters*—is now known only in the edition of 1605, but references in the text suggest that it was written around the time an invasion of England was threatened by the Spanish Armada in 1588. It was registered with the STATIONERS' COMPANY in 1594, but if an edition was published at that time, no copy has survived. Some scholars believe that Shakespeare knew the play from the stage and simply recalled the elements he employed in *Lear.* He clearly knew the play before 1594, in any case, for several minor details in *Richard III* (ca. 1591) can be traced to *King Leir.* In fact, Shakespeare may have acted in *King Leir,* playing the character that corresponds to the Earl of Kent, for a number of passages in the old play that are echoed in *Lear* are spoken while that character is onstage. It is conceivable that Shakespeare consulted the 1605 edition of *King Leir,* though it appeared only very shortly before *Lear* itself, and it is just as likely that it was republished in order to capitalize on the forthcoming appearance of a new play by Shakespeare.

King's Men   Acting company in which Shakespeare was a partner, the successor to the CHAMBERLAIN'S MEN. When King JAMES I acceded to the throne of England in 1603, the Chamberlain's Men's patron, George Carey, Baron HUNSDON, surrendered his position to the new king, an enthusiast of the stage. The number of performances at court was much higher for the troupe under James—an average of 12 times a year in Shakespeare's lifetime, versus four during the reign of Queen Elizabeth—and after 1608, the King's Men had a new winter home, the BLACKFRIARS THEATRE, with a different, more sophisticated audience. Under these influences, a new sort of play evolved and JACOBEAN DRAMA emerged, led by the King's Men.

At the time of the change of patron, the partners in the company were Shakespeare, Robert ARMIN, Richard BURBAGE, Henry CONDELL, Richard COWLEY, John HEMINGE, Augustine PHILLIPS, and William SLY. Joining them was Laurence FLETCHER, a member of the king's household. Fletcher had a theatrical background but seems not to have been an active participant in the King's Men. By 1605 three more members were added, probably Alexander COOKE, Samuel CROSSE, and John LOWIN. In 1619 the company's royal patent was renewed, and its members were named in a surviving official document. Only Burbage, Heminge, and Condell remained of the original eight; the other nine partners listed were Lowin, Nathan FIELD, John UNDERWOOD, Nicholas TOOLEY, William ECCLESTONE, Robert BENFIELD, Robert GOUGH, Richard ROBINSON, and John SHANK, Burbage died in the same month and was replaced by Joseph TAYLOR. The company's business manager was Heminge until his death in 1630, after which it was run by Lowin and Taylor.

The King's Men performed at the GLOBE TREATRE in the summer and, after 1608, at the Blackfriars in the winter. The company was universally regarded as England's best. Their many appearances at court were a measure of their prestige; especially noteworthy is the fact that they performed 20 plays—eight of them Shakespeare's—during the weeks-long celebration of the marriage of the princess ELIZABETH STUART in 1613. The King's Men's principal playwrights were Shakespeare and later John FLETCHER—often in collaboration with Francis BEAUMONT—and Philip MASSINGER. The King's Men also staged works by other dramatists, including Ben JONSON and John WEBSTER.

King's Revels See CHILDREN'S COMPANIES.

Kingston portrait See ASHBOURNE PORTRAIT.

Kirkham, Edward (active 1586–1617) English theatrical entrepreneur. Kirkham was a subordinate to the MASTER OF THE REVELS and was therefore involved in the regulation of ELIZABETHAN THEATER. He also invested in the profession. Between 1603 and 1608 he was a partner of Henry EVANS in the productions of the Children of the Queen's Revels (see CHILDREN'S COMPANIES) at the BLACKFRIARS THEATRE, which Evans leased from Richard BURBAGE, Shakespeare's associate in the KING'S MEN. When the boys' company lost its royal patronage in 1608, Evans relinquished his lease on the Blackfriars to Burbage, who thereupon sold shares in the theater to a number of people, including Shakespeare and a relative of Evans. Kirkham was effectively abandoned. He sued Evans, Burbage, and others in unsuccessful attempts to gain a share of their profits. Modern scholars find in the records of these suits a number of clues as to the nature of the early-17th-century theater, including the information that the Blackfriars was much more profitable to the King's Men than was the GLOBE THEATRE.

Kirkman, Francis (1632–after 1674) English writer and publisher. In 1662 Kirkman's collection of DROLLS—the brief dramas performed illicitly when the English theaters were closed in 1642–60—was published by Henry MARSH, his business partner, as *The Wits: or Sport upon Sport.* Kirkman himself published a second edition in 1672 and a supplementary volume in 1673. He also compiled and published a *Catalogue of English Stage Playes,* which listed 690 dramas in its first edition (1661) and added 116 more in the second (1671). Kirkman also published an edition of THE BIRTH OF MERLIN (1662), which he attributed to Shakespeare and William ROWLEY. He translated and published romantic tales from French and Spanish and wrote several of his own, as well as at least one play.

Kittredge, George Lyman (1860–1941) American scholar. Kittredge, a longtime professor at Harvard University (1888–1936), was a respected authority on both Shakespeare and CHAUCER. He is best known as a teacher who influenced generations of students to a greater appreciation of English literature in general and Shakespeare's plays in particular. He also edited an edition of Shakespeare's *Complete Works* (1936) and wrote books on Shakespeare, Chaucer, and other subjects ranging from *Sir Thomas Malory* (1925) to *Witchcraft in Old and New England* (1929).

Knell, William (d. 1587) English actor, a member of the QUEEN'S MEN. Knell is known to have played Prince Hal in THE FAMOUS VICTORIES, but his significance rests on his place in a theory about Shakespeare's early years. Knell was killed in a fight while the Queen's Men were playing in STRATFORD in June 1587, and some scholars speculate that the young Shakespeare was hired to replace him and accompanied the troupe to LONDON, thus beginning his theatrical career. This intriguing hypothesis is entirely unprovable, but Knell has nonetheless found a niche in literary history. His widow married John HEMINGE.

Knight, Edward (active 1623–1633) Bookkeeper for the KING'S MEN. As the bookkeeper for Shakespeare's theater company, Knight was responsible for maintaining the PROMPTBOOK of each play the company performed. He must therefore have known their repertoire quite well, and for this reason some scholars believe he may have done much of the actual editorial work on the FIRST FOLIO edition of Shakespeare's plays. Some of the correspondence he carried on with the MASTER OF THE REVELS has survived, and it sheds light on the business side of the theatrical world in Shakespeare's day.

Knight, G. Wilson (1897–1985) English literary critic. Knight boldly interpreted Shakespeare's plays as mystical poems that express their ideas through the symbolic use of imagery and themes in meaningful configurations. This view has influenced both commentary and theatrical production beginning in the 1930s. He is regarded as one of the most important 20th-century Shakespearean critics, but his emphasis on religion is not always accepted. For example, he saw *King Lear* as similar to the Book of Job and Lear himself as symbolic of the crucified Christ. His best-known works are *The Wheel of Fire* (1930, 1949), *The Imperial Theme* (1931), *The Shakespearean Tempest* (1932), *The Crown of Life* (1947); and *The Sovereign Flower* (1958).

Knollys, Sir William (ca. 1547–1632) High official in the court of Queen Elizabeth I (see Elizabeth I in *Henry VIII*) and possibly a satirical model for Malvolio in *Twelfth Night*. After a successful military career, Knollys succeeded his father, Sir Francis Knollys (ca. 1514–96), as comptroller, and later treasurer, of the royal household, a position analogous to that of steward, the office held by Malvolio in the household of Olivia. In the late 1590s Knollys was the subject of amused court gossip as he pursued a much younger woman, Mary FITTON, going so far as to dye his beard—a young man's fashion of the day—perhaps suggesting Malvolio's laughable courtship of Olivia. Fitton, however, had another lover, William Herbert, Earl of PEMBROKE, by whom she became pregnant in 1600, bringing the gossip to a peak at about the time *Twelfth Night* was written. The theory linking Knollys and Malvolio was introduced by Professor Leslie HOTSON; detractors think that Shakespeare would have been unlikely to pillory a man who remained powerful at court throughout the playwright's career, particularly if *Twelfth Night* were written for a courtly occasion, as Hotson also proposed. (For other possible Malvolios, see FFARINGTON, WILLIAM; HOBY, SIR THOMAS POSTHUMOUS; WILLOUGHBY, SIR AMBROSE.)

Komisarjevsky, Theodore (1882–1954) Russian director. A major figure in the theater and opera of prerevolutionary Russia, Komisarjevsky came to Britain in 1919. He is best known in the West for his stagings of Chekhov and for a series of avant-garde Shakespearean productions in STRATFORD in the 1930s. Especially notable were *Macbeth*, played in a severely abstract metallic set (1933); a highly praised *King Lear* (1936); and *The Comedy of Errors*, presented as a COMMEDIA DELL'ARTE play (1939).

Kozintsev, Grigori (1903–1973) Russian stage and FILM director. Kozintsev is best known in the West for his films of *Hamlet* (1964) and *King Lear* (1970). During the shooting of the latter, Kozintsev corresponded with Peter BROOK, who was simultaneously making his film of the play. Both movies are characterized by the intimacy of the acting and the epic grandeur of their landscapes, interiors, and costumes. Kozintsev also wrote an influential book, *Shakespeare: Time and Conscience* (1967).

Kurosawa, Akira (1910–1998) Japanese FILM director, maker of famed adaptations of *Macbeth* and *King Lear*. Kurosawa's *Throne of Blood* (1957) is based on *Macbeth*, and his *Ran* (1985) is derived from *King Lear* (*ran* means "chaos"). These films are set in medieval Japan, and they employ many aspects of Japanese Noh drama and samurai films, unfamiliar genres in the West. Moreover, Shakespeare's tales are altered considerably (for instance, the children of Kurosawa's Lear equivalent are male, and his Lady Macbeth has a miscarriage), none of the names are the same, and the language is not at all Shakespearean, even in translation. However, these works are nonetheless powerful evocations of Shakespeare's themes, and unlike virtually all other Shakespearean adaptations, they are regarded as great works of art in their own right by nearly unanimous critical consent.

Kyd, Thomas (1558–1594) English playwright, author of an important influence on *Hamlet* and of minor sources for other plays. Some commentators believe that many of Shakespeare's plays were written in part by other playwrights (see, e.g., FLEAY, FREDERICK GARD; ROBERTSON, JOHN MACKINNON) and have attributed passages and scenes in several plays, especially *Hamlet* and *Titus Andronicus*, to Kyd. Modern scholars, however, dispute most such attributions.

With Christopher MARLOWE, Kyd was the most important English playwright when Shakespeare began his career, and he was immensely influential on both the younger playwright and on ELIZABETHAN DRAMA in general. With *The Spanish Tragedy* (ca. 1588), he virtually invented the REVENGE PLAY, a genre that was to be immensely popular. It and its probable companion piece, the now-lost play known as the UR-HAMLET, provided the apparent inspiration—as well as many details—for *Hamlet*. *The Spanish Tragedy* was also the source of minor elements of *Titus Andronicus*, *Richard III*, and *3 Henry VI*; the latter play also owes some details to Kyd's *Soliman and Perseda* (1590).

Kyd, the son of a scribe, was not university-educated, but he attended an excellent secondary school, where Edmund SPENSER was a classmate. He was at least conversant with Latin literature, for SENECA's influence on his work is great (though he would have known the Roman playwright in English translations as well). He was a close friend and probable collaborator of Marlowe, and when Marlowe was prosecuted for "atheism and immorality" in 1593, Kyd was also arrested. Under torture, he recanted and was released, but he received no patronage thereafter and died in deep poverty.

L

Lacy, John (d. 1681) English actor and playwright, author of an adaptation of *The Taming of the Shrew*. Lacy's *Sauny the Scot* (1667) was a farcical revision in which the comical servant Grumio—renamed Sauny—was the principal character. The play was written in prose and set in England. Extremely popular, *Sauny* was revived periodically for a century.

Originally a dancing instructor, Lacy turned to the theater in the 1660s and achieved fame as a comic actor in Thomas KILLIGREW's company. He was particularly noted for his Falstaff, and he played the title role in the original production of *Sauny*. He wrote three other comedies.

Lady Elizabeth's Men Seventeenth-century LONDON theatrical company (see ELIZABETHAN THEATER). Founded in 1611 and named for their patron, the princess ELIZABETH STUART, Lady Elizabeth's Men spent a year touring the provinces before coming to London and playing under contract to Philip HENSLOWE. Among the members were William ECCLESTONE, John RICE, and Joseph TAYLOR. They performed at the ROSE, SWAN, and WHITEFRIARS THEATRES. In 1613 they absorbed the Children of the Queen's Revels (see CHILDREN'S COMPANIES) and, with them, Nathan FIELD, who became their leader. After two seasons at the HOPE THEATRE, the company sued Henslowe in 1615; some of the records of the case survive and provide a glimpse of the theater world's business side. Sometime just before or after Henslowe's death in 1616, the company formed an alliance with PRINCE CHARLES' MEN, but Field had already left and soon the company failed, though it seems to have existed in the provinces for several years. In 1622 a new company called Lady Elizabeth's Men was formed by Christopher BEESTON, and it prospered briefly, but it was stricken by plague in the epidemic of 1625 and was not re-founded. Princess Elizabeth had long been gone from England, and Beeston replaced Lady Elizabeth's Men with Queen Henrietta's Men, named for the new queen.

Lamb, Charles (1775–1834) English essayist, best known for his whimsical essays written under the pseudonym Elia. Lamb also wrote commentary on Shakespeare's plays, and with his sister Mary (1764–1847), he compiled prose renditions of the comedies and tragedies in *Tales from Shakespeare* (1807). Lamb's most influential critical work was his *Specimens of English Dramatic Poets who lived about the time of Shakespeare* (1808), which did much to revive interest in ELIZABETHAN DRAMA. He also wrote a notorious essay, "On the Tragedies of Shakespeare" (1811), in which he contended that the plays—especially *King Lear*—were unsuited for performance, though he also insisted that if they were staged, it should be done using Shakespeare's texts rather than adaptations. Lamb wrote essays on contemporary Romantic poetry as well; he was one of the first critics to recognize the genius of John KEATS, and Samuel Taylor COLERIDGE and William Wordsworth (1770–1850) were close friends. He wrote poetry himself, but neither it nor his fiction is widely read today, whereas *Tales from*

Shakespeare and the collected *Essays of Elia* (1823, second series 1833) have continued to be popular.

Lamb's life was stricken by personal tragedy. Mental illness ran in his family; Lamb himself was briefly hospitalized for insanity in his youth and suffered from alcoholism all his life. In 1796 his sister Mary Lamb killed their mother in a fit of temporary madness; Lamb refused to have Mary institutionalized and cared for her the rest of his life.

Lamb, George (1784–1834) British politician, playwright, and poet, author of an adaptation of *Timon of Athens*. In 1816 Lamb composed an adaptation of Shakespeare's play with the intention of restoring the original text, which was heavily altered in presentations at the time. While Lamb's *Timon* retained some features of its immediate predecessors and failed to restore some omissions, it did employ most of Shakespeare's text. Produced by Edmund KEAN, who also took the title role, it was only moderately successful but may have paved the way for the first staging of the complete text, by Samuel PHELPS, a generation later.

Lamb had a varied career. After briefly practicing law, he shared in the management of the Drury Lane Theatre in London. He staged two of his own plays—an operetta and a farce—besides *Timon*. He was probably best known for his translation of the poems of Catullus (ca. 84–ca. 54 B.C.), though both it and his own poetry are generally regarded as mediocre. Introduced into politics by his brother William Lamb, Lord Melbourne (1779–1848), twice prime minister, George Lamb was a member of parliament in 1819–20 and again from 1826 to his death. He also served briefly as undersecretary of state.

Lambert, John (active 1587–1602) Shakespeare's first cousin and opponent in litigation. In 1588 John SHAKESPEARE—acting for himself, his wife Mary Arden SHAKESPEARE, and his son William—sued his nephew John Lambert (the son of Mary Arden Shakespeare's sister and Edmund Lambert [ca. 1525–87]) for the return of a piece of property—a house on 56 acres of land near STRATFORD—which Lambert had inherited from his father. This property had been mortgaged to Edmund by John Shake-

speare in 1578, in return for a loan of £40 to be repaid in two years. The money was never repaid, and Edmund still owned the land at his death. According to the Shakespeares' complaint, John Lambert had agreed to accept £20 in return for clear title to the land, but Lambert denied this and won his case. John and Mary sued again in 1597 on different grounds but again lost. Lambert sold part of the property in 1602. The naming of William Shakespeare in the legal papers of 1588 is the only surviving mention of the playwright between the baptism of Hamnet and Judith SHAKESPEARE in Stratford in 1585 and the mocking reference by Robert GREENE to the young LONDON playwright in 1592. This mention has sometimes been thought to indicate that Shakespeare was in residence in Stratford or its environs at the time, but scholars generally agree that his technical involvement in the suit has little significance.

Lancaster family Branch of the PLANTAGENET FAMILY, major figures in Shakespeare's HISTORY PLAYS. The Lancastrian kings were descended from John of Gaunt, Duke of Lancaster, the third son of King Edward III. Gaunt had inherited the title from his father-in-law, Henry of Lancaster, the Earl of Derby in *Edward III*. In 1399 Gaunt's son, Henry Bolingbroke, deposed King Richard II and ruled as Henry IV. He bequeathed the throne to his son, Henry V, in 1413. These events are dealt with in the major TETRALOGY of history plays, comprising *Richard II*, *1* and *2 Henry IV*, and *Henry V*. When Henry V died in 1422, his son, Henry VI, was an infant. In the absence of a strong monarch, opposition to the illegal deposition of Richard II revived, and the YORK branch of the dynasty successfully pressed its claim to the throne, overthrowing Henry VI in 1461 (he was briefly reinstated in 1470–71). The rivalry between Lancaster and York, culminating in the WARS OF THE ROSES, is the principal subject of the minor tetralogy, consisting of *1*, *2*, and *3 Henry VI* and *Richard III*. The Yorkists were finally defeated in 1485 by the last Lancastrian, the Earl of Richmond. This distant cousin of Henry VI, who ruled England as Henry VII, founded the TUDOR DYNASTY.

Lane, John (1590–1640) Resident of STRATFORD who was sued for slander by Shakespeare's daughter, Susanna SHAKESPEARE Hall. In June 1613 Lane allegedly declared that Mrs. Hall had committed adultery with a local hatter, Raphael Smith (1577–1621). She promptly sued him, and when he failed to appear for the trial on July 15, she was formally declared innocent of any impropriety and he was excommunicated. Lane was apparently a difficult man; he was tried in 1619 for riot and libel after he attacked—presumably by public verbal abuse—the vicar and aldermen of Stratford, and in the same year he was declared a drunkard by the churchwardens. Stratford was a small town, and the Shakespeare and Lane families were acquainted in other contexts. Lane's uncle, Richard LANE, was a business partner of Shakespeare's, and his first cousin Thomas NASH later married Susanna's daughter Elizabeth HALL.

Lane, Richard (ca. 1556–1613)   Resident of STRATFORD, a business acquaintance of Shakespeare. Lane was a friend of Shakespeare's father, John SHAKESPEARE, who chose him in 1599 to help gather depositions in a lawsuit. In 1611 Lane joined William Shakespeare in a complicated lawsuit over tithe holdings (see COMBE, WILLIAM). In his will Lane appointed Shakespeare's son-in-law Dr. John HALL as trustee for his children, just a few days before Susanna SHAKESPEARE Hall sued his nephew John LANE for libel.

Laneman, Henry (Henry Lanman) (1536–ca. 1592)   English theatrical entrepreneur, owner and probably the founder of the CURTAIN THEATRE. Laneman was the owner of the Curtain during the period 1585–92, when he and James BURBAGE, owner of the neighboring playhouse, THE THEATRE, agreed to pool the profits of both theaters. In 1581 he was the lessor of the land on which the Curtain stood, and so he is presumed to have built it in 1577. Nothing else is known of him.

Langbaine, Gerard (1656–1692)   English scholar and writer, the author of the first account of Shakespeare's sources. Langbaine's *Momus Triumphans, or the Plagiaries of the English Stage exposed* (1687) is a catalogue of the sources used by various Elizabethan and Jacobean playwrights, including Shakespeare.

However, his treatment was brief and pedantic and was superseded by the work of Charlotte LENNOX and more modern scholars.

Langley, Francis (1550–1601)   Goldsmith and theatrical entrepreneur in LONDON, owner of the SWAN THEATRE. Langley's name is linked with Shakespeare's in a mysterious lawsuit. Langley bought land on the south bank of the Thames near the ROSE THEATRE in 1595 and built the Swan, despite the opposition of the London government. However, in the summer of 1597, in the theater's second season, PEMBROKE'S MEN staged Thomas NASHE's allegedly "seditious" play *Isle of Dogs,* with the result that the royal CENSORSHIP closed all the London theaters for four months. After that Langley kept his theater open only with difficulty. Upon his death, the Swan Theatre was sold to another London investor.

Records show that another company played at the Swan before Pembroke's Men, and the scholar Leslie HOTSON has established a relationship between Langley and Shakespeare, which suggests that the company was probably the CHAMBERLAIN'S MEN. The owner of the Swan and the playwright were named jointly in a legal paper, though their connection is unknown (see GARDINER, WILLIAM). The most plausible relationship between the two is that of theater owner and representative of an acting company, so it is concluded that Shakespeare's troupe probably performed at the Swan.

Lanier, Emilia (1570–1654)   Mistress of theatrical patron Henry Carey, Lord HUNSDON, and possibly the Dark Lady of the *Sonnets.* Emilia Bassano was the illegitimate daughter of an Italian musician at the court of Queen Elizabeth I and became the mistress of Lord Hunsdon, when she was in her teens. In 1593 she became pregnant and was given some money and married to Alphonse Lanier, another court musician. The next year Hunsdon became the patron of Shakespeare's theatrical company, and it is possible that Emilia Lanier might have known Shakespeare through this connection. She might also have known the playwright through her husband's place in the world of court entertainment. The possibility that she was Shakespeare's

Dark Lady rests chiefly on these connections, plus a description of her—by the astrologer, Simon FORMAN, with whom she may have had an affair—as a witch-like "incuba," a characterization thought to accord well with the poet's "female evil . . . [who can] corrupt [a] saint to be a devil" (Sonnet 144.5–7).

Lanier's husband Alphonse was a wastrel, and they were soon impoverished. She published a book—a long poem on the women of the Bible—but it was not popular, and when Alphonse died in 1613, she was very poor. She opened a school, but it failed. Her son, Henry, a court musician to King Charles I, may have provided for her, but he died in 1633, and Lanier was left with the responsibility for his two children. She received a pension from the crown but died in near poverty.

Laplace, Pierre-Antoine de (1707–1793)   French translator of Shakespeare. Laplace, under the influence of a concern to revitalize the French theater, wrote a book, *A Discourse on English Theatre* (1745), and translated 23 English plays, 10 of them by Shakespeare, the first renderings of the playwright into French. These adaptations, though they were significantly adulterated versions, introduced French readers to ELIZABETHAN DRAMA and inspired the adaptations of Jean-François DUCIS and, later, their own surpasser, the translations of Pierre LE TOURNEUR. (See also TRANSLATION OF SHAKESPEARE.)

Laughton, Charles (1899–1962)   British actor. Laughton, who studied acting under Theodore KOMISARJEVSKY, is probably best known for his performance in the title role of the 1933 film *The Private Lives of Henry VIII* (not based on Shakespeare's play)—for which he won an Academy Award—and other movie roles, such as Captain Bligh in *The Mutiny on the Bounty* (1935) and the *Hunchback of Notre Dame* (1939). However, in the 1930s, Laughton succeeded in a variety of Shakespearean roles at the OLD VIC THEATRE, including Prospero (*The Tempest*), Angelo (*Measure for Measure*), and Macbeth. Also, after years in Hollywood—he became an American citizen in 1941—he returned to England in 1959 and played

Bottom (*A Midsummer Night's Dream*) and Lear at the Shakespeare Memorial Theatre in STRATFORD.

Law, Matthew (active 1599–1629)   Publisher and bookseller in LONDON. Law bought the rights to three of Shakespeare's plays from Andrew WISE and then produced the third through sixth editions of *1 Henry IV* (1603, 1608, 1613, 1622), the fourth and fifth editions of *Richard II* (1608, 1615), and the fourth through sixth editions of *Richard III* (1605, 1612, 1622). Errors in the printing of each of these plays in the FIRST FOLIO (1623) point to delays in the setting of type for them; scholars attribute this delay to difficulties involved in securing Law's permission to republish them. Originally a draper, Law joined the STATIONERS' COMPANY in 1599; he had two bookshops for much of his career. He was fined several times for selling books on Sundays and for selling pirated texts.

Law Against Lovers, The   Play by William DAVENANT based loosely on *Measure for Measure* and *Much Ado About Nothing*. Produced in 1662, *The Law Against Lovers* has a main plot that is a much-altered version of *Measure for Measure*, combined with some material from the Beatrice and Benedick plot of *Much Ado* and much that had nothing to do with Shakespeare's plays. Most of the dialogue is by Davenant, who declared his intention to "save" Shakespeare by making the plays palatable to a new audience. This play, however, was unsuccessful, receiving only a few performances and remaining unrevived thereafter. Though Samuel PEPYS liked it, an anonymous satirical poet of the day differed, saying of Davenant that ". . . only he the Art of it had / Of two good Playes to make one Bad." *The Law Against Lovers* nevertheless inspired an imitation, Charles GILDON's *Measure for Measure, or Beauty the Best Advocate* (1699), in which much of Davenant's text was retained, but the material from *Much Ado* was replaced by an operatic MASQUE.

Leake, William (d. 1633)   London publisher of several editions of *Venus and Adonis*. After buying the rights to Shakespeare's poem from John HARRISON in 1596, Leake, a prosperous bookseller and officer of the STATIONERS' COMPANY, published six editions (Q5–Q10) between 1599 and 1617.

Lee, Sidney (1859–1926)   British scholar, author of a standard biography of Shakespeare. Lee, an editor and writer of the *Dictionary of National Biography*, elaborated his dictionary article on the playwright into his *Life of William Shakespeare* (1898), which remained the definitive biography for decades. He wrote other books on Shakespeare, including *Shakespeare and the Modern Stage* (1906) and *Shakespeare and the Italian Renaissance* (1915); he also edited a facsimile edition (1902) of the FIRST FOLIO.

Legh, Gerard (d. 1563)   English antiquarian, author of a minor source for *The Taming of the Shrew* and *King Lear*. Legh's book on heraldry, *Accedens of Armory* (1562), contains a story that probably inspired the episode of the Tailor in 4.3 of *Shrew*; it also includes one of many versions of Lear's story and provided some minor details for Shakespeare's play on the subject. A prosperous draper, Legh was largely self-taught. The *Accedens*, his only work, is a compendium of miscellaneous heraldic lore in the form of a dialogue between a herald named Gerard and a knight named Legh.

Leicester, Robert Dudley, Earl of (1532–1588)   English nobleman and theatrical patron. As patron of the acting company called LEICESTER'S MEN, Leicester was an important figure in the early history of ELIZABETHAN THEATER, even though he merely gave the troupe the legal standing they needed and did not actively engage in the production of plays. Leicester was a favorite of Queen Elizabeth I (see Elizabeth I in *Henry VIII*) and may have been her lover, but the evidence is uncertain. Though already married, he was thought to aspire to a royal wedding; when his wife died suspiciously in 1560, rumor called it murder (historians generally disagree), so it may have been impossible for the queen to marry him even if she had wished to. She continued to demonstrate her favor in any case, giving him KENILWORTH Castle and making him earl of Leicester.

Leicester became leader of an important political faction and intrigued against the queen's chief minister, Lord BURGHLEY. When he remarried in 1578, he acquired a stepson, Robert Devereux, Earl of ESSEX, who came to share his hostility to Burghley. His marriage offended the queen, and Leicester was out of favor for several years, but he resumed his position when given the command of English forces aiding the Dutch rebellion against Spain. The actor William KEMPE was in Leicester's retinue in the Netherlands, and some scholars speculate that the young Shakespeare may have been as well, though no confirming evidence exists. Leicester returned to England to take a high command in the army assembled to resist the Spanish Armada in 1588 and died of an illness soon after the crisis ended.

Leicester's Men   Early English theatrical company. From at least 1559, the nobleman Robert Dudley, later Earl of LEICESTER, patronized a company of actors. Known as Dudley's Men until 1564, when their patron received his title, this troupe mostly toured the provinces. It did, however, play at the court of Queen Elizabeth I several times between 1560 and 1562, perhaps because their patron was the queen's favorite, possibly her lover.

In 1572, when actors were declared vagrants unless supported by a nobleman (see ELIZABETHAN THEATER), Leicester's Men was formally defined and its players named, including James BURBAGE and Robert WILSON. In 1574 the queen declared Leicester's Men her own employees as well, licensing them to play anywhere in England, including LONDON. This challenged for the first time the London government's puritanical opposition to public theater, an important watershed in the history of English drama.

For a decade Leicester's Men were the most important theatrical troupe in England, performing at Elizabeth's court and (after 1577) at Burbage's THEATRE. However, with the creation in 1583 of the QUEEN'S MEN, which was permitted to raid some of Leicester's best performers, their prominence diminished. In the summer of 1586, one of Leicester's Men, William KNELL, died while the troupe was performing in STRATFORD. This fact has prompted speculation that the young Shakespeare joined them at this time and returned with them to London to begin his career, although no other evidence supports this proposition. Upon Leicester's death in 1588, the company dissolved; some scholars believe that its members joined STRANGE'S MEN.

Leigh, Vivien (1913–1967)   English actress. Leigh, the wife of Laurence OLIVIER, was best known as a movie actress, though she also performed a number of major Shakespearean roles on the stage, usually opposite her husband. Her most notable performances were as Cleopatra (1951) and Lady Macbeth (1955).

Le Maçon, Antoine (active ca. 1550–1580) French writer and translator. Le Maçon's translation of BOCCACCIO's *Decameron* was probably a subsidiary source for *All's Well That Ends Well* and a major source for *Cymbeline*. Shakespeare's chief source for *All's Well* was William PAINTER's translation of a tale from Boccaccio in his *The Palace of Pleasure*, but the playwright probably used Le Maçon's text also. Painter himself used it, alongside the original. The "wager" plot of *Cymbeline* derives from a *Decameron* tale that was not translated into English before 1620, and Le Maçon's translation is one of several possible versions of the story that Shakespeare may have encountered.

Le Maçon was a courtier at the court of Princess Marguerite of Valois. His translation of Boccaccio was extremely popular throughout Europe as soon as it appeared in 1545; it was reissued 16 times during the 16th century. He also wrote a prose romance, published in 1550. Little else is known of his life.

Lennox, Charlotte (1720–1804)   English writer, author of the first substantial analysis of Shakespeare's sources. Lennox, who was also a novelist, wrote *Shakespear* [sic] *Illustrated; or, the Novels and Histories on which the Plays are founded* (1753), which covered more than half of Shakespeare's plays, thus improving greatly on its only predecessor, the work of Gerard LANGBAINE.

Leo Africanus (Joannes Leo) (active ca. 1520) Moorish traveler and writer whose work may have influenced *Othello* and *Antony and Cleopatra*. Leo translated his writings on the regions now known as North, West and East Africa from Arabic into Italian. John PORY translated them into English in 1600 as *A Geographical History of Africa*, but they had been well known in England in Italian (and a French translation) since about 1550. Leo was among the first writers to replace ancient and medieval legends with real facts about the nations south of the Sahara (a word that Pory's translation introduced into English). His writings are still valuable for modern historians, providing a rare source of reliable information on precolonial sub-Saharan Africa. Pory's translation was a celebrated work in its day, and surely provided part of Shakespeare's background knowledge of North Africa (see, e.g., *Antony and Cleopatra*, 2.7.17–23). Moreover, Pory's preface included an account of Leo's life that is thought to have inspired Othello's autobiographical remarks in 1.3.134–145. Leo's works also informed a number of other English writers, including PUTTENHAM, Richard EDEN, and Ben JONSON.

Leo Africanus, or Leo of Africa, was a North African Moor who crossed the Sahara a number of times as a freelance soldier and scholar. He was captured ca. 1520 by Christian naval forces in the Mediterranean and presented to Pope Leo X, who converted him to Christianity from Islam and gave him the baptismal name Joannes Leo.

Lessing, Gotthold Ephraim (1729–1781)   German playwright and critic, the first important appreciator of Shakespeare in Germany. In 1767–68 Lessing wrote a series of articles on German theater that denounced its dependence on French plays and recommended the adoption of the ancient Greek dramatists and Shakespeare as primary models. These articles were extremely influential; they helped popularize the translations of Christoph WIELAND, and the critic J. G. Herder (1744–1803), a follower of Lessing, introduced Shakespeare to GOETHE, whose writings secured the playwright's place in German literary history. Germany's great enthusiasm for Shakespeare is often said to have begun with Lessing.

Lessing studied theology, literature, and philosophy before taking up journalism to make a living while he wrote plays, poems, and essays. He was greatly celebrated in his own time as Germany's leading man of letters. His plays *Miss Sarah Sampson* (1755), *Minna von Barnheim* (1767, considered one of the finest comedies in all literature), *Emilia Galotti* (1772), and *Nathan the Wise* (1769) are still performed in Germany and elsewhere. Lessing was the greatest representative of the German Enlightenment, and the first German writer to establish an international reputation.

Le Tourneur, Pierre (1736–1788) French translator of Shakespeare. Le Tourneur, who also translated English novels and poetry, is best known for producing the first complete edition of Shakespeare's plays in French, published in 20 volumes between 1776 and 1783. Though in prose, his renderings were much more accurate than those of his predecessor, Pierre-Antoine de LA PLACE, and they, along with the contemporary stage productions of Jean-François DUCIS, presented Shakespeare convincingly to the French public for the first time. In an essay of appreciation that he appended to his translations, he criticized the French critics who found Shakespeare a "barbarian" because he did not follow the neoclassical theories that informed French drama, and this work inspired VOLTAIRE's famous excoriation of both Le Tourneur and Shakespeare in his "Letter to the *Académie Français*" (1776). (See also TRANSLATION OF SHAKESPEARE.)

Leveridge, Richard (ca. 1670–1758) English singer and composer. Leveridge, a noted bass of his day, mostly composed SONGs, including music for several songs from Shakespeare's plays. He also wrote a burlesque of Italian OPERA, *The Comick Masque of Pyramus and Thisbe* (1716), that took its plot from the PYRAMUS AND THISBE episode in *A Midsummer Night's Dream*. He is one of several composers whom scholars believe may have written the incidental music for *Macbeth* traditionally attributed to Matthew LOCKE.

Leveson, William (active 1580–1612) English merchant, a trustee for Shakespeare's interest in the ground lease for the GLOBE THEATRE. The lease for the land on which the Globe stood was entered into by two parties: the BURBAGE brothers and five members of the CHAMBERLAIN'S MEN acting jointly—Shakespeare, John HEMINGE, William KEMPE, Augustine PHILLIPS, and Thomas POPE. To make their shares independently salable, the actors assigned their half to two trustees—Leveson and Thomas SAVAGE—who then regranted a fifth to each.

Leveson probably got this job through Heminge, whom he knew as a fellow parishioner of a LONDON church. Leveson was an investor in overseas expeditions, serving at different times as a member of the Muscovy Company (which traded to Russia), the Virginia Company, and the North-West Passage Company. Dudley DIGGES, stepson of Shakespeare's friend Thomas RUSSELL, was Leveson's fellow investor in all of these enterprises.

Lillo, George (1693–1739) British dramatist, creator of a crude adaptation of *Pericles*. In his *Marina* (1738), Lillo used only the last two acts of Shakespeare's play, and he altered those almost beyond recognition. The moderate success of Lillo's version of *Pericles* does not attest to any popularity for the original play; on the contrary, it was the only production of *Pericles* (or rather, related to *Pericles*) during the 18th century.

Lillo was among the leading British playwrights of his day. His best-known work, *George Barnwell* (1731), is a melodramatic tale of a young Londoner led by passion to murder, which ends with a morally proper punishment. It is considered a good example of the 18th-century vogue for sentimental dramas set among the urban bourgeoisie.

Lily, William (William Lilly, William Lyly) (ca. 1468–1522) English scholar and coauthor of the standard Latin textbook of Shakespeare's day, known as *Lily's Latin Grammar*, which is quoted several times in the plays—e.g., in 4.1 (the "Latin" scene) of *The Merry Wives of Windsor*, 1.1. 162 of *The Taming of the Shrew*, and 4.2.20–21 of *Titus Andronicus*. Lily's book, written in collaboration with the famous humanist scholar John Colet (ca. 1467–1519), was the basic text used at the Grammar School in STRATFORD, where Shakespeare was educated. Lily was a close friend of Sir Thomas MORE and the grandfather of playwright and novelist John LYLY.

Ling, Nicholas (active 1570–1607)   Printer, publisher, and bookseller in LONDON who produced the first two editions of *Hamlet*. In 1603 Ling and John TRUNDELL published the QUARTO edition known as Q1. It is a BAD QUARTO version of the play, recorded from the memories of actors, probably for this pirated edition. James ROBERTS had registered the play earlier, but he probably sold his rights to Ling, who also produced the first legitimate edition of *Hamlet*—employing Roberts as the printer—in 1604. In November 1607, shortly before his death, Ling sold John SMETHWICK the rights to *Hamlet*, along with those to *Love's Labour's Lost*, *Romeo and Juliet*—which he had bought from Cuthbert BURBY but never used—and *The Taming of a Shrew* (a Bad Quarto of *The Taming of the Shrew*). Ling had also bought *A Shrew* from Burby, but he produced an edition of it (Q3, 1607) before selling the rights.

Livy (Titus Livius) (59 B.C.–A.D. 17)   Ancient Roman author of a Latin history of ROME, a minor source for *Coriolanus* and possibly an inspiration for *The Rape of Lucrece*. Livy's *Ab urbe condita* was translated by Philemon HOLLAND as *The Romane Historie* (1600), and a passage from Holland's book is echoed in Menenius's famous "belly speech" in *Coriolanus* (1.1.95–153). Livy's history also contains the story of Lucrece and was probably consulted by Shakespeare in writing his poem on the subject, though whether it initially inspired him is unknown.

Livy was a prominent member of the literary circle surrounding the emperor Augustus. His only major work was his immense history, covering Rome from its mythical beginnings until 9 B.C. He began it at the age of 30 and worked on it for 40 years. Of the 142 books that composed the work, only 35 survived into the Middle Ages, though summaries of most of the others were compiled by other Latin authors. The book made Livy famous even before it was completed, and it dominated the Western world's knowledge of Roman history until the RENAISSANCE. Modern scholars, however, give him more credit for his fine literary style than for the accuracy of his account.

Locke, Matthew (ca. 1630–1677)   English composer of church and theater music, including incidental music for John DRYDEN and William DAVENANT's 1667 version of *The Tempest*. Locke was long believed to have written the once-famous incidental music to Davenant's *Macbeth* (1663), on the strength of an attribution published in 1708. Modern musicologists disagree, believing on stylistic grounds that the music was probably written by a later composer. (It is in any case based on the much older work of Robert JOHNSON for Thomas MIDDLETON's *The Witch* [ca. 1610–20]; scholars attribute the revision to any of several composers, including Richard LEVERIDGE and Henry PURCELL.) Locke had a highly successful career before his early death. He wrote some of the music for the first English OPERA, Davenant's *Siege of Rhodes* (1656), and in 1661 he was named composer to the newly restored King Charles II.

Locrine   Anonymous play sometimes attributed to Shakespeare, part of the Shakespeare APOCRYPHA. *Locrine*, a melodrama of ancient kings, was published by Thomas CREEDE in 1595 and credited to "W. S.," possibly in the hope that the public would believe it was by Shakespeare. In 1664 it was published in the Third FOLIO, but modern scholars are confident that Shakespeare did not write the play, for it is very different from Shakespeare's work in style and content. However, a positive attribution has not been agreed upon. On stylistic grounds, Robert GREENE, Christopher MARLOWE, and various others have been nominated, while W. W. GREG discovered a copy of the 1595 edition with early-17th-century notes that ascribe it to one Charles Tilney (d. 1586). Tilney is otherwise unknown as a writer.

Lodge, Thomas (ca. 1557–1625)   English writer, creator of the major source for *As You Like It*. Lodge, one of the UNIVERSITY WITS who dominated ELIZABETHAN DRAMA in the 1580s, wrote only two plays—one in collaboration with Robert GREENE. He was best known for his lyric poetry and a prose romance, *Rosalynde* (1590), that provided the central elements of *As You Like It*. Shakespearean scholars who believe many of Shakespeare's early plays were written collaboratively (see, e.g., FLEAY, FREDERICK GARD; ROBERTSON, JOHN MACKINNON) have often cited Lodge as a possible coauthor of *1 Henry VI*, *The Taming of the Shrew*, and others, but this theory is now generally deprecated. Lodge's very popular romantic poetry may have influenced Shakespeare in the writing of *Venus and Adonis*, though specific connections are absent.

Lodge is regarded as a minor writer whose work was chiefly derived from that of others; *Rosalynde*, for instance, is an imitation of John LYLY's novels. Son of the Lord Mayor of London, Lodge attended Oxford University and the INNS OF COURT, before commencing his literary career with a defense of poetry and drama against the attacks of Stephen GOSSON. He produced most of his literary work during the 1580s, after which he lived abroad and traveled—he was part of an expedition that explored South America in 1591 to 1593, for example. On his return, he practiced medicine and wrote an account of his travels (now lost). A convert to Catholicism, he faced religious persecution and briefly fled the country in 1616. He died in near poverty.

London Principal city of England, a location in each of Shakespeare's HISTORY PLAYS and his residence for much of his life. In Shakespeare's time London was not only the great metropolitan center of England, home to about 300,000 people (almost 10 percent of the nation's population), it was also the third-largest city in Europe (behind Naples and Paris) and was soon to be the largest. Outside the medieval walled city were new suburban expansions; to the south, across the Thames River via London Bridge, was SOUTHWARK, where the GLOBE THEATRE and several other theaters were established during Shakespeare's residency in the city (see ELIZABETHAN THEATER).

Shakespeare lived in a number of known locales in London. In October 1596 he was assessed for taxes as a resident of Bishopsgate. This neighborhood was near the northeasternmost city gate, beyond which, in the suburb of Shoreditch, was the THEATRE, where his acting company, the CHAMBERLAIN'S MEN, performed. However, by November he

had apparently moved to the southern suburbs, for he was subject to the jurisdiction of the county of Surrey when he was involved in litigation between Francis LANGLEY and William GARDINER. The move probably reflects a season spent at the SWAN THEATRE by the Chamberlain's Men in the winter of 1596–97. Shakespeare's tax bill followed him and was forwarded in 1600 to the diocese of Winchester, which governed the Clink, a neighborhood in Southwark near the Globe, so Shakespeare probably lived there at the close of the 16th century.

The playwright can next be located in 1604 as the tenant of Christopher MOUNTJOY in Cripplegate, at the northwest corner of the city. He was probably there as early as 1602 and may have remained for some years after 1604, though no later evidence of a London address for him exists. After 1608 his principal theatrical venue was the BLACKFRIARS THEATRE, north of the river near the western wall of the city. Shakespeare probably moved back to Stratford by about 1610. His connections with the city were still strong, however, and he visited London several times after that, possibly staying at the MERMAID TAVERN, whose manager was his friend William JOHNSON. In 1613 he invested in London real estate, buying the BLACKFRIARS GATEHOUSE. Both the Blackfriars Theatre and the Blackfriars Gatehouse were on the grounds of the former BLACKFRIARS ABBEY.

London's buzzing life is frequently manifested in Shakespeare's work. In the English history plays, Shakespeare was dealing with events that often occurred in London, as many scenes are set there. Numerous buildings and other landmarks familiar to his London audiences are presented, including the TOWER OF LONDON, the INNS OF COURT, PARLIAMENT HOUSE, BAYNARD CASTLE, and Blackfriars Abbey. Especially common are interiors of WESTMINSTER PALACE, where the political leaders often assembled.

Some scenes in the histories are particularly noteworthy for their vivid glimpses of the London populace. In Act 4 of *2 Henry VI* Jack Cade's rebellion spreads to the city from KENT and we see the citizenry rise up in support of rebellion, as they did historically, not only for Cade but on other occasions as well. Incidents of Cade's rebellion occur at BLACKHEATH and SMITHFIELD, semirural areas adjacent to the city. Another aspect of civil disorder that London knew all too well was the helplessness of the common people in the face of aristocratic quarrels and civil war. This is well exemplified in 2.3 of *Richard III*, where several Londoners discuss the political situation in resigned tones. Another view of such politics is given in 5.2.1–40 of *Richard II*, where the Duke of York describes a triumphal entrance into London, in which the assembled people hail the conqueror, Henry Bolingbroke, and ridicule the fallen Richard II. Shakespeare's most famous depiction of the life of London is in the *Henry IV* plays, where much of the action is centered on the BOAR'S HEAD TAVERN in the neighborhood of EASTCHEAP. There a colorful subsection of city life, the world of petty thieves and slumming aristocrats, is presented with infectious gusto.

Sometimes scenes in plays set elsewhere in Europe reflect the realities of life in London in a manner familiar to London audiences. For instance, the VENICE of *The Merchant of Venice* offers a satirical slant on the business world of Shakespeare's London, and the VIENNA of *Measure for Measure* includes a sort of Eastcheap underworld. The outbreak of plague in VERONA, with its "searchers of the town" (*Romeo and Juliet* 5.2.8), reflects a disaster that was common in London. Further, the politically unruly commoners of London seem to inhabit the ROME of *Julius Caesar* and *Coriolanus*.

London Prodigal, The   Play formerly attributed to Shakespeare, part of the Shakespeare APOCRYPHA. *The London Prodigal*, a domestic comedy of a prodigal husband's reformation by his wife, was published in 1605 by Nathaniel BUTTER, who ascribed it to Shakespeare. This was probably a conscious fraud, for *The London Prodigal* is totally unlike Shakespeare's plays. Its characters are uniformly shallow, its poetry is weak, and it is of a genre unused by Shakespeare—a comedy set in contemporary LONDON. Though the editors of the FIRST FOLIO rejected it, the play was again published as Shakespeare's in the Third and Fourth Folios (see FOLIO) and in the editions of Nicholas ROWE and Alexander POPE. The authorship of *The London*

Prodigal remains unknown, though some scholars attribute it to Thomas MARSTON.

Longleat manuscript   Single page containing the earliest known illustration from Shakespeare, a scene taken from *Titus Andronicus*. This document, in the library at Longleat, the estate of the Marquess of Bath, bears a semi-legible date, generally held to be 1594 or 1595, and is signed by Henry Peachem (ca. 1576–1643), an artist and writer. The illustration, at the top of the page, depicts Tamora on her knees before Titus Andronicus, with two bound figures behind her on the right and Aaron behind them. At the left, behind Titus, are two soldiers bearing halberds. Below the picture is a text consisting of Tamora's plea for mercy when her son is to be sacrificed (1.1.104–120) and the captive Aaron's defiant proclamation of his own evil (5.1.125–144). These speeches are linked by three lines not from the play, presumably composed by Peachem. It is speculated that the Longleat manuscript may have been created for a private, amateur theatrical production.

Lopez, Roderigo (d. 1594)   Contemporary of Shakespeare, a Portuguese doctor living in England whose trial and execution for treason may have helped inspire the composition of *The Merchant of Venice*. Lopez, born Jewish but a Christian convert, fled the Portuguese Inquisition in 1559 and by 1586 was appointed physician to Queen Elizabeth I (see Elizabeth I in *Henry VIII*). In 1592 he entered into a dangerous intrigue involving a pretender to the Portuguese throne, and he appears to have antagonized the powerful Robert Devereux, Earl of ESSEX, who accused him of plotting to poison the Queen. Although it has long been generally held that Lopez was almost certainly innocent, since the prosecution depended heavily on torture-induced testimony, recent scholarship has cast doubt on history's "innocent" verdict. In any case, he was hanged on June 7, 1594. His trial stimulated an outbreak of anti-Semitic feeling in London and also spurred a series of revivals of *The Jew of Malta*, by Christopher MARLOWE. It has often been thought that when Gratiano insultingly tells Shylock that his soul is that of "a wolf . . . hanged for human slaughter" (*The Merchant of Venice* 4.1.134), he was punning on Lopez's name, which means "wolf."

Lord Howard's Men   See ADMIRAL'S MEN.

Love in a Forest   Play by Charles JOHNSON based loosely on *As You Like It*. Produced in 1723, *Love in a Forest* was the first version of Shakespeare's play to appear for more than a century, but it was a radically changed text. It incorporated elements from several of Shakespeare's other plays—including *A Midsummer Night's Dream, Much Ado About Nothing, Twelfth Night,* and even *Richard II*—and eliminated a number of characters, among them Touchstone, Audrey, William, Phebe, and Corin. Colley CIBBER played Jaques. Popular for a time, *Love in a Forest* was superseded in the 1740s by a production of *As You Like It* itself.

Love's Martyr   A long allegorical poem by Robert Chester, published in 1601 in a book of the same name with a collection of shorter poems by other poets, including Shakespeare's "The Phoenix and Turtle." Nothing is known of Chester except that he was a member of the household of Sir John SALUSBURY, whose marriage in 1586 this book commemorates. An allegory, the poem tells of a mystical love between two birds—the turtledove (commonly called "turtle" in Elizabethan English), a symbol of fidelity, and the mythological phoenix, an ancient emblem of immortality. The allegory is, however, interspersed with discourses on King Arthur, precious stones, natural history, and so on. Eventually, the phoenix and the turtle decide to die together, and they construct a funeral pyre and burn to death.

The love between phoenix and turtledove is also the theme of the poems later added to Chester's, including "The Phoenix and Turtle." Salusbury was knighted in 1601, and this was probably the occasion for the poem's publication, with the addition of work by much better-known writers, several of them Salusbury's friends; *Love's Martyr* also includes contributions by George

CHAPMAN, Ben JONSON, and John MARSTON, among others. Shakespeare's "Phoenix" is now the only well-known piece in the book.

Love's Martyr was first published in 1601 by Edward BLOUNT in a QUARTO edition printed by Richard FIELD. Ten years later it was republished with a new title, *The Annals of Great Britain,* but only the title page varied from the original quarto. The 1601 edition has therefore been the basis of all subsequent editions of both Chester's poem, which was not republished until 1878, and of "The Phoenix and Turtle."

Lowin, John (John Lowen) (1576–1653)   English actor. One of the 26 men listed in the FIRST FOLIO as the "Principall Actors" of Shakespeare's plays, Lowin was one of the most noted members of the KING'S MEN in the early 17th century. A very large man, he was famous for his Falstaff (see *1 Henry IV*), and he may have originated the part of Henry VIII (although this report—that Lowin learned the part from Shakespeare himself—dates from 1708 and is suspect).

Lowin was apprenticed to a goldsmith as a boy, but as soon as he was free he turned to the stage. He was a member of WORCESTER'S MEN in 1602–03, but in 1603 he joined the King's Men, becoming a partner in 1604. After 1630 he was a comanager of the company, with Joseph TAYLOR, and he remained with them until the closing of the theaters by the revolution in 1642. After retirement he owned a small tavern, but he died in poverty.

Lucian (ca. A.D. 120–180)   Greek satirist, author of a probable source for *Timon of Athens*. Lucian's *Timon the Misanthrope* is a satirical dialogue that contains numerous elements of Shakespeare's plot and clearly was known to Shakespeare in some form. Though no English translation of this work existed in Shakespeare's day, he may have known it in Latin, French, or Italian. Alternatively, he may have used another source based on Lucian, perhaps an anonymous English play known as the "old *Timon*" (ca. 1580–1610), or perhaps some work now lost, possibly a source for the "old *Timon*" that derived from Lucian.

Lucian was originally from a Greek-speaking settlement in what is now Syria. He traveled around the Roman Empire lecturing on philosophy and rhetoric. He settled in Athens around the age of 40, and there wrote the dialogues that made him famous throughout the Mediterranean as a clever satirist of philosophical and religious ideas.

Lucy, Sir Thomas (1532–1600)   Contemporary of Shakespeare, a WARWICKSHIRE landowner sometimes identified with Justice Shallow, a comic character in *2 Henry IV* and *The Merry Wives of Windsor*. According to a local tradition—first published by Nicholas ROWE in 1709—the young Shakespeare was caught poaching deer on Lucy's estate near STRATFORD; he was prosecuted for the crime and took vengeance by writing an insulting ballad about Sir Thomas. The same tradition was also recorded at about the same time by Richard DAVIES, testifying to its currency in the 17th century. In the 18th century several versions of the scurrilous ballad were published by various antiquarians.

Sir Thomas Lucy's heraldic emblem of three vertical white fish (luces—i.e., pike) resembles that of Shallow, as described with comic solemnity and confusion in *The Merry Wives*, 1.1.15–25, and Shallow threatens Falstaff with a lawsuit for having killed his deer. It thus appears that, if the tale of young Shakespeare and Lucy is true, the playwright could have been mocking his old enemy. However, there are a number of reasons to doubt that this is the case. No further resemblance to Lucy can be found in *The Merry Wives* or *2 Henry IV*. The heraldic luces may be found in other coats of arms—in fact, they support the argument in favor of a different identification of Shallow (see GARDINER, WILLIAM). Further, *The Merry Wives* was first presented at the Queen's court, where it would have been foolish of Shakespeare to pillory a powerful nobleman, supposing—improbably—that his audience would have understood the allusions, and pointless if they would not. Lastly, the story itself is subject to considerable doubt. It is impossible to rely on a tale whose earliest known recounting dates from more than a century after the events it describes. Lucy may not have kept deer; he did not have the required license to do so, although unlicensed deer parks were known in Elizabethan times, and his grandson later took out a license for the same land. In any case, the poaching tale could well have arisen from the play, rather than vice versa, the seeming allusions to Lucy perhaps being associated with his grandson's recorded prosecution of poachers in 1610. However, perhaps significantly, Lucy himself in 1584 introduced a bill in Parliament that would have made poaching a felony. Incidentally, a separate tradition tells that the grandson, another Thomas Lucy (1585–1640), was a friend of Shakespeare after the playwright's retirement.

Sir Thomas was one of the richest landlords in Warwickshire; in 1572, when Shakespeare was eight years old, Queen Elizabeth visited his estate. He would have been a powerful enemy. A zealous Protestant, he was a local leader in the persecution of Catholics. Sir William Lucy, who appears in *1 Henry VI*, was his great-great-great-grandfather.

Lupton, Thomas (active 1570s and 1580s)   English writer, author of a minor source for *Measure for Measure*. Lupton's collection of political anecdotes and utopian tales, *The Second Part and knitting up of the booke entitled Too Good to be True* (1581; *Too Good to be True* appeared in 1580), contains an account of the Italian judicial scandal of 1547 that was the original source of Shakespeare's play, though the playwright also knew of this event from several other sources that were more important. From Lupton came the germ of the encounters between Angelo and Isabella and, perhaps, the sense of urgency conveyed by repeated, precise references to the scheduling of the imminent execution of Claudio.

Though Lupton is today remembered chiefly for his contribution to *Measure for Measure*, he also wrote one of the last English MORALITY plays and a number of anti-Catholic religious tracts. However, he was best known in his own time for a layman's health manual, a collection of recipes and cures entitled *A Thousand Notable Things of Sundry Sorts* (1579), which was immensely popular and was republished at intervals until 1793.

Lydgate, John (ca. 1370–ca. 1451)   English poet, author of a source of *Troilus and Cressida*. Inspired by Guido delle COLONNE's *Historia destructionis Troiae* (1287), Lydgate wrote a long poem on the TROJAN WAR, entitled *Troy Book* (1420, publ. 1512, 1555), which influenced Shakespeare's play, especially in its emphasis on the chivalric aspects of the war.

Though an ordained priest, Lydgate spent much of his life staging pageants for the guilds of London. He was a friend of the great poet Geoffrey CHAUCER, and he enjoyed the patronage of Humphrey, Duke of Gloucester, who appears in four Shakespearean plays and through whom Lydgate became the official poet of the court of King Henry VI. Though his reputation was quite good in his own day, Lydgate is now generally regarded as a bad poet whose medieval religiosity and prosaic language are no longer of interest. However, his translation of BOCCACCIO's *The Fate of Illustrious Men* (1355–74)—published as *Falls of Princes* (1431–38, publ. 1494)—was an influence on the compilers of A MIRROR FOR MAGISTRATES, a prominent work in Shakespeare's day that was also a source for the playwright.

Lyly, John (ca. 1554–1606)   English novelist and playwright, a major influence on Shakespeare's early plays. Lyly's extravagant novels and courtly comedies were quite fashionable in LONDON in the 1580s, and they evidently fascinated the young Shakespeare. In elaborate language Lyly's plays presented tales of conflicting love and friendship often involving journeys to exotic climates frequented by outlaws. Their tone, combining sentimentality and sharp wit, seems to have contributed much to Shakespeare's early comedies—especially *Love's Labour's Lost*, but also *The Comedy of Errors*, *The Two Gentlemen of Verona*, and *A Midsummer Night's Dream*. Literal borrowings, however, are rare and minor.

Lyly, grandson of the humanist scholar William LILY, was the oldest member of the UNIVERSITY WITS, who revolutionized ELIZABETHAN DRAMA in the 1580s. He first achieved fame as the author of a romantic novel of courtly love and genteel adventure, *Euphues, the Anatomy of Wit* (1578), whose extravagant prose style startled readers with its novelty. *Euphues* was studded with puns, repetitions, alliterations, high-flown rhetorical digressions, and fanciful references to classical mythology and natural history (often invented). So distinctive was the style that it became known (and is still known) as euphuism. It was highly fashionable for years and was much imitated. Shakespeare was as likely to mock euphuism as imitate it, and in *1 Henry IV* 2.4.393–426, Falstaff indulges in a delightful parody of it.

After publishing a second volume of his novel—*Euphues and his England* (1580)—Lyly turned to the theater. He wrote numerous elegant comedies for two CHILDREN'S COMPANIES, primarily between 1584 and 1590 but also occasionally until 1602. He was also associated with Henry EVANS and William HUNNIS in the first BLACKFRIARS THEATRE. He then turned to politics and the court of Queen Elizabeth I. He was several times a Member of Parliament, and for years he unsuccessfully pursued an appointment as the queen's MASTER OF THE REVELS.

M

Mabbe, James (1572–1642) English writer, possibly the author of one of the introductory poems to the FIRST FOLIO edition (1632) of Shakespeare's plays. Mabbe is best known as the translator of a major work of the Spanish RENAISSANCE, the novel *La Celestina*, by Fernando de Rojas (d. ca. 1541). He was a longtime friend of Leonard DIGGES, who knew Shakespeare, and scholars generally believe he is the author of "To the memorie of M. W. Shakespeare," a poem of four rhymed couplets that is signed "I. M." in the FOLIO (but see MAYNE, JASPER).

Machiavel Villainous but humorous character type of ELIZABETHAN DRAMA, a sly cynic who loves evil for its own sake. A Machiavel is characterized by a delight in evil that makes other motivation unnecessary, the habit of commenting on his own activities in humorous soliloquies, treachery to his own allies, a tendency to lewdness, and a cynical contempt for goodness and religion. By convention, the good characters never recognize the Machiavel's evil intentions until it is too late. Othello's extraordinary gullibility is paradoxically explained, in part, by Iago's obvious villainy, for its very obviousness to the audience presumes its invisibility to the characters.

Shakespeare's principal Machiavels besides Iago—who is probably the most famous of all such characters—were Aaron *(Titus Andronicus)*, Edmund *(King Lear)*, and Richard III. A number of other Shakespearean characters display the features of the type to a lesser degree—for example, the Bishop of Winchester in *1 Henry VI* and Cassius in *Julius Caesar*. The first famous Machiavel—who doubtless influenced Shakespeare—was Barabas, the villain of *The Jew of Malta* by Christopher Marlowe; also, a character named Machiavel speaks the PROLOGUE to the play. Other dramatists of the period employed the figure as well.

The Machiavel takes his name from the Italian political philosopher Niccolò Machiavelli (1469–1527), who was (and is) popularly misunderstood to have advocated atheism, treachery, and criminality as preferable to other means of statecraft. This model was applied to an already-existing character type, the VICE, a humorous villain from the medieval MORALITY PLAY. Machiavelli added elements of intelligence, craftiness, and political ambition. Shakespeare's Richard, who identifies himself as a superior Machiavel in *3 Henry VI* 3.2.193 (probably referring to Marlowe's prologue speaker), also describes his methods: "Plots have I laid, inductions dangerous," and adds for good measure that he is "subtle, false, and treacherous" *(Richard III* 1.1.32–37).

Macklin, Charles (ca. 1700–1797) Irish actor, a notable Shylock *(The Merchant of Venice)*. Macklin is best known as the actor who restored Shakespeare's Shylock after the part had for at least a generation been customarily played for laughs by crude comedians. After Macklin, the dignity and pathos of the figure never again lapsed so far, though even Macklin played him as a melodramatic villain. Macklin played many comic parts in Shakespeare, and in 1754 he delivered a series of lectures on the playwright that are the earliest ever recorded. He was also a playwright who wrote two successful comedies. He retired in 1789, at about age 90, after forgetting his lines while playing Shylock.

Macready, William Charles (1793–1873) British actor and producer. Macready, one of the great tragedian of the 19th century, played all of Shakespeare's great protagonists, as well as numerous other figures, such as Hotspur, Iago, and Jaques (in *1 Henry IV, Othello,* and *As You Like It,* respectively). He often played opposite Helen FAUCIT. He helped pioneer the period's return to genuine Shakespearean texts, removing the accretions of earlier centuries, especially in his productions of *King Lear, Coriolanus,* and *The Tempest.* However, Macready's versions were themselves abridgments, in part to make room for the spectacular tableaus for which he was well known, and in part to censor Shakespeare, removing, for instance, the grisly fate of Gloucester from *King Lear.* With Edmund KEAN, Macready dominated the English theater of the 1820s and was alone its major figure in the following decade. His diaries, published in 1875, offer a lively picture of the theater of his day. Macready played in New York in 1826 and 1848–49; on the latter occasion, the rivalry of Edwin FORREST led to the notorious Astor Place riot.

Malipiero, Gian Francesco (1882–1973) Italian composer, creator of several OPERAs based on Shakespeare. A champion of modern music in Italy in the 1920s, Malipiero later came to be better known for his large part in the introduction of the music of the RENAISSANCE to modern ears. His own works tended to combine an antique flavor derived from that source, with the complex, sometimes dissonant idiom of early modern music. He was noted for operas based on a remarkable range of subject matter, from VIRGIL to the bizarre etchings of the 17th-century French artist Jacques Callot (1592–1635), and including a paradoxical libretto by the Italian modernist writer Luigi Pirandello (1867–1936). The latter offended Benito Mussolini, Italy's dictator (1883–1945; ruled 1922–43), and Malipiero dedicated his next opera to the ruler. Mussolini was unappeased, perhaps because the work, *Giulio Cesare* (1934), derived from a play about a tyrannicide, Shakespeare's *Julius Caesar.* However that may be, Malipiero's next opera was also Shakespearean, *Antonio e Cleopatra* (1938), and he also included some Shakespearean material in a later work, *Mondi celeste e infernali* (1948).

Malone, Edmond (1741–1812) English scholar. Malone was probably the greatest of 18th-century Shakespearean scholars, and one of the greatest of all time. His *Attempt to ascertain the Order in which the Plays of Shakespeare were written*—the first such effort—was published in George STEEVENS's 1778 edition of the plays, and he edited two volumes added in 1780 to Steevens's collection, containing the poems, the doubtful plays of the third FOLIO, and Malone's history of ELIZABETHAN THEATER. In 1790 he brought out his own edition of the plays, incorporating a tremendous amount of scholarship, including his massive *Life* of Shakespeare, the basis for all subsequent biographies. In 1796 he led the exposure of the forgeries of William Henry IRELAND, and when he died he was at work on a new edition of the plays. This was eventually completed by James BOSWELL the Younger. Known as the "Third Variorum" (see VARIORUM EDITION) or "Boswell's Malone," it has been the foundation of modern Shakespeare studies.

Manningham, John (ca. 1576–1622) English diarist. Manningham, a lawyer and minor official, was an avid theatergoer who recorded the earliest known performance of *Twelfth Night,* in 1602. In the same year he also preserved the only surviving contemporary anecdote of Shakespeare's life. He had been told, he wrote in his diary, that the playwright, during a performance of *Richard III,* had overheard a message from a female admirer to its star, Richard BURBAGE, inviting him to a dalliance later that evening. Shakespeare, according to the story, arrived at the appointment before Burbage and was enjoying the company of the young woman when a servant brought word that "Richard III" was at the door. Shakespeare then sent back a message that "William the Conqueror was before Richard III." While a student at the

INNS OF COURT, Manningham knew William COMBE, and through him he may have been personally acquainted with Shakespeare.

Mantell, Robert Bruce (1854–1928)   Scottish-American actor. Mantell began his career in Ireland and went to America in 1878, joining Helena MODJESKA's company. After a brief return to Britain, Mantell remained in New York for good. A romantic leading man early in his career and a character actor as an older man, he played many Shakespearean parts.

Mantua   City in northern Italy, a location in *Romeo and Juliet*. Romeo flees to Mantua when banished from VERONA, and he is seen there in 5.1. Shakespeare took this incident from his source, the poem *Romeus and Iuliet*, by Arthur BROOKE. The same source accounts for a reference to the city in *The Two Gentlemen of Verona*, in which Silvia asserts (mistakenly) that Valentine is in exile there (4.3.23). The city is also named in *The Taming of the Shrew* (4.2.77–85); it is referred to as a port, and this has often been cited as an error on Shakespeare's part. But in the 16th century Mantua, situated on the Mincio River, participated in the considerable river-and-canal trade that was prominent in northern Italy until the advent of the railroads in the 19th century.

March, Earl of   Historically, the hereditary title of the head of the Mortimer family. Several earls of March laid claim to the English throne by virtue of their descent from a daughter of Lionel Plantagenet, Duke of Clarence, the oldest brother of the deposed King Richard II. In *1 Henry VI*, this claim is transmitted to the family of Richard Plantagenet, Duke of York, by Edmund Mortimer, thus helping to lay the groundwork for the WARS OF THE ROSES. Due to confusion in his sources, in *1 Henry IV* Shakespeare gave the title to a different Edmund Mortimer, who was historically a younger brother and thus neither an Earl of March nor in the royal line of descent.

In *3 Henry VI*, Edward of York, soon to be King Edward IV, is referred to as the Earl of March, at 2.1.179 and 2.1.192, in connection with his allies among the Welsh, for the Earldom's lands bordered

Wales. The word *march*, meaning "border region," had been added to the title generations earlier.

Markham, Gervase (Jervis Markham) (ca. 1568–1637)   English poet and author, writer of possible minor sources for Shakespeare's plays, and perhaps a model for the boastful soldier Armado of *Love's Labour's Lost* or the "rival poet" of the *Sonnets*. Markham was a noted soldier and horseman—he probably introduced the Arabian horse to England—who turned to hack literature after his military career. He wrote copiously on a variety of subjects, especially military tactics, falconry, fishing, housekeeping, and all aspects of owning and breeding horses. His easy, colloquial style made him popular, and he still offers readers a pleasant introduction to the Elizabethan age. Scholars believe that some of his practical information is echoed in Shakespeare's plays, for instance in Petruchio's elaborate description of falcon training in *The Taming of the Shrew* (4.1.175–198). Markham's confidence in his own infallibility suggests he may have been satirized in Shakespeare's Armado, though the point cannot be proven with existing evidence.

Markham was an extremely prolific author who sometimes issued almost identical texts under different titles to increase sales. At one point a group of London booksellers, seeing that he was flooding his own market, persuaded him to sign an agreement not to write any more books on blacksmithing, but he soon violated the pact. He occasionally aspired to more serious literature, and because he dedicated one such work to Shakespeare's patron, Henry Wriothesley, Earl of SOUTHAMPTON, he has been associated with the "rival poet," though most scholars find the identification extremely dubious.

Marlowe, Christopher (1564–1593)   English playwright, Shakespeare's immediate predecessor as leading English dramatist and a considerable influence on his work. Marlowe, with Thomas KYD, virtually invented Elizabethan TRAGEDY, and Marlowe's influence on ELIZABETHAN DRAMA in general was great. In his *Tamburlaine* (1587) he successfully established BLANK VERSE as the standard medium for drama, and the grandeur of his protagonists and themes elevated his successors' aspirations.

Many passages in Shakespeare's early works are clearly modeled on Marlowe; scholars who believe that many of Shakespeare's plays were written in part by other playwrights have even attributed parts of the *Henry VI* plays, *Richard III*, *Titus Andronicus*, and others to Marlowe, though modern scholars mistrust most of these attributions. In *As You Like It*, Phebe quotes a line from a Marlowe poem, ascribing it to a "dead shepherd" (3.5.81–82), Shakespeare's only certain reference to a contemporary poet. Further quotations from and allusions to Marlowe's work abound in the plays (e.g., *A Midsummer Night's Dream*, 1.1.170; *Merry Wives of Windsor*, 3.1.16–35; *Much Ado About Nothing*, 5.2.29), attesting not only to Shakespeare's admiration but also to his confidence that his audiences knew and appreciated Marlowe's work. In addition, Marlowe's *The Jew of Malta* (1589) probably helped inspire Shylock in Shakespeare's *The Merchant of Venice*; similarly, Marlowe's *Edward II* (1592) probably informed *Richard II*'s presentation of a flawed ruler, and his poem "Hero and Leander" offered a model for *Venus and Adonis*. (Marlowe's poem was unfinished at his death and published posthumously—with additions by George CHAPMAN—in 1598, but Shakespeare knew it earlier, in manuscript.)

Marlowe led a violent, dissolute, and dramatic life. A notorious drinker and brawler, he flaunted his homosexuality at a time when homosexuality was a capital crime. He was a soldier in the Netherlands, from which he was deported for counterfeiting gold coins, and he was probably a spy for the government of Queen Elizabeth I (see Elizabeth I in *Henry VIII*)—both abroad and in England. In 1589 he was involved in a street fight in which a man was killed. He was one of the earliest Englishmen to publicly admit to atheism, and in 1593 he was charged with blasphemy—along with Kyd—but before he could be tried, he was stabbed to death, reportedly in a dispute over a tavern bill. Some historians believe he was murdered, silenced by a government agent; in any case, his killer, who is known to have been a fellow spy, was immediately pardoned. (Marlowe's death may be alluded to in *As You Like It* 3.3.9–12.)

The son of a shoemaker, Marlowe nevertheless received a good education, graduating from Cambridge University in 1587, in the same year that his first play, *Tamburlaine*, became the talk of LONDON. He followed it with *Tamburlaine, Part 2* (1588), *The Jew of Malta* (1589), *Doctor Faustus* (1592), *Edward II* (1592)—the first English historical play—and *The Massacre at Paris* (1593). Most of his plays were probably commissioned by the ADMIRAL'S MEN, and his heroic protagonists were first played by Edward ALLEYN. At his death Marlowe left another play unfinished—*Dido, Queen of Carthage*, completed by Thomas NASHE and staged in 1594—along with "Hero and Leander." His oeuvre was completed by two other short poems (one of them, the delightful "Passionate Shepherd to his Love," was falsely attributed to Shakespeare in THE PASSIONATE PILGRIM). While the body of work is small, it encompasses at least three great plays—*Tamburlaine*, *The Jew of Malta*, and *Doctor Faustus*—and a magnificent lyric poem, "Hero and Leander." Marlowe, who was born the same year as Shakespeare, was only 29 when he was killed. This fact has not prevented conspiracy theorists from supposing that Marlowe may have been the "real" Shakespeare (see AUTHORSHIP CONTROVERSY).

Marlowe, Julia (1865–1950) American actress. Born in Britain, Marlowe came to America at age four, began acting with a touring company at 12, and made her New York debut at 21. She quickly established herself as a leading actress, especially in Shakespearean comedy, playing Viola (*Twelfth Night*), Rosalind (*As You Like It*), Beatrice (*Much Ado About Nothing*), and Portia (*The Merchant of Venice*). She also excelled as Juliet. In 1904 Marlowe founded a Shakespearean repertory company with E. H. SOTHERN, whom she later married. She took on more tragic roles, including Lady Macbeth. Just after her retirement in 1924, she and Sothern staged 10 Shakespearean performances whose proceeds were donated to the Shakespeare Memorial Theatre in STRATFORD.

Marseilles City in southern FRANCE, setting for one scene in *All's Well That Ends Well*. Helena announces her intention to leave FLORENCE and find the King of France at "Marcellus" (4.4.9)—indicating the Elizabethan pronunciation of the name—

and in 5.1 she is said in the stage directions to be there, only to discover that the King has left for ROSSILLION. No characteristics of Marseilles or southern France are alluded to, but the setting is apt because Marseilles is the major city on either a land or land-and-sea route from Florence to Rossillion.

Marsh, Henry (d. 1665) English publisher. Marsh published the first edition of a famous collection of DROLLs, *The Wits, or Sport upon Sport* (1662), assembled by his partner, Francis KIRKMAN. He may have been a royalist and in exile during the period of the Puritan revolutionary government (1642–60), for he is absent from the publishing records from 1642 to 1658. When he died he left his business to Kirkman.

Marston, John (ca. 1575–1634) English dramatist. Marston abandoned a legal education to be a writer. In 1598 he established himself in the literary world with two long poems, one erotic (*The Metamorphosis of Pygmalion's Image*) and one satiric (*The Scourge of Villainy*). In 1599 he wrote for Philip HENSLOWE and the ADMIRAL'S MEN, but in the same year he began writing for the CHILDREN'S COMPANIES, where he spent the rest of his short career. He is chiefly remembered for bitter satirical COMEDY, but he also specialized in the REVENGE PLAY. With his best-known work, *The Malcontent* (1604), he managed to combine the two genres. Writing for the Children of Paul's, Marston began the WAR OF THE THEATERS with his *Historio-Mastix* (1599), a comedy containing a satire on Ben JONSON. In reply to Jonson's responses, he added *Jack Drum's Entertainment* (1600) and *What You Will* (1601) to the fray, as well as collaborating with Thomas DEKKER on *Satiromastix* (1601). He was on good terms with Jonson by 1604, when he dedicated *The Malcontent* to his one-time rival. In that year Marston began writing for the Children of the Queen's Revels, and in 1605 he collaborated with Jonson and George CHAPMAN on *Eastward Ho!* King JAMES I deemed the play seditious, with the result that Marston's collaborators were jailed, though Marston fled LONDON until the affair blew over, thereby igniting Jonson's enmity anew. In 1608, however, Marston was imprisoned for offending the king again, with a play now lost,

and he abandoned the theater, leaving a final play unfinished. By 1616 he was a Protestant minister.

masque Courtly entertainment that evolved into a drama-like theatrical genre. Masques appear in various forms in a number of Shakespeare's plays. Originally an amateur masquerade in which members of the court put on masks and costumes and feted the monarch with dancing on holiday occasions, the masque evolved under King JAMES I into a theatrical presentation with extremely elaborate sets and costumes, many professional musicians and dancers in support of the aristocratic amateurs, and highly literary scripts by such writers as Francis BEAUMONT, Samuel DANIEL, and most notably Ben JONSON. These productions were staged on significant royal occasions, such as weddings and birthdays. (Nonroyal aristocrats also staged masques on such occasions.) The masques were allegorical in nature, with mythological or emblematic characters who represented particular virtues and vices or more or less clearcut ideas, such as marriage or PASTORAL contentment. The great expense of such extravaganzas eventually became a significant political issue, and the courtly masque did not survive the revolution that began in 1642.

The 17th-century masque exerted considerable influence on JACOBEAN DRAMA. Shakespeare's last works—the ROMANCES plus *Henry VIII*, which were written for the aristocratic audiences at the BLACKFRIARS THEATRE—all contain elaborate masquelike elements. Masques also appear in several earlier Shakespeare plays: Simple maskings of a social sort are enacted in *Love's Labour's Lost*, *Romeo and Juliet*, and *Much Ado About Nothing*, while more formal stagings, featuring named mythological characters, occur in *As You Like It* and *Timon of Athens*. In addition, there are masquelike elements in other plays, most strikingly in *A Midsummer Night's Dream*.

As in movies that contain scraps of older movies as part of the characters' experience, the appearance of masques in plays amused their audiences with enactments of familiar—or at least notorious—pleasures while also furthering the play's developments. For instance, in *The Winter's Tale*, a masquelike "dance of twelve Satyrs" (4.4.343) is presented at a sheep-shearing festival. A delightful theatrical spectacle in itself, it demonstrates the vitality of pastoral life and at the same time, by evoking an aristocratic entertainment, expresses the hidden nobility present, for the leading shepherdess is actually the lost princess Perdita. In *Timon of Athens*, Cupid's brief masque in 1.2 displays the aristocratic elegance of the title character's household while providing an occasion for an irascible complaint against extravagant vanity by the play's philosopher-jester, Apemantus. An actual royal masque of 1527 is reenacted in 1.4 of *Henry VIII*, and the betrothal masque in 4.1 of *The Tempest* resembles contemporary (ca. 1611) masques and lends grandeur to the proposed marriage of Ferdinand and Miranda, whose status as future royalty has significance in the play's scheme of things. The masque in 3.5 of *The Two Noble Kinsmen* was in fact a scene from a real masque, Beaumont's *Masque of the Inner Temple and Gray's Inn* (1613) (see INNS OF COURT), though this borrowing was the work of Shakespeare's collaborator, John FLETCHER.

The masque was known at least as far back as the 14th century, during the reign of Richard II. It was formalized, with prepared scenarios, under Queen Elizabeth I, but it only became a literary, quasi-dramatic genre under James. However, even Jacobean masques always contained large elements of dance, the original masque medium, and—at least in life, if not always on the stage—masques were normally preludes to social dancing, in which the participants joined the spectators at a ball. A masque was accordingly an occasion for coquetry and sexual intrigue, as is quite clear in Shakespeare.

Masques were influential on literature, as well as drama. Masquelike elements appear in such works as *The Faerie Queene* by Edmund SPENSER, and some late masques are significant literary works in their own right, most notably John MILTON's *Comus* (performed 1634; published 1637). The courtly masque did not reappear after the Puritan revolution; the last known script was written by William DAVENANT in 1640.

Massinger, Philip (1583–1640) English playwright, a secondary figure of JACOBEAN DRAMA. Massinger's plays are characterized by his imitation of Shakespeare's verse style, to the extent that though no known work of Massinger's can be dated before 1616, he is sometimes thought to have written the parts usually assigned to Shakespeare in his collaborations with John FLETCHER, *The Two Noble Kinsmen* and possibly *Henry VIII*. Most scholars, however, deem Massinger's involvement extremely unlikely, though he did collaborate with Fletcher, his close friend, on many plays. He also worked with numerous other playwrights. After Fletcher's death, Massinger became the chief playwright for the KING'S MEN.

Massinger wrote a variety of works. He is best remembered for his satirical comedies, especially *A New Way to Pay Old Debts* (1621) and *The City Madam* (1632). He also wrote tragedies. His *Duke of Milan* (1621), which is based on *Othello*, is regarded as among the better Jacobean tragedies. In the late 17th century, Massinger's *The Roman Actor* (1626) was thought to be by Shakespeare. Massinger often faced governmental CENSORSHIP, for he frequently touched on such sensitive issues as Catholicism (he was himself a Catholic convert), foreign policy, and various public figures.

Master of Revels English official of the 16th and 17th centuries who regulated the theater. The Master headed the Revels Office, a department of the royal household that originally dealt with the annual royal entertainments during the Revels season, from All Saints' Day (November 1) to the beginning of Lent in the following spring. The position of Master of Revels was created in 1545 under King Henry VIII. At first the Master was simply responsible for hiring and paying entertainers, but gradually the powers of the office were expanded. By Shakespeare's time the Revels Office consisted of the Master and four full-time subordinates, and it not only hired theatrical companies to perform at court but provided them with scenery and costumes from its own stores. It also selected the plays they were to perform and oversaw the content of the plays. The Master thus had the authority of a censor (see CENSORSHIP), especially after the passage of the 1606 antiblasphemy statute, "Act to Restrain Abuses of Players," which enlarged his authority to cover the publication of plays as well.

The Master collected various fees as he issued licenses for provincial acting companies, for the performance and publication of individual plays, and for dispensations to companies who wished to perform during Lent. In addition, he was frequently bribed. The office of Master of Revels was accordingly an extremely profitable one. The nominal salary was only £10 a year, but it is known that in 1603 the Master made about £100. Beginning in 1623, Sir Henry HERBERT paid the ostensible Master £150 a year to perform the office and collect the income, which must have been considerably greater. The office of Master of Revels fell into disuse when the theaters were closed at the outset of the civil war in 1642. Herbert tried to revive it upon the restoration of the monarchy in 1660, but his attempt failed, and the office was formally eliminated.

Mayne, Jasper (1604–1672)   English writer, possibly the author of one of the introductory poems to the FIRST FOLIO edition (1623) of Shakespeare's plays. Mayne published several poems and two plays (both written ca. 1638), one of which contains a scene apparently inspired by the interrogation of Parolles in 4.3 of *All's Well That Ends Well*. He also translated the Latin author LUCIAN. After 1660 he was chaplain to King Charles II. Some scholars attribute to him the poem "To the memorie of M. W. *Shake-speare*," a poem of four rhymed couplets that is signed "I. M." in the Folio. However, because Mayne was quite young in 1623, James MABBE is more commonly believed to be its author.

McKellen, Ian (b. 1935)   English actor. McKellen is noted for a variety of roles, having played most of Shakespeare's protagonists. He played Macbeth in Trevor NUNN's 1976 staging of *Macbeth* in STRATFORD and in the subsequent TELEVISION presentation. He also played the title role in the first known professional performance of *Sir Thomas More* in 1964. Perhaps his finest performance was in the title role of the National Theatre's Fascist-themed production of *Richard III* and the subsequent film version in 1995.

Mendelssohn, Felix (1809–1847)   German composer of music for *A Midsummer Night's Dream*.

Mendelssohn, a major figure of the Romantic movement in music, is perhaps best known today for his "Wedding March," written, along with a full array of incidental music, for Ludwig TIECK's 1827 German-language production of the *Dream*, the first in centuries to employ Shakespeare's full text (albeit translated; see TRANSLATION OF SHAKESPEARE). Mendelssohn's music also accompanied the first English revival of the play in 1840, as well as many, probably most, subsequent 19th- and 20th-century productions.

Though he died young, Mendelssohn was a prolific composer and wrote important works in every form but OPERA. Besides the Overture and Incidental Music for *A Midsummer Night's Dream*, his best-known works include his Fingal's Cave Overture, Italian Symphony, and the oratorio *Elijah*.

Meres, Francis (1565–1647)   English writer, author of a contemporary assessment of Shakespeare's early career. Meres is considered a pioneer literary critic, for in his *Palladis Tamia: Wit's Treasury*, an anthology of philosophical and literary maxims, he compares the English writers of his day with classical models. He declares that OVID's soul lives in Shakespeare, citing "his *Venus and Adonis*, his *Lucrece*, his sugred Sonnets among his private friends." Thus we know that by 1598, at least some of the *Sonnets* had been written and circulated in manuscript among Shakespeare's friends. Meres thought Sir Philip SIDNEY was the greatest English poet, but he proclaimed Shakespeare the equal of PLAUTUS in COMEDY and SENECA in TRAGEDY, and "among the English . . . the most excellent in both kinds for the stage." Here he cited six comedies and six tragedies: "his *Gentlemen of Verona*, his *Errors*, his *Loue labours lost*, his *Loue labours wonne*, his *Midsummers night dreame*, & his *Merchant of Venice* . . . his *Richard the 2*, *Richard the 3*, *Henry the 4*, *King John*, *Titus Andronicus* and his *Romeo and Juliet*." This list names all of Shakespeare's plays that other evidence indicates had been written by this time, except the *Henry VI* plays and *The Taming of the Shrew* (though the latter may be the mysterious *Love's Labour's Won*). Meres's remarks have helped scholars date the early works and offer evidence of the great respect commanded by Shakespeare among his contemporaries, even early in his career. Meres had only a brief career in LONDON as a writer—he also wrote devotional works—before he became a rural minister and schoolmaster.

Mermaid Tavern   Tavern in LONDON, meeting place of a literary club thought to have included Shakespeare. The Friday Street Club, named for the Mermaid's address, was a famous convivial gathering of London writers. Among its members were Francis BEAUMONT, John FLETCHER, and Ben JONSON. Shakespeare is traditionally counted a member as well, but this is not confirmed in any surviving contemporary accounts, and the club's great days came after the playwright had probably retired to STRATFORD. However, the idea is supported by Shakespeare's close connections with Jonson and Fletcher and his acquaintance at least with the innkeeper at the Mermaid, William JOHNSON.

Merry Devil of Edmonton, The   Anonymous play formerly attributed to Shakespeare, part of the Shakespeare APOCRYPHA. *The Merry Devil of Edmonton* is a comedy about lovers who elope to escape the bride's parents' plans for a mercenary marriage. It was published in six 17th-century editions, beginning with that of Arthur JOHNSON (1608). It was also popular on the stage, as is shown by many contemporary references to performances. It was first ascribed to Shakespeare by Francis KIRKMAN in 1661, but almost no later scholars have accepted this suggestion. Though *The Merry Devil* is one of the few apocryphal plays that commentators agree is an excellent drama, modern scholars are confident that it is not by Shakespeare. It is not like his work stylistically, and it was never associated with the playwright when it was new, despite the well-established commercial value of his name. Some scholars speculate that it was written by Michael DRAYTON or Thomas HEYWOOD, but its authorship remains uncertain.

Messina   City in Sicily, setting for *Much Ado About Nothing* and one scene of *Antony and Cleopatra*. Although there is nothing particularly Sicilian—let alone Messinian—about the events or locations in *Much Ado*, one of Shakespeare's sources for the play, Matteo BANDELLO's novella, is set in Messina, where an Aragonese army is celebrating its conquest of Sicily. Sicily was ruled by the kings of Aragon—and later Spain—from 1282 until 1713. Messina was the site of the first Aragonese victory, in 1282, against the French, who ruled the island until then. This doubtless accounts for Bandello's location, which Shakespeare simply adopted.

In 2.1 of *Antony and Cleopatra* Pompey confers with Menas and Menecrates about their war against Octavius Caesar, Lepidus, and Mark Antony. Shakespeare did not indicate the locale of this conference, but scholars have identified it. Beginning with Edward CAPELL in 1768, editors have generally provided a stage direction that places this scene in Messina. This follows Shakespeare's source, PLUTARCH's *Lives*, which locates Pompey's headquarters there. Sicily was Pompey's principal base for much of his rebellion against Rome, and his occupation of Messina, which commanded the strait between the island and mainland Italy, was strategically important. His final defeat was only possible through Caesar's blockade of Messina in 36 B.C., in a very difficult campaign that is casually referred to in 3.5.4. of the play.

meter (metre)   Regular rhythmic pattern in poetry. While some poetry lacks meter—this is called free verse—almost all premodern poetry, including Shakespeare's, is metrical; the words are arranged in a definite measurable pattern. The term *meter* derives from the Greek word for "measure." Some meters are *syllabic*, measuring simply the number of syllables in a line; some are *accentual*, measuring only the syllables that are stressed or accented when the poetry is read. *Quantitative* meters measure the duration of the sounds as they are spoken; ancient Greek, Latin, and Sanskrit verse usually follow this pattern. Most English poetry, including Shakespeare's, is composed in accentual-syllabic meters; that is, both the stresses and the syllables are counted.

These patterns of stresses and syllables are generally organized into elements known as feet. Six types of feet are most common in English poetry, though very rarely others—usually taken from quantitative systems—are used. The six feet are the iamb, consisting of an unstressed syllable followed by a stressed one, as in the word *delight*; the anapest, consisting of two unstressed syllables followed by one stressed one, as in the word *intervene*; the trochee, one stressed syllable followed by an unstressed one, as in *hotter*; the dactyl, one stressed syllable followed by two unstressed ones, as in *lovingly*; the spondee, two stressed syllables, as in *amen*; and the pyrrhic, two unstressed syllables, as in the syllables "-es of," in the line "I'll gild the faces of the grooms withal" (*Macbeth*, 2.2.55), where all the other feet are iambs. As this last example demonstrates, a foot does not necessarily correspond to a word or phrase; also, the same word or words may comprise different sorts of foot, depending on the feet surrounding it in the line.

Meters are named according to the number of feet in a line, using the Greek prefixes for numbers—*dimeter* for two feet, *trimeter* for three, *tetrameter* for four, *pentameter* for five, *hexameter* for six, and so on—and according to the kind of foot that dominates in the line: iambic, anapestic, trochaic, dactylic, spondaic, or pyrrhic. Variation is necessary; a poem of any length consisting solely of one sort of foot would sound intolerably mechanical. Thus an iambic pentameter line—typical in Shakespeare's poetry (see BLANK VERSE)—does not always consist only of iambs, and all the lines of an iambic pentameter poem or passage need not have five feet. However, throughout a work that is said to be written in iambic pentameter, iambs will dominate, and almost all the lines will have five feet.

Middleham Castle   Heavily fortified and moated castle in northern England, a location in *3 Henry VI*. The grounds of Middleham Castle, home to the brother of the Duke of Warwick, are the setting for 4.5, in which the Duke's captive, King Edward IV, is rescued by his allies.

Middleton, Thomas (1580–1627)   English playwright, a prolific writer of JACOBEAN DRAMA and a probable collaborator with Shakespeare. As a young man, Middleton worked for Philip HENSLOWE, turning out plays in collaboration with Thomas DEKKER, Michael DRAYTON, and Anthony MUNDAY. Recent scholarship has attracted much support for the proposition that Middleton collaborated on *Timon of Athens*, at least to the extent of having written an earlier text that Shakespeare adapted, but perhaps having written almost a third of the play himself, chiefly in 1.2 and Act 3, episodes focusing on the treacherous debtors of Timon. Middleton was also a satirist, and among other works he wrote a takeoff on *The Rape of Lucrece* (*The Ghost of Lucrece*, 1600). He wrote comedies for various CHILDREN'S COMPANIES between 1602 and 1608, then worked with Dekker on *The Roaring Girl* (1610), a highly successful COMEDY of the period.

In the 1620s Middleton collaborated with William ROWLEY, who wrote comic SUBPLOTS, on several plays for PRINCE CHARLES' MEN. These included his greatest play, *The Changeling* (1622), a TRAGEDY of murder, madness, and obsessive love that was frequently revived in the 20th century. Another of his best works, *Women Beware Women* (ca. 1625), is also a tragedy of perverse attractions and grave moral sickness. One of Middleton's last works, *A Game at Chess* (1624), is a boldly anti-Catholic, anti-Spanish allegory that blatantly alluded to King JAMES I's pursuit of a marital alliance with the Spanish Hapsburgs. It was a huge success at the GLOBE THEATRE, running for nine days—two days would have been unusual at that time (see ELIZABETHAN THEATER)—before the government prohibited it and briefly imprisoned its author.

Two SONGs from Middleton's tragedy *The Witch* (ca. 1610–20) were printed in the first edition of *Macbeth*, having been interpolated in Shakespeare's play for some early performance. Middleton may have written THE PURITAN and collaborated with William ROWLEY on THE BIRTH OF MERLIN, both plays at one time ascribed to Shakespeare. Also, he probably wrote "The Second Maiden's Tragedy" (1611), which was published in 1994 (probably mistakenly) as the missing *Cardenio*.

Milan   City in Italy, possibly the setting of several scenes in *The Two Gentlemen of Verona*. These scenes involve the members of the court of the Duke of Milan, but the geography of the play is confused at best, and it is difficult to know where the characters are much of the time. The actual city of Milan is in no way depicted in any case. Elsewhere in Shakespeare's works, Milan is referred to a number of times, though it is nowhere significant. It is most prominent in *The Tempest,* where the magician Prospero has been deposed as Duke of Milan and in the course of the play recovers that position. However, the whole play takes place on the magic island where Prospero rules in exile, and Milan is merely mentioned.

Miles Gloriosus   Traditional character type, dating from ancient Roman drama, that influenced several Shakespearean characters, most notably Armado in *Love's Labour's Lost.* The Miles Gloriosus, a foolish, bragging soldier, was well known in Shakespeare's day through Latin texts and, more important, through the braggart captain of Italian COMMEDIA DELL'ARTE. This *capitano* was usually a Spaniard, a reflection of the Spanish role in the wars that ravaged Italy in the 16th century. His nationality was naturally adopted by Shakespeare, for hostility toward Spain was also a central element of the contemporary English worldview. Besides Armado, the Shakespearean characters who partake of the same ancestry include Ajax and Thersites in *Troilus and Cressida* and Parolles in *All's Well That Ends Well.* Although Falstaff is often cited in this connection, he transcends the empty vainglory of the traditional type. Maurice MORGANN—the 18th-century writer on Falstaff—observed that the Miles Gloriosus provides the fat knight with no more than a trace of flavor.

Miller, James   (1706–1744)   Eighteenth-century playwright, author of *The Universal Passion* (1737), a popular adaptation combining Shakespeare's *Much Ado About Nothing* and Molière's *La Princesse d'Élide.* Miller, who became famous for a satire he wrote while he was still a student, later became a clergyman but continued to write plays—generally adaptations of French works. Several of these, including *The Universal Passion,* were successfully produced.

Miller, Jonathan   (b. 1934)   British director, creator of many modern productions of Shakespeare's plays, including a powerful *Merchant of Venice* (1970), with Laurence OLIVIER as Shylock. He is also noted for his numerous Shakespearean TELEVISION productions in the early 1980s, as part of the BBC's complete cycle of the plays. In 2002 Miller was acclaimed for a stunning production of *King Lear* at Stratford, Ontario, starring Christopher PLUMMER.

Miller was a medical student when he and friends at Cambridge University amused themselves with a comic revue, *Beyond the Fringe,* that became a theatrical blockbuster and established its authors in highly successful careers. He is perhaps best known for his versatility, having produced everything from grand opera through Shakespeare and contemporary theater to science shows for television. He has also written popular books on medicine and other subjects.

Millington, Thomas   (active 1583–1603)   Publisher and bookseller in LONDON, producer of first editions of several Shakespeare plays. In 1594 Millington joined with Edward WHITE to publish the first edition of *Titus Andronicus,* a QUARTO (Q1). The same year, on his own, he published Q1 of *2 Henry VI* (known as *The Contention*), and in 1595 he produced Q1 of *3 Henry VI* (*The True Tragedy*). In 1600 he published a second edition of both these works and, in partnership with John BUSBY, the first edition of *Henry V.* Each of these editions was pirated, for each is a BAD QUARTO, assembled from the memories of actors and published without permission of the acting company that owned the rights.

Milton, John   (1608–1674)   Major English poet, author of *Paradise Lost, Paradise Regained, Samson Agonistes,* and many shorter works, including a well-known EPITAPH on Shakespeare. The first of Milton's poems to be published was "An Epitaph on the admirable Dramaticke Poet, W. Shakespeare," which appeared anonymously among the introductory verses in the second FOLIO (1632). It also appeared in the third and fourth Folios (1663, 1685). It is considered one of the poet's best short works (16 lines), an elegiac lyric reflecting on the power of Shakespeare's art to outlast his death. Milton also mentions Shakespeare, in another early work, *L'Allegro*, calling him "Fancy's child," whose plays "warble his native wood-notes wild."

Mirror for Magistrates, A   English anthology of biographies in verse (published in seven versions, from 1559 to 1619) that influenced Shakespeare, especially in the writing of the HISTORY PLAYS. Originally intended as a sequel to John LYDGATE's *Falls of Princes* (1431–38, publ. 1494)—a translation of BOCCACCIO's *The Fate of Illustrious Men* (1355–74)—*A Mirror* reflects the RENAISSANCE interest in individual lives, along with a traditional concern for the fates of kings and other monumental figures. Most tales told of the dire fate, usually ending in violent death, of a villainous tyrant or would-be tyrant, for, as its title suggests, the book was intended to exercise a moral influence. The first edition was compiled in 1555, but it was suppressed by the government of Queen Mary and not published until 1559 under Queen Elizabeth (see Elizabeth I in *Henry VIII*), and it contained 19 such "tragedies" (see TRAGEDY) by various authors. In 1563 a second edition appeared that featured seven more biographies and included Thomas SACKVILLE's *Induction* and his *Complaint of Buckingham*, the only material in *A Mirror* that has been considered fine literature by later ages.

The material in these first two compilations dealt chiefly with English history from Richard II onward, and it provided Shakespeare with details for most of his history plays. John HIGGINS, whose interests were more antiquarian, issued the third and fourth editions of *A Mirror* (1574, 1578), to which he contributed 16 poems about heroes of ancient Britain. One of these was consulted by Shakespeare in writing *King Lear*. In 1587 a fifth edition (the one Shakespeare knew) appeared. It incorporated with the earlier material new work that included another major contribution from Higgins—an additional 24 lives, all but one from the classical world. His biography of Julius Caesar provided material for Shakespeare's *Julius Caesar*. Two later editions of *A Mirror*—in 1610 and 1619—included tales of virtue rewarded and added positive lessons to the older accounts of villainy punished.

Misenum   Ancient Italian town, location for two scenes in *Antony and Cleopatra*. In 2.6 the corulers of Rome—Octavius Caesar, Lepidus, and Mark Antony—meet with Pompey, whose naval forces have been pillaging Italian coastal towns, and negotiate a peace treaty. Pompey accepts the rule of Sicily and Sardinia in exchange for which he will "rid all the sea of pirates" (2.6.36), that is, his own followers, represented by Menas and Menecrates. In 2.7 the negotiators celebrate their agreement with a drunken banquet aboard Pompey's ship, anchored off Misenum. During the banquet, the true colors of several of the participants are revealed.

Located on the northern headland of the Bay of Naples, Misenum was the site of a meeting such as is seen in the play, and it resulted in a pact known as the Treaty of Misenum in 39 B.C. Essentially, Pompey was added to the Roman Triumvirate, but the peace did not last long. Pompey renewed his raids on the Italian coast and provoked Caesar to invade his base at MESSINA and to destroy him for good in 36 B.C., a conquest that is referred to in 3.5.4–12.

Misery of Civil War, The   Seventeenth-century adaptation of *2* and *3 Henry VI*. See CROWNE, JOHN.

Modjeska, Helena (1844–1909)   Polish-born American actress. Born Helena Opid in Cracow, she followed her brother into the local theater, where she got her stage name from a brief first marriage. She became a leading actress in Warsaw and then, in 1876, was forced to flee from Russian-governed Poland with her second husband, who was a Polish nationalist. They went to San Francisco, where Modjeska quickly learned English and played Juliet and *Hamlet*'s Ophelia, among other parts. Immediately recognized as a superior actress, she made her New York debut the next year and for almost 30 years, despite suffering a stroke in 1897, she was among the most popular of American actresses. Among Shakespearean roles, she was best known for Viola (*Twelfth Night*), Isabella (*All's Well That Ends Well*), and Lady Macbeth, playing the latter several times in the 1880s opposite Edwin BOOTH.

Mohun, Michael (ca. 1625–1684)   English actor. Mohun was a boy actor (see CHILDREN'S COMPANIES) in Christopher BEESTON's company in the 1630s. He fought with distinction for the royalists in the Civil Wars, and when the theaters were reopened upon the restoration of the monarchy in 1660, he joined the King's Company under Thomas KILLIGREW. He was among the most admired actors of the period, though he mostly played secondary roles, usually opposite Charles HART. He was particularly noted for his portrayals of Iago and Cassius (in *Othello* and *Julius Caesar*, respectively).

Mömpelgard, Frederick, Count of Württemberg (later Duke of Württemberg) (d. 1608)   Contemporary of Shakespeare, alluded to in *The Merry Wives of Windsor*. As part of a sequence of anti-German jokes associated with the theft of horses from the Host in Act 4, several references are made to German travelers in England and particularly to a German Duke who is *not* expected to come to Windsor (4.3.4–5; 4.5.81–84). These obscure allusions have a particular connection both to Mömpelgard and to the occasion for which the play was written.

Frederick of Mömpelgard was heir apparent to the Duchy of Württemberg, then an independent country in what is now southwestern Germany. In 1592 he visited Windsor and other English cities (those specified in 4.5.73) and developed an enthusiasm for the Order of the Garter. He repeatedly solicited Queen Elizabeth I for membership in the knightly order; finally, after he had inherited the duchy and achieved some importance in European affairs, she admitted him. However, in what appears to have been a calculated slight, he was not notified of his admission in time for him to attend the investment ceremonies in the spring of 1597. *The Merry Wives* was written for precisely those ceremonies, and thus the references to Mömpelgard's earlier visit, and to a German Duke who is *not* visit-

ing, are quite evidently inside jokes intended for the play's first audience, the knights of the Garter, who will have been well aware of the Queen's action. These references appear only in the FIRST FOLIO edition of the play, which reflects the initial, private performance, and not in the 1602 QUARTO that is derived from early theatrical productions.

Monarcho (d. before 1580)   The nickname given to a well-known London lunatic of Shakespeare's day. Monarcho's mad claims to be ruler of the world inspired comment in contemporary documents, including a published epitaph titled "The Phantasticall Monarke." Armado, the braggart Spaniard in *Love's Labour's Lost*, is thought to have been based in part on this figure, for he is referred to as "A phantasime, a Monarcho" (4.1.100). Shakespeare can never have seen Monarcho, who died when the playwright was still a teenager in STRATFORD, but he had clearly heard enough to be impressed.

Monck, Nugent (1877–1958)   British theatrical producer. In 1911 Monck founded an important theatrical company for the production of ELIZABETHAN DRAMA in Norwich, England. In 1921, he converted a 16th-century Norwich house into the Maddermarket Theatre, the first modern replica of an Elizabethan playhouse. There he staged many influential productions of Shakespeare's plays, in the crisp, spare manner of William POEL.

Montaigne, Michel de (1533–1592)   French essayist, author of minor sources for *The Tempest* and perhaps for *Hamlet* and *King Lear*. Shakespeare knew Montaigne's essays in the translation by John FLORIO, *Essayes on Morall, Politike, and Militarie Discourses* (1603). A passage in Montaigne's essay "Of Cannibals" is echoed in Gonzalo's praise of primitive societies in *The Tempest* 2.1.143–164, and another essay, "Of Crueltie," probably inspired Prospero's praise of reconciliation in 5.1.25–30. Montaigne's influence is less direct in the two tragedies. His views seem to inform some aspects of Hamlet's thought, as when he compares death to sleep and calls it a "consummation" (*Hamlet* 3.1.63), or when he appraises man as "this quintessence of dust"

(2.2.308). In *King Lear* the villainous Edmund's cynical notions probably reflect Montaigne's scepticism.

For the most part, however, Montaigne's sceptical, "modern" attitudes are rejected in Shakespeare's work. Gonzalo's theory is decidedly refuted by the play as a whole, Hamlet's musings are obviously the product of despair, and the arguments of so villainous a figure as Edmund can only be disdained by a sympathetic audience. In the playwright's deployment of Montaigne's thought—as in his work in general—we can see that his allegiance lay with the old world of social hierarchy and unquestioned Christianity whose attitudes and customs Montaigne was prepared to question and often rejected. On the other hand, the two writers have in common a tolerant, accepting attitude toward humanity's foibles—reflected more in the use of Montaigne in *The Tempest* than elsewhere. That the playwright should have felt an affinity for the essayist's work is not surprising.

Montaigne was the son of a nobleman and government official of southern France. He became a lawyer in Bordeaux and frequently visited the royal court in Paris on business, once for 18 months. He pursued political ambitions at the court but was unsuccessful, and after his father's death in 1568, he retired to his estate and began writing. Literature occupied much of his time in the 1570s and again between 1586 and his death, but he also traveled, engaged in diplomacy on behalf of Henri of Navarre (later King Henri IV of FRANCE), and was twice elected mayor of Bordeaux. His *Essays* were first published in 1580, with a considerably enlarged collection appearing in 1588; his last work was published posthumously. He also published a travel journal and a translation of a work by the Spanish philosopher Raimundo Sebonde (d. 1436), which sparked his longest and best-known essay, "Apology for Raimond de Sebonde."

Montaigne's essays record in an intimate, gossipy style his opinions on a wide range of subjects from minor domestic matters to political issues and philosophical topics. This sort of literary work was previously unknown, and Montaigne indicated the experimental nature of his writings by designating them *essais* (attempts), thus naming the genre as well as inventing it. His scepticism,

curiosity, and amiable tolerance yielded essays of a philosophical ambiguity that is reflected in the wide range of critical interpretation they have inspired. Politically, Montaigne has been regarded as reactionary, liberal, and revolutionary, and in religion as both a devout practitioner and an agnostic; in a famous remark the 19th-century critic Charles-Augustin Sainte-Beuve declared him a good Catholic but not a Christian. In any case, the *Essays* constitute a self-portrait of a reflective man whose concerns are universal and whose witty and intelligent style has charmed generations of readers. Still regarded as among the greatest works of European literature, Montaigne's essays offer one of the first examples of the individualism that was to dominate Western culture in subsequent centuries.

Montemayor, Jorge de (ca. 1521–1561) Portuguese-born author of a famous romance that was a source for several of Shakespeare's plays. Montemayor spent most of his life in Spain and wrote in Spanish. Though he was also a poet and composer, his fame rests entirely on his long prose romance, *Diana Enamorada*, which was published in Valencia ca. 1559. It soon became popular throughout Europe; Bartholomew YONG translated it into English in 1582. Though this work was not published until 1598, Shakespeare knew the book in manuscript or by hearsay and was able to make use of it in that form. It was among the playwright's chief sources for *The Two Gentlemen of Verona* and *A Midsummer Night's Dream*, and it also probably influenced the writing of *As You Like It* and *Twelfth Night*.

Montgomery, Philip Herbert, Earl of (Philip Herbert, Lord Pembroke) (1584–1650) English aristocrat and co-dedicatee of the FIRST FOLIO (1623) of Shakespeare's plays. Montgomery had no connection with Shakespeare and was doubtless included in the dedication—made by John HEMINGE and Henry CONDELL—as a compliment to the other dedicatee, his brother, William Herbert, Earl of PEMBROKE, who as Lord Chamberlain was responsible for the publication of plays. Also, the publishers may have anticipated Montgomery's becoming Lord Chamberlain himself, which he did three years later.

Montgomery was a model of the irresponsible aristocrat. He was a courtier from the age of 15, and he became a favorite of King JAMES I, who frequently had to extract him from violent quarrels and extravagant debts. He succeeded his brother as Earl of Pembroke in 1630, but he was offended that James's son, King Charles I (ruled 1625–49), did not appreciate him sufficiently, and he retired to his country estate, nursing his hostility and eventually joining the Parliamentarian cause in the Civil Wars.

morality play   Medieval dramatic genre that features allegorical characters who face and overcome personified moral problems or temptations. Morality plays employ one-dimensional characters who represent abstract concepts from which they take their names—Charity, Everyman, Understanding, Perseverance, etc. The plays are constructed with alternating serious and comic scenes that are intended to entertain while they instruct. They use plots that depict the conflict between vice and virtue for the possession of the hero's soul, with virtue triumphant at the close. The moral lesson is uncomplicated and is presented in a direct manner. The best-known surviving morality plays are *Mankind* (ca. 1470) and *Everyman* (ca. 1500). The genre arose in the 14th century as a combination of religious sermon and festive entertainment, and morality plays were still performed in Shakespeare's day, though their popularity was rapidly fading.

In their structure, devices, and themes, morality plays were influential upon ELIZABETHAN DRAMA. *Doctor Faustus*, by Christopher MARLOWE, is regarded as the Elizabethan play most similar to a morality play (though Marlowe pointedly gives the triumph to vice, rather than virtue), but the genre is reflected in a number of Shakespeare's plays as well. For instance, a number of his villains—perhaps most notably Aaron (of *Titus Andronicus)* and Richard III—display the traits of a stock character from the genre, the VICE. The abstract personages of the genre also appear here and there—for instance, in the disguises of Tamora and her sons as Revenge, Rape, and Murder (*Titus Andronicus,* 5.2), and in the Son That Hath Killed His Father and the Father That Hath Killed His Son (*3 Henry VI,* 2.5). More significantly, one of the major

themes found in morality plays, the social evil represented by sin, was to be explored repeatedly by Shakespeare, especially in the HISTORY PLAYS. Other plays where commentators find the particular influence of the genre include *Measure for Measure* and *Timon of Athens.*

More, Sir Thomas (1478–1535)   English writer, author of a source for *Richard III* and the subject of a play on which Shakespeare collaborated, *Sir Thomas More.* More is best known for his *Utopia* (1516)—a Latin account of an ideal country, whose name provided our word *utopia.* He also wrote a *History of King Richard the thirde* (written in 1513 and first published, in part, in Richard GRAFTON's 1543 chronicle; published in full only in 1557). More's account was incorporated by both Edward HALL and Raphael HOLINSHED in their histories, which were Shakespeare's chief sources for his HISTORY PLAYS. Thus, More's account was an important influence on the creation of Shakespeare's villainous Richard III. More's chief source for the history of the period was the manuscript of his friend Polydore VERGIL's *Historia Anglia* (1505–33, published 1534), but he created his own King Richard. It was he who first established the popular image of a cynical and witty villain, a cripple who proves himself through ruthless ambition. More's ironic narrative plainly influenced Shakespeare's similar treatment.

As a youth, More was a page to Cardinal John Morton (1420–1500), who had known King Richard—he appears in *Richard III* as the Bishop of Ely. The son of a judge, More became a successful lawyer as a young man, but he was also interested in humanism and literature, becoming the intimate friend of such RENAISSANCE luminaries as William LILY, John Colet (1466–1519), and Desiderius Erasmus (ca. 1467–1536). He became an adviser to King Henry VIII and rose quickly in the court hierarchy. In 1529 he succeeded Cardinal Wolsey as Lord Chancellor (as is mentioned in *Henry VIII* 3.2.393–399, where well-wishing sentiments ring highly ironic, given his ultimate fate). He resigned the post in 1532 and retired, engaging in literary disputes over the emerging doctrines of Protestantism. Unwilling to support either King Henry's divorce from Queen Katherine or his assumption of the pope's authority in religious matters, More was tried for treason, convicted, and executed. He is considered a saint by the Catholic Church, having been canonized in 1935. His life was the subject of *A Man for All Seasons*, a popular play (1960) and movie (1966), both written by Robert Bolt (1924–95).

Morgan, McNamara (d. 1762)   Irish lawyer and playwright, author of an adaptation of *The Winter's Tale*. Morgan's *The Sheep-Shearing: or, Florizel and Perdita* (1754) focused on Act 4 of Shakespeare's play, omitting the plot concerning Leontes' jealousy. In 1761 it was produced as an operetta, with music by Thomas ARNE. Morgan was principally a Dublin barrister who wrote plays as a sideline; both *The Sheep-Shearing* and his tragedy *Philoclea* (1754, based on part of SIDNEY's *Arcadia*) were produced by his friend Spranger BARRY.

Morgann, Maurice (1726–1802)   Eighteenth-century English civil servant and writer, author of an influential essay on Falstaff. In his *Essay on the Dramatic Character of Sir John Falstaff* (1777), Morgann initiated a style of impressionistic Shakespearean criticism, centered on a quasi-psychological interpretation of the characters that was popular throughout the 19th century into the 20th. Essentially Morgann ignores the actual evidence of the plays and emphasizes one's emotional response to Falstaff. His essay strongly influenced the inclination—powerful ever since in many readers—to defend the fat knight as a bold and courageous character and to fault Prince Hal for rejecting his old companion.

Although one of Morgann's purposes in writing was to refute Voltaire, who had called Falstaff a "drunken savage," his defense of the fat knight displays the humanitarian influence of the French Enlightenment, which valued sentiment as evidence of a humane sensibility and opposed the Machiavellian values of statecraft.

Morley, Thomas (1557–1603)   English composer, possibly a friend of Shakespeare, who probably wrote music for two of the playwright's songs. Shakespeare's SONG "It was a lover and his lass" (*As You Like It* 5.3.14–37) was published with Morley's music in the composer's *First Book of Ayres* (1600), but it is

uncertain whether he set the playwright's words to music or Shakespeare wrote words to match Morley's tune. Another Morley tune, in his *First Book of Consort Lessons* (1599), bears the title of a Shakespeare song, "O Mistress mine" (*Twelfth Night* 2.3.40–53); scholars generally believe the song in the play is meant and that this tune was used on stage. However, the composer may have adapted it from an earlier version by his onetime teacher, the notable composer William Byrd (ca. 1543–1623).

Morley and Shakespeare were neighbors in 1596 and may have been acquainted. Morley was an organist for St. Paul's Cathedral and a musician for the court of Queen Elizabeth I. He is best known as a composer of madrigals, contrapuntal songs for several voices that had been introduced into England from ITALY by Byrd. He also composed church music, solo songs with lute accompaniment, and compositions for strings and keyboard. He published five books on music, including *A Plain and Easy Introduction to Practical Music* (1597), the first work of its kind in English.

Mortimer's Cross   Location in *3 Henry VI*, an English village near WALES and a battle site of the WARS OF THE ROSES. A plain near Mortimer's Cross is the setting of 2.1, although the battle itself is not referred to. However, an incident from that conflict is depicted; a transient atmospheric effect causes an apparent tripling of the sun in the sky. This omen appears to Edward (Edward IV) and Richard (Richard III), who take it to signify future success. This improbable but historical phenomenon, a type of high-latitude mirage, was indeed seen during the battle, and it inspired Edward to adopt a stylized sun as his emblem.

Shakespeare omitted the battle, which Edward's forces won in February 1461 (historically, Richard was not present, being only nine years old), because he wished to present a string of Yorkist losses, to be reversed by the battle of TOWTON, which closes the act.

Moseley, Humphrey (d. 1661)   English bookseller and publisher. In 1653 Moseley claimed the copyrights to a number of old plays whose manuscripts he had collected, including THE MERRY DEVIL

OF EDMONTON, *Cardenio*, HENRY I AND HENRY II. In 1660 he added DUKE HUMPHREY, *King Stephen*, and *Iphis and Iantha, or a marriage without a man.* Only *The Merry Devil of Edmonton* has survived, but scholars agree almost unanimously that of these works, only *Cardenio* and possibly *Duke Humphrey* are connected with Shakespeare.

Moseley was a successful publisher, becoming a high officer in the STATIONERS' COMPANY. He published the first collection of the plays of Francis BEAUMONT and John FLETCHER, along with works by John MILTON and others.

Mountjoy, Christopher (active 1598–1613) Wigmaker in LONDON, Shakespeare's landlord and the defendant in a lawsuit in which Shakespeare testified. In 1612 Mountjoy was sued by his son-in-law and former apprentice, Stephen BELOTT, who claimed that he had not been paid money promised him in his marriage agreement. Belott claimed that in 1604, in the course of the marriage negotiations, Shakespeare, then a lodger in the Mountjoy household, had told him on Mountjoy's behalf that his bride would receive a dowry of £60 plus household goods and that he would inherit £200 on Mountjoy's death. Shakespeare was summoned from STRATFORD in May 1612 to affirm or deny these assertions. He confirmed his residency with the Mountjoys in 1604 (he was probably there a year or two earlier, since he declared that he had first known both Mountjoy and Belott around 1602). He said that he had solicited Belott to marry Mountjoy's daughter at the request of the father, but that he did not remember the amount of the proposed dowry and that he knew nothing of a promised inheritance. The court turned the case over to the arbitration of the men's parish church, which criticized both men but awarded Belott a token payment, though Mountjoy evidently refused to pay it. The records of this episode reveal Shakespeare's London residence around 1602–04 and that he had returned to Stratford by the spring of 1612, as well as offering a glimpse of the private life of the playwright at the period when he was writing *Othello*, *King Lear*, and the PROBLEM PLAYS.

Mountjoy was a French Huguenot refugee who was a "tire-maker," or specialist in the elaborate bejewelled ornamental headgear worn by aristocratic women. He was a skilled craftsman in a rich and prestigious trade; he once made a tire for Queen Elizabeth I. His wife, Marie, also a Huguenot, was having an affair with a neighboring cloth dealer during the period that Shakespeare was a lodger, as we know from the diary of the astrologer and physician Simon FORMAN, whom she consulted about a suspected pregnancy. The pregnancy may have been a false alarm or aborted, for she had no child. Shakespeare may have met the couple through his friend Richard FIELD, whose wife was also a Huguenot and who lived nearby.

After Marie's death in 1616, Mountjoy evidently took up "a dissolute and unregulated life," as recorded by the French church. He feuded with his daughter and son-in-law, threatening them with disinheritance, thus sparking the lawsuit that involved Shakespeare.

Mousetrap, The See MURDER OF GONZAGO, THE.

Mucedorus Anonymous play formerly attributed to Shakespeare, part of the Shakespeare APOCRYPHA. *Mucedorus* is a comedy that burlesques pastoral romance and tales of chivalry. It was first published in 1598 by William JONES. It was extremely popular and was printed more often than any other work of ELIZABETHAN or JACOBEAN DRAMA, yielding at least 17 editions by 1668. The play was sometimes ascribed to Shakespeare in the late 17th century, and it was included with FAIR EM and THE MERRY DEVIL OF EDMONTON in King Charles II's specially prepared collection of Shakespeare's plays. Apparently this ascription is made on the strength of the title pages beginning with the third edition (1610), which stated that the play had been staged by the KING'S MEN. Shakespeare therefore knew the work, and its depiction of a forest-dwelling "wild man" may have influenced the creation of Caliban, in *The Tempest*.

However, no modern scholar believes Shakespeare wrote *Mucedorus*, for it is a crude drama that is beneath the standard of even the least of Shakespeare's work. Its authorship remains uncertain, though it is perhaps most frequently given to Thomas LODGE.

Munday, Anthony (ca. 1560–1633) English playwright, author of a possible influence on Shakespeare and a coauthor of *Sir Thomas More*. Munday, originally a printer apprenticed to John ALLDE, turned to acting but was unsuccessful; he appeared with OXFORD'S MEN in the late 1570s and early 1580s. He began a notorious career as a hack writer with a series of anti-Catholic tracts (ca. 1578–80). His first book was *Zelauto* (1580), a novel written in imitation of John LYLY's famed *Euphues*. Its treatment of usury and Jews may have influenced *The Merchant of Venice*. Between 1594 and 1602 he wrote plays for the ADMIRAL'S MEN. Three of these works have survived: *John à Kent and John à Cumber* (1594) may have suggested elements of the comic subplot of *A Midsummer Night's Dream*, and a pair of plays on Robin Hood (both 1598) may have influenced *As You Like It*. Francis MERES referred to Munday as one of England's leading comic dramatists. Munday also wrote numerous plays, including SIR JOHN OLDCASTLE, in collaboration with others. He was probably the principal author of *Sir Thomas More*, which contains a scene by Shakespeare.

Murder of Gonzago, The Playlet presented within *Hamlet*. In 3.2 Prince Hamlet arranges for the Players to perform *The Murder of Gonzago* for his uncle, the King. The plot of the playlet resembles the actual murder of Hamlet's father by the King, and Hamlet expects the King's response to reveal his guilt. For this reason, he refers to the brief play as *The Mousetrap* (3.2.232).

First, in a DUMB SHOW, a man pours poison in the ear of a sleeping king and then consoles his grieving queen, exiting with her. Then, in dialogue, the Player King denies the Player Queen's assertion that she would not remarry if he died. In the next scene, Lucianus, said by Hamlet to be "nephew to the King" (3.2.239), poisons the sleeping Player King in his ear, just as the real King had poisoned Hamlet's father. The play has its intended effect at this point, as the King flees the room; the performance is never completed.

Hamlet speaks of a source for *The Murder of Gonzago*—which he calls "the image of a murder done in Vienna" (3.2.233)—as "extant, and written in very choice Italian" (3.2.256–257), but if such a document existed, scholars have not discovered it. However, the murder of Hamlet's father—and thus the playlet—is clearly based on a real murder, committed in Italy in 1538 (see *Hamlet*, "Sources of the Play").

Mytilene City on the Greek island of Lesbos, a location for several scenes of *Pericles*. Marina, the lost daughter of Pericles, is sold to a brothel in Mytilene in 4.2, and she remains there in 4.5 and 4.6. In 5.1, when she has escaped the brothel but remains in Mytilene, her father arrives there and they are reunited. Marina later marries the Governor of Mytilene, Lysimachus. Shakespeare followed his sources in placing these episodes in Mytilene, but no specific attributes of the city are referred to in the text. The historical Mytilene was a minor port city of the Aegean Sea, famous chiefly as the home of the poet Sappho (active ca. 590 B.C.).

N

Nabokov, Nicolas (1903–1978) Russian-born American composer, creator of an OPERA based on *Love's Labour's Lost*. Best known as a composer for ballet and as a writer on music and musicians, Nabokov (a cousin of the famous novelist Vladimir Nabokov [1899–1977]) also wrote the music for the opera *Love's Labour's Lost* (1973), whose libretto was written by W. H. AUDEN and Chester Kallman (1921–75).

Nash, Anthony (d. 1622) Farmer in STRATFORD and friend of Shakespeare. Nash was a wealthy farmer who witnessed several business deals made by Shakespeare and managed some of his farm lands. He and his innkeeper brother John (d. 1623) were among the seven close friends to whom the playwright willed money to buy a commemorative ring. His eldest son was Thomas NASH, later the husband of Shakespeare's granddaughter.

Nash, Thomas (1593–1647) First husband of Shakespeare's granddaughter Elizabeth HALL. The son of Shakespeare's friend Anthony NASH, Thomas Nash may have been acquainted with the playwright as a child. He married Elizabeth Hall in 1626. They probably lived at first in his home, next door to the Shakespeare-Hall home at NEW PLACE. (Known as Nash's House, it is today maintained as a museum by the Shakespeare BIRTHPLACE Trust.) The couple were living in New Place, however, at the time of Nash's death. Nash was a lawyer, but he did not practice after inheriting his father's fortune. He also owned an inn in STRATFORD, inherited from

an uncle. He was a committed Royalist in the Civil Wars. At their outset in 1642, he was noted as by far the greatest Stratford contributor of money to the king's cause, and in 1643 he hosted the harried Queen Henrietta Marie at New Place. At his death he willed Nash's House to his wife; he bequeathed New Place to another relative, but Elizabeth and her mother, Susanna SHAKESPEARE Hall, fought the will in court and won.

Nashe, Thomas (Thomas Nash) (1567–ca. 1601) English writer and a possible collaborator with Shakespeare on *1 Henry VI*. Nashe was the author of the earliest specific reference to a Shakespeare play and of minor sources for *Hamlet* and *All's Well That Ends Well*. In addition, he may be a model for the character Moth in *Love's Labour's Lost*. An episode in Nashe's novel *The Unfortunate Traveller* (1594) may have influenced the exposure of Parolles in 4.3 of *All's Well That Ends Well*. Nashe's popular satirical pamphlet *Pierce Penniless His Supplication to the Devil* (1592) influenced several passages in *Hamlet*, especially Hamlet's remarks on drunkenness in 1.4.16–38. *Pierce Penniless* also contains a reference to the popularity of Talbot in *1 Henry VI*, the earliest surviving literary remark on a particular Shakespearean work, though Nashe does not mention either title or playwright (*1 Henry VI* may well have been written collaboratively— possibly with Nashe's participation—but Talbot is considered Shakespeare's creation.)

As the first English picaresque novel, *The Unfortunate Traveller* is an important literary monument, but Nashe is probably best known for his biting satirical pamphlets. Nashe was also the anonymous author of several government counterblasts to the rebellious religious tracts of the pseudonymous Puritan Martin Marprelate (see Martext, Sir Oliver, in *As You Like It*). In the course of the Marprelate controversy, Nashe's avid anti-Puritanism earned him the enmity of Gabriel HARVEY, and the two pamphleteers conducted a long feud in print, which may be the subject of a number of obscure topical jokes in *Love's Labour's Lost*. Moreover, many scholars believe that the diminutive Nashe was satirized as the sharp-tongued and tiny youth Moth.

Nashe was one of the UNIVERSITY WITS, the playwrights who dominated ELIZABETHAN DRAMA in the 1580s, but he wrote only two plays of his own—a satirical MASQUE entitled *Summer's Last Will and Testament* (1592) and *The Isle of Dogs* (1597)—though he also collaborated with Robert GREENE and Christopher MARLOWE. The *Isle of Dogs*, whose text is now lost, was among the most controversial of Elizabethan plays, a notable subject of government CENSORSHIP. The government found it "seditious" and not only suppressed it but closed all the LONDON theaters for several months; three of the actors in the play—Ben JONSON, Robert SHAW, and Gabriel SPENCER—were jailed briefly, though Nashe fled London and escaped punishment. He only returned in 1599, to face a blanket condemnation of his works by the government. His last years are obscure, and we know of his death only through an elegy published some time later, in 1601.

Neilson, Adelaide (1746–1840) British actress. Neilson was best known for her dramatic adaptations of stories from the works of Sir Walter Scott (1771–1832), but she also played many Shakespearean roles, including Viola (*Twelfth Night*), Isabella (*Measure for Measure*), Imogen (*Cymbeline*), and Juliet. She was noted for her great beauty.

Neilson, Julia (1868–1957) British actress, the wife of Fred TERRY. A comic actress who played Rosalind and other Shakespearean parts, Neilson is best known as the costar and comanager, with her husband, of a theater company that presented a variety of plays between 1900 and 1930.

Newington Butts Suburb of LONDON, site of an early theater. Little is known of the theater, which was located near an archery practice field—archery targets were called butts—in the village of Newington (then a distant suburb, now well within London). The theater was in existence by 1580, when it was ordered closed during a plague epidemic. At some point it was apparently bought or leased by Philip HENSLOWE, who hired troupes to play there in June 1594, including the earliest known performance by the CHAMBERLAIN'S MEN, Shakespeare's company. However, the only later record of this theater is a 1631 reference to its former existence.

New Place Shakespeare's home in STRATFORD from 1597 until his death, and that of his descendants until 1649. The purchase of New Place had considerable personal significance for Shakespeare, advertising to Stratford that his success as a LONDON playwright had restored the family fortune after the financial collapse suffered by his father, John SHAKESPEARE, some years earlier. It was the second-largest residential building in the town, built around 1490 by one of Stratford's most famous citizens, Hugh Clopton (d. 1496), a onetime lord mayor of London. Shakespeare bought it from William UNDERHILL in 1597, and despite difficulties created when Underhill was murdered by his son, took possession and began making repairs. Documents relating to the sale reveal that the house was 60 by 70 feet in area and that it had 10 fireplaces (and surely more rooms than fireplaces, as the latter were taxed as luxuries). On its property were two barns, two gardens, and two orchards. An 18th-century drawing shows a three-storied, five-gabled mansion. In 1602 Shakespeare added the nearby CHAPEL LANE COTTAGE to the New Place property, perhaps as housing for a gardener.

Shakespeare did not live at New Place full-time until he retired from the theater, around 1611, but his wife, Anna HATHAWAY Shakespeare, and his daughters doubtless moved in as soon as the repairs were completed, probably in 1598. Mary Arden SHAKESPEARE, the playwright's mother, may have lived at New Place after her husband's death in 1601. Shakespeare retired to New Place and died there in 1616.

Shakespeare left New Place to his daughter Susanna SHAKESPEARE Hall, who lived there until her death in 1649. She in turn left it to her daughter, Elizabeth HALL, who had lived there with her first husband, Thomas NASH, and did so briefly with her second, John Bernard, whom she married just before her mother died. However, she soon moved to Northamptonshire with Bernard, and the house may have been vacant for some years. Elizabeth left New Place to her husband when she died in 1670, and on his death in 1674 the house was sold to one Edward Walker, whose daughter married a Clopton in 1699, so the house returned to the family of its builder.

The Cloptons altered the house, virtually rebuilding it to a different ground plan. In 1756 the property was sold to the Reverend Francis Gastrell, who demolished the house in 1759, reportedly because he felt its taxes were too high. Today the site of New Place, encompassing the foundations of the house and a series of gardens, is owned by the Shakespeare BIRTHPLACE Trust and is open to the public.

Nicolai, Karl Otto (1810–1849)   German composer best known for an OPERA based on *The Merry Wives of Windsor*. Nicolai was a well-known opera composer and conductor in both Italy and Germany when he wrote *Die lustigen Weiber von Windsor*, which premiered two months before his tragically early death. With a libretto by poet Hermann von Mosenthal (1821–77) based on the TRANSLATION by SCHLEGEL, it still delights opera audiences.

Noble, Adrian (b. 1951)   English theater director, former head of the ROYAL SHAKESPEARE COMPANY (RSC). Well known as an innovative director of classical drama before becoming a member of the RSC in 1980, he became its director in 1991. His accomplishments include the overseeing of the company's recovery from a staggering debt, as well as directing a number of acclaimed productions, including a chronologically ordered presentation of the HISTORY PLAYS, from *Richard II* to *Richard III*; a *Hamlet* starring Kenneth BRANAGH (1992); and notable renderings of *King Lear* (1993) and *A Midsummer Night's Dream* (1994, a production that went on to a successful run in New York and was the basis for a FILM directed by Noble). However, in

2002 Noble resigned the RSC's directorship amid controversy over his considerable changes in the company, including an emphasis on commercial theatrical projects and plans for the demolition of its STRATFORD playhouse in favor of a more elaborate theater complex to be built in its place. His successor was Michael BOYD.

Nonpareille   Name of a ship mentioned in *Edward III*, whose use offers a clue about one of the play's sources and a hint as to its date. The *Nonpareille* is named in 3.1.177 as one of the ships at the battle of SLUYS. The name does not appear in the principal sources for the play and was probably taken by the playwright (whether Shakespeare or a collaborator [see *Edward III*, "Commentary"]), along with other details, from an account, published in 1590 by Petruccio UBALDINO, of the English victory over the Spanish Armada in 1588. Scholars conclude from this and other evidence that the play was written in the early 1590s (see *Edward III*, "Text of the Play").

North, Sir Thomas (ca. 1535–ca. 1601)   English translator of PLUTARCH's *Lives*. North's *Lives of the Noble Grecians and Romans* (1579)—a retranslation of Jacques AMYOT's French rendering of Plutarch's original Greek—became Shakespeare's primary source for *Antony and Cleopatra, Coriolanus, Julius Caesar,* and *Timon of Athens* and a source for minor elements in other plays. North, a nobleman educated at Cambridge and the INNS OF COURT, translated various works from Spanish, French, and Italian, but he is chiefly known for his Plutarch translation, which, besides having inspired Shakespeare, also influenced several generations of English prose writers; it is regarded as one of the major works of 16th-century English literature.

Nunn, Trevor (b. 1940)   British theatrical director and producer. As the artistic director of the Royal Shakespeare Company from 1968 to 1986, Nunn was responsible for numerous notable Shakespearean productions, including a cycle of the ROMAN PLAYS in 1972, a 1973 *Coriolanus* starring Nicol WILLIAMSON, a 1976 *Macbeth* with Ian MCKELLEN and Judi DENCH, and a 1981 *All's Well That*

Ends Well that was successful in STRATFORD, London, and New York. Beginning in the late 1970s, Nunn's career centered on contemporary theater, as he produced such transatlantic hits as *Nicholas Nickleby*, *Cats*, and *Les Misérables*. But he continued to work on Shakespearean projects as well. His 1990 *Othello* is regarded as one of the best TELEVISION presentations of Shakespeare, though his FILM of *Twelfth Night* (1996), set in the 1890s, was not as well received.

Okes, Nicholas (active 1596–1639) Printer in LONDON, producer of two editions of works by Shakespeare. Okes printed the fifth edition of *The Rape of Lucrece* (Q5, 1607) for the publisher John HARRISON and the first edition of *Othello* (Q1, 1622) for Thomas WALKLEY. In the 1620s Okes was prosecuted several times for publishing forbidden political satires.

Old Vic Theatre London theater, famous for its tradition of Shakespearean productions. The Old Vic was built in south London as the Coburg Theatre in 1818. For years it was noted for extravagant melodrama and staged little or no Shakespeare. In 1833 it was renamed the Victoria Theatre after Princess Victoria (later Queen, ruled 1837–1901) attended a performance. In 1871 the Victoria, by now familiarly known as the Old Vic, became a music hall. In 1880 Emma Cone, a prominent opponent of alcohol, bought it and reopened it as a temperance hall. Her niece, Lilian BAYLIS, joined her in 1898 and introduced to the repertoire first OPERA and then, beginning in 1914, Shakespeare. By 1923, under the leadership of Baylis, Ben GREET, and Robert ATKINS, the entire CANON of Shakespeare's plays had been performed at the Old Vic, for the first time in any theater. Under the direction of Atkins (1919–25), Harcourt WILLIAMS (1929–33), and Tyrone GUTHRIE (1933–45), most of the leading actors and actresses of prewar Britain performed in Shakespeare's plays at the Old Vic. In 1940 a German bomb destroyed the theater. It was reopened in 1950, and between 1953 and 1958 the entire canon

was again staged. In 1963 the Old Vic Drama Company was reorganized as the National Theatre, and in 1976 this company moved to the new National Theatre building. The Old Vic Theatre remains in use as a successful repertory theater.

Olivier, Laurence (1907–1989) British actor and director. Olivier—whose career covered a wide range of roles, both classical and modern, on stage and in FILM and TELEVISION—is often regarded as the greatest actor of the 20th century. Only John GIELGUD and Ralph RICHARDSON are ranked with him among the great Shakespearean actors of the age. Among Olivier's best-known Shakespearean roles are Hamlet, Richard III, Henry V, Sir Toby Belch *(Twelfth Night)*, and Titus Andronicus, and he played many other Shakespearean characters.

At the age of nine, playing Brutus in a schoolboy production of *Julius Caesar*, Olivier was by chance observed by Sybil THORNDIKE and Lewis CASSON, who recorded their opinion that he was clearly a great actor. Similarly, he attracted rave reviews playing Katherina in *The Taming of the Shrew* at 14. In 1926 he joined the Birmingham Repertory Company, under Barry JACKSON, where he mostly played non-Shakespearean parts. His fame as a Shakespearean actor began in 1935, when he and Gielgud alternated roles as Romeo and Mercutio in a famous production of *Romeo and Juliet*. In 1936 he played Orlando in a movie version of *As You Like It* and then, in a remarkable 1937–38 season at the OLD VIC THEATRE, he played Hamlet, Sir Toby, Henry V, Macbeth, and *Hamlet*'s Iago. He also played Hamlet at ELSINORE in 1937. In the late 1930s Olivier made a number of popular and critically acclaimed movies, such as *Wuthering Heights* (1939) and *Pride and Prejudice* (1940). His romance with Vivien LEIGH began in 1936—a subject of extensive gossip, since both were married to others—and they married in 1940.

In 1944 Olivier returned to the Old Vic, where he played Richard III to great acclaim and began directing plays. In the same year he produced, directed, and starred in a film of *Henry V.* He made two more Shakespearean films, *Hamlet* (1948) and *Richard III* (1955), starring in each. *Hamlet* won two Academy Awards, for best film and best actor. (Olivier's *Hamlet* was a radically abridged version of Shakespeare's play, however, eliminating almost half the text, including all of Rosencrantz and Guildenstern's part.) In 1947 Olivier was knighted, and in 1948 he was awarded another Oscar for his achievement throughout his career.

Olivier starred in the *Titus Andronicus* of Peter BROOK (1955), a production that is credited with creating a renewed interest in the play. In 1961, divorced from Vivien Leigh, he married Joan PLOWRIGHT. From 1963 to 1972 he was the founding director of the British National Theatre Company, producing notable stagings of *Othello* and *The Merchant of Venice*—with himself as Othello and Shylock—and many other plays, both Shakespearean and otherwise. Suffering from a degenerative muscle disease, Olivier gave his last stage performance in 1974, but he continued working in films and television. He won an Emmy for his performance in the 1983 television production of *King Lear.* His last role was a cameo appearance in a 1988 television show, *War Requiem,* based on a work by Benjamin BRITTEN. Olivier published an autobiography, *Confessions of an Actor* (1982), and another book, *On Acting* (1986).

opera Theatrical performance in which a play is entirely set to music, numerous examples of which are adapted from the plays of Shakespeare. For centuries, composers and librettists (the authors of opera scripts) have recognized the affinity between the works of Shakespeare and the theatrical qualities of grand opera. Both are highly rhetorical media, glowing with the heat of larger-than-life protagonists who are driven by larger-than-life emotions toward love or death, often both. In the best of both opera and Shakespeare, a variety of entertainments—SUBPLOTS, comic and otherwise; processions and tableaus; eccentric secondary characters—combine with the plot to lead to resounding emotional climaxes in theatrical set pieces capable, when performed well, of providing an audience with a true catharsis, a sense of having experienced an extremity of human possibility. The best Shakespearean operas are able, as the librettist Arrigo BOITO put it, "to extract all of the juice from that great Shakespearean orange."

Accordingly, the plays have been much the most frequently used source for operas. Yet commentators agree that few of the approximately 270 operas based on Shakespeare are very good, and still fewer are in the repertoires of modern opera companies. The wordplay and rapid-fire conversation that characterize much of Shakespeare's dialogue is difficult to translate into a musical idiom. Only six Shakespearean operas—Benjamin BRITTEN's *A Midsummer Night's Dream;* Giuseppi VERDI's three great masterpieces *Macbeth, Otello,* and *Falstaff;* Karl Otto NICOLAI's version of *The Merry Wives of Windsor;* and the *Hamlet* of Ambroise THOMAS— are regularly performed, though revivals of several others appear periodically, and new adaptations continue to be created.

Opera began around the 15th century in Italy, rising from various other sorts of theatrical events, such as the MORALITY PLAY and the MASQUE. Theatrical music was commonplace in the ELIZABETHAN THEATER and is often called for in Shakespeare's play (see SONG), but opera had not yet been developed in England in Shakespeare's time. By mere chance, the first composer of music for a Shakespearean opera was Matthew LOCKE, whose incidental music to *The Tempest* was used when that play was made into an opera, *The Enchanted Island,* by the producer Thomas SHADWELL in 1674. Other composers, including Robert JOHNSON, were also commissioned to write for this work, but it was all replaced by Henry PURCELL's music in a new production of 1690. Purcell's *Enchanted Island* was highly popular in England for generations. John

Weldon (1676–1736) wrote another musical staging of William DAVENANT and John DRYDEN's *Tempest,* which was staged in 1712. Purcell also wrote music for *The Fairy Queen* (1692), derived from *A Midsummer Night's Dream* with a (very non-Shakespearean) libretto by Thomas BETTERTON, and passages from Purcell's opera *Dido and Aeneas* were incorporated into both Shadwell's 1694 adaptation of *Timon of Athens* and Charles GILDON's *Measure for Measure* (1699). These baroque productions were merely forerunners of the genre we now know as "grand opera," dramas in which all dialogue is sung, not spoken, and in which the music is preeminent.

Opera became a major form of entertainment in Europe in the course of the 18th century, at a time when translations and adaptations of Shakespeare into French and German were beginning to be made (see TRANSLATION OF SHAKESPEARE). The affinity of Shakespeare's creations with this mode of presentation was quickly recognized, but most 18th-century operas purporting to be adapted from Shakespeare were actually based on secondary sources and often had little or nothing to do with the playwright's work. Late in the century, the arts of Europe underwent a major shift in emphasis, as the neoclassical aesthetic was overtaken by the Romantic Movement, with its interest in individual psychology, the picturesque, and expressive variations in the forms of literature and music. Shakespeare became a cultural hero for many (but see VOLTAIRE), and Shakespearean operas that were much truer to their source became popular. In 1786, in Vienna, the English composer Stephen STORACE wrote music for an Italian libretto by Lorenzo da Ponte (1749–1838; Mozart's librettist) based on *The Comedy of Errors.* A leading Austrian composer, Carl Dittersdorf (1739–99), adapted *A Midsummer Night's Dream,* in 1796.

The 1816 *Otello* of Gioachimo ROSSINI is considered the first great opera based on Shakespeare (in this case on a version by Jean-François DUCIS). It was soon followed by Vincenzo BELLINI's very loose adaptation of *Romeo and Juliet,* titled *I Capuleti e i Montecchi* (1830), and then by Verdi's three great masterpieces: *Macbeth* (1847), *Otello* (1887), and *Falstaff* (1893). German opera also utilized Shakespeare: The young Richard WAGNER adapted *Measure for Measure* as *Das Lieberverbot* in 1836, and Nicolai wrote *Die lustigen Weiber von Windsor* (1849). In France, Hector BERLIOZ, in addition to several works of orchestral music inspired by the plays, wrote *Béatrice et Bénédict* (1867), based on *Much Ado About Nothing,* and Charles François GOUNOD adapted *Romeo and Juliet* in the same year. Thomas's *Hamlet,* one of the most popular operas of the century, premiered the next year.

In the 20th century, opera composers continued to turn to Shakespeare. The Hungarian-German composer Karl Goldmark (1830–1915) adapted *The Winter's Tale,* his last opera, in 1908. Ernst BLOCH adapted *Macbeth* early in his career. Ottorino RESPIGHI wrote *Lucrezia* (1937), based on *The Rape of Lucrece,* and it was in turn the inspiration for a smaller-scale, chamber-opera version by Benjamin Britten, *The Rape of Lucretia* (1946). Britten wrote both music and libretto for his *Midsummer Night's Dream* (1960), which is the only major Shakespearean opera that employs only Shakespeare's words (but for a single line, needed to establish facts lost when a scene was cut). Mario CASTELNUOVO-TEDESCO, who composed numerous works based on Shakespearean texts, wrote two operas based on Shakespeare's plays. The first, *All's Well That Ends Well,* was written, to an Italian libretto, in the mid-1920s, but it was suppressed by the Fascist government and was not performed until 1958; the second, his popular *Merchant of Venice,* had premiered in 1956. Other 20th-century operas include Carl ORFF's *Ein Sommernachtstraum* of 1962 (from *A Midsummer Night's Dream*), Samuel BARBER's *Antony and Cleopatra* (1966), Nicholas NABOKOV's *Love's Labour's Lost* (1973; libretto by W. H. AUDEN), Aribert REIMANN's *Lear* (1978), and several by Gian Francesco MALIPIERO.

Orff, Carl (1895–1982) German composer of *Ein Sommernachtstraum,* an OPERA of 1962 based on *The Midsummer Night's Dream* (in the German translation by SCHLEGEL; see TRANSLATION OF SHAKESPEARE). Best known for his *Carmina Burana* (1938), a song cycle in a rhythmic, declamatory modern style, Orff also wrote many other choral and orchestral works and was a well-known conductor. He was particularly distinguished as a teacher of music to children, on which he wrote extensively.

Orléans Location in *1 Henry VI*, a city in FRANCE. The English siege of Orléans, part of the HUNDRED YEARS' WAR, is the subject of 1.2 and 1.4–2.2. Although Joan La Pucelle (Joan of Arc) arrives among the French and inspires them, and the English commander, Thomas Montague, Earl of Salisbury, is killed, the English, led by Talbot, take the city in a nighttime attack.

Shakespeare's treatment of the siege of Orléans was intended to expand Talbot's role and exalt his heroism, and the playwright took extraordinary liberties with the historical record. Most strikingly, the English never actually took Orléans; besieged for six months, the city withstood the English troops. The English were led by Salisbury for only the first few weeks of the siege, and Talbot was not with the army at the time. After Salisbury's death, command was assumed by William de la Pole, Earl of Suffolk, a much less competent general; 10 days after Joan arrived, the revived French drove his forces away. Neither Charles VII nor Reignier was present. Talbot's nighttime attack was derived from accounts of another battle—the capture of Le Mans.

Ostler, William (ca. 1588–1614) English actor, a member of the KING'S MEN. One of the 26 men listed in the FIRST FOLIO as the "Principall Actors" in Shakespeare's plays, Ostler began his career as a boy actor (see CHILDREN'S COMPANIES). He and John UNDERWOOD probably became members of the King's Men at the same time, replacing William SLY and Laurence FLETCHER upon their deaths in 1608. John DAVIES called Ostler "sole King of Actors" in a poem (1611) that also implied that he had been involved in a brawl. In 1611 Ostler married Thomasine, daughter of John HEMINGES, and at the same time became a partner in the BLACKFRIARS THEATRE; a year later he acquired a share in the GLOBE THEATRE as well. After Ostler's early death, Heminges claimed Ostler's shares in the theaters, despite a lawsuit by Thomasine.

Otway, Thomas (1652–1685) English playwright, author of an adaptation of *Romeo and Juliet*.

Otway's *History and Fall of Caius Marius* (1670) combined elements of Shakespeare's play with a drama based on a biography in PLUTARCH's *Lives*. Set in ancient ROME, *Caius Marius* tells of two lovers on opposite sides of a political conflict between patricians and plebeians. His Romeo was Caius Marius (157–86 B.C.), a historical Roman commoner who rose to high political rank, marrying the daughter of a consul, one Julia (Otway's Juliet), the aunt of Julius Caesar. He later led one side in the first Roman civil war. Otway's *Marius* was so popular that *Romeo and Juliet* was not revived until well into the 1740s.

Otway was best known for two works that dominated the age of Restoration TRAGEDY: *The Orphan* (1680) and *Venice Preserved* (1682). Both are still revived occasionally. Though he was prolific, and his plays were produced by Thomas BETTERTON, Otway ended in poverty, dying quite suddenly at 33 after a short but dramatic life consumed by an unrequited love for Elizabeth BARRY. According to one report, he died in a pub; according to another, in a debtor's prison.

Ovid (Publius Ovidius Naso) (43 B.C.–A.D. 17) Roman poet, author of sources for many of Shakespeare's works. The story of Philomel, in Ovid's *Metamorphoses*, a collection of poems telling tales from Greek and Roman mythology, provided the germ of Lavinia's fate in *Titus Andronicus*, and in fact Ovid's work is explicitly cited in 4.1.42. *The Metamorphoses* was also the source for *Venus and Adonis*, which has a couplet from Ovid's *Amores* (love poems) as an epigraph. Another work by Ovid—the *Fasti*, an almanac in verse with legends and historical anecdotes for each month—was the principal source for *The Rape of Lucrece*. In addition, many references to and quotations from Ovid are scattered throughout the plays, particularly the early ones. Shakespeare undoubtedly read Ovid in school, as his work figured largely in the Latin curriculum of the times, but he also made use of Arthur GOLDING's translation of *The Metamorphoses*. A Latin copy of *The Metamorphoses* in the BODLEIAN LIBRARY bears a note declaring that it was once owned by Shakespeare, but the accompanying Shakespearean signature is rejected as inauthentic by scholars and handwriting experts.

Ovid, a minor aristocrat who abandoned the practice of law for poetry, lived comfortably in Rome. He was respected for his poetry and patronized by the emperor Augustus Caesar, until he was suddenly exiled in A.D. 8, partly for having written some erotic poems (his *Ars Amatoria*, or *Arts of Love*), which allegedly led the emperor's daughter to promiscuity, and partly for some other, now obscure scandal. He spent the remainder of his life in a remote colonial outpost on the Black Sea. His boast at the close of *The Metamorphoses* that "immortality is mine to wear" has proven justified, for that work has inspired poets and artists ever since.

Oxford, Edward de Vere, Earl of (1550–1604) English aristocrat, poet, and playwright. Oxford was a patron of poets and players (see OXFORD'S MEN) and wrote verse and plays himself. John LYLY was his secretary and wrote plays for his boys' company (see CHILDREN'S COMPANIES). Oxford's own plays are lost, but he was ranked with Shakespeare by Francis MERES as a good COMEDY writer.

Oxford was renowned as a violent and irresponsible nobleman. Orphaned at 12, he was raised in the household of Lord BURGHLEY, the chief minister of Queen Elizabeth I, and he married Burghley's daughter, though against her father's will. He may have killed a servant when he was 17, though the affair was hushed up, and his brawling was notorious. However, he was also an accomplished musician and dancer, and he was a favorite courtier of the queen, until he converted to Roman Catholicism. He then made one of the queen's ladies-in-waiting pregnant, for which he was imprisoned in 1581. After his release, he brawled and dueled with the woman's family, finally leaving the country to fight for the Dutch Republic and incurring Elizabeth's wrath for doing so without seeking her permission. By 1590 he had spent his fortune, but when his wife died and he remarried—to another of the queen's ladies—the queen granted him a pension. Though Oxford died years before Shakespeare's career was complete, some conspiracy theorists regard him as the favorite candidate for "the real Shakespeare" (see AUTHORSHIP CONTROVERSY).

Oxford's Men   Acting company of the ELIZABETHAN THEATER. In 1580 a troupe of players previously patronized by Ambrose Dudley, Earl of Warwick (brother of Robert Dudley, Earl of LEICESTER's) transferred their allegiance to Edward de Vere, Earl of OXFORD, though it is unclear whether they joined an extant company or constituted the founding members of Oxford's Men. Their best-known member was Laurence DUTTON. They do not seem to have been successful—mostly touring in the provinces and playing at the court of Queen Elizabeth I only occasionally. Their history, however, is not clear, for Oxford also patronized a CHILDREN'S COMPANY managed by Henry EVANS and a troupe of tumblers and acrobats. In some cases the surviving records are unclear about which of Oxford's groups they refer to. In 1602 Oxford's Men—the troupe of adult actors—received a license to join WORCESTER'S MEN and were absorbed by that company, probably in the same year.

P

Padua City in northern Italy, setting for *The Taming of the Shrew*. Shakespeare transferred the scene of his story from Ferrara, where it is set in his source, GASCOIGNE's play *Supposes*, for Padua was better known to his audience, enjoying a reputation as a major seat of learning. In fact, many English students of Shakespeare's day attended the university at Padua, which had been founded in the 13th century. The town's academic ambience is not important to the play—although in 1.1.1–24 Lucentio speaks of the desire for learning that has brought him to Padua—but a university town seems an apt setting for a tale of young love.

In *The Merchant of Venice*, Padua is the home of Portia's cousin, a scholar known for his legal wisdom, and it thus figures in the heroine's presentation of herself as a lawyer. It is also the hometown of Benedick in *Much Ado About Nothing*.

Shakespeare's apparent assumptions that Padua was a port (*Shrew*, 1.1.42, 4.2.83) and in Lombardy (1.1.3) have often been cited as serious errors, since Padua is neither on the coast nor in Lombardy. However, while the playwright's European geography is sometimes mistaken, here he may be excused: In his day the term *Lombardy* was often taken to refer to all of northern Italy, and Padua, while it is some 20 miles from the Adriatic, was a 16th-century canal port of some significance. An intricate canal network covered much of northern Italy in the Middle Ages and Renaissance; it operated until it was superseded by railroads in the 19th century. In fact, Padua can still be reached by water in small craft.

Painter, William (ca. 1525–1590) English translator, creator of source material for several of Shakespeare's works. Painter produced an anthology of more than 100 tales from Italian and Latin authors, including LIVY, PLUTARCH, BOCCACCIO, and CINTHIO, in his *Palace of Pleasure* (1566–67). A Boccaccio story from Painter was the principal source for *All's Well That Ends Well*, and other tales provided material for *Romeo and Juliet*, *Timon of Athens*, and *The Rape of Lucrece*. Many other Elizabethan and Jacobean playwrights turned to Painter as well, and he may deserve credit for the abundance of Italian settings and stories in their plays. Painter was a government official in charge of military supplies at the TOWER OF LONDON.

Palsgrave's Men Theatrical company in LONDON, previously known as PRINCE HENRY'S MEN and the ADMIRAL'S MEN. When Prince HENRY FREDERICK died in November 1612, the patronage of his theater company was taken over by Frederick V, Elector Palatine, the German fiancé of Princess ELIZABETH STUART. The couple married early in 1613, and the actors took one of Frederick's titles. A palsgrave, literally "palace count," was a noble of the Holy Roman Empire who ruled with imperial powers within his own territories. The new royal patent for the Palsgrave's Men listed the members of the company, including Samuel ROWLEY—who also wrote plays for the company—Thomas DOWNTON, Humphrey JEFFES, and John SHANK. They continued to play at the FORTUNE THEATRE and at the royal court, but in 1621 the Fortune burned to the ground, and the company lost all its costumes and props, and even many play scripts. The company struggled along for several years but never completely recovered. After a bad season in 1625—complicated by the combination of a plague epidemic and the death of King JAMES I—the company disbanded.

Papp, Joseph (1921–1991) American theatrical producer. Papp's New York Shakespeare Festival—originally (1953) the Shakespeare Workshop—had produced almost all of Shakespeare's plays before he relinquished its helm shortly before his death. This included a six-year cycle, begun in 1986, of the 36 plays in the FIRST FOLIO. Early in the Festival's existence, Papp often worked virtually without pay, until the endeavor was firmly established. For many years he produced and directed most of the festival's plays. Since 1962 the Festival has offered summer performances free of charge in the Delacorte Theater in New York City's Central Park. In 1967 Papp founded the New York Shakespeare Festival Public Theater, in order to produce contemporary, often experimental drama as well.

Paris Capital of FRANCE and a location in several of Shakespeare's plays. In 3.4 and 4.1 of *1 Henry VI*, English forces occupy Paris, and King Henry VI of England is crowned King of France there as part of the English diplomatic effort in the HUNDRED YEARS' WAR. A number of scenes in *All's Well That Ends Well* (1.2, 2.1, 2.3, 2.4, 2.5) are located in the Paris palace of the King of France. One scene of *3 Henry VI* (3.3) is set at the court of King Lewis, which is most plausibly assumed to be in Paris. As presented on stage, none of these venues is at all distinctively Parisian; the location is simply established in each case for its value to the plot.

Parliament House Building housing the English Parliament in London, a location in one scene each of *1* and *3 Henry VI*. A part of WESTMINSTER PALACE, this structure was a predecessor to the present Houses of Parliament, which were built in the 19th century. In 3.1 of *1 Henry VI*, an episode in the feud between Gloucester and Winchester occurs in the Parliament House; and in 1.1 of *3 Henry VI* York claims the crown of Henry VI

there, preempting a meeting of Parliament called by Queen Margaret.

In Shakespeare's day, as in the times he depicted in the HISTORY PLAYS, Parliament did not play the important policy-making and legislative role that we associate with the institution today. Although Parliament's power to levy taxes made it a necessary nuisance to the monarch, the aristocracy largely controlled elections to the Commons, and in any case the actual administration of government was entirely in the hands of the royal ruler and his or her advisers. The first great advances toward modern representative government were to come in the quarter-century following the playwright's death.

Parnassus plays Group of three amateur plays containing several references to Shakespeare and the LONDON theatrical world. These anonymous works are titled *The Pilgrimage to Parnassus*, *The Return from Parnassus* (Part 1), and *The Return from Parnassus* (Part 2), and they are referred to as *1*, *2*, and *3 Parnassus*. They were performed at Cambridge University, probably on Christmas 1598, 1599, and 1601. *1 Parnassus* is an allegory of travel to Mt. Parnassus, sacred to the Muses; *2* and *3 Parnassus* are set in London. In *2 Parnassus* a lover quotes from *Venus and Adonis* and declares, "I'le worshipp sweet Mr Shakspeare, and to honoure him will lay his *Venus and Adonis* under my pillowe." In *3 Parnassus* Richard BURBAGE and Will KEMPE appear as characters. Burbage auditions someone who recites the opening lines of *Richard III*, and another character praises both *Venus and Adonis* and *The Rape of Lucrece*. Most strikingly, Kempe declares of inferior playwrights that "our fellow Shakespeare puts them all downe . . . and Ben Ionson too," adding that Ben JONSON "is a pestilent fellow . . . but our fellow Shakespeare hath given him a purge." The play's date, 1601, suggests a reference to the WAR OF THE THEATERS, in which Jonson figured, but except for an obscure allusion in *Twelfth Night* (3.1.60), Shakespeare took no part in this exchange of satires. No "purge" he might have given Jonson has been identified. The remark may merely express the author's preference for Shakespeare, or it may reflect some lost piece of theater gossip.

Passionate Pilgrim, The   Collection of poems published as Shakespeare's in 1599, though only a quarter of the works in the anthology are known to have been written by him. William JAGGARD assembled this miscellany, apparently without Shakespeare's participation or knowledge, presumably to capitalize on the popularity of *Venus and Adonis* and *The Rape of Lucrece*. All of the poems deal with love; the title refers to a commonplace image of the seeker of love as a worshipper at a sacred shrine.

The first two poems in *The Passionate Pilgrim* are by Shakespeare (Sonnets 138 and 144), and Nos. 3, 5, and 16 (in the modern numbering of the *Pilgrim's* poems) are versions of passages from *Love's Labour's Lost* (4.3.57–70; 4.2.101–114; 4.3.98–118). Most scholars believe that Shakespeare wrote none of the remaining poems (there are 21 poems in the early editions, in which one poem is broken into two, and 20 in modern editions, in which the reassembled poem is No. 14).

Several of the remaining poems are attributable, with varying degrees of certainty, to other poets. No. 19 combines four stanzas from a poem by Christopher MARLOWE, "The Passionate Shepherd to his Love," with one from Walter RALEIGH's "The Nymph's Reply to the Shepherd"; these were not published until 1600, but they circulated in manuscript, a common practice at the time. No. 11 had already been published (1598) as the work of Bartholomew GRIFFIN, and Nos. 4, 6, and 9, similar in content and style, are usually attributed to him as well. Nos. 8 and 20 had already been published as the work of Richard BARNFIELD.

Seven of the remaining eight poems are generally considered by critics and scholars to be grossly inferior, unlikely to have been written by Shakespeare, even in his earliest years; only one, No. 12, seems possibly authentic, and although it has charm, it differs considerably from known Shakespearean poems in its simple assertiveness and unsophisticated poetic technique. In 1631 it appeared as one stanza of a Thomas DELONEY poem.

Two editions of *The Passionate Pilgrim* were published by Jaggard in 1599; they are known conventionally as Q1 and Q2, although they appeared in octavo, not QUARTO, format. Q1 is known only through the existence of isolated pages, bound with pages from Q2 in a single surviving copy, and its date is uncertain. Q2 appears to have been printed from Q1, and it is dated. Modern editions follow the combined texts.

Jaggard published a third edition, Q3 (also an octavio), in 1612 with additional material—also ascribed to Shakespeare—that he had culled from a book by Thomas HEYWOOD, which he had published three years earlier. Heywood protested publicly, asserting that not only he, but also Shakespeare, was "much offended" by Jaggard's high-handedness. Jaggard then issued Q3 with a new title page omitting Shakespeare's name.

Pasternak, Boris (1890–1960)   Russian novelist and translator of Shakespeare. Pasternak, renowned for his novel *Dr. Zhivago*, rendered seven of the best-known of Shakespeare's plays into Russian (published between 1941 and 1951) from the German of SCHLEGEL. His translations of these works remain standard for most Russian readers and audiences, supplementing the 19th-century translation of the complete works by Nicolai Gerbel (1827–83) (see TRANSLATION OF SHAKESPEARE).

The son of a well-known painter, Pasternak studied law, music, and philosophy before turning to literature, becoming a noted poet in his 20s. Following the Russian Revolution, he made a living as a librarian and continued to write. He wrote many stories in the 1920s, but during the grimmest years of the Stalinist repression, he became an official translator, producing his renderings of Shakespeare, GOETHE, and others while also beginning work on the book that was to make him famous around the world. Rejected by Soviet authorities, *Dr. Zhivago* was published abroad in 1957 in Italian and in English in 1958. It was immediately acclaimed as one of the great works of world literature. However, its tale of a disillusioned Communist of the 1920s was anathema to the Soviet government, and Pasternak was deprived of employment, sent into internal exile in the Russian countryside, and forced to refuse the Nobel Prize offered him in 1958. He died soon thereafter.

pastoral   Popular RENAISSANCE literary genre that influenced a number of Shakespeare's works, especially *As You Like It* and *The Winter's Tale*. The term may be used as either an adjective or a noun. In general, pastoral literature encompasses all works that depict an idealized vision of rural life, usually within the context of a love story. Such works are frankly escapist, though they are occasionally vehicles for more elevated literary aims.

The pastoral originated in a genre of ancient Greek poetry that dealt with the supposedly idyllic lives of shepherds, beginning with the work of Theocritus (ca. 308–240 B.C.). It was continued in ancient Roman poetry that contrasted the urban and the rural in order to satirize the sophisticated life of urban courtiers, most famously in the *Eclogues* of VIRGIL. In this form the genre was rediscovered and imitated by Italian poets in the Renaissance. The pastoral romance, a long tale in verse or prose, began with BOCCACCIO and was widely popular throughout Europe. In English, Sir Philip SIDNEY's *Arcadia* is among the greatest of pastorals, and Thomas LODGE's *Rosalynde*, the source of *As You Like It*, is a lesser example.

In the English pastoral dramas of Shakespeare's age, the delights of rustic life are conventionally idealized, and the amorous shepherds and shepherdesses are often portrayed as natural philosophers, Many dramatists essayed the genre in one form or another, notably Ben JONSON, John FLETCHER, and Samuel DANIEL. *As You Like It* gently parodies the conventions of the pastoral, but in Act 4 of *The Winter's Tale* they are treated more seriously, as a demonstration of human potentiality.

Pater, Walter (1839–1894)   English essayist and novelist, author of several significant essays on Shakespeare. An apologist for the "aesthetic" point of view represented by the phrase "art for art's sake," which he helped introduce into the language, Pater was among the most noted writers of his day and an acknowledged master of English prose. He was best known for his *Studies in the History of the Renaissance* (1873)—the book that made him famous—and a novel. *Marius the Epicurean* (1885). Three notable essays on Shakespeare—on *Measure for Measure* (1874), *Love's Labour's Lost*

(1878), and the HISTORY PLAYS (1889)—were highly influential, contributing to a revaluation of the playwright's work during the period.

Pavier, Thomas (d. 1625)   English bookseller and publisher associated with the publication of several of Shakespeare's plays. Pavier is notorious for his involvement in the FALSE FOLIO of Shakespeare's works (1619), to which he contributed pirated texts of *2* and *3 Henry VI* (jointly, as *The Whole Contention*), *Henry V, Pericles*, and two plays not actually by Shakespeare, SIR JOHN OLDCASTLE and A YORKSHIRE TRAGEDY. Pavier had earlier published the first editions of *Sir John Oldcastle* (1600) and *A Yorkshire Tragedy* (1608), attributing the latter to Shakespeare at that time. In 1600 Pavier purchased the "rights" to a pirated edition of *Henry V* from Thomas MILLINGTON and John BUSBY, and he reissued their BAD QUARTO as Q2 of the play in 1602. Though Pavier's practices seem dubious from a modern point of view, the evolving world of 17th-century publishing was not so strict, and Pavier was an honored member of the STATIONERS' COMPANY.

Peele, George (ca. 1557–1596)   English playwright, a possible collaborator with Shakespeare. Peele was one of the UNIVERSITY WITS, the group of dramatists that dominated the LONDON theater in the 1580s. After attending Oxford, Peele pursued an impecunious and dissipated life in London, writing plays and other works. His most successful work was *The Old Wives' Tale*, a romantic play based on folk stories. Most modern scholars, beginning with Frederick Gard FLEAY and John Mackinnon ROBERTSON, have come to believe that many of Shakespeare's earliest (and latest) plays were collaborative efforts, and scenes or passages in them are sometimes attributed to Peele, especially in *Edward III, 1 Henry VI*, and *Titus Andronicus*.

Pembroke, Henry Herbert, Earl of (ca. 1534–1601)   English aristocrat and theatrical patron. Pembroke was the patron of PEMBROKE'S MEN, with whom Shakespeare may have acted early in his career. Though willing to lend his name to the players who sometimes performed at his estate, Pembroke took no active part in their operations. His interests were chiefly political and military. An important figure in the court of Queen Elizabeth I (see Elizabeth I in *Henry VIII*), he was president of the council of WALES and spent much time in that land. He also took part in several important treason trials under Elizabeth, including that of Mary, Queen of Scots (see JAMES I). He was married to Mary Sidney, sister of Sir Philip SIDNEY, but he did not share the literary interests of that great patron of the arts. If Shakespeare was a member of the Pembroke's Men, it is possible that Pembroke was acquainted with the young playwright, though there is no specific evidence for any personal relationship. Some scholars believe that a continuing connection between Shakespeare and Pembroke may account for the pointed interest in Wales that appears in some of the plays. Also, there is a posthumous connection between the family and Shakespeare, for Pembroke's sons, William and Philip (see PEMBROKE, WILLIAM HERBERT, EARL OF; MONTGOMERY, PHILIP HERBERT, EARL OF), were co-dedicatees of the FIRST FOLIO.

Pembroke, William Herbert, Earl of (1580–1630)

English aristocrat, one of the dedicatees of the FIRST FOLIO of Shakespeare's plays and a possible model for the young man to whom the *Sonnets* are addressed. Pembroke's father, Henry Herbert, Earl of PEMBROKE, may have been acquainted with Shakespeare in the 1590s; this, along with Pembroke's known rejection of possible brides in 1595 and 1597, and the match between his initials and the "Mr. W. H." of Thomas THORPE's dedication to the *Sonnets*, has suggested to some commentators that he may have been the young man whose marriage is advocated in *Sonnets* 1–17. However, no certain connection between Shakespeare and Pembroke is known—the dedication of the Folio (to Pembroke and his brother Philip Herbert, Earl of MONTGOMERY) was made long after Shakespeare's death, by John HEMINGE and Henry CONDELL, doubtless because Pembroke was the lord chamberlain and therefore responsible for the publication of plays. In the absence of new evidence, Pembroke's association with the *Sonnets* must remain purely speculative.

Pembroke had other literary connections from an early age, however. His mother was the sister of Sir Philip SIDNEY and the patron of Edmund SPENSER and others. Samuel DANIEL was among his tutors, and as a young man, Pembroke wrote poetry himself. In the 1590s he was a courtier to Queen Elizabeth I (see Elizabeth I in *Henry VIII*), but he lost her favor in 1600 when he refused to marry his pregnant mistress, Mary FITTON. He was imprisoned for this offense, but Elizabeth's successor returned him to favor, and he became a prominent member of the new court. Pembroke was a patron of Ben JONSON and the poet George Herbert (1593–1633), a distant cousin; he was also an active investor in colonial development. He was a longtime chancellor of Oxford University—Pembroke College there is named in his honor—and he contributed many volumes to the BODLEIAN LIBRARY (there is still a statue of him outside it).

Pembroke's Men

Acting company of the ELIZABETHAN THEATER, possible employer of the young Shakespeare. In late 1592 a troupe of actors sponsored by Henry Herbert, Earl of PEMBROKE, performed at the court of Queen Elizabeth I, and the following year, with the LONDON theaters closed by the plague, the company toured England. The tour was a financial failure, however, and in September 1593 their rival Philip HENSLOWE recorded that they were forced to sell costumes to pay their debts. A number of plays known to have been in their repertoire were published by other people in 1594, suggesting that they were forced to sell their rights in them as well.

A revived Pembroke's Men played in the provinces from 1595 to 1597, and in the latter year they began a year's engagement in London, at Francis LANGLEY's new SWAN THEATRE. However, their July production of Thomas NASHE's allegedly seditious play, *Isle of Dogs*, resulted in the brief imprisonment of three members of the company— Gabriel SPENCER, Ben JONSON, and Robert SHAW— and the enforced closure of all the theaters for the summer. When they reopened in October, several actors had left Pembroke's for the ADMIRAL'S MEN. Soon the remnant of Pembroke's returned to the provinces, no longer able to compete in London. In 1600 two performances at Henslowe's ROSE THEATRE were flops, spelling the end of the company.

The repertoire of Pembroke's Men can be deduced in part. We know from the title page of the

BAD QUARTO of *3 Henry VI* (published as *The True Tragedy* in 1595) that this play—and, by implication, its companion, *2 Henry VI*—were staged by the company. As in any Bad Quarto, the actors' faulty memories have been supplemented by their recollections of performances in other plays. Thus, the other works echoed in these texts were probably part of the company's repertoire, including *1 Henry VI* as well as works by Christopher MAR-LOWE, Thomas KYD, and others. The title pages of *Titus Andronicus* and *The Taming of a Shrew* (1594)—a Bad Quarto of *The Taming of the Shrew*—declare that Pembroke's Men also performed these works. The association of Pembroke's Men with five of Shakespeare's early works has led scholars to assume that the young playwright was himself part of the company at some point during the mysterious beginnings of his career, leaving them before their collapse in 1593. The extremely poor quality of *The Taming of a Shrew* suggests that he was no longer with Pembroke's Men when it was prepared in the summer of 1592.

Pentapolis   Ancient Mediterranean land, the setting for most of Act 2 of *Pericles*. Pentapolis is the domain of King Simonides, whose daughter Thaisa marries Pericles. At the end of the play, Pericles learns of Simonides' death and announces that he and Thaisa shall rule in Pentapolis. Pericles' encounter with three Fishermen in 2.1 establishes that Pentapolis has a seacoast, but the country is otherwise undistinctive and serves purely as an exotic locale.

In classical times, Pentapolis—Greek for "five cities"—referred to any of five different locales, all of them political entities centered on five towns. None of them were independent kingdoms at the time of the play's only historical figure, Antiochus the Great, and it is impossible to be certain which of them Shakespeare had in mind. He may not have considered the matter, for he simply took the name from a source, the *Confessio Amantis* of John GOWER.

In an early Latin version of the tale—unknown to the playwright—the term clearly refers to the region also known as Cyrenaica, a Greek colony on the shores of North Africa in what is now eastern Libya. Since this was much the best known ancient Pentapolis, scholars generally associate it with the "country of Greece" (2.1.64) of *Pericles*. (However, it could also be the Pentapolis of Greek Asia Minor, on the Aegean coast of what is now Turkey, rather closer to the other territories represented in the play.)

Pepys, Samuel (1633–1703)   Seventeenth-century diarist and longtime administrator of the Royal Navy. Pepys kept his famous diary between 1660 and 1669. An inveterate theatergoer, he recorded his impressions of many Restoration period adaptations of Shakespeare's plays.

Phelps, Samuel (1804–1878)   British actor and producer. Phelps was among the most influential of 19th-century producers of Shakespeare's plays, restoring much of the original text to plays encumbered by two centuries of adaptations. In an age of lavishly spectacular sets and scenic effects, which often required Shakespeare's texts to be cut to allow time for them, Phelps introduced relative simplicity. His followers William POEL and Harley GRANVILLE-BARKER transmitted these ideas to the 20th century.

Originally a journalist, Phelps moved from amateur theatricals to the professional theater. He was well established in the British provinces as a tragic actor before triumphing in London as Shylock in an 1837 production of *The Merchant of Venice*. After several years under Benjamin WEBSTER and W. C. MACREADY, Phelps became manager of the SADLER'S WELLS THEATRE, where in 18 years (1844–62) he staged most of Shakespeare's plays. In 1845 he presented the first staging of Shakespeare's text of *King Lear* in almost 200 years, finally superseding the radical adaptation of Nahum TATE, and his 1847 presentation of *Macbeth* did away with William DAVENANT's operatic additions. Similarly, he revived *Antony and Cleopatra* in 1849, and his 1851 *Timon of Athens* is believed to have been the initial staging of the play, which was apparently not produced in Shakespeare's time. Phelps was the leading player of his company, and he continued to act under various directors after he left Sadler's Wells. He portrayed most of the great tragic protagonists—Othello and Lear were thought to be his best parts—while also playing many other characters, such as Malvolio

(*Twelfth Night*), Shallow (*1 Henry IV*), and Pericles. He was particularly acclaimed as Bottom, in *A Midsummer Night's Dream*.

Philippi   Ancient city in what is now northern Greece, a battle site in the Roman civil wars and a location in *Julius Caesar*. The armies of Brutus and Cassius on one hand, and Antony and Octavius on the other, meet at Philippi in Act 5. Brutus risks all on this battle, against the advice of the more experienced Cassius, but he attacks too early and leaves Cassius without support, as Titinius remarks in 5.3.5–8 Brutus and Cassius are defeated, and both commit suicide rather than be captured. The battle of Philippi provides the climax wherein Antony avenges Brutus's murder of Caesar.

Shakespeare altered the account of the battle that he found in his source, PLUTARCH's *Lives*. In 5.1 he invented the prebattle meeting of the opposing generals, at which they trade insults and challenges. This exchange follows a well-known convention of medieval and Renaissance battle accounts, in which the credentials, as it were, of the warriors are established. More important, the playwright also compressed the events of several weeks into a single day to provide a dramatically more cohesive chain of events, as he had done in the HISTORY PLAYS.

There were in fact two battles at Philippi. In the first, fought on October 23, 42 B.C., the forces of Brutus and Cassius won a slight advantage. Antony's forces routed some of Cassius's troops and raided his headquarters, as is reported in 5.3.10; however, as Shakespeare also recounts, Brutus's premature attack was successful, and Octavius's men were defeated. Nevertheless, Cassius, believing mistakenly that all was lost, killed himself; an early account attributed the error to his defective eyesight. The loss was crucial, for Brutus was a bad general. Although Antony's and Octavius's forces were short of supplies in enemy country, Brutus could not control his impatience, and after 20 days he fought the second battle of Philippi, which in the play takes place on the same afternoon as the first, as per Brutus's order in 5.3.109–110. This second encounter, a bloody, day-long battle, resulted in Brutus's defeat and suicide.

The combined battles were decisive; the civil war that followed the assassination of Julius Caesar had been won by the supporters of his style of dictatorial government. Moreover, the remnants of the old Roman aristocracy were largely wiped out in this campaign, which was particularly bloody by the standards of the day. Although more strife was to follow between the victors of Philippi (as is enacted in *Antony and Cleopatra*), the stage was set for the establishment of the Roman Empire under Octavius Caesar.

Phillips, Augustine (d. 1605)   One of the 26 men listed in the FIRST FOLIO as "Principall Actors" in Shakespeare's plays, though not identified with any particular Shakespearean role. Phillips was in STRANGE'S MEN from about 1590 to 1593 and was probably an original member of the CHAMBERLAIN'S MEN. He was one of the original partners in the GLOBE THEATRE in 1599, and he was still with the Chamberlain's Men when it became the KING'S MEN in 1603. Thus, most of his professional life was spent with this troupe. This is reflected in his will, which has survived. The executors were John HEMINGE, Richard BURBAGE, and William SLY, all King's Men, and he left small bequests to many of his fellow actors, including Shakespeare. Also, Phillips's sister married another member, Robert GOUGH, who witnessed the will just days before Phillips died. Among the items Phillips bequeathed were several musical instruments, suggesting that he had been a musician as well as actor. His widow, who inherited his share in the Globe, married John WITTER.

Phoenix   Name of a house, one of three onstage, in *The Comedy of Errors*. The Phoenix, which may be distinguished in a stage set by a sign above its door, is the home of Antipholus of Ephesus and Adriana. The other houses that comprise the setting are the PORCUPINE and the PRIORY. This arrangement of three structures, each with an entrance onto the stage, was standard in ancient Roman stage design as it was understood in Shakespeare's time, and it is quite appropriate to this play, which, of all Shakespeare's works, most closely resembles Roman drama.

Picardy   Region in northern FRANCE, location of the battle of AGINCOURT and the setting of several scenes in *Henry V.* In 3.6 and 3.7 the English and French armies, respectively, are shown in camp prior to the crucial battle, which itself occupies all of Act 4. Picardy is the historical term for an area north and east of the River Seine along the English Channel.

"Pied Bull" Quarto See "Text of the Play," *King Lear.*

Planché, James Robinson (1796–1880) British playwright and theatrical designer. Planché wrote many successful burlesques and pantomimes, as well as a few legitimate dramas, over a period of 50 years, beginning in 1818. He was also a serious antiquarian—a founder of the British Archaeological Association—specializing in the history of costume. His *History of British Costume* (1834) was a standard work in the field for many years. In this capacity he helped create the 19th-century enthusiasm for historically accurate productions of Shakespeare's plays. He designed the costumes for the first such staging, the *King John* staged by Charles KEMBLE in 1823. He also was credited with much of the success of the 1840 *Midsummer Night's Dream* of Charles Mathews and Elizabeth VESTRIS; he designed the Athenian costumes and a famous finale featuring dozens of twinkling lights. Lastly, he designed the 1844 production by Benjamin WEBSTER of *The Taming of the Shrew,* which is said to have legitimized the presentation of Shakespeare's plays in their original form.

Planché, the son of a watchmaker of Huguenot descent, had many other talents. He was a good professional musician and a respected authority on heraldry; he wrote OPERA librettos; and, following the unauthorized production of one of his plays, he became largely responsible for the first law granting modern copyright protection to dramatists.

Plantagenet family English ruling dynasty from 1154 to 1485, parts of whose history form the subject matter of most of Shakespeare's HISTORY PLAYS. *King John* deals with an early Plantagenet monarch, and *Edward III* presents the earliest phase of the HUNDRED YEARS' WAR, as conducted by the last Plantagenet ruler to govern before the feud between the YORK and LANCASTER branches of the family,

which culminated in the WARS OF THE ROSES. This nation-sundering disaster is the subject of two sequences of four plays each (see TETRALOGY) that cover the reigns of the last Plantagenet rulers.

The earliest Plantagenet was a French nobleman, Geoffrey, Count of Anjou, and the family was originally known as the Angevin dynasty. Geoffrey's badge was a representation of a white flower, *planta argent,* from which the later family name derives. (The use of this name began only in the 1460s, when Richard, Duke of York, assumed it as part of his campaign to claim the throne for his branch of the family.)

In 1127 Geoffrey of Anjou married the daughter of Henry I of England, a younger son of William the Conqueror; Geoffrey's son, Henry II, became the first Plantagenet king in 1154, ruling both England and territories in FRANCE, a situation that eventually resulted in the Hundred Years' War. As in most medieval dynasties, the ancient rule of primogeniture provided that the crown was to be inherited by an eldest son or his descendants, or by a next-eldest son if the eldest had no sons or had died before the king. This eventually caused great difficulties for England, but for two centuries the Plantagenets transmitted their power peacefully.

Richard I, the Lionhearted, succeeded his father, Henry II. Dying childless, Richard was succeeded by his younger brother, John, in 1199. King John, who may have been insane, was at least highly temperamental and made enemies easily. His reign was accordingly distinguished by repeated wars and political skirmishes with rebellious barons, with France, with the pope, and others. The most famous of these conflicts, in modern eyes, resulted in the signing of the Magna Carta in 1215, but this did not yet have great symbolic value in Elizabethan times, and Shakespeare's *King John* concerns another dispute, which ended with John's death (though not by poison, as in the play). Beginning with John's son, the Henry of *King John,* who ruled (1216–72) as King Henry III, son succeeded father for four generations. But Henry III's great-grandson King Edward III, though victorious in France, saw his son and heir, the "Black Prince," die there. He was therefore succeeded by his grandson, Richard II, in 1377. The dynasty subsequently broke down.

The York and Lancaster branches of the Plantagenet family descended from two of the seven sons of Edward III. Richard II's father, the "Black Prince," had been the first of the them. King Edward's second son, the Duke of Clarence, did not have a son; his daughter married into the Mortimer family. The third son was John of Gaunt, Duke of Lancaster, whose son, Henry Bolingbroke deposed his cousin Richard in 1399 and ruled as Henry IV, the first Lancastrian king. The fourth son of King Edward, Edmund Langley, Duke of York, could entertain no claim to rule under a normal succession. However, after Richard's deposition, the Mortimers attempted to claim the throne by virtue of their relation to King Edward's second son, who would have succeeded Richard under any circumstances but usurpation; and York's son, the Earl of Cambridge in *Henry V*, married a Mortimer and inherited their claim. Thus, by the mid-15th century the Yorkist faction was the chief rival to the Lancastrians. The remaining sons of Edward III had no importance in the Plantagenet succession, though the murder of one of them, Thomas, Duke of Gloucester, helped spark the fall of Richard II, which, along with the reigns of the first two Lancastrian monarchs, is dealt with in *Richard II*, *1 and 2 Henry IV*, and *Henry V*.

Henry IV might have been a strong monarch, but he spent much of his time putting down revolts by Richard's supporters, including Owen Glendower and the Archbishop of York. These conflicts are enacted in *1 and 2 Henry IV*, where another plot line concerns the development of the King's son, Prince Hal, who overcame a tendency to dissipation (much exaggerated in Shakespeare) to become, upon being crowned as King Henry V, a charismatic military leader who triumphed over the French in the battle of AGINCOURT, as enacted in *Henry V*. This victory was followed by further campaigning in which Henry was close to seizing PARIS when he died of dysentery. His triumphs were the last of England's successes in the Hundred Years' War, because the country was soon engulfed in the Wars of the Roses.

When Henry V died in 1422, his son, Henry VI, was an infant, and the illegality of Richard II's deposition was still a living issue that only a strong monarch could silence. The Yorkist claim was pressed, and the resulting wars are the principal subject of *1, 2,* and *3 Henry VI* and *Richard III*. Beginning in 1461, three members of the York family ruled England: Edward IV, Edward V, and Richard III. In 1485, as enacted in *Richard III*, Richard III was overthrown by a distant cousin of Henry VI, the Earl of Richmond, who ruled as King Henry VII, the founder of the TUDOR DYNASTY.

Two Plantagenets survived the Wars of the Roses, a boy and a girl, great-great-grandchildren of the original Duke of York. The boy, Edward, Earl of Warwick, was imprisoned for most of his brief life to prevent him from claiming the crown; Henry VII executed him in 1499, after rebels had made several attempts to impersonate him and seize the throne. His sister, Margaret, the last Plantagenet, lived until 1541, when she was beheaded, at the age of 68, by Henry VIII, who also feared a rebellion in favor of the former dynasty.

Platter, Thomas (1574–1628) Swiss doctor from Basel who traveled widely in 1595–1600 and published an account of his journeys (in German) in 1604. He was in England in September–October 1599 and recorded a performance of *Julius Caesar* at the GLOBE THEATRE and an unnamed play at the CURTAIN THEATRE. His remarks are among the few sources of detail about the ELIZABETHAN THEATER.

Plautus, Titus Maccius (ca. 254–184 B.C.) Ancient Roman dramatist, author of sources for *The Comedy of Errors* and *The Taming of the Shrew*. Plautus's *Menaechmi* was the principal source for *The Comedy of Errors*, providing the central plot of long-lost twins who are farcically mistaken for each other; another of his works, *Amphitryon*, provided the second set of twins. Numerous details in *The Shrew*, including the names of Grumio and Tranio, came from Plautus's *Mostellaria* (*The Haunted House*). Minor elements in other plays also reflect Shakespeare's knowledge of Plautus.

Moreover, many other writers and dramatists had relied on Plautus's plays as sources, so elements from Plautus could have reached Shakespeare indirectly. For instance, one of the main sources for *The Shrew*, ARIOSTO's *I Suppositi* (1509), was itself based on Plautus's *Captivi*. The first English comedy, *Ralph Roister Doister* (ca. 1553) by Nicholas UDALL, is based on Plautus's *Miles Gloriosus* (after whose hero the character type MILES GLORIOSUS is named). Plautus was still very well known in Shakespeare's day, and the playwright clearly assumed that his audience was familiar with his work, as when he had Polonius tritely observe that "Plautus [cannot be] too light" (*Hamlet*, 2.2.396–397). Plautus continues to provide stimulation to writers of COMEDY; for instance, elements from several of his comedies were incorporated in the American musical *A Funny Thing Happened on the Way to the Forum* (1962).

Plautus wrote many plays, of which 21 survive, all of them comedies and all free translations of older Greek works, especially those of Menander (ca. 342–292 B.C.), some of whose plays are known only through their Plautine versions. Plautus's works are generally characterized by a casually cynical tone, complicated plots, and stereotyped characters (his character types helped stimulate the 17th-century COMEDY OF HUMOURS). Some works are merely farcical (see FARCE), while others have sentimental or social themes. He was highly popular in the Roman world, and his plays continued to be produced for centuries after his death. Many later plays were falsely ascribed to him—more than 100 have been reattributed by modern scholars. Plautus was ignored during the Middle Ages, and his rediscovery was an important stimulus to RENAISSANCE literature and drama throughout Europe.

Pliny the Elder (ca. A.D. 23–79) Roman author of an encyclopaedia of natural history that served as a minor source for *Othello*. Pliny's *Naturalis Historia*, translated by Philemon HOLLAND as *Natural History* (1601) provided several details for Othello's description of his adventures in 1.3.

Pliny's vast work assembles a tremendous body of lore, and though much of it is inaccurate, it remained an important reference into the RENAISSANCE. A career military officer and a close friend of the emperor Vespasian (ruled A.D. 69–79), he wrote many books, mostly on military subjects, but only the *Natural History* survives. His scientific curiosity was so great that during the eruption of Vesuvius in A.D. 79, he traveled to Pompeii and was killed. His death is described by his nephew Pliny the Younger (A.D. 61–ca. 114) in a famous passage from his *Letters*.

Plowright, Joan (b. 1929) English actress, widow of Laurence OLIVIER. Plowright often played opposite her husband, perhaps most notably as Portia to his Shylock in his 1970 London production of *The Merchant of Venice* and again in the 1974 TELEVISION version. Her most striking Shakespearean part was also on television, the double role of Sebastian and Viola in a 1969 production of *Twelfth Night*.

Plummer, Christopher (b. 1929) Canadian actor. Plummer has played many Shakespearean roles in Stratford, Ontario, and elsewhere. At Stratford in 1972, he starred opposite Zoë CALDWELL in a memorable *Antony and Cleopatra*. He also won particular acclaim for his Iago, opposite James Earl JONES, in Nicol WILLIAMSON's 1982 New York production of *Othello*. More recently, he triumphed as King Lear in the 2002 Stratford (Ontario) production by Jonathan MILLER.

Plutarch (ca. A.D. 46–ca. 130) Greek philosopher and biographer whose *Lives*—as translated by Sir Thomas NORTH—was Shakespeare's primary source for *Antony and Cleopatra, Coriolanus, Julius Caesar,* and *Timon of Athens* and a source of minor elements in other plays. Plutarch, after studying in Athens, became a teacher of philosophy in Rome, where he received the patronage of the emperors Hadrian and Trajan and wrote (in Greek) many works on ethical, religious, and political questions. Following Trajan's death, Plutarch returned to Greece, where he wrote his famous biographies of Greek and Roman heroes of history and legend. These works, intended as moral lessons in greatness and failure, have inspired many generations of readers. Among Plutarch's most important admirers, besides Shakespeare, have been Michel de MONTAIGNE, Ralph Waldo Emerson, and Napoleon Bonaparte.

Poel, William (1852–1934) English theatrical producer. Beginning in 1894, with the founding of the Elizabethan Stage Society, Poel revolutionized the theatrical presentation of Shakespeare's plays with productions that attempted to replicate the experience of 16th- and 17th-century playgoers. Using a projecting stage, very little scenery, and original texts, his group staged numerous works by Shakespeare (including the first modern presentation of any part of *Edward III*, a 1911 performance of Act 2), Christopher MARLOWE, Francis BEAUMONT and John FLETCHER, Ben JONSON, Thomas MIDDLETON, and others. Financial losses closed the society in 1905, but Poel continued to produce such works elsewhere, including DER BESTRAFTE BRUDERMORD in 1924 (its first English production) and ARDEN OF FEVERSHAM in 1925. His work influenced others, notably Nugent MONCK and Harley GRANVILLE-BARKER, and furthered a long-lasting trend toward scrupulously preserved texts produced in rigorously simple stagings that countered extravagant spectacles of the late 19th century. His work also influenced critical attitudes toward Shakespeare's work; for instance, he was the first director to stage all three PROBLEM PLAYS, thereby helping to stimulate their acceptance in a world that had previously spurned them (Poel had been instructed in college never to read *Measure for Measure* or *Troilus and Cressida* because of their gross impropriety). Poel also wrote several plays himself and a number of books on the theater.

Poetomachia   See WAR OF THE THEATERS.

Poitiers   Location in *Edward III*, a town in central FRANCE, the site of a battle of the HUNDRED YEARS' WAR. As enacted in 4.4–4.7 of the play, the battle of Poitiers is won by the valor and effort of King Edward's son, the Prince. In 4.4 the Prince and his follower Lord Audley find themselves surrounded and outnumbered by the French forces. Three French messengers appear, one after the other, with increasingly insulting demands for surrender, but the Englishmen refuse and declare their willingness to die fighting. In 4.5 the French commanders, King John and his son Charles hear of a panic in their ranks inspired by a dense flock of ravens—as predicted in a prophecy recounted before the battle, in 4.3—and issue orders designed to counter it.

King John grants a safe-conduct to the English Lord Salisbury and sends him to the English with a gloating message about the coming English defeat. In 4.6 a series of three battlefield vignettes represent the actual fighting: first (4.6.1–17), the Prince and his ally Artois observe the success of the English archers but note that they are running out of arrows. The Prince declares they'll fight on with stones (thereby, unconsciously, fulfilling another element of the prophecy). Then, in 4.6.18–52 the French leaders face the fact that their army is in full retreat; they vow to fight on if they can find troops enough to do so. Lastly, in 4.6.53–62 the wounded Audley is carried from the field by two soldiers; though mortally wounded, he exults in an English victory. In 4.7 the triumphant Prince speaks to his captives, King John and Charles, as Artois appears with another prisoner, the French Prince Philip. Audley and his Esquires arrive and are munificently rewarded by the Prince, and all rejoice patriotically in the English success.

Shakespeare and/or his collaborators (see *Edward III*, "Commentary") took great liberties with their presentation of this battle, beginning with its place in the chronology of events. It did not occur simultaneously with Edward's siege of CALAIS, as the play has it, but took place 10 years later. This rearrangement tightens the dramatic action. The events of the battle itself are also distorted. Most significant, the English Prince was never surrounded by French troops and never in serious danger of catastrophe; Audley's elaborate account of the disposition of the French forces in 4.4.10–39 is entirely fictional, as are the taunting Heralds. These alterations increase suspense. The flight of ravens (predicted by the prophecy—a fiction common in medieval and Elizabethan accounts of battles) occurred at CRÉCY, not Poitiers, and was not consequential. Moreover, the French Prince Charles was not captured; Prince Philip did not command troops; and Artois was not in the battle, having been dead 13 years at the time. These and other such discrepancies simply demonstrate differences in the intentions of dramatists and military historians. As rendered, the battle of Poiters adds to *Edward III*'s patriotic presentation of English triumphs.

The historical battle was almost lost by the English before it began: The Prince, seeing himself badly outnumbered, offered to surrender to King John and promised to sign a seven-year truce if permitted to withdraw from France. However, the French monarch, too confident of victory, refused this offer and insisted on a complete surrender of the English forces. In the event, English archery won the day, as it had earlier at Crécy and would later at AGINCOURT (as depicted in *Henry V*). Success at Poitiers sealed England's triumph in the first phase of the Hundred Years' War.

Pollard, Alfred William (1859–1944) British scholar, a founder of modern textual criticism. Pollard's major contributions to Shakespearean scholarship were his *Shakespeare's Folios and Quartos 1594–1685* (1909), a groundbreaking consideration of the various texts of the plays, and *Shakespeare's Fight with the Pirates* (1917), a study of the illicit publication of play texts in Shakespeare's time. He helped establish that Shakespeare was a collaborator on *Sir Thomas More*. He was also a major authority on Geoffrey CHAUCER.

Pomfret Castle (Pontefract Castle) Strong fortress in northern England, the site of a number of political murders and executions in the 14th and 15th centuries, two of which are presented in Shakespeare's HISTORY PLAYS. Richard II is murdered in his cell by Exton in 5.5 of *Richard II*, and Lords Rivers, Grey, and Vaughan are led to execution in 3.3 of *Richard III*. The historical Earl of Salisbury was also executed at Pomfret. Lord Rivers refers to the castle's bloody history when he exclaims, just before his death in *Richard III*, "O Pomfret, Pomfret! O thou bloody prison, / Fatal and ominous to noble peers!" (3.3.9–10).

Pope, Alexander (1688–1744) British poet and editor of Shakespeare. Best known as a poet, Pope also produced the second scholarly edition of Shakespeare's plays in 1725. He is regarded by modern scholars as a bad editor, however. He claimed to have corrected, by following QUARTO texts, many instances in which the playwright's words had been corrupted by the FOLIO editors; in

fact, he mostly followed the 1709 edition of Nicholas ROWE (based on the Fourth Folio), though he did make numerous "improvements" in his own words. Lewis THEOBALD, the first great Shakespearean scholar, pointed out many of Pope's errors in a 1726 book, for which he was pilloried in Pope's famous literary satire, *The Dunciad* (1728). Pope, however, did incorporate many readings from Theobald's critique when he reissued his own collection in 1728. Moreover, Pope is credited with some scholarly accomplishments: he first established firmly the locations of many scenes, and he corrected the rhythm of many lines that had been improperly printed. He was also the first commentator to recognize that THE TROUBLESOME RAIGNE OF KING JOHN was derived from Shakespeare's *King John* rather than the other way around.

A childhood disease left Pope a hunchback, and he was embittered by it, once describing his life as one long disease. His sharp wit and penchant for invective made him a close friend of the satirist Jonathan Swift (1667–1745), but his social relations tended to end in mutual hostility. His talent for recrimination against former friends earned him the epithet "The Wicked Wasp of Twickenham" (after the town where he lived). He was England's leading poet in the first half of the 18th century, with such works as *An Essay on Criticism* (1711), *The Rape of the Lock* (1712), translations of *The Iliad* and *The Odyssey* (1720, 1725), *Moral Essays* (1731–35), and *An Essay on Man* (1732–34).

Pope, Thomas (d. ca. 1603) English actor, member of the CHAMBERLAIN'S MEN. Though he is one of the 26 men listed in the FIRST FOLIO as the "Principal Actors" in Shakespeare's plays, it is not known what roles he played. They must have been comic parts, for he was a clown and acrobat. He toured DENMARK and Germany with William KEMPE and others in 1586–87, and he was a member of STRANGE'S MEN beginning in about 1591. He was probably an original member of the Chamberlain's Men, with whom he remained until at least 1599, when he became an original partner in the GLOBE THEATRE. He was not part of the troupe when it became the KING'S MEN in 1603, having probably retired. He died in late 1603 or early

1604. As late as 1612 he was still described as a memorable actor.

Porcupine (Porpentine) Name of a house, one of three on stage, in *The Comedy of Errors*. The Porcupine, which may be distinguished in a stage set by a sign above its door, is the home of the Courtesan. The other houses that comprise the setting are the PHOENIX and the PRIORY. This arrangement of three structures, each with an entrance onto the stage, was a standard device of ancient Roman stage design as it was understood in Shakespeare's time, and it is quite appropriate to this play, which, of all Shakespeare's works, most closely resembles Roman drama. It has been speculated that Shakespeare called the Courtesan's house "Porcupine" ("Porpentine" in Elizabethan English) after a well-known London brothel in an inn of that name.

Porter, Henry (d. 1599) English dramatist. Porter wrote at least six plays for Philip HENSLOWE and the ADMIRAL'S MEN, some of them in collaboration with Henry CHETTLE and Ben JONSON. He was praised by Francis MERES as being among the best English writers of COMEDY. Only one play written solely by Porter has survived: *The Two Angry Women of Abingdon* (ca. 1596), a comedy that resembles *The Merry Wives of Windsor*. Though greatly inferior, it was very popular in its day, and it may have stimulated Shakespeare's interest in writing a busy comedy of town life. Porter was perennially poor, and he died deep in debt. He was stabbed to death in a fight by fellow playwright John DAY.

portraits of Shakespeare Only two depictions of Shakespeare—both posthumous—are believed to have been based on genuine portraits: the DROESHOUT engraving, which illustrates the title page of the FIRST FOLIO, and the sculptural bust by Gheerart JANSSEN that is part of the poet's memorial in Holy Trinity Church, in STRATFORD. However, numerous other images have been thought of as portraits of Shakespeare, though modern scholars generally reject them. The most significant of these is probably the CHANDOS PORTRAIT,

The title page of the First Folio has on it what is probably a reliable likeness of Shakespeare, an engraving by Martin Droeshout.

which was accepted as genuine for many years; it was the basis for the sculpture by Peter SCHEEMAKERS in WESTMINSTER ABBEY. Other portraits of note include the ASHBOURNE PORTRAIT, the ELY PALACE PORTRAIT, the FLOWER PORTRAIT, the KESSELSTADT DEATH MASK, and works by Nicholas HILLIARD and Cornelis JANSSEN.

Pory, John (1572–1636) English writer, the translator of the work of LEO AFRICANUS, a possible influence on *Othello*. Pory was an associate of Richard HAKLUYT, who suggested he translate Leo's Italian account of his African travels. The translation was published as *A Geographical History of Africa* (1600), and Pory's prefatory biography of Leo probably influenced Othello's autobiographical remarks in 1.3.

Pory also produced a version of a famous early atlas, *The Epitome of Ortelius* (1602), but until 1612 he made his living publishing newsletters, accounts of parliamentary and court events that he sent to private subscribers, a practice that preceded the development of modern newspapers. He was a very widely traveled man. From 1612 to 1617 he traveled in Ireland and Europe as an agent for Sir George CAREW, from 1617 to 1619 he was employed by an English diplomat in Constantinople, and in 1619 he went to Virginia as secretary to the governor. Pory was on the governing council of the colony and served as the speaker of the initial session of the Burgesses, the first legislative assembly in the New World. He returned to England in 1623—after being shipwrecked and imprisoned in the Azores—and resumed his newsletter business, retiring a few years before his death.

Preston, Thomas (1537–1598) Sixteenth-century playwright parodied by Shakespeare. Preston's play *Cambyses* (1569), whose full title described it as "A lamentable Tragedie, mixed full of pleasant mirth . . .," is mocked in the comical presentation of PYRAMUS AND THISBE in *A Midsummer Night's Dream* (1.2.11–12) and by Falstaff in *1 Henry IV* (2.4.382–389). *Cambyses*, though highly bombastic and melodramatic, represents a significant development from the MORALITY PLAY toward TRAGEDY. Preston was primarily an educator; he served as vice chancellor of Cambridge University.

Prince Charles' Men Seventeenth-century LONDON theatrical company. Prince Charles' Men were organized in 1608 as a provincial company called the Duke of York's Men in honor of their patron, King JAMES I's younger son, later King Charles I (ruled 1625–49). The company began staging plays at the royal court in London in 1610. Among their members were the dramatist William ROWLEY, who wrote most of their plays and directed the company, and Joseph TAYLOR, their leading actor. In 1612, when Charles's older brother, Prince HENRY FREDERICK, died, Charles became the heir apparent and was known as the Prince of Wales; the company he patronized changed its name accordingly. Around 1614–16 the company was briefly allied with LADY ELIZABETH'S MEN. They played at a variety of London playhouses as well as at the court. In 1619 Christopher BEESTON joined the company as its manager, and for several years they played regularly at his theater, the Phoenix and then, after 1621, at the CURTAIN THEATRE. Taylor left for the KING'S MEN in 1619, and in 1623 Rowley followed him. The company dispersed when Prince Charles became king in 1625 and transferred his patronage to the King's Men.

Prince Henry's Men Seventeenth-century LONDON theatrical company, formerly the ADMIRAL'S MEN. In 1603, after King JAMES I succeeded to the crown of England, his son Prince HENRY FREDERICK assumed patronage of the company, which changed its name accordingly. Their new royal patent lists the members of the company, including Edward ALLEYN—their longtime leader—Thomas DOWNTON, Humphrey JEFFES, and Samuel ROWLEY, who also wrote plays for the company. By 1606 Alleyn had retired, though he kept a financial interest in the company and was part owner of the FORTUNE THEATRE, where they appeared, so he probably retained some influence on the company's affairs. In November 1612 Prince Henry died, and his patronage was taken up by the German fiancé of Princess ELIZABETH STUART, Frederick V the Elector Palatine. When the royal couple married in early 1613, the company formally took on one of Frederick's titles and was known as the PALSGRAVE'S MEN.

Priory Name of a house, one of three on stage, in *The Comedy of Errors*. The Priory, which may be distinguished in a stage set by a cross or other sign above its door, is the religious house headed by Emilia, its Abbess. Antipholus and Dromio of Syracuse take refuge there early in 5.1. (Until well into the 17th century in England, a criminal or a defendant in a civil suit could take sanctuary from the law in a church or other sacred building.)

The other houses that comprise the setting are the PHOENIX and the PORCUPINE. This arrangement of three structures, each with an entrance onto the stage, was standard in ancient Roman stage design as it was understood in Shakespeare's time, and it is quite appropriate to this play, which, of all Shakespeare's works, most closely resembles Roman drama.

Pritchard, Hannah (1711–1768) British actress. Pritchard began her career as a fairground singer and was recruited for the stage by Theophilus CIB-BER. She went on to achieve fame playing with David GARRICK. She played many Shakespearean roles and was acclaimed for her comedic heroines—especially Rosalind in *As You Like It*—which she continued to play well into middle age. She also played tragic roles, and her greatest fame came as Lady Macbeth, which she played opposite Garrick for many years. After her death, he never played Macbeth again.

problem plays Three of Shakespeare's comedies that present difficulties to audiences and readers due to sometimes unpleasant characters and situations, clashes of mood and tone, and uncertainty as to the playwright's viewpoint. The problem plays—*All's Well That Ends Well*, *Measure for Measure*, and *Troilus and Cressida*—are potent satires characterized by disturbingly ambiguous points of view and seemingly cynical attitudes toward sexual and social relations. These plays—all written around 1602–04—are concerned with basic elements of life, sex, and death, and the psychological and social complications they give rise to. These issues are problematic, and the plays further stress this by pointedly offering no clear-cut resolutions, leaving audiences with a painful awareness of life's difficulties.

Many people find the plays difficult to enjoy because of various other disturbing qualities. All three feature a number of unpleasant characters, villainous or misanthropic or both, such as Thersites and Pandarus of *Troilus and Cressida*, Parolles and Bertram of *All's Well That Ends Well*, and Angelo of *Measure for Measure*. The plays all end unsatisfactorily to most tastes, with a bleak and inconclusive denouement for *Troilus and Cressida*, and with arbitrary and unconvincing "solutions" imposed on the other two. Perhaps most dismaying

to modern tastes, psychologically astute characterizations clash with extremely artificial plotting in a disjunction that seems to weaken both the realism and the fantasy in all three plays.

The unpleasant aspects of the problem plays have led some commentators to suggest that they reflect some corresponding unpleasantness in Shakespeare's life, and that they were written by an embittered man who had recently undergone some psychological trauma, the nature of which can only be guessed at. Lack of evidence has not inhibited speculation, and a romantic crisis such as that described in the *Sonnets*, the execution of Robert Devereux, Earl of ESSEX, and the death of Shakespeare's father in 1601 have all been suggested as causes of the playwright's presumed unhappiness. However, most scholars believe that no such personal explanation is necessary. The problem plays are not so much sad as they are scathing; each is placed in a distinctive and highly stylized social milieu, and their plots do not present realistic personal situations. In all these respects it seems more likely that their peculiar nature was generated by dramatic considerations rather than personal ones. The period saw a strong fashion for social satire, led by the biting comedies of Ben JONSON, and the problem plays are clearly part of this trend in JACOBEAN DRAMA. Moreover, the accession of JAMES I in 1603 stimulated a lot of theorizing about society that is reflected in the problem plays, especially *Measure for Measure*.

The origin of the term *problem play* lends support to the view that the plays were conceived as public discourse rather than private lament. The phrase was first applied to these plays—plus the slightly earlier TRAGEDY, *Hamlet*—by the Shakespearean scholar Frederick S. BOAS in his book *Shakspere and his Predecessors* (1896). He took the term from the contemporary theater of his day. In the 1890s "problem play" was a new expression coined to deal with a new sort of drama—for example, the work of Ibsen, George Bernard SHAW, and others—that dealt frankly and purposefully with social problems. Thus, the term as applied to Shakespeare's plays has implications about the playwright's intentions: These works are, indeed, profoundly concerned with society and its discontents.

At the close of both *All's Well* and *Measure for Measure*, villainy is exposed, its effects are corrected, and faults are forgiven in an air of general reconciliation. The effect is one of moral instruction, and, in fact, all three plays are distinguished by a pronounced emphasis on ethical questions. In *All's Well* the native worth of an individual is valued above aristocratic social standing, and the value of forgiveness is stressed in its conclusion. *Measure for Measure* addresses the nature of good and bad governance, the evils of extreme and inflexible moral positions, and, again, the value of forgiveness. *Troilus and Cressida* offers a scathing critique of the soldierly pretensions to honor and of the dishonesties of fashionable courtship in a context that exposes the futility of war.

Less baldly satirical than Jonson's work, the problem plays were perhaps found too serious and troubling by their original audiences, for all three plays were badly received when they were new, and they continued to be decidedly unpopular for three centuries thereafter. They have only been widely accepted in recent times, perhaps because the modern era is inclined both to the analysis of human problems and to a fear that they may not be easily solved. Commentators such as Shaw and Walter PATER instituted a reappraisal of the problem plays in the 1870s and 1880s, and William POEL's productions of all three, between 1895 and 1905, began a process of theatrical rediscovery that has not stopped. Since the 1930s the plays have been staged regularly, and they will doubtless continue to attract producers and audiences. Their problematic aspects seem fitted to our problematic times; Shaw, writing in 1907, said that in these works Shakespeare was "ready and willing to start at the twentieth century if the seventeenth would only let him."

With greater acceptance, the positive aspects of the problem plays have become more evident. Certain seeming defects have more virtue than is immediately apparent. For instance, the employment of the "bed trick" by Helena in *All's Well* and Isabella in *Measure for Measure*, along with Cressida's hasty abandonment of Troilus, are often seen as ill-motivated perversions of the characters' personalities. However, these events have significant symbolic functions, though they may not make sense psychologically. In the problem plays the point is not simply personality but also situation, not merely reality but also ideas. These intellectual aspects need not inhibit theatrical pleasure, for all three plays contain inspiring parts for actors. These include some unattractive figures, such as Thersites and Parolles, and also such splendid non-villains as Isabella, Helena, and Ulysses (*Troilus and Cressida*). Even some of the lesser parts, such as the Countess of *All's Well*, are notable for fine speeches and a sympathetic presence. Moreover, all three plays offer genuinely funny passages, and several roles—such as Lucio (in *Measure for Measure*); Ajax, Thersites, and Pandarus (in *Troilus and Cressida*); and Parolles (in *All's Well That Ends Well*)—that are fine vehicles for good comic actors. Especially in performance, the plays have a comedic focus that makes them less dark than the ideas they deal with.

This bright aspect lends its emotional tone to another important factor, one that was more popular in the 17th century than it is today. Except in the case of *Troilus and Cressida*, the plays display marked religious overtones, specifically suggestive of Christian redemption. Both Helena and Isabella have been seen as intentionally symbolic of God's grace, and the title of *Measure for Measure* alludes to the Sermon on the Mount. The appallingly deficient moral character of Bertram and Angelo, the male protagonists of these two plays, is also a powerful symbol in such a context, for these undeserving cads have but one purpose: to sin and be forgiven. These characters are similar to the central figures in medieval MORALITY PLAYS, which were still a living tradition for Shakespeare and his original audiences.

Once we understand that moral issues are the plays' raison d'être, we can adjust to the symbolic aspects of character and the allegorical nature of some of the plotting. The extent to which moral questions are stressed makes clear their importance to Shakespeare, and his refusal to provide easy answers to them makes them particularly potent. Shakespeare recognizes, as always, the complexity of life and the difficulty in making moral judgments. The capacity of these plays to disturb causes us to be more engaged in these questions; we become aware of the need to strive after ideals, to pursue and believe in virtue even though we, like the figures in the plays, may not fully achieve it.

prologue Dramatic device in ELIZABETHAN DRAMA, a speech introducing a play. Sixteenth-century plays often opened with a prologue spoken by an allegorical figure—sometimes actually called the Prologue (as in *Henry V*)—commonly dressed in a distinctive black velvet cloak. He remarked briefly on the action to come, preparing the audience to respond appropriately. Elizabethan playwrights borrowed the prologue from Roman drama, which in turn had taken it from ancient Greek drama. Five of Shakespeare's plays begin with a prologue: *Romeo and Juliet* (see CHORUS); *Henry V, Troilus and Cressida, Pericles* (see GOWER, JOHN); and *The Two Noble Kinsmen*. In addition, three plays within a play present brief prologues, those in *A Midsummer Night's Dream* (5.1.108–117), *Hamlet* (3.2.143–146), and *The Two Noble Kinsmen* (3.5.101–133).

promptbook Copy of a play used during performances by the prompter, called the book-holder in ELIZABETHAN THEATER. A promptbook contained notes for entrances and exits, music cues, cuts in the text made by the company during rehearsals, and so on. Because the author's manuscript, or FOUL PAPERS, was often difficult to use in this way, a promptbook was usually a transcript made for the purpose and then annotated. Sometimes, however, if a play was already published when a promptbook was required, a printed copy would be annotated. The promptbook was usually the text presented to the MASTER OF REVELS for approval, before a play could be staged. Since the promptbook was the acting company's official copy of a play—and probably the only one—its loss was too dangerous to risk by lending it to a publisher to be printed from. Thus only a few of Shakespeare's plays were first printed from a promptbook, presumably when another version was not available. Texts printed from promptbooks are characterized by the appearance of actors' names for those of characters, the placing of stage directions a few lines before they are needed, instructions for sound effects, and warnings of upcoming requirements for stage properties.

Prynne, William (1600–1669) Puritan pamphleteer and opponent of the theater. In his *Histriomastix, The Players Scourge* (1633), Prynne declared that "popular stage-plays . . . are sinfull, heathenish, lewde, ungodly Spectacles" and called people who wrote, acted in, or attended plays "unlawful, infamous and misbeseeming Christians." Prynne's attack was only one example of Puritan hostility toward drama, and Puritan culture increasingly dominated English life from the 1580s on. After 1642, as the civil wars began and a revolutionary government controlled first London and later the country, the theaters of England were closed for 18 years (but see DROLL).

Prynne's career also offers an impressive demonstration of the barbarous rigor of the law in 17th-century England. *Historiomastix* contained references to the just downfalls of monarchs, and insulted the queen for appearing in MASQUES. Because of this, Prynne was imprisoned for life, fined a huge amount of money, and had his ears cut off. He managed to publish from prison a pamphlet that attacked English bishops, and was therefore branded on both cheeks with the letters "S. L." (for "seditious libeller"). With the approach of the revolution, he was freed in 1640. He was elected to Parliament, but he continued to attack various aspects of the revolution itself, and in 1650 he was again imprisoned for three years. Prynne finally mellowed somewhat and avoided further prosecution, though he did not cease his public commentaries. In the course of his career he published over 200 books and pamphlets. He supported the restoration of the monarchy in 1660, served again in Parliament, and was appointed to a clerical position at the TOWER OF LONDON, where he had once been imprisoned.

Purcell, Henry (ca. 1659–1695) English composer, creator of music for several adaptations of Shakespeare's plays. Perhaps the greatest English composer, Purcell led the creation of an English baroque style in music. He is best known today for two OPERAS: *The Fairy Queen* (1692), with a libretto taken by Thomas BETTERTON from *A Midsummer*

Night's Dream (but which contains none of Shakespeare's lines); and *Dido and Aeneas* (1689), parts of which were incorporated in Charles GILDON's 1699 adaptation of *Measure for Measure*. He also composed music for a 1690 revival of Thomas SHADWELL's *The Enchanted Island,* an operatic version of *The Tempest* (as adapted by John DRYDEN and William DAVENANT), and Shadwell's 1694 adaptation of *Timon of Athens.* However, in all these works, the only words of Shakespeare set to music by Purcell are two SONGs in *The Tempest,* "Come unto these yellow sands" (1.2.377–389) and "Full fadom five" (1.2.399–407).

Puritan, The Anonymous play formerly attributed to Shakespeare, part of the Shakespeare APOCRYPHA. *The Puritan,* sometimes called *The Puritan Widow* (its full title was *The Puritan or The Widdow of Watling-Streete*), is a farce with a pointed anti-Puritan bias. It was published by George ELD in 1607 as "written by W. S.," possibly with the intention of associating the play with Shakespeare. It was also included among Shakespeare's plays in the Third and Fourth FOLIOS and in the editions of Nicholas ROWE and Alexander POPE. Scholars are confident, however, that *The Puritan* was not written by Shakespeare. Although it is a better drama than most of the apocryphal plays, it bears no resemblance to Shakespeare's known works as it is a topical satire set in contemporary London and written mostly in prose. Stylistically, it is tentatively ascribed by many scholars to John MARSTON or Thomas MIDDLETON.

Puttenham, George (ca. 1529–1590), or **Puttenham, Richard** (ca. 1520–1601) English writer, author of a book of literary theory that is parodied in *King Lear. The Arte of English Poesie* (1589) appeared anonymously; William CAMDEN referred to it as the work of "Maister Puttenham," but it is not known which of the two Puttenham brothers, George or Richard, wrote the book, so it is traditionally ascribed to "Puttenham." Puttenham's manual of style critiques the best-known English poets and is considered the first impor-

tant work of English poetry criticism. It also analyzes rhetorical and poetic devices and advises on language usage. Puttenham inveighs against the use of archaic or foreign terms and suggests adopting the accents of LONDON and the royal court. Several passages in Shakespeare's plays (e.g., *All's Well* 2.3.293–294) echo Puttenham's wording, and the prophecy of the Fool in *King Lear* (3.2.79–96) is a parody of some lines attributed to CHAUCER in the book. *The Arte of English Poesie* was published by Shakespeare's friend, Richard FIELD, and it is possible the playwright knew its author.

Pyramus and Thisbe Title of the play within *A Midsummer Night's Dream,* an INTERLUDE performed at the wedding of Duke Theseus and Queen Hippolyta. The play is enacted in 5.1 by a group led by Peter Quince, artisans of ATHENS whom Shakespeare portrays as humorous English rustics. Nick Bottom, an excellent Shakespearean CLOWN, plays the romantic lead in a comic manner. Theseus generously gives a dignified reception to the preposterous production, although his bride is less tolerant, declaring the play to be ridiculous, which of course Shakespeare meant it to be.

The story of Pyramus and Thisbe was familiar to Shakespeare through OVID's *Metamorphoses,* but even illiterate members of his audience will have known it, for Pyramus and Thisbe figured in several Elizabethan popular songs. The ancient Greek myth tells of the love of a boy and girl, Pyramus and Thisbe, who live in neighboring buildings but whose parents have forbidden them to meet. Able to communicate only through a hole in the wall between their homes, the lovers agree to elope. Thisbe arrives at their rendezvous early. Frightened by a lion, she hides in a cave but loses her cloak as she flees. The lion has just eaten and has a bloody mouth; nuzzling her garment, he bloodies it. When Pyramus arrives, he sees the bloodstained cloak and lion's tracks and concludes that Thisbe has been killed by the animal. Heartsick, he kills himself with his sword. When Thisbe reappears and sees what has happened, she seizes his sword and kills herself.

This tale, although burlesqued by the artisans' production, provides an illuminating counterpart to the elopement of Lysander and Hermia earlier in *A Midsummer Night's Dream.* It demonstrates, in a harmless context, the potential for tragedy that the lovers' predicament harbored. The contrast heightens our pleasure in the benevolent outcome that has actually occurred.

Shakespeare's parody is not directed at Ovid's classic version, but rather at the bombast and theatrical heroics in 16th-century drama, especially that of Thomas PRESTON. In addition, two minor modifications of Ovid's tale stand out. Quince's original casting of the interlude (1.2.56–59) includes the lovers' parents, who are merely mentioned in Ovid, and Bottom's assertion that the wall had "parted their fathers" (5.1.338) introduces an interfamily feud that does not exist in Ovid. Both additions suggest aspects of *Romeo and Juliet,* and it is thought that Shakespeare's use of the legend in this fashion reflects his recent composition of that play.

Q

quarto Format for a book or page. A quarto is a sheet of paper that is folded in half twice, yielding four leaves or eight pages. It is also a book composed of such pages (see FOLIO). Most of the early editions of Shakespeare's plays were produced in this format, and the term is often used to refer to these editions. Some of these came from authoritative sources that accurately reflected what Shakespeare wrote, such as his FOUL PAPERS; these are known as GOOD QUARTOS. Others, whose text was reconstructed by actors from memory, are seriously flawed in various ways and are known as BAD QUARTOS. Of the 38 plays in the CANON, 22 were initially published as quartos. However, there are 10 Bad Quartos and 14 Good Quartos, for *Romeo and Juliet* and *Hamlet* appeared in both Good Quarto and Bad Quarto editions.

Quayle, Anthony (1913–1989) British actor and director. On both stage and screen, Quayle played a variety of Shakespearean parts—including Bottom, Pandarus, Othello, and Falstaff—as well as other roles in both classic and modern drama. He was director of the Shakespeare Memorial Theatre at STRATFORD from 1948 to 1956. He wrote two novels—*Eight Hours from England* (1945) and *On Such a Night* (1947)—based on his wartime service as a leader of guerrilla bands behind Nazi lines in Europe. Quayle is probably most widely remembered for several non-Shakespearean movie roles, in *The Guns of Navarone* (1961), *Lawrence of Arabia* (1963), and *Anne of a Thousand Days* (1970). In the latter he played Cardinal Thomas Wolsey.

Queen's Men (Queen Elizabeth's Men) Acting company of the ELIZABETHAN THEATER, possibly Shakespeare's first theatrical home. The Queen's Men were created by order of Queen Elizabeth I (see Elizabeth I in *Henry VIII*) in 1583; at the queen's command, her MASTER OF REVELS raided other acting companies for some of their finest players. The Queen's Men consequently became the most popular and important LONDON acting company for almost a decade. Its original members included John BENTLEY (who killed a man at an early Queen's Men performance), the great comic actor Richard TARLTON, John SINGER (another comic actor), and Robert WILSON. The Queen's Men performed in London in the winter, at the THEATRE and at the court, and toured the provinces in the summer. In the summer of 1587, they played in STRATFORD, a fact that has encouraged speculation that Shakespeare may have gone with them to London to begin his career (see KNELL, WILLIAM).

After Tarlton's death in 1588, the fortunes of the Queen's Men declined, and two newer companies, the ADMIRAL'S MEN and STRANGE'S MEN, began to dominate the theatrical scene. Between 1591 and 1594 the Queen's Men performed only twice at court, a measure of their declining prestige. In the latter year, they allied themselves with SUSSEX'S MEN, but to no avail; unable to compete in London, they converted themselves into a full-time provincial touring company, surviving until the queen's death in 1603.

Queen's Men Seventeenth-century LONDON theatrical company, successor to WORCESTER'S MEN.

Upon the accession of King JAMES I in 1603, his family assumed the patronage of the three London theater companies. His queen, Anne of Denmark (1574–1619), gave her name to Worcester's Men, the least important of the three, whose chief members were the actor Christopher BEESTON and the playwright Thomas HEYWOOD. When the company's royal patent was issued the next year, they were said to perform regularly at an inn, where they had existed as Worcester's, and at the CURTAIN THEATRE, a new venue for them. In 1609, when the patent was renewed, the locations named are the Curtain and the Red Bull Theatre, a new playhouse. After 1617 they performed at the Phoenix Theatre, owned by Beeston. Beeston managed the company from 1612—ineptly and perhaps dishonestly, as the records of several lawsuits reveal—until the company dissolved on the death of Queen Anne in 1619.

Queen's Revels   See CHILDREN'S COMPANIES.

Quin, James (1693–1766) British actor. The chief rival to David GARRICK in the 1730s and 1740s, Quin was renowned for his portrayal of Falstaff, though he also played Brutus, Othello, Macbeth, the Ghost in *Hamlet,* and other parts. He is considered the last great representative of the formal and declamatory school of acting that had been popular in the second half of the 17th century but was supplanted by the more naturalistic and active mode of Garrick. Quin appears in Tobias Smollett's great novel *Humphrey Clinker* (1771).

Quiney, Judith Shakespeare   See SHAKESPEARE, JUDITH.

Quiney, Richard (before 1557–1602) Businessman in STRATFORD, an acquaintance of Shakespeare. Quiney was a dealer in fine cloth, a partner with his father, Adrian (d. 1607; a friend of Shakespeare's father, John SHAKESPEARE). He was evidently a respected businessman, for he represented the town of Stratford at the court of Queen Elizabeth I on several occasions, and sought government relief for the town after the great fires of 1594 and 1595.

Quiney's surviving correspondence contains several references to Shakespeare as well as the only extant letter addressed to the playwright (though it was apparently never delivered). While in LONDON in January 1598, Quiney received a letter from another Stratford businessman suggesting that he try to interest Shakespeare in a real-estate deal they were contemplating, and in October, again in London, he wrote a letter to the playwright asking for a loan to cover extra expenses resulting from an unforeseen delay. He apparently did not deliver this missive, which remained among his papers still sealed, probably because he was able to make his request in person; another letter of the same date, to Abraham STURLEY, reports that Shakespeare promised assistance. Later during the same visit, Quiney received a letter from his father that mentions Shakespeare in connection with an otherwise obscure business deal. In addition to establishing Shakespeare's presence in London at these times, these letters also make clear the playwright's continuing involvement with the affairs of his home town.

Quiney opposed the attempt of a neighboring nobleman, Sir Edward Greville, to enclose the town commons for sheep grazing. A drunken group of Greville's followers roughed him up one night in May 1602, and he died from his injuries. His widow was left with nine children under the age of 20, one of whom, Thomas QUINEY, became Shakespeare's son-in-law.

Quiney, Thomas (1589–ca. 1652) Vintner in STRATFORD and Shakespeare's son-in-law. Quiney, the son of Richard QUINEY, ran a tavern and apparently had a reputation as a rake when he married Judith SHAKESPEARE in February 1616. They were wed during Lent without obtaining the necessary special license, for which he was briefly excommunicated. Within a month he was in worse trouble, for when one Margaret Wheeler died in childbirth in March, Quiney was named as the father of the child (who also died). He was ordered to appear as a penitent, wearing a white sheet, in the parish church on three successive Sundays, though he avoided this public disgrace by paying a fine. It has been speculated that this scandal may have hastened Shakespeare's death, for he died a few weeks later, after changing his will to protect Judith's inheritance from Quiney. Quiney established a wine and tobacco shop, but he was an unsuccessful businessman, and the shop was eventually run by trustees who assigned him a yearly allowance. The Quineys' three sons all died young. Quiney is thought to have died while visiting a brother in London sometime after 1655, though no record of his death has survived.

R

Raleigh, Walter (Walter Ralegh) (ca. 1552–1618) English soldier, seaman, explorer, and writer. Raleigh, son of an obscure country gentleman, became a favorite of Queen Elizabeth I (see Elizabeth I in *Henry VIII*) through a combination of personal charm and a successful military career, including naval raids against Spanish overseas territories. During the 1580s Raleigh organized and financed several colonizing expeditions to the New World—including the famous lost colony on Roanoke Island, North Carolina—but no successful settlements resulted. He also explored the Orinoco River in South America, in search of El Dorado, the legendary city of gold.

In addition Raleigh was a poet, accepted as a literary equal by his friends Edmund SPENSER and Christopher MARLOWE. He wrote many poems that were circulated in manuscript, and those that have survived place him among the better poets of his day. (At least one of Raleigh's poems, "The Nymph's Reply to the Shepherd," was attributed to Shakespeare in the *Poems* published by John BENSON in 1640; also, one stanza of it—linked with the Marlowe poem to which it replies—was attributed to Shakespeare in THE PASSIONATE PILGRIM.)

A man of great intellectual curiosity, Raleigh dabbled in the magical doctrines and esoteric knowledge that were part of the budding science of the RENAISSANCE. These activities raised widespread suspicion that he was an atheist; combined with his arrogant disdain for other people's opinions, this made him generally unpopular. In 1597 he quarreled with Robert Devereux, Earl of ESSEX, over the conduct of the naval war against Spain, and they remained enemies thereafter. This feud aggravated Raleigh's unpopularity. Shakespeare may have subtly sided against Raleigh in the obscure jests of *Love's Labour's Lost*, where he seemingly parodies the circle of George CHAPMAN—which included Raleigh—for its interest in magic. The playwright may have taken such a position on behalf of his patron, Henry Wriothesley, Earl of SOUTHAMPTON, a follower of Essex, but he may also have felt a personal aversion to the reputedly irreligious and arrogant Raleigh.

King JAMES I certainly felt such an aversion, and he accepted the accusations of conspiracy brought by Raleigh's enemies, especially Robert CECIL, and imprisoned him. Raleigh was held in the TOWER OF LONDON from 1603 to 1616, during which time he began his *History of the World*, which, though incomplete, is now considered to be one of the best prose works of the day. He was released in order to conduct another search for El Dorado on the king's behalf, but with the condition that he not attack the Spanish, whom James was pursuing as allies. However, while in South America, Raleigh raided a Spanish settlement, and on his return he was executed for treason.

Ratsey, Gamaliel (d. 1605) English highwayman and theatergoer. Ratsey was hung for his crimes in March 1605, and later in the year an anonymous biography of him, *Ratseis Ghost*, appeared, of which a single copy survives. In one episode of it, Ratsey displays a fondness for theater and an awareness of current LONDON enthusiasms.

The highwayman reportedly hired a traveling company of actors to perform for him at an inn. He delivered a detailed critique of their profession in which he complained of actors who "are grown so wealthy that they have expected to be knighted"—a possible reference to Shakespeare's acquisition of a COAT OF ARMS. Nevertheless, he paid his players 40 shillings, twice what they expected. However, the next day he robbed them on the highway, getting back his 40 shillings and more. Before he left them he amused himself by advising the leading actor to go to London to pursue his career. He remarked on the fame of "one man"—meaning Richard BURBAGE—as Hamlet and elaborated on the possibility of earning enough money to "buy thee some place or lordship in the country." He was perhaps referring to the success of Shakespeare—who had bought NEW PLACE in STRATFORD eight years earlier—or, more probably, that of William ALLEYN, who had bought a country manor in 1603.

Redgrave, Michael (1908–1985) British actor. Redgrave, the son of actors, was briefly a teacher before turning to the theater in 1934. After World War II he divided his time between stage and FILM. His Shakespearean parts included Hamlet—on several stages, including that at ELSINORE—Lear, Macbeth, Antony, and Shylock (The Merchant of Venice). He also wrote two plays and a book on acting. He was knighted in 1959. His daughters Vanessa (b. 1937) and Lynn (b. 1943) are well-known actresses of stage and film.

Reed, Isaac (1742–1807) British scholar, editor of the First VARIORUM EDITION of Shakespeare's works. Reed, the son of a London baker, became a lawyer but eventually focused largely on literature. He published editions of old plays and wrote Biographia Dramatica (1782), a collection of critical biographies of English playwrights. Reed was a close friend of the Shakespearean scholar George STEEVENS, and he helped edit Steevens's 1785 edition of Shakespeare's works. As his friend's literary executor, he posthumously expanded his 1778 edition of Shakespeare into the First Variorum, and he revised and augmented Steevens's already copious annotations.

Rehan, Ada (1860–1916) American actress. Born Ada Crehan (a printer's error in a playbill gave her a stage name), Rehan was for many years the leading actress in Augustin DALY's New York company. She specialized in classical comedy and played several of Shakespeare's heroines, including Rosalind in As You Like It, Viola in Twelfth Night, and the part for which she was best known, Katherina in The Taming of the Shrew.

Reimann, Aribert (b. 1936) German composer of a modern OPERA based on King Lear. Reimann, a composer of complex music much influenced by Alban Berg (1885–1935), has written a number of operas on texts ranging from Euripides to Kafka, including Lear (1978; libretto based on the translation by J. J. ESCHENBURG; see TRANSLATION OF SHAKESPEARE). His Lear is a powerful work featuring explosive orchestral effects, passages of string-quartet music, and elements from jazz.

Reinhardt, Max (1873–1943) German theatrical producer. In the early 20th century, after 10 years as a notable character actor (specializing in old men), Reinhardt began his career as a leading avant-garde director of the classics, especially Shakespeare and the ancient Greek drama. To involve the spectators more closely than before, he extended the stage into the auditorium, where it was surrounded on three sides by seats, and he used rhythmic movements of crowds of players to sweep the audience into the world of the play. (He is still considered the greatest master of crowd scenes.) His use of a revolving stage quickened the pace and variety of scenes; he also added dramatic lighting and scenic effects.

Reinhardt worked mostly in Berlin until 1920 and in Vienna until 1933, but he periodically produced plays in London and New York as well. In 1933 he fled the Nazi regime and lived in America for the rest of his life. Reinhardt's revolutionary techniques were both acclaimed and condemned. Particularly notable among his Shakespearean productions were his 1912 staging of A Midsummer Night's Dream (which he later made as a FILM starring James Cagney and Mickey Rooney [1935]) and his 1921 presentation of The Merchant of Venice in a notorious blue and white cubist set.

Renaissance Period of rich development in European culture that marked the end of the Middle Ages and the beginning of the modern era. The Renaissance arose in ITALY in the 14th century and spread throughout Europe over the next 300 years, continuing its development in peripheral regions such as England through the first half of the 17th century. Characterized by humanism, which proposed a focus on human nature and individual expression in art and literature, the Renaissance was sparked by an enthusiasm for the newly rediscovered cultural worlds of classical Greece and Rome. The period saw extraordinary developments in more mundane areas as well, as secular governments emerged from the dominance of the medieval church, the modern commercial world of banks and debt-financed development arose, and Europe's expansion into the New World, southern Africa, and Asia began. Printing magnified all these effects by permitting an unprecedented diffusion of ideas. The Reformation translated the age's spirit into new religious movements in many parts of northern Europe, including England, and a revitalized Counter-Reformation Catholic Church elsewhere.

In England the Renaissance began in the early 16th century, though its greatest development was during the reign of Queen Elizabeth (1558–1603). The grandest accomplishments of the English Renaissance were in literature, especially in poetry and ELIZABETHAN DRAMA. Its leading figures in poetry were Edmund SPENSER, Philip SIDNEY, and Shakespeare, and in drama, Shakespeare, Christopher MARLOWE, and Ben JONSON. The leading writers of prose included Thomas MORE and Francis Bacon (1561–1626). A flood of translations from Latin, Greek, and contemporary European languages enlivened England's intellectual life. John FLORIO's translation of MONTAIGNE, Arthur GOLDING's version of OVID's *Metamorphoses,* and Thomas NORTH's rendering of PLUTARCH stand out. In philosophy, *The Laws of Ecclesiastical Polity* (1593–97) by Richard Hooker (ca. 1554–1600) established a Protestant doctrine of religious government in elegant prose.

Respighi, Ottorino (1879–1936) Italian composer of an OPERA based on *The Rape of Lucrece.* Best known for the immensely popular orchestral work, *The Fountains of Rome* (1915–16), Respighi wrote several operas, among them *Lucrezia,* the only full-scale work based on Shakespeare's poem. Begun in 1933, it was not quite finished at his death but was completed by his widow and a student of his and premiered in 1937. It has rarely been performed since, but Benjamin BRITTEN was to base his own small-scale version, the chamber opera *The Rape of Lucrece* (1946), on it.

revenge play Genre of ELIZABETHAN and JACOBEAN DRAMA, represented in Shakespeare's work by *Titus Andronicus* and *Hamlet.* A revenge play is a drama of retribution in which an evil is avenged—and often the vengeance itself repaid—in a series of bloody and horrible deeds. Often called the horror movies of their time, revenge plays were intended to be spectacular theatrical events, and they were extremely popular. On stage they typically featured murders and physical mutilations, insanity (or feigned insanity), and supernatural visitations, all enacted in a bravura style colored by extravagant imagery and bold rhetoric. Thomas KYD, with his *The Spanish Tragedy* (ca. 1587), led English playwrights in the development of the genre, which was based largely on the works of the Roman dramatist SENECA. Other notable revenge plays include *The White Devil* (1612) and *The Duchess of Malfi* (1613–14) by John WEBSTER, George CHAPMAN's *Bussy D'Ambois* (ca. 1604), and the mysterious UR-HAMLET.

Of Shakespeare's two full-scale revenge plays, *Titus* is a perfect example of the genre, but *Hamlet* is somewhat restrained by a more complex attitude toward retribution. Shakespeare also included elements from the genre in other works, especially *Richard III, Julius Caesar,* and *Macbeth.*

Reynolds, Frederick (1764–1841) English playwright and theatrical entrepreneur, producer of operatic versions of several of Shakespeare's plays. Reynolds altered Shakespeare's texts freely, cutting large sections and often combining elements from several plays. Most of the scores for these light operas were written by Henry Rowley BISHOP, though he sometimes employed music written for other purposes by such composers as Mozart and

Thomas ARNE. Reynolds's Shakespearean productions were *A Midsummer Night's Dream* (1816), *The Comedy of Errors* (1819), *Twelfth Night* (1820), *Two Gentlemen of Verona* (1821), *The Tempest* (1821), *The Merry Wives of Windsor* (1824), and *The Taming of the Shrew* (1828). As a young man, Reynolds was educated as a lawyer but turned to the theater instead. He wrote more than 200 plays, the first of which was produced in 1785. They were mostly light comedies and melodramas; his most popular work, *The Caravan* (1803), featured a live dog that performed an onstage rescue of a child from a tank of water.

Reynolds, William (1575–1633)   Resident of STRATFORD and friend of Shakespeare. In his will, Shakespeare left Reynolds money to buy a memorial ring, a common gesture of friendship, but no more is known of their relationship. Reynolds was a Catholic whose family sheltered a Jesuit priest in the dangerous days of the early 17th century, when anti-Catholic feeling ran high in England. He prospered, however, and died one of the principal landowners of Stratford.

rhyme royal   Verse pattern in which a stanza has seven lines, each in iambic pentameter (see METER), rhyming *ababbcc*. Rhyme royal is used in *The Rape of Lucrece* and *The Lover's Complaint*; each of these works is a COMPLAINT, a genre for which the pattern was recommended by 16th-century treatises on poetry. This practice was doubtless inspired by CHAUCER's great use of rhyme royal, which is still sometimes called the Chaucerian stanza. Rhyme royal dominated English poetry in the 15th and 16th centuries. It went out of style entirely in the early 17th century, although it has reappeared occasionally in recent times—e.g., in long poems by John Masefield and W. H. AUDEN. Rhyme royal is a form of great flexibility and power, capable of carrying a sustained narrative without becoming monotonous, and its subtle rhyming is well suited to a wide range of effects, from simple description to ironic witticism.

Rice, John (active 1607–1630)   English actor, a member of the KING'S MEN and one of the 26 men listed in the FIRST FOLIO as the "Principall Actors" in Shakespeare's plays. As a boy actor, Rice was the apprentice of John HEMINGE in 1607. He is thought to have been considered the best boy actor in the company, for twice, in 1607 and 1610, the King's Men paired him with their leading actor, Richard BURBAGE, when they provided players for ceremonial occasions. In 1611 Rice was a member of the LADY ELIZABETH'S MEN, but he rejoined the King's Men in 1619. No record of Rice as an actor has survived after 1625, but he is probably the "John Rice, clerk of St Saviour's" mentioned by Heminge in his will (1630), so it appears that he retired from the stage and became a church official.

Rich, Barnabe (Barnaby Riche) (ca. 1540–1617)   Contemporary of Shakespeare, author of the principal source of *Twelfth Night*. Rich was a soldier who retired from a career of active campaigning in Europe and Ireland and turned to literature. He wrote several tracts on military and political matters, but he is best known for a collection of romantic tales, derived mostly from Italian originals. One, entitled "Apolonius and Silla"—taken from a tale by François BELLEFOREST, who had it from an anonymous Italian play, *Gl'Ingannati*—provided Shakespeare with the main plot of *Twelfth Night*. Another of Rich's tales may have inspired Falstaff's departure in a laundry basket in 3.3 of *The Merry Wives of Windsor*.

Rich, John (1692–1761)   British theatrical producer. Rich was a comic actor who popularized the COMMEDIA DELL'ARTE character Harlequin in England, but he is much better known as a theatrical entrepreneur. Rich staged a number of Shakespeare's plays with a company whose leading player was James QUIN. Rich's productions of *Measure for Measure* (1720) and *Much Ado About Nothing* (1721) were especially important, in that they restored much of Shakespeare's text after William DAVENANT's radical alterations. Rich was the founder of London's Covent Garden Theatre in 1733. In the 1750s he produced *Romeo and Juliet* with Spranger BARRY as Romeo, in rivalry with David GARRICK's presentation, in the "*Romeo and Juliet* war."

Richard II, King of England   See Richard II, King of England, in *Richard II*.

Richard III, King of England   See Richard III, King of England, in *Richard III*; Gloucester, Richard Plantagenet, Duke of, in *Henry VI, Part 3*.

Richardson, John (d. 1594)   Farmer near STRAT- FORD, a friend of Anne HATHAWAY's family. In 1581 Richardson witnessed the will of Anne's father, Richard Hathaway, and in November 1582 he and Fulk SANDELLS posted a bond necessary for Anne's marriage to Shakespeare, who was a minor; they agreed to pay £40 to the church if the wedding proved unlawful. Nothing more is known of Richard- son, except that he was a prosperous husbandman who owned £87 and 130 sheep when he died.

Richardson, Ralph (1902–1983)   British actor. Richardson began his career in 1921, playing Lorenzo in *The Merchant of Venice*. By 1926 he was acting under Barry JACKSON in the Birmingham Repertory Theatre. In 1930 he joined the OLD VIC THEATRE, with which he was chiefly associated until 1949. Among his best-known Shakespearean roles were Falstaff, Bottom, and Sir Toby Belch, though he also played a wide range of other parts. He appeared as Buckingham in Laurence OLIVIER's FILM of *Richard III*. With Olivier and John GIELGUD, Richardson is considered one of the greatest Shakespearean actors of the 20th century.

Roberts, James (active 1564–1608)   Printer and publisher in LONDON, producer of several editions of Shakespeare's plays. Roberts's play publications are complicated by unusual circumstances and have been the subject of much scholarly controversy. As a publisher, he specialized in almanacs and playbills but otherwise mostly printed for other publishers. In his long career he only registered five (possibly nine) plays with the STATIONERS' COMPANY—all within five years and all belonging to Shakespeare's CHAMBERLAIN'S MEN. Four of them were registered as "to be stayed" (i.e., explicitly not to be published without further authorization); in any event, he did not publish any of them. Scholars speculate that Roberts was attempting either to protect the plays from piracy on behalf of the Chamberlain's Men or to pirate them himself, though both theories are dif- ficult to sustain. One of the five plays (two if he reg- istered nine) was in fact pirated, so the first theory seems weak. Yet since Roberts himself didn't publish any and printed only two—both from reliable and thus presumably unpirated texts—the second idea seem misplaced. The problem is probably insoluble without further evidence.

In 1598 Roberts registered *The Merchant of Venice* to be stayed; in 1600 he transferred his rights in the play to Thomas HEYES, who then hired him to print an apparently legitimate edition of the play (Q1, 1600). Also in 1600 the printer registered two more Chamberlain's Men plays to be stayed, neither of them by Shakespeare and neither eventually printed by Roberts. (An adjoining entry names four other Chamberlain's Men plays—including *As You Like It*, *Henry V*, and *Much Ado About Nothing*—that may or may not have been registered by Roberts. One was immediately pirated, one was legitimately published in the same year, and one remained unpublished until the FIRST FOLIO [1623].) In 1602 Roberts registered *Hamlet*, and though no staying order is recorded, he did not publish the play. A BAD QUARTO was put out by Nicholas LING in 1603, and then Roberts printed a GOOD QUARTO for Ling (Q2, 1604). In 1603 Roberts registered one more Shakespeare play, *Troilus and Cressida*; it too was to be stayed, and it too was neither published nor printed by him.

In 1600, in a straightforward, uncontroversial arrangement that is unrelated to the others, Roberts printed the second edition of *Titus Andron- icus* (Q2) for Edward WHITE. In 1619 Thomas PAVIER's FALSE FOLIO erroneously ascribed a back- dated edition of *A Midsummer Night's Dream* to Roberts, though he is not otherwise associated with that play. Roberts sold his business to William JAG- GARD in 1608 and is not recorded thereafter.

Robertson, John Mackinnon (1856–1933)   En- glish literary critic. Robertson was a leading member of the school of so-called disintegrators among Shakespearean scholars. He thought that passages he considered to be of inferior quality must have been written by other, lesser authors, most frequently Christopher MARLOWE or George CHAPMAN. Robertson thought that only one play, *A Midsummer Night's Dream,* was entirely by Shakespeare. He expressed his views in his five-volume *The Shakespeare Canon,* published over 10 years beginning in 1922, and a smaller work, *The Genuine in Shakespeare* (1930). While Robertson's work has been valuable to later scholars, his overall thesis is generally thought to be exaggerated. Robertson was first a journalist and later a leading Member of Parliament. His enthusiasm for Shakespeare led him to scholarship.

Robeson, Paul (1898–1976) African-American actor. Robeson played only one Shakespearean part, Othello, but his American appearances as the Moor were significant to the history of 20th-century theater. Robeson was already well known—both as an actor and singer and as a committed socialist and opponent of racism—when he triumphed in a 1930 London production of *Othello* opposite Peggy ASHCROFT as Desdemona. However, American racism blocked a tour of the United States. Eventually, in 1942 Margaret WEBSTER directed a Robeson *Othello* in America. It played in several cities before it ran for almost 300 performances on Broadway in 1943, then an American record for a Shakespeare play. The production, which was widely publicized

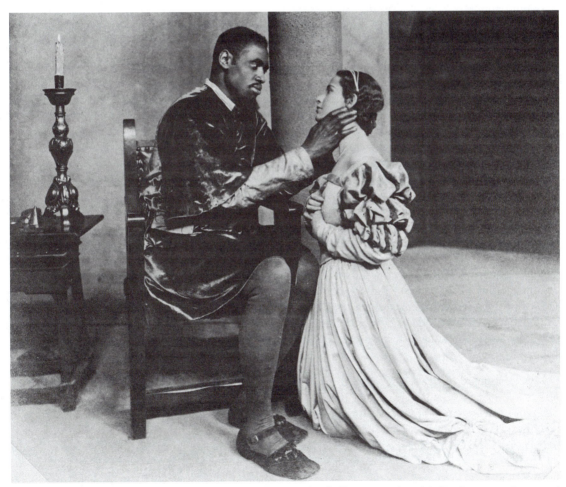

Paul Robeson in the title role of the 1930 London production of *Othello.* Peggy Ashcroft is Desdemona. *(Courtesy of Billy Rose Theatre Collection; New York Public Library at Lincoln Center; Astor, Lenox and Tilden Foundations)*

in *Life* magazine and elsewhere, sparked controversy as bigots objected to interracial casting, and it considerably advanced the cause of civil rights in the American theater. Robeson again played the part in 1950 at STRATFORD.

Robinson, John (active 1616)   Witness to Shakespeare's will. A number of John Robinsons appear in STRATFORD records, but no information—save that one was a "laborer"—is provided about any of them. Like another of the will's witnesses, Robert WHATCOTT, Robinson may have been a servant in the household of either Shakespeare or his daughter Susanna SHAKESPEARE Hall. In LONDON a John Robinson leased Shakespeare's BLACKFRIARS GATEHOUSE in 1616; possibly he was visiting his landlord when the will was signed. In any case, nothing more is known of him.

Robinson, Mary ("Perdita") (1758–1800)   English actress. After a short but successful career on the stage, Mary Robinson became the mistress of the Prince Regent, later King George IV (ruled 1820–30), in 1779. He became infatuated with her when she played Perdita in David GARRICK's version of *The Winter's Tale*, and their love affair—he referred to himself as her Florizel—was followed with delight by the public, who gave her the name by which she is still best known. After Garrick, struck by her great beauty, trained her for a 1776 debut as Juliet, she played several other parts, including Rosalind in *As You Like It*, before her fateful encounter with the prince. When he deserted her after two years, she did not return to the stage for fear of public ridicule. She soon contracted rheumatic fever and lived the rest of her life in various spas, supporting herself with hack literary work.

Robinson, Richard (active ca. 1577–1600)   Contemporary of Shakespeare, a writer and translator. Robinson's translation of the famous *Gesta Romanorum*, a medieval collection of Latin tales, was published in 1577 and 1595 and may have been a source for *The Comedy of Errors* and *The Merchant of Venice*. Robinson was an unsuccessful and impoverished writer who composed many minor works in verse and prose, chiefly on religious subjects.

Robinson, Richard (d. 1648)   English actor, member of the KING'S MEN. Robinson is one of the 26 men listed in the FIRST FOLIO as the "Principall Actors" in Shakespeare's plays, though it is not known which Shakespearean roles he played. He was in part a comedian, though he played straight dramatic roles as well. Robinson first appeared with the King's Men in 1611 as a boy playing women's roles. He was still known as a "lad" in 1616, when Ben JONSON praised his impersonation of a woman in what was apparently a practical joke. By 1619, however, he was old enough to be a witness to the will of Richard BURBAGE, and in the same year he succeeded Richard COWLEY as a partner in the King's Men. He was noted for his collection of "pictures and other rarities." Sometime before 1635, he married Burbage's widow.

Roche, Walter (ca. 1540–after 1604)   Schoolmaster, lawyer, and clergyman in STRATFORD. Roche was master of the Stratford grammar school between 1569 and 1571, before resigning to practice law; he was replaced by Simon HUNT. Roche almost certainly did not teach Shakespeare, who was still one of the younger students and thus taught by an assistant, or usher, when Roche resigned. Nevertheless, Shakespeare certainly knew him in later years, for he remained in Stratford and lived near the Shakespeare household, even during his rectorship of a church in a nearby town (1574–78). He mostly practiced law (on one occasion representing a cousin of the Shakespeares). Later, when Shakespeare was a successful LONDON playwright whose Stratford home was NEW PLACE, Roche lived only three doors away.

Rochester   City in southeastern England, setting of 2.1 of *1 Henry IV*. In an inn in Rochester, the highwayman Gadshill learns from two Carriers that rich Travellers are soon leaving for London, and he gets further details on these potential victims from an accomplice, the Chamberlain of the inn. In 2.2 Gadshill, Falstaff, and others rob the Travellers at nearby GAD'S HILL and are then robbed themselves by Prince Hal and Poins. Rochester was the halfway point on the pilgrims' route between London and Canterbury and was thus fruitful territory for highwaymen.

Rogers, John (active 1605–1619) Vicar in STRATFORD during Shakespeare's later years. Rogers came to Stratford in 1605, after serving in a church in nearby Warwick. After 1611 he lived near Shakespeare's home at NEW PLACE. He was probably the "Jo. Rogers" who witnessed Shakespeare's contract with Arthur Mainwaring during the WELCOMBE enclosures crisis in October 1614. In 1615 the town asked Rogers to intercede with one of the enclosers, William COMBE, but he was unsuccessful. He probably presided at Shakespeare's funeral, though no record has survived. In 1618 the town awarded Rogers a gift of a fur-lined robe but at the same time hoped that he would "amend his former faultes and faylinges." This may be a reference to a scandal alluded to in Francis COLLINS's will, written in 1617, in which he declares that he and Rogers had been cotrustees of a legacy left for the poor, but that the vicar and another lawyer had looted it. On the other hand, when Rogers was removed from office in 1619, public outrage led to riots and accusations of Puritan influence.

Rogers, Phillip (active 1603–1604) Apothecary in STRATFORD, a debtor to Shakespeare. Rogers, a neighbor of the Shakespeares, bought 20 pounds of malt from the household supply of NEW PLACE between March and May of 1604, agreeing to pay later. He also borrowed a small amount of money. The total debt came to a little over £2. He repaid only sixpence, and Shakespeare, at an unknown date, sued him to collect. No record of the outcome has survived. At his apothecary shop, Rogers sold drugs, tobacco, and—after getting a license in 1603—ale, for which he presumably used the playwright's malt.

Rollins, Hyder E. (1889–1958) American Shakespearean scholar. Best known for his massive volumes on the *Sonnets* and other poems (1938–44) in the New VARIORUM EDITION of Shakespeare's works, Rollins was also a respected authority on Elizabethan poetry in general, the popular ballads of early modern Britain, and the work and life of John KEATS. A longtime professor at Harvard, he was the successor to the chair in English literature held by George Lyman KITTREDGE.

romances Shakespeare's late comedies—*Pericles, Cymbeline, The Winter's Tale,* and *The Tempest*—considered as a group. *The Two Noble Kinsmen* is also often considered a Shakespearean romance, although it is largely the work of John FLETCHER and deviates strongly from the group's general pattern. Written between about 1607 and 1613 (1611, if *The Kinsmen* is disregarded), the romances, with *Henry VIII* (which itself has many features in common with them) and the lost *Cardenio,* are the works of the playwright's final period. Each is a TRAGICOMEDY, in the broadest sense of the term: elements of TRAGEDY find their resolution in the traditional happy ending of COMEDY.

All of the romances share a number of themes, to a greater or lesser degree. The theme of separation and reunion of family members is highly important. Daughters are parted from parents in *Pericles, Cymbeline, The Winter's Tale,* and *The Two Noble Kinsmen,* and wives from husbands in the first three; sons are also lost, to a father in *The Winter's Tale* (permanently) and *The Tempest* (temporarily), and to parents of each sex in *Cymbeline.* The related idea of exile also features in the romances, with the banished characters—usually rulers or rulers-to-be—restored to their rightful homes at play's end. Another theme, jealousy, is prominent in *The Winter's Tale, Cymbeline,* and *The Two Noble Kinsmen,* and it has minor importance in *Pericles* and *The Tempest.* Most significantly, the romances all speak to the need for patience in adversity and the importance of providence in human affairs. This visionary conception outweighs any given individual's fate or even the development of individual personalities.

Compared with earlier plays, realistic characterization in the romances is weak; instead, the characters' symbolic meaning is more pronounced. The plots of these plays are episodic and offer improbable events in exotic locales. Their characters are frequently subjected to long journeys, often involving shipwrecks. Seemingly magical developments arise—with real sorcery in *The Tempest*—and supernatural beings appear. These developments are elaborately represented, and all of the romances rely heavily on spectacular scenic effects.

In all these respects, *Henry VIII* resembles Shakespeare's more exotic work of the same period.

In its episodic plot structure; in its elaborate processions and tableaux; in the prominence of King Henry VIII's family concerns, especially the birth of an heir; and in its emphasis on the importance of providence in human affairs, it offers a strong flavor of the romances to go with its historical subject matter.

The romances are based on a tradition of romantic literature going back at least to Hellenistic Greece, in which love serves as the trigger for extraordinary adventures. In this tradition love is subjected to abnormal strains—often involving jealous intrigues and conflicts between male friendship and romantic love—and there are fantastic journeys to exotic lands, encounters with chivalric knights, and allegorical appearances of monsters, supernatural beings, and pagan deities. Absurdly improbable coincidences and mistaken identities complicate the plot, though everything is resolved in a conventional happy ending. The protagonists are also conventional, their chief distinction being their noble or royal blood. They lack believable motives and are merely vehicles for the elaborate plot, whose point is frankly escapist. Such tales were extremely popular in Shakespeare's day, especially in the increasingly decadent world of the court of King JAMES I, who succeeded Queen Elizabeth I (see Elizabeth I in *Henry VIII*) in 1603.

The genre had long influenced the stage, but its impact was particularly strong in the early-17th-century MASQUE, a form of drama that was popular at James's court. In the masque, lush and exotic settings framed strange, often magical tableaus and episodes. With the advent of JACOBEAN DRAMA, the taste for such allegorical presentations expanded beyond the court to the so-called private theaters. These differed from the "public" playhouses, such as the GLOBE THEATRE, in being enclosed against the weather. They were smaller and more intimate, lit by candles and equipped with the mechanical apparatus necessary for elaborate scenic effects. To support all this, they charged a much higher admission price, and they attracted wealthier, better-educated, and more sophisticated audiences.

Shakespeare had made use of romance material throughout his career—*The Two Gentlemen of Verona* is based on a famous romance, for instance, and small-scale masques are performed in a number of plays, while others contain masquelike elements. He had not, however, applied it so fully and systematically before. Any personal motives the playwright may have had for turning to romance late in his career cannot be known, but adequate reasons were available in the theatrical world. Around 1608, his acting company, the KING'S MEN, took over the BLACKFRIARS THEATRE, a private playhouse, and began to produce plays in this new, more remunerative but more demanding venue. Shakespeare was a thoroughgoing theatrical professional—he made his living from the success of every aspect of the company's business, not simply from writing plays for pay—and he responded to the new situation by creating a drama to match it. The exotic locales, supernatural phenomena, and elaborate masques of the romances are clearly intended to satisfy the tastes of the time, and they succeeded. However, though the playwright considered popular demand, he also followed his own artistic sensibility. Unlike many similar works of the period, Shakespeare's plays build a meaningful symbolic world on the escapist premises of romance literature.

In the romances, Shakespeare returned to an idea that had been prominent in his earlier comedies: young lovers are united after various tribulations. Now, however, the focus is not only on the young lovers; it also encompasses the older generation, once the opponents of love. At the end of these plays, the emphasis is not on reward and punishment—with the young lovers wed and the obstructive elders corrected—but rather on the reunion of parents and children and the hopeful prospect of new generations to come. The romances concern themselves with the lovers not for their own sake but for their effect on the whole continuum of life. The focus is on family groupings rather than on individuals or couples, and the action is spread over many years (except in *The Two Noble Kinsmen*), making this aspect especially clear. (*The Tempest* and *Cymbeline* take place over shorter periods—*The Tempest* within a single day—but narrations of pre-play events produce the same effect.) This broader canvas is enlarged even further with its many images of the supernatural—gods and goddesses, rituals and oracles, apparent resurrections—which add a sense of infinite mystery.

The prominence of resurrection as a motif in the romances points to their similarity to the ancient festivals celebrating the rebirth of spring each year. The mock death and staged resurrection so common in such rites are reenacted in each of the romances. In *The Two Noble Kinsmen* the reference is oblique, but Palamon, sentenced to death, is reprieved, and the Gaoler's Daughter is restored to normal life from her descent into insanity, an emblematic death. In *Pericles* the prince undergoes a similar restoration from catatonia, and two reported deaths, Marina's and Thaisa's, prove false. Similarly, in *The Tempest*, Ferdinand and Alonso each mistakenly believe the other is dead, as do Imogen and Posthumus in *Cymbeline* (Posthumus's very name suggests resurrection). Also, Perdita and Hermione are believed dead in *The Winter's Tale*, where an elaborate resurrection scene is staged by Paulina.

Winter is represented as well as spring. Compared to the earlier comedies, increased importance is given to separation and bereavement, to error and conflict, in short to the anxieties associated with tragedy. A tone of resignation and grief prevails until a sudden reversal brings an ending of joy and renewal that had seemed impossible. Pericles, Leontes (*The Winter's Tale*), Cymbeline, and Prospero (*The Tempest*) all suffer grievously. Each experiences a painful separation from all he holds dear (while Prospero, unlike the others, retains his daughter, he is isolated from everything else in his once-secure world). Each then undergoes a penance before the final reconciliation (except Pericles, an omission that Shakespeare may have consciously corrected in the subsequent plays). Here, too, the play encompasses the entire community, for each sufferer is also a ruler, so his welfare has great symbolic resonance. His winter of struggle gives way to the spring of resurrection—and regeneration, through the marriage of the young people who have been resurrected. As in ancient ritual, temporary death turns to hope for the future.

The pagan religious component of these plays is quite overt, with the appearances of Diana in *Pericles* and Jupiter in *Cymbeline*, the vivid evocation of Apollo's oracle in 3.1 of *The Winter's Tale*, the goddesses enacted in the betrothal masque in *The Tempest* (4.1), and the stunning scenes of worship at the altars of Mars, Venus, and Diana in 5.1 of *The Two Noble Kinsmen*. Even in *Henry VIII*, Queen Katherine's dying vision (see 4.2.83 S.D.), while not expressly pagan, is certainly not Christian and is redolent with exotic religiosity. In such an ambience, the merits of the characters are generally of less importance than the good will of the gods—or of Prospero, their surrogate (and even Prospero is dependent on "bountiful Fortune" [1.2.178] to bring his enemies within range of his magic).

The plays insist that a patient acceptance of the accidents of fate is necessary to survive. The several shipwrecks in these plays and their imagery of the ocean's power make this point clear, for the impersonal violence of the sea is beyond humanity's influence. The characters are often passive and in any case are helpless to improve their situations. Their strength in adversity is supported by faith—not that the gods will save them but that the gods are great—and therein lies their eventual salvation. As Paulina puts it, "It is requir'd / You do awake your faith" (*Winter's Tale*, 5.3.94–95). Only providence can bring about the destined resolution through strange turns of fate, whose very improbability stresses the irrelevance of human desires. In the unreal world of the romances, the characters—and we as spectators—must, like Pericles, make our "senses credit . . . points that seem impossible" (*Pericles* 5.1.123–124).

However, more is also required. It is necessary for humankind to act with mercy, in emulation of the gods. Imogen accepts Posthumus despite his viciousness toward her; Hermione also forgives Leontes; and Prospero's forgiveness motivates the entire action of *The Tempest*. Even where repentance is not offered, most flagrantly in the case of Antonio in *The Tempest*, vengeance—even justice—is foresworn. All of the romances—like many of Shakespeare's comedies—have points in common with the medieval MORALITY PLAY, in which a sinful human receives God's mercy through no merit of his own. Although the romances are secular works (their pagan gods were presumed by Shakespeare and his audiences to be fictional), their Christian content is nonetheless clear. Our receptivity to such abstract philosophical concerns is eased by the fantasy inherent in the romance genre, for it offers a different level of imagination from which to view the complexities of life.

The romances conclude in a spirit of hope, as the main characters are reunited in an aura of reconciliation—a favorite motif throughout Shakespeare's career. Wrongs are righted and errors amended, exiles return to their homes, and even death is frustrated. The natural good in humanity is put under pressure but preserved through the action of providence. An emphasis on the cycle of regeneration—both in the traditional comedic emphasis on marriage and in the theme of reunited families—offers a guarantee that the preservation will be lasting.

Romano, Giulio See GIULIO ROMANO.

Roman plays Shakespeare's three plays set in ancient ROME. In the order in which they were written, the Roman plays are *Julius Caesar, Antony and Cleopatra,* and *Coriolanus.* The much earlier *Titus Andronicus,* though Roman in setting, is generally excluded from this classification because it is a timeless tale that neither needs nor involves any real, historical world. Each of the Roman plays is a TRAGEDY, but they are unlike the other tragedies, which are placed in virtually imaginary historical situations. These works are complicated by the history of ancient Rome, which is reasonably accurately presented, and they are thus similar to the HISTORY PLAYS. The first two plays depict episodes of the civil wars that sundered the Roman Republic in the first century B.C., while the third involves legendary events of the republic's first days, about 450 years earlier.

Julius Caesar deals with the assassination of the title character, Caesar, by Marcus Brutus, and with Brutus's defeat at the battle of PHILIPPI (42 B.C.) by Caesar's followers, led by his nephew Octavius and Mark Antony. At the play's close the victors rule Rome and its territories. However, the play is less concerned with this development than with the moral ambivalence of Brutus, a highly righteous man whose action—the killing of his ruler and personal benefactor—is intended to produce good for Rome but yields instead the evil of civil war.

Antony and Cleopatra, set about a decade later, tells of Antony's love affair with Cleopatra, queen of Egypt; of the enmity this arouses in Antony's coruler, now known as Octavius Caesar; of Antony's defeat at the battle of ACTIUM (31 B.C.); and of the subsequent suicides of the title characters. More clearly a tragedy, *Antony and Cleopatra* centers on the moral conflict in Antony as he is torn between the stern call of Roman duty and the irresistible compulsion of love for Cleopatra and her opulent life. At the play's climax, Cleopatra's suicide transfigures both lovers as she seems to transcend the play's world by approaching death as intensely as she had lived.

Coriolanus enacts the rejection of a great warrior, Coriolanus, by the people of Rome, who are provoked by his prideful arrogance. It goes on to tell of his desertion to the enemy Volscians, with whom he attacks the city, and of his submission to his mother's entreaties that he spare the city, after which he is killed by the Volscians. On one hand, *Coriolanus* is the most distinctly personal tragedy of the Roman plays—from beginning to end, the psyche of the doomed warrior is the central concern. On the other, it offers a broader political canvas as background for its story and features a sharply drawn struggle between aristocrats and plebeians, where *Julius Caesar* and *Antony and Cleopatra* deal only with the high politics of the ruling class.

When he wrote plays about ancient Rome, Shakespeare dealt with material that was highly meaningful to his age, and this fact is reflected in the works. Due to the RENAISSANCE rediscovery of classical literature and art, the Roman era in the Mediterranean world was seen as the high-water mark of Western culture, and the general outlines of its history were familiar to all educated people. Thus, the politics of that world, and the lives of its illustrious personages, were viewed with great interest. The moral questions found in the careers of Coriolanus, Brutus, and Antony had particular importance as they were examples taken from the most important epoch in the development of Western politics.

Rome's history also had importance to Christians because it was thought of as the period of Christianity's birth. In particular, the establishment of the empire was often perceived as evidence of God's intervention in human affairs. It provided a period during which the birth of Christ and the early growth of the religion named for him could take place in relative peace and stability. This belief is acknowledged in *Antony and Cleopatra*, 4.6.5–7. Thus, the events depicted held additional meaning for the original audiences.

In fact, it is important to the Roman plays that the Roman Republic was pre-Christian. Shakespeare's repeated allusions to suicide as an honorable alternative to defeat marks a striking difference in pre-Christian morality. The allusions were unavoidable in light of Roman history, but the playwright's emphasis on it suggests that these deaths had particular significance. They point to the most important distinction of the Roman tragedies: they lack Christianity's belief in divine providence as a final arbiter of human affairs. This was a very important aspect of ancient history as it was understood in Shakespeare's day. Without God's promised redemption, the moral questions of the classical world had to be resolved within an earthbound universe of references. The protagonists of the Roman plays look to their relations with Rome and its history and cannot consider the more "cosmic" viewpoint to which we are accustomed—and that we see in such other tragic figures as Hamlet, Lear, and Othello. Thus, Brutus's course of action can only be ambiguous; he cannot recognize an error and gain divine forgiveness, nor can he be confident that he is right in the face of worldly defeat. Similarly, the final transfiguration of Cleopatra does not involve the presumption of divine judgment that attends, say, Othello's conviction that he faces eternal punishment, or Hamlet's dying confidence that Horatio can justify his life. Cleopatra's achievement is especially admirable for its dependence on pure human spirit.

The consequence is that Rome's conflicts are never clearly organized on lines of good and evil; each side contains elements of both. We cannot identify individual figures of pure evil, like Iago, or of complete good, like Desdemona (both in *Othello*), because, from the Christian point of view shared by Shakespeare and his audiences, these categories simply could not exist prior to God's illumination of the world through Christ. Volumnia,

for instance, is not evil but is merely blind to the effects of her actions, and Brutus is a wholly moral man who even so cannot be seen as good, either by himself or by others. The deaths in defeat of Brutus, Antony, and Coriolanus all leave us aware of the limited spiritual possibilities they have had available to them, and Cleopatra's death offers only a partial exception. The Roman tragedies elicit sympathy for their protagonists because they cannot achieve fulfillment, as that idea is understood in the world of Shakespeare's plays as a group.

Surprisingly, the moral ambiguity found in the Roman plays makes them excellent for ethical discussion. In the absence of absolute values, comparisons must be made, and the three plays present a considerable range of political conduct. *Julius Caesar* simply and boldly presents a conflict of opinions about the government and the morality of resistance to despotism. It also offers a demonstration of the differing political techniques of Brutus and Antony. *Antony and Cleopatra* opposes the concerns of the government with the individualism of its protagonists, who insist on the value of private aspirations and satisfactions. In *Coriolanus* an individualist revolts against the demands of the state to the extent of treason, but in this pessimistic work neither the state nor the individual is strong, and a failure to achieve wholeness constitutes both the private tragedy and the public disaster.

Like the histories, the Roman plays reflect a widespread enthusiasm in Shakespeare's England for the study of the past. However, because they were set in remote times and places, they offered the playwright an opportunity to speculate broadly on political possibilities that English settings actually inhibited. *Coriolanus* is particularly noteworthy in this respect, for its picture of class conflict is more realistic and sober than are the glimpses of it that occur in the histories (see, e.g., Jack Cade in *2 Henry VI*). The government CENSORSHIP that loomed over Shakespeare's theater would probably have found English class relations too sensitive a subject to discuss seriously in public. Ancient Rome, however, presented a more intellectual, and therefore discreet, context in which to contemplate an event such as the corn riots, similar to those found in *Coriolanus*, that raged in England not long before the play was written. Similarly, *Julius Caesar*'s central—and unresolved—moral debate on assassination is not found in the histories, nor is Cleopatra and Antony's sexual immorality observed among Shakespeare's English rulers—Prince Hal's rejection of Falstaff's world at the end of *2 Henry IV* confirms this.

Commentators have often remarked that the Roman plays have points in common with two other Shakespearean genres, the tragedies and the history plays. In the tragedies a distinctively great person, because of some aspect of that greatness, suffers a crushing downfall. This causes us to reflect on the vulnerability of human existence. In the histories the uses and abuses of government are demonstrated in various ways. This causes us to consider the exercise of power and the value of political loyalty. The Roman plays' greatest strength lies in their combination of these themes. They raise important issues about the individual and society while they stimulate our awareness of both disturbing political questions and profound social ideals.

Rome   Capital city of the ancient Roman Empire and the setting for much of *Julius Caesar, Antony and Cleopatra,* and *Coriolanus*—collectively called the ROMAN PLAYS—as well as all of *Titus Andronicus* and three scenes of *Cymbeline*. Especially in the Roman plays, Shakespeare places great importance on the idea that ancient Rome relied on a highly developed ethic of public duty. Conflicts between the demands of Roman government and the personal motives of individuals are central to the Roman plays. Though less dominant, the empire is significant in *Titus Andronicus* and *Cymbeline*, as well.

The early *Titus Andronicus* is not classed among the Roman plays, for it does not deal with a factual Rome. However, even in this melodrama, Shakespeare deals with the clash between individual drives and public issues that Rome's significance evoked. Titus Andronicus insists on pursuing what he sees as the correct moral action for a Roman, and the result is tragic chaos. Titus's unquestionable ethic has failed, and for him, Rome itself has failed. He declares that "Rome is but a wilderness of tigers" (3.1.54), a line that has often been quoted as a con-

demnation of vicious power-seeking. The hero's inability to reconcile the Roman ideal with political reality drives him insane. Because the ideal is specifically Roman, an element of grandeur is added to his plight. The significance of Rome was much greater to RENAISSANCE audiences than it is today.

In *Julius Caesar,* the civil order of Rome is disturbed by Brutus, whose personal morals lead him to kill Caesar. Civil war ensues; thus, society suffers because an individual is unwilling to compromise. On the other hand, it is evident that Brutus also represents a traditional model of Roman political morality. The individual is thus seen to relate to the state in an ambiguous manner. Here, too, the play's themes are given resonance by the fact that the state is Rome, an age-old symbol of authority. The city is the location for all of the scenes prior to 4.2, and actual sites in ancient Rome are evoked—the Forum, the Capitol, the Senate, etc.—though the people of Rome seem comparable to the populace of Shakespeare's LONDON.

In *Antony and Cleopatra,* Rome is contrasted with another political venue, the luxurious court of Cleopatra. The demanding ethic of Rome is set against the sensual indolence of Egypt. Antony finds himself wavering between a Roman ideal—rigorous response to "the strong necessity of time" (1.3.42)—and an alien one, "the love of Love, and her soft hours" (1.1.44). This conflict is seen immediately, in 1.1, as Antony rejects the call of duty—represented by messages from Rome—in favor of the irresponsible pastimes of Cleopatra. The city is less in evidence than in *Caesar,* for fewer scenes are set there—1.4, 2.2–2.4, 3.2, and 3.6—and they are located on anonymous streets or in interiors. However, the symbolic weight of Roman power and the energy and rigor of the men who wield it is omnipresent.

Another aspect of classical Rome as it was understood by 17th-century English audiences is important in *Antony and Cleopatra.* The Roman Empire was regarded as not only a great achievement in political history but as a significant phenomenon theologically as well. Christian doctrine held that God permitted Rome to rule the Mediterranean world in order that its power might provide peace for a long period, during which Christ was to be sent to humankind and the Christian church established. Caesar makes a reference to this doctrine that would have been unmistakably clear in Shakespeare's day. He observes of his imminent victory over Antony, "The time of universal peace is near" (4.6.5). Thus, the power of Rome was considered a manifestation of God's will. This theme recurs in *Cymbeline*.

Coriolanus takes place in the legendary early days of the Roman Republic as the city is convulsed by the rise of the common people to political power. The conflict between aristocrats and plebeians permits a more detailed depiction of the city's people than in the other plays. In about half of the play's scenes, the setting is stated to be Rome, but the physical city is left to the imagination of the reader or theatrical producer. The domestic life of the city is alluded to, as in 4.6.8–9, and the commoners are vividly present in the form of several well-drawn minor figures, but they are essentially no different from the common folk of the English HISTORY PLAYS.

The glory of Rome is much less evident in *Coriolanus*. The idea of a great power is evoked when Menenius says, ". . . you may as well / Strike at the heaven with your staves, as lift them / Against the Roman state . . ." (1.1.66–68), but in fact Rome does not fare well here. Its messy politics encompasses the cynicism of tribunes and aristocrats, and the thoughtless unreliability of the common people. The result is the expulsion of the city's greatest warrior, Coriolanus, who joins Rome's enemies, the Volscians. He brings defeat to the city and—because he refuses to destroy Rome utterly—death for himself. The tragedy of *Coriolanus* offers a sense of Rome's greatness in Coriolanus's power and pride, and its later corruption and fall in his foolish politics and ultimate fate. As he is driven from Rome, Coriolanus hurls a curse upon the city that predicts its history—which was entirely familiar to Shakespeare's audiences. He says, ". . . here remain with your uncertainty! / . . . [until you become] captives to some nation / that won you without blows!" (3.3.124–133). The fall of Rome is invoked, which increases the grandeur of the hero's tragic collapse.

Rome has less importance in *Cymbeline*, but the city nevertheless has two different and interesting historical aspects. Though we see only a domestic interior, 1.5 and 2.4 are set in Rome. We meet there the villainous Iachimo, whose delight in deceit along with his decadent world of duels and drink were probably intended to suggest an idea commonly held by 17th-century English playgoers. The home of Machiavelli and of Reformation England's enemy the Catholic Church, contemporary Rome was seen as a sink of duplicity and corruption. In this light, Cymbeline's Rome is closer to Shylock's VENICE than to the ancient imperial capital. On the other hand, we see the familiar toga-clad officials of ancient Rome in 3.8, and we also know from developments at the court of King Cymbeline that the play's Rome is the capital of Augustus Caesar, the Caesar of *Antony and Cleopatra*, whose name is pointedly repeated. Caesar's representative in Britain is the courtly Lucius, who is clearly a sympathetic character. Here, as in *Antony and Cleopatra*, Shakespeare invokes the Rome that was admired by Christian humanism, the powerful provider of good government and peace appropriate to the birth of Christianity. In this light, the brief war between Britain and Rome that takes place in *Cymbeline* has great symbolic significance. British patriotism is valued only by villains, the Queen and Cloten, and though (unhistorically) the Britons successfully resist Rome, they finally yield anyway. Part of the play's joyful conclusion in 5.5 is the king's decision to "submit to Caesar, / And to the Roman empire" (5.5.461–462), for Rome's peace must be accepted by Britain. Thus, here as in the other plays, Shakespeare gilds his drama with the glory of ancient Rome as understood by the Renaissance humanism of his own time.

Roses, Wars of the   See WARS OF THE ROSES.

Rose Theatre   Playhouse built by Philip HENSLOWE in 1587, whose recently discovered ruins reveal much information about ELIZABETHAN THEATER. The Rose was the first theater south of the River Thames, in what later became the most important theater district of LONDON. Henslowe leased a property that had formerly been a rose garden, in partnership with a grocer named Cholmley, who put up capital in exchange for the food concession at the theater. The theater was built by early 1588, but the earliest surviving records of the Rose date only to its repair in 1592, from which it has long been known that it was built of timber and plaster on a brick foundation.

Henslowe's *Diary* records the companies that played for him, presumably at the Rose, after 1592 STRANGE'S MEN—possibly including the young Shakespeare—were there that spring and during the next winter season; *1 Henry VI* and *Titus Andronicus* may have premiered during this period. SUSSEX'S MEN played there briefly during 1593, when the theaters were mostly closed by a plague epidemic, and shared the stage with the QUEEN'S MEN in the spring of 1594. In that season the ADMIRAL'S MEN, led by Henslowe's son-in-law and partner William ALLEYN, moved to the Rose for a seven-year stay. PEMBROKE'S MEN gave their final two performances at the Rose, just after the Admiral's Men departed in 1600, and WORCESTER'S MEN played there in 1602–03. The *Diary* goes no further, but it is known that Henslowe did not renew his ground lease in 1605. Authorities differ on the Rose's later history, but it was probably torn down around 1606.

In 1989 the foundations of the Rose were accidentally uncovered during the construction of a modern office building. After a preliminary archaeological survey, they were reburied in a slurry of sand and concrete, to conserve them during the construction of the new building. During the brief interval of its exposure, archaeologists discovered that the remains were quite well preserved since the site, which is very close to the Thames, is often waterlogged; organic material, such as timber, cherry stones, and thatch fallen from the roof, had been covered by river silt and thereby kept from oxidation. Also, numerous small artifacts were recovered, including a small trove of straight pins that were probably used in fitting costumes.

Much of the theater's foundations remain, including about 70 percent of the outlines of the stage and the galleries, of both the original building and its remodeled—probably substantially rebuilt—successor of 1592. Presumptions and surmises based on surviving records have had to be revised. It had been supposed that the diameter of the Rose might be a great as 90 feet, but it was in fact only 72 feet; and speculation as to the shape of the near-circular polygonal building was settled: It had 14 short sides,

rather than a few long ones, and it was an irregular shape, with longer sides toward the rear of the building. Perhaps most significantly, the trapezoidal shape of both the Rose's stages raised questions about contemporary stages elsewhere, generally thought to have been rectangular. Moreover, the theater may originally have been built without a stage—that is, as an arena rather than a theater. This is one of many questions theater historians hope to be able to address if new excavations are undertaken. The site was reopened as a public exhibit in 1999, but it is unclear when or if a full excavation of the site will be begun.

The Rose Theatre existed for fewer than 20 years, but the discovery of its ruins, combined with its status as the only Elizabethan theater for which much contemporary documentation exists, make it one of the most interesting of England's archaeological sites. Moreover, its discovery immediately sparked a search for the remains of its more illustrious neighbor, the GLOBE THEATRE, which have also been uncovered.

Rossillion (Rousillon) Region in southwestern FRANCE, a location in *All's Well That Ends Well.* The castle of the Countess of Rossillion is the setting for many scenes in the play, but no specific characteristics of the region are mentioned; Shakespeare simply took the location from his sources, translations from BOCCACCIO. The Countess's son, Bertram, is the Count of Rossillion, and he is occasionally called this, as in 4.3.39.

Rossillion is an anglicization of the French Rousillon, a medieval state whose capital was Perpignan, the present-day capital of the province of Pyrénées-Orientales. Independent until 1172, Rousillon was then governed at various times by France and Aragon (later Spain), before finally becoming French in 1659. In Shakespeare's day it had been Aragonese since 1493. His placement of it under French rule derives from Boccaccio, but it may also have been designed to emphasize that the action takes place in a remote time and thus, perhaps, to make the play's improbable elements more plausible. Another Count of Rossillion was a familiar legendary figure, a follower of Charlemagne who appeared in the play *Orlando Furioso* (1594), by Robert GREENE.

Rossini, Gioachimo (1792–1868)   Italian composer, creator of an OPERA based on *Othello*. Rossini, the giant of Italian opera until supplanted by VERDI, and still one of the major figures in opera history, was a popular composer but not yet recognized as a great one when he produced *Otello* (1816), with an Italian libretto based on the French adaptation by Jean-François DUCIS. A simple tale of sexual rivalry lacking the subtlety of Shakespeare's characterizations (the English poet, Lord Byron [1788–1824], wrote of Rossini's "crucifying Othello"), it is nevertheless considered one of the great operas of the 19th century.

Rossini went on to success after success, in Naples and then Paris, until 1829, when he suddenly ceased composing and retired, to the consternation of the musical world. He lived almost 40 years more, writing only a few scattered pieces of music until his last years, when he composed a group of over 150 short pieces in various forms, which he called "The Sins of Old Age." He did not publish them, and they were largely unperformed until the 1950s, when they were recorded. Since then they have entered the modern repertoire.

Rouen   French city occupied by the English during the HUNDRED YEARS' WAR, the site of a battle in *1 Henry VI* and a location for two interior scenes in *Henry V*. In *1 Henry VI* the French take the city through a ruse by Joan La Pucelle (Joan of Arc), and then the English, led by Talbot, take it back by assault the same day (3.2). Historically, Rouen remained under English rule from 1419, when Henry V conquered it, until 1449, 18 years after Joan had been burned there. The French retook it only when the English were driven from Normandy for good; Talbot was actually captured at the fall of Rouen in 1449 and was not ransomed until a year later. Although the incident in the play is wholly fictional, it includes details of other battles, which Shakespeare based on the chronicles of Edward HALL and Robert FABYAN. The episode was created to heighten the contrast between the heroic Talbot and the cowardly Fastolfe, and to emphasize Joan's trickery.

In 3.4 of *Henry V*, Princess Katharine is comically instructed in the English language by Alice, and in the next scene the French leaders demonstrate overconfidence about facing the English in battle. Both of these interior scenes take place in Rouen, not long before its conquest by the English.

Rowe, Nicholas (1674–1718)   First critical editor of Shakespeare's works. Rowe, a successful though minor playwright, issued an edition of Shakespeare's plays in 1709; a second edition in 1714 included the poems. Working from the highly corrupt text of the Fourth FOLIO, Rowe made many emendations, and he also created lists of the dramatis personae and act and scene divisions, the first time these features were provided for most of the plays. While many of Rowe's textual emendations continue to be accepted, he was at times rather arbitrary and intrusive in a manner not tolerated by modern scholarship. For instance, where Shakespeare has Hector cite ARISTOTLE in *Troilus and Cressida* (2.2.167), Rowe—offended by the anachronism (for Aristotle lived centuries after the TROJAN WAR)—substituted the phrase *graver sages* for the philosopher's name. Rowe introduced his collection with a brief biography, which he acknowledged was based largely on the lore collected by Thomas BETTERTON. Though filled with anecdotal information that modern scholars reject, Rowe's biography remained the standard life of the playwright until Edmond MALONE's work.

Rowley, Samuel (d. ca. 1630)   English playwright, author of a possible precursor of *Henry VIII*. Rowley wrote plays for the ADMIRAL'S MEN (later PRINCE HENRY'S MEN and the PALSGRAVE'S MEN), for whom he was also an actor. He mostly worked collaboratively with a variety of playwrights, including John DAY and Thomas DEKKER. The only play known to have been written wholly by him was *When you see me, You know me* (1605), a comic history play dealing with the reign of King Henry VIII. Scholars believe Shakespeare may have been alluding to Rowley's play in *Henry VIII* when the Prologue promises the audience that they will see a serious work and not "a merry bawdy play" (Prologue.14). The possible subtitle to *Henry VIII*—*All Is True*—may have been intended to make the same comparison. Rowley may have written some of the comic prose that was added in 1602 to *Doctor Faustus* by Christopher MARLOWE, and he may have written similar scenes in *The Taming of a Shrew* and *THE FAMOUS VICTORIES*.

Rowley, William (ca. 1585–1626)   English actor and playwright, sometimes held to have been a collaborator with Shakespeare. Between 1607 and 1625, Rowley appeared with or wrote for the QUEEN'S MEN, PRINCE CHARLES' MEN, and the KING'S MEN. Rowley was best known in his own time as an actor, and playwriting seems to have been a sideline. He generally provided low comedy scenes in prose. He collaborated several times with Thomas MIDDLETON, most successfully on *The Changeling* (1622). He has been nominated as a coauthor of *Pericles* and of *THE TROUBLESOME RAIGNE OF KING JOHN*, though most scholars dismiss both attributions. In 1662 Francis KIRKMAN published *THE BIRTH OF MERLIN* as the work of Shakespeare and Rowley, but the ascription to Shakespeare was false; scholars believe that the play is by Rowley alone or by Rowley and Middleton.

Roxborough Castle   Location in *Edward III*, a grand fortification in what is today southeast SCOTLAND (though it was in English territory at the time of the play), the home of the English Countess of Salisbury. In 1.1 Sir William Montague reports to King Edward that King David of Scotland has "begirt with siege / The castle of Roxborough, where enclosed / The Countess Salisbury is like to perish" (1.1.129–131). King Edward declares that he will take his army and rescue the Countess, who commands the castle in the absence of her husband, the Earl of Salisbury. In 1.2 and 2.1, which take place at the castle, the King becomes obsessed with the Countess's beauty, pursues her, is rejected, and learns from her a lesson in proper conduct. The physical castle, a famously secure redoubt, is not made evident in any respect except that, as 1.2 opens, the Countess is said to be "above" [1.2.0, stage directions], meaning on the stage's upper level or balcony, a common feature of 16th-century stages (see ELIZABETHAN THEATER), which here represents the battlements, or defensive wall of the castle.

That the actual Roxborough Castle was not the scene of the historical events depicted was known to Shakespeare from his chief source, the history by Jean FROISSART, though he was probably unconcerned by this inaccuracy, for he merely required a famous castle known to have been at one time owned by the Salisbury family and been besieged by the Scots. Froissart's account of the relationship of the King and Countess is unconnected to a siege. And while a woman had been chatelaine at Roxborough Castle during a siege by the Scots, this had occurred at an earlier time, and she was not the Countess of Salisbury but the wife of the play's Montague, who, as a vassal of Salisbury, was the castle's governor.

Although inaccurate, the situation enacted in the play reflects the frequent exchanges of this border castle between England and Scotland over many centuries, until the English finally tore it down in 1550, in accordance with a peace treaty. The picturesque ruins of several walls and gateways are all that remain.

Royal Shakespeare Company   Modern British theatrical company famous for productions of Shakespeare's plays. In existence since the 1879 founding of the Shakespeare Memorial Theatre in STRATFORD, the Company assumed its present name in 1961. Led by such major Shakespearean directors as Frank BENSON, Barry JACKSON, Anthony QUAYLE, and Glen Byam SHAW, the Company achieved international fame, and since 1961, during the directorships of Peter HALL, Trevor NUNN, Terry HANDS, Adrian NOBLE, and Michael BOYD, it has continued to play a leading role in world theater, with remarkable productions of both Shakespeare and a wide range of classical and contemporary playwrights. It employs several theaters in both Stratford and London.

Russell, Thomas (1570–1634)   Landowner in WARWICKSHIRE and a friend of Shakespeare. In his will Shakespeare left Russell the sizable token of £5 and appointed him an overseer of the will. Russell's first wife was a cousin of Henry WILLOUGHBY, who may thereby have known Shakespeare and thus possibly written about him in his mysterious poem

"Willobie his Avisa." Russell may well have known Shakespeare in LONDON, where he lived in 1599. At this time a widower, he was courting his second wife, who lived near the playwright. She was the widowed mother of Dudley and Leonard DIGGES, whom Shakespeare almost certainly did know; the former may have provided information used in writing *The Tempest*, and the latter contributed dedicatory verses to the FIRST FOLIO edition of the plays. After marrying Mrs. Digges in 1603, Russell lived with her at her estate near STRATFORD. The couple had already lived together for three years, marrying only when their lawyers could devise a way to break certain provisions in her late husband's will, intended to discourage remarriage. Dudley Digges later came to resent this and harried Russell for years with a long, acrimonious lawsuit.

Rutland, Francis Manners, Earl of (1578–1632) English aristocrat, a minor patron of Shakespeare. Rutland's records reveal payments to Shakespeare and Richard BURBAGE for the preparation of a ceremonial shield that the earl used at a tournament held on the 10th anniversary of King JAMES I's accession in 1613. This type of coat of arms bore a painted allegorical composition called an *impresa*, or emblem. It was not used in fighting but was carried by a knight's page, who recited a poetic interpretation of the emblem when the nobleman presented himself for the joust. Each Knight in 2.2 of *Pericles* bears such a shield, and the emblems are interpreted by Thaisa. Presumably Shakespeare wrote the poetic interpretation for Rutland's emblem, and Burbage painted the image, for which each man received 44 shillings in gold. This was a substantial

sum of money in the 17th century, at least several month's wages for most workmen.

Rylance, Mark (b. 1960) British actor and director, artistic director of the Shakespeare's Globe Theatre (see WANAMAKER, SAM). In 1995 Rylance, whose varied career has encompassed the foundation of two independent theater companies, was appointed the first artistic director of the company occupying London's replica of the 16th-century GLOBE THEATRE. Directing and starring in numerous productions in the new theater, Rylance was especially acclaimed for his portrayals of Richard II and, in an all-male cast, Viola of *Twelfth Night*, both in 2003. In September 2004 he announced his intention to resign as the Globe's director at the end of the following year.

Ryther, Augustine (active 1576–1580) English engraver, illustrator, and publisher of a source for *Edward III*. Ryther, who was one of the first engravers on copper in England, provided maps for several well-known 16th-century atlases. He made a free translation of Petruccio UBALDINO's Italian account of the English defeat of the Spanish Armada and had it published, in 1590, as *A Discourse Concerninge the Spanish Fleet Invadinge Englande, in the Year 1588*, apparently as a vehicle for his numerous accompanying charts and illustrations. It was one of the most widely read contemporary accounts of the English defeat of the Armada, and scholars find its influence on several details of *Edward III*. This suggests that the play was written in the first years of the 1590s, after the work's publication but before accounts of the Armada became old news.

S

Sackville, Thomas (1536–1608)   English author and statesman, coauthor of the first English TRAGEDY and the author of a source for Shakespeare's HISTORY PLAYS. Sackville's literary activity came early in his career. With Thomas Norton (1532–84), the first English translator of Calvin and later a Puritan opponent of the theater, Sackville wrote *Gorbuduc* (1562), the first tragedy written in English. He also wrote poetry and contributed two essays, the "Induction" and "Complaint of Buckingham," to the second edition (1563) of *A MIRROR FOR MAGISTRATES*, a collection of biographies from which Shakespeare derived material for several of the histories. Sackville's work was especially important for *2 Henry VI*.

Sackville was an extravagant young nobleman, and around 1563 he had to flee England to avoid imprisonment for debt. In Rome he was briefly jailed on suspicion of espionage. He returned after inheriting a fortune. A cousin and favored courtier of Queen Elizabeth I (see Elizabeth I in *Henry VIII*), he was granted an estate at Knole in KENT, which he renovated into what is now one of the grandest of surviving English homes. As a diplomat, he represented the queen in several important matters, including her relations with Mary, Queen of Scots. He eventually became her lord treasurer, and he was kept in this position by her successor, King JAMES I. However, in 1608 he was accused of taking excessive bribes, and he died suddenly at his trial on these charges.

Sadler, Hamnet (d. 1624), and **Sadler, Judith** (d. 1614)   Couple in STRATFORD, probable godparents of Hamnet and Judith SHAKESPEARE. Hamnet Sadler was a baker and a lifelong friend of Shakespeare. The Sadlers' son, born in 1598, was named William. In Shakespeare's will, which Hamnet Sadler witnessed, the baker was one of seven friends to whom the playwright left money to buy a commemorative ring (though his name appears to have been inserted as an afterthought, replacing that of Richard TYLER). Sadler's family had been in Stratford for more than two centuries. Hamnet and Judith Staunton were married between 1578—when Hamnet inherited his bakery—and 1580. They had 14 children, of whom seven survived to adulthood. Sadler suffered severe losses in the Stratford fire of 1595, from which he never entirely recovered; several subsequent lawsuits by creditors are recorded. Sadler appears in the records as both Hamnet and Hamlet—he is named Hamlet in Shakespeare's will, but he witnessed it as Hamnet—suggesting that the two names were actually variants of one. (In any case Shakespeare took the name for his great tragic hero from his sources, not from his friend or his son.)

Sadler's Wells Theatre   London theater, once a center of Shakespearean productions. In 1684 an ancient medicinal spring was discovered on a plot of land in open country north of London. Its owner, one Mr. Sadler, created on the site a "pleasure garden," or private park where refreshments and light entertainment were sold. A few years later he built a theater, where a variety of entertainment was offered. In 1765 a stone theater was built—it was managed in the 1770s by Tom KING—but it was not particularly distinguished until Samuel PHELPS leased it in 1844 and used it for 20 years to stage his famous and influential series of Shakespearean productions. After subsequent service as a part-time skating rink and boxing arena, as well as, from time to time, a legitimate stage, the theater became a virtual ruin early in the 20th century. In 1931 Lilian BAYLIS bought and refurbished it, and Shakespearean productions were again resumed, though since 1934 it has chiefly been associated with opera and ballet.

St. Albans   Village near London, near which several scenes of *2 Henry VI* occur. Now a city of more than 50,000 people, St. Albans was in Shakespeare's day a small village whose chief attraction was a shrine to St. Alban, the first British martyr. In 2.1 the imposter Simpcox, having staged a "miraculous" cure at the shrine, is encountered by King Henry VI's hawking party near St. Albans. In 5.2 and 5.3 the fields near the town are the scene of the first battle of St. Albans, which began the WARS OF THE ROSES in 1455. The Duke of York, attempting to enforce his claim to the crown, defeats the forces of the king and forces him to retreat to London, closing the play. The battle is then alluded to in *3 Henry VI* (1.1). The second battle of St. Albans occurred in 1461, and it is described in *3 Henry VI* (2.1.95–141).

St. Edmundsbury   English town in Suffolk, the setting for 5.2 of *King John*. The French camp here is the site of the treasonous alliance between the Dauphin Lewis and several English noblemen, led by the Earl of Salisbury, who are rebelling against King John.

St. Edmundsbury was the location of an assembly of John's rebellious nobles in 1214, as Shakespeare knew from HOLINSHED's history. The lords swore an oath to oppose the king—a prelude to the signing of the Magna Carta the next year; it was entirely unrelated to the French invasion of 1216. However, Shakespeare associated the two, both to compress the sequence of events in the interest of fast-moving drama, and in order to identify treason with the threat of foreign conquest.

As BURY ST. EDMUNDS, the town is a location in *2 Henry VI*.

Sainte-Maure, Benoît de (Benoît, Sainte-More) (active ca. 1150–1175)   French poet, author of a source of *Troilus and Cressida*. In about 1160 Sainte-Maure (also known as Sainte-More or Benoît) wrote his *Roman de Troie*, a very long poem (30,000 verses) on the history of TROY. This work, which derived from a sixth-century account by the pseudonymous Dares Phrygius (Dares the Trojan), was translated into Latin prose by Guido delle COLONNE, and, as his *Historia destructionis Troiae* (pub. 1270–87), it became the standard work on the TROJAN WAR throughout the Middle Ages, until the rediscovery of HOMER in the RENAISSANCE restored the oldest account of the war to its current prominence. Colonne's *Historia* influenced Shakespeare's Greek and Trojan warriors through two English works—William CAXTON's *The Recuyell of the Historyes of Troye* (1471) and John LYDGATE's long poem *Troy Book* (1420, publ. 1512, 1555). Further, Sainte-Maure's poem inspired BOCCACCIO's *Filostrato* (1338), which, through CHAUCER's *Troilus and Criseyde* (ca. 1482), gave the playwright the story of his ill-fated title characters. Sainte-Maure's work was the first to introduce this tale, which is not in Dares Phrygius or Homer.

Sainte-Maure is thought to have been a wandering troubadour, serving as court poet in one aristocratic household after another. He spent many years in England at the court of King Henry II (1133–89). He probably wrote the *Roman de Troie* there, for it is dedicated to Henry's queen, Eleanor of Aquitaine.

Salusbury, John (John Salisbury) (ca. 1566–1612) Contemporary of Shakespeare, minor nobleman whose marriage was the subject of an allegorical poem, LOVE'S MARTYR (1601), that was published with Shakespeare's "The Phoenix and Turtle." Originally from Denbighshire, in WALES, Salusbury studied law in London and remained there in the court of Queen Elizabeth I (see Elizabeth I in *Henry VIII*). He became friends with a number of writers and dramatists, including Ben JONSON, John MARSTON, and probably Shakespeare. Salusbury was knighted by the queen in 1601, possibly for his loyalty during the attempted rebellion by Robert Devereux, Earl of ESSEX. This honor is thought to have been the occasion for the publication of *Love's Martyr*, written 15 years earlier by a member of Salusbury's household, with additional works by his more illustrious literary friends.

Salvini, Tommaso (1829–1915) Italian actor. Salvini was Italy's leading Shakespearean actor of the 19th century, playing most of the tragic heroes but specializing in Othello. In the 1870s and 1880s Salvini, a massive man with a booming voice, achieved great success touring Britain and America as Othello (with Edwin BOOTH as Iago in 1886). Until 1880 these productions were wholly in Italian, and later he continued to perform in Italian while the rest of the company spoke English, but this did not interfere with his great popularity with English-speaking audiences, who admired his stage presence and great vocal power.

Sams, Eric (b. 1926) English musicologist and Shakespeare scholar. Probably best known as an authority on the relationship between words and music in SONG, especially in 19th-century German *lieder*, Sams has also written extensively on Shakespeare, focusing on the dating and identifying of possibly Shakespearean material among the apocryphal works (see APOCRYPHA). He has published editions of EDMUND IRONSIDES (1986) and *Edward III* (1996), both as Shakespeare's work. While numerous scholars believe the playwright may have collaborated on the latter play, few accept the former as Shakespeare's. Sams has also written *The Real Shakespeare: Retrieving the Early Years, 1564–1594*, in which he argues that during the so-called lost years, Shakespeare was in fact a busy apprentice playwright, writing early versions of the masterpieces generally considered to be later works.

Sandal Castle Castle in Yorkshire, location in *3 Henry VI*. Now a total ruin, in the 15th century Sandal Castle was a fortification belonging to the Duke of York. In 1.2 York's sons persuade him to renew his claim to the crown, just as an army led by Queen Margaret approaches, intending to besiege them in the castle. A battle is fought over the next several scenes at nearby WAKEFIELD.

Sandells, Fulk (1551–1624) Farmer near STRATFORD, a friend of Anne HATHAWAY's family. In 1581 Sandells was made supervisor of the will of Anne's father, Richard Hathaway, in which he was described as Hathaway's "Trustee friend and neighbour." He was responsible for paying Anne her inheritance "at the day of her marriage." In November 1582 he and John RICHARDSON posted a bond guaranteeing the legality of Anne's intended marriage to Shakespeare, who was a minor; they agreed to pay £40 to the church if the wedding were not properly conducted.

Sardis Ancient city in Greek Asia Minor, in what is now western Turkey, a location in *Julius Caesar*. A few days before the fatal battle of PHILIPPI, the rebel generals Brutus and Cassius meet at Sardis, where they argue over dominance and where Brutus is visited by the Ghost of Julius Caesar. Historically the meeting at Sardis took place many months before Philippi, but Shakespeare compressed events for dramatic purposes.

Sardis was an important city at least as early as the sixth century B.C.; it was ruled by ROME and then the Byzantine Empire from 133 B.C. until the Turks conquered it in the late 11th century A.D. In 1402 the Mongols, under Tamurlane, destroyed the city, which has been a ruin ever since.

Saunderson, Mary (d. 1712) English actress. Wife of the leading actor of the time, Thomas BETTERTON, Mrs. Saunderson, as she was known, was generally considered the leading actress. She was the first woman to play many Shakespearean parts after the legalization of women on stage in 1660, and she was particularly notable as Ophelia in *Hamlet*, Juliet, and Lady Macbeth.

Savage, Thomas (ca. 1552–1611) English businessman, a cotrustee with William LEVESON of Shakespeare's interest in the ground lease for the GLOBE THEATRE. Half of the lease for the land on which the Globe stood was entered into jointly by five actors in the CHAMBERLAIN'S MEN: Shakespeare, John HEMINGE, William KEMPE, Augustine PHILLIPS, and Thomas POPE. To make their shares independently salable, the actors assigned their half to two trustees—Leveson and Savage—who then regranted a fifth of it to each of them.

Savage, a goldsmith whose principal occupation was as a minor official governing the coal trade, was Heminge's neighbor and landlord, which is probably why he was one of the trustees. He was also a close friend of Shakespeare's friend John JACKSON.

Saxo Grammaticus (Saxo Lange) (ca. 1150–ca. 1206) Danish poet and historian, author of a remote source of *Hamlet*. Saxo Lange—known posthumously as Grammaticus for his scholarship—wrote in Latin a quasi-mythical history of the Danes, called the *Historiae Danicae*, which contains the earliest complete version of the legendary tale of Amleth, the predecessor of Hamlet, though earlier fragments appear in the Icelandic sagas. Saxo was a monk, the secretary of an archbishop who was chief minister for the king of DENMARK; little more is known of him. His history, though well known in medieval times through manuscript copies, was not published until 1514, in Paris. The Amleth material was then used by a French writer, François BELLEFOREST, in a story that subsequently influenced the author of the UR-HAMLET, Shakespeare's immediate source.

Scarlet, Thomas (d. 1596) LONDON printer who produced the first edition of *Edward III*. Little is known of Scarlet except that he printed a number of plays for Cuthbert BURBY, including the first QUARTO (Q1) of *Edward III*. Even given the difficulties to be expected in printing from a manuscript in several hands, as he probably did in this case, Scarlet seems to have been a poor worker, perhaps accounting for his obscurity.

Scheemakers, Peter (1691–1770) Flemish sculptor, creator of the statue of Shakespeare in WESTMINSTER ABBEY. In 1740 Scheemakers was commissioned to sculpt Shakespeare in the Abbey's "Poet's Corner"

as part of a memorial designed by the architect William Kent (1684–1748) and financed by a public subscription. He based his depiction of the playwright on the CHANDOS PORTRAIT.

Scheemakers spent most of his career in London, where he was among the most popular sculptors of the mid-18th century. Fourteen of the other Westminster Abbey memorial sculptures are his work. His brother Henry (d. 1748) and nephew Thomas (1740–1808) were also well-known London sculptors.

Schiller, Johann Christoph Friedrich (1759–1805) German poet, dramatist, and philosopher, creator of an adaptation of *Macbeth*. In 1800, at GOETHE's Weimar theater, Schiller staged his own translation of *Macbeth*. He altered the play radically, making Shakespeare's grand villain into a noble victim of the malignant Witches. For the sake of "purity," the humorous monologue of the Porter was replaced by a pious hymn. For all his own dramatic genius, Schiller could not accept the complex, full-blooded world of Shakespeare. This reflected the limitations of the developing German theater of the day.

Schiller is generally regarded as second only to Goethe among German writers. His first play, *The Robbers* (1781), is about a brave man who unsuccessfully defies tyranny. It established Schiller as a defender of liberty in a revolutionary age, and its dramatic virtues—it remains popular today—marked him as a leading literary figure. He also wrote poetry: his "Ode to Joy" (1785) was used by BEETHOVEN in the chorale movement of his Ninth Symphony. In 1787 he settled in Weimar, where he taught history and developed an aesthetic philosophy. Influenced by his friendship with Goethe and his study of the philosopher Kant, he stressed the sublime nature of creativity and was a formative influence on the Romantic movement. He continued to write plays, and many of them were staged at Goethe's theater. The most notable of these were *Mary Stuart* (1800), *Wilhelm Tell* (1804), and his greatest masterpiece, a trilogy of historical plays about a famous general, *Wallenstein* (1798–99).

Schlegel, August Wilhelm von (1767–1845) German scholar and poet, the most important translator of Shakespeare into German. With his wife, Karoline Michaelis Schlegel (best known as Karoline Schelling; 1763–1809), also a notable writer, Schlegel translated 16 of Shakespeare's plays (published 1797–1801; a 17th was issued in 1810). Following the Schlegels' divorce in 1803, the remaining plays were translated by a group led by Ludwig TIECK. The complete set was published between 1823 and 1829. It immediately became the standard German Shakespeare, replacing the prose versions of J. J. ESCHENBURG. The Schlegel-Tieck Shakespeare is considered to be one of the masterpieces of German literature, and it confirmed the stature that Shakespeare has since held among Germans as history's premier poet and dramatist.

Though best known for his Shakespeare translations, Schlegel also wrote poetry—some of it set to music by Franz SCHUBERT—and translated from Italian and Spanish. He produced the definitive German text of the plays of the great Spanish dramatist Pedro Calderón (1600–81), as well as works by Dante Alighieri (1265–1321), Ludovico ARIOSTO, and Miguel de CERVANTES. He and his brother, the philosopher Friedrich von Schlegel (1772–1829), are regarded as among the most important founders of German Romanticism, a literary and artistic movement that swept Europe in the early 19th century. (See also TRANSLATION OF SHAKESPEARE.)

Schoenbaum, S. (1927–1996)   American scholar, biographer of Shakespeare. Born Samuel Schoenbaum. S. Schoenbaum (as he signed his works), long a professor at Northwestern University, was best known for his *Shakespeare's Lives* (1970), an historical account of biographies of the playwright; and *William Shakespeare: A Documentary Life* (1975), a scholarly and readable biography that consists of a commentary on the extant documents of Shakespeare's life, with facsimiles of them. This book was also published in a popular, condensed version, *William Shakespeare: A Compact Documentary Life*. Schoenbaum also edited the authoritative revised editions of *Annals of English Drama 975–1700* (1964, 1970), a record of all known English plays before the 18th century.

Schröder, Friedrich Ludwig (1744–1816)   German actor and producer. In a series of productions

beginning in 1776, Schröder introduced Shakespeare to the German theater; except for an occasional flawed adaptation, such as DER BESTRAFTE BRUDERMORD, the playwright's works had not been performed in Germany since the early 17th century, when English touring companies may have presented some of them. However, beginning with Schröder's *Hamlet* (in which the producer played the Ghost), Shakespeare became a staple of the German stage. Schröder was one of the leading lights of the German theater, as both an actor and a producer. Born into a family of traveling players, he began his career at the age of three and eventually became a major figure in German cultural affairs of the late 18th and early 19th centuries.

Schubert, Franz (1797–1828)   German composer of the Romantic movement whose many famous works include settings for three of the best-known songs from Shakespeare's plays (see SONG). In the summer of 1827 Schubert composed music for a *Standchen*, or "Serenade," a translation of "Hark, Hark, the Lark" (*Cymbeline*, 2.3.19–25); a *Trinklied*, or "Drinking Song" (*Antony and Cleopatra*, 2.7.111–116); and, the most famous of the three, *An Sylvia*, or "Who Is Silvia?" (*The Two Gentlemen of Verona*, 4.2.38–52). The first of these was translated by August Wilhelm von SCHLEGEL; the others by a friend of the composer, Edouard von Bauernfeld. According to a famous—though probably untrue—story, Schubert wrote *An Sylvia* on the back of a menu during a meal.

Schubert, a very prolific and highly influential composer, also set to music a great deal of poetry by J. W. von GOETHE, Friedrich SCHILLER, and Schlegel, as well as German translations of the work of such varied authors as Aeschylus, Petrarch, Alexander POPE, and Sir Walter Scott. Best known for his songs and chamber music, he also wrote important symphonic works.

Schücking, Levin Ludwig (1878–1964)   German scholar. Schücking was a leading member of the so-called realist school of Shakespearean criticism, which attempted to relate the plays to the traditions and practices of ELIZABETHAN DRAMA and ELIZABETHAN THEATER, rather than simply analyzing the characters and their actions. Schücking's most influential work, translated as *Character Problems in Shakespeare's Plays* (1922), deals with the techniques the playwright inherited from earlier drama, such as having characters comment on the play's developments in the manner of a CHORUS.

Scofield, Paul (b. 1922) British actor. Scofield is especially noted for his portrayals of King LEAR, directed by Peter BROOK, both in the 1962 stage production and the 1970 FILM. As a young man, Scofield joined the Birmingham Repertory Theatre under Barry JACKSON, and he went with Jackson to the Shakespeare Memorial Theatre in STRATFORD in 1945. There he established himself as a classical actor, playing Armado (*Love's Labour's Lost*), Feste (*Twelfth Night*), Mercutio (*Romeo and Juliet*), and Hamlet, among others. He has since played many classical and modern parts. He has only taken movie roles occasionally, but in addition to his *King Lear* for Brook, he has played the French King in Kenneth BRANAGH's *Henry V* (1989) and the Ghost in Franco ZEFFERELLI's 1990 *Hamlet*. He is probably most widely known as Sir Thomas MORE in the film *A Man for All Seasons*, a part he had previously played on the stage and for which he won an Academy Award in 1966.

Scot, Reginald (Reginald Scott) (ca. 1538–1599) English writer, author of a source for *A Midsummer Night's Dream*, *Macbeth*, and *The Tempest*. Scot's *The Discovery of Witchcraft* (1584) provided Shakespeare with items of folklore about witches and fairies that he used in his plays, especially in his depictions of Puck in *Dream*, the Witches in *Macbeth*, and Ariel in *The Tempest*. Scot himself, however, derided the information as silly superstitions.

Scot, a country gentleman and justice of the peace for KENT, was appalled by the persecution of "witches"—mostly poor or retarded people—that was raging in his time, and he wrote his book against the practice, attempting to disprove the existence of witchcraft. He was a century ahead of his time, for witches continued to be persecuted in England until the early 18th century. Scot's work was attacked by "authorities" on witchcraft, including King JAMES I. Scot also wrote a pioneering technical manual on the growing of hops, a major Kentish industry.

Scotland Country to the north of England, setting for most of *Macbeth* and an enemy of England in *Edward III*. The importance of the Scottish nation is stressed at the beginning of *Macbeth*. Act 1 details the suppression of a revolution supported by foreigners from Norway and Ireland, Macbeth's murder of King Duncan is repeatedly associated with a catastrophic decline in Scotland's fortunes, and the rebellion against him is specifically intended to restore "a swift blessing [to the] suffering country" (3.6.47–48). The trials of the nation, especially as described in the conversations of the exiled lords in 4.3, demonstrate the growth of evil that Macbeth's deed triggers. As ROSSE puts it, Scotland under Macbeth seems no longer "our mother, but our grave" (4.3.166). Shakespeare had a specific lesson in mind here: that immortality in the leaders of a country leads to its social and political disruption. This is a lesson that is also very prominent in the HISTORY PLAYS.

Scotland loomed large in English political considerations in Shakespeare's day. It was traditionally allied with England's enemy, FRANCE, a circumstance that looms large in the first act of *Edward III*. Scotland's ruling family was Catholic, and Scottish plots were feared throughout the reign of Queen Elizabeth I (see Elizabeth I in *Henry VIII*). Mary, Queen of Scots, was imprisoned in England for many years and eventually executed. However, her son King James VI of Scotland was a Protestant, and he succeeded Elizabeth as JAMES I in 1603 and united the two lands under a single ruler for the first time (though a full merger was still a century away).

James's accession was probably the reason that Shakespeare wrote a play set in Scotland, and allusions to James's reign are scattered throughout *Macbeth*. Some scholars believe that the playwright may also have been inspired by a trip to Scotland as an actor. He and other members of the CHAMBERLAIN'S MEN may have fled to Scotland in the wake of their seeming involvement in the rebellion of Robert Devereux, Earl of ESSEX, in February 1601. They may have performed with Laurence FLETCHER in Aberdeen. John Dover WILSON went so far as to propose that *Macbeth* was written in Scotland and first performed in Edinburgh. However, these theories cannot be convincingly supported with any known evidence.

Segar, William (d. 1633) Contemporary of Shakespeare, a scholar of chivalric lore and heraldry. Segar's treatise *The Booke of Honour and Armes* (1590) probably influenced Shakespeare's humorous parodies of dueling in *Love's Labour's Lost* (1.2.167–170), *Romeo and Juliet* (2.4.19–26), and *As You Like It* (5.4.67–102), as well as his more serious treatment of trial by combat in *Richard II* (1.3.1–122). Segar held several important positions as a herald, including that of Garter King of Arms, the chief herald of England. As a result, he played an important part in arranging entertainments at the courts of Queen Elizabeth I (see Elizabeth I in *Henry VIII*) and King JAMES I and may thus have been personally acquainted with Shakespeare.

Seneca, Lucius Annaeus (ca. 4 B.C.–A.D. 65) Roman philosopher and playwright, an important influence on Shakespeare and ELIZABETHAN DRAMA in general. Seneca wrote nine tragedies that were widely adapted in 16th-century England. He followed ancient Greek TRAGEDY in his subject matter and his effort to produce a catharsis through pity and terror (see ARISTOTLE), but his focus on bloody incidents and his attention to ghosts and magic rather than divinity gave his works a very different tone. He did not intend his plays for performance, but rather as moral lessons to be read and studied, but his English followers did not know this. In 16th-century England, ancient Greek plays were almost unknown, and Seneca was taken as a model of the classical drama.

The REVENGE PLAY constitutes the purest Elizabethan use of Seneca, for his works generally center on vengeance taken for the murder of a parent or child and depict bloody killings and physical mutilations. A number of other Senecan devices were popular with Elizabethan playwrights, including Shakespeare: soliloquies, exaggerated rhetoric, insanity and feigned insanity, and the use of ghosts. After the 1560s Seneca's plays were staged infre-

quently, but Shakespeare assumed his audiences were at least familiar with their reputation and general character, for he has *Hamlet*'s Polonius, tritely evaluating theatrical styles, remark that "Seneca cannot be too heavy" (2.2.396).

Highly organized and formal, Seneca's plays observe the classical unities—that is, the events take place within a few hours and occur in a single location. There are five acts, which progress from exposition to anticlimax in a prescribed sequence. The plays are filled with moralizing and instructive passages and employ formal devices such as the PROLOGUE and the CHORUS. Seneca concentrated on the failings of the evil and powerful; as Sir Philip SIDNEY remarked of his works, "high and excellent Tragedie . . . maketh kings fear to be tyrants." *Titus Andronicus* is very Senecan in subject matter and tone, and Shakespeare employed Senecan elements in many other works, especially *Richard III*, *Hamlet*, and *Macbeth*. Later in his career, however, Seneca's influence diminished.

Seneca, the aristocratic son of a famous rhetorician and historian, also became a famous orator and writer. In A.D. 41 he was exiled by the emperor Claudius, for reasons that are not known; called back in 49, he became tutor to the future emperor Nero. He was probably mentally ill to some extent, as the content of his plays suggests. He nevertheless wrote a number of works on law and philosophy—the plays themselves were meant as works of moral philosophy—but many have been lost. He advocated a stoic detachment and contempt for death that was later praised by Christian thinkers. As a minister under Nero, Seneca was reluctantly involved in the emperor's crimes. For instance, he composed a defense for Nero's murder of his own mother. Implicated in a conspiracy against Nero—probably unjustly—Seneca was sentenced to death. He was permitted to commit suicide, which he did with a serenity that became legendary.

Shadwell, Thomas (1642–1692) English playwright and theatrical entrepreneur, producer of adaptations of *Timon of Athens* and *The Tempest*. Shadwell was a successful writer of comedies, usually modeling his work on that of Ben JONSON. He undertook to make an OPERA of William

DAVENANT's and John DRYDEN's adaptation of *The Tempest*. The result, *The Enchanted Island* (1674), employed music by several composers, including Matthew LOCKE, though in 1690 Henry PURCELL composed a new score. In this form the work remained popular for well over a century, influencing subsequent adaptations of Shakespeare's play. Shadwell also wrote a dramatic adaptation of *Timon of Athens*. His *Timon of Athens, the Man-Hater* (1678) altered the tone of Shakespeare's play considerably, chiefly by adding two lovers—one faithful, one not—for the title character. It was popular for more than 50 years.

Shakespeare, Anne (1571–1579)   Shakespeare's sister. Anne Shakespeare was born when the future playwright was seven and died when he was 14. There is evidence that her loss may have been particularly grievous to the family, for the record reveals that her funeral was unusually elaborate and costly, although the financial difficulties of John SHAKESPEARE were great at the time. Nothing else is known of her.

Shakespeare, Anne Hathaway   See HATHAWAY, ANNE.

Shakespeare, Edmund (1580–1607)   Shakespeare's brother, probably an actor in LONDON. The playwright's brother is only recorded as such at his christening, but he is thought to have been the "Edmund Shakespeare, a player" who was buried in St. Saviour's Church, SOUTHWARK, on December 31, 1607. In addition to the coincidence of name, his very expensive funeral, presumably unaffordable by the estate of an unknown actor, suggests a prosperous relative such as the playwright. Four months earlier, the burial of an illegitimate child, "Edward, sonne of Edward Shackspeere" was recorded at a different London church; the father may be Edmund, mistakenly given the boy's name (similar errors are known in this parish register). Edmund was probably named for his uncle Edmund Lambert (father of John LAMBERT).

Shakespeare, Gilbert (1566–1612)   Shakespeare's brother. Gilbert Shakespeare was recorded as a haberdasher in LONDON in 1597, but he also lived in STRATFORD, or at least had returned there by 1602, when he stood in for William by receiving a deed to land the playwright had bought from John and William COMBE. In 1609 he was summoned to appear in a Stratford court concerning a lawsuit, though neither its subject nor Gilbert's connection to it is known, and in 1610 he witnessed a document in Stratford. He was buried there and was recorded as a bachelor.

Shakespeare, Hamnet (1585–1596)   Shakespeare's son. The birth of Hamnet and his twin sister, Judith SHAKESPEARE, around the end of January 1585 (they were christened on February 2), offers a datable association of the future playwright with STRATFORD before he left to pursue his career in LONDON, for they must have been conceived around April 1584. Their father is next known as an established actor and playwright in London in 1592. Hamnet's death at age 11 must have been shattering to his father, but there is no certain trace of it in the playwright's work (except possibly in the touching response of Hubert to the death of Prince Arthur in 4.3.105–106 of *King John*; under a generally discredited but still possible hypothesis, this play could have been written as late as 1596). Hamnet was probably named for Shakespeare's friend (and the boy's likely godfather) Hamnet SADLER.

Shakespeare, Henry (d. 1596)   Shakespeare's uncle. Henry, the brother of the playwright's father, John SHAKESPEARE, was a tenant farmer on a manor near STRATFORD. He was sued several times over money matters; in 1587 John, as his guarantor, was sued as well, at a time when his own finances were in trouble. Henry was in trouble with the law on several occasions. He was fined for fighting in 1574 and in 1583 for improper garb in church, and he was jailed in 1591 for trespass and in 1596 for debt—three months before his death. At this time his creditor went to his farm and confiscated a team of oxen. This may have paid the debt and secured his release, but he was fined a month later for not properly maintaining his land and the neighboring highway, as he was required to do. However, despite such problems, he was reported to have been a prosperous man at his death, with money and a barn full of fodder.

Shakespeare, Joan (1558–before 1569) Shakespeare's sister. Nothing is known of this Joan Shakespeare except her christening date, but she certainly died before the birth of the second Joan SHAKESPEARE in 1569. She was probably named for her mother's sister Joan Arden Lambert (mother of John LAMBERT).

Shakespeare, Joan (Joan Shakespeare Hart) (1569–1646) Shakespeare's sister. Joan Shakespeare was the only one of the playwright's siblings to survive him, and she was apparently the only one who married. Her husband was a hatter, William Hart (d. 1616, a week before Shakespeare), about whom no more is known. In his will Shakespeare left his sister £20, all of his clothes, and a lifetime lease on the house in which she lived (the playwright's BIRTHPLACE, which he left to his daughter Susanna SHAKESPEARE Hall). She lived there for the rest of her life, and her only surviving child (of four), Thomas Hart (1605–before 1670), lived there after her. Her descendants lived there until 1806.

Shakespeare, John (before 1530–1601) Shakespeare's father. John Shakespeare left the farm of his father, Richard SHAKESPEARE, and became an apprentice glover and tanner of fine leathers in STRATFORD. He prospered; he is recorded as a householder in 1552 and had bought more property by 1556 (possibly including the house that was to be the playwright's BIRTHPLACE). Between 1556 and 1558 he married Mary Arden (see SHAKESPEARE, MARY ARDEN), the youngest daughter of his father's landlord. He inherited his father's leasehold on the land, but he sold it to a brother-in-law of Mary, preferring his shop in Stratford. He eventually became a broker of wool and other commodities, in addition to his leather business. He was respected among his fellow citizens and was appointed and elected to a variety of increasingly important civic positions, including that of chamberlain, supervising the town's finances. In 1565, the year after William's birth, he was elected an alderman—entitling his children to a free education at the Strat-

ford Grammar School—and in 1568 he became bailiff of Stratford, the equivalent of mayor. (As bailiff he issued the license for the first traveling theatrical company to play in Stratford, in 1569.) He always signed his name with a mark, but this did not necessarily signify illiteracy (literate men of the time are known to have signed in this fashion). Given John Shakespeare's success as a town official, he was almost certainly literate, though he may have been able to read only. Around 1570 he began the process of applying for a COAT OF ARMS and establishing a position in the gentry.

In 1575 he bought two more houses in Stratford, but thereafter his fortunes declined. After 1577 he stopped attending the aldermen's meetings, at which he had regularly been present. In 1578 he was delinquent in taxes, and in the same year he mortgaged an estate Mary Shakespeare had inherited and sold other property that she owned. In 1580 he was fined the considerable amount of £40—more than his father had possessed at his death—for failure to appear in court and guarantee that he would keep the peace. The cause of this proceeding is unknown—it was a routine legal maneuver in a litigious age—but the size of the fine suggests the court's opinion that he was still a man of wealth. In 1586 he was finally removed from the board of aldermen because of inattendance. By 1590 his real estate holdings had been reduced to the Henley Street house, and in 1592 he was fined for not attending church, with the notation that he was thought to be staying home in fear of arrest for debt (though some take this as evidence that John Shakespeare was a "crypto-Catholic"; see SPIRITUAL TESTAMENT OF JOHN SHAKESPEARE). On the other hand, he was still a valued neighbor, and he was several times called on to evaluate people's estates, a position of trust.

It has been speculated that John Shakespeare succumbed to alcoholism in this period, but this cannot be confirmed. In any case the family's situation improved only after 20 years, presumably in consequence of Shakespeare's success in the theater. In 1596 John was finally awarded his coat of arms. In 1597 John and William attempted unsuccessfully to recover Mary's mortgaged estate (see LAMBERT, JOHN), but William bought NEW PLACE in the same year. Just before his death, John Shakespeare reappeared on the town council.

Shakespeare, Judith (Judith Shakespeare Quiney)
(1585–1662) Shakespeare's daughter. The birth of Judith and her twin brother, Hamnet SHAKE-SPEARE, in late January 1585 offers evidence that Shakespeare was in STRATFORD around the previous April, when they were conceived. He must soon thereafter have left to pursue a career in LONDON, but no record of him between then and 1592 has survived.

Judith, who was probably named for Judith SADLER, married at 31, rather late by the standards of the day. She and a locally notorious rake, Thomas QUINEY, who was four years younger, were wed in February 1616. Her father evidently disapproved of the match, for he changed his will to protect her portion from her husband (though the marriage is not mentioned in the will). Dying two months later, he left Judith £100 as a dowry, but a further £150 was held in reserve, and she received only the interest on it as long as Quiney lived. If she died, the sum would revert to Susanna SHAKE-SPEARE and her heirs and not to Quiney, unless he had by then legally endowed his and Judith's children with land.

Judith and Thomas Quiney were married during Lent without obtaining the special license required, and he, at least, was briefly excommunicated (the record is unclear about her). In November their first child, Shakespeare Quiney, was born, but he lived only five months. Their two subsequent children also died young, at 11 and 19, both in 1639. After surviving her children by more than 20 years, her sister Susanna by 13, and her husband by 10, Judith died at the age of 77 and was buried in Stratford, though the location of her grave has been lost.

Shakespeare, Mary Arden (ca. 1540–1608)
Shakespeare's mother. Mary Arden was the youngest of the eight daughters of Robert ARDEN, a gentleman farmer who owned land in several villages near STRATFORD. In 1556 she was the executor of her father's will, though she was 16 and probably illiterate, suggesting her recognized capabilities.

Her father left her some money, an estate that included a farmhouse and about 60 acres of land, and a share in another property, part of which was leased for farming by Richard SHAKESPEARE. He had also already given her other properties before he died. When she married John SHAKESPEARE sometime between 1556 and 1558 (no record has survived), she moved from the Arden farm to the town of Stratford, where she lived for the remainder of her life. She had two children who died in infancy before William was born in 1564. Of five later children, four lived to adulthood (see Anne, Edmund, Gilbert, Joan, and Richard SHAKESPEARE). All of her inherited property was lost in the course of her husband's financial difficulties. After John's death in 1601, she either lived with her married daughter Joan in the playwright's BIRTHPLACE, her home for more than 40 years, or at NEW PLACE with William's family. Little more is known of her life.

Shakespeare, Richard (d. 1561) Shakespeare's
paternal grandfather. Richard Shakespeare was a farmer in Snitterfield, a village a few miles from STRATFORD. Nothing is known of him before 1529 (though a Richard "Shakyspere" was resident in another village, eight miles away, in 1524). He was a tenant farmer working land on several different manors (as was common), one of which was owned by Shakespeare's maternal grandfather, Robert ARDEN. The records mentioning Richard Shakespeare reveal the ordinary life of an English yeoman: he was frequently fined for failure to attend a manor court held twice a year—rather than travel six miles there and back, he, like many farmers, preferred to pay the nominal fine—and for grazing too many cattle on the commons (though the vicar of Snitterfield was also fined for forcibly removing them).

Richard Shakespeare was a solid citizen who was several times called on to value the estates of his deceased neighbors, a position of trust. When he died, his property was valued at more than £38, making him a prosperous though not wealthy husbandman. Richard's wife is unknown, but with her he had at least two sons (records on two other Shakespeares of the neighborhood are unclear): John SHAKESPEARE, the playwright's father, and Henry SHAKESPEARE, his uncle.

Shakespeare, Richard (1574–1613)   Shakespeare's brother. Nothing is recorded of this younger brother of the playwright between his christening and his burial. He was presumably named for his paternal grandfather, Richard SHAKESPEARE. He probably lived in STRATFORD all his life and apparently did not marry.

Shakespeare, Susanna (Susanna Shakespeare Hall) (1583–1649)   Shakespeare's daughter. Susanna Shakespeare was born only six months after her parents' marriage (see HATHAWAY, ANNE). Her name, taken from the biblical Apocrypha, had only recently appeared in STRATFORD and was associated with strong religious sentiment, especially Puritan leanings. Twenty-four years later, she married a man of strong Puritan sentiments, Dr. John HALL. (However, a year earlier, she was cited as absent from church on Easter, a criminal offense that was associated with Catholic dissent. The case was dropped, either because she was deemed innocent or because she had formally repented.) Susanna's only child, Elizabeth HALL, was born in February 1608, eight and a half months after her wedding. The Halls are only known to have lived at NEW PLACE, which Shakespeare bequeathed to Susanna, but another STRATFORD house, Hall's Croft (now owned by the Shakespeare BIRTHPLACE Trust) is traditionally regarded as the couple's first home. In 1613 Susanna successfully sued John LANE for libel when he declared in public that she had committed adultery, but otherwise she appears only in business records associated with her inheritance. Shakespeare left her most of his estate: New Place (where she lived for the rest of her life), the family home on Henley Street (the "birthplace"), the BLACKFRIARS GATE-HOUSE, and several leases on other properties. She and Hall were also residuary legatees. She survived her husband by 14 years and was buried with a gravestone declaring that she was "witty above her sex" and attributing that quality to her father.

"Shall I Die?"   Ninety-line poem controversially attributed to Shakespeare. "Shall I Die?" was stated to be an early Shakespearean work by Professor Gary Taylor in November 1985. Professor Taylor was coeditor of the 1986 Oxford University Press edition of the complete works of Shakespeare, where "Shall I Die?" is included under the title "A Song," in its first publication anywhere. The poem was first designated as Shakespeare's in a manuscript anthology of poems—such as were commissioned by many wealthy patrons of the 16th and 17th centuries—dated 1630. (It is only known to appear in one other such manuscript, also of the 1630s, where it is unattributed.) Earlier scholars were aware of this attribution but felt that the source was unreliable: such manuscripts commonly contain misattributed poems and were compiled by unknown anthologists whose knowledge was often limited.

Taylor's attribution generated much controversy. Some commentators felt that the poem bore no resemblance to any of Shakespeare's known work and was itself decidedly bad poetry; defenders pointed out the marked presence of words Shakespeare was fond of using. However, continuing studies have yielded a scholarly consensus: while its authorship remains uncertain, "Shall I Die?" is generally felt to be clearly non-Shakespearean, and it remains absent from the CANON.

Shank, John (ca. 1565–1636)   English actor, a member of the KING'S MEN, one of the 26 men listed in the FIRST FOLIO as the "Principall Actors" in Shakespeare's plays. Shank was a veteran comedian, especially noted for his antic dancing, when he joined the King's Men. Earlier, he had performed with PEMBROKE'S MEN, the QUEEN'S MEN, and PRINCE HENRY'S MEN (later the PALSGRAVE'S MEN). Though he does not appear in documents as a King's Man before 1619, he may have joined the company in 1615 upon the death of Robert ARMIN, whose roles he presumably played. He seems to have acted very little after 1629, and in 1631 he disappears from the cast lists. In 1635 he was successfully sued by several members of the company for having illegally acquired shares in the GLOBE and BLACKFRIARS THEATRES; in a countersuit, he claimed that the company was punishing him by keeping him off the stage. However, it is likely that he had simply been retired because of his age.

Sharpham, Edward (1576–1608)   English playwright. Edward Sharpham wrote several plays, two of which have survived: *The Fleir* (1606) and *Cupid's Whirligig* (1607). The former includes a passage that echoes dialogue from *King Lear,* and this fact helps date Shakespeare's play, which had to have been written before Sharpham's work was registered with the STATIONERS' COMPANY in May 1606.

Shaw, George Bernard (1856–1950) British playwright and essayist. As part of his persona as a crusty opponent of hidebound orthodoxy, Shaw adopted a disparaging tone toward the conventionally admired Shakespeare. He coined the term *bardolatry* to mock the attitude of such hero-worshippers as the poet Algernon SWINBURNE, and he delighted in such observations as, "With the single exception of Homer, there is no eminent writer, not even Sir Walter Scott, whom I despise so entirely as I despise Shakespeare." Moreover, he rewrote the final scene of *Cymbeline* (as *Cymbeline Refinished* [1937]), declaring that Shakespeare's version was simply too poor to be tolerated any longer.

However, Shaw could not help admiring Shakespeare; for instance, he wrote that *As You Like It,* though a "cheap and pleasant falsehood," was "one of the most effective samples of romantic nonsense in existence." He purported to admire Shakespeare's poetry while deprecating his intellect. He wrote that "Shakespeare's power lies in his enormous command of word-music, which gives fascination to his most blackguardly repartees, and sublimity to his hollowest platitudes." Essentially, his attitude is egotistical, for in making Shakespeare seem both magnificent and ludicrous, he could claim him as an artistic equal while appearing to be his intellectual superior. This attitude is perhaps best represented in his one-act play *The Dark Lady of the Sonnets* (1910) and his puppet play *Shakes versus Shav* (1949).

While Shaw has been considered Shakespeare's equal by no one but himself, he was nevertheless a very good dramatist and a highly important writer. His criticism, mostly of drama and music, was a strong influence in late-19th- and early-20th-century Britain, helping to introduce modernism to a wide audience. A grand eccentric, he made himself as prominent as possible while advocating vegetarianism, antivivisection, a mystical religion based on evolutionary theory, and spelling reform. He was also an active socialist who promoted his political ideals in all his works, including a body of explicitly political essays. However, his most important role was as a dramatist. Shaw wrote more than 50 plays, among the best known of which are *Mrs. Warren's Profession* (1898), *Caesar and Cleopatra* (1901), *Man and Superman* (1903), *Major Barbara* (1905), *Androcles and the Lion* (1912), *Pygmalion* (1913), *Heartbreak House* (1919), and *Saint Joan* (1923). Following the great Norwegian playwright Henrik Ibsen (1828–1906), Shaw dealt with such modern issues as the status of women and the problems of the poor, employing barbed wit and an elegant prose style. He was awarded the Nobel Prize in literature in 1925.

Shaw, Glen Byam (1904–1996) British actor and producer. Director of the Shakespeare Memorial Theatre in STRATFORD from 1952 to 1959 (with Anthony QUAYLE until 1956), Shaw mounted a number of noteworthy productions of Shakespeare's plays, including a particularly acclaimed *Antony and Cleopatra* of 1953, starring Michael REDGRAVE and Peggy ASHCROFT.

Shaw, July (Julian Shaw) (1571–1629) Wool trader in STRATFORD, a friend of Shakespeare's and a witness to his will. Shaw's first name was recorded as July at his christening, his marriage, and his burial, though he signed himself "July," "Julynes," "Julyns," and "Julyne" (the *n*'s approximate the Latin rendering "Julianus" or "Julinus"). He leased a house near NEW PLACE and was thus Shakespeare's neighbor. He prospered trading wool and malt, becoming an important Stratford landowner, and he served in many public offices in the town, being bailiff, or mayor, at the time he witnessed Shakespeare's will. He was a stepson of Alexander ASPINALL.

Shaw, Robert (Robert Shaa) (d. 1603) English actor. Shaw was one of the three members of PEMBROKE'S MEN imprisoned for staging the allegedly seditious *Isle of Dogs* in July 1597. Upon his release he joined the ADMIRAL'S MEN, with whom he remained until 1602. He played a major role in the company's business affairs while he performed in minor parts. In 1602 he joined WORCESTER'S MEN, though in the same year he sold a play—*The Four Sons of Aymon*—to the Admiral's Men, who performed it in 1603; however, this work may have been an old text rather than Shaw's creation.

Sheridan, Thomas (1719–1788)   Irish actor. Sheridan played numerous Shakespearean parts in London, beginning in 1744. He especially distinguished himself as Hamlet, and was generally regarded as second only to David GARRICK among the actors of the day. In 1754 Sheridan adapted Shakespeare's *Coriolanus* by combining it with another play of the same title—an entirely independent work by James Thomson (1700–48)—and played the title role himself, to great acclaim. His production was quite popular, was frequently revived for almost 15 years, and was later adapted by J. P. KEMBLE. In the 1770s Sheridan was a notable worker for educational reform.

Shirley, Anthony (1565–ca. 1635)   English traveler and adventurer alluded to in *Twelfth Night*. Shirley, originally a soldier and a follower of Robert Devereux, Earl of ESSEX, was famous for his unofficial embassy in 1598 to the court of the shah (or sophy) of Persia, Abbas the Great (1571–1629). Shirley made the treacherous overland voyage from the Mediterranean to Isfahan and negotiated rights for Christian merchants in Persia in exchange for assistance in building a modern army for the Sophy's government. (Shirley's brother Robert [ca. 1581–1628] served the shah as a military adviser for 20 years.) Shirley conducted several unsuccessful diplomatic missions on behalf of the shah between 1599 and 1601, before moving on to other adventures, chiefly as a mercenary soldier fighting for Spain against the Turks. In the meantime, two books on his adventures in Persia were published in London in 1600 and 1601. These were extremely popular, and Shakespeare included two references to the sophy in *Twelfth Night* (2.5.181, 3.4.284).

Short, Peter (d. 1603)   English printer, producer of several editions of Shakespeare's plays and poems. In 1594 Short printed *The Taming of a Shrew*—a BAD QUARTO of Shakespeare's *The Taming of the Shrew*—for Cuthbert BURBY, and in 1595 he printed the *True Tragedy*—a bad quarto of *3 Henry VI*—for Thomas MILLINGTON, but in both cases the piracy was the publisher's doing, not Short's. Short also printed the first edition of *1 Henry IV* (1598) for Andrew WISE, the second through fourth editions of *The Rape of Lucrece* (1599, 1600) for John HARRISON and his brother, and the third and fourth editions of *Venus and Adonis* (both 1599) for William LEAKE. He also printed the *Palladis Tamia* of Francis MERES. Little is known of his life.

Shrewsbury   Town in western England, site of a battle that occupies much of Acts 4–5 of *1 Henry IV*. The battle of Shrewsbury was fought between King Henry IV and rebellious noblemen led by Hotspur, allied with Scotsmen under Douglas. In 4.1 Hotspur receives news that his armies will not be reinforced by the troops of his father, Northumberland, nor by those of his Welsh ally Owen Glendower. However, the fiery warrior insists on fighting anyway. In 4.3 the rebels accept an offer to negotiate, and in 5.1 Hotspur's uncle, Worcester, meets with the king, who offers clemency. Worcester, fearful of treachery after a truce, does not convey this message to Hotspur, however, and the battle begins. In 5.3 and 5.4 several hand-to-hand combats take place, climaxing with a fight between Hotspur and King Henry's son, Prince Hal. Hotspur's death at Hal's hands demoralizes the rebels, and they flee, as is reported in 5.5.17–20.

Shakespeare followed his sources in relating the general course of the battle, and his account largely agrees with those of modern scholars, but he invented the close combat between Hal and Hotspur, along with other, less important details. Although Hotspur would not withdraw his outnumbered army, he did not start the battle; King Henry began the fight by breaking off the negotiations that preceded it. Hotspur's death did precipitate the rout; the two sides are thought to have sustained about the same number of casualties, and had their leader survived, the rebels might have won.

Sicilia   Latin for Sicily, the Italian island that is the setting for much of *The Winter's Tale*. Acts 1–2 and 3.1–2 are all set in Sicilia, where King Leontes unjustly accuses his wife of adultery, leading to a tragic aftermath. Eventually the action returns to Sicilia in Act 5, when a resolution is achieved. Sicilia is merely specified as Leontes' kingdom, and nothing Sicilian, or even Italian, about the realm is suggested in the text or stage directions. Shakespeare simply took the name from his source, *Pandosto* by Robert GREENE, though there Sicilia was the place of exile (not BOHEMIA, as in Shakespeare). Sicilia was suitable for use in a romantic drama (see ROMANCES) because it was on the fringe of familiar European geography and was thus appropriately exotic.

Siddons, Sarah (1755–1831) British actress, sister of Charles, John Philip, and Stephen KEMBLE and the leading tragic actress of the late 18th and early 19th centuries. Daughter of the manager of a traveling acting company, Mrs. Siddons, as she was known throughout her career, was a child actress who at 18 married a member of the troupe. An early attempt at success in London failed, but in 1782 she triumphed in a non-Shakespearean play and was quickly regarded as the finest tragic actress of the day, a position she never relinquished. Her most famous Shakespearean parts were Constance (*King John*), Queen Katherine of Aragon (*Henry VIII*), Desdemona (*Othello*), Ophelia (*Hamlet*), Volumnia (*Coriolanus*), and, most of all, Lady Macbeth. In 1775, while still touring the provinces, Mrs. Siddons became the first of many actresses to play Hamlet, initiating a vogue that has lasted 200 years. She continued to play the Prince of Denmark periodically until she was almost 50, though her evident age and increasing girth provoked some ridicule. She retired in 1812, after a farewell performance as Lady Macbeth, though she briefly returned to the stage several times—to terrible reviews—the last in 1819.

Sidney, Philip (1554–1586) English poet, author, and soldier, whose works influenced several of Shakespeare's plays. Sidney's massive PASTORAL, *Arcadia* (ca. 1580, published 1590), introduced romantic literature, a genre of the Italian RENAISSANCE, to England. It was widely influential and helped inspire a number of Shakespeare's works, notably *Two Gentlemen of Verona*, *As You Like It*, and the ROMANCES. It provided the SUBPLOT concerning

Edmund and Edgar, along with various details, to *King Lear*, and one of its heroes, Pyrocles, is thought to have inspired the name of Shakespeare's Pericles. Sidney also wrote one of the most famous SONNET sequences, *Astrophel and Stella* (ca. 1580–84; published 1591), a work that inspired the great vogue for the genre in the 1590s, when Shakespeare wrote his sonnets. *Astrophel and Stella* probably influenced *Romeo and Juliet* as well.

Sidney was widely regarded in his own day as an ideal Renaissance gentleman. Born into the aristocracy, he was one of the most admired gentlemen at the court of Queen Elizabeth I (see Elizabeth I in *Henry VIII*). Sidney went to war in the Low Countries, on the staff of his uncle Robert Dudley, Earl of LEICESTER, and he was killed there. His death sparked general mourning in England; one result was a great poem, "Astrophel," by his friend Edmund SPENSER.

Simmes, Valentine (active 1576–1622) Printer of a number of early editions of Shakespeare's plays. Simmes, the best of the early LONDON printers of Shakespeare, printed nine of his plays in seven years. He printed the first edition of *Richard III* (Q1, 1597) and the first three editions of *Richard II* (Q1, 1597; Q2 and Q3, 1598), all for Andrew WISE. In 1600, working for the partnership of Wise and William ASPLEY, Simmes printed the first editions of *2 Henry IV* and *Much Ado About Nothing* (both Q, 1600). In the same year he printed Q2 of *2 Henry VI* (see *The Contention*) for Thomas MILLINGTON. In 1603 he printed the first edition of *Hamlet* (Q1) for Nicholas LING and John TRUNDELL. This was a BAD QUARTO or pirated edition, though the printer was not responsible for that. In 1604 Simmes printed the third edition (Q3) of *1 Henry IV* for Matthew LAW, and in 1607, another bad quarto for Ling, Q3 of *The Taming of a Shrew*.

Simmes was often in trouble with the law. In 1589, only four years after completing his apprenticeship, he was arrested for assisting in the printing of the seditious "Martin Marprelate" tracts (see Martext, Sir Oliver in *As You Like It*), and in 1595 for pirating books. His press was seized and his type melted down, but he somehow got back in business, for in 1599 he was one of a group of printers expressly forbidden to print satires. In 1622 he was finally forbidden to work at all, though he received a pension from the STATIONERS' COMPANY.

Simpson, Richard (1820–1876) British scholar. Simpson was a Protestant clergyman who converted to Catholicism and became a literary scholar. He wrote *An Introduction to the Philosophy of Shakespeare's Sonnets* (1868), and he pioneered the study of the playwright's politics in *The Politics of Shakespeare's Historical Plays* (1874). He also edited a series of plays not usually attributed to Shakespeare (see APOCRYPHA) that he nonetheless felt the playwright had written, at least in part. Simpson was the first to suggest that part of *Sir Thomas More* was Shakespeare's, an idea that is now generally accepted. On the other hand, his elaborate analysis of FAIR EM as Shakespeare's allegorical attack on Robert GREENE has been universally rejected.

Sinklo, John (John Sinklo, John Sincler) (active 1590–1604) English actor who originated several Shakespearean roles. The inclusion of Sinklo's name in stage directions or speech headings of various texts reveals that he played a Keeper in *3 Henry VI*, one of the Players in *The Taming of the Shrew*, and a Beadle in *2 Henry IV*. The Beadle's extraordinary thinness is a source of humor in 5.4.8–30, and it has thus been concluded that Sinklo was notable for this feature and may therefore have been cast as particularly thin men. Indeed, it is possible that Shakespeare wrote extremely thin men into his plays because he knew that Sinklo would be impressive in the parts. A number of characters that he may have played include Dr. Pinch in *A Comedy of Errors* ("a hungry, lean-fac'd villain . . . A needy-hollow-ey'd-sharp-looking-wretch" [5.1.238–241]); Feeble, a tailor, and Shadow, both in *2 Henry IV* (Shadow is compared to "the edge of a pen-knife" [3.2.262], and tailors were proverbially skinny, but Sinklo could only have played one of them since they appear together); the Tailor in *Shrew*; the Apothecary in *Romeo and Juliet*; Starveling in *A Midsummer Night's Dream*; and Robert Faulconbridge in *King John*.

Singer, John (d. ca. 1605) English actor, a noted CLOWN. A member of the QUEEN'S MEN from their founding in 1583, and after 1594 a member of the ADMIRAL'S MEN, Singer was regarded by his contemporaries as the equal of such better-known theatrical clowns as Richard TARLTON and William KEMPE. He also wrote at least one play, for which the Admiral's Men paid him in 1603, but no other record of it survives.

Sir John Oldcastle Play formerly attributed to Shakespeare, part of the Shakespeare APOCRYPHA. Thomas PAVIER first published *The First Part of Sir John Oldcastle* as an anonymous play in a QUARTO edition known as Q1 (1600). Later in the same year, however, he released a second edition (Q2) in which the play was credited to Shakespeare, as it also was in Pavier's notorious FALSE FOLIO (1619). Pavier's false attribution also led to the play's inclusion in the Third and Fourth FOLIOS. The records of Philip HENSLOWE, who produced the play, reveal that its authors were Michael DRAYTON, Richard HATHWAY, Anthony MUNDAY, and Robert WILSON. *The Second Part of Sir John Oldcastle*, which is now lost, was written by Drayton alone.

Sir John Oldcastle concerns an historical figure, a proto-Protestant religious martyr. It was conceived in response to a controversy surrounding Shakespeare's great character, Falstaff. In *1* and *2 Henry IV*, Falstaff had originally been named Oldcastle. The historical Oldcastle's descendants were horrified, and their influence was such that the name was changed. Henslowe presumably saw a way to capitalize on the popularity—and notoriety—of Falstaff, and at the same time ingratiate himself with the historical Oldcastle's chief defender, William Brooke, Lord COBHAM. The prologue of *Sir John Oldcastle* expressly contrasts its hero with Shakespeare's "pampered glutton," and Falstaff himself is twice mentioned in the play in disapproving terms.

Slater, Martin (Martin Slaughter) (active 1594–1625) English actor. A leading member of the ADMIRAL'S MEN from 1594–1597, Slater was then associated with Laurence FLETCHER in England and

Scotland, and with other provincial companies. In 1608 he was comanager with Michael DRAYTON of a CHILDREN'S COMPANY that performed at the WHITE-FRIARS THEATRE. In the records of a lawsuit that resulted from this enterprise, Slater is described as an ironmonger with eight children, which suggests that he had need of a sideline. He had returned to touring companies by 1610, and in 1616 he was cited for staging plays without a license. He continued to perform with provincial troupes until at least 1625.

Sluys, Battle of   Naval battle between England and FRANCE that figures in *Edward III*. In 3.1.62–78, a Mariner tells King John of France of the approach of the English fleet bearing King Edward's army of invasion. King John and his entourage hear the sounds of battle, before the Mariner reappears to inform them woefully, in 3.1.141–184, of the unexpected English victory. The English army is now free to march inland, to the battle of CRÉCY, which occurs over the next several scenes.

This naval battle, the first important action of the HUNDRED YEARS' WAR, was named for the nearby harbor of Sluys, now in the Netherlands. Shakespeare and his collaborators (see *Edward III*, "Commentary") presented very little of the detail available from their historical sources (see *Edward III*, "Sources of the Play"). In fact, the Mariner's descriptions derive in good part from Petruccio UBALDINO's account of the still-recent English defeat of the Spanish Armada, a feature that will have emphasized, for its original audience, the play's patriotic character. Within the dramatic action, the events of 3.1 simply further the account of Edward's advance to Crécy (whose battle did not in fact occur until six years later).

Historically, in June 1340 King Edward commanded in person a large fleet, which may have numbered up to 250 vessels (though many of them were small transport vessels not used in combat). The French fleet was larger yet but under the command of admirals with little combat experience. They anchored their ships in defensive rows outside the harbor, lashing them together to construct floating walls, in the hope that this would keep an English frontal attack from separating them. Instead Edward simply attacked the end of each line with ships full of infantrymen, who were sent aboard their quarry and fought their way from vessel to vessel, while English archers, shooting from the relative safety of their own rigging, swept the French decks with a deadly barrage. The French fleet was almost entirely destroyed, with a great slaughter of its sailors. This battle established English control of the English Channel and was thus of great importance. However, unlike in *Edward III*, it was immediately followed by the inconclusive siege of Tournai, not enacted in the play, and a complicated series of truces and skirmishes before the next major encounter, on land, at Crécy in 1346.

Sly, William   (d. 1608)   English actor, member of the CHAMBERLAIN'S MEN and the KING'S MEN. Sly is one of the 26 men listed in the FIRST FOLIO as "Principall Actors" in Shakespeare's plays. He was with either STRANGE'S MEN or the ADMIRAL'S MEN around 1590, for he appears in the combined company of that year. Between 1592 and 1594, he was probably associated with PEMBROKE'S MEN, for he apparently helped compile their text for *The Taming of a Shrew*, a BAD QUARTO (text assembled from memory) of *The Taming of the Shrew*. Sly played—and was presumably the namesake of—Christopher Sly in *The Shrew*, and that part is fairly accurately reproduced in *A Shrew*. His next documented appearance was with the Chamberlain's Men in 1598, though he may have been a member of the company at its inception in 1594. He remained a member after it became the King's Men, until his death. He may have played Osric in *Hamlet*, though except for Christopher Sly, no Shakespearean role can be assigned with certainty to him. He was not an original partner in the GLOBE THEATRE, but he had acquired a share by 1605. In 1608 he was an original shareholder in the BLACKFRI-ARS THEATRE, but he died a week after the agreement was signed, and his share was redistributed among the other partners. He left his share in the Globe to Robert BROWNE, who was probably his brother-in-law.

Smethwick, John (John Smithweeke)   (d. 1641) English bookseller and publisher, producer of several editions of Shakespeare's plays and a partner in the FIRST FOLIO. In 1607 Nicholas LING sold Smethwick the rights to *Hamlet, Romeo and Juliet, Love's Labour's Lost*, and *The Taming of a Shrew*. Smethwick is only known to have produced editions of two of these, however: Q3 of *Romeo and Juliet* (1609) and Q3–5 of *Hamlet* (1611, 1622, 1637). He had a share in both the First and Second Folios of Shakespeare's collected plays (1623, 1632).

Smethwick finished nine years of apprenticeship and became a member of the STATIONERS' COMPANY in 1597. Early in his career, he was fined several times for pirating copyrighted books, but he presumably changed his ways, for he eventually became a high officer in the Stationers' Company.

Smith, Morgan (ca. 1833–1882) African-American actor in Britain. Like Ira ALDRIDGE before him, Smith made a living in the English theater at a time when black American actors could not surmount racial prejudice at home. Though not the major figure Aldridge was, he had a successful career as a touring performer, often reading a miscellany of speeches in lieu of a play production. A native of Philadelphia, Smith trained with a Welsh actor in Boston, but, when he was refused employment there, he emigrated. Four days after his arrival in England in 1866, never having appeared in public before, Smith performed successfully as Othello. He also played Richard III, Macbeth, Hamlet, Shylock (*The Merchant of Venice*), Iago (*Othello*), and Romeo, as well as a range of non-Shakespearean roles, until ill health compelled him to retire in about 1879.

Smithfield An open field to the north of London, the location, in 4.7 of *2 Henry VI*, of a skirmish won by Jack Cade's rebels, after which they execute Lord Say. This choice of location, not necessitated by Shakespeare's sources, was appropriate: Smithfield, which was London's great livestock market, was frequently the site of public executions.

Smithson, Harriet (1800–1853) Irish actress, successful in France. Smithson was a relatively unknown London actress when she played Ophelia in a production of *Hamlet* mounted in Paris by William Charles MACREADY in 1827. She was a

great success, both in this role and others, notably Othello's Desdemona, and she toured Europe to continued acclaim. A leading Parisian critic of the day declared that she had introduced Shakespeare to France. She soon abandoned her career, however, to marry the composer Hector BERLIOZ in 1833. It was an unhappy marriage, and he eventually left her for another woman, though when she became an invalid in her last years, he returned and stayed with her until her death.

Snodham, Thomas (d. 1625) London printer. Snodham, who established his printing business in 1603, printed an edition of THOMAS LORD CROMWELL—a play spuriously attributed to Shakespeare—in 1613, and in 1616 he printed Q6 of *The Rape of Lucrece* for publisher Roger JACKSON. Snodham was a brother-in-law of publisher Cuthbert BURBY.

soliloquy Speech made by a character, usually when alone on the stage, revealing his or her inner thoughts. Originally a device of ancient Greek and Roman drama, the soliloquy was popular in the REN-AISSANCE and was widely used in ELIZABETHAN DRAMA. Shakespeare frequently used this device to present the audience with material that could not be realistically delivered in dialogue. Sometimes the soliloquy simply provides information on the plot—as when villains such as Aaron (*Titus Andronicus*), Iago (*Othello*), and Richard III comment on their own schemes—but more often it functions to reveal character through the expression of private emotional drives. This technique is particularly striking in *Hamlet* and *Macbeth*, whose soliloquies are among Shakespeare's greatest poetic achievements. The two uses can of course apply simultaneously, as when Iago both directs our knowledge of the central plot and displays his own tortuous nature. While Shakespeare's most famous soliloquies are given to his great tragic characters, the effect of a soliloquy can also be comic, as in those of Malvolio (*Twelfth Night*) and Benedick (*Much Ado About Nothing*).

Though artificial, the soliloquy nevertheless supports our sense of the play's truth to reality, for we recognize that a character has no motive for lying in a soliloquy and accordingly accept the passage as a legitimate revelation. In Shakespeare, a character's use of soliloquy often in itself demonstrates an introspective personality; Hamlet and Macbeth are actively molding their psychological and spiritual natures, whereas others, such as Coriolanus and Antony, do not concern themselves with these matters and seldom reveal themselves to the audience.

song   Short poem accompanied by music, often used in Shakespeare's plays, though not always written by the playwright. Many of these songs are versions or fragments of popular songs known from other sources, a few were probably written by collaborators, and some may have been inserted into a play by someone other than the playwright, in the course of a theatrical run. However, scholars generally believe that the following songs (in approximate order of composition) were written by Shakespeare: "Who Is Silvia?" (*Two Gentlemen of Verona*); "When daisies pied" (*Love's Labour's Lost*); "You spotted snakes" (*A Midsummer Night's Dream*); "Tell me, where is fancy bred" (*The Merchant of Venice*); "Sigh no more, ladies" and "Pardon, goddess of the night" (*Much Ado About Nothing*); "Under the greenwood tree," "Blow, blow, thou winter wind," "What shall he have that killed the deer?", and "It was a lover and his lass" (*As You Like It*); "O mistress mine," "Come away, death," and "When that I was and a little tiny boy" (*Twelfth Night*); "Take, O take those lips away" (*Measure for Measure*); "Hark, hark, the lark" and "Fear no more the heat o' the sun" (*Cymbeline*); "When daffodils begin to peer," "Get you hence, for I must go," and "Lawn as white as driven snow" (*The Winter's Tale*); "Come unto these yellow sands," "Full fadom five thy father lies," and "Where the bee sucks" (*The Tempest*); "Orpheus with his lute" (*Henry VIII*); and "Roses, their sharp spines being gone" (*The Two Noble Kinsmen*).

Shakespeare's early songs mostly served to adorn a COMEDY and generally had little if any importance to the plot or characterizations. However, beginning with the songs of Amiens and Touchstone in *As You Like It* (1599), the songs begin to relate to character and to the play's theme. This change probably reflects the talents of Robert ARMIN; before he joined the CHAMBERLAIN'S MEN, the availability of a

A 17th-century setting of Desdemona's song in *Othello*. Songs were elements in many of Shakespeare's plays, whether written by the playwright himself or, like this one, taken from popular ballads of the day. (*Courtesy of the Trustees of the British Museum*)

good singer for a play was uncertain, so the playwright may have been reluctant to give a song much significance. Shakespearean TRAGEDY uses song dramatically—as in the songs of the Fool in *King Lear*, Ophelia in *Hamlet*, and Desdemona in *Othello*—but these were popular ballads of the day, recognizable by the original audiences and thus even more potent dramatically. In the last plays, the ROMANCES and *Henry VIII*, the influence of the MASQUE demanded songs, most of which Shakespeare wrote.

Little of the original music for Shakespeare's plays has survived. The tunes of currently popular songs were doubtless used for at least some of the songs, even among those Shakespeare wrote, but other melodies were composed by Robert JOHNSON, Thomas MORLEY, John WILSON, and possibly others. Shakespeare was plainly conscious of the composer's task, for he was careful to write lyrics with short, rhymed lines of varying lengths, and he emphasized vowel sounds rather than consonants, especially at the ends of lines. Many notable composers have subsequently set Shakespeare's songs to music (see, e.g., ARNE, THOMAS AUGUSTINE; SCHUBERT, FRANZ; SULLIVAN, ARTHUR SEYMOUR).

sonnet Verse form, a 14-line poem, usually in iambic pentameter (see METER) and with any of several traditional rhyme schemes. The sonnet has been widely popular ever since its evolution from medieval Italian verse and is still used by poets in most European languages. Shakespeare's *Sonnets* are among the best known, and he also employed sonnets in several of his plays, most notably in *Romeo and Juliet* and *Love's Labour's Lost.*

A sonnet usually consists of two parts, an eight-line section (the octet) followed by a six-line section (the sestet). Three rhyme schemes are most commonly employed in English sonnets: the Shakespearean sonnet (abab cdcd efef gg), which is named for Shakespeare's use of it to the exclusion of other schemes; the Spenserian sonnet (abab bcbc cdcd ee), which was developed by Edmund SPENSER; and the Italian sonnet (abba abba cdecde; the sestet may have a different arrangement as long as it does not end with two rhyming lines, a couplet). The Italian sonnet, the oldest variety, is also called the Petrarchan sonnet, after its most famous exponent, Petrarch (1304–74).

In the Petrarchan sonnet, the pattern of rhymes changes completely in the sestet. This arrangement encourages a two-part division of content; an important component of the Petrarchan sonnet is the *volta* (an Italian musical term), or "turn of thought," the change of direction that often occurs in line 9. This change may be a feature of non-Petrarchan sonnets as well, as in Shakespeare's "But thy eternal summer shall not fade" (Sonnet 18.9). However, the Spenserian and Shakespearean schemes—which are more appropriate to English, a language with fewer rhymes than Italian—offer

another pattern of development: a progression through three quatrains to a concluding or summarizing couplet. These two developments are not, of course, mutually exclusive. Sonnet 18, in fact, exemplifies both: Its quatrains lead like stepping-stones to a strong concluding couplet.

The sonnet, which developed in medieval Italy, first became known to English poets in the love poems of Dante (1265–1321) and Petrarch. Thomas WYATT is commonly credited with introducing the form to England, though CHAUCER had translated a sonnet by Petrarch and incorporated it in his *Troilus and Criseyde,* without acknowledging it. But it was Henry Howard, Earl of SURREY, who popularized the English quatrains-and-couplet arrangement. Spenser's rhyme scheme compromises between the stricter Italian and the looser English. In Elizabethan England, sonnets were a fashionable pastime, and sonneteers flourished (they are amiably satirized in *Love's Labour's Lost*). In Elizabethan poetry the sonnet was conventionally associated with love poetry; John Donne, in the early 17th century, expanded its range to encompass religious themes, and John MILTON continued this development, composing sonnets on various personal and public matters. In the 18th century, the form fell into disuse. Revived with the rise of romanticism, the sonnet has adapted well to the less-formal modern world. Today it is often used with less rigorously prescribed rhyme and meter, for every imaginable subject.

Sothern, Edward Hugh (1859–1933) British-born American actor. At 20 Sothern began his career by joining his father, a comedian who was performing in America. Himself a comedian and romantic leading man, he was best known as Malvolio, in *Romeo and Juliet,* and also played Hamlet. From 1904 to 1926 he and Julia MARLOWE headed a Shakespearean company; they married in 1911.

Southampton Seaport in southern England, a location in *Henry V.* In 2.2, just before invading FRANCE, King *Henry V* entraps three treacherous noblemen—the Earl of Cambridge, Lord Scroop, and Sir Thomas Grey—who have conspired with the enemy and plan to assassinate him. Shakespeare himself did not indicate the setting, but the historical event took place in Southampton, and modern editors have generally followed Alexander POPE in placing the scene there.

Southampton, Henry Wriothesley, Earl of (1573–1624) Contemporary of Shakespeare, a patron of the arts to whom Shakespeare dedicated *Venus and Adonis* (1593) and *The Rape of Lucrece* (1594). These two dedications are the only certain connection between Shakespeare and Southampton; they were written in the hope of patronage (i.e., financial support) from the young nobleman. The first dedication is an ordinary approach by a poet seeking backing from someone he does not know well, but the second reflects considerable friendship between patron and poet. Unlike any other dedication of the period, it is confident of the support it seeks and radiates an air of intimacy. The poet may have spent some time during the plague years of 1592 to 1594—the period during which he wrote the poems—at Southampton's estate. An 18th-century account attributes to William DAVENANT the information that Southampton had given Shakespeare £1000, and though the amount is much too large to be believed—perhaps 10–20 times Shakespeare's annual income at the time—there may be a germ of truth to the story. Some scholars believe that Southampton may be the young man to whom most of the *Sonnets* are addressed, or the mysterious "Mr. W. H." to whom they are dedicated by the publisher. This cannot be proven, but that the two men were friends is accepted by most scholars.

A favorite courtier of Queen Elizabeth I (see Elizabeth I in *Henry VIII*), Southampton was a patron of John FLORIO and other writers. He became a follower of Robert Devereux, Earl of ESSEX, and accompanied him on his successful expeditions to Cadiz and the Azores in 1595 and 1596. Essex's cousin was his mistress, and he married her in 1598, when she became pregnant. The queen was angered at the match and briefly imprisoned him; he never recovered the monarch's favor. In 1599 he joined Essex on his ill-fated mission to Ireland and shared in his subsequent disgrace. He helped plan Essex's rebellion and with him was condemned to death on its failure, but his sentence was commuted to life imprisonment

on the intervention of Robert CECIL. Southampton spent the rest of Elizabeth's reign in the TOWER OF LONDON. King JAMES I released him and made him a favored courtier. He became a promoter of colonizing enterprises and was an important member of the Virginia Company. In 1624, commanding English troops against the Spanish in the Netherlands, he died of plague. His family name is pronounced "Risley."

Southwark Southern suburb of LONDON, the location of a scene in *2 Henry VI*, and Shakespeare's residence between 1597 and sometime before 1602. In Shakespeare's day, Southwark was a raw, newly developed area, with crude roads and a nearby swamp. Beginning in 1587 several theaters—including the SWAN THEATRE, the ROSE THEATRE, and Shakespeare's GLOBE THEATRE—were built in Southwark because it was outside the jurisdiction of London, whose Puritan government was opposed to professional drama. Shakespeare probably moved there when his company, the CHAMBERLAIN'S MEN, left the THEATRE, to the north of London, and began to perform at the Swan. His exact residence in the district is unknown.

Southwark is also the setting for 4.8 of *2 Henry VI*, the depiction of an historical event that took place there in 1450. In 4.8 the rebellion led by Jack Cade has been driven from London across the Thames into Southwark, and the rebels are offered amnesty if they will disband, which most of them do, ending the uprising.

Spalding, William (1809–1859) Scottish scholar. Spalding was a professor of logic at the University of Edinburgh, but early in his career he published an essay that assigned authorship of different parts of *The Two Noble Kinsmen* to Shakespeare and John FLETCHER by studying the verse techniques employed in the play. This groundbreaking study of 1833 contributed greatly to the use of the VERSE TEST in the study of Shakespeare plays.

Spencer, Gabriel (d. 1598) English actor, a colleague of Shakespeare. Spencer was one of three members of PEMBROKE'S MEN—another was Ben JONSON—imprisoned briefly for staging the allegedly seditious play *Isle of Dogs* in July 1597. Upon his release he joined the ADMIRAL'S MEN as a principal actor. In September 1598 Jonson killed Spencer in a rapier duel. Little more is known of Spencer's life except that he himself had killed a man in a fight two years earlier.

Spencer is probably referred to in the FIRST FOLIO text of *3 Henry VI*, where a stage direction at 1.2.47 refers to the Messenger as "Gabriel," apparently meaning Spencer, who must have played the part. The title page of the 1595 edition of the play states that it had been performed by Pembroke's Men, so we may conclude that Spencer was with them before that date. However, it is possible that the stage direction was written for a later production by the CHAMBERLAIN'S MEN, in which case Spencer may have been a member of that troupe between 1594 and 1597.

Spenser, Edmund (ca. 1552–1599)

English poet, a major figure in English literature, the first great writer to succeed CHAUCER and the author of works that influenced Shakespeare. Spenser's monumental epic poem *The Faerie Queene* (published 1590, 1598) provided the playwright with the inspiration for many passages, especially in the earlier plays and poems. The PASTORAL poems in Spenser's *Shepheardes Calendar* (1579), and possibly his great wedding poem *Epithalamion* (1595), did the same for *A Midsummer Night's Dream*. Another of Spenser's poems, "The Teares of the Muses" (1591), may be alluded to in the *Dream* (5.1.52–53).

The son of a LONDON merchant, Spenser attended Cambridge University, where he met Gabriel HARVEY, through whom he was introduced to the literary circle centered on Sir Philip SIDNEY, whose close friend he became. His *Faerie Queene* has been recognized since its first appearance as one of the greatest accomplishments of English poetry. A vast tapestry of chivalry and adventure, it is simultaneously a nationalistic epic, a mythic romance, and an allegory on the human soul. Spenser was also an important influence on the development of the English SONNET.

Spiritual Testament of John Shakespeare

Document purporting to be a declaration of Catholic faith by Shakespeare's father, John SHAKESPEARE.

Reportedly found in 1757 in the roof of the Shakespeare BIRTHPLACE in STRATFORD, the Spiritual Testament was a six-page booklet, published in the 16th century, consisting of a statement of belief in various Catholic doctrines (the English translation of an Italian text, as scholars have discovered), with a signature line. It bears John Shakespeare's name. Such documents were provided to English Catholics by the Catholic Church in exile during the early days of the English Reformation, when Catholics were persecuted by the government, sometimes with great ferocity. A believing Catholic who felt compelled to maintain a public persona as a Protestant—and there were many—could sign such a testament and feel they were still, secretly, members of their original faith.

In recent decades a number of scholars have explored the question of whether or not William Shakespeare was a secret Catholic—or at the least, a Catholic sympathizer—and his father's religion has accordingly come under scrutiny. John Shakespeare was born a Catholic, before the English Reformation took place; he was married in the Catholic Church (during the reign of the Catholic queen Mary I); and he may, like many English people of his generation, have maintained his Catholic faith surreptitiously. Such "crypto-Catholicism" seems strongly suggested by the existence of the Testament, though scholars remain uncertain of its import, as well as of its legitimacy.

The Testament apparently remained in Stratford, a local curiosity, for 30 years, before finding its way to the great Shakespearean scholar, Edmond MALONE, who published it with his 1790 edition of the plays. However, he subsequently declared that it did not relate to Shakespeare's father, stating that he had found further documentary evidence disassociating the Testament from the playwright's family. He proposed to publish this evidence with his forthcoming biography of Shakespeare. Unfortunately, he died before doing so, and his successor, James BOSWELL, never found the evidence. It is speculated that Malone's proof may have associated the document with a different John Shakespeare (others are known) or may have faulted the tale of its discovery in the birthplace rafters, but no one now knows.

The document itself has been lost, though the copy Malone made survives, as do other instances of the printed form. Scholars dispute both the legitimacy of the find in the first place and its import for the life or beliefs of Shakespeare's father in the second. While the document itself is assumed to have been genuine (others like it have surfaced both in England and other countries), that Shakespeare's father was its signer is not self-evident, and its discovery might have been misunderstood or the document may even have been "planted" by 18th-century Catholic sympathizer. Further, even supposing the document completely genuine—completed by Shakespeare's father and hidden by him in the rafters—one may still suggest that he may have signed it under pressure from a fellow Catholic, or in a mere momentary effusion of enthusiasm that did not reflect his actual way of life, and then, fearful of the authorities but reluctant to simply destroy a religious document, hidden it.

In any case, there is no real evidence in William Shakespeare's works or in the records of his life to suggest that he felt any great inclination toward his father's hidden religious beliefs, if any; he might conceivably not have known of them. A number of Stratfordians—including John COTTAM and his brother, William REYNOLDS, and (possibly) Simon HUNT—were associated with underground Catholicism during these years, but the Shakespeares themselves were never so identified during their lifetimes, and the question of John's religion—and William's—remains unresolved.

Spread of the Eagle, The   TELEVISION production based on Shakespeare's ROMAN PLAYS. The British Broadcasting Corporation presented *The Spread of the Eagle* in 1963, combining *Coriolanus*, *Julius Caesar*, and *Antony and Cleopatra* in a nine-segment depiction of Roman history from the fifth century B.C. to the defeat of Mark Antony by Octavius Caesar in 31 B.C.

Spurgeon, Caroline (1869–1941)   British scholar. A longtime professor of English literature at the Uni-

versity of London, Spurgeon is best known for her book *Shakespeare's Imagery and What It Tells Us* (1935). This groundbreaking study examines the patterns of images in certain plays and attempts to determine aspects of Shakespeare's personality by analyzing the imagery he was most inclined to use. Spurgeon also edited *Keats' Shakespeare* (1928), a seven-volume edition of Shakespeare's works as annotated by the poet John KEATS.

Stafford, Simon (active 1596–1626)   LONDON printer who produced editions of several of Shakespeare's plays. Stafford, who mostly printed ballads and sermons, also printed the second QUARTO (Q2) of *1 Henry IV* (1599) for Andrew WISE, Q2 of *Edward III* for Cuthbert BURBY, and Q3 of *Pericles* (1611) for an unknown publisher. He also printed the 1605 edition of KING LEIR, a possible source for *King Lear*.

Stanley, Ferdinando, Lord Strange   See STRANGE, FERDINANDO STANLEY, LORD.

Stationers' Company   English guild of booksellers, publishers, and printers, an organization licensed by the government to protect the interests of its members by policing the publishing industry (with the exception of the university presses of Oxford and Cambridge). For such offenses as printing outlawed works or publishing works properly claimed by another member, the company could fine a printer or publisher, seize his press and type, suspend his right to conduct business, or even, in extreme cases, revoke it altogether (see DANTER, JOHN; SIMMES, VALENTINE). A member of the company could secure the rights to a work once it was licensed by the government—by the MASTER OF REVELS, in the case of plays—by registering it for a fee with the company. Where the publisher got his text was immaterial to the company, for the point was not to prevent piracy but to create copyright for the members. Also, it was not necessary to register a work with the company to publish it; however, an unregistered work could be freely reprinted by anyone. The Stationers' Company made no effort to protect the rights of an author, and even so far as it went it was inefficient—many violaters of the system went unpunished—but it marks the crude beginning of English copyright law.

Steevens, George (1736–1800) English scholar. Steevens published the texts of 20 QUARTO editions of the plays in 1766, and his edition of the collected plays came out in 1773. This edition was based on the text published by Samuel JOHNSON, with the addition of his own corrections and notes. It was reprinted with revisions in 1778 and 1785, with the assistance of Isaac REED. In response to Edmond MALONE's 1790 edition, Steevens undertook a final edition of his own in 1793. His 1778 edition was the basis for the first two VARIORUM EDITIONS. To his assiduous scholarship Steevens added a sardonic wit—inventing scholarly sources to which he attributed indecent interpretations, for instance. For this he is known as "the Puck of Commentators."

Stevens, R. J. S. (1757–1837) English composer, creator of several perennially popular glees, or unaccompanied SONGS, with lyrics from Shakespeare. Among the best-known of Stevens's works, "Ye spotted snakes" employs the fairies' song in 2.2.9–24 of *A Midsummer Night's Dream*, and "From Oberon in fairyland" uses other lines from that play. "The Cloud-capt towers" extracts lines from Prospero's famous valedictory speech, beginning at *The Tempest* 4.1.152, and "Crabbed age and youth" presents Poem No. 12 from THE PASSIONATE PILGRIM, a text that is probably not actually by Shakespeare, though Stevens would have thought it was.

Stoll, Elmer Edgar (1874–1959) American scholar. E. E. Stoll, as he is generally known, was a leading Shakespearean critic of the so-called realist school, which focused on the relationship of Shakespeare's plays to the playwright's times, especially to the practices of the ELIZABETHAN THEATER. Stoll was a longtime professor at the University of Minnesota; his best-known work is *Art and Artifice in Shakespeare* (1933).

Storace, Stephen (1762–1796) English composer of an OPERA based on *The Comedy of Errors*. The son of an Italian musician employed in England, Storace studied music in Italy and produced operas in Vienna (where he was a friend of Mozart), before he returned to England. His career as a composer lasted only a few years before his

early death. In 1786, while in Vienna, he wrote music for the opera *Gli equivoci*, to a libretto by Lorenzo Da Ponte (1749–1838; Mozart's frequent librettist) based on Shakespeare's comedy, which premiered at the Burgtheatre just after Mozart's *Le Nozze di Figaro*.

Stow, John (ca. 1525–1605) English historian whose works provided Shakespeare with minor details for the HISTORY PLAYS, perhaps especially influencing *King John*. Stow, a self-educated tailor, became an antiquarian under the influence of his friend William CAMDEN. He published a collection of the works of CHAUCER and a summary of early English chronicles, but his major work was his *Annales* (1580), a history of Britain from its mythological foundations to the year of publication. This popular work was reissued five times by 1631, with new additions by other authors. Stow also helped prepare the 1587 edition of Raphael HOLINSHED's *Chronicles*, Shakespeare's most important historical source. He also wrote a book on the LONDON of his day, *Survey of London* (1598), that offers scholars many telling glimpses of Shakespeare's world.

Strachey, Lytton (1880–1932) English biographer and critic. Strachey wrote *Shakespeare's Final Period* (1906), an important work that helped revolutionize Shakespearean criticism in the early 20th century. He influenced subsequent commentators—such as E. E. STOLL and Levin SCHÜCKING—to consider the plays in light of the circumstances under which they were produced, rather than by focusing exclusively on the worlds of the characters. A major figure of the famed Bloomsbury group—along with novelist Virginia Woolf (1882–1941) and economist John Maynard Keynes (1883–1946)—Strachey is best known for his biographies, such as *Eminent Victorians* (1918), *Queen Victoria* (1921), and *Elizabeth and Essex* (1928).

Strachey, William (ca. 1567–ca. 1634) English colonial entrepreneur and author, writer of sources for *The Tempest* and possibly *King Lear*. In June 1609 Strachey sailed for Virginia as part of a group of investors and adventurers involved in the newly established colony in Jamestown. One of the three ships in the expedition was wrecked in Bermuda, and Strachey, with Sylvester JOURDAIN, was marooned for 10 months before going on to Virginia. From Jamestown he wrote to England of his experiences. His letter was circulated among interested investors, and Shakespeare saw it, probably through Dudley DIGGES. It provided the playwright with details of the shipwreck in *The Tempest* 1.1 and Ariel's description of St. Elmo's fire in 1.2.196–206. Perhaps more important, it emphasized the providential survival of the voyagers and stressed the fact that an island previously notorious for evil spirits turned out to be a pleasant and productive place. (Partly in consequence Bermuda was soon settled by the English and is now the oldest British colony.) Both the role of providence and the sequence of deviltry succeeded by blessedness are paralleled in Shakespeare's depiction of Prospero's realm. Strachey's letter was eventually published in *Purchas his Pilgrimes* (1625), a famous anthology of exploration literature (see HAKLUYT, RICHARD).

Strachey was acquainted with Ben JONSON and wrote a laudatory poem for the preface to Jonson's *Sejanus* (1605). This poem may have influenced some of the wording in *King Lear*. Strachey's connection with *Sejanus*, a work Shakespeare acted in, suggests that he may well have known the playwright personally.

Strachey returned to England in 1611 and helped write the first code of laws for Virginia. By 1613 he had completed a *Historie of Travell into Virginia Britania*, but this work, valued by modern historians, was not published until 1849.

Strange, Ferdinando Stanley, Lord (ca. 1559–1594)   English theatrical patron, the sponsor of a theatrical company, STRANGE'S MEN, with whom Shakespeare may have been associated. Lord Strange (the name rhymes with "sang") was a courtier and minor poet. He patronized a provincial company of acrobats and tumblers that eventually evolved into an important theatrical company, though his involvement was not an influence on its development. As his "servants," the performers were protected from antitheatrical legislation (see ELIZABETHAN THEATER), and he could call on the company for private performances, but the personnel and repertoire of the

company were determined by its members. Strange's Men visited their patron's Lancashire home often, and Lord Strange may thus have known the young Shakespeare personally, though doubtless distantly. Some scholars believe that the visits (or accounts of them from other players) later influenced Shakespeare to create his comic stewards Malvolio (of *Twelfth Night*) and Oswald (of *King Lear*), who may have been modeled on Strange's steward, William FFARINGTON.

Strange succeeded his father as Earl of Derby (and the company therefore took the name DERBY'S MEN) in 1593. Now that he was a leading nobleman, a conspirator against Queen Elizabeth I approached him to suggest that he seize the crown on the strength of his mother's descent from Henry VII. Derby, as Strange was now known, denounced the traitor, who was executed. When the earl died a few months later, it was rumored that he had been killed in revenge, though modern scholars believe he died naturally. He was succeeded as earl by his younger brother, William Stanley, Earl of DERBY.

At Tong, in Shropshire, is the tomb of some of Lord Strange's relatives; on it are two epitaphs said to have been written by Shakespeare. This tradition, however, was first recorded years after Shakespeare's death and seems highly doubtful. Only one of the two epitaphs is of a literary quality that can plausibly be associated with Shakespeare, and in any case the occupants of the tomb died either long before or long after the playwright's connection with the family, which existed only through Strange's Men. The traditional attribution of these texts is probably a product of local pride.

Strange's family had long been prominent in the English aristocracy, and Shakespeare depicted several of his ancestors in the HISTORY PLAYS. Ferdinando Stanley, Lord Strange, was the great-great-grandson of Sir Thomas Stanley, who appears in *Richard III*, and thus Thomas and William Stanley, in *2 and 3 Henry VI*, respectively, were also his relatives.

Strange's Men   Acting company of the ELIZABETHAN THEATER, possible employer of the young Shakespeare and predecessor of the CHAMBERLAIN'S MEN (later the KING'S MEN), undeniably the playwright's longtime professional home. Named for its patron, Ferdinando Stanley, Lord STRANGE (the name rhymes with "sang"), Strange's Men was apparently a troupe of acrobats and tumblers when it first appeared in LONDON in the early 1580s, but in 1588, when its leader joined the QUEEN'S MEN, the company was reorganized; henceforth it emphasized acting over acrobatics.

By 1590 Strange's Men was allied with the other major London troupe, the ADMIRAL'S MEN, performing at the THEATRE, owned by James BURBAGE, whose son, Richard BURBAGE, was to become the company's leading tragedian. Strange's and the Admiral's Men were associated off and on for several years; the former often played at the CURTAIN THEATRE, whose owner, Henry LANEMAN, was James Burbage's partner at the time. A cast list of 1591 shows that among the members of Strange's—or at least acting with them—were Richard Burbage, George BRYAN, Richard COWLEY, Thomas GOODALE, John HOLLAND, Augustine PHILLIPS, Thomas POPE, John SINCKLO, and William SLY. Bryan, Phillips, Pope, and Cowley are also recorded as members in 1593, and these four plus Burbage were charter members of the Chamberlain's Men, when Strange's was reorganized under a new patron following Lord Strange's death in the spring of 1594. Less than a year earlier, Strange had become the Earl of Derby, so the company was also known briefly as DERBY'S MEN.

Scholars believe that Shakespeare was involved with Strange's Men, probably as both actor and playwright. (He may, however, have been associated with other companies as well. See ADMIRAL'S MEN; LEICESTER'S MEN; PEMBROKE'S MEN; QUEEN'S MEN; SUSSEX'S MEN.) The troupe produced *Titus Andronicus* and *Harey vj* (almost certainly *1 Henry VI*); the combined Strange's-Admiral's company probably staged both *2* and *3 Henry VI*. Further, though the earliest surviving documentary evidence linking Shakespeare with the company dates only from December 1594, after Strange's Men's demise, the playwright was already a leading figure in the Chamberlain's Men when first mentioned, receiving the company's fee for a performance at court, suggesting that he had already been involved with them for some time.

Stratford Town in WARWICKSHIRE, England, Shakespeare's hometown and his residence upon retirement from LONDON. Stratford-upon-Avon, to give it its full name, was a simple market town of 1,500–2,000 people in Shakespeare's day. It was the center of a rich farming area and the locus of its trade. Its population consisted largely of farmers, the artisans and craftsmen who served them, and the businessmen who ran stores and inns, retailed manufactured goods, and marketed the farmer's crops. John SHAKESPEARE, the playwright's father, advanced economically through all of these groups. The son of a farmer, he became a tanner of fine leathers, a maker and seller of gloves, and a trader in various commodities such as grain and wool. Stratford's principal industry in Shakespeare's day (and until the 20th century) was the brewing of beer and ale. (Among the commodities John Shakespeare traded was barley, the brewer's basic raw material.) At the top of the social scale were wealthy landowners, the class to which Shakespeare advanced when he returned to Stratford a rich man after his career in the theater.

Stratford was a very ancient rural center. Taking its name from its location where an ancient road—a *straet* in Anglo-Saxon—crossed the Avon River at a *ford*, it was first settled by Bronze Age Celts. It was recognized as an independent market town in medieval times. A religious organization, the Guild of the Holy Cross, provided its government and a variety of civil services, including its schools. The guild was abolished in 1547, after the coming of Protestantism under King Henry VIII (see Henry VIII in *Henry VIII*), and a secular government with elected officials was established in its place. During the 1560s and 1570s, Shakespeare's father was among those officials. The guild's headquarters, the Guild Hall, built in 1417, still survives. A two-story half-timbered structure, it was the central building of the town in Shakespeare's day, with the meeting rooms of the town government on the street floor and the Stratford grammar school above, in a single large classroom. Shakespeare must have attended the grammar school between approximately 1570 and 1580, though the records for these years have not survived.

The future playwright will also have seen theatrical performances during his youth, for Stratford was large and prosperous enough that professional

Shakespeare's birthplace, Stratford-upon-Avon. *(Courtesy of British Tourist Authority)*

acting companies found audiences there (see ELIZA-BETHAN THEATER; QUEEN'S MEN; WORCESTER'S MEN). In fact, such performances were first licensed in the town during John Shakespeare's term as bailiff, the equivalent of mayor.

The Shakespeares lived in a neighborhood of prosperous tradesmen on the northern side of the town, in a house that was composed of two modest buildings joined to make a more substantial dwelling. Because the playwright was probably born in this house, it is known as the BIRTHPLACE, and it has been renovated as a museum. Shakespeare's later home in Stratford, the mansion called NEW PLACE, no longer survives. It was the second-largest house in the town (the largest had once been a dormitory for the medieval guild). Shakespeare subsequently

added an adjacent property, the CHAPEL LANE COTTAGE, to New Place.

At the south end of the town was Stratford's most important institution, the Church of the Holy Trinity. The most prominent building in Stratford, then and now, Holy Trinity is regarded as among the loveliest of England's small medieval churches. Its construction began around A.D. 1200, with different parts being added on over the centuries. Indeed, the prominent spire that tops its square tower was built long after Shakespeare's day. At the time of Shakespeare's birth, the rector of Holy Trinity was John BRETCHGIRDLE, who bequeathed to the grammar school much of its library. The first rector that Shakespeare could have known was Henry HEICROFT, who arrived when the future playwright was five and was still there to christen Susanna SHAKESPEARE in 1583. The rector for most of the period after Shakespeare's return from London until after his death was John ROGERS. Another important man at Holy Trinity was its longtime curate, or assistant to the rector, William GILBARD, a possible model for Nathaniel in *Love's Labour's Lost*.

Soon after Shakespeare's death, Stratford's fame as the playwright's home became central to its existence. As early as 1630, a visitor described it as "most remarkable for the birth of famous William Shakespeare." In the centuries since, it has become a mecca for greater and greater numbers of Shakespeare enthusiasts. In 1847 a nonprofit organization was formed to buy and maintain the birthplace, which was then a butcher's shop. In 1891 the Shakespeare Birthplace Trust was incorporated to care for this building and New Place. The Trust later acquired Anne HATHAWAY's cottage, the supposed ARDEN home, the home of Shakespeare's son-in-law Dr. John HALL, and other properties related to the playwright.

Stratford also became a center for the performance of Shakespeare's plays. In 1769 David GARRICK held a "Jubilee" of performances there, and in 1827 a series of festivals was instituted, though the financial failure of the first one killed the idea. However, as an outgrowth of the elaborate 1864 celebration of Shakespeare's 300th birthday, the Shakespeare Memorial Theatre was created, opening its own building in 1879 with a performance of *Much Ado About Nothing* starring Barry SULLIVAN and Helen FAUCIT. A permanent company evolved under the leadership of Frank BENSON from 1886 to 1919, and Stratford today enjoys an annual theater season running from April to November. Reorganized in 1961 as the ROYAL SHAKESPEARE COMPANY, the troupe performs in London in the winter and sends road companies on tour as well, producing Shakespeare's works and other plays, both classical and modern.

Stuart dynasty   Ruling dynasty in England from 1603 to 1714 (except from 1649 to 1660). King JAMES I (ruled 1603–25), the first Stuart monarch to govern England, ruled during the last 13 years of Shakespeare's life. James, already King James VI of

SCOTLAND, succeeded to the English throne when his cousin Queen Elizabeth I (see Elizabeth I in *Henry VIII*), the last monarch of the TUDOR DYNASTY, died childless. Although the Scottish dynasty, which dated to the 14th century, spelled their name Stewart, James VI's mother, Mary Queen of Scots (1542–87), married a cousin whose branch of the Stewart family resided in FRANCE and had adopted the French spelling Stuart.

James's ascension provided a Protestant ruler for England and offered the prospect of unity for the two kingdoms he ruled (though the formal union of England and Scotland did not come until 1707). Thus, in the early 17th century, Stuart rule was generally welcomed by the English. Shakespeare reflected this attitude in *Henry VIII*, where a prediction is made that James shall rule with "Peace, plenty, love, truth, terror" (5.4.47, where *terror* simply means "awe-inspiring power").

However, after Shakespeare's time the Stuart dynasty had a difficult history, in good part because of religious disputes. Though James was strongly Protestant, the next three kings were more sympathetic to Catholicism, and all three married Catholic princesses from European countries. English Protestants, a vast and often militant majority, distrusted them. James's son Charles I (ruled 1625–49) proved unable to prevent the Civil Wars of 1642–51, in the course of which he was executed and a revolutionary government was established in Britain. When the new government eventually collapsed, however, Charles's exiled son was called back and ruled as Charles II from 1660 to 1685. His reign was marked by strong anti-Catholic sentiment in English politics, and while generally popular, he was suspected of pro-Catholic leanings. He was thought to have secretly converted on his deathbed, and his successor, his brother James II (ruled 1685–89), was suspected of practicing Catholicism even before he acceded. James's first wife was a Protestant, and their children, Mary and Anne (later to rule), were raised as Protestants, but his second wife was an Italian Catholic. Popular opinion suspected Vatican-inspired plots to impose Catholicism on the country. For this and other reasons, James was deposed and exiled in the Glorious Revolution of 1689, so called for its bloodlessness.

The thoroughly Protestant Mary Stuart and her Dutch husband, William of Orange, were installed as Mary II and William III, known jointly as William and Mary (ruled 1689–1702). They were succeeded by Mary's sister Anne, during whose reign England and Scotland were formally united as the Kingdom of Great Britain. Anne died childless in 1714, the last Stuart monarch in Britain. However, the Catholic branch of the Stuarts had not yet disappeared. On three occasions—in 1689–91, 1715, and 1745–46—rebellions were launched in favor of the former monarch James II, his son, and his grandson, respectively. All were suppressed. Finally, with the defeat of James's grandson "Bonnie Prince Charlie" at the battle of Culloden (1746), all hope of restoring the dynasty was abandoned, even by its most fanatical adherents.

Sturley, Abraham (d. 1614) Businessman of STRATFORD and an acquaintance of Shakespeare. Sturley, an investor in real estate and tithes (the right to collect the taxes on a given property—a marketable commodity in Shakespeare's day and one in which the playwright also invested), settled in Stratford after a period spent working for Sir Thomas LUCY. Part of his correspondence with Richard QUINEY, his nephew, has survived, in which he writes on several occasions of dealings with Shakespeare, at one point doubting that the playwright would make a requested loan ("I will like it [the loan], as I shall hear when, and where, and how"). The accuracy of his prediction is unknown, and his other references to Shakespeare's business affairs are equally obscure.

subplot Sequence of developments secondary in importance to the main line of action in a drama. The subplot is a common feature of ELIZABETHAN DRAMA and JACOBEAN DRAMA—indeed, of virtually all premodern English drama—and few of Shakespeare's plays lack one. Sometimes his subplots offer a pointed contrast with the central material, as in *Love's Labour's Lost,* where the buffoonery of Costard and the other rustic characters emphasizes the elegance of Berowne and the other courtiers. On the other hand, a subplot can parallel a main plot, offering different angles on the same theme, as in the subplot involving Gloucester in *King Lear.*

Sugarsop Name mentioned in *The Taming of the Shrew.* Sugarsop is cited by Grumio as one of the servants of Petruchio in 4.1.80, but he never appears or is referred to again. This may reflect an abbreviated text, from which roles were cut because of a shortage of actors, but it is more probable that Grumio was being humorous; a sugarsop was a piece of bread soaked in a sweet or spiced sauce.

Sullivan, Arthur Seymour (1842–1900) English composer. Best known as the collaborator of W. S. Gilbert (1836–1911) in their famous operettas, Sullivan first achieved renown with his incidental music for *The Tempest* (1862). For the tercentenary celebrations of Shakespeare's birth in 1864, he wrote the *Kenilworth Cantata,* which incorporates Lorenzo's lovely speech on the beauties of the night (*Merchant of Venice* 5.1.54–65). He also wrote accompaniments for several of Shakespeare's songs and composed incidental music for *Henry VIII* (1877) and *Macbeth* (1888).

Sullivan, Barry (1821–1891) Irish actor. Sullivan played in more than 300 Shakespearean productions. He was best known as Hamlet and Richard III. In 1879 he played Benedick opposite the Beatrice of Helen FAUCIT in *Much Ado About Nothing,* the premiere performance at the Shakespeare Memorial Theatre in STRATFORD.

Surrey Horse belonging to King Richard III in *Richard III,* his mount at the battle of BOSWORTH FIELD. In 5.3.65, Richard calls for "white Surrey," who is reported killed in battle in 5.4, before the king's famous cry, "My kingdom for a horse" (5.4.13). Surrey's presence is based on several references in the chronicles to a great white charger ridden by Richard, but the name appears to be an invention of Shakespeare's.

Surrey, Henry Howard, Earl of (ca. 1517–1547) English poet, important developer of the English SONNET and the introducer of BLANK VERSE into English poetry. Surrey studied the poets of the Italian RENAISSANCE, especially Petrarch (1301–74), and shortly after his close friend Thomas WYATT introduced the sonnet into English, Surrey developed a variant more appropriate to the relatively rhyme-poor English language. This was the rhyme scheme that Shakespeare was to use in his *Sonnets*, the so-called English, or Shakespearean sonnet. In his partial translation of VIRGIL's *Aeneid* (published 1557), Surrey first used blank verse in English.

Surrey was a cousin of King Henry VIII and a close friend of his illegitimate son. As a young man, he naturally became involved in the political intrigue of the court. In 1540 he helped his father—the Surrey of *Henry VIII*—bring about the downfall of Thomas Cromwell. Surrey fell victim to the increasing paranoia of King Henry, who was dying and feared that a promising young man of royal blood might want to hasten the process. Surrey was tried for treason on trumped-up charges and executed, only a few days before the king's death.

Sussex's Men   Acting company of the ELIZABETHAN THEATER, possibly employers of Shakespeare early in his career. An acting company employed by Robert Radcliffe, Earl of Sussex (1573–1629), Sussex's Men performed at the court of Queen Elizabeth I in 1592. In the winter of 1593–94, Sussex's Men performed for Philip HENSLOWE, probably at the ROSE THEATRE, for a short interval when plays were permitted during the plague year. *Titus Andronicus* was in their repertoire at that time; some scholars think the young Shakespeare may have been a member of the company and may have written it expressly for them. In the spring of 1594, Sussex's Men performed jointly with the QUEEN'S MEN, and the two may have coalesced at this time, for Sussex's Men disappear from the record until 1602, when they reappear as a provincial touring company.

An earlier Sussex's Men had been employed by Robert's father, Thomas Radcliffe (ca. 1530–83), and they had appeared regularly at court, as well as on tour in the provinces, between 1572 and 1583. Because Thomas was Elizabeth's chamberlain after 1572, the company was sometimes called the Chamberlain's Men, but they are not to be confused with the later CHAMBERLAIN'S MEN, Shakespeare's company for many years.

Swan Theatre   Playhouse in LONDON built by Francis LANGLEY around 1595 and depicted in the only surviving drawing of a 16th-century English theater interior. Johannes de Witt, a Dutch traveler who visited London around 1596, made a drawing of the Swan, of which a copy has survived. Its accuracy has been questioned, but its major features are probably correct. They include a circular building with three stories of seats, each containing three rows, overlooking an unroofed central area into which a stage thrusts. The stage is half-covered by a canopy extending from its rear wall and supported by massive columns on stage; there are two doors in the back wall of the stage, with a set of box seats above these doors, behind the stage. At the top of this rear structure is a roofed hut, from which a flag flies and a man blows a trumpet, both signs that a play is scheduled. On the stage are three performers.

This drawing of the Swan Theatre by Johannes de Witt is the only known contemporary image of the interior of an Elizabethan theater.

The circularity of the theater in de Witt's drawing reflects the reality of a building in the shape of a many-sided polygon. A 1628 map of the neighborhood shows the Swan as a 14-sided building, and this evidence seems confirmed by the archaeological excavation of the ROSE THEATRE, which proves to have been 14-sided. Similarly, the GLOBE THEATRE was a 20-sided polygon. Plastering in the angles where the sides met would have made these theaters appear circular to the casual observer.

If de Witt was in fact in London in 1596—the record is obscure—then the performers on the stage in his drawing may be members of Shakespeare's company, the CHAMBERLAIN'S MEN, who probably played at the Swan for a season that year. In 1597 the PEMBROKE'S MEN came to London and engaged the theater for a year, but their production of an allegedly seditious play, *Isle of Dogs* by Thomas NASHE, resulted in the government's closure of all the London theaters for four months. When the theaters reopened, Langley was unable to recruit another company, and the Swan was not used regularly thereafter. After Langley's death in 1601, the theater was sold to another London investor, who had no greater success. Only one play besides *Isle of Dogs* is known to have been staged there. Miscellaneous entertainments—a fencing match, a poetry improvisation contest—are also recorded, but in 1632, a writer declared the Swan was "now fallen to decay."

Swinburne, Algernon Charles (1837–1909) English poet. Best known as a major late-Victorian poet, Swinburne also wrote literary criticism and enthusiastically encouraged a renewed interest in ELIZABETHAN DRAMA. Swinburne's Shakespearean commentary is regarded as more of a curiosity than a resource, however, for his adulation was extreme. For instance, he called *Cymbeline*'s Imogen "the woman best beloved in all the world of song and all the tide of time." Such sentimentality spurred a response led by George Bernard SHAW, who coined the word *bardolatry* to mock it.

Swinstead Abbey (Swineshead Abbey) Religious establishment in Lincolnshire, setting for 5.6–7 of *King John,* the site of the death of King John. Sick and dispirited, John withdraws from the fighting against the French and is poisoned by a monk. He dies the next day, and the Bastard leads the other noblemen in swearing allegiance to his successor, Henry.

Swinstead Abbey, which Shakespeare misnamed following John FOXE, was not the historical site of John's death, nor was the King poisoned, although Shakespeare took the tale from Raphael HOLINSHED and Foxe. John, stricken with dysentery while battling the French-supported rebels, spent a few days at Swineshead Abbey in October 1216, but he died several days later in nearby Newark.

T

Tamworth Village in central England, about 10 miles from BOSWORTH FIELD, setting for 5.2 of *Richard III*. As the Earl of Richmond approaches the forces of Richard III, he mentions the hamlet (in 5.2.13).

Tarlton, Richard (d. 1588) English comic actor, a leading figure in ELIZABETHAN THEATER when Shakespeare's career began. Tarlton was a member of the QUEEN'S MEN from its foundation in 1583 until his death. He was a particular favorite of Queen Elizabeth and served also as her personal jester or FOOL, though she began to dislike him when he went too far in jokes about her favorites. He also wrote plays, and his *The Seven Deadly Sins* (1585) may have been revived in the 1590s by Shakespeare's STRANGE'S MEN. His greatest accomplishment, however, was the establishment of a popular style for the stage CLOWN—earthy, awkward, comically confused in speech—that became standard. He was a great influence on William KEMPE, for whom Shakespeare wrote a number of parts. Tarlton was especially noted for his ability to improvise, and Hamlet's complaint about "clowns [who] speak . . . more than is set down for them" (*Hamlet* 3.2.39) was a joke at the expense of Tarlton and his successors. The great clown became something of a cult figure after his death; taverns were named for him, and ballads and joke books about him—or allegedly by him—appeared for at least 40 years. An unproven tradition holds that Shakespeare was thinking of Tarlton when he had Hamlet reminisce fondly of the jester Yorick.

Tate, Nahum (1652–1715) English poet and playwright, best known for his adaptations of Shakespeare's plays. Tate wrote a number of plays, most of them based on the works of various Elizabethan dramatists, but he is chiefly remembered for his version of *King Lear*. His *History of King Lear* (1681) retained some of Shakespeare's dialogue, but only in a drastically revised play. Tate eliminated the blinding of Gloucester and his suicide attempt, and he added a love affair between Edgar and Cordelia. He deleted the king's Fool, and, most notoriously, he provided a happy ending in which Lear is restored to his throne, abdicating in favor of Edgar and Cordelia. Though modern commentators condemn Tate's adaptation as a travesty, it was one of the most successful plays in the history of the English theater, performed for over 150 years in successive revivals and published in 22 editions. (Shakespeare's text was restored in bits and pieces by various producers, but his ending was not again enacted until 1823, by Charles KEAN; and the original play as a whole was staged only in 1838, by W. C. MACREADY.)

Tate's play was not simply a tasteless avoidance of the tragic; composed in the wake of a revolution and civil war, it carried a strong moralizing endorsement of civil order, which doubtless accounted in part for its original popularity. His Lear, in being both martyred and restored, recalled the recent history of the STUART DYNASTY and assured its partisans—the establishment of the day—that disaster could be overcome. Later, its generally optimistic stance, combined with the power of Shakespeare's poetry, endeared it to generations; it continued to be staged as late as 1843.

In 1680 Tate also adapted *Richard II*, but the state CENSORSHIP was even more nervous about this story of a king's deposition than it had been in Shakespeare's day—for in the interval the reality had occurred in England. Though Tate changed the scene and characters, calling it *The Sicilian Usurper*, it was suppressed by the government. In 1681, just after his *Lear* was staged, Tate took on *Coriolanus*, again making great alterations. His *The Ingratitude of a Commonwealth* retained some of Shakespeare's text, but it was essentially a different play, most conspicuously in its passages of sensationalistic violence. It too addressed the conservative political sensibility of the day, stressing the value of respectful loyalty, supporting Coriolanus's complaints about rebellious commoners, and de-emphasizing the hero's faults. However, unlike *The History of King Lear*, it was a commercial failure.

Taylor, Joseph (d. 1652) English actor, a member of the KING'S MEN. Though Taylor only joined the King's Men in 1619, he is listed among the "Principall Actors" of Shakespeare's plays in the FIRST FOLIO of 1623. He was hired away from PRINCE CHARLES' MEN to replace Richard BURBAGE within a few weeks of that star's death. He took over Burbage's most famous role, Hamlet, and was acclaimed in it. He was also noted as Iago, in *Othello*. In 1630 he became a partner in both the BLACKFRIARS and GLOBE THEATREs. In the same year he became a comanager of the company, with John LOWIN, and remained in that position until the theaters were closed down by the Puritan revolution in 1642.

Tchaikovsky, Peter Ilyich (1840–1893) Russian composer. One of the most popular and influential composers of the 19th century, Tchaikovsky was inspired by Shakespeare on several occasions. He wrote brief symphonic pieces for both *Hamlet* and *The Tempest*, and his symphonic fantasy *Romeo and Juliet* (1864) is one of his best-known works.

Tearle, Godfrey (1884–1953) British actor. The son of theatrical entrepreneurs who had staged Shakespeare at STRATFORD in the late 19th century,

Tearle had a long and illustrious career on stage and screen. He was especially noted for his portrayals of Hamlet, Othello, and the Antony of *Antony and Cleopatra*.

television Entertainment medium. All of Shakespeare's plays (except *The Two Noble Kinsmen*, which many people do not admit to the CANON of the playwright's works) have been produced for television. Many of the plays have been produced several times. Since the earliest days of the medium, television executives have been frank about using Shakespeare to provide a veneer of high seriousness to their operations, but it is also clear that there is a widespread audience for the plays. The British Broadcasting Corporation, at the forefront of Shakespeare production for television, has broadcast the standard canon of plays more than once, including special series such as THE SPREAD OF THE EAGLE and AN AGE OF KINGS.

Temple Grafton Village in WARWICKSHIRE, possibly the site of Shakespeare's marriage to Anne HATHAWAY. Shakespeare's marriage license identifies his bride as Anne Whately of Temple Grafton, a small farming village about five miles from STRATFORD. The misnomer of Whately for Hathaway seems due to clerical error—a Whately appears nearby in the records, though without a connection to Temple Grafton—but Anne was from Shottery, closer to Stratford. Commentators speculate that Anne may have been temporarily resident in Temple Grafton, or fallaciously so (to evade Shottery gossip about the pregnancy that apparently precipitated the wedding; see RICHARDSON, JOHN; SANDELLS, FULK; WHITGIFT, JOHN), or that Temple Grafton was the site of the wedding, chosen for the local minister, John FRITH, whom Puritan authorities called "an old priest and unsound in religion" who had apparently come to their attention earlier for laxity in accepting such hurried marriages. Some scholars have surmised, in the absence of any other data, that by coincidence another, otherwise unknown William Shakespeare married an otherwise unknown Anne Whately at about the same time the playwright married Anne Hathaway. This is, of course, highly unlikely, but what is certain is that this minor mystery cannot be unraveled with the existing evidence.

Terence (Publius Terentius Afer) (ca. 185–ca. 159 B.C.)   Ancient Roman dramatist well known to Shakespeare and a major influence on a source for several of his plays. Terence (with his contemporary, PLAUTUS) was an important figure in the early development of Latin literature, especially in transmitting ancient Greek COMEDY to the nascent Roman theater of his day. He was much later to be an important model for Ludovico ARIOSTO, whose work, through the translations of George GASCOIGNE, provided material for several of Shakespeare's plays, especially *The Taming of the Shrew*. Also, Shakespeare will have read Terence in school in STRATFORD, for selections from the Roman's plays were part of the ordinary Latin curriculum at that time.

Terry, Ellen (1848–1928)   British actress. Terry, the daughter of actors, was the leading Shakespearean actress of the last quarter of the 19th century and the first years of the 20th. She began her career at the age of eight, as Mamillius in *The Winter's Tale* of Charles KEAN, and she retired after playing the Nurse in a 1919 production of *Romeo and Juliet*. Between, she was chiefly associated with the company led by Henry IRVING, opposite whom she played many of Shakespeare's most important female roles, as well as many other parts, between 1878 and 1902. She was particularly noted as Beatrice *(Much Ado About Nothing)*, Imogen *(Cymbeline)*, Portia *(The Merchant of Venice)*, and Lady Macbeth, but in all her roles she was acclaimed as one of the great actresses of all time. After a brief early marriage, she lived for a number of years with the famed architect and designer Edward Godwin (1833–86), with whom she had two children, Gordon CRAIG and the actress Edith Craig (1869–1947). She also had two later, childless marriages. Terry was a member of a sprawling theatrical family. Both her parents and her eight siblings—including Fred TERRY—were in the theater, and when she celebrated her 50th year on the stage, 24 relatives appeared with her in a special performance. John GIELGUD was her great-nephew.

Terry, Fred (1863–1933)   British actor, brother of Ellen TERRY and husband of Julia NEILSON. Terry

established himself as an actor playing Sebastian opposite his sister's Viola in *Twelfth Night*, but he is best known as the costar and comanager, with his wife, of a popular theatrical company that performed in London and the British provinces between 1900 and 1930.

tetralogy   Either of two groupings of four HISTORY PLAYS that together deal with English dynastic history from just before the fall of King Richard II in 1399 until the battle of BOSWORTH FIELD on August 22, 1485, when the rule of the PLANTAGENET FAMILY ended and that of the TUDOR DYNASTY began. The two tetralogies are usually distinguished as the "major" and the "minor," one being regarded as much superior to the other, both as literature and as drama. The minor tetralogy, which was written in 1590 and 1591, consists of *1, 2*, and *3 Henry VI* and *Richard III*, and covers the later part of the historical period, from 1422 on. The major tetralogy is composed of *Richard II, 1* and *2 Henry IV*, and *Henry V*, and it is concerned with the earlier history. It was written between 1595 and 1599.

Tewkesbury (Tewksbury)   Location in *3 Henry VI*, a town near Gloucester and a battle site in the WARS OF THE ROSES. The army of Queen Margaret is defeated at Tewkesbury by that of King Edward IV. The battle takes place between 5.4 and 5.5; the fighting itself is not staged. In the former scene, the queen delivers a stirring speech to her followers, and in the latter they are all captives of Edward, who, with his brothers, kills Margaret's son, the Prince of Wales. This incident is taken from the chronicle by Edward HALL, but earlier accounts report the prince was killed in combat. The battle, which was fought in May 1471, three weeks after the battle of BARNET, marked the end of Lancastrian hopes and firmly secured Edward on the throne of England.

Tharsus   Ancient river port, the present-day Turkish city Tarsus, the setting for a number of scenes in *Pericles*. Governed by Cleon, Tharsus is saved from imminent starvation when Pericles arrives with supplies, in 1.4. In 3.3 Pericles leaves his infant daughter, Marina, in the care of Cleon and his wife Dionyza, and in 4.1 Dionyza attempts to murder the child, who is now 14 years old. The location was provided by Shakespeare's sources, and the actual city is not in evidence.

The historical Tarsus was a wealthy city, the center of a prosperous linen industry. First important as part of the Persian Empire and later a wealthy Hellenistic and Roman center, it was a commercial center of the Seleucid Empire at the time of the play. It straddled the Cydnus River and was the site of the first meeting of Mark Antony and Cleopatra (described in *Antony and Cleopatra*, 2.2.186 ff.), and the hometown of St. Paul. It was notorious in classical literature for the luxurious lifestyle of its upper class, as is reflected in 1.4.21–31 of *Pericles*.

Theatre, the First LONDON playhouse, built by James BURBAGE in 1576. The Theatre was built on leased land in Shoreditch, a northern suburb just beyond the jurisdiction of the London city government, which was controlled by Puritans who were opposed to theatrical entertainment on moral grounds. Before the Theatre was built, plays were performed in inn yards or other buildings not intended for the purpose. No reliable image of Burbage's theater exists, but it was apparently a polygonal, roughly cylindrical, three-story structure built around an open, unroofed central space. There were rows of galleries overlooking the center at each level. The stage projected from one sector of the building into the center, with the building above it reserved for backstage areas (see ELIZABETHAN THEATER). A number of acting companies played at the Theatre during its lifetime: LEICESTER'S MEN from 1576 to 1578, one of the groups known as OXFORD'S MEN on occasions between 1579 and 1582, the QUEEN'S MEN between 1583 and 1589, both the ADMIRAL'S MEN and STRANGE'S MEN in 1590–91, and the CHAMBERLAIN'S MEN after 1594. The Theatre was also used for fencing competitions and other activities. When the theaters were closed by the royal government in July 1597 after the *Isle of Dogs* scandal (see NASHE, THOMAS; PEMBROKE'S MEN; CENSORSHIP), the Theatre did not reopen. Burbage's ground lease had expired the previous April, just after he had died and left the Theatre and its lease to his son Cuthbert BURBAGE. After long negotia-tions, Cuthbert could not come to terms with the landowner, and in December 1598 he and a group of associates disassembled the building and used the lumber to build the GLOBE THEATRE.

Thebes Ancient Greek city, setting for several scenes of *The Two Noble Kinsmen*. In 1.2 the noblemen Palamon and Arcite contemplate the evils of life at the court of King Creon of Thebes and decide to leave the city. However, before they can do so, Theseus, Duke of ATHENS, attacks Thebes, and the two young men are honor-bound to fight. Thus, they become prisoners of war in Athens, where most of the play takes place. In 1.4–5 Theseus permits Creon's victims to bury their dead, presumably outside the walls of the city.

There is nothing specifically Theban, or even Greek, about any of these scenes. Shakespeare took the location, along with the idea of Theban corruption, from his source, Geoffrey CHAUCER's "The Knight's Tale"; Chaucer in turn was responding to an ancient tradition of conflict between the heroic Theseus and the villainous Creon over the latter's refusal to allow the burial of his slain foes.

Theobald, Lewis (1688–1744) English scholar, the third editor of Shakespeare's collected works. A hack writer, translator, and minor producer of theatrical pantomimes, Theobald wrote the first book devoted to Shakespeare, a critique of the edition of the plays published by Alexander POPE, titled, in the grandiloquent manner of the period, *Shakespeare Restored: or, a Specimen of the Many Errors, as Well Committed, as Unamended, by Mr. Pope in His Late Edition of the Poet* (1726). For this he was made the butt of Pope's scathing satire *The Dunciad* (1728). Theobald went on to produce his own edition in 1733. He was the first scholar to point to the importance of PLUTARCH and Raphael HOLINSHED as sources for the plays, and he introduced the practice of using "parallel readings" in other Elizabethan authors to deduce the meanings of obscure words and idioms. Though Theobald's work was superseded later in the century by such great scholars as Edward CAPELL and Edmond MALONE, his work was extremely valuable, and many of his emendations have remained standard.

Third Folio   See FOLIO.

Thomas, Ambroise (1811–1896)   French composer of two Shakespearean OPERAs. Thomas, one of the most popular composers of the 19th century and the subject of a considerable revival at the end of the 20th, is best known for two works still in the operatic repertoire: *Mignon* (1866, based on Johann Wolfgang von GOETHE's *Wilhelm Meister's Apprenticeship*) and *Hamlet* (1868). The latter, based on a version of the play by Alexandre DUMAS, featured exotic and controversial instrumentation (mostly newly developed horns, such as a bass saxophone) and, following Dumas, an equally controversial conclusion, in which the Ghost reappears, visible to all, and tells his tale publicly, whereupon Hamlet kills King Claudius and is himself triumphantly crowned. (In a LONDON production soon following, however, Shakespeare's ending was restored.) Thomas's *Hamlet* became one of the most-performed operas of the late 19th century, though it is much less popular today.

Thomas had earlier written an opera entitled *Le songe d'une nuit d'été* (1850), which humorously purports to derive from *A Midsummer Night's Dream*. But it is largely a series of drinking songs, featuring an assemblage of Shakespearean characters, notably Falstaff, and Shakespeare himself. The central action concerns the playwright becoming drunk in the presence of Queen Elizabeth, who forgives him and encourages him in his art. This *jeu d'esprit* was not successful and is no longer performed.

Thomas Lord Cromwell   Anonymous play formerly attributed to Shakespeare, part of the Shakespeare APOCRYPHA. *Thomas Lord Cromwell* is a historical drama set in the time of King Henry VIII. It was published by William JONES in 1602 as "written by W. S.," possibly with the intention of associating the play with Shakespeare. It was also included among Shakespeare's plays in the Third and Fourth FOLIOs and in the editions of Nicholas ROWE and Alexander POPE. Scholars are certain, however, that Shakespeare did not write it, for it is a badly structured, poorly written drama that is

clearly not as good as even the least of Shakespeare's genuine work. Its authorship remains uncertain, though Michael DRAYTON and Thomas HEYWOOD are often nominated.

Thorndike, Sybil (1882–1976)   British actress. Thorndike was noted for a number of Shakespearean roles, especially Lady Macbeth, Queen Katherine (*Henry V*), Constance (*King John*), and Volumnia (*Coriolanus*). Much of her career was spent on tour, from her travels to America with Ben GREET's company in the early days of the century to her performances in occupied Europe in 1945. She also played often with the OLD VIC THEATRE company, perhaps most memorably during World War I, when she portrayed a number of male characters, including Prince Hal of *1* and *2 Henry IV*, *The Tempest's*, Ferdinand, and the Fool in *King Lear*. She also coauthored a book on Lilian BAYLIS. With her husband, Lewis CASSON, she was especially associated with the production of Shakespeare and ancient Greek drama.

Thorpe, Thomas (active 1584–1625)   Bookseller and publisher in LONDON, producer of the first edition of Shakespeare's *Sonnets*. Thorpe's 1609 QUARTO edition of the *Sonnets*, known as Q, bears the obscure dedication to "Mr. W. H." that has baffled commentators ever since. Signed "T. T.," this gnomic utterance seems to justify Thorpe's nickname, "Odd." Thorpe published a variety of other works, including John MARSTON's *The Malcontent* (1604).

Tieck, Ludwig (1773–1853)   German poet, novelist, and literary critic, editor of the German TRANSLATION OF SHAKESPEARE's plays begun by A. W. SCHLEGEL. The Schlegel-Tieck translation, as it is known in Germany, was not actually translated by Tieck. The 19 plays left undone by Schlegel were translated by his daughter, Dorothea Tieck, and another translator, Wolf Baudisson; they produced German texts which Tieck edited. The plays were published between 1823 and 1829. The completed collection is still regarded as a major masterpiece of German literature. Tieck was considered the leading German scholar of Shakespeare and ELIZA-BETHAN DRAMA, and his *Anglisches Theatre* (1811) was for many years a basic text. He was called upon to participate in productions of English plays, and in 1827 he staged *A Midsummer Night's Dream* in Schlegel's translation. This was the first presentation of the complete play since Shakespeare's time.

As a creative writer, Tieck was an important figure in the German Romantic movement and was especially noted for stories dealing with horror and the supernatural, as well as with the glorification of art as the only thing in life worth pursuing. He was at one time considered the equal of GOETHE, though his reputation declined before his death, and little of his work has appeal for modern readers.

Tiger   Ship whose mention in *Macbeth* offers a clue to the play's date of composition. In 1.3 the Witches demonstrate their malevolence by casting a spell against the captain of the ship *Tiger*, whose wife has offended them. The First Witch says she will cause the vessel to suffer a storm lasting "sev'n-nights nine times nine" (1.3.7)—that is, 81 weeks. Contemporary records tell of a ship named *Tiger* that returned to port after a storm-tossed voyage of exactly that length, in June 1606, suggesting that the play was written (or at least scene 1.3 completed) not long after that date, while this news was still current, and certainly not before it.

Tillyard, E. M. W.   (1889–1962)   English scholar. Tillyard is best known for *The Elizabethan World Picture* (1943), an analysis of the political thought underlying the HISTORY PLAYS and Shakespeare's work in general. He argued that the plays endorse the pervasive ideas of Shakespeare's period, offering a conservative view of society and placing a high value on an orderly hierarchical system guaranteed by divine authority. More recent scholars tend to find this view too rigid in light of the rapidity of change in 16th-century England. Tillyard also wrote other influential works on both Shakespeare and John MILTON.

Tonson, Jacob   (1656–1737)   English publisher of the first "modern" editions of Shakespeare's plays. At the turn into the 18th century, an age of extrava-gant adaptations of Shakespeare, in which the playwright's actual text was increasingly ignored, Tonson adopted a course of preservation. After buying the copyrights to the plays in the Fourth FOLIO, he commissioned the editions of, first, Nicholas ROWE (1709) and next Alexander POPE. These landmarks opened an era of exploration of Shakespeare's works and world that still continues.

Tooley, Nicholas   (ca. 1575–1623)   English actor, member of the KING'S MEN. Tooley was one of the 26 "Principall Actors" of Shakespeare's plays listed in the FIRST FOLIO, though no important role is associated with him. He may have played the Servant in *The Taming of the Shrew*, who is designated as "Nicke" in a speech heading in the first edition of the play. He is known to have played a madman in a non-Shakespearean play. He was a member of the King's Men from 1605 until his death, but he had probably appeared with the company earlier, for he was apprenticed to Richard BURBAGE. When he died, he was lodging in the home of Cuthbert BURBAGE, who was executor of his will, along with Henry CONDELL.

Tower of London   Fortification and prison, a famous London landmark and a setting in several of the HISTORY PLAYS. Originally a military base built by the Norman conquerors of England, the Tower, actually a complex of several buildings, was a combination of prison, warehouse, and royal residence by the 15th century, when the plays are set. The sinister reputation of the Tower is reflected in (and to some extent inflated by) its role in Shakespeare's plays as the site of Richard III's notorious political murders. Richard kills Henry VI in his Tower cell in 5.6 of *3 Henry VI*. He arranges for the imprisonment of his own brother the Duke of Clarence, and then hires murderers who kill the prisoner in 1.4 of *Richard III*. Later in the same play, though not on stage, a similar fate befalls Richard's young nephews the Prince of Wales and the Duke of York. In 2.5 of *1 Henry VI*, another political prisoner, Edmund Mortimer, dies in the Tower, though of old age. Also, in *Richard II*, a later play, the deposed King Richard II is condemned to the Tower, although his subsequent murder occurs elsewhere.

Aside from its use as a prison, the Tower was a military storehouse and, as such, an important center of royal power. In Shakespeare's earliest depiction of it, in 1.3 of *1 Henry VI*, two feuding aristocrats dispute its control, and, during Jack Cade's rebellion, depicted in Act 4 of *2 Henry VI*, the commander of the Tower, Lord Scales, plays a leading role in driving the rebels from London in 4.5.

Towton   Location in *3 Henry VI*, a town near YORK, a battle site of the WARS OF THE ROSES. The battle of Towton constitutes the action of 2.3–2.6. Although Shakespeare includes several fictitious incidents, such as the death of Clifford and the response of Warwick to his dying brother's call for revenge, he nonetheless accurately depicts the battle as by far the bloodiest battle of the civil war. In 2.5, a major scene, King Henry VI withdraws from the fray and comments on its fury, its confusion, and the uncertainty of its outcome. The actual battle was fought in a raging snowstorm on the afternoon of Palm Sunday in 1461, and by the time it ended hours later, about 40,000 men had been slaughtered. Its violence remained a byword in Shakespeare's time, and it was commonly asserted that soldiers had killed their own fathers or sons in the fight, a tradition that the playwright used in King Henry's moving encounters with the Son That Hath Killed His Father and the Father That Hath Killed His Son, also in 2.5.

tragedy   Drama dealing with a noble protagonist placed in a highly stressful situation that leads to a disastrous, usually fatal conclusion. The 10 plays generally included among Shakespeare's tragedies are, in approximate order of composition, *Titus Andronicus, Romeo and Juliet, Julius Caesar, Hamlet, Othello, Macbeth, King Lear, Antony and Cleopatra, Coriolanus,* and *Timon of Athens*. A central group of four plays—*Hamlet, Othello, Macbeth,* and *King Lear*—offer Shakespeare's fullest development of tragedy, and they are sometimes collectively labeled the great or major tragedies. These plays focus on a powerful central character whose most outstanding personal quality—his tragic flaw, as it is often called—is the source of his catastrophe. He is the victim of his own strength, which will

not allow accommodation with his situation, and we are appalled at this paradox and at the inexorability of his fate. These works—sometimes with the addition of *Antony and Cleopatra*—are often thought to constitute Shakespeare's greatest achievement as a playwright.

Naturally, Shakespeare wrote his tragedies concurrently with other plays, and the group is not isolated within his oeuvre. In fact, its boundaries are not clear-cut. *Timon of Athens* is sometimes classed as a COMEDY, and the FIRST FOLIO edition of the plays (1623) listed *Cymbeline* and *Troilus and Cressida*, usually thought of as comedies, as among the tragedies. Moreover, two of the HISTORY PLAYS, *Richard III* and *Richard II*, offer protagonists who have tragic aspects, though the plays themselves, with their pronounced political and social aspects, are not tragedies. Also, three of the tragedies—*Julius Caesar, Antony and Cleopatra,* and *Coriolanus*—are similarly historical in orientation and may be separately grouped as the ROMAN PLAYS.

Shakespeare's tragedies developed out of earlier 16th-century tragedies, which had antecedents in the "tragedies" of medieval poetry—verse accounts of disaster, suffering, and death, usually of mighty rulers. The poems emphasized the fate of kings and emperors partly because of their importance in a hierarchical society, but also because, from a purely literary point of view, the contrast between their good and bad fortune was highly dramatic. These tragedies, however, did not lend themselves to the stage because they simply made a simple point—that suffering and death come even to the great, without regard for merit or station—in the same fashion every time. The emotional tone remained in accord with the doctrine voiced by Aelius Donatus, a fourth-century Roman critic who was influential throughout the Middle Ages: "The moral of tragedy is that life should be rejected."

However, at least as early as BOCCACCIO's *The Fate of Illustrious Men* (1355–74), RENAISSANCE authors, imbued with a sense of the value of human experience, began to alter the pattern. A wider range of subjects was assembled, and, more important, moral lessons were adduced from their lives. A good instance, and an important inspiration for Shakespeare, is the English biographical compilation *A MIRROR FOR MAGISTRATES*, in which the settings range from the classical and biblical worlds to quite recent history. The typical subject is a villainous tyrant whose fall is obviously and amply deserved. Retribution becomes the theme rather than simple inevitability. This material lent itself to dramatic development, as the tables were turned on the villain. It also lent itself to theatrical effect, as the villainy and the retribution alike were generally bloody. The ancient plays of SENECA were similar in subject and tone; already a part of the Renaissance fascination with the classical world, these works were exploited by 16th-century playwrights. The immediate result was the REVENGE PLAY, which offered the spectacle of the avenger being bloodily dispatched along with the original villain. Christopher MARLOWE and Thomas KYD pioneered this development.

However, the emphasis on evil figures was gradually eroded by an awareness of the dramatic value of virtue, providing the moral contrasts so important to Shakespearean tragedy. The medieval heritage of the MORALITY PLAY was an important influence on this development. Sometimes the good were simply victims, as in *Titus Andronicus;* sometimes virtuous deeds resulted in death or disaster, as in the story of Lucrece, which Shakespeare treated poetically in *The Rape of Lucrece* and which others dramatized; and sometimes the two motifs combined in virtuous victims whose deaths are redemptive, spiritually cleansing the world of the play. *Romeo and Juliet* offers a fine example.

Shakespeare's first tragedy, *Titus Andronicus,* is a simple melodrama, frankly imitative of Seneca. With *Romeo and Juliet,* the young playwright advances considerably, developing humanly credible protagonists, virtuous young lovers who are ennobled as love triumphs over death. An essential tragic theme is established in *Romeo and Juliet:* the superiority of the human spirit to its mortal destiny. At about the same time, Shakespeare takes another important step. In Richard III he first creates a mighty protagonist who can dominate a play by force of personality, though Richard's features are somewhat stereotyped and his tragic defect is simply a given of the plot rather than a plausibly developed personal trait. However, Richard II constitutes a new phenomenon,

a hero who is not merely "star-cross'd" (*Romeo,* Prologue 6) but, rather, psychologically flawed. His inner conflicts are exposed in his introspective soliloquies and self-revealing actions, and we see a complex consciousness tragically unable to deal with external circumstances. Nevertheless, Richard's fall depends chiefly on those circumstances. It is in *Julius Caesar* that Shakespeare first achieves the distinctive element of the major tragedies, a protagonist, Brutus, who is undone precisely by his own virtues, as he pursues a flawed political ideal. A paradoxical sense of the interconnectedness of good and evil permeates the play, as the hero's idealism leads to disaster for both him and his world.

Only with *Hamlet* does the hero's personal sense of that paradox become the play's central concern. In *Hamlet* and its three great successors, Shakespeare composes four variations on the overarching theme that humanity's weaknesses must be recognized as our inevitable human lot, for only by accepting our destiny can we transcend our mortality. Hamlet, unable to alter the evil around him because of his fixation on the uncertainties of moral judgment, falls into evil himself in killing Polonius and rejecting Ophelia, but he finally recovers his humanity by recognizing his ties to others. He accepts his own fate, knowing that "readiness is all" (*Hamlet* 5.2.218). Lear, his world in ruins of his own making, can find salvation only through madness, but in his reconciliation with Cordelia, he too finds that destiny can be identified with, "As if we were God's spies" (*Lear* 5.3.17). As Edgar puts it, sounding very like Hamlet, "Ripeness is all" (5.2.11). Othello, drawn into evil by an incapacity for trust, recognizes his failing and, acknowledging that he "threw a pearl away" (*Othello* 5.2.348), kills himself, "to die upon a kiss" (5.2.360). The power of love—the importance of our bonds to others—is again upheld. In *Macbeth* the same point is made negatively, as the protagonist's rejection of love and loyalty leads to an extreme human isolation, where "Life's but a walking shadow" (5.5.24). In each of the four major tragedies, a single protagonist grows in self-awareness and knowledge of human nature, though he cannot halt his disaster. Hamlet's thoughtfulness, Lear's emotional intensity, Othello's obsessive love, Macbeth's ambition—each could be a positive feature, but each is counter to the forces of the hero's world. We find human dignity in a tragic protagonist's acceptance of a defeat made necessary by his own greatest strengths.

In the later Roman tragedies, *Antony and Cleopatra* and *Coriolanus,* we see the same pattern. Both Cleopatra and Coriolanus face their ends with equanimity. For the Egyptian queen, death is "as sweet as balm, as soft as air, as gentle" (*Antony* 5.2.310); Coriolanus in his more stoical way, says only, "But let it come" (*Coriolanus* 5.3.189). However, these plays differ from their predecessors in that the central figures are placed in a complex social and political context, and the plays are strongly concerned with the relationship between the individual and society, with correspondingly less focus on the emotional development of the tragic hero. *Timon of Athens,* considered the last tragedy (though perhaps written at the same time as *Coriolanus*) is a flawed effort that Shakespeare left incomplete. Also quite socially oriented, it has a strong satirical quality that allies it as much with the comedies known as PROBLEM PLAYS as with the great tragedies. Nevertheless, as in the other tragedies, Timon is a central figure whose decline stems from a mistaken sense of virtue. Shakespeare's attempt to integrate elements of tragedy and comedy was to be more successful in the later ROMANCES.

Shakespeare's tragedies are disturbing plays. We feel horror at the stories—a horror that is aggravated by such scenes as the blinding of Gloucester in *King Lear*—and we feel pity for the victims. That this pity extends to doers of evil as well—Macbeth, Othello, Lear, Coriolanus—attests to Shakespeare's power. We recognize the nobility of the human spirit, which may err catastrophically but does so through an excess of strength, challenging its own limits. Hamlet loses his humanity before he learns to accept destiny; Lear in his madness assumes the burden of his evils and thus achieves remission. Othello, recognizing the evil he has fallen to, uses his strength to compensate in the only way remaining to him. Even Macbeth, the most explicitly villainous of the tragic protagonists, resumes his humanity at the play's close and seizes his sole virtue, courage, to face his end with vigor. The essence of these plays is that blame is not the appropriate response to evil that derives from human weakness. In a tragic universe, we are all flawed precisely because we are human, and Shakespeare's tragic heroes embody this inexorable feature of life.

tragicomedy   Genre of drama combining elements of TRAGEDY and COMEDY, especially when a tragic plot results in a happy ending. The genre was popular in JACOBEAN DRAMA, for its odd composition lent an ironic distance from its themes—usually a combination of sexual love and violent death in a socially significant setting—that appealed to the age's audiences. John FLETCHER, an accomplished practitioner of the genre, provided a neat formulation of it: "A tragicomedy is not so called [because it combines] mirth and killing, but [because] it wants [i.e., lacks] deaths, which is enough to make it no tragedy, yet brings some [characters] near it, which is enough to make it no comedy." Though most Jacobean tragicomedies are obsessed with grotesque rhetoric and bizarre acts of violence, in a fashion far removed from Shakespeare's work, a number of his plays may nevertheless be classed as tragicomedies in a structural sense, especially *Measure for Measure, Cymbeline,* and *The Winter's Tale.*

Traïson   Abbreviated title of an early-15th-century French prose work that may have influenced the writing of *Richard II.* The anonymous *Chronicque de la Traïson et Mort de Richart Deux* may have been written by a member of the household of Queen Isabel. It records the last three years of the reign of Richard II, closing with his murder and burial. It includes the only early account of Sir Piers Exton, who is otherwise unknown. (Shakespeare probably took the tale from HOLINSHED, who had it from *Traïson.*) If Shakespeare did know this work, which existed only in manuscript in his day (though at least a partially complete copy is known to have circulated among his contemporaries), he took from it directly only a few minor elements; however, its positive attitude toward Richard may have helped to shape the playwright's portrait of the king.

translation of Shakespeare   Shakespeare's works have been rendered, at least in part, into scores of languages, although they are quite difficult to translate. The playwright's immense vocabulary and frequently obscure allusions; his use of both newly minted words and archaisms; his puns and malapropisms, slang, dialect, and passages in other languages; frequent use of technical, legal, and commercial argot; and occasional outright nonsense all combine to challenge the most capable translators. And of course, the music of the verse, both in the poems and in the plays, does not often survive into another tongue. But the charisma of his characters and the strength of his plots; the humor, romance, and grandeur of the plays; his subtle conceptions and splendid evolutions of thought—these have proven strong enough to flourish in the seemingly alien soil of other languages.

Shakespeare translation had its beginnings in the efforts of English traveling theater companies who toured in Germany and the Low Countries (see, e.g., Robert BROWNE and John GREEN) to employ such proven hits as Shakespeare's plays, However, these translations (see, e.g., BESTRAFTE BRUDERMORD, DER) were crude ones, intended only for the use of the players. They were not published and did not contribute to the eventual worldwide accessibility of Shakespeare. Further efforts awaited the Enlightenment in the 18th century, when writers in Germany and France, determined to expand cultural horizons by vitalizing their national repertoire of dramas, discovered Shakespeare.

In France the famed philosopher VOLTAIRE, who lived in exile in England for a period, first introduced Shakespeare to continental readers, writing about him throughout the 1730s, in essays and in the prefaces to his own plays—some of them derived from Shakespeare's—but he did not translate the English playwright. This task was first undertaken by Pierre-Antoine LAPLACE, who attempted to revitalize what he saw as an old-fashioned French theater with a book, A Discourse on English Theatre (1745), and translations of 23 English plays, 10 of them by Shakespeare. In the 1770s and 1780s, Jean-François DUCIS adapted a number of these for the stage, and French theatergoers were first exposed to Shakespeare, who proved wildly popular. The first translation of the complete plays was published between 1776 and 1783 by Pierre LE TOURNEUR.

François Guizot (1787–1874), most famous as an historian, revised Le Tourneur's translations in 1821, and many other translations into or adaptations in French of Shakespeare plays were published in the 19th century. However, the translation of the complete works by François-Victor HUGO, published from 1859 to 1866, quickly became the standard French Shakespeare, and it remains so for many readers.

In the 20th century, numerous famed French writers translated Shakespeare in part, among them Yves Bonnefoy (b. 1923), Jean Cocteau (1889–1963), and André Gide (1869–1951); and, for Quebecois speakers in Canada, Michel Garneau (b. 1939). Also, several versions of the complete works were published, including most recently the edition of 1993–2000 by Jean-Michel Déprats (b. 1949).

Germany is the only other European literature that absorbed Shakespeare as early as the 18th century. Germans have adopted an enthusiasm for the playwright that has, perhaps, only been exceeded by English speakers. The first serious, published, German translations of Shakespeare were undertaken by C. M. WIELAND, who published 22 of the plays, in prose versions, between 1762 and 1766. The appearance of these works inspired the scholar J. J. ESCHENBURG, who produced the first German edition of the complete plays, between 1775 and 1782. This version informed the increasing German enthusiasm for Shakespeare for several decades, until A. W. von SCHLEGEL translated 16 of the plays, leaving the task of a complete works to Ludwig TIECK, who completed the job in 1829. The Schlegel-Tieck translation, as it is known, is considered a great masterpiece of German literature in its own right, and it is still the standard Shakespeare for German readers and audiences.

Early translators of Shakespeare into most other languages did not translate from the original English texts, because they did not know English. Rather, they worked from the already existing German (especially in Eastern and Northern Europe) or French (in much of the rest of the world, where, prior to the 20th century, French was the dominant language of trade and diplomacy).

In Russia, which like Germany adopted Shakespeare with tremendous enthusiasm, the earliest adaptations of Shakespeare—including two (the oddly matched *Merry Wives of Windsor* and *Timon of Athens*) by the Empress Catherine the Great (ruled 1762–96)—were taken from Ducis's French, but the translations still in use today were made from the German. The poet Nicolai Gerbel (1827–83), who also translated GOETHE and SCHILLER, published his Shakespeare in 1865, and this remains the standard translation, supplemented by those plays rendered by Boris PASTERNAK, published in the 1940s and 1950s. Other translations still in use that were based on German include those into Polish by the poet Józef Ignacy Kraszewski (1812–87); into Hungarian by Karoly Kisfaludy (1788–1830) and Dezso Kosztolányi (1885–1936); and into Swedish by Carl August Hagberg (1810–64).

Spain first became aware of Shakespeare in versions derived from the French adaptations of Ducis; a *Hamlet* was published as early as 1772. Diplomat Leandro Fernández de Moratín (1760–1828) published a prose translation in 1798 (under the pseudonym Inarco Celenio) that remained the standard version for a century. Moratín had served as Spain's ambassador to England, where he had studied Shakespeare with the aid of the actor John Philip KEMBLE. His translations were only superceded by the prose translations of Luis Astrana Marín (1889–1959), published in 1929, which remain the most familiar version of Shakespeare for many Spaniards, though the complete plays translated by José María Valverde (1926–96) and published in 1967 is also popular. Spain has four official languages, and the other three—Catalan, Basque, and Galician—found their Shakespeare translators rather later. The 27 plays translated by Josep María de Sagarra (1894–1961), beginning in 1941, are the standard for performance and reading in Catalan. In Basque, Bedita Larrakoetxea (1894–1990) produced a translation of the complete plays between 1957 and 1970. Only a few plays have been translated into Galician, beginning around 1920.

In Italy, where there were no translations of Shakespeare before the 19th century, Ducis and Le Tourneur were the principal source for early translators. A prose version by Carlo Rusconi (1819–89) published in 1831, remained the most familiar Italian Shakespeare until the publication of a modern

translation by scholar Mario Praz (1896–1982), in the 1940s. In the 1980s the scholar Giorgio Melchiori (b. 1920) (also the editor of an English-language edition of *Edward III*) offered a newer one.

Beyond Europe, the coverage of Shakespeare by literary translators is of course less comprehensive, but in several parts of the world, many readers have texts of the playwright's works in their native languages. Arabic, a language that is used over a large portion of the globe, has a tradition of Shakespeare translation that begins with the Egyptian writer Najib El Haddad (1867–99) and frequent translations and adaptations (often quite radically un-Shakespearean, frequently as musicals) were made throughout the 20th century. Serious scholarly translations were also undertaken, notably by Lebanese poet and dramatist Khalil Mutran (1879–1949), Palestinian novelist Jabra Ibrahim Jabra (1920–94), and the famed blind Egyptian writer and activist Taha Hussein (1898–1973), who oversaw the Arab League's project, begun in the 1940s, to publish all of Shakespeare's works in Arabic.

Not surprisingly, given the long presence of British institutions in India, Shakespeare has been an important presence not just in Anglo-Indian literature, written in English, but in numerous of the other languages of South Asia. Although literate Indians tend to speak and write English, over a thousand adaptations of Shakespeare plays in Indian languages have been made, most of them into Bengali, Marathi, Tamil, and Hindi (in that order). The majority of these, however, are extravagantly free, often bearing little or no resemblance to their originals. Among the most notable Indian translators of Shakespeare are Girishchandra Ghosh (1844–1912), whose 1893 translation of *Macbeth* is regarded as a treasure of Bengali literature; Harana Chandra Rakskit (active 1900), who translated the complete works into Bengali (1896–1902); the Hindi poet Harivansh Rai Bachchan (1907–2003); and Kandukuri Veeresalingam (1848–1919), writing in Telugu. Since India's independence in 1947, translation or close adaptations of Shakespeare in Indian languages are rare, as the literatures of India emphasize more contemporary and home-grown work.

In Japan, Shakespeare was virtually unknown until the 1870s, when dramatists began to exploit his plots in free adaptations, most often based on *Tales from Shakespeare* by Charles LAMB and Mary Lamb, extracts from which had been published in some form more than 100 times by 1930. Between 1909 and 1928, Tsubouchi Shoyo (1859–1935) translated the complete plays from Shakespeare's texts; not satisfied with his work, he did it again (dying just before completing the second version). His has been the standard Japanese Shakespeare. Since 1992 Matsuoka Kazuko (b. 1942) has been working on a new version. Hers will be the first 21st-century Japanese translation of the complete works.

In China, as in Japan, acquaintance with Shakespeare came late and was first made through Lamb. However, all of the plays have been translated, perhaps most notably in editions of the complete works begun by Zhu Shenghao (1912–44), whose early death prevented his completion of the project, but whose work is regarded as the finest of Chinese efforts; and Liang Shiqui (1902–87), who first accomplished a complete translation of the plays, published in Taiwan in 1967. In 2000 the scholar Fang Ping published, both in Taiwan and on mainland China, a new version in which a Chinese equivalent to blank verse attempts to provide a sense of the rhythm of Shakespeare. Some of the plays have also been adapted by the famous Peking Opera company, for performance in the traditional Chinese musical theater.

The continuing prominence of English in international commercial, scientific, and diplomatic discourse guarantees that awareness of English literature, and of Shakespeare in particular, will continue to expand across the globe. In the 21st century the works of the playwright will find their way into the published literature of new languages, and literatures in which there already are translations will doubtless receive new ones.

Tree, Herbert Beerbohm (1853–1917) British actor and producer. Born Herbert Beerbohm, Tree was a successful actor when he became manager of London's Haymarket Theatre in 1887. There, he staged several of Shakespeare's plays, including *The Merry Wives of Windsor*, in which he played Falstaff, and *Hamlet*, with himself in the title role. He built a new playhouse, Her (later His) Majesty's Theatre,

and in 1897 he began to put on extravagant productions in the tradition of Charles KEAN and Henry IRVING, with lavish sets and costumes and spectacular processions and tableaus. For *Julius Caesar* he employed elaborate scenic designs by the most prominent (and expensive) British artist of the day, Sir Lawrence Alma-Tadema (1836–1912). His *Midsummer Night's Dream* (1900) featured live rabbits and birds on stage, and the coronation parade in 4.1 of his *Henry VIII* (1910, 1916 in New York) was so time-consuming that he had to cut Act 5 entirely. He is the last major exponent of this characteristically 19th-century style, and it was in

Beerbohm Tree—seen here in his role as Benedick, the confirmed bachelor who comes to marry Beatrice in *Much Ado About Nothing*—was a prominent actor and manager of the late 19th century. *(Courtesy of Culver Pictures, Inc.)*

part rebellion against his work that inspired such modern pioneers as William POEL and Harley GRANVILLE-BARKER.

Trojan War Legendary conflict between the ancient Greeks and the Trojans, often mentioned in Shakespeare's works, most notably in *Troilus and Cressida*, which enacts part of it. In classical myth and legend, beginning with the *Iliad* of HOMER, the Trojan War was fought by the city of TROY against invaders from Greece, who were attempting to avenge the abduction of a Greek queen, Helen, by a Trojan prince, Paris. The story was quite familiar to Shakespeare's audiences.

As the Prologue declares, *Troilus and Cressida* begins well into the conflict, with the Greeks continuing a seven-year-long siege of Troy, and it ends with the Trojan forces in disarray, facing apparent defeat. However, as the playwright and his audience both knew, that defeat was to be deferred until, in a later episode, Greek troops were smuggled into the city inside the famed Trojan Horse, ostensibly a gift signifying the Greeks' abandonment of their siege. The subsequent sack of Troy is described in a long passage in *The Rape of Lucrece* (lines 1366–1533). Another striking use of the war occurs in *Hamlet*, where the First Player delivers a dramatic account of the killing of King Priam of Troy and the grief of Queen Hecuba (2.2.448–514).

According to Greek mythology, Zeus arranged the Trojan War as a cure for overpopulation. With the assistance of Eris, goddess of discord, he sparked a dispute among three goddesses as to which was the most beautiful. Paris was appointed to decide; bribed with the promise of the world's most beautiful woman as a bride, he chose Aphrodite. She rewarded him by helping him to kidnap Helen. Though this well-known legend arose before Homer's time, he ascribes Paris's abduction of Helen to his love for her beauty, with no mention of divine aid.

Troublesome Raigne of King John, The Anonymous Elizabethan play published in 1591, probably derived from Shakespeare's *King John* but traditionally regarded as its source. It was long argued that *The Troublesome Raigne*, as the play is known, was adapted by Shakespeare in writing *King John*, but modern scholars—and others, beginning with Alexander POPE—have challenged this assumption, noting the many respects in which the anonymous play resembles a BAD QUARTO: It contains echoes of other plays, including *3 Henry VI*, *Richard III*, and works by MARLOWE and PEELE; its published text is riddled with errors, including ambiguous or missing stage directions; and it contains passages in which stage directions summarize and describe missing dialogue. Moreover, the 1591 title page associates *The Troublesome Raigne* with an acting company, the QUEEN'S MEN, that is known to have put on a number of such derivative plays, including *The Taming of a Shrew*.

Troy Ancient city of Asia Minor, the site of the TROJAN WAR of Greek legend and the setting for *Troilus and Cressida*. In the play, Troy and its people are decadent and immoral. Although they know that Helen is a worthless prize, the aristocratic warriors carry on a costly conflict simply because they wish to achieve military renown. Love in Troy is represented by the sexual encounter of Cressida and Prince Troilus as arranged by the voyeuristic Pandarus. Once the Trojans' great hero Hector is killed, the city is helpless, and at the play's bleak close the Greeks are on the verge of victory.

While the Troy of the play is seen as corrupt, the leaders of Troy are distinctly less evil than the Greeks, and it is clear that the playwright felt a bias in favor of the Trojans. This may seem surprising to modern readers familiar with the pro-Greek sentiments of Troy's first chronicler, HOMER. However, like most western Europeans at the end of the Middle Ages, the English identified with Troy, believing themselves the descendants of Trojan refugees scattered by the defeat of the city. This legend sprang from the ancient Roman belief found in the *Aeneid* of VIRGIL that Rome had been founded by Aeneas. In English tradition the British Isles were first colonized by a great-grandson of Aeneas named Brut, who was said to have founded London, naming it New Troy, and for whom Britain was believed to be named. Accordingly, the English derived the history of Troy from pro-Trojan accounts.

All histories of Troy are legendary—Homer composed his work centuries after its fall—and the historical city is known only through archaeology, principally the famous excavations by Heinrich Schliemann (1822–90). In the northwest corner of what is now Turkey, Troy occupied a strategically important location overlooking the Dardanelles, a strait that provided access to the Black Sea and was a major route for trade. Troy's location is thought to have been likeliest stimulus for a Greek invasion. A long succession of ancient cities stood on the same site from as early as 5,000 years ago. Each of these was a rich and heavily fortified town, presumably the capital of the surrounding territory. The seventh of these settlements is believed to have been the one besieged by the Greeks because it was destroyed by a great fire and because it existed at the right time, ca. 1200 B.C. Other cities continued to occupy the site until early Christian times.

Troyes   City in eastern FRANCE, location for 5.2 of *Henry V*. In 1420 the treaty that confirmed King Henry V's conquest of France was signed at Troyes, located in the domains of the Duke of Burgundy, England's ally. This event is presented in the play, though the principal action in the scene is Henry's courtship of Princess Katharine. The only clause of the treaty alluded to, besides the marriage of Henry and Katharine, is the declaration of Henry as the heir to the French crown, pronounced in French and Latin, in 5.2.356–360.

Historically the treaty of Troyes did not result from the English victory at AGINCOURT, as the play suggests. Simplifying his drama, and emphasizing the glory of Agincourt, Shakespeare omitted the events that actually produced the treaty: several years of campaigning in Normandy and, crucially, Burgundy's alliance with England. In the play the Duke of Burgundy appears to speak for the French King at Troyes.

Trundell, John (active 1603–1626)   London publisher and bookseller. Trundell copublished the first edition (Q1) of *Hamlet* with Nicholas LING in 1603. Little else is known of him.

Tuckfeild, Thomas (active 1624)   English actor who may have performed in early productions of *The Two Noble Kinsmen*. In the first edition of the play (Q1, 1634), the stage direction opening 5.3 names the Attendants called for; one of them is named "T. Tucke." Scholars believe that this refers to Tuckfeild, indicating that he played the part in an early production by the KING'S MEN. Tuckfeild was with the company in 1624, so this clue (with similar evidence concerning Curtis GREVILLE) suggests that Q1 was printed from a PROMPTBOOK of the 1620s. Tuckfeild is known from a single document, listing him among the King's Men's "musicians and other necessary attendants."

Tudor dynasty   Ruling family in England from 1485 to 1603. The first Tudor monarch was King Henry VII, who seized the throne after winning the final phase of the WARS OF THE ROSES by defeating Richard III at the battle of BOSWORTH FIELD. This event is the climax of the long period of conflict dealt with in Shakespeare's HISTORY PLAYS. Henry VII appears in *Richard III* as the Earl of Richmond. His son, King Henry VIII, who ruled from 1509 to 1547, is depicted in *Henry VIII* as a symbol of good kingship in a play that emphasizes his part in introducing Protestantism to England. Henry's son ruled as King Edward VI from 1547 to 1553 but died at 15. His half sister Mary was queen from 1553 to 1558; a Catholic, she persecuted Protestants, and it was only under her younger half sister, Elizabeth, that English Protestantism was finally and firmly established. Queen Elizabeth I (see Elizabeth I in *Henry VIII*), who reigned during most of Shakespeare's lifetime, was the last Tudor monarch; upon her death in 1603, the STUART DYNASTY came to the throne. The 16th century saw the country emerge from medieval economic and political practices into the early modern period. Thus, the Tudors presided over a crucial transition in the country's history.

Twine, Laurence (active 1564–1576)   English translator, creator of a source for *Pericles*. In his prose romance *The Patterne of Painefull Adventures . . . That Befell unto Prince Apollonius*, Twine translated the tale of Apollonius of Tyre from a French version of an ancient story found in the *Gesta Romanorum*, a medieval Latin collection. Shakespeare drew from Twine's book in composing his play. *The Patterne of Painefull Adventures* was written ca. 1576, but if it was published then, no copy has survived; Shakespeare probably knew it in either an undated edition of ca. 1594 or a reprint of 1607.

Tyler, Richard (1566–1636) Resident of STRATFORD and friend of Shakespeare. Tyler, two years younger than Shakespeare, probably knew Shakespeare at the Stratford grammar school, for his father, as an alderman, was entitled to send his children there without charge. However, his most significant connection with Shakespeare lies in his removal from the playwright's will. Though he was originally one of seven close friends given bequests of money to buy a commemorative ring, Tyler's name was scratched out and replaced with that of Hamnet SADLER. This may have been Shakespeare's response to Tyler's involvement in a scandal: As a collector of relief funds after the great Stratford fire of 1614, Tyler was charged with enriching himself. However, he apparently continued to be a friend of the family, participating in the transfer of the BLACKFRIARS GATEHOUSE to Susanna SHAKESPEARE Hall in 1618.

Tyler, Thomas (1826–1902) British scholar. Tyler was best known as a biblical scholar, but he also wrote several works on Shakespearean topics, most notably *The Philosophy of Hamlet* (1874). In his edition of the *Sonnets* (1890), Tyler identified Mary FITTON as Shakespeare's "Dark Lady." This theory was popularized by Frank HARRIS, but scholars now generally reject it.

Tyre City of the ancient Seleucid Empire on the coast of what is now Lebanon, the setting for three scenes of *Pericles, Prince of Tyre*. The title character is the ruler of Tyre, and 1.2–3 and 2.4 are set within interiors located in the city. Shakespeare simply followed his source in placing his hero in Tyre, and the actual Mediterranean seaport is in no way present in the text of the play.

Of cities surviving today, Tyre is among the most ancient, as it has existed since prehistoric times. A famous producer of dyes—"Tyrian purple" cloth was proverbially rich and fashionable—and a significant port, Tyre was a wealthy city-state that maintained its independence while paying tribute to the succession of empires that ruled the region after its conquest by Alexander the Great in 332 B.C. At the time of Antiochus—the play's only historical figure—Tyre was actually a republic, but Shakespeare was not concerned with Middle Eastern history, and his Tyre is merely an exotic locale, appropriate to a tale of romantic adventures.

U

Ubaldino, Petruccio (Petruccio Ubaldini) (ca. 1525–ca. 1600)   Italian writer, author of a source for *Edward III*. Immediately after England's successful resistance to the Spanish Armada in 1588, Ubaldino wrote a brief treatise—originally a synopsis, in Italian, of a set of reports compiled for the admiral who had commanded England's resistance to the Armada—titled *A Discourse Concerning the Spanish Fleet Invadinge Englande, in the Year 1588*, in the translation published by Augustine RYTHER in 1590. It was one of the most widely read contemporary accounts of the event. Scholars find its influence on *Edward III* in the account of the naval battle of SLUYS, given by the Mariner in 3.1.62–78 and 3.1.141–184. Mention of the ship NON-PAREILLE, and a striking emphasis on the crescent-shaped formation taken by the vessels (the latter also, perhaps, influential on Audley's description of the land battle of POITIERS, in 4.4.31–32), are thought to have been taken, by Shakespeare or a collaborator (see *Edward III*, "Commentary"), from Ubaldino. This supposition suggests that the play was written in the first years of the 1590s, after the publication of Ubaldino's work but before accounts of the Armada would have receded from the immediate recollection of the play's potential audience.

Ubaldino, born into the Florentine nobility, first came to England in 1545 and lived there, with intervals abroad, for the rest of his life. He managed a living as a writer and translating into Italian for Italian patrons and English for English ones. He also illustrated manuscripts and wrote essays and poems, as well as memoirs of his life in England. In addition, he was something of an aristocratic jack-of-all-trades, essentially working for gifts, serving as an aide to noble patrons and possibly as a spy for England and/or Florence or Venice. He may even have practiced some medicine. He submitted essays to Queen Elizabeth on such subjects as Italian military affairs, philosophy, and tax policy in exchange for gifts of jewelry and silver. However, his account of the Armada is thought to have been written originally for the government of Venice.

Udall, Nicholas (1504–1556)   English author and playwright, author of the earliest English COMEDY. Udall translated the Latin plays of TERENCE (with John HIGGINS) and essays of the great humanist Erasmus (ca. 1456–1536). He also wrote theological works, along with a number of plays, all but one of them lost. His *Ralph Roister Doister* (ca. 1553, published 1566) is generally considered the earliest English comedy; only a single copy of it was still in existence in 1825, when its importance was recognized by John Payne COLLIER. In boisterous rhymed dialogue, Udall borrowed elements from Terence, PLAUTUS, and crude English farces to create a distinctively original work. Among other comic touches, Udall invented a device—the mischievously mispunctuated reading of a document—that Shakespeare used in *A Midsummer Night's Dream* (5.1.108–117). Udall was discharged from his position as headmaster of Eton for homosexuality, but he recovered his social standing sufficiently to find favor with Queen Mary (ruled 1553–58), who collaborated with him in a translation, licensed him to write plays, and provided him with another head-mastership, shortly before his death.

Underhill, William (1556–1597) Landowner in and around STRATFORD, the seller of NEW PLACE to Shakespeare. Underhill was a member of the gentry who held a remunerative position in the county court at Warwick and had inherited New Place and much other land at the age of 14. He sold New Place to Shakespeare in May 1597, but in July he was poisoned by his eldest son, Fulke (b. 1579), who was executed for the murder in 1599. The Underhill properties were sequestered by the state, and when the second son, Hercules (b. 1581), came of age in 1602, he had to reconfirm the sale of New Place to Shakespeare.

Underwood, John (d. 1624) English actor, member of the KING'S MEN. Underwood was one of the 26 men listed in the FIRST FOLIO as "Principall Actors" in Shakespeare's plays, though no specific Shakespearean role is associated with him. He and William OSTLER probably became members of the King's Men at the same time, replacing William SLY and Laurence FLETCHER, who died in 1608. When Underwood died, he held shares in the GLOBE, CURTAIN, and BLACKFRIARS THEATREs. He left them to his five children, all minors, for whom his fellow actor Henry CONDELL acted as trustee.

University Wits Group of English playwrights credited with the development of ELIZABETHAN DRAMA in the 1580s. Called the University Wits by modern scholars, these men were distinguished by their superior educations in a profession that had always been somewhat disreputable at best (see ELIZABETHAN THEATER). The most notable of them were Oxford graduates Thomas LODGE, John LYLY, and George PEELE, and Cambridge alumni Robert GREENE, Thomas NASHE, and Christopher MARLOWE. These men purposefully went beyond the didactic chronicles and shapeless, knockabout farces of the existing English stage. They combined the influences of ancient Roman drama, the medieval MORALITY PLAY, ACADEMIC DRAMA, and contemporary Italian and French drama, to create

plays with intelligible structure, vigorous plotting, and vital poetry. The plays of the University Wits were very popular and helped establish the flourishing theatrical world that Shakespeare entered as a young man.

Ur-Hamlet Name given to a lost Elizabethan play resembling *Hamlet* and believed to have been used by Shakespeare as a source. Several references prove that there was an earlier play involving *Hamlet*. In 1589 Thomas NASHE, mocking plays derived from SENECA and especially those of Thomas KYD, referred to ". . . whole Hamlets, I should say handfuls of tragical speeches." The context of this remark leads most scholars to conclude that Kyd wrote the *Ur-Hamlet*. A performance of a play called *Hamlet* by Shakespeare's acting company, the CHAMBERLAIN'S MEN, is recorded in 1594, and a famous reference by Thomas LODGE printed two years later implies that the work was still current and provides an image from it: ". . . ghost which cried so miserably . . . *Hamlet, revenge.*"

Little more is known of the play's contents, for no text survives. However, it presumably followed the tale by François BELLEFOREST that was probably its major source. It seems it included most, if not all, of the following elements: Hamlet seeking revenge against his uncle for the murder of his father and the seduction of his mother; his feigned madness and his romantic involvement with a woman; his dramatic encounter with his mother during which he kills a spy; his exile to England and the trick whereby he arranges for the execution of his escorts instead of himself; and his killing of his uncle in a long-deferred vengeance.

Thus the *Ur-Hamlet* was plainly a REVENGE PLAY like Kyd's *The Spanish Tragedy* (1588–89), to which it may have been a companion piece. Scholars comparing *Hamlet* and *The Spanish Tragedy* find further clues concerning the *Ur-Hamlet*: some elements of *The Spanish Tragedy*, a play that also centers on a postponed revenge, suggest themes found in Shakespeare's *Hamlet* in more developed forms, and it is thought these elements may also have been used by Kyd in the *Ur-Hamlet*. Thus, the *Ur-Hamlet* may have included a procrastinating Hamlet who dies at the play's close, a heroine whose love for Hamlet is opposed by her family and who eventually becomes insane and commits suicide, and a play within a play, all of which resemble components of *The Spanish Tragedy* yet are not present in Belleforest. Further, the sub-plot in which Hamlet kills the father of the man who kills him and of the woman who loves him is not Belleforest and thus may have been in the *Ur-Hamlet*. However, Shakespeare may very well have devised this himself, and *The Spanish Tragedy* may simply have been an influence on *Hamlet* rather than containing the same ideas as the *Ur-Hamlet*.

One further minor source of information may exist. DER BESTRAFTE BRUDERMORD, a German version of *Hamlet* gleaned from the recollections of English actors who toured Germany in the 17th century, offers certain minor details that do not come from *Hamlet* yet correspond to Belleforest, and it is thought these may have been remembered by actors who had also performed in the *Ur-Hamlet*.

Ur-Shrew   Hypothetical play sometimes assumed to be the source for both *The Taming of the Shrew* and *The Taming of a Shrew*. The *Ur-Shrew* is usually attributed to Shakespeare, but it is presumed to have been revised by the playwright in order to incorporate the SUBPLOT involving Bianca and her suitors. The revised play, according to this theory, is *The Taming of the Shrew*, whereas *The Taming of a Shrew* is a BAD QUARTO of the *Ur-Shrew*, whose original text has been lost. The *Ur-Shrew* hypothesis exists to account for inconsistencies between *A Shrew* and *The Shrew*, especially the differences between their subplots. However, most recent scholarship finds that these questions can be resolved without assuming the existence of a play for which no other evidence exists, and the *Ur-Shrew* theory has generally been rejected in favor of the idea that *The Shrew* is Shakespeare's original play and *A Shrew* a Bad Quarto of it.

variorum edition Annotated edition of an author's work. The name comes from the Latin *cum notis variorum*, meaning "with the notes of various [people]." Several editions of Shakespeare's works are so designated, but in the 20th century the term usually refers to the New Variorum, edited by H. H. FURNESS and his successors, and published beginning in 1871.

The First Variorum was based on the 1778 edition of George STEEVENS's Shakespeare, which was posthumously expanded and published by Isaac REED in 1803. The collected essays and notes included in this 21-volume work offer a copious representation of 18th-century Shakespearean scholarship, though the edition omits the playwright's poems. The Second Variorum (1813) was simply a reprint of the First, but the Third Variorum incorporated the work of Edmond MALONE. James BOSWELL the younger completed Malone's second edition of Shakespeare's works after the older scholar's death in 1812 and grafted it onto Reed's work. The Third Variorum, also known as "Boswell's Malone," was published in 1821, also in 21 volumes. It encompasses annotated texts of all the plays and the poems, Malone's life of the playwright (a basic reference for all subsequent biographers of Shakespeare), his history of the English stage, and other materials.

The New Variorum consists of one or more volumes per play, two for the *Sonnets*, and one for the other poetry. Furness had produced 18 volumes before he died in 1912. The work was completed in 1953 by a series of successors, including his son H. H. Furness Jr., and J. Q. ADAMS.

Vaughan Williams, Ralph (1872–1958) English composer. Best known for his symphonies and choral works, Vaughan Williams also wrote several operas, among them *Sir John in Love* (1929), based on *The Merry Wives of Windsor*. He often set poetry to music, including many passages from Shakespeare. Among his best-known Shakespearean works is a 1951 setting for Prospero's famous "revels" speech (*Tempest* 4.1. 148–158), and he declared that the last movement of his famous Sixth Symphony was based on this passage. He composed music for many of Shakespeare's songs, beginning as early as 1891 and returning to them often. In 1913 he composed incidental music for *2 Henry IV*, *Henry V*, *The Merry Wives of Windsor*, *Richard II*, and *Richard III*, and in 1944 he wrote the score for a radio play of *Richard II*.

Vaux, Sir Thomas (1509–1556) English poet. Vaux was a cultivated aristocrat who was a member of the courts of several English monarchs, beginning with Henry VIII. Although his poetry was superior to that of most of his fellow courtiers, he is noteworthy today only for having written "The aged lover renounces love," which appears, in a very garbled form, as the Grave-digger's song in *Hamlet* (5.1.61–64, 70–73, 92–95). Vaux's poem, said to have been written on his deathbed, was still well known in Shakespeare's day as a popular song.

Vaux's father, Sir Nicholas Vaux, likewise a courtier, appears in *Henry VIII*, and his grandfather, Sir William Vaux, has a role in *2 Henry VI*.

Venice City in northern Italy, setting for *The Merchant of Venice* and the opening scenes of *Othello*. In Shakespeare's day Venice was already famous for the sumptuous beauty that still astonishes the world today. A great commercial center, it stood for luxuriant culture and the power of money, and Shakespeare pictures it vividly—without describing it—by presenting his audience with its wealthy and self-confident citizens and exotic foreign figures. Significantly, in both *The Merchant* and *Othello* the prosperous society of Venice relies on an outsider—one a Jew and the other a Moor—who is not fully admitted to the society's fellowship and whose alien status is important to the drama's central conflict.

Venice was present in Shakespeare's sources, but he may also have been influenced by the image Elizabethans had of the fabled city in developing his themes of generosity and greed in *The Merchant,* and of human dignity versus envy and malice in *Othello.* Venice is frequently presented in Elizabethan literature as a symbol for a hypercommercial society in which the acquisitive instinct rules to the detriment of finer impulses. Shakespeare was not concerned with presenting an accurate Venetian setting, and he plainly invoked this stereotype, especially in *The Merchant of Venice,* where all of his Venetians express themselves in financial and commercial terms. For example, the clown Launcelot employs legalistic language in 2.2.1–30; Bassanio claims Portia in mercantile terms in 3.2.140, 149; and Portia can remark of her lover, "Since you are dear bought, I will love you dear" (3.2.312). The point is less prominent in *Othello,* but the envious Iago "know[s his] price" (1.1.11), and Roderigo's mode of courtship consists of conspicuous expense. Even the despairing Othello compares his dead Desdemona to "a pearl . . . Richer than [a] tribe" (5.2.348–349), and the saintly Desdemona says of the crucial loss of Othello's love token, "I had rather lose my purse / Full of crusadoes" (Portuguese gold coins) (3.4.21–22).

Of course, such characteristics are not difficult to find in any cosmopolitan society. Venice was certainly a colorful and exotic locale with its commercial connections to the remote and glamorous East. It was a likely place to encounter such strange sights as a Rialto moneylender in his "Jewish gaberdine" (*Merchant,* 1.3.107) or a Moorish general, but it surely seemed familiar in its vices to the Londoners of Shakespeare's day. In fact, Venice's success as a commercially based empire was about to be imitated on a larger scale by England. The wealthy and cultivated classes in 16th-century London regarded Venice as something of a prototype of their own developing society, and the satirical thrust of *The Merchant'*s Venice was surely not lost on its original audiences.

Verdi, Giuseppe (1813–1901) Italian composer of several OPERAs inspired by Shakespeare's plays. After creating his first Shakespearean opera, *Macbeth* (1847), Verdi declared his intention of composing for all of the playwright's major works. He planned a *King Lear* but never actually wrote it, for lack of an adequate libretto. Although his ambition was unfulfilled, his two remaining Shakespearean operas, *Otello* (1887) and *Falstaff* (1893)—the latter based on *The Merry Wives of Windsor,* with additions from the *Henry IV* plays—are great accomplishments in themselves. With libretti by Arrigo BOITO, they are the twin masterpieces of Verdi's old age and in the opinion of most commentators, two of the best operas ever written.

Vergil, Polydore (1470–1555) Italian-born English author, writer of a history of England that informed Shakespeare's sources for the HISTORY PLAYS. Vergil's *Historia Anglia,* a Latin history commissioned by King Henry VII, focused on the WARS OF THE ROSES and emphasized the influence of divine providence in punishing Henry IV's sin in usurping the crown from Richard II with the civil conflicts. Thus, he aggrandized the TUDOR DYNASTY by presenting its founder, Henry VII, as an instrument of God. This point of view was adopted by Edward HALL and Raphael HOLINSHED, Shakespeare's chief sources, and so became the dominant theme of the history plays.

Vergil, born in Urbino, came to England in 1501 as a representative of the pope. Henry commissioned the *Historia Anglia* in 1505, and the Italian became an English citizen in 1510, though he returned to Urbino in 1551. He was a friend of Sir

Thomas MORE, who read Vergil's history in manuscript and was influenced by it in writing his biography of Richard III, which was also influential on Shakespeare through Hall and Holinshed.

Verona   City in Italy, the setting for *Romeo and Juliet*. The Prince of Verona is named Escalus, a Latinization of Della Scala, the name of the princely family that ruled the city in the late Middle Ages, but there is nothing specifically Veronese in the play, and Shakespeare simply took the location from his source.

The feud between the Montague and Capulet families was long thought to have been historical, but in fact it never occurred. The root of the error, which first appears in a story published in 1530 (see *Romeo and Juliet*, "Sources of the Play") may be a line in Dante's *Inferno*, in which two families, the Capelleti and the Montecchi, are cited for fomenting civil disorders. However, while the Montecchi lived in Verona, the Capelletti came from Cremona, and there was no connection between them.

While the title of *The Two Gentlemen of Verona* suggests that the title characters come from that city, and several scenes (1.1–2.3 and 2.7) are presumed to take place there for the same reason, there is no textual reference to confirm these suppositions. On the other hand, at 3.1.81 and 5.4.127 it is suggested that the court of the Duke of Milan is in Verona, clearly an error. The geography of this play is confused at best, and its settings have no specificity.

Verona is mentioned in passing elsewhere in the plays. It is the home of Petruchio in *The Taming of the Shrew*, and several scenes take place in his nearby country house. It may also be the home of Cassio, though the reference, if it is one, is made in an apparently corrupt line (*Othello*, 2.1.26).

verse test   Scholarly method used to determine the authenticity and the chronological order of Shakespeare's plays. The verse test is a statistical analysis of the playwright's use of poetic devices. At its simplest, a verse test of a work determines the relative quantities of prose and poetry, and of rhymed and unrhymed lines within the poetry, and it compares the result to other plays. Additional elements that are generally noted are the number of lines with feminine endings (i.e., that do not end on a stress; see METER), the number of speeches that end in the middle of a line; and the quantitative ratio of BLANK VERSE to rhymed verse.

Verse tests were first applied by Edmond MALONE and others in the late 18th century, but they were most important in the Shakespearean studies of the 19th century, when a body of comparisons was developed by such scholars as Frederick FURNIVALL, G. G. GERVINUS, F. G. FLEAY, and William SPALDING. In the 20th century verse tests are much less important to scholars, who apply other concepts to the same questions and find the results of verse tests to be inconclusive.

Vestris, Elizabeth (1797–1856)   British actress. Madame Vestris, as she was known, was born Lucia Elizabeth Bartolozzi. She kept the name of her first husband, a ballet dancer who deserted her, and became a successful comic actress, specializing in farces and burlesques. She married the actor Charles James Mathews (1803–78). Beginning in 1839, they managed a theatrical company at the Covent Garden Theatre. They began by presenting the first performances of *Love's Labour's Lost* since the early 17th century—Madame Vestris played Rosaline—followed by *The Merry Wives of Windsor*, in which she played Mistress Page and used her fine voice to sing a number of interpolated songs. In 1840 Vestris and Mathews presented *A Midsummer Night's Dream*, and though their version was abridged, it was entirely Shakespearean, again for the first time in 200 years. It was also the first English production to use the famous incidental music by Felix MENDELSSOHN. Unfortunately, these productions were not financially successful, and the couple went bankrupt. Though they never again produced Shakespeare, they continued to perform—indeed, they had to, for Madame Vestris died before their finances were restored. Mathews eventually recovered and followed a less demanding career as a minor comic actor.

Vice, the   Conventional figure from the medieval MORALITY PLAY, an influence upon the development of both Shakespeare's villains and his comic figures. The Vice attempts to seduce the soul of the protagonist, who represents mankind, into evil ways. A hypocrite, deceit and guile are his weapons—he is able to weep at will—and he employs them with great pleasure. At the same time, the Vice is a comic figure, designed to entertain while he instructs. He typically makes lewd jokes, puns outrageously, engages in physical horseplay, and brandishes his wooden sword with comic ineffectuality (both Falstaff [in *1 Henry IV*, 2.4.133] and Pistol [in *Henry V*, 4.4.73–74] are associated with this feature). Especially in the more sophisticated 16th-century morality plays, he resembles the FOOL. The Vice also evolved into another, more distinctly Elizabethan character type, the MACHIAVEL.

At his most striking, the Vice advertises his villainy to the audience. He revels in viciousness in extravagant, humorous asides filled with demonic laughter. It is a convention of the morality plays that his victims are the only ones who cannot see through his obvious dishonesty; thus, the Vice demonstrates the habitual blindness of the sinner. A number of Shakespeare's early villains are distinctly Vice-like. The most notable of these, perhaps, is Richard III, who in fact describes himself as " . . . like the formal Vice, Iniquity" (*Richard III*, 3.1.82). The character's influence is still detectable in the later Shakespearean figure Iago of *Othello*.

Vienna City in Austria, the setting for *Measure for Measure*. Dramatic convention called for a foreign locale for Shakespeare's sensational tale, and he probably chose Vienna because it was much better known to an English audience than its neighbor, Innsbruck, where the story takes place in his chief source, CINTHIO's novella. Much of the play occurs indoors—mostly in a prison, where local color is distinctly lacking—and no Viennese ambience is achieved or even attempted.

In fact, Shakespeare's Vienna—presented chiefly in the comic SUBPLOT—resembles Shakespeare's LONDON, by no coincidence, for the play's satirical edge is intended to expose the immorality and cynicism of "modern" life of the early 17th century. The humorous catalogue of petty criminals recited by Pompey, in 4.3.1–20, offers a sampling of current London stereotypes. The idle, war-loving noblemen who condemn peace and laugh at venereal disease are our introduction to Vienna's streets in 1.2, and they probably reflect the negotiations for peace with Spain that were held in London from May to August 1604. During this time the citizenry were troubled with the presence of disorderly soldiers, and professional officers bemoaned the prospective interruption of their careers. Similarly, Mistress Overdone's complaint about "the war . . . the sweat . . . the gallows" (1.2.75–76) reflects the same situation, as well as a plague that raged in London over the winter of 1603–04 and a series of treason trials and executions that enlivened the news. Further, the proclamation for the destruction of brothels, reported by Pompey in 1.2, corresponds to a London law of 1603 ordering the razing of whole districts inhabited by "dissolute and idle persons"—ostensibly an antiplague effort, but one that was especially directed at whorehouses and gambling dens.

Virgil (Vergil) (70–19 B.C.) Ancient Roman poet, an important influence on Shakespeare's art in general—indeed, on all of Western literature—whose works were also a source for details in a number of Shakespeare's plays and poems. For instance, Virgil's *Aeneid*, an epic poem on the founding of ROME, provided imagery and occasional episodes, most prominently in *The Rape of Lucrece*, *Hamlet*, and *The Tempest*. When the Archbishop of Canterbury compares society to a beehive in *Henry V* (1.2.187–204), he is echoing a famous passage in Virgil's *Georgics*, a collection of hymns to the traditional rural life of Italy. Virgil's PASTORAL *Eclogues* were among the finest examples of a genre that particularly influenced *As You Like It* and *The Winter's Tale*.

However, the general impact of Virgil on the playwright's age is more important than any specific contributions. In the RENAISSANCE the works of Virgil, especially the *Aeneid*, were regarded as literature's highest achievement, and every 16th-century writer felt their impact. The stately, measured pace of Virgil's verse was an important influence on the tone of Shakespeare's poetry and that of all his contemporaries. In fact, BLANK VERSE was introduced to England in the translations of Virgil by Henry Howard, Earl of SURREY. Virgil's themes—the patriotism of the *Aeneid* and the rustic beauties of the *Eclogues* and the *Georgics*—informed Elizabethan notions of genre.

Moreover, Virgil was a great literary nationalist—not only in the *Aeneid*'s grand history, but in the local pride of place displayed in the *Eclogues* and *Georgics*. As England emerged from the Middle Ages to find itself a distinctive nation, Virgil's nationalistic vision seemed remarkably appropriate. As if to demonstrate this, more than 50 English writers translated some part of Virgil's works during the 16th and 17th centuries. Shakespeare may have read the renderings of Surrey, Thomas Phaer (ca. 1510–60), or Richard Stanyhurst (1545–1615), but he surely knew Virgil's works best in the original Latin, in which he had studied them in school.

Virgil was born near MANTUA, the son of a prosperous peasant—a potter and beekeeper, according to some traditions. He studied rhetoric and philosophy in Milan and Rome from 55 to around 42 B.C. At this time he began writing, and he also made friends with the poet Gallus, who introduced him to a patron, Maecenas, the friend and adviser of Augustus Caesar (all three of whom appear in *Antony and Cleopatra*). Maecenas probably encouraged the publication of the *Eclogues,* which appeared around 39 B.C., and he definitely urged the poet to compose the *Georgics,* which are written in honor of Maecenas, though they contain many passages eulogizing Augustus. The poet read the *Georgics* to Augustus upon his return from the campaign of ACTIUM in 29 B.C. and sparked the future emperor's enthusiasm and support. Both the *Eclogues* and the *Georgics* reflect their troubled times in a nostalgia for a simpler world combined with a hopeful anticipation of better times in the peace that has been wrought by Rome's new ruler. Their patriotic tone anticipates the *Aeneid*, on which Virgil worked for the last 10 years of his life. He died with the epic still incomplete and left instructions in his will that it be burned, but the emperor overruled this stipulation and had the poem published in its unfinished state.

Voltaire (1694–1778) Pen name of François-Marie Arouet, famed French novelist, playwright, and philosopher, who introduced Shakespeare to

France and later disparaged him. The best-known of the *philosophes*, Voltaire lived in exile in England between 1726 and 1729, where he was introduced to English literature by such literary lights as Alexander POPE. He wrote in praise of Shakespeare in several works: his *Essay on Epic Poetry* of 1726, the preface to his own tragedy *Oedipus* (1730), *The Discourse on Tragedy* (1731), and elsewhere. He cited Shakespeare's full-blooded genius, though with the qualification that, being unaware of classical aesthetics, the unfortunate Englishman had no taste. He ascribed to the plays "coarse but appealing irregularities." This reflected the neoclassical bent of French literature at the time, but it also echoed much English sentiment of the same period, which delighted in the extreme adaptations of Nahum TATE, for example. Despite his reservations in writing about Shakespeare, Voltaire introduced him to the world of French letters, indeed of European culture, for the English playwright was virtually unknown on the continent before this time.

Voltaire thought Shakespeare's influence could be enlivening, and he undertook to present it to France in the carefully adulterated form of his own derivative plays, such as *Eryphile* (1732), an adaptation of *Hamlet;* his *Zaïre* (also 1732, from *Othello*); and *La Mort de César* (1735; *Julius Caesar*). However, as the century wore on, Shakespeare became more and more popular, and the aging Voltaire saw a threat to the neoclassical aesthetics that governed his own art and taste. He lashed out at the playwright and the barbarities that admiration of him was introducing into French culture, being especially enraged by the plays of Jean-François DUCIS and the TRANSLATION of the complete plays by Pierre LE TOURNEUR. When Le Tourneur criticized him in turn, Voltaire responded with a famous open letter, his "Letter to the *Académie Français*" (1776), in which he excoriates Shakespeare at great length. Thus, ironically, the expanding influence of the English playwright on European literature was deplored by the very man who had introduced him to the continent.

Wagner, Richard (1813–1883) German composer, a major figure in the history of OPERA and the creator of an opera based on *Measure for Measure*. In the 1830s the young Wagner, under the influence of "Young Germany," a radical movement for political and cultural reform, wrote *Das Liebersverbot (The Ban on Love)*, his third opera. Writing his own libretto (as he did for all his operas), the composer moved Shakespeare's tale of moral corruption from VIENNA to Palermo, suffusing it in a Mediterranean atmosphere of hedonism and sensuality, in reaction against what he thought of as a conventionally sentimental German opera tradition and a puritanical German attitude toward sex. As musical director of a traveling theater company, Wagner was able to direct and conduct the first performance of his opera in 1836, its only performance in his lifetime. Regarded today as mere student work, uncharacteristic of Wagner's distinctive style, and overshadowed by his many more famous works, *Das Liebersverbot* has been performed only rarely since.

Wagner became perhaps the best-known opera composer of all, and his operas were probably among the most influential works of art in Europe for several generations. They are still much loved and frequently performed. He envisioned opera productions that would encompass all arts—painting and sculpture as well as literature and music. In this quest for a supreme art, he saw the universality of Shakespeare as a model. Though Wagner only turned to the playwright once for a subject, he appreciated the plays greatly: He wrote about the music of his idol, BEETHOVEN, that "applying Beethovenian music to the Shakespearean drama might lead to the utmost perfecting of musical form."

Wagner wrote several books on opera and music, including the notorious *Judaism in Music*, a relentlessly anti-Semitic tract of 1850 that established his deserved reputation as a bigot, an aspect of his life that has received great emphasis ever since Hitler and the Nazis adopted him as an icon of German culture.

Wakefield Location in *3 Henry VI*, a town in Yorkshire and a battle site during the WARS OF THE ROSES. The battle, fought in December 1460 between the army of the Duke of York and a considerably larger force led by Queen Margaret, takes place in 1.3–1.4. It results in the capture and death of York and a catastrophic loss for his troops. In depicting the conflict, Shakespeare took considerable liberties with the recorded accounts. York's son Rutland, who died in combat, is incorrectly depicted as a child and a brutally murdered noncombatant. York's oldest son Edward (Edward IV), whose exploits the playwright describes, was not present at the battle; he was with another armed force, one that might have relieved York had he been patient and waited for it. However, the Duke undertook to fight despite the odds, probably underestimating the leadership of Queen Margaret, and suffered the loss, which is accurately portrayed. Another son, Richard (Richard III), is made to encourage the hasty decision to fight; in reality, Richard was only eight years old at the time and lived in exile in Burgundy. The playwright made these alterations for various reasons: Rutland's murder emphasizes the theme of revenge; the presence of Edward and Richard tightens the succession of incidents that the play must depict; and Richard's role further reflects his importance as a major character.

Wales Ancient kingdom to England's west, a location used in *Cymbeline* and *Richard II,* and an important subject in *1* and *2 Henry IV* and *Henry V.* A Welsh character appears in *The Merry Wives of Windsor,* and Wales is referred to occasionally in other plays as well.

In the HISTORY PLAYS Wales is strategically important in the civil conflicts fought by King Henry IV. In *Richard II,* when Henry Bolingbroke (the future king) arrives in England with an army, intent on challenging King Richard II, Richard is in Ireland. Bolingbroke therefore marches to Wales to intercept him upon his return. Scenes 2.4, 3.2, and 3.3 take place in this important location, although no fighting takes place. In 2.4 Shakespeare first presents, in the person of the Captain, the archetypal Welshman who appears in these plays, a cautious and superstitious figure. The Captain deserts Richard's cause, and he may represent Owen Glendower, a famous Welsh warrior who appears in 3.1 of *1 Henry IV,* where his superstition is a significant factor in the unfolding of the plot.

Wales became a part of Britain by conquest over the course of the 11th to 13th centuries, but periodic revolts lasted until the time of the history plays, when Glendower led a rebellion that produced the last few years of Welsh independence, ca. 1405–09. In both of the *Henry IV* plays, the political importance of Wales is apparent: As well as being a hotbed of rebellion, it was a fertile source of soldiers. The courage and military prowess of the Welsh were well known, as was their inclination toward feuding and personal disputes. Other characteristics of the archetypal Welshman of Shakespeare's day are embodied in Glendower and his daughter, Lady Mortimer: a sentimental streak and a love of music. Also, various peculiarities of spelling and syntax in Glendower's speeches, as they were originally published, probably reflect a Welsh accent.

Shakespeare was clearly aware of the popular English stereotype of the Welsh as distinctly foreign, but in *Henry V* Wales is specifically included in a united Britain. Shakespeare depicted Henry V as a king of all the British peoples, especially in the so-called international scene (3.2). Here the Welsh representative is Captain Fluellen, who is notable for his comically powerful Welsh accent. Fluellen is a hot-tempered but honest and courageous soldier; in 5.1, when Pistol mocks him by saying he smells of leeks—the Welsh national symbol—Fluellen forces him to eat one.

Another Welsh character appears in *The Merry Wives of Windsor,* the village clergyman and schoolmaster, Sir Hugh Evans. He also has a pronounced accent and a tendency toward clichés, another allegedly Welsh characteristic. Also, he is partly responsible for a theft of horses, an episode that reflects another, less attractive English stereotype of the Welsh as inveterate thieves. In the famous "Latin scene" of *The Merry Wives* (4.1), Evans comically drills a student in the ancient language. This perhaps reflects the playwright's own experience at STRATFORD, where he may have had a schoolmaster of Welsh ancestry, Thomas JENKINS. In any case, the creation of Evans, Glendower, Lady Mortimer, and Fluellen indicates that in the late 1590s Shakespeare's acting company, the CHAMBERLAIN'S MEN, included one or more Welshmen.

In *Cymbeline,* a much later play, Wales is the location for most of Acts 3 and 4 of the play. It is the land of exile for Belarius, who has been unjustly exiled from the court of King Cymbeline. In addition to being a wilderness, Wales is again a military venue, as the Romans use Milford Haven, a Welsh port, as their point of invasion (though the ensuing battle takes places over the border in England). However, these features are not developed in the play, and the only specifically Welsh element in *Cymbeline* is a minor one: the pseudonym, Morgan, taken by Belarius. Since Belarius/Morgan, like Evans, is given to clichés, he may also have been intended to suggest a comic Welsh stereotype.

Welsh material crops up elsewhere in the plays as well. For instance, the fairy lore of *A Midsummer Night's Dream* probably came from Wales, perhaps through the traditions of WARWICKSHIRE, Shakespeare's home, but perhaps also through the Welsh players in the Chamberlain's Men. The *Dream* was written around the same time as *Richard II*, where matters Welsh are first found in Shakespeare. In an intriguing sidelight, it is often thought that "Ducdame, Ducdame, Ducdame" (*As You Like It*, 2.5.51), the mysterious "nonsense" refrain in the parody song by Jaques, is a version of a phrase in Cymric, the Welsh language, that means "Come to me," and which was used in a well-known children's game. The date of *As You Like It* is uncertain, but it is thought to have been written in the same period as *The Merry Wives of Windsor, 1 Henry IV*, and *Henry V*.

Walker, Henry (d. 1616)   Musician in LONDON, seller of the BLACKFRIARS GATEHOUSE to Shakespeare. Walker bought the gatehouse for £100 in 1604 and sold it to Shakespeare for £140 in 1613, issuing a short-term mortgage for £80 of it. Like Shakespeare, he had owned the house as an investment and had not lived in it. He was a musician by trade—a "Minstrel" in the language of the deed—though he also had a shop and apprentices and was a wealthy man.

Walker, William (1608–1680)   Shakespeare's godson. Walker, the son of a prosperous cloth dealer who had served three times as bailiff, or mayor, of STRATFORD, received a cash bequest in his namesake's will. Little more is known of him, except that he too was elected bailiff, in 1649.

Walkley, Thomas (active 1618–1649)   London bookseller and publisher. Walkley published the first QUARTO edition of *Othello*, hiring printer Nicholas OKES. He owned two London bookstores, but little more is known of him except that he published Royalist propaganda during the civil wars.

Walley, Henry (active 1608–1655)   London publisher and bookseller, copublisher of the first edition of *Troilus and Cressida*. With Richard BONIAN, Walley published the QUARTO edition of the play in 1609. When the FIRST FOLIO edition of Shakespeare's works was produced in 1623, Bonian had died and Walley alone held the rights to *Troilus*

and Cressida. Textual evidence reveals that printing of the play was delayed once begun, and scholars conclude that Walley drove a difficult bargain with the Folio publishers, led by Isaac JAGGARD. Walley enjoyed a long career; he entered the STATIONERS' COMPANY in 1608 and was elected its master, or chief officer, in 1655.

Walton, William (b. 1902)   British composer, creator of music for several FILMS of Shakespeare's plays. Walton, one of Britain's most highly regarded 20th-century composers, is best known for symphonic works and for orchestral settings of modern literary readings, but he also wrote numerous film scores, including music for Paul CZINNER's *As You Like It* (1936) and all three of Laurence OLIVIER's Shakespeare films: *Henry V* (1944), *Hamlet* (1947), and *Richard III* (1955). He also composed the theme music for the BBC's *Shakespeare Series* (1977). Walton composed several well-known operas, including a *Troilus and Cressida*, though it is based on CHAUCER's version of the tale rather than Shakespeare's.

Wanamaker, Sam (1919–1993)   American actor and principal creator of the Shakespeare's Globe Theatre, a London cultural complex that includes a replica of the 16th-century GLOBE THEATRE, where many of Shakespeare's plays were first performed. Sam Wanamaker, an actor from Chicago, Illinois, made his career and home in Britain after being blacklisted during the McCarthyist hysteria of the 1950s. When he found that the only relic of Shakespeare's old playhouse was a vaguely worded plaque, he determined that something more fitting should be done. He was the director of an art and performance center at the Shakespeare Theatre in Liverpool when he founded the Shakespeare Globe Trust in 1970. The Trust was a charitable organization dedicated to building and operating a replica of the Globe Theatre in London. The Trust—initially using Wanamaker's own money—began by buying real estate near the original Globe's location. Over 20 years, Wanamaker and others continued pursuing funds and political backing for his project. In 1987 construction began on the new Globe, intended to approximate the original as much as scholarship and adherence to modern safety regulations permitted. The project has grown to be a complex of buildings, including the Globe replica, formally called the Shakespeare's Globe Theatre; a replica of a 17th-century indoor playhouse, approximating the BLACKFRIARS THEATRE; and exhibition space. Wanamaker witnessed the first trial performances, held before the construction was complete, but he died four years before the Shakespeare's Globe Theatre held its first premiere in 1997.

Warburton, John (1682–1759) English antiquarian and manuscript collector. Warburton recorded his ownership of many play manuscripts, including copies of DUKE HUMPHREY (by "Will. Shakespear") and *Henry I* (by "Will. Shakespear and Rob. Davenport"; see HENRY I AND HENRY II). Neither manuscript survives—most of Warburton's collection was destroyed by a servant who mistook it for wastepaper—but scholars doubt that either was by Shakespeare.

Warkworth Castle Fortified dwelling in northern England, a setting in *1* and *2 Henry IV*. The principal home of the Percy family, this castle served as a headquarters for the rebellion against King Henry IV led by Hotspur and his uncle Worcester. In 2.3 of *1 Henry IV* Hotspur here prepares for the forthcoming campaign and bids an affectionate farewell to his wife, Lady Percy. In *2 Henry IV* the INDUCTION, in which Rumour tells of the contrary reports that the Earl of Northumberland will soon receive, and 1.1, in which they arrive, are both set at Warkworth, as is 2.3, in which Northumberland is persuaded by Lady Northumberland and Lady Percy to abandon the rebels' hopeless cause.

Warkworth Castle was built in the 12th century and remodeled in the 14th by the Earl of Northumberland of the play. A strategically important fort on England's northern border, Warkworth saw much warfare and was often besieged. In 1405 Henry IV, mopping up the Percy rebels, damaged the castle considerably with his artillery. Today, still owned by the Percy family, it is a picturesque ruin (though still habitable in part) that is open to the public.

Warner, William (ca. 1558–1609)   English author whose translation of *The Menaechmi* by PLAUTUS, the principal source for *The Comedy of Errors*, may have been known by Shakespeare. Although Warner's translation was not published until 1595, somewhat later than the presumed date of composition of Shakespeare's play, the playwright may have read it in manuscript, a common practice at that time. This speculation is strengthened by the fact that Warner's book was dedicated to Henry Carey, Lord HUNSDON, the patron of the CHAMBERLAIN'S MEN, Shakespeare's theatrical company.

War of the Theaters (Poetomachia)   Rivalry between playwrights—Ben JONSON versus John MARSTON and Thomas DEKKER—marked by satirical plays written and produced between 1599 and 1602. Also called the Poetomachia—Dekker's comical Greek term for "combat of the poets"—the War of the Theaters involved seven plays produced by three acting companies. It is difficult to tell whether the rivalry was based on real animosity or was a publicity stunt. Jonson later remembered his hatred for Marston, but he was peacefully collaborating with him just a few years after this conflict, and by all accounts no one felt hostile toward the genial Dekker, either then or ever. The contest certainly did generate publicity for the CHILDREN'S COMPANIES as they recovered their position in the public theaters in the early years of the 17th century.

The War of the Theaters began with Marston's *Histrio-mastix* (1599), staged by the Children of Paul's, which contained a humorous character modeled on Jonson. Though Marston may have meant no offense, Jonson replied by satirizing his bombastic style in *Every Man out of His Humour* (1599), produced by Shakespeare's CHAMBERLAIN'S MEN (who were otherwise uninvolved in the fray). Marston countered by portraying Jonson as a cuckold in *Jack Drum's Entertainment* (1600), a Paul's play. Jonson's reply encompassed Dekker, Marston's fellow writer for Paul's, in *Cynthia's Revels* (1601) (he depicted himself in it as "a creature of a most perfect and divine temper"); this work was staged by the Children of the Chapel. Marston immediately replied with an uncomplimentary Jonson-figure in *What You Will* (1601), and Dekker and Marston together began to write another satire. Jonson learned of this, however, and rushed out *The Poetaster* (1601), in which Dekker is presented as a "play-dresser [i.e., reviser of other people's dramas] and plagiary" and Marston as a "poetaster and plagiary." This time Jonson depicted himself as the Roman poet Horace (65–8 B.C.), and in Dekker and Marston's *Satiromastix* (1601), Horace is ridiculed. The battle of plays ended at this point, as the participants moved on to other work. By 1604 Marston had even dedicated a play to Jonson.

Shakespeare alluded to the War of the Theaters twice in the plays he was writing at the time. In *Hamlet* the children's companies of DENMARK are said to "berattle the common stages," with "much to do on both sides" and "much throwing about of brains" (2.2.340, 350, 356). In *Twelfth Night* Feste's remark that the word *element* is "overworn" (3.1.60) alludes to Dekker's satire in *Satiromastix* on Jonson's use of the word.

Wars of the Roses   English dynastic wars of 1455–85, in which are set the first four of Shakespeare's HISTORY PLAYS: *1, 2,* and *3 Henry VI* and *Richard III.* The wars were a struggle between two branches of the PLANTAGENET FAMILY, the houses of YORK and LANCASTER. Traditionally (though unhistorically), the Yorkists were thought to have used white roses as their emblem and the Lancastrians to have worn red ones.

In the mid-15th century a Lancastrian, Henry VI, ruled England. A weak king, crowned while only an infant and heavily influenced by aristocratic cliques, Henry lost most of England's conquests in FRANCE in the last phase of the HUNDRED YEARS' WAR—the principal subject of *1 Henry VI.* These losses, along with evident corruption and extravagance at the royal court, resulted in recurring popular unrest. An opposition party of aristocrats arose, led by the Duke of York. In the political maneuvering depicted in *2 Henry VI,* York gained ascendancy over the faction led by Queen Margaret, and he ruled the country while the king was temporarily insane in 1453–54 (Shakespeare does not mention this episode). York was excluded from power when Henry recovered, and he resorted to

war, winning the battle of ST. ALBANS, with which *2 Henry VI* closes, in 1455.

York reclaimed power, but the rivalry continued, and the two sides resumed warfare in 1459. After a Yorkist victory in July 1460, the duke claimed the throne. However, this action produced resistance among the aristocracy, and York had to accept a compromise, as is enacted in 1.1 of *3 Henry VI:* Henry was permitted to continue ruling, though York would succeed him. Queen Margaret retaliated by raising an army; she won the battle of WAKEFIELD in December 1460, in which York was killed. However, her triumph was short-lived: she alarmed the aristocracy by claiming the right to dispossess her enemies of their estates, and she alienated the common people by permitting her army to loot and pillage after the battle. York's son, soon to be Edward IV, assumed his father's claim to the throne, and after a bloody victory at TOWTON in March 1461, he was crowned, ending the first phase of the Wars of the Roses.

Edward ruled England with considerable success for 22 years, though his reign was interrupted in 1470 by a Lancastrian invasion, led by Margaret and the Earl of Warwick, a onetime Yorkist. They placed Henry VI back on the throne for six months, but Edward recaptured the crown in 1471 after winning the battles of BARNET and TEWKESBURY, completing the second cycle of the wars. These events occupy Acts 3–5 of *3 Henry VI.*

Richard III deals with the last stage of the Wars of the Roses. Edward died in April 1483. In his will he appointed his brother Richard as Protector, ruling for the 12-year-old Prince of Wales. However, Edward's widow, Queen Elizabeth, led an attempt to displace Richard, and he responded by seizing the throne in July 1483. He probably had the prince and his younger brother murdered, although the evidence is inconclusive. In any event, his coup spurred the last, brief campaign of the Wars of the Roses: The only surviving Lancastrian claimant to the crown, the Earl of Richmond, invaded England and defeated Richard at the battle of BOSWORTH FIELD. Richmond took the throne as Henry VII and established the TUDOR DYNASTY.

The Wars of the Roses constituted an important historical watershed, bringing feudalism to an end in England. The feudal aristocracy, exhausted by the conflict, was unable to resist the establishment of a strong, centralized monarchy by the Tudors, who, under Richmond's granddaughter Queen Elizabeth I (see Elizabeth I in *Henry VIII*), still ruled England in Shakespeare's day. One consequence of the Tudors' consolidation of power was the development of a bias in the subsequent writing of English history. Shakespeare's principal sources, the histories by HALL and HOLINSHED and Thomas MORE's biography of Richard III, are fairly reliable with respect to the chronology of the wars, but they are markedly prejudiced in favor of the winning side, depicting Richmond's predecessors, especially Richard, as particularly vicious and villainous.

Shakespeare followed his sources in this respect, but he took important liberties with their account of the wars. In general he altered history in two chief ways: He compressed the time scale during which events occurred, and he exaggerated the ambitions of the Yorkists. The compression, eliminating the long stretches when the conflict was on hold, serves to maintain a high level of dramatic excitement, but it also virtually eliminates the successful reign of King Edward and thereby overstates the extent of England's disruption and overemphasizes the importance of the Tudor "rescue" of the country. In the plays the conflict seems both horrifying and relentless, though in fact it consisted of only four campaigns, widely scattered over 30 years, and included only one episode of civil plundering, that of Margaret's army after Wakefield, and only one strikingly bloody battle, Towton.

Furthermore, Shakespeare stresses the evil of the Duke of York's attempt to rebel against an anointed king. York is shown conspiring for many years to seize the throne, when in fact his attempted usurpation was almost impulsive. Similarly, Richard III is depicted as scheming to wear the crown at a time when he was actually an infant, and his villainy, although derived from the sources, is magnified to spectacular effect. Thus sinful human greed is presented as the cause of grievous social disruption, when the actual situation, even as reported in the biased sources, was much more complex.

Warwickshire   County in England, location of STRATFORD, Shakespeare's home, and a setting in

3 Henry VI. In 4.2 the Duke of Warwick comes to Warwickshire, his home territory, with a French army, judging his own locality to be the safest place to commence a conquest of England on behalf of the deposed King Henry VI. One of the chief towns of Warwickshire, COVENTRY, also figures as a location in several of the HISTORY PLAYS. In addition, in the INDUCTION to *The Taming of the Shrew*, there are numerous references and allusions to the Stratford neighborhood. This suggests that the play may have been written shortly after Shakespeare's arrival in LONDON.

Waterson, John (active 1634)   Publisher in LONDON, producer of the first edition of *The Two Noble Kinsmen*. In 1634 Waterson published *The Two Noble Kinsmen* as a work by Shakespeare and John FLETCHER, in a QUARTO edition (known as Q1). Waterson is known to have been a reputable publisher who handled other plays in the repertoire of the KING'S MEN; these factors support the attribution of the play to Shakespeare and Fletcher, a point that is disputed by some scholars.

Webster, Benjamin (1797–1882)   British actor, playwright, and producer. Webster was a successful playwright and character actor, but he is most remembered for a single production from his equally successful career as a theater manager. In 1844, in collaboration with J. R. PLANCHÉ, he staged *The Taming of the Shrew* and made history by presenting the uncut text of Shakespeare's play. The experiment was well received by the public, and the use of legitimate Shakespearean texts eventually became the norm. Webster's great-granddaughter was Margaret WEBSTER.

Webster, John (d. 1634)   English dramatist, a leading figure of JACOBEAN DRAMA. Webster is chiefly known for two plays that are generally considered the greatest Jacobean tragedies after Shakespeare's: *The White Devil* (1612) and *The Duchess of Malfi* (1614). These striking REVENGE PLAYS, which feature obsessed and passionate heroines, are still frequently performed. Webster's poetry, filled with leitmotifs and entrancing imagery, is more finely crafted than that of any dramatist of the period except Shakespeare. Only two other plays by Webster—lesser works—can be surely identified, but he may also have written *The Revenger's Tragedy* (1606), a gruesome and bizarre revenge play that ranks with *The White Devil* and *The Duchess of Malfi*. Published anonymously, it is sometimes attributed to Thomas MIDDLETON or, following a late-17th-century ascription, to Cyril Tourneur (d. 1626), a much lesser talent.

Webster, Margaret (1905–1972) British actress and producer, active in the United States. The daughter of two well-known actors and the great-granddaughter of Benjamin WEBSTER, Margaret Webster made her professional debut as an actress with Sybil THORNDIKE and Lewis CASSON. She subsequently toured with Ben GREET and performed at the OLD VIC THEATRE in the early 1930s. In 1936 she moved to New York and became a leading director, especially of Shakespeare. Often employing Maurice EVANS as leading man, Webster mounted many noteworthy productions, including *1 Henry IV* and *Hamlet* in 1939, *Macbeth* in 1941—with Judith ANDERSON as Lady Macbeth—and a controversial *Othello* starring Paul ROBESON in 1942. She also lectured widely in America and supervised the Shakespearean productions at the New York World's Fair in 1939. While she popularized Shakespeare to a great extent, she was also criticized for tampering with his texts, perhaps most notoriously when she replaced the EPILOGUE of *The Tempest* with Prospero's famous "revels" speech, relocated from 4.1.148–158, in her otherwise well-received production of 1945. She wrote on her experiences as a director in *Shakespeare without Tears* (1942).

Weelkes, Thomas (ca. 1575–1623) Composer of madrigals, the text to one of which was ascribed to Shakespeare in William JAGGARD's spurious anthology THE PASSIONATE PILGRIM (1599). "My flocks feed not," published in Weelkes's *Madrigals to 3, 4, 5 & 6 Voices* (1597), appears as poem no. 17 in Jaggard's collection. However, since madrigalists did not usually write the lyrics to their songs, the creator of this poem remains unknown; scholars agree that it—like many of the poems in the *Pilgrim*—is definitely not Shakespearean.

Weelkes was one of the leading composers of his day, but little is known about him. He was also a noted organist, playing at Chichester Cathedral for the last two decades of his life. He published four collections of songs before 1608 but later devoted himself chiefly to church music.

Welcombe Village near STRATFORD, the site of a real-estate investment of Shakespeare's and the center of a political crisis that gripped Stratford from 1614 to 1616. Shakespeare owned property near Welcombe, and he also subleased tithes to lands in the village, in partnership with Thomas GREENE. That is, he paid a fee for the right to collect the taxes—a percentage of the profits—on specified fields, to a man who had purchased a long-term lease on these rights from the town of Stratford.

In August 1614 a proposal was made by Arthur Mainwaring, a nobleman from Shropshire who owned a large tract of land in Welcombe, to enclose the farmlands in the area and use them to raise sheep. This idea, known as enclosure, was one of the major sources of conflict in 16th- and 17th-century England. Under the traditional medieval system, agricultural lands were owned in units no larger than a few acres and were generally much smaller, organized in clusters within which a given owner's or renter's holdings were scattered randomly. This system was extremely uneconomic, for such techniques as crop rotation were impractical, and no one would introduce capital improvements such as irrigation when his neighbors would benefit as much or more than he. Under enclosure, these units were grouped together in larger lots that were "enclosed" by ditches and hedges and used for grazing sheep, whose wool was sold to the burgeoning cloth industry. Though grazing was less productive per acre, it required much less labor, and when enough acres were involved, it was extremely profitable. Its eventual widespread adoption boosted England's economy into the modern world. However, the conversion of lands from agriculture to pasturage was invariably fiercely resisted, for its immediate, local effects were negative. It raised the price of grain by reducing its supply, and it produced unemployment, since herding sheep required only a few shepherds for hundreds of acres.

In 1614 in Stratford, Mainwaring was joined by a local landowner, William COMBE, in promoting enclosure, against the opposition of the town of Stratford, which was protecting the majority of its citizens. Shakespeare's opinion was doubtless ambivalent, for as a tithe holder he stood to gain if the overall productivity of the area rose, yet he might take immediate losses as arable land was converted to pasture. In any case he had the foresight to strike a deal with Mainwaring's agent, who guaranteed him and Greene against any such losses, thus forestalling their potential opposition. Greene, however, was the town clerk of Stratford and as such was opposed anyway. His correspondence on the matter has survived, and his continuing attempts to recruit Shakespeare to his side reflect the playwright's cool distance from the subject. In November 1614 he records a conversation in which Shakespeare assured him that Mainwaring's proposal would probably be dropped and need not be worried about.

However, Mainwaring and Combe proceeded, evicting tenant farmers from their lands and preparing ditches and hedges for sheep fields. They countered opposition with violence, Combe being particularly arrogant in his encounters with opponents. In March 1615 the WARWICKSHIRE court issued an injunction against the enclosure, and Mainwaring withdrew, but Combe, incensed, appealed the case and continued to persecute the tenant farmers, destroying their crops, seizing their livestock, beating them, and even briefly imprisoning some of them. He bought up lands and houses in an express attempt to depopulate Welcombe. The crisis dragged on for another year before the chief justice of England ruled firmly against Combe, only refraining from punishing him because he was the sitting sheriff of Warwickshire at the time. Combe finally dropped his efforts, though he was to reinstitute the proposal several times.

Welles, Orson (1915–1985) American actor, director, and producer of stage and FILM. Welles is probably best remembered for his movies—especially his first, *Citizen Kane* (1940)—and his panic-inducing radio play *The War of the Worlds* (1938), but he was also a significant Shakespearean actor and director. He established himself as an actor playing Mercutio in Katherine CORNELL's *Romeo and Juliet* (1933).

Working for the depression-era Negro Theatre Project, Welles directed a controversial *Macbeth* (1936), with an all-black cast, that was set in 18th-century Haiti and featured a gigantic mask as Banquo's Ghost, a Hecate with a 12-foot bullwhip, and a band of onstage drummers. In 1937 he and John Houseman (1902–88) founded the Mercury Theatre—having lost their federal financing for political reasons—and their first production was a famous, politically oriented, modern-dress *Julius Caesar* (1938), directed by Welles, who also played Brutus. The Mercury Theatre successfully presented many modern and classic plays and is regarded as a milestone in Broadway history, but Welles turned his attention to films. He went to Hollywood, where he directed several masterpieces of American cinema, including *Citizen Kane*, *The Magnificent Ambersons* (1941), and *Lady from Shangai* (1948). In 1948 he also filmed *Macbeth*, with himself in the title role. However, these movies were not successful at the box office, and Welles went abroad to make low-budget films, including *Othello* (1952), shot in Morocco. In 1956 he returned to the Shakespearean stage a final time, to direct and star in *King Lear*. Perhaps his finest Shakespearean film was his last one, *Chimes at Midnight* (1965; known as *Falstaff* in Europe) a combination of Falstaff's episodes from the *Henry IV* plays and *The Merry Wives of Windsor*, and his companions' mournful account of his last days, from *Henry V*.

Westminster Abbey   London church, the location for 1.1 of *1 Henry VI* and 4.4 of *2 Henry IV*, and the site of a well-known monument to Shakespeare. A masterpiece of Gothic architecture, the abbey contains memorials to many famous English men and women, including, in the "Poet's Corner," a monument incorporating a statue of Shakespeare by Peter SCHEEMAKERS. Westminster Abbey has been the traditional setting for British royal ceremonies since long before 1425, when the funeral of Henry V took place there, as depicted in the opening scene of *1 Henry VI*. In *2 Henry IV*, 4.4–4.5, the dying King Henry IV is housed in the JERUSALEM CHAMBER of the abbey.

Westminster Hall   Room in WESTMINSTER PALACE, LONDON, location in *Richard II*. King Richard II is forced to abdicate in Westminster Hall in 4.1. This

Orson Welles directed and starred in a film version of *Macbeth* as well as another movie, *Chimes at Midnight,* which followed the career of Falstaff through three plays. Welles brought a new, expressionistic language to Shakespeare films. *(Courtesy of Culver Pictures, Inc.)*

massive chamber (70 by 240 feet) was already famous in Shakespeare's day as the site of many famous trials, including the historical deposition of Richard, although the king was not present on the actual occasion. Shortly after the play was written, Robert Devereux, Earl of ESSEX, was sentenced to death in the same room. Its famous timber roof, still one of the grandest sights in London, was commissioned in 1394 by Richard himself, following flood damage. Ironically, the work was still in progress when Richard was deposed.

Westminster Palace   Complex of buildings constituting the seat of England's royal government and the setting for many scenes in Shakespeare's HISTORY PLAYS. Often the events depicted in Westmin-

ster Palace are of a governmental nature, whether confidential, as when William de la Pole, Earl of Suffolk, persuades King Henry VI to marry the future Queen Margaret in 5.5 of *1 Henry VI*, or public, as when Richard III is crowned in 4.2 of *Richard III*. However, since the palace was also a royal residence in the era depicted—as it was in Shakespeare's day—some of the events set within it are private. For instance, in 2.4 of *Richard III*, Queen Elizabeth prepares to flee with her young sons into the sanctuary of a church, and in 4.5 of *2 Henry IV*, Prince Hal encounters his father, King Henry IV, on his deathbed.

The following scenes—some of them only specified by such stage directions as "a room in the Queen's apartments" (*Henry VIII* 3.1.1) but some more specifically—take place in Westminster Palace: *Edward III*, 1.1; *1 Henry IV*, 1.1–1.2, 3.2, *2 Henry IV*, 3.1, 5.2; *Henry V*, 1.1–1.2; *1 Henry VI*, 3.1 (in PARLIAMENT HOUSE, a separate building within the palace), 5.1, 5.5; *2 Henry VI*, 1.1, 1.3, 4.4; *3 Henry VI*, 1.1 (in Parliament House), 3.2, 4.1, 4.4, 5.7; *Henry VIII*, 1.1–1.3, 2.2–2.3, 3.1–3.2, 5.1–5.4; *Richard II*, 4.1 (in WESTMINSTER HALL); and *Richard III*, 2.1, 4.2–4.4.

The palace at Westminster was a principal residence of English monarchs from the time of Edward the Confessor (ruled 1043–66) until the 16th century. The original medieval structure was added to and embellished over the centuries, gradually disappearing under the rebuilding. At the time of the history plays, England's monarchs knew Westminster Palace as a warren of buildings that included offices, churches, residences, and meeting halls. In 1834 a disastrous fire, which spared only the famous timber roof of Westminster Hall, necessitated the construction of the present-day Westminster Palace, home of the Houses of Parliament, one of the masterpieces of 19th-century architecture designed by Charles Barry (1795–1860) and A. W. N. Pugin (1812–52).

Whatcott, Robert (active 1613–1616)   Witness to Shakespeare's will. In 1613 Whatcott appeared as a witness for Susanna SHAKESPEARE Hall in her libel suit against John LANE. He may have been a servant in the Hall household.

Whately, Anne   See TEMPLE GRAFTON.

Whetstone, George (ca. 1544–ca. 1587)   English author and playwright whose works were sources for Shakespeare. Whetstone's play *Promos and Cassandra* (1578), based on a novella by the Italian writer CINTHIO, was a principal source for *Measure for Measure*. A story in his *The Rocke of Regard* (1576) may have inspired an aspect of *Much Ado About Nothing*, the fact that Hero is rejected at her own wedding.

Whetstone, the son of a London haberdasher, was best known for *Promos and Cassandra* and for *An Heptameron of Civil Discourse*, a prose work which describes his travels in Italy in 1580 and

includes a version of the Cinthio tale the play was based on (though Shakespeare apparently used only the play in writing *Measure for Measure*). His later works, including *A Mirrour for Magistrates of Cityes* (1584), an account of the vices of LONDON, which also may have had some influence on *Measure for Measure*, were more didactic and sermonizing as he came under the influence of Puritanism. An adventurous man, he sailed on an abortive expedition to America in 1578, and he entered the military in 1587, serving under Robert Dudley, Earl of LEICESTER, in the Low Countries, where he was killed in a duel with another English officer.

White, Edward (active 1577–1612)   London publisher of early editions of *Titus Andronicus*. Chiefly a publisher of ballads, White joined Thomas MILLINGTON in publishing the first edition (Q1) of *Titus* in 1594, and he published Q2 (1600) and Q3 (1611) himself. The son of a Suffolk retailer, White was a successful publisher, becoming an officer of the STATIONERS' COMPANY.

White, William (active 1583–1615)   LONDON printer, White printed plays by Shakespeare and others, as well as numerous ballads. He printed first editions of *Love's Labour's Lost* (1598, for publisher Cuthbert BURBY) and *Pericles* (1609, for Henry GOSSON), and later editions of *3 Henry VI* (Q2, 1600, for Thomas MILLINGTON), *Richard II* (Q4, 1608, for Matthew LAW), *Pericles* (Q2, 1609, for Gosson), and *1 Henry IV* (Q5, 1613, for Law).

Whitefriars Theatre   Seventeenth-century LONDON playhouse. The Whitefriars Theatre, named for its site on the grounds of a former priory of the Carmelite, or White Friars, was established by Michael DRAYTON and others in 1608, as a venue for the short-lived King's Revels Company (see CHILDREN'S COMPANIES). The Queen's Revels, another boys' troupe, played there from 1609 to 1613, and an adult company, LADY ELIZABETH'S MEN, in 1613–14, after which Drayton's lease expired. PRINCE CHARLES' MEN may have played there occasionally until at least 1621, but the later history of the theater is obscure. It was replaced in 1629 by another theater on the same site.

Whitgift, John (ca. 1530–1604) English clergyman, issuer of Shakespeare's marriage license and later a powerful leader of the Church of England. As Bishop of Worcester, the diocese that included STRATFORD, Whitgift signed the license authorizing the marriage of Shakespeare and Anne Whateley— a clerical error for Anne HATHAWAY—without the usual three banns or formal announcements of intention to marry. This dispensation was required because Advent season was beginning, during which time banns could not be declared, and a quick marriage was desired, for Anne was pregnant. Whitgift was a famously stern churchman, and that he approved the avoidance of banns indicates that it was not a shady procedure, as some have thought.

Whitgift was shortly to occupy the most powerful position in the English church. A graduate and longtime professor and administrator of Cambridge University, Whitgift forcefully opposed a strong strain of Puritanism among the faculty and students. Queen Elizabeth was pleased with his opinion on this subject, which was becoming increasingly divisive in the nation, and she appointed Whitgift Bishop of Worcester in 1577 and then Archbishop of Canterbury in 1583. As archbishop, he was most noted for his repressive campaign against Puritanism, but he was also a highly competent administrator and instituted valuable reforms. He became a close adviser to the queen and later officiated at the coronation of her successor, King JAMES I.

Whittington, Thomas (d. 1601) Husbandman of STRATFORD who mentioned Shakespeare in his will. Thomas Whittington, a shepherd who was employed by Anne HATHAWAY Shakespeare's father, stipulated in his will that his executors should collect from Shakespeare a debt of 40 shillings he was owed by Anne and donate it to the poor people of Stratford. Elsewhere in the will, Whittington left a similar amount to the poor people of Stratford, so his separate mention of Shakespeare stands out. It may reflect no more than that when Whittington began preparing his will, this small matter crossed his mind first, but it has also been interpreted as evidence that the shepherd wanted to insinuate that Shakespeare was a miser, perhaps one who had reduced his wife to borrowing from her father's

hired hand while he was in London. On the other hand, the will also mentions several other financial relationships between Whittington and the Hathaway family, and perhaps they were the informal equivalent of bankers for him.

Wieland, Christoph Martin (1733–1813) German poet and translator. Wieland produced the first German TRANSLATION OF SHAKESPEARE, rendering 22 of the plays into prose between 1762 and 1766. His work inspired and was superseded by that of J. J. ESCHENBURG.

As a young man, Wieland was known for poetry that supported Pietism, a popular religious and esthetic cult of the day. He later achieved a European reputation as the creator of sophisticated, elegant, and mildly erotic verses and novels that celebrated an ideal of the Enlightenment movement, the combination of intellect and sensuality. He was regarded for a time—until the advent of GOETHE—as Germany's greatest writer. However, with the rise of Romanticism in the early 19th century, Wieland's reputation declined catastrophically, and it is only in recent years that critics have once again taken him seriously.

Wilkins, George (active 1603–1608) English author and dramatist, a possible collaborator with Shakespeare. Wilkins was a hack writer who penned pamphlets, plays, and a novel; virtually nothing more is known of his life. As a playwright he collaborated with John DAY, Thomas DEKKER, Samuel ROWLEY, and others, and some scholars attribute parts of *Timon of Athens* or *Pericles* to him. Though the first of these suggestions is very uncertain and much disputed, the second has received considerable support from scholars. Wilkins's novel *The Painful Adventures of Pericles Prince of Tyre* (1608) was written to capitalize on the popularity of Shakespeare's *Pericles*. This was the principal stimulus for speculation that he wrote parts of the play, and recent studies, comparing details of the styles of the two playwrights, have convinced a number of scholars that he did indeed do so. Wilkins also wrote a play on his own, *The Miseries of Enforced Marriage* (1607), which dealt with the same notorious murder that was the subject of A YORKSHIRE TRAGEDY.

Williams, Harcourt (1880–1957) English actor and director. Williams, a successful actor who appeared mostly in modern plays—although he was the First Player in John BARRYMORE's LONDON presentation of *Hamlet* (1925)—was the director of the OLD VIC THEATRE from 1929 to 1934. A follower of Harley GRANVILLE-BARKER, he insisted on staging the full texts of Shakespeare's plays, with little or no scenery. He encouraged rapid speaking of Elizabethan English, both to make clear its colloquial nature in the characters' mouths and to keep the performances from flagging. In 1935 he published a memoir of his directorate, *Four Years at the Old Vic.* He resumed his acting career and returned to the Old Vic as an actor in 1946.

Williamson, Nicol (b. 1938) British actor and director. Williamson has been acclaimed in a number of major Shakespearean performances, most notably perhaps as Coriolanus in Trevor NUNN's 1973 Royal Shakespeare Company production; as Macbeth on stage in 1974 and 1982 and on TELEVISION in 1983; and as Hamlet in London and New York, on an American tour in 1968–69, and on FILM in 1969. In 1982 he directed a highly successful *Othello*, with James Earl JONES in the title role.

Willoughby, Sir Ambrose (active 1598) High official in the court of Queen Elizabeth I (see Elizabeth I in *Henry VIII*) and possibly a satirical model for Malvolio in *Twelfth Night.* Willoughby was the queen's chief sewer, the official in charge of the service of meals at court. In 1598 Willoughby had a dispute with Shakespeare's patron, the Earl of SOUTHAMPTON, that has been proposed as the source of Malvolio's famous encounter with Sir Toby, Sir Andrew, and Feste in 2.3. After having chastised the earl and Sir Walter RALEIGH for their noisy midnight carousing in the queen's courtyard, Willoughby was physically accosted by Southampton but successfully drove the earl from the palace. The queen later publicly thanked Willoughby for the deed.

This incident's resemblance to the one in the play is the basis for the link between Willoughby and Malvolio that some scholars make. Others, however, point out that Elizabeth supported Willoughby very strongly and that the playwright was therefore unlikely to pillory him. (For other possible Malvolios, see FFARINGTON, WILLIAM; HOBY, SIR THOMAS POSTHUMOUS; KNOLLYS, SIR WILLIAM.)

Willoughby, Henry (Henry Willobie) (b. ca. 1575) English poet and possibly the "Mr. W. H." of the *Sonnets.* Willoughby is believed to have been the author of the poem "Willobie his Avisa" (1594), a long account of the attempts of various suitors, including the poet, to seduce the chaste Avisa. In an anonymous commendatory poem published with "Willobie," Shakespeare is named as the author of *The Rape of Lucrece,* in the earliest surviving reference to him as a poet. In "Willobie" itself, the poet, "H. W.," tells of his conversations with his friend, the "old player," "W. S.," who has similarly fallen a victim to passion. Some commentators believe that Shakespeare was W. S., that the frustrating love affair of W. S. is that described in the *Sonnets,* and that H. W. is the Mr. W. H. of Thomas THORPE's dedication to the *Sonnets.* Further, Avisa is sometimes held to be the "Dark Lady" of the *Sonnets* (although it is unclear in "Willobie" whether W. S. has loved Avisa or another woman). However, both W. S. and Avisa are unidentified—even Willoughby is hardly known—and these speculations remain entirely unprovable. Willoughby may conceivably have known Shakespeare, however, for he was a cousin by marriage of the playwright's friend Thomas RUSSELL.

Wilson, Jack (ca. 1585–ca. 1641) Singer and actor who may have played Balthasar in *Much Ado About Nothing.* A stage direction in the FOLIO edition of the play (1623) refers to "Iacke Wilson," plainly an actor who played the part—though perhaps not in the original production. Although an otherwise unknown Wilson may have been the man, Jack Wilson is known to have been an actor and singer and is thus generally favored (but see WILSON, JOHN). He was the son of a traveling minstrel but was probably a lifelong resident of LONDON himself. Little more is known of him, though he is recorded as a singer whom the city of London hired on ceremonial occasions.

Wilson, John (1595–1674) Noted composer, musician, and singer. Early in his career Wilson composed music for the stage, including settings for two Shakespearean songs, "Take, o take those lips away" (*Measure for Measure*, 4.1.1–6) and "Lawn as white as driven snow" (*The Winter's Tale*, 4.4.220–232). He may have been the "Iacke Wilson" who played Balthasar, according to a stage direction in the FIRST FOLIO edition of *Much Ado About Nothing* (1623). Though he was too young to have originated the part, he could have taken the role in a later production (but see WILSON, JACK). In 1635 he became a royal musician under King Charles I; in 1642, at the beginning of the Civil Wars, he fled with the king to Oxford, where he received a doctorate in music, becoming a professor of music in 1656. He published a collection of English songs, *Cheerful Ayres or Ballads* (ca. 1660), which contains the pieces mentioned above, along with works by Robert JOHNSON and others. Upon his death Wilson was buried in WESTMINSTER ABBEY, a measure of his eminence.

Wilson, John Dover (1881–1969)   English scholar. Editor of many of the plays in the New Cambridge edition of Shakespeare's plays, Dover Wilson also wrote a number of books on the playwright and his works, including *The Essential Shakespeare* (1932), *What Happens in Hamlet* (1935), and *The Fortunes of Falstaff* (1943).

Wilson, Robert (ca. 1550–ca. 1600)   English actor and dramatist. Wilson, associated with LEICESTER'S MEN and the QUEEN'S MEN, was highly respected as an actor—he was classed with the great Richard TARLTON in his ability to extemporize witty verse—and he was also noted as a playwright. He apparently retired from the stage before 1594 to concentrate exclusively on writing. He probably wrote *The Three Ladies of London* (1584), *The Three Lords and Three Ladies of London* (1590), and *The Cobbler's Prophecy* (1594), and he collaborated with others on SIR JOHN OLDCASTLE. He is also known to have written or collaborated on a number of other plays that are now lost, many of them created for the ADMIRAL'S MEN.

Windsor   Town west of LONDON, setting for *The Merry Wives of Windsor*, several scenes in *Richard II*, and one scene in *1 Henry IV*. In *The Merry Wives*

the town is a typical English rural community in which the intrusion of a comical but cynical and exploitative outsider, Falstaff, is defeated by the homespun wiles of the title characters. *The Merry Wives* was written for a ceremonial occasion at the court of Queen Elizabeth I, a banquet in honor of new members of the Order of the Garter. The banquet was held in London, but the formal induction ceremonies were scheduled for a later date at Windsor Castle—an occasion referred to in 5.5.56–74—and this doubtless accounts for the use of Windsor as the setting.

Modern scholars have determined that the events enacted in certain scenes of the HISTORY PLAYS actually took place in Windsor Castle, a home for British sovereigns since the days of William the Conqueror, who began its construction; thus, in many modern editions the castle is designated as the setting for scenes that are not explicitly located in the original texts. These scenes are 1.1, 2.2, 5.3, 5.4, and 5.6 of *Richard II* and 1.3 of *1 Henry IV*.

Wise, Andrew (active 1580–1603)   London publisher and bookseller. Wise published five of Shakespeare's plays. He produced the first three editions of *Richard III* (1597, 1598, 1602) and *Richard II* (1597, 1597, 1598), and the first two of *1 Henry IV* (1598, 1599). He sold the rights to these plays to Matthew LAW in 1603. In partnership with William ASPLEY he also published the first editions of *2 Henry IV* and *Much Ado About Nothing* (both 1600). Aspley alone held these rights when the FIRST FOLIO was published in 1623, and Wise may have been dead by that date. After nine years of apprenticeship, Wise became a member of the STATIONERS' COMPANY in 1589, but little more is known of him.

Witter, John (active 1605–1619)   Shareholder in the GLOBE THEATRE and litigant against John HEMINGES and Henry CONDELL. Witter, who had no known occupation, acquired a partial share in the Globe when he married the widow of Augustine PHILLIPS. The share she inherited reverted to the other shareholders when she remarried, but Heminges leased a share to the couple. Witter had abandoned his wife, and she had subsequently died, by the time the Globe burned down in 1613. Witter, already in arrears to Heminges, could not pay his portion of the repairs, and his share reverted to Heminges, who gave or sold part of it to Condell. In 1619 Witter sued unsuccessfully for its return, and with this he disappears from history. He is obviously unimportant in himself, but the records of this case have provided scholars with much of our knowledge of financial arrangements in the ELIZABETHAN THEATER.

Woffington, Peg (Margaret Woffington) (1714–1760) English actress. Born in Ireland, Woffington was a child actress who went on to become the leading comedienne of her day. She was famous for a male part, the hero of a popular contemporary comedy, which she repeatedly revived to great enthusiasm, but she also played most of Shakespeare's comedic heroines, including Portia, Rosalind, Viola, and Helena (in *The Merchant of Venice, As You Like It, Twelfth Night,* and *All's Well That Ends Well,* respectively). In addition, she took some non-comic parts, such as Constance in *King John* and Portia in *Julius Caesar.* She was David GARRICK's mistress for a number of years and had many other lovers in a notorious life that still enthralled the public a century later, when it was the subject of a popular novel of 1853 (*Peg Woffington* by Charles Reade [1814–84]). She became ill in 1757, during her last performance (as Rosalind), and never recovered.

Wolfit, Donald (1902–1968) British actor and director. Wolfit's long career was spent chiefly as a performer and director of Shakespeare's plays. He made his debut in 1920 as Biondello in *The Taming of the Shrew* and in 1929 joined the OLD VIC THEATRE company, with whom he played many major parts, including Hamlet, King Claudius, and Othello. He played Antony in Theodore KOMISARJEVSKY's 1936 production of *Antony and Cleopatra.* In 1937 he formed a touring company and traveled in Canada and the British provinces, performing mostly Shakespeare and other 16th- and 17th-century English dramas. In 1960 he toured around the world, giving recitals of famous Shakespearean passages.

Woodstock (Thomas of Woodstock) Anonymous play, written ca. 1592–95, that was a source for *Richard II* and *1 Henry IV. Woodstock* deals with earlier events than does *Richard II,* focusing on the murder of Thomas of Woodstock, Duke of Gloucester. It is sometimes referred to as *1 Richard II;* Shakespeare did not write it, but it has been speculated that he may have known a sequel to *Woodstock*—now lost, if it ever existed—on which he based his own play. The influence of *Woodstock* on *Richard II* is most evident in 2.1, which echoes the earlier work's emphasis on Richard's extravagance and extortionate financial measures. It is also thought that *Richard II's* John of Gaunt is derived from *Woodstock's* Duke of Gloucester; both are depicted as wise elders and exemplary patriots.

Woodstock has a comic SUBPLOT involving a corrupt chief justice who is also a cowardly highwayman, a possible prototype of Falstaff. In its relationship of subplot to main plot, the play may also have influenced the structure of *1 Henry IV.* In any case, a number of wordings found in *Woodstock* are apparently echoed in Shakespeare's highway robbery scene in *1 Henry IV,* 2.2.

Worcester's Men Seventeenth-century LONDON theatrical company. Worcester's Men was originally a provincial company, sponsored by the Earl of Worcester, that toured intermittently between 1555 and 1585. They played in STRATFORD several times during Shakespeare's youth. In 1584 William ALLEYN was a teenage member of the troupe, though he soon left for London. In 1589, under a new earl, the company renewed its existence, and in 1602, they staged a play at the court of Queen Elizabeth I. William KEMPE and Thomas HEYWOOD, who wrote the play, were its leading members. In the same year, Worcester's Men absorbed OXFORD's MEN, and the enlarged troupe received a license to play before the public at an inn. Thus they became the third theater company of London, after the ADMIRAL's MEN and Shakespeare's CHAMBERLAIN's MEN. Christopher BEESTON, the company's future manager, joined them at this point. In February 1603 they performed a Heywood play at Philip HENSLOWE's ROSE THEATRE. Upon Queen Elizabeth's death in March

1603, Worcester's Men came under the patronage of Anne of Denmark (1574–1619), the wife of England's new ruler, King JAMES I, and were known thereafter as the QUEEN'S MEN.

Worthies, Nine Traditional array of medieval heroes, often presented in dramas or tableaux at fairs and festivals. The comical characters in *Love's Labour's Lost* enact such a tableau (5.2.541–717). Traditionally, the Nine Worthies were divided into three groups of three, representing Old Testament leaders, pre-Christian warriors, and medieval notables. They were, respectively: Joshua, David, and Judas Maccabeus; Hector of Troy, Alexander the Great, and Julius Caesar; and King Arthur, Charlemagne, and Godfrey of Bouillon (in England, Godfrey was sometimes replaced by Guy of Warwick). The lineup of Worthies in *Love's Labour's Lost* is quite different, which Shakespeare probably intended as a humorously ignorant error on the part of his unsophisticated characters.

Wyatt, Thomas (ca. 1503–1542) English poet, generally regarded as the introducer of the SONNET into English and possibly the author of a minor source for *Twelfth Night*. Wyatt, while serving as a diplomat in Italy, translated some of the sonnets of Petrarch (1304–74), producing the first English sonnets, around 1530 (but see CHAUCER). Wyatt and his friend Henry Howard, Earl of SURREY, subsequently became the first English poets to compose their own poems in this form. Wyatt also wrote in other forms and may have written the SONG sung by Feste in *Twelfth Night* 4.2.75–82, though some scholars dispute the attribution.

Wyatt was a successful courtier who achieved high office under King Henry VIII (see Henry VIII in *Henry VIII*) despite two periods of imprisonment in the TOWER OF LONDON. He was probably an early lover of the king's wife Anne Boleyn (see Anne Bullen in *Henry VIII*), and his incarceration in 1536, as part of Queen Anne's trial for adultery, may have been connected with this.

Y

Yates, Mary Ann (1728–1787) English actress, wife of Richard YATES. Mrs. Yates, as she was known, succeeded Susannah CIBBER as London's favorite tragic actress, though she also played comedic heroines, including Viola, Rosalind, and Isabella (in *Twelfth Night*, *As You Like It*, and *Measure for Measure*, respectively). She was a famous Lady Macbeth, and she played Cleopatra opposite David GARRICK in the first recorded performance of *Antony and Cleopatra* since Shakespeare's day; she was thus the first woman to play the part.

Yates, Richard (ca. 1706–1796) English actor, husband of Mary Ann YATES. Yates, who was considered the finest comedian of his day, specialized in his version of the COMMEDIA DELL'ARTE figure Harlequin. He also played many of Shakespeare's comic characters, including Touchstone (of *As You Like It*), Autolycus (of *The Winter's Tale*), and Feste and Malvolio (of *Twelfth Night*).

Yong (Yonge, Young), Bartholomew (ca. 1555–ca. 1612) English translator, creator of a work that was a source for *Two Gentlemen of Verona* and *A Midsummer Night's Dream* and may have influenced *As You Like It* and *Twelfth Night*. Yong's version of the Spanish prose romance *Diana enamorada* by Jorge de MONTEMAYOR was not published until 1598, but it was completed in 1582 and circulated widely in manuscript. Shakespeare knew it well, as its importance to *Two Gentlemen* indicates. Yong, an alumnus of one of the INNS OF COURT, spent two years in Spain, 1577 and 1578,

and became familiar with the language, though he apparently encountered Montemayor's *Diana* only after his return. His patron was Penelope Rich (1563–1607), the sister of Robert Devereux, Earl of ESSEX. Yong also translated BOCCACCIO's *Fiammetta* from Italian, as *Amorous Fiammetta* (1587).

York City in northern England, a location in *3 Henry VI* and *1* and *2 Henry IV*. Second in economic and political power only to LONDON during the Middle Ages, York figured heavily in the history of the time and thus naturally appears in the HISTORY PLAYS.

In 2.2 of *3 Henry VI* Queen Margaret and King Henry VI march their army to the walls of York, and the queen points out the severed head of the Duke of York, which has been placed above the city gate. In 4.7 the duke's son Edward (King Edward IV) comes to York after the reinstatement of Henry, whom he had earlier deposed. The Mayor declares the city's loyalty to Henry, and Edward is admitted only after he swears he is not pursuing the Crown. Once within the walls, he reneges on his pledge and declares himself king. The incident illustrates the treachery and dishonesty of the period's political life, an important theme of the *Henry VI* plays.

In the *Henry IV* plays, York is important as the headquarters of the Archbishop of York, a leading rebel against King Henry IV. In 4.4 of *1 Henry IV* the Archbishop, at his home in York, plans to continue the failing rebellion, thus anticipating the events of *Part 2*. In 1.3 of *2 Henry IV* the rebels hold a council of war and formulate their strategy in the same location.

York family Branch of the PLANTAGENET FAMILY, major figures in Shakespeare's HISTORY PLAYS. The Yorkist kings were descended from Edmund, Duke of York (who figures in *Richard II*), the fourth son of King Edward III. In the WARS OF THE ROSES the house of York fought for control of the throne with another line of the Plantagenets, the house of LANCASTER.

Three members of the York family ruled England: Edward IV, from 1461 to 1483; Edward V, briefly and only nominally in 1483; and Richard III, from 1483 to 1485. When the Earl of Richmond overthrew Richard III, he married Richard's niece, the daughter of Edward IV and Queen Elizabeth, incorporating the York lineage into the new TUDOR DYNASTY.

The rivalry between York and Lancaster is the subject of Shakespeare's earliest history plays, the minor TETRALOGY, consisting of *1, 2,* and *3 Henry VI* and *Richard III*. The roots of the conflict lie further back in history, and Shakespeare used this material in the major tetralogy—*Richard II, 1* and *2 Henry IV,* and *Henry V.* Although the Yorks are less important in this historical period, several members of the family figure in these plays as well.

Yorkshire Tragedy, A Play formerly attributed to Shakespeare, part of the Shakespeare APOCRYPHA. *A Yorkshire Tragedy* was published by Thomas PAVIER in 1608 and again in 1619 (in the FALSE FOLIO) as a play by Shakespeare that had been performed by the KING'S MEN. It was also published in the Third and Fourth FOLIOS of Shakespeare's plays, and in the editions of Nicholas ROWE and Alexander POPE. However, although it is a respectable play—unlike most of the apocryphal works—scholars agree that it is not in fact by Shakespeare. This very brief play is quite dissimilar from the playwright's known works in its setting and its subject. It is set in contemporary England and concerns a sensational murder case of 1605 in which a man killed two of his children and attempted to kill his wife and a third child. Moreover, the play's poetry is distinctly inferior to Shakespeare's—especially his late work—and its only important characters, the murderer and his wife, are two-dimensional caricatures who are not even given names and are thus entirely beneath the level of Shakespeare's characterizations. Its actual authorship remains unknown.

Z

Zeffirelli, Franco (b. 1923)   Modern stage, FILM, and OPERA director, creator of a number of noteworthy productions of Shakespeare's plays. Although he has produced many plays and operas, Zeffirelli is most widely known for his films. He produced *Romeo and Juliet* on the stage in 1960 and the screen in 1968; his film of *The Taming of the Shrew* (1967) was extremely popular. He also filmed *Hamlet* (1990) and VERDI's opera *Otello* (1986). He produced *Much Ado About Nothing* on stage in 1965 and for TELEVISION two years later. He is often criticized for the lavish spectacle of his productions (e.g., see BARBER, SAMUEL), which are said to distract from the underlying play, but he has undeniably brought Shakespeare to a very wide audience.

PART IV

Appendices

A COLLECTION OF QUOTATIONS FROM SHAKESPEARE'S WORKS

All's Well That Ends Well

Helena: Oft expectation fails, and most oft there
Where most it promises, and oft it hits
Where hope is coldest and despair most fits.

—2.1.141–143

First Lord: The web of our life is of a mingled
yard, good and ill together [. . .]

—4.3.68–69

King: The bitter past, more welcome is the sweet.

—5.3.328 (last line of the play)

Antony and Cleopatra

Enobarbus: Age cannot wither her, nor custom stale
Her infinite variety: other women cloy
The appetites they feed, but she makes hungry,
Where most she satisfies. For vilest things
Become themselves in her, that the holy priests
Bless her, when she is riggish.

—2.2.235–240 (speaking of Cleopatra)

Antony: Sometime we see a cloud that's dragonish,
A vapour sometime, like a bear, or lion,
A tower'd citadel, a pendent rock,
A forked mountain, or blue promontory
With trees upon 't, that nod unto the world,
And mock our eyes with air.

—4.14.2–7

Cleopatra: Let's do it after the high Roman fashion,
And make death proud to take us.

—4.15.87–88 (as she proposes suicide)

As You Like It

Duke: Sweet are the uses of adversity,
Which like the toad, ugly and venomous,
Wears yet a precious jewel in his head[.]

—2.1.12–14

Jaques: All the world's a stage,
And all the men and women merely players.
They have their exits and their entrances,
And one man in his time plays many parts,
His acts being seven ages. At first the infant,
Mewling and puking in the nurse's arms.
Then the whining school-boy with his satchel
And shining morning face, creeping like snail
Unwillingly to school. And then the lover,
Sighing like furnace, with a woeful ballad
Made to his mistress' eyebrow. Then, a soldier,
Full of strange oaths, and bearded like the pard,
Jealous in honour, sudden, and quick in quarrel,
Seeking the bubble reputation
Even in the cannon's mouth. And then, the justice,
In fair round belly, with good capon lin'd,
With eyes severe, and beard of formal cut,
Full of wise saws, and modern instances,
And so he plays his part. The sixth age shifts

Into the lean and slipper'd pantaloon,
With spectacles on nose, and pouch on side,
His youthful hose well sav'd, a world too wide
For his shrunk shank, and his big manly voice,
Turning again toward childish treble, pipes
And whistles in his sound. Last scene of all,
That ends this strange eventful history,
Is second childishness and mere oblivion,
Sans teeth, sans eyes, sans taste, sans everything.

—2.7.139–166

Rosalind: But these [tales] are all lies. Men have
died from time to time and worms have eaten
them, but not for love.

—4.1.101–103

The Comedy of Errors
Antipholus of Syracuse: [T]here's many a man
hath more hair than wit.

—2.2.81–82

Abbess (Emilia): The venom clamours of a jealous
woman
Poisons more deadly than a mad dog's tooth.

—5.1.69–70

Coriolanus
Sicinius: Nature teaches beasts to know their
friends.

—2.1.5

Sicinius: What is the city but the people?

—3.1.197

Aufidius: So our virtues
Lie in th'interpretation of the time,
And power, unto itself most commendable,
Hath not a tomb so evident as a chair
T'extol what it hath done.

—4.7.49–53

Cymbeline
Guiderius: Fear no more the hear o'th' sun,
Nor the furious winter's rages,

Thou thy worldly task has done,
Home art gone and ta'en thy wages.
Golden lads and girls all must,
As chimney-sweepers, come to dust.

—4.2.258–263 (a funeral SONG)

Pisanio: Fortune brings in some boats that are not
steer'd.

—4.3.46

Cymbeline: By med'cine life may be prolong'd, yet
death
Will seize the doctor too.

—5.5.29–30

Edward III
King Edward: Like as the wind doth beautify a sail
And as a sail becomes the unseen wind,
So do her words her beauty, beauty, words.

—2.1.280–282 (on the Countess of Salisbury)

Hamlet
Hamlet: O that this too too sullied flesh would melt,
Thaw and resolve itself into a dew,
Or that the Everlasting had not fix'd
His canon 'gainst self-slaughter. O God! God!
How weary, stale, flat, and unprofitable
Seem to me all the uses of this world!
Fie on't, ah fie, 'tis an unweeded garden
That grows to seed; things rank and gross in nature
Possess it merely.

—1.2.129–137

Hamlet: I have of late, but wherefore I know not,
lost all my mirth, forgone all custom of exercises;
and indeed it goes so heavily with my disposition
that this goodly frame the earth seems to me a
sterile promontory, this most excellent canopy
the air, look you, this brave o'er hanging firma-
ment, this majestical roof fretted with golden
fire, why, it appeareth nothing to me but a foul
and pestilent congregation of vapours. What
piece of work is a man, how noble in reason,
how infinite in faculties, in form and moving

how express and admirable, in action how like an angel, in apprehension how like a god: the beauty of the world, the paragon of animals— and yet, to me, what is this quintessence of dust?

—2.2.295–308

Hamlet: To be, or not to be, that is the question:
Whether 'tis nobler in the mind to suffer
The slings and arrows of outrageous fortune,
Or to take arms against a sea of troubles
And by opposing end them. To die—to sleep,
No more; and by a sleep to say we end
The heart-ache and the thousand natural shocks
That flesh is heir to: 'tis a consummation
Devoutly to be wish'd. To die, to sleep;
To sleep, perchance to dream—ay, there's the rub:
For in that sleep of death what dreams may come,
When we have shuffled off this mortal coil,
Must give us pause—there's the respect
That makes calamity of so long life.
For who would bear the whips and scorns of time,
Th'oppressor's wrong, the proud man's contumely,
The pangs of dispriz'd love, the law's delay,
The insolence of office, and the spurns
That patient merit of th'unworthy takes,
When he himself might his quietus make
With a bare bodkin? Who would fardels bear,
To grunt and sweat under a weary life,
But that the dread of something after death,
The undiscover'd country, from whose bourn
No traveller returns, puzzles the will,
And makes us rather bear those ills we have
Than fly to others that we know not of?
Thus conscience does make cowards of us all,
And thus the native hue of resolution
Is sicklied o'er with the pale cast of thought,
And enterprises of great pitch and moment
With this regard their currents turn awry
And lose the name of action.

—3.1.56–88

Hamlet: Get thee to a nunnery. Why, wouldst thou be a breeder of sinners? I am myself indifferent honest, but yet I could accuse me of such things that it were better my mother had not borne me. I am very proud, revengeful,

ambitious, with more offences at my beck than I have thoughts to put them in, imagination to give them shape, or time to act them in. What should such fellows as I do crawling between earth and heaven? We are arrant knaves all, believe none of us. Go thy ways to a nunnery.

—3.1.121–130 (to Ophelia)

Hamlet: Our indiscretion sometime serves us well
When our deep plots do pall; and that should learn us
There's a divinity that shapes our ends,
Rough-hew them how we will—

—5.2.8–11

Hamlet: We defy augury. There is a special providence in the fall of a sparrow. If it be now, 'tis not to come; if it be not to come, it will be now; if it be not now, yet it will come. The readiness is all. Since no man, of aught he leaves, hows aught, what is't to leave betimes? Let be.

—5.2.215–220

Horatio: Now cracks a noble heart. Good night, sweet prince,
And flights of angels sing thee to thy rest.

—5.2.364–365 (as Hamlet dies)

Henry IV, Part 1

Falstaff: Now, Hal, what time of day is it, lad?
Prince Hal: Thou art so fat-witted with drinking of old sack, and unbuttoning thee after supper, and sleeping upon benches after noon, that thou hast forgotten to demand that truly which thou wouldst truly know. What a devil hast thou to do with the time of day? Unless hours were cups of sack, and minutes capons, and clocks the tongues of bawds, and dials the signs of leaping-houses, and the blessed sun himself a fair hot wench in flame-coloured taffeta, I see no reason why thou shouldst be so superfluous to demand the time of the day.

—1.2.1–12

Falstaff: No, my good lord; banish Peto, banish
Bardolph, banish Poins—but for sweet Jack
Falstaff, kind Jack Falstaff, true Jack Falstaff,
valiant Jack Falstaff, and therefore more
valiant, being as he is old Jack Falstaff, banish
not him thy Harry's company, banish not him
thy Harry's company, banish plump Jack, and
banish all the world.
Prince Hal: I do, I will.

—2.4.468–475

Falstaff: The better part of valour is discretion, in
the which better part I have saved my life.

—5.4.119–120 (remarks after having
played dead in battle)

Henry IV, Part 2

Falstaff: I am not only witty in myself, but the
cause that wit is in other men.

—1.2.8–9

Feeble: [A] man can die but once, we owe God a
death. [. . .] and let it go which way it will, he
that dies this year is quit for the next.

—3.2.229–233 (as he volunteers for the army)

Henry IV: Be it thy course to busy giddy minds
With foreign quarrels, that action hence borne out
May waste the memory of the former days.

—4.5.213–215 (the king recommends
"wagging the dog")

Henry V

Prologue: O, for a Muse of fire, that would ascend
The brightest heaven of invention [. . .]

—PROLOGUE, 1–2

Henry V: This story shall the good man teach
his son;
And Crispin Crispian shall ne'er go by,
From this day to the ending of the world,
But we in it shall be remembered;
We few, we happy few, we band of brothers;
For he today that sheds his blood with me

Shall be my brother; be he ne'er so vile
This day shall gentle his condition:
And gentlemen in England now a-bed
Shall think themselves accurs'd they were not here,
And hold their manhoods cheap whiles any speaks
That fought with us upon Saint Crispin's day.

—4.3.56–67 (speech before the battle of
AGINCOURT)

Henry VI, Part 1

Bedford: Hung be the heavens with black, yield
day to night!
Comets, importing change of times and states,
Brandish your crystal tresses in the sky,
And with them scourge the bad revolting stars,
That have consented unto Henry's death—
Henry the Fifth, too famous to live long!
England ne'er lost a king of so much worth.

—1.1.1–7

Warwick: Between two hawks, which flies the
higher pitch;
Between two dogs, which hath the deeper mouth;
Between two blades, which bears the better temper;
Between two horses, which doth bear him best;
Between two girls, which hath the merriest eye—
I have perhaps some shallow spirit of judgment;
But in these nice sharp quillets of the law,
Good faith, I am no wiser than a daw.

—2.4.11–18

Henry VI, Part 2

Henry VI: O Lord, that lends me life,
Lend me a heart replete with thankfulness!

—1.1.19–20

Duchess: Could I come near your beauty with my
nails
I'd set my ten commandments in your face.

—1.3.141–142 (to Queen Margaret)

Cade: [W]hen I am king, as king I will be,—
All: God save your Majesty!
Cade: I thank you, good people—there shall be no
money; all shall eat and drink on my score, and I

will apparel them all in one livery, that they may
agree like brothers, and worship me their lord.
Dick the Butcher: The first thing we do, let's kill
all the lawyers.

—4.2.66–73

Henry VI, Part 3

Henry VI: O God! methinks it were a happy life
To be no better than a homely swain;
To sit upon a hill, as I do now,
To carve out dials quaintly, point by point,
Thereby to see the minutes how they run—
How many makes the hour full complete,
How many hours brings about the day,
How many days will finish up the year,
How many years a mortal man may live,
When this is known, then to divide the times—
So many hours must I tend my flock;
So many hours must I take my rest;
So many hours must I contemplate;
So many hours must I sport myself;
So many days my ewes have been with young;
So many weeks ere the poor fools will ean;
So many years ere I shall shear the fleece:
So minutes, hours, days, weeks, months, and years,
Pass'd over to the end they were created,
Would bring white hairs unto a quiet grave.
Ah, what a life were this! how sweet! how lovely!
Gives not the hawthorn bush a sweeter shade
To shepherds looking on their silly sheep,
Then doth a rich embroider'd canopy
To kings that fear their subjects' treachery?

—2.5.21–45 (the king regrets his royal status)

Henry VIII

Wolsey: I have touch'd the highest point of all my
greatness,
And from that full meridian of my glory
I haste now to my setting. I shall fail
Like a bright exhalation in the evening,
And no man see me more.

—3.2.223–227 (on his fall from power)

Wolsey: Had I but serv'd my God with half the zeal
I serv'd my king, he would not in mine age
Have left me naked to mine enemies.

—3.2.455–457

Julius Caesar

Cassius: Why, man, he doth bestride the narrow
world
Like a Colossus, and we petty men
Walk under his huge legs, and peep about
To find ourselves dishonorable graves.
Men at some time are master of their fates:
The fault, dear Brutus, is not in our stars,
but in ourselves, that we are underlings.

—1.2.133–139 (on Caesar)

Caesar: Cowards die many times before their
deaths;
The valiant never taste of death but once.
Of all the wonders that I yet have heard,
It seems to me most strange that men should fear,
Seeing that death, a necessary end,
Will come when it will come.

—2.2.32–37

Antony: Friends, Romans, countrymen, lend me
your ears;
I come to bury Caesar, not to praise him.
The evil that men do lives after them,
The good is oft interred with their bones;
So let it be with Caesar.

—3.2.75–79 (the funeral oration)

Antony: This was the noblest Roman of them all.
[. . .]
His life was gentle, and the elements
So mix'd in him, that Nature might stand up
And say to all the world, "This was a man!"

—5.5.68–75 (on Brutus)

King John

Bastard: Well, whiles I am a beggar, I will rail
And say there is no sin but to be rich;
And being rich, my virtue then shall be
To say there is no vice but beggary.

—2.1.593–596

Lewis: There's nothing in this world can make me
joy:

Life is as tedious as a twice-told tale
Vexing the dull ear of a drowsy man[.]

—3.3.(3.4.)106–108 (For double citation
see *King John*, "Synopsis.")

Bastard: [I]f you be afeard to hear the worst,
Then let the worst unheard fall on your head.

—4.2.135–136

King Lear

Lear: Blow, winds, and crack your cheeks! rage!
    blow!
You cataracts and hurricanoes, spout
Till you have drench'd our steeples, drown'd the
    cocks!
You sulph'rous and thought-executing fires,
Vaunt-couriers of oak-cleaving thunderbolts,
Singe my white head! And thou, all-shaking
    thunder,
Strike flat the thick rotundity o'th'world!
Crack Nature's moulds, all germens spill at once
That makes ingrateful man!

—3.2.1–9 (in the storm)

Lear: Poor naked wretches, whereso'er you are,
That bide the pelting of this pitiless storm,
How shall your houseless heads and unfed sides,
Your loop'd and window'd raggedness, defend you
From seasons such as these? O! I have ta'en
Too little care of this. Take physic, Pomp;
Expose thyself to feel what wretches feel,
That thou mayst shake the superflux to them,
And show the Heavens more just.

—3.4.28–36 (realizing his insensitivity as king)

Lear: Thou wert better in a grave than to answer
    with thy uncover'd body this extremity of the
    skies. Is man no more than this? Consider him
    well. Thou ow'st the worm no silk, the beast no
    hide, the sheep no wool, the cat no perfume.
    [. . .] thou art the thing itself; unaccommodat-
    ed man is no more but such a poor, bare, forked
    animal as thou art.

—3.4.99–106 (on "Tom O'Bedlam")

Edgar: Men must endure
Their going hence, even as their coming hither:
Ripeness is all.

—5.2.9–11

Lear: Come, let's away to prison;
We two alone will sing like birds i'th'cage:
When thou dost ask me blessing, I'll kneel down,
And ask of thee forgiveness: so we'll live,
And pray, and sing, and tell old tales, and laugh
At gilded butterflies, and hear poor rogues
Talk of court news; and we'll talk with them too,
Who loses and who wins; who's in, who's out;
And take upon's the mystery of things,
As if we were Gods' spies: and we'll wear out,
In a wall'd prison, packs and sects of great ones
That ebb and flow by th'moon.

—5.3.8–19 (speaking to Cordelia)

Lear: Howl, howl, howl! O! you are men of stones:
Had I your tongues and eyes, I'd use them so
That heaven's vault should crack. She's gone for
    ever.
I know when one is dead, and when one lives;
She's dead as earth.

—5.3.256–260 (carrying the dead Cordelia)

EDGAR: The weight of this sad time we must obey;
Speak what we feel, not what we ought to say.
The oldest hath borne most: we that are young
Shall never see so much, nor live so long.

—5.3.322–325 (last lines of the play)

Love's Labour's Lost

Berowne: This wimpled, whining, purblind, way-
    ward boy,
This signor junior, giant-dwarf, dan Cupid;
Regent of love rhymes, lord of folded arms,
The anointed sovereign of sighs and groans,
Liege of all loiterers and malcontents,
Dread prince of plackets, king of codpieces,
Sole imperator and great general
Of trotting paritors[.]

—3.1.174–181

Holofernes: This is a gift that I have, simple, simple; a foolish extravagant spirit, full of forms,
figures, shapes, objects, ideas, apprehensions,
motions, revolutions: these are begot in the
ventricle of memory, nourished in the womb of
pia mater, and delivered upon the mellowing of
occasion. But the gift is good in those in whom
it is acute, and I am thankful for it.

—4.2.64–70 (congratulating himself on his
talent for poetry)

Berowne: O! never will I trust to speeches penn'd,
Nor to the motion of a school-boy's tongue,
Nor never come in visor to my friend,
Nor woo in rhyme, like a blind harper's song,
Taffeta phrases, silken terms precise,
Three-pil'd hyperboles, spruce affection,
Figures pedantical; these summer flies
Have blown me full of maggot ostentation:
I do forswear them; and I here protest,
By this thing white glove (how white the hand,
   God knows),
Henceforth my wooing mind shall be express'd
In russet yeas and honest kersey noes[.]

—5.2.402–413

Macbeth
Malcolm: Nothing in his life
Became him like the leaving it: he died
As one that had been studied in his death,
To throw away the dearest thing he ow'd,
As 'twere a careless trifle.

—1.4.7–11 (of the first Thane of Cawdor)

Macbeth: Is this a dagger, which I see before me,
The handle toward my hand? Come, let me clutch
   thee:—
I have thee not, and yet I see thee still.
Art thou not, fatal vision, sensible
To feeling, as to sight? or art thou but
A dagger of the mind, a false creation,
Proceeding from the heat-oppressed brain?

—2.1.33–39 (before he kills Duncan)

First Witch: Round about the cauldron go;
In the poison'd entrails throw.—
Toad, that under cold stone
Days and nights has thirty-one
Swelter'd venom, sleeping got,
Boil thou first i'th'charmed pot.
All: Double, double toil and trouble:
Fire, burn; and, cauldron, bubble.
Second Witch: Fillet of a fenny snake,
In the cauldron boil and bake;
Eye of newt, and toe of frog,
Wool of bat, and tongue of dog,
Adder's fork, and blind-worm's sting,
Lizard's leg, and howlet's wing,
For a charm of powerful trouble,
Like a hell-broth boil and bubble.
All: Double, double toil and trouble:
Fire, burn; and, cauldron, bubble.
Third Witch: Scale of dragon, tooth of wolf;
Witches' mummy; maw, and gulf,
Of the ravin'd salt-sea shark;
Root of hemlock, digg'd i'th'dark;
Liver of blaspheming Jew;
Gall of goat, and slips of yew,
Sliver'd in the moon's eclipse;
Nose of Turk, and Tartar's lips;
Finger of birth-strangled babe,
Ditch-deliver'd by a drab,
Make the gruel thick and slab:
Add thereto a tiger's chaudron,
for th'ingredient of our cauldron.
All: Double, double toil and trouble:
Fire, burn; and, cauldron, bubble.
Second Witch: Cool it with a baboon's blood:
Then the charm is firm and good.

—4.1.4–38 (as the Witches prepare a potion)

Lady Macbeth: Out, damned spot! out, I say!—
   One; two: why, then 'tis time to do't.—Hell is
   murky.—Fie, my Lord, fie! a soldier, and
   afeard?—What need we fear who knows it,
   when none can call our power to accompt?—
   Yet who would have thought the old man to
   have had so much blood in him?
[. . .]

The Thane of Fife had a wife: where is she now?
  What, will these hand ne'er be clean?—No
  more o'that, my Lord, no more o'that: you mar
  all with this starting.
[. . .]
Here's the smell of the blood still: all the perfumes
  of Arabia will not sweeten this little hand. Oh!
  oh! oh!
[. . .]
Wash your hands, put on your night-gown; look
  not so pale.—I tell you yet again, Banquo's
  buried: he cannot come out on's grave.
[. . .]
To bed, to bed: there's knocking at the gate. Come,
  come, come, come, give me your hand. What's
  done cannot be undone. To bed, to bed, to bed.

  —5.1.33–65 (sleepwalking, she reveals her guilt)

Macbeth: To-morrow, and to-morrow, and to-
  morrow,
Creeps in this petty pace from day to day,
To the last syllable of recorded time;
And all our yesterdays have lighted fools
The way to dusty death. Out, out, brief candle!
Life's but a walking shadow; a poor player,
That struts and frets his hour upon the stage,
And then is heard no more: it is a tale
Told by an idiot, full of sound and fury,
Signifying nothing.

  —5.5.19–28

Measure for Measure

Duke: Heaven doth with us as we with torches
  do,
Not light them for themselves; for if our virtues
Did not go forth of us, 'twere all alike
As if we had them not.

  —1.1.32–35

Isabella: [M]an, proud man,
Dress'd in a little brief authority,
Most ignorant of what he's most assur'd—
His glassy essence—like an angry ape
Plays such fantastic tricks before high heaven
As makes the angels weep[.]

  —2.2.118–123

Boy: Take, o take those lips away
that so sweetly were forsworn,
And those eyes, the break of day
lights that do mislead the morn:
But my kisses bring again,
bring again;
Seals of love, but seal'd in vain,
seal'd in vain.

  —4.1.1–6 (SONG)

Mariana: They say best men are moulded out of
  faults,
And, for the most, become much more the better
For being a little bad. So may my husband.

  —5.1.437–439 (asking mercy for Angelo)

The Merchant of Venice

Shylock: I am a Jew. Hath not a Jew eyes? hath
  not a Jew hands, organs, dimensions, senses,
  affections, passions? fed with the same food,
  hurt with the same weapons, subject to the
  same diseases, healed by the same means,
  warmed and cooled by the same winter and
  summer as a Christian is?—if you prick us do
  we not bleed? if you tickle us do we not laugh?
  if you poison us do we not die? and if you
  wrong us shall we not revenge?—if we are like
  you in the rest, we will resemble you in that. If
  a Jew wrong a Christian, what is his humility?
  revenge! If a Christian wrong a Jew, what
  should his sufferance be by Christian example?—why revenge! The villainy you teach me
  I will execute, and it shall go hard but I will
  better the instruction.

  —3.1.52–66

Portia: The quality of mercy is not strain'd,
It droppeth as the gentle rain from heaven
Upon the place beneath: it is twice blest,
It blesseth him that gives, and him that takes,
'Tis mightiest in the mightiest, it becomes
The throned monarch better than his crown.
His sceptre shows the force of temporal power,
The attribute to awe and majesty,
Wherein doth sit the dread and fear of kings:

But mercy is above this sceptred sway,
It is enthroned in the hearts of kings,
It is an attribute to God himself;
And earthly power doth then show likest God's
When mercy seasons justice: therefore Jew,
Though justice by thy plea, consider this,
That in the course of justice, none of us
Should see salvation: we do pray for mercy,
And that same prayer, doth teach us all to render
The deeds of mercy.

—4.1.180–198 (to Shylock)

Lorenzo: How sweet the moonlight sleeps upon
   this bank!
Here will we sit, and let the sounds of music
Creep in our ears—soft stillness and the night
Become the touches of sweet harmony:
Sit Jessica,—look how the floor of heaven
Is thick inlaid with patens of bright gold,
There's not the smallest orb which thou behold'st
But in his motion like an angel sings,
Still quiring to the young-ey'd cherubins;
Such harmony is in immortal souls,
But whilst this muddy vesture of decay
Doth grossly close it in, we cannot hear it[.]

—5.1.54–65

Lorenzo: The man that hath not music in himself,
Nor is not moved with concord of sweet sounds,
Is fit for treasons, stratagems, and spoils,
The motions of his spirit are dull as night,
And his affections dark as Erebus:
Let no such man be trusted[.]

—5.1.83–88

The Merry Wives of Windsor

Mistress Page: We'll leave a proof, by that which
   we will do,
Wives may be merry and yet honest too.

—4.2.95–96 (the wives plot revenge on Falstaff)

Falstaff: Have I lived to be carried in a basket, like
   a barrow of butcher's offal, and to be thrown in
   the Thames? Well, if I be served such another
   trick, I'll have my brains ta'en out and but-

tered, and give them to a dog for a New Year's
gift. The rogues slighted me into the river with
as little remorse as they would have drowned a
blind bitch's puppies, fifteen i' th'litter; and you
may know by my size that I have a kind of
alacrity in sinking: if the bottom were as deep
as hell, I should down. I had been drowned but
that the shore was shelvy and shallow—a death
that I abhor: for the water swells a man; and
what a thing should I have been when I had
been swelled! I should have been a mountain of
mummy.

—3.5.4–17

Mistress Page: There is an old tale goes that
   Herne the hunter,
Sometime a keeper here in Windsor Forest,
Doth all the winter time, at still midnight,
Walk round about an oak, with great ragg'd horns,
And there he blasts the tree, and takes the cattle,
And makes milch-kine yield blood, and shakes a
   chain
In a most hideous and dreadful manner.
You have heard of such a spirit, and well you know
The superstitious idle-headed eld
Receiv'd, and did deliver to our age,
This tale of Herne the hunter for a truth.

—4.4.28–38

A Midsummer Night's Dream

Lysander: Ay me! For aught that I could ever read,
Could ever hear by tale or history,
The course of true love never did run smooth[.]

—1.1.132–134

Bottom: I have had a most rare vision. I have had
   a dream, past the wit of man to say what dream
   it was. Man is but an ass if he go about to
   expound this dream. Methought I was—there is
   no man can tell what. Methought I was—and
   methought I had—but man is but a patched
   fool if he will offer to say what methought I had.
   The eye of man hath not heard, the ear of man
   hath not seen, man's hand is not able to taste,
   his tongue to conceive, nor his heart to report,
   what my dream was. I will get Peter Quince to

write a ballad of this dream: it shall be called
'Bottom's Dream', because it hath no bottom;
and I will sing it in the latter end of a play [. . .]

—4.1.203–216 (upon awakening from
his enchantment)

Theseus: Lovers and madmen have such seething
brains,
Such shaping fantasies, that apprehend
More than cool reason ever comprehends.
The lunatic, the lover, and the poet
Are of imagination all compact:
One sees more devils than vast hell can hold;
That is the madman: the lover, all as frantic,
Sees Helen's beauty in a brow of Egypt:
The poet's eye, in a fine frenzy rolling,
Doth glance from heaven to earth, from earth to
heaven;
And as imagination bodies forth
The forms of things unknown, the poet's pen
Turns them to shapes, and gives to airy nothing
A local habitation and a name.

—5.1.4–17

Puck: Now the hungry lion roars,
And the wolf behowls the moon;
Whilst the heavy ploughman snores,
All with weary task fordone.
Now the wasted brands do glow,
Whilst the screech-owl, screeching loud,
Puts the wretch that lies in woe
In remembrance of a shroud.
Now it is the time of night
That the graves, all gaping wide,
Every one lets forth his sprite
In the church-way paths to glide.
And we fairies, that do run
By the triple Hecate's team
From the presence of the sun,
Following darkness like a dream,
Now are frolic; not a mouse
Shall disturb this hallow'd house.
I am sent with broom before
To sweep the dust behind the door.

—5.1.357–376 (introducing the
fairies' midnight revels)

Much Ado About Nothing

Don John: I had rather be a canker in a hedge
than a rose in his [Don Pedro's] grace, and it
better fits my blood to be disdained of all than
to fashion a carriage to rob love from any: in
this, though I cannot be said to be a flattering
honest man, it must not be denied but I am a
plain-dealing villain.

—1.3.25–30 (the villain proclaims himself)

Benedick: They say the lady is fair—'tis a truth, I
can bear them witness; and virtuous—'tis so, I
cannot reprove it; and wise, but for loving
me—by my troth, it is no addition to her wit,
nor no great argument of her folly, for I will be
horribly in love with her. I may chance have
some odd quirks and remnants of wit broken on
me because I have railed so long against marriage: but doth not the appetite alter? A man
loves the meat in his youth that he cannot
endure in his age. Shall quips and sentences
and these paper bullets of the brain awe a man
from the career of his humour? No, the world
must be peopled. When I said I would die a
bachelor, I did not think I should live till I were
married. Here comes Beatrice. By this day, she's
a fair lady! I do spy some marks of love in her.

—2.3.222–235 (comments after having been tricked
into believing Beatrice has said she loves him)

Don Pedro: Officers, what offence have these men
done?
Dogberry: Marry, sir, they have committed false
report, moreover they have spoken untruths,
secondarily they are slanders, sixth and lastly
they have belied a lady, thirdly they have veri-
fied unjust things, and to conclude, they are
lying knaves.

—5.1.210–214 (the constable brings in the villains)

Othello

Iago: Were I the Moor, I would not be Iago:
In following him, I follow but myself.
Heaven is my judge, not I for love and duty,
But seeming so, for my peculiar end.

For when my outward action does demonstrate
The native act, and figure of my heart,
In complement extern, 'tis not long after,
But I will wear my heart upon my sleeve,
For doves to peck at: I am not what I am.

—1.1.57–65

Iago: A double knavery . . . how, how? . . . let me
    see,
After some time, to abuse Othello's ear,
That he [Cassio] is too familiar with his wife:
He has a person and a smooth dispose,
To be suspected, fram'd to make women false:
The Moor a free and open nature too,
That thinks men honest that but seems to be so:
And will as tenderly be led by the nose . . .
As asses are.
I ha't, it is engender'd; Hell and night
Must bring this monstrous birth to the world's light.

—1.3.392–402 (thoughts as he plots against
Cassio and Othello)

Emilia: 'Tis not a year or two shows us a man:
They are all but stomachs, and we all but food;
They eat us hungerly, and when they are full,
They belch us.

—3.4.100–103 (to Desdemona)

Othello: Had it pleas'd heaven
To try me with affliction, had he rain'd
All kinds of sores and shames on my bare head,
Steep'd me in poverty, to the very lips,
Given to captivity me and my hopes,
I should have found in some part of my soul
A drop of patience; but, alas, to make me
A fixed figure, for the time of scorn
To point his slow unmoving fingers at . . . oh, oh,
Yet could I bear that too, well, very well:
But there, where I have garner'd up my heart,
Where either I must live, or bear no life,
The fountain, from the which my current runs,
Or else dries up, to be discarded thence,
Or keep it as a cistern, for foul toads
To knot and gender in!

—4.2.48–63

Emilia: [. . .] I do think it is their husbands' faults
If wives do fall: say, that they slack their duties,
And pour our treasures into foreign laps;
Or else break out in peevish jealousies,
Throwing restraint upon us: or say they strike us,
Or scant our former having in despite,
Why we have galls: and though we have some grace,
Yet have we some revenge. Let husbands know,
Their wives have sense like them: they see, and
    smell,
And have their palates both for sweet, and sour,
As husbands have. What is it that they do,
When they change us for others? Is is sport?
I think it is: and doth affection breed it?
I think it doth. Is 't frailty that thus errs?
It is so too. And have not we affections?
Desires for sport? and frailty, as men have?
Then let them use us well: else let them know,
The ills we do, their ills instruct us so.

—4.3.86–103 (to Desdemona)

Othello: I pray you in your letters,
When you shall these unlucky deeds relate,
Speak of them as they are; nothing extenuate,
Nor set down aught in malice; then must you speak
Of one that lov'd not wisely, but too well:
Of one not easily jealous, but being wrought,
Perplex'd in the extreme; of one whose hand,
Like the base Indian, threw a pearl away,
Richer than all his tribe: of one whose subdued eyes,
Albeit unused to the melting mood,
Drops tears as fast as the Arabian trees
Their medicinal gum; set you down this,
And say besides, that in Aleppo once,
Where a malignant and a turban'd Turk
Beat a Venetian, and traduc'd the state,
I took by the throat the circumcised dog,
And smote him thus.[*stabs himself.*]

—5.2.341–357 (Othello's suicide speech)

Pericles, Prince of Tyre

Third Fisherman: I marvel how the fishes live in
    the sea.
First Fisherman: Why, as men do a-land: the great
    ones eat up the little ones. I can compare our
    rich misers to nothing so fitly as to a whale: a'

plays and tumbles, driving the poor fry before
him, and at last devours them all at a mouthful.
Such whales have I heard on a'th'land, who
never leave gaping till they swallow'd the whole
parish, church, steeple, bells, and all.

—2.1.28–34

Simonides: Opinion's but a fool, that makes us scan
The outward habit by the inward man.

—2.2.55–56

Marina: If you were born to honour, show it now;
If put upon you, make the judgement good
That thought you worthy of it.

—4.6.91–93

Richard II

Henry Bolingbroke: O, who can hold a fire in his
hand
By thinking on the frosty Caucasus?
Or cloy the hungry edge of appetite
By bare imagination of a feast?
Or wallow naked in December snow
By thinking on fantastic summer's heat?
O no, the apprehension of the good
Gives but the greater feeling to the worse.
Fell sorrow's tooth doth never rankle more
Than when he bites, but lanceth not the sore.

—1.3.294–303

Gaunt: This royal throne of kings, this scept'red isle,
This earth of majesty, this seat of Mars,
This other Eden, demi-paradise,
This fortress built by Nature for herself
Against infection and the hand of war,
This happy breed of men, this little world,
This precious stone set in the silver sea,
Which serves it in the office of a wall,
Or as a moat defensive to a house,
Against the envy of less happier lands;
This blessed plot, this earth, this realm, this
England [. . .]

—2.1.40–50

Richard II: For God's sake let us sit upon the
ground
And tell sad stories of the death of kings:
How some have been depos'd, some slain in war,
Some haunted by the ghosts they have deposed,
Some poisoned by their wives, some sleeping kill'd,
All murthered—for within the hollow crown
That rounds the mortal temples of a king
Keeps Death his court, and there the antic sits,
Scoffing his state and grinning at his pomp,
Allowing him a breath, a little scene,
To monarchize, be fear'd, and kill with looks;
Infusing him with self and vain conceit,
As if this flesh which walls about our life
Were brass impregnable; and, humour'd thus,
Comes at the last, and with a little pin
Bores thorough his castle wall, and farewell king!
Cover your heads, and mock not flesh and blood
With solemn reverence; throw away respect,
Tradition, form, and ceremonious duty;
For you have but mistook me all this while.
I live with bread like you, feel want,
Taste grief, need friends—subjected thus,
How can you say to me, I am a king?

—3.2.155–170

Richard II: I have been studying how I may compare
This prison where I live unto the world;
And, for because the world is populous
And here is not a creature but myself,
I cannot do it. Yet I'll hammer it out.
My brain I'll prove the female to my soul,
My soul the father, and these two beget
A generation of still-breeding thoughts,
And these same thoughts people this little world,
In humours like the people of this world;
For no thought is contented.

—5.5.1–11

Richard III

Richard III: I do the wrong, and first begin to brawl:
The secret mischiefs that I set abroach
I lay unto the grievous charge of others
[. . .]
But then I sigh, and, with a piece of Scripture,

Tell them that God bids us do good for evil:
And thus I clothe my naked villainy
With odd old ends stol'n forth of Holy Writ,
And seem a saint, when most I play the devil.

—1.3.324–338

Second Murderer: I'll not meddle with it [i.e.,
  conscience]; it makes a man a coward. A man
  cannot steal but it accuseth him; a man cannot
  swear but it checks him; a man cannot lie with
  his neighbour's wife but it detects him. 'Tis a
  blushing, shamefaced spirit, that mutinies in a
  man's bosom. It fills a man full of obstacles; it
  made me once restore a purse of gold that by
  chance I found. It beggars any man that keeps
  it; it is turned out of towns and cities for a dangerous thing; and every man that means to live
  well endeavours to trust to himself, and live
  without it.

—1.4.128–138

[Stage direction:] *Richard starteth up out of a dream*
Richard III: Give me another horse! Bind up my
  wounds!
Have mercy, Jesu!—Soft, I did but dream.
O coward conscience, how dost thou afflict me!
The lights burn blue; it is now dead midnight.
Cold fearful drops stand on my trembling flesh.
What do I fear? Myself? There's none else by;
Richard loves Richard, that is, I and I.
Is there a murderer here? No. Yes, I am!
Then fly. What, from myself? Great reason why,
Lest I revenge? What, myself upon myself?
Alack, I love myself. Wherefore? For any good
that I myself have done unto myself?
O no, alas, I rather hate myself
For hateful deeds committed by myself.
I am a villain—yet I lie, I am not!
Fool, of thyself speak well! Fool, do not flatter.
My conscience hath a thousand several tongues,
And every tongue brings in a several tale,
And every tale condemns me for a villain:
Perjury, perjury, in the highest degree;
Murder, stern murder, in the direst degree;
All several sins, all us'd in each degree,
Throng to the bar, crying all, 'Guilty, guilty!'

I shall despair. There is no creature loves me,
And if I die, no soul will pity me—
And wherefore should they, since that I myself
Find in myself no pity to myself?
Methought the souls of all that I had murder'd
Came to my tent, and every one did threat
Tomorrow's vengeance on the head of Richard.

—5.3.178–207 (waking from a ghostly visitation,
  the night before the Battle of BOSWORTH FIELD)

Richard III: Go, gentlemen: every man unto his
  charge!
Let not our babbling dreams affright our souls;
Conscience is but a word that cowards use,
Devis'd at first to keep the strong in awe.
Our strong arms be our conscience, swords our law.
March on! Join bravely. Let us to it pell-mell—
If not to Heaven, then hand in hand to hell!

—5.3.308–314 (to his officers, as the battle opens)

Richard III: A horse! A horse! My kingdom for a
  horse!
Catesby: Withdraw, my Lord; I'll help you to a
  horse.
Richard III: Slave! I have set my life upon a cast,
And I will stand the hazard of the die.
[. . .]
A horse! A horse! My kingdom for a horse!

—5.4.7–13 (Richard's last words)

Romeo and Juliet
Mercutio: O then I see Queen Mab hath been
  with you.
She is the fairies' midwife, and she comes
In shape no bigger than an agate stone
On the forefinger of an alderman,
Drawn with a team of little atomi
Over men's noses as they lie asleep.
Her chariot is an empty hazelnut
Made by the joiner squirrel or old grub,
Time out o' mind the fairies' coachmakers;
Her waggon-spokes made of long spinners' legs,
The cover of the wings of grasshoppers,
Her traces of the smallest spider web,
Her collars of the moonshine's watery beams,

Her whip of cricket's bone, the lash of film,
Her waggoner a small grey-coated gnat,
Not half so big as a round little worm
Prick'd from the lazy finger of a maid;
And in this state she gallops night by night
Through lovers' brains, and then they dream of love;
O'er courtiers' knees, that dream on curtsies
   straight;
O'er lawyers' fingers who straight dream on fees;
O'er ladies' lips, who straight on kisses dream,
Which oft the angry Mab with blisters plagues
Because their breaths with sweetmeats tainted are.
Sometime she gallops o'er a courtier's nose
And then dreams he of smelling out a suit;
And sometime comes she with a tithe-pig's tail,
Tickling a parson's nose as a lies asleep;
Then dreams he of another benefice.
Sometime she driveth o'er a soldier's neck
And then dreams he of cutting foreign throats,
Of breaches, ambuscados, Spanish blades,
Of healths five fathom deep; and then anon
Drums in his ear, at which he starts and wakes,
And being thus frighted swears a prayer or two
And sleeps again. This is that very Mab
That plaits the manes of horses in the night
and bakes the elf-locks in foul sluttish hairs,
Which, once entangled, much misfortune bodes.
This is the hag, when maids lie on their backs,
That presses them and learns them first to bear,
Making them women of good carriage.
This is the—
Romeo: Peace, peace, Mercutio, peace.
Thou talk'st of nothing.

                   —1.4.53–96

Romeo: O, she doth teach the torches to burn
   bright.
It seems she hangs upon the cheek of night
As a rich jewel in an Ethiop's ear—
Beauty too rich for use, for earth too dear.
So shows a snowy dove trooping with crows
As yonder lady o'er her fellows shows.
The measure done, I'll watch her place of stand,
And touching hers, make blessed my rude hand.
Did my heart love till now? Forswear it, sight.
For I ne'er saw true beauty till this night.

      —1.5.43–52 (on first seeing Juliet)

Romeo: But soft, what light through yonder win-
   dow breaks?
It is the east and Juliet is the sun!
Arise fair sun and kill the envious moon
Who is already sick and pale with grief
That thou her maid art far more fair than she.

      —2.2.2–6 (on seeing Juliet at her balcony)

Romeo: Courage, man, the hurt cannot be much.
Mercutio: No, 'tis not so deep as a well, nor so
   wide as a church door, but 'tis enough, 'twill
   serve. Ask for me tomorrow and you shall find
   me a grave man. I am peppered, I warrant, for
   this world. A plague o'both your houses.

   —3.1.96–101 (Mercutio is mortally wounded)

Romeo: O my love, my wife,
Death that hath suck'd the honey of thy breath
Hath had no power yet upon thy beauty.
Thou art not conquer'd. Beauty's ensign yet
Is crimson in thy lips and in thy cheeks,
And death's pale flag is not advanced there.
[. . .]
Ah, dear Juliet,
Why art thou yet so fair? Shall I believe
That unsubstantial Death is amorous,
And that the lean abhorred monster keeps
Thee here in dark to be his paramour?
For fear of that I still will stay with thee,
And never from this palace of dim night
Depart again. Here, here, will I remain
With worms that are thy chambermaids. O here
Will I set up my everlasting rest
And shake the yoke of inauspicious stars
From this world-wearied flesh. Eyes, look your last.
Arms, take your last embrace! And lips, O you
The doors of breath, seal with a righteous kiss
A dateless bargain to engrossing Death.
Come, bitter conduct, come unsavoury guide,
Thou desperate pilot now at once run on
The dashing rocks thy seasick weary bark.
Here's to my love! [*He drinks.*] O true apothecary,
Thy drugs are quick. Thus with a kiss I die.

     —5.3.91–120 (Romeo's suicide speech)

Prince: A glooming peace this morning with it
  brings:
The sun for sorrow will not show his head.
Go hence to have more talk of these sad things.
Some shall be pardon'd and some punished,
For never was a story of more woe
Than this of Juliet and her Romeo.

—5.3.304–309 (last lines of the play)

The Taming of the Shrew
Petruchio: I come to wive it wealthily in Padua;
If wealthily, then happily in Padua.
Grumio: Nay, look you, sir, he tells you flatly what
  his mind is. Why, give him gold enough and
  marry him to a puppet or an aglet-baby, or an
  old trot with ne'er a tooth in her head, though
  she have as many diseases as two and fifty horses. Why, nothing comes amiss, so money comes
  withal.

—1.2.73–81 (Petruchio's servant sums up
his master's intention)

Petruchio: Good Lord, how bright and goodly
  shines the moon!
Katherina: The moon? The sun! It is not moon-
  light now.
Petruchio: I say it is the moon that shines so bright.
Katherina: I know it is the sun that shines so bright.
Petruchio: Now by my mother's son, and that's
  myself,
It shall be moon, or star, or what I list,
Or e'er I journey to your father's house.—
[To Servants.] Go on, and fetch our horses back
  again.—
Evermore cross'd and cross'd, nothing but cross'd.
Hortensio: Say as he says, or we shall never go.
Katherina: Forward, I pray, since we have come so
  far,
And be it moon, or sun, or what you please.
And if you please to call it a rush-candle,
Henceforth I vow it shall be so for me.
Petruchio: I say it is the moon.
Katherina: I know it is the moon.
Petruchio: Nay, then you lie. It is the blessed sun.
Katherina: Then, God be blest, it is the blessed sun.
But sun it is not, when you say it is not,
And the moon changes even as your mind.

What you will have it nam'd, even that it is,
And so it shall be so for Katherine.

—4.5.2–22

Katherina: Thy husband is thy lord, thy life, thy
  keeper,
Thy head, thy sovereign; one that cares for thee,
And for thy maintenance; commits his body
To painful labour both by sea and land,
To watch the night in storms, the day in cold,
Whilst thou liest warm at home, secure and safe;
And craves no other tribute at thy hands
But love, fair looks, and true obedience;
Too little payment for so great a debt.
Such duty as the subject owes the prince
Even such a woman oweth to her husband.
And when she is froward, peevish, sullen, sour,
And not obedient to his honest will,
What is she but a foul contending rebel,
And graceless traitor to her loving lord?
I am asham'd that women are so simple
To offer war where they should kneel for peace,
Or seek for rule, supremacy, and sway,
When they are bound to serve, love, and obey.
Why are our bodies soft, and weak, and smooth,
Unapt to toil and trouble in the world,
But that our soft conditions and our hearts
Should well agree with our external parts?
Come, come, you froward and unable worms,
My mind hath been as big as one of yours,
My heart as great, my reason haply more,
To bandy word for word and frown for frown.
But now I see our lances are but straws,
Our strength as weak, our weakness past compare,
That seeming to be most which we indeed least are.
Then vail your stomachs, for it is no boot,
And place your hands below your husband's foot.
In token of which duty, if he please,
My hand is ready, may it do him ease.

—5.2.147–180 (her speech of submission)

The Tempest
Caliban: You taught me language; and my profit
  on't
Is, I know how to curse. The red plague rid you
For learning me your language!

—1.2.365–367

Ariel: Full fadom five thy father lies;
Of his bones are coral made;
Those are pearls that were his eyes:
Nothing of him that doth fade,
But doth suffer a sea-change
Into something rich and strange.
Sea nymphs hourly ring his knell:
Burthen: Ding-dong.
[. . .] Ding-dong, bell

—1.2.399–407 (SONG)

Caliban: Be not afeard; the isle is full of noises,
Sounds and sweet airs, that give delight, and hurt
    not.
Sometimes a thousand twangling instruments
Will hum about mine ears; and sometime voices,
That, if I then had wak'd after long sleep,
Will make me sleep again: and then, in dreaming,
The clouds methought would open, and show riches
Ready to drop upon me; that, when I wak'd,
I cried to dream again.

—3.2.133–141

Prospero: Our revels now are ended. These our
    actors,
As I foretold you, were all spirits, and
Are melted into air, into thin air:
And, like the baseless fabric of this vision,
The cloud-capp'd towers, the gorgeous palaces,
The solemn temples, the great globe itself,
Yea, all which it inherit, shall dissolve,
And, like this insubstantial pageant faded,
Leave not a rack behind. We are such stuff
As dreams are made on; and our little life
Is rounded with a sleep.

—4.1.148–158

Miranda: O wonder!
How many goodly creatures are there here!
How beauteous mankind is! O brave new world,
That has such people in 't!

—5.1.181–184

Timon of Athens
Apemantus: *[Apemantus' Grace]*
Immortal gods, I crave no pelf;

I pray for no man but myself.
Grant I may never prove so fond,
To trust man on his oath or bond;
Or a harlot for her weeping,
Or a dog that seems a-sleeping,
Or a keeper with my freedom,
Or my friends, if I should need 'em.
Amen, So fall to't:
Rich men sin, and I eat root.

—1.2.62–71

Timon: Why, I was writing of my epitaph;
It will be seen to-morrow. My long sickness
Of health and living now begins to mend,
And nothing brings me all things.

—5.1.184–187

Titus Andronicus
Titus: In peace and honour rest you here, my
    sons;
Rome's readiest champions, repose you here in rest,
Secure from worldly chances and mishaps.
Here lurks no treason, here no envy swells,
Here grow no damned drugs, here are no storms,
No noise, but silence and eternal sleep.
In peace and honour rest you here, my sons.

—1.1.150–156 (eulogizing his sons)

Aaron: Ah, why should wrath be mute, and fury
    dumb?
I am no baby, I, that with base prayers
I should repent the evils I have done;
Ten thousand worse than ever yet I did
Would I perform, if I might have my will.
If one good deed in all my life I did,
I do repent it from my very soul.

—5.3.184–190

Troilus and Cressida
Cressida: Yet hold I off. Women are angels, wooing:
Things won are done; joy's soul lies in the doing.
That she belov'd knows naught that knows not
    this:
Men prize the thing ungain'd more than it is.

—1.2.291–294

Ulysses: Take but degree away, untune that string,
And hark what discord follows. Each thing melts
In mere oppugnancy; the bounded waters
Should lift their bosoms higher than the shores,
And make a sop of all this solid globe;
Strength should be the lord of imbecility,
And the rude son should strike his father dead;
Force should be right—or rather, right and wrong,
Between whose endless jar justice resides,
Should lose their names, and so should justice too.
Then everything includes itself in power,
Power into will, will into appetite,
And appetite, an universal wolf,
So doubly seconded with will and power,
Must make perforce an universal prey,
And last eat up himself.

—1.3.109–124 (in praise of social hierarchy)

Cressida: If I be false, or swerve a hair from truth,
When time is old and hath forgot itself,
When water-drops have worn the stones of Troy,
And blind oblivion swallow'd cities up,
And mighty states characterless are grated
To dusty nothing—yet let memory,
For false to false, among false maids in love,
Upbraid my falsehood. When they've said 'As false
As air, as water, wind, or sandy earth,
As fox to lamb, or wolf to heifer's calf,
Pard to the hind, or stepdame to her son'—
Yea, let them say, to stick the heart of falsehood,
'As false as Cressid'.

—3.2.182–194 (unknowingly foretelling
her own fate)

Ulysses: Fie, fie upon her!
There's language in her eye, her cheek, her lip—
Nay, her foot speaks; her wanton spirits look out
At every joint and motive of her body.

—4.5.54–57 (on Cressida)

Thersites: Here's Agamemnon: an honest fellow
   enough, and one that loves quails, but he has
   not so much brain as ear-wax[.]

—5.1.50–52

Twelfth Night

Orsino: If music be the food of love, play on,
Give me excess of it, that, surfeiting,
The appetite may sicken, and so die.
That strain again, it had a dying fall:
O, it came o'er my ear like the sweet sound
That breathes upon a bank of violets,
Stealing and giving odour. Enough, no more;
'Tis not so sweet now as it was before.

—1.1.1–8

Viola: Make me a willow cabin at your gate,
And call upon my soul within the house;
Write loyal cantons of contemned love,
And sing them loud even in the dead of night;
Halloo your name to the reverberate hills,
And make the babbling gossip of the air
Cry out 'Olivia!' O, you should not rest
Between the elements of air and earth,
But you should pity me.

—1.5.272–280 (Viola, disguised as a man, declares
      how she would woo Olivia, if she loved her.)

Feste: What is love? 'Tis not hereafter,
Present mirth hath present laughter:
What's to come is still unsure.
In delay there lies no plenty,
Then come kiss me, sweet and twenty:
Youth's a stuff will not endure.

—2.3.48–53 (SONG)

Sir Toby: Dost thou think because thou art virtuous, there shall be no more cakes and ale?

—2.3.95–115

Viola: This fellow is wise enough to play the fool,
And to do that well, craves a kind of wit:
He must observe their mood on whom he jests,
The quality of persons, and the time,
And like the haggard, check at every feather
That comes before his eye. This is a practice
As full of labour as a wise man's art:
For folly that he wisely sows is fit;
But wise men, folly-fall'n, quite taint their wit.

—3.1.61–69 (on Feste's being a FOOL)

Sebastian: What relish is in this? How runs the
    stream?
Or I am mad, or else this is a dream:
Let fancy still my sense in Lethe steep;
If it be thus to dream, still let me sleep!

—4.1.59–62 (on encountering Olivia)

Sebastian: This is the air, that is the glorious sun,
This pearl she gave me, I do feel't, and see't,
And though 'tis wonder the enwraps me thus,
Yet 'tis not madness.

—4.3.1–4

The Two Gentlemen of Verona

Valentine: Cease to persuade, my loving Proteus;
Home-keepingg youth have ever homely wits.
Were't not affection chains thy tender days
To the sweet glances of thy honour'd love,
I rather would entreat thy company
To see the wonders of the world abroad
Than (living dully sluggardis'd at home)
Wear out thy youth with shapeless idleness.

—1.1.1–8

Proteus: O, how this spring of love resembleth
The uncertain glory of an April day,
Which now shows all the beauty of the sun,
And by and by a cloud takes all away.

—1.3.84–87

Launce: Nay, 'twill be this hour ere I have done
    weeping. [. . .] I think Crab my dog be the
    sourest-natured dog that lives: my mother weep-
    ing; my father wailing; my sister crying; our maid
    howling; our cat wringing her hands, and all our
    house in a great perplexity; yet did not this cruel-
    hearted cur shed one tear. He is a stone, a very
    pebble stone, and has no more pity in him than
    a dog. A Jew would have wept to have seen our
    parting. Why, my grandam, having no eyes, look
    you, wept herself blind at my parting. [. . .] Now
    the dog all this while sheds not a tear; nor speaks
    a word; but see how I lay the dust with my tears.

—2.3.1–32

The Two Noble Kinsmen

Hippolyta: They two have cabined
In many as dangerous as poor a corner,
Peril and want contending; they have skiffed
Torrents whose roaring tyranny and power
I'th'least of these was dreadful; and they have
Fought out together where death's self was lodged;
Yet fate hath brought them off. Their knot of love,
Tied, weaved, entangled, with so true, so long,
And with a finger of so deep a cunning,
May be outworn, never undone. I think
Theseus cannot be umpire to himself,
Cleaving his conscience into twain and doing
Each side like justice, which he loves best.

—1.3.35–47 (on the friendship of Theseus
and Pirithous)

Arcite: O Queen Emilia,
Fresher than May, sweeter
Than her gold buttons on the boughs, or all
Th'enamelled knacks o'th'mead or garden—yea,
We challenge too the bank of any nymph
That makes the stream seem flowers—thou, O
    jewel
O'th'wood, o'th'world, has likewise blessed a place
With thy sole presence.

—3.1.4–11 (on his love for Emilia)

Theseus: O you heavenly charmers
What things you make of us! For what we lack
We laugh; for what we have are sorry; still
Are children in some kind. Let us be thankful
For that which is, and with you leave dispute
That are above our question. Let's go off,
And bear us like the time.

—5.4.131–137 (addressing the gods; last lines
of the play)

The Winter's Tale

Polixenes: We were as twinn'd lambs that did frisk
    i'th' sun,
And bleat the one at th' other: what we chang'd
Was innocence for innocence: we knew not
The doctrine of ill-doing, nor dream'd
That any did. Had we pursu'd that life,

And our weak spirits ne'er been higher rear'd
With stronger blood, we should have answer'd
  heaven
Boldly 'not guilty', the imposition clear'd
Hereditary ours.

> —1.2.67–75 (on his childhood friendship
> with Leontes)

Shepherd: I would there were no age between ten
  and three-and-twenty, or that youth would
  sleep out the rest; for there is nothing in the
  between but getting wenches with child, wrong-
  ing the ancientry, stealing, fighting—Hark you
  now! Would any but these boiled-brains of nine-
  teen and two-and-twenty hunt this weather?
  They have scared away two of my best sheep,
  which I fear the wolf will sooner find than the
  master: if anywhere I have them, 'tis by the sea-
  side, browsing of ivy. [*Seeing the babe*] Good
  luck, and't be thy will, what have we here?
  Mercy on 's, a barne! A very pretty barne! A
  boy or a child, I wonder? A pretty one; a very
  pretty one. . . . I'll take it up for pity[.]

> —3.3.59–76 (on finding the abandoned
> infant Perdita)

Autolycus: My father named me Autolycus; who,
  being as I am, littered under Mercury, was likewise a snapper-up of unconsidered trifles. [. . .]
  beating and hanging are terrors to me: for the
  life to come, I sleep out the thought of it.

> —4.3.24–30 (boasting of his life as a petty thief)

Perdita: I would I had some flowers of the spring,
  [. . .] daffodils,
That come before the swallow dares, and take
The winds of March with beauty; violets, dim,
But sweeter than the lids of Juno's eyes
Or Cytherea's breath; pale primroses,
That die unmarried [. . .]
  [. . .] lilies of all kinds,
The flower-de-luce being one. O, these I lack,
To make you garlands of; and my sweet friend,
To strew him o'er and o'er!
Florizel: What, like a corpse?

Perdita: No, like a bank, for love to lie and play
  on:
Not like a corpse; of it—not to be buried,
But quick, and in my arms.

> —4.4.113–132 (the lovers at the
> shepherds' festival)

Shepherd: Come, boy; I am past moe children, but
  thy sons and daughters will be all gentlemen
  born.
Clown: [to Autolycus] You are well met, sir. You
  denied to fight with me this other day, because
  I was no gentleman born. See you these
  clothes? say you see them not and think me
  still no gentleman born: you were best say these
  robes are not gentleman born: give me the lie;
  do; and try whether I am not now a gentleman
  born.
Autolycus: I know you are now, sir, a gentleman
  born.
Clown: Ay, and have been so any time these four
  hours.
Shepherd: And so have I, boy.
Clown: So you have: but I was a gentleman born
  before my father; for the king's son took me by
  the hand, and called me brother; and then the
  two kings called my father brother; and then
  the prince, my brother, and the princess, my
  sister, called my father after; and so we wept;
  and there was the first gentleman-like tears
  that ever we shed.
Shepherd: We may live, son, to shed many more.
Clown: Ay; or else 'twere hard luck, being in so
  preposterous estate as we are.

> —5.2.127–148 (the rustics on their new status)

Venus and Adonis

'Fondling,' she saith, 'since I have hemm'd thee
  here
Within the circuit of this ivory pale,
I'll be a park, and thou shalt be my deer:
Feed where thou wilt, on mountain or in dale;
  Graze on my lips, and if those hills be dry,
  Stray lower, where the pleasant fountains lie.
'Within this limit is relief enough,

Sweet bottom grass and high delightful plain,
Round rising hillocks, brakes obscure and rough,
To shelter thee from tempest and from rain:
    Then be my deer, since I am such a park,
    No dog shall rouse thee, though a thousand
bark.'

          —ll. 229–240 (Venus describes herself
                           seductively)

'Love comforteth like sunshine after rain,
But lust's effect is tempest after sun;
Love's gentle spring doth always fresh remain,
Lust's winter comes ere summer half be done;
    Love surfeits not, lust like a glutton dies;
    Love is all truth, lust full of forged lies.[']

                —ll. 799–804 (Adonis)

[']For he being dead, with him is beauty
slain,
And beauty dead, black Chaos comes
again.[']

        —ll. 1019–1020 (Venus mourns Adonis)

The Rape of Lucrece

As the poor frighted deer that stands at gaze,
Wildly determining which way to fly,
Or one encompass'd with a winding maze,
That cannot tread the way out readily;
    So with herself is she in mutiny,
    To live or die which of the twain were better,
    When life is sham'd and death reproach's debtor.

                —ll. 1149–1155

For men have marble, women waxen, minds,
And therefore are they form'd as marble will;
The weak oppress'd, th' impression of strange kinds
Is form'd in them by force, by fraud, or skill.
Then call them not the authors of their ill,
    No more than wax shall be accounted evil,
    Wherein is stamp'd the semblance of a devil.
Their smoothness, like a goodly champaign plain,
Lays open all the little worms that creep;
In men as in a rough-grown grove remain
Cave-keeping evils that obscurely sleep;

Through crystal walls each little mote will peep;
    Though men can cover them with bold stern
looks,
    Poor women's faces are their own faults' books.
No man inveigh against the withered glower,
But chide rough winter that the flower hath kill'd;
Not that devour'd, but that which doth devour
Is worthy blame; O let it not be hild
Poor women's faults, that they are so fulfill'd
    With men's abuses! those proud lords to blame
    Make weak-made women tenants to their
shame.

                —ll. 1240–1260

Sonnets

Shall I compare thee to a summer's day?
Thou art more lovely and more temperate:
Rough winds do shake the darling buds of May,
And summer's lease hath all too short a date [. . .]

                —No. 18, ll. 1–4

Sonnet 29

When in disgrace with fortune and men's eyes
I all alone beweep my outcast state,
And trouble deaf heav'n with my bootless cries,
And look upon myself, and curse my fate,
Wishing me like to one more rich in hope,
Featured like him, like him with friends possessed,
Desiring this man's art and that man's scope,
With what I most enjoy contented least;
Yet in these thoughts myself almost despising,
Haply I think on thee, and then my state,
Like to the lark at break of day arising,
From sullen earth sings hymns at heaven's gate;
    For thy sweet love remembered such wealth
      brings
    That then I scorn to change my state with kings.

Not marble, not the gilded monuments
Of princes, shall outlive this powerful rhyme [. . .]

                —No. 55, ll. 1–2

That time of year thou mayst in me behold,
When yellow leaves, or none, or few do hang
Upon those boughs which shake against the cold,

Bare ruined choirs where late the sweet birds
   sang;
   [. . .]
This thou perceiv'st, which makes thy love
   more strong,
To love that well, which thou must leave ere
   long.

—No. 73, ll. 1–4, 13–14

How like a winter hath my absence been
From thee, the pleasure of the fleeting year!
What freezings have I felt, what dark days seen,
What old December's bareness everywhere!

—No. 97, ll. 1–4

Sonnet 116

Let me not to the marriage of true minds
Admit impediments; love is not love
Which alters when it alteration finds,
Or bends with the remover to remove.
O no, it is an ever-fixed mark,
That looks on tempests and is never shaken;
It is the star to every wand'ring bark,
Whose worth's unknown, although his height be
   taken.
Love's not Time's fool, though rosy lips and
   cheeks
Within his bending sickle's compass come;
Love alters not with his brief hours and weeks,
But bears it out even to the edge of doom.
   If this be error and upon me proved,
   I never writ, nor no man ever loved.

Sonnet 129

Th'expense of spirit in a waste of shame
Is lust in action; and till action, lust
Is perjured, murd'rous, bloody, full of blame,
Savage, extreme, rude, cruel, not to trust;
Enjoyed no sooner but despised straight;
Past reason hunted, and no sooner had,
Past reason hated as a swallowed bait,
On purpose laid to make the taker mad;

Mad in pursuit, and in possession so,
Had, having, and in quest to have, extreme;
A bliss in proof, and proved, a very woe;
Before, a joy proposed; behind a dream.
   All this the world well knows, yet none knows
      well
   To shun the heaven that leads me to this hell.

Sonnet 130

My mistress' eyes are nothing like the sun;
Coral is far more red than her lips' red;
If snow be white, why then her breasts are dun;
If hairs be wires, black wires grow on her head;
I have seen roses damasked, red and white,
But no such roses see I in her cheeks;
And in some perfumes is there more delight
Than in the breath that from my mistress reeks.
I love to hear her speak, yet well I know
That music hath a far more pleasing sound;
I grant I never saw a goddess go;
My mistress when she walks treads on the ground.
   And yet, by heaven, I think my love as rare
   As any she belied with false compare.

When my love swears that she is made of truth,
I do believe her, though I know she lies,
That she might think me some untutored youth
Unlearned in the world's false subtleties.
Thus vainly thinking that she thinks me young,
Although she knows my days are past the best,
Simply I credit her false-speaking tongue;
On both sides thus is simple truth suppressed.

—No. 138, ll. 1–8

A Lover's Complaint

O father, what a hell of witchcraft lies
In the small orb of one particular tear!
But with the inundation of the eyes
What rocky heart to water will not wear?
What breast so cold that is not warmed here?

—lines 288–292

SHAKESPEAREAN TIME LINE

Events in **bold type** are from Shakespeare's personal life. References to entries in this book are in SMALL CAPITALS.

Note: Dates for the composition of plays are often doubtful. See the entry for each play for further information.

ca. 1200 B.C.
Probable period of the TROJAN WAR, enacted in *Troilus and Cressida*

509 B.C.
Establishment of the Roman Republic, following the events narrated in *The Rape of Lucrece*

493 B.C.
Roman capture of CORIOLES, enacted in *Coriolanus*

ca. 450–404 B.C.
Lifetime of ALCIBIADES, and thus an approximate date for the events in *Timon of Athens*

187 B.C.
Death of ANTIOCHUS "the Great," and thus an approximate date for the events in *Pericles, Prince of Tyre*

184 B.C.
Death of PLAUTUS

44 B.C.
Assassination of Julius Caesar, enacted in *Julius Caesar*

31 B.C.
Battle of ACTIUM and death of Mark Antony, enacted in *Antony and Cleopatra*

19 B.C.
Death of VIRGIL

A.D. 14
Death of Augustus Caesar, who appears in *Antony and Cleopatra*

ca. A.D. 40
Death of Cunobelinus, British tribal ruler, the original of Cymbeline

A.D. 130
Death of PLUTARCH

Ninth century
Composition of the earliest known fragments of the story of Hamlet, in the Icelandic sagas

1039
Murder of King Duncan of Scotland, enacted in *Macbeth*

1167
Birth of King John

1312
Birth of King Edward III

1337–1453
The HUNDRED YEARS' WAR

1346
Battle of CRÉCY, enacted in *Edward III*

1366
Birth of Henry of Bolingbroke, later King Henry IV, of *Richard II* and *1* and *2 Henry IV*

1377
Death of King Edward III; accession of King Richard II

1381
The Peasant's Rebellion in England

1387
Birth of Prince Hal (later King Henry V), of *1* and *2 Henry IV* and *Henry V*

1399
Deposition of King Richard II and accession of King Henry IV, enacted in *Richard II*

1400
Death of Geoffrey CHAUCER

1413
Death of King Henry IV and accession of King Henry V, enacted in *2 Henry IV*

1415
Battle of AGINCOURT, enacted in *Henry V*

1420
Treaty of TROYES
Marriage of King Henry V and Princess Katharine of France, enacted in *Henry V*

1422
Death of King Henry V; accession of King Henry VI (born 1421), of *1*, *2*, and *3 Henry VI*

1431
Death of Joan of Arc (Joan La Pucelle), of *1 Henry VI*

1442
Birth of King Edward IV, of *2* and *3 Henry VI* and *Richard III*

1453
Battle of BORDEAUX, enacted in *1 Henry VI*, ending the HUNDRED YEARS' WAR

1455–1485
The WARS OF THE ROSES, enacted in *1*, *2*, and *3 Henry VI* and *Richard III*

1457
Birth of the Earl of Richmond, later King Henry VII, of *Richard III*

1471
Battle of TEWKSBURY, enacted in *3 Henry VI*
Death of King Henry VI; accession of King Edward IV

1483
Death of King Edward IV; accession of King Edward V; murder of Edward V and accession of King Richard III, all enacted in *Richard III*

1485
Battle of BOSWORTH FIELD, ending the WARS OF THE ROSES; death of King Richard III and accession of King Henry VII, the first monarch of the TUDOR DYNASTY, all enacted in *Richard III*

1491
Birth of King Henry VIII

1509
Death of King Henry VII; accession of King Henry VIII and his marriage to Katherine of Aragon

before 1530
Birth of Shakespeare's father, John SHAKESPEARE

ca. 1530
Composition of the first English SONNETs by Thomas WYATT

1531
Separation of King Henry VIII from his wife, Katherine of Aragon, and his secret marriage to Anne Boleyn, enacted in *Henry VIII*

1532–1534
Birth of Queen Elizabeth I (1532); excommunication of King Henry VIII (1533); formal institution of the Church of England as a Protestant denomination (1534), all enacted in *Henry VIII*

ca. 1540
Birth of Shakespeare's mother, Mary Arden SHAKESPEARE

1547
Death of King Henry VIII; accession of King Edward VI

1548
Publication of *The Union of the Two Noble and Illustre Families of Lancaster and York*, a history of the WARS OF THE ROSES by Edward HALL

1553
Death of King Edward VI; accession of Queen Mary I and reinstitution of Catholicism as the English church
Production of *Ralph Roister Doister*, by Nicholas UDALL, the first English COMEDY

ca. 1556
Birth of Anne HATHAWAY, later the wife of William Shakespeare

1557
Publication of the (partial) translation of VIRGIL's *Aeneid* by the Earl of SURREY, the first use of BLANK VERSE in English

1558
Death of Queen Mary I; accession of Queen Elizabeth I and reinstatement of the Anglican (Protestant) Church

1564
Birth of William Shakespeare
Plague in STRATFORD
Birth of Christopher MARLOWE

1566
Birth of Shakespeare's brother, Gilbert SHAKESPEARE

1568
Birth of Richard BURBAGE

1569
Birth of Shakespeare's sister, Joan SHAKESPEARE
Birth of John FLETCHER

1570
Birth of Emilia LANIER, possible "Dark Lady" of the *Sonnets*

1571
Birth of Shakespeare's sister, Anne SHAKESPEARE

1571–1575
Simon HUNT a teacher at Stratford Grammar School

1572
Birth of Ben JONSON

1574
Birth of Shakespeare's brother, Richard SHAKESPEARE

1575
Festival held at KENILWORTH by Queen Elizabeth I

1576
Construction of the THEATRE, London's first playhouse

1578
Publication of Raphael HOLINGSHED's *Chronicles of England, Scotland, and Ireland*

1579
Death of Shakespeare's sister, Anne SHAKESPEARE
Arrival of John COTTAM in Stratford
Publication of Thomas NORTH's translation of PLUTARCH's *Lives*
Death of Katherine HAMLETT

1580
Birth of Shakespeare's brother, Edmund SHAKESPEARE
Publication of John STOW's *Annales*

1582
Marriage of Shakespeare and Anne HATHAWAY

1583
Birth of Shakespeare's daughter, Susanna SHAKESPEARE

1585
Birth of Shakespeare's twins Hamnet and Judith SHAKESPEARE
Formation of the ADMIRAL'S MEN

1587
Establishment of BLANK VERSE as a theatrical medium with the success of *Tamburlane*, by Christopher MARLOWE

1588
Attempted invasion of England by the Spanish Armada

ca. 1589–1594
Composition of *The Comedy of Errors, The Taming of the Shrew,* and *Titus Andronicus*

1590–1591
Composition of *1, 2,* and *3 Henry VI*

1590–1595
Composition of *The Two Gentlemen of Verona*

1591
Composition of *Richard III*

1592
Publication of *Greene's Groatsworth of Wit*, by Robert GREENE, first literary reference to Shakespeare

1592–1594
Plague in London closes theaters

1592–1593
Composition of *Venus and Adonis*

1592–1595
Composition of *Edward III*

1593
Death of Christopher MARLOWE

1593–1594
Composition of *The Rape of Lucrece* and *Love's Labour's Lost*

1594
Organization of the CHAMBERLAIN'S MEN, with Shakespeare a partner
Execution of Roderigo LOPEZ, possible model for Shylock

1594–1595
Composition of *Romeo and Juliet* and *King John*

1595–1596
Composition of *A Midsummer Night's Dream* and *Richard II*

1596
Death of Hamnet Shakespeare
Composition of *1 Henry IV*
Award of a COAT OF ARMS to Shakespeare's father
Legal action involving Shakespeare and William GARDINER
Death of Shakespeare's uncle, Henry SHAKESPEARE
Shakespeare taxed as resident of Bishopsgate in LONDON

1596–1597
Composition of *The Merchant of Venice* and *The Merry Wives of Windsor*

1597
Shakespeare's purchase of NEW PLACE

1597–1598
Composition of *2 Henry IV*

1598
Composition of *Much Ado About Nothing*
First publication of Shakespeare's work in Shakespeare's name (*Love's Labour's Lost*)
Publication of Francis MERES's comments on Shakespeare

1599
Construction of the GLOBE THEATRE; Shakespeare a partner

Publication of THE PASSIONATE PILGRIM, containing poems by Shakespeare

ca. 1599
Composition of *Julius Caesar, Henry V,* and *As You Like It*

1599–1601
Composition of *Twelfth Night*

1599–1602
The WAR OF THE THEATERS

ca. 1600
Composition of *Hamlet* and "The Phoenix and Turtle"
Shakespeare a resident of SOUTHWARK
Hundred-mile dance of Will KEMPE

1601
Death of Shakespeare's father, John SHAKESPEARE
Failed rebellion by Robert Devereux, Earl of ESSEX
Publication of LOVE'S MARTYR, with Shakespeare's "The Phoenix and Turtle"

1602
Composition of *Troilus and Cressida*
Shakespeare's purchase of the CHAPEL LANE COTTAGE

1603
Death of Queen Elizabeth I; accession of King JAMES I
The CHAMBERLAIN'S MEN become the KING'S MEN
Shakespeare's last recorded appearance as an actor (in Ben JONSON's *Sejanus*)

ca. 1603–1606
Composition of *Othello, King Lear,* and *Macbeth*

1604
Death of Edward de Vere, Earl of OXFORD

ca. 1604
Composition of *All's Well That Ends Well* and *Measure for Measure*
Shakespeare a tenant of Christopher MOUNTJOY, in Cripplegate, LONDON

1605
Shakespeare buys tithing rights to land in WELCOMBE, in partnership with Thomas GREENE
Execution of Gamaliel RATSEY

ca. 1605–1610
Composition of *Coriolanus*

1606
Execution of Henry GARNET

ca. 1606
Composition of *Antony and Cleopatra*

1606–1608
Composition of *Timon of Athens*

1607
Marriage of Shakespeare's daughter Susanna SHAKESPEARE to Dr. John HALL
Death of Shakespeare's brother, Edmund SHAKESPEARE
Composition of *Pericles, Prince of Tyre*

1608
Death of Shakespeare's mother, Mary Arden SHAKESPEARE
Birth of Shakespeare's granddaughter, Elizabeth HALL

ca. 1608–1610
Composition of *Cymbeline*

1609
The KING'S MEN begin performing in BLACKFRIARS THEATRE
Shipwreck of William STRACHEY and Sylvester JOURDAIN on Bermuda
Publication of Shakespeare's *Sonnets* by Thomas THORPE

1610–1611
Composition of *The Winter's Tale* and *The Tempest*

1611
Shakespeare involved in lawsuit concerning his tithing rights in WELCOMBE

1612
Death of Shakespeare's brother, Gilbert SHAKESPEARE
Shakespeare testifies in the MOUNTJOY lawsuit

1612–1613
Composition (in collaboration with John FLETCHER) of *Henry VIII, Cardenio*, and *The Two Noble Kinsmen*

1613
Death of Shakespeare's brother, Richard SHAKESPEARE
Burning and rebuilding of the GLOBE THEATRE
Shakespeare buys the BLACKFRIARS GATEHOUSE
Marriage of Princess ELIZABETH STUART

1614
Enclosure controversy at WELCOMBE

1616
Marriage of Judith SHAKESPEARE
Death of William Shakespeare

1619
Death of Richard BURBAGE
Publication of the FALSE FOLIO

1623
Publication of the FIRST FOLIO

1642
Theatrical performances outlawed by the English revolutionary government

1660
Restoration of the English monarchy and reopening of the theaters
Margaret HUGHES the first woman to act in Shakespeare (as Desdemona) in Thomas KILLIGREW's *Othello*

1667
John DRYDEN's *The Tempest, or the Enchanted Island*

1670
Death of Shakespeare's last surviving descendant, his granddaughter, Elizabeth HALL

1681
Premiere of Nahum TATE's *History of King Lear*

1692
Henry PURCELL's OPERA *The Fairy Queen*, based on *A Midsummer Night's Dream*

1709
Publication of Shakespeare's plays by Nicholas ROWE

1725
Publication of Shakespeare's plays by Alexander POPE

1726
Publication of the first book devoted to Shakespeare, Lewis THEOBALD's *Shakespeare Restored*

1730s
VOLTAIRE's essays on Shakespeare

1757
Discovery of the SPIRITUAL TESTAMENT OF JOHN SHAKESPEARE in Shakespeare's BIRTHPLACE

1769
The Shakespeare Jubilee is held at STRATFORD, organized by David GARRICK

1775
Sarah SIDDONS the first woman to play Hamlet

1782
Completion of the first German translation of Shakespeare's complete plays, by J. J. ESCHENBURG

1783
Completion of the first French translation of the complete plays, by Pierre LE TOURNEUR

1790
Publication of Edmond MALONE's edition of the plays

1796
W. H. IRELAND's Shakespearean forgeries published

1802
Composition of Beethoven's *Tempest* Sonata

1802–1818
Samuel Taylor COLERIDGE's lectures on Shakespeare

1803
Publication of the first VARIORUM EDITION of Shakespeare's plays

1807
Publication of *Tales from Shakespeare*, by Charles LAMB and Mary Lamb

1818
Publication of Thomas BOWDLER's censored version of Shakespeare's works

1820s
Edmund KEAN performs as Shylock, Hamlet, and Othello

1827
Premiere of Felix MENDELSSOHN's Overture and Incidental Music for *A Midsummer Night's Dream*

1844
First modern staging of an uncut Shakespearean play, *The Taming of the Shrew*, directed by Benjamin WEBSTER

1849
Astor Place riot (see FORREST, EDWIN)

1859
Shakespeare forgeries of J. P. COLLIER exposed by C. M. INGLEBY

1879
Founding of the Shakespeare Memorial Theatre in STRATFORD

1882
Henry IRVING's production of *Romeo and Juliet*

1891
Formation of the Shakespeare BIRTHPLACE Trust in STRATFORD

1893
Premiere of Giuseppe VERDI's opera *Falstaff*

1899
First filming of Shakespeare: scenes from Beerbohm TREE's stage production of *King John*

1900
First staging of the complete *Hamlet*, by Frank BENSON
First FILM of *Hamlet*, starring Sarah BERNHARDT

1911
William POEL's staging of the second act of *Edward III*, the first modern presentation of the play

1912
Max REINHARDT's production of *A Midsummer Night's Dream*
Harley GRANVILLE-BARKER's productions of *The Winter's Tale* and *Twelfth Night*

1921
Max REINHARDT's notorious "cubist" production of *The Merchant of Venice*

1922
John BARRYMORE performs as Hamlet

1930
Foundation of the FOLGER SHAKESPEARE LIBRARY

1933
Paris production of *Coriolanus* sparks pro- and anti-Nazi riots
Theodore KOMISARJEVSKY's staging of *Macbeth*

1935
Max REINHARDT's film of *A Midsummer Night's Dream*, featuring Mickey Rooney as Puck

1936
Orson WELLES's "voodoo" *Macbeth*
Theodore KOMISARJEVSKY's *King Lear*

1938
Theatrical musical comedy *The Boys from Syracuse*, adaptation of *The Comedy of Errors*

1939
Film *Swinging the Dream,* based on *A Midsummer Night's Dream,* featuring the Benny Goodman Sextet and Louis Armstrong as Bottom
Theodore KOMISARJEVSKY's staging of *The Comedy of Errors*

1941–1951
Boris PASTERNAK's translations of seven of Shakespeare's plays

1944
Film of *Henry V* by Laurence OLIVIER

1946
Publication of W. H. AUDEN's *The Sea and the Mirror*

1948
Laurence OLIVIER wins two Oscars, for best actor and best film, for his *Hamlet*

1953
Tyrone GUTHRIE's Stratford, Ontario, production of *All's Well That Ends Well,* as a farce

1955
Laurence OLIVIER's film of *Richard III*

1957
Akira KUROSAWA's film *Throne of Blood,* based on *Macbeth*
STRATFORD production of *The Tempest,* starring John GEILGUD

1960
Premiere of Benjamin BRITTEN's opera *The Midsummer Night's Dream*
Film of *Macbeth* starring Maurice EVANS and Judith ANDERSON

1961
The Shakespeare Memorial Theatre becomes the ROYAL SHAKESPEARE COMPANY.

1964
Simultaneous filmings of *Hamlet* by Peter BROOK and Grigori KOZINTSEV

1965
Orson WELLES's film *Chimes at Midnight,* with himself as Falstaff

1966
Premiere of Samuel BARBER's opera *Antony and Cleopatra*

1967
Franco ZEFFIRELLI's film of *The Taming of the Shrew,* starring Elizabeth Taylor and Richard Burton
Completion of first complete TRANSLATION OF SHAKESPEARE's works into Chinese
Publication of Grigori KOZINTSEV's book *Shakespeare: Time and Conscience*

1970
Uncut production of *Hamlet* by Peter HALL

1973
Joseph PAPP's production of *King Lear,* starring James Earl JONES
Premiere of Nicholas NABOKOV's *Love's Labour's Lost,* with a libretto by W. H. AUDEN

1978
Premiere of Aribert REIMANN's opera *Lear*

1981
University of Illinois adaptation of *Macbeth* as a Japanese *kabuki* theater production

1983
Laurence OLIVIER's *King Lear* wins TELEVISION's Emmy Award

1985
Akira KUROSAWA's film *Ran* ("Chaos"), based on *King Lear*

1989
Film of *Henry V* by Kenneth BRANAGH

1991
First performances in Sam WANAMAKER's replica of the GLOBE THEATRE in LONDON

1993
Film of *Much Ado About Nothing* by Kenneth BRANAGH

1994
Adrian NOBLE's production of *A Midsummer Night's Dream*

1996
Film of *Hamlet* by Kenneth BRANAGH

1997
Formal opening of the new GLOBE THEATRE in LONDON

2000
Michael Almereyda's film of *Hamlet*, set in midtown Manhattan

Film of *Love's Labour's Lost* by Kenneth BRANAGH
Publication of W. H. AUDEN's *Lectures on Shakespeare*

2001
ROYAL SHAKESPEARE COMPANY production of *The Tempest*, directed by Michael BOYD

2002
ROYAL SHAKESPEARE COMPANY production of *Edward III*

2004
Trevor NUNN's production of *Hamlet*, at the Old Vic

SUGGESTED READING

A comprehensive bibliography on Shakespeare would be many times the size of this book. The following is simply a selection of particularly interesting and appealing books.

Adams, Joseph Quincy. *Shakespearean Playhouses: A History of English Theatres from the Beginning to the Restoration.* Magnolia, Mass.: Peter Smith, 1959.

Alexander, Peter. *Shakespeare's Life and Art.* Westport, Conn.: Greenwood Press, 1979.

Alvis, John, and Thomas G. West, eds. *Shakespeare as Political Thinker.* Wilmington, Del.: ISI Books, 2000.

Auden, W. H. *Lectures on Shakespeare.* Princeton, N.J.: Princeton University Press, 2000.

Baldwin, Thomas Whitfield. *The Organisation and Personnel of the Shakespearean Company.* Princeton, N.J.: Princeton University Press, 1927.

Barber, Cesar Lombardi. *Shakespeare's Festive Comedy.* Princeton, N.J.: Princeton University Press, 1972.

Barton, John. *Playing Shakespeare: An Actor's Guide.* New York: Knopf, 2001.

Bentley, Gerald Eades. *The Profession of Player in Shakespeare's Time, 1590–1642.* Princeton, N.J.: Princeton University Press, 1984.

———. *Shakespeare: A Biographical Handbook.* New Haven, Conn.: Yale University Press, 1974.

Boas, Frederic Samuel. *Shakspere and His Predecessors.* Brooklyn, N.Y.: Haskell, 1969.

Bradbrook, Muriel C. *The Artist and Society in Shakespeare's Time.* Totowa, N.J.: Barnes & Noble, 1982.

———. *Elizabethan Stage Conditions.* Hamden, Conn.: Archon, 1962.

———. *The Rise of the Common Player.* Cambridge, Eng.: Cambridge University Press, 1979.

———. *Shakespeare and Elizabethan Poetry.* London: Chatto & Windus, 1951.

Bradley, Andrew Cecil. *Shakespearean Tragedy.* Cleveland: World, 1964.

Brennecke, Ernest. *Shakespeare in Germany 1590–1700: With Translations of Five Early Plays.* Chicago: University of Chicago Press, 1964.

Bristol, Michael, et al., eds. *Shakespeare and Modern Theatre: The Performance of Modernity.* London: Routledge, 2001.

Brode, Douglas. *Shakespeare in the Movies: From the Silent Era to Shakespeare in Love.* New York: Oxford University Press, 2000.

Brown, Ivor. *How Shakespeare Spent the Day.* London: Bodley Head, 1963.

———. *Shakespeare.* Garden City, N.Y.: Doubleday, 1949.

Brown, John Russell, and Bernard Harris, eds. *Early Shakespeare.* New York: Schocken, 1966.

Bullough, Geoffrey. *Narrative and Dramatic Sources of Shakespeare.* 8 vols. New York: Columbia University Press, 1957–1975.

Cavell, Stanley. *Disowning Knowledge: In Seven Plays of Shakespeare.* 2d ed. Cambridge, Eng.: Cambridge University Press, 2003.

Chambers, Sir Edmund Kerchever. *The Elizabethan Stage.* 4 vols. Oxford: Clarendon Press, 1961.

———. *William Shakespeare: A Study of Facts and Problems.* 2 vols. Oxford: Oxford University Press, 1989.

Chute, Marcel. *Shakespeare of London.* New York: Dutton, 1957.

Clemen, Wolfgang H. *The Development of Shakespeare's Imagery.* Cambridge, Mass.: Harvard University Press, 1951.

Coleridge, Samuel Taylor. *Coleridge's Criticism of Shakespeare.* Edited by R. A. Foakes. Detroit: Wayne State University Press, 1989.

Colie, Rosalie. *Shakespeare's Living Art.* Princeton, N.J.: Princeton University Press, 1974.

Cooper, Duff. *Sergeant Shakespeare.* New York: Haskell, 1972.

Craig, Hardin. *The Enchanted Glass: The Elizabethan Mind in Literature.* Westport, Conn.: Greenwood Press, 1975.

Day, Barry. *This Wooden "O": Shakespeare's Globe Reborn: Achieving an American's Dream.* London: Oberon Books, 1997.

Dean, Leonard Fellows, ed. *Shakespeare: Modern Essays in Criticism.* New York: Oxford University Press, 1967.

Dessen, Alan C. *Rescripting Shakespeare: The Text, the Director, and Modern Productions.* Cambridge, Eng.: Cambridge University Press, 2002.

Drakakis, John, ed. *Alternative Shakespeares.* New York: Routledge, Chapman & Hall, 1985.

Duncan-Jones, Katherine. *Ungentle Shakespeare: Scenes from His Life.* London: Arden Shakespeare, 2001.

Eccles, Mark. *Shakespeare in Warwickshire.* Madison: University of Wisconsin Press, 1963.

Edwards, Philip. *Shakespeare: A Writer's Progress.* Oxford: Oxford University Press, 1987.

———, ed. *Shakespeare's Styles: Essays in Honour of Kenneth Muir.* Cambridge, Eng.: Cambridge University Press, 1980.

Empson, William. *Essays on Shakespeare.* Cambridge, Eng.: Cambridge University Press, 1986.

Fischlin, Daniel, and Mark Fortier. *Adaptations of Shakespeare: A Critical Anthology of Plays from the Seventeenth Century to the Present.* London: Routledge, 2000.

Foakes, R. A. *Illustrations of the English Stage 1580–1642.* Stanford, Calif.: Stanford University Press, 1985.

Ford, Boris, ed. *The Age of Shakespeare.* New York: Penguin, 1982.

Fripp, Edgar I. *Shakespeare, Man and Artist.* 2 vols. London: Oxford University Press, 1938.

———. *Shakespeare's Stratford.* 1928. Reprint, Salem, N.H.: Ayer, n.d.

Frye, Northrop. *Fools of Time: Studies in Shakespearean Tragedy.* Toronto: University of Toronto Press, 1967.

———. *The Myth of Deliverance: Reflections on Shakespeare's Problem Comedies.* Toronto: University of Toronto Press, 1983.

Gesner, Carol. *Shakespeare and the Greek Romance: A Study of Origins.* Lexington: University Press of Kentucky, 1970.

Granville-Barker, Harley. *Prefaces to Shakespeare.* 2 vols. Princeton, N.J.: Princeton University Press, 1978.

Greenblatt, Stephen. *Hamlet in Purgatory.* Princeton, N.J.: Princeton University Press, 2001.

———. *Renaissance Self-Fashioning.* Chicago: University of Chicago Press, 1980.

Greg, Walter Wilson. *The Editorial Problem in Shakespeare.* Oxford: Clarendon Press, 1954.

———. *The Shakespeare First Folio.* Oxford: Clarendon Press, 1955.

Gross, John. *Shylock: A Legend and Its Legacy.* New York: Simon and Schuster, 1993.

———, ed. *After Shakespeare: An Anthology.* New York: Oxford University Press, 2002.

Gurr, Andrew. *Playgoing in Shakespeare's London.* New York: Cambridge University Press, 1987.

———. *The Shakespearean Stage 1574–1642.* Cambridge, Eng.: Cambridge University Press, 1981.

Halliday, F. E. *Shakespeare and His Critics.* London: Duckworth, 1958.

———. *A Shakespeare Companion: 1564–1964.* Baltimore: Penguin, 1964.

———. *Shakespeare in His Age.* London: Duckworth, 1956.

Harbage, Alfred. *As They Liked It: A Study of Shakespeare's Moral Artistry.* Philadelphia: University of Pennsylvania Press, 1972.

———. *Conceptions of Shakespeare.* Cambridge, Mass.: Harvard University Press, 1966.

———. *Shakespeare and the Rival Traditions.* New York: Macmillan, 1952.

———. *Shakespeare's Audience.* New York: Columbia University Press, 1961.

Harrison, George Bagshawe. *Elizabethan Plays and Players.* Ann Arbor: University of Michigan Press, 1956.

———. *Shakespeare at Work.* London: Routledge, 1933.

Hartnoll, Phyllis, ed. *The Oxford Companion to the Theatre.* London: Oxford University Press, 1983.

Henken, Elissa R. *National Redeemer: Owain Glyndwr in Welsh Tradition.* Ithaca, N.Y.: Cornell University Press, 1996.

Hill, Errol. *Shakespeare in Sable: A History of Black Shakespearean Actors.* Amherst: University of Massachusetts Press, 1986.

Hillebrand, Harold Newcomb. *The Child Actors.* Urbana: University of Illinois Press, 1926.

Hodges, Cyril W. *The Globe Restored.* New York: Somerset, 1973.

Honan, Park. *Shakespeare: A Life*. New York: Oxford University Press, 1998.

Honigmann, E. A. J. *Shakespeare: The "Lost Years."* Totowa, N.J.: Barnes & Noble Books, 1985.

———. *The Stability of Shakespeare's Text*. London: Arnold, 1965.

Hotson, Leslie. *Shakespeare's Motley*. Brooklyn, N.Y.: Haskell, 1970.

———. *Shakespeare's Sonnets Dated and Other Essays*. New York: Oxford University Press, 1949.

———. *Shakespeare's Wooden O*. London: Hart-Davis, 1959.

Hunter, George K. *Dramatic Identities and Cultural Tradition: Studies in Shakespeare and His Contemporaries*. Liverpool: Liverpool University Press, 1978.

Jones, Emrys. *The Origins of Shakespeare*. Oxford: Oxford University Press, 1977.

Jones, Ernest. *Hamlet and Oedipus*. New York: Norton, 1976.

Joseph, Sister Miriam. *Shakespeare's Use of the Arts of Language*. New York: Columbia University Press, 1947.

Kennedy, Dennis. *Looking at Shakespeare: A Visual History of Twentieth-Century Performance*. 2d ed. Cambridge, Eng.: Cambridge University Press, 2001.

Kinney, Arthur F. *Shakespeare by Stages: An Historical Introduction*. Oxford: Blackwell, 2003.

Kirschbaum, Leo. *Shakespeare and the Stationers*. Columbus: Ohio State University Press, 1955.

Knight, George Wilson. *The Crown of Life: Essays in Interpretation of Shakespeare's Final Plays*. London: Methuen, 1947.

———. *The Wheel of Fire: Essays in Interpretation of Shakespeare's Sombre Tragedies*. New York: Routledge, Chapman & Hall, 1949.

Knights, Lionel Charles. *How Many Children Had Lady Macbeth?* New York: Haskell, 1973.

———. *Shakespeare's Politics*. London: Oxford University Press, 1957.

Laslett, Peter. *The World We Have Lost: England before the Industrial Age*. 3d ed. London: Routledge, 2003.

Lee, Sidney. *A Life of William Shakespeare*. New York: Macmillan, 1931.

———. *Shakespeare and the Modern Stage*. New York: AMS, 1974.

Leech, Clifford. *Twelfth Night and Shakespearean Comedy*. Toronto: Dalhousie University Press/ University of Toronto Press, 1965.

Levin, Harry. *Shakespeare and the Revolution of the Times*. New York: Oxford University Press, 1976.

Mahood, M. M. *Bit Parts in Shakespeare's Plays*. Cambridge, Eng.: Cambridge University Press, 1992.

Merchant, William Moelwyn. *Shakespeare and the Artist*. London: Oxford University Press, 1959.

Mirsky, Mark Jay. *The Absent Shakespeare*. Rutherford, N.J.: Fairleigh Dickinson University Press, 1994.

Morozov, Mikhail Mikhailovich. *Shakespeare on the Soviet Stage*. London: Soviet News, 1947.

Muir, Kenneth. *Last Periods of Shakespeare, Racine, and Ibsen*. Liverpool, Eng.: Liverpool University Press, 1961.

———. *Shakespeare's Sonnets*. London/Boston: Allen & Unwin, 1979.

———. *The Sources of Shakespeare's Plays*. London: Methuen, 1977.

Mulryne, J. R., and Margaret Shewring. *Shakespeare's Globe Rebuilt*. Cambridge, Eng.: Cambridge University Press, 1997.

Nagler, Alois M. *Shakespeare's Stage*. New Haven, Conn.: Yale University Press, 1981.

Naylor, Edward Woodall. *Shakespeare and Music*. London: Dent, 1931.

Neill, Michael. *Putting History to the Question: Power, Politics, and Society in English Renaissance Drama*. New York: Columbia University Press, 2001.

Nevo, Ruth. *Comic Transformations in Shakespeare*. New York: Routledge, Chapman & Hall, 1981.

———. *Tragic Form in Shakespeare*. Princeton, N.J.: Princeton University Press, 1972.

Noble, Richmond Samuel Howe. *Shakespeare's Biblical Knowledge*. 1935. Reprint, New York: Gordon, n.d.

Odell, George C. D. *Shakespeare from Betterton to Irving*. 2 vols. New York: Dover, 1966.

Onions, Charles Talbut. *A Shakespeare Glossary*. Oxford: Clarendon Press, 1986.

Orell, John. *The Quest for Shakespeare's Globe*. Cambridge, Eng.: Cambridge University Press, 1983.

Palmer, Alan, and Veronica Palmer. *Who's Who in Shakespeare's England*. New York: St. Martin's, 1981.

Parker, Patricia, and Geoffrey Hartman, eds. *Shakespeare and the Question of Theory*. New York/London: Methuen, 1985.

Partridge, Eric. *Shakespeare's Bawdy*. London: Routledge & Kegan Paul, 1968.

Quennell, Peter. *Shakespeare: The Poet and His Background*. London: Weidenfeld & Nicolson, 1963.

Rabkin, Norman. *Shakespeare and the Common Understanding*. Chicago: University of Chicago Press, 1984.

———. *Shakespeare and the Problem of Meaning*. Chicago: University of Chicago Press, 1982.

Reese, Max Meredith. *Shakespeare: His World and His Work*. New York: St. Martin's, 1980.

Ribner, Irving. *The English History Play in the Age of Shakespeare*. New York: Barnes & Noble, 1965.

Richmond, Velma Bourgeois. *Shakespeare, Catholicism, & Romance*. New York: Continuum International Publishing, 2000.

Righter, Anne. *Shakespeare and the Idea of the Play*. Westport, Conn.: Greenwood Press, 1977.

Rothwell, Kenneth S. *A History of Shakespeare on Screen: A Century of Film and Television*. Cambridge, Eng.: Cambridge University Press, 1999.

Saccio, Peter. *Shakespeare's English Kings*. Oxford: Oxford University Press, 1977.

Sams, Eric, ed. *Shakespeare's* Edmund Ironside: *The Lost Play*. Aldershot, Eng.: Wildwood House, 1985.

———. *The Real Shakespeare: Retrieving the Early Years, 1564–1594*. New Haven, Conn.: Yale University Press, 1995.

Schmidgall, Gary. *Shakespeare and Opera*. New York: Oxford University Press, 1990.

Schoenbaum, Samuel. *Shakespeare's Lives*. New York: Oxford University Press, 1970.

———. *William Shakespeare: A Compact Documentary Life*. New York: Oxford University Press, 1987.

———. *William Shakespeare: A Documentary Life*. New York: Oxford University Press, 1975.

Shapiro, James. *Shakespeare and the Jews*. New York: Columbia University Press, 1996.

Siegel, Paul N. *Shakespearean Tragedy and the Elizabethan Compromise: A Marxist Study*. Lanham, Md.: University Press of America, 1983.

Simmons, Joseph Larry. *Shakespeare's Pagan World: The Roman Tragedies*. Charlottesville: University Press of Virginia, 1973.

Sisson, Charles Jasper. *Lost Plays of Shakespeare's Age*. Cambridge, Eng.: Cambridge University Press, 1936.

———. *The Mythical Sorrows of Shakespeare*. London: Milford, 1934.

———. *New Readings in Shakespeare*. Cambridge, Eng.: Cambridge University Press, 1956.

Smith, Hallett. *Shakespeare's Romances*. San Marino, Calif.: Huntington Library, 1972.

Smith, Irwin. *Shakespeare's Blackfriars Playhouse*. New York: New York University Press, 1964.

———. *Shakespeare's Globe Playhouse*. New York: Scribner's, 1956.

Smith, Logan Piersall. *On Reading Shakespeare*. 1933. Reprint, New York: Somerset, n.d.

Snyder, Susan. *The Comic Matrix of Shakespeare's Tragedies*. Princeton, N.J.: Princeton University Press, 1979.

Speaight, Robert. *Shakespeare on the Stage: An Illustrated History of Shakespearean Performance*. Boston: Little, Brown, 1973.

Spencer, Theodore. *Shakespeare and the Nature of Man*. New York: Macmillan, 1942.

Spivack, Bernard. *Shakespeare and the Allegory of Evil*. New York: Columbia University Press, 1958.

Sprague, Arthur Colby. *Shakespeare and the Actors*. New York: Russell & Russell, 1963.

Spurgeon, Caroline. *Shakespeare's Imagery*. Cambridge, Eng.: Cambridge University Press, 1975.

Thomson, Peter W. *Shakespeare's Theatre*. London/Boston: Routledge & Kegan Paul, 1983.

Tilley, Morris Palmer. *A Dictionary of the Proverbs in England in the Sixteenth and Seventeenth Centuries*. New York: AMS, 1982.

Tillyard, E. M. W. *The Elizabethan World Picture*. New York: Random House, 1959.

Traversi, Derek. *Shakespeare, The Last Phase*. Stanford, Calif.: Stanford University Press, 1955.

Trewin, John Courtenay. *Shakespeare on the English Stage 1900–1964*. London: Barrie & Rockliff, 1964.

Vaughan, Alden T., and Virginia Mason Vaughan. *Shakespeare's Caliban: A Cultural History*. Cambridge, Eng.: Cambridge University Press, 1991.

Vendler, Helen. *The Art of Shakespeare's Sonnets*. Cambridge, Mass.: Harvard University Press, 1997.

Vickers, Brian. *The Artistry of Shakespeare's Prose*. London: Methuen, 1968.

———. *Classical Rhetoric in English Poetry*. Carbondale: Southern Illinois University Press, 1989.

———. *Shakespeare, Co-Author*. New York: Oxford University Press, 2002.

Walker, Alice. *Textual Problems of the First Folio*. Cambridge, Eng.: Cambridge University Press, 1953.

Welch, James M., et al., eds. *Shakespeare into Film*. New York: Checkmark Books, 2002.

Wells, Stanley, ed. *The Cambridge Companion to Shakespeare Studies*. Cambridge, Eng.: Cambridge University Press, 1986.

Wells, Stanley, and Lena Cowen Orlin, eds. *Shakespeare: An Oxford Guide*. New York: Oxford University Press, 2003.

Welsford, Enid. *The Court Masque*. Cambridge, Eng.: Cambridge University Press, 1927.

———. *The Fool: His Social and Literary History*. Garden City, N.Y.: Anchor, 1961.

Whitaker, Virgil Keeble. *Shakespeare's Use of Learning: An Inquiry into the Growth of His Mind and Art.* San Marino, Calif.: Huntington Library, 1953.

Wickham, Glynne. *Early English Stages.* 2 vols. New York: Columbia University Press, 1980.

Wilson, Jean. *The Archaeology of Shakespeare: The Material Legacy of Shakespeare's Theatre.* Phoenix Mill, Eng.: Alan Sutton Publishing, 1995.

Wilson, J. Dover. *The Essential Shakespeare.* New York: Haskell, 1977.

Wright, Louis B. *Middle Class Culture in Elizabethan England.* New York: Hippocrene, 1980.

Yates, Frances. *Majesty and Magic in Shakespeare's Last Plays.* Boulder, Colo.: Shambhala, 1978.

CONTENTS BY CATEGORY

To find the page numbers for the entries below, use the index at the back of the book.

Wanamaker, Sam
Webster, Benjamin
Webster, Margaret
Weelkes, Thomas
Welles, Orson
Williams, Harcourt
Williamson, Nicol
Wilson, Jack
Wilson, John
Wilson, Robert
Woffington, Peg
Wolfit, Donald
Worcester's Men
Yates, Mary Ann
Yates, Richard
Zeffirelli, Franco

Contemporaries and Near-Contemporaries of Shakespeare

Addenbrooke, John
Allde, Edward
Alleyn, Edward
Amyot, Jacques
Annesley, Brian
Armin, Robert
Aspinall, Alexander
Aspley, William
Atkinson, William
Bandello, Matteo
Barents, Willem
Barkstead, William
Barnes, Barnabe
Barnfield, Richard
Barton, Richard
Basse, William
Beaumont, Francis
Bedford, Lucy, Countess of
Beeston, Christopher
Belleforest, Francois de
Belott, Stephen
Benfield, Robert
Benson, John
Bentley, John
Berners, John Bouchier, Lord
Blount, Edward
Bonian, Richard
Bradock, Richard
Bretchgirdle, John
Bright, Timothy
Brooke, Arthur

Browne, Robert
Bryan, George
Buchanan, George
Burbage, Cuthbert
Burbage, James
Burbage, Richard
Burby, Cuthbert
Burghley, Lord
Busby, John
Butter, Nathaniel
Camden, William
Carew, Richard
Cecil, Robert, Earl of Salisbury
Cecil, Thomas
Cervantes Saavedra, Miguel de
Chapman, George
Chester, Robert
Chettle, Henry
Cinthio
Cobham, William Brooke, Lord
Collins, Francis
Combe, John
Combe, Thomas
Combe, Thomas
Combe, William
Combe, William
Condell, Henry
Cooke, Alexander
Cottom, John
Covell, William
Cowley, Richard
Cox, Robert
Crane, Ralph
Creede, Thomas
Crosse, Samuel
Daniel, Samuel
Davenant, William
Davies, John of Hereford
Davies, Sir John
Day, John
Dekker, Thomas
Deloney, Thomas
Dennis, John
Derby, William Stanley, Earl of
Dethick, Sir William
De Witt, Johannes
Digges, Dudley
Digges, Leonard
Downton, Thomas
Drayton, Michael
Droeshout, Martin

Dryden, John
Du Bartas, Guillaume de Sallust
Dutton, Laurence
Ecclestone, William
Eden, Richard
Edwards, Richard
Eld, George
Eliot, John
Elizabeth I, Queen of England
Elizabeth Stuart, Queen of Bohemia
Epenow
Essex, Robert Devereux, Earl of
Evans, Henry
Farrant, Richard
Fenton Geoffrey
Ffarington, William
Field, Nathan
Field, Richard
Fisher, Thomas
Fitton, Mary
Fletcher, Giles
Fletcher, John
Fletcher, Laurence
Florio, John
Ford, John
Forman, Simon
Foxe, John
Frith, John
Gardiner, William
Garnet, Henry
Gascoigne, George
Gibborne, Thomas
Gilbard, William
Gilburne, Samuel
Giles, Nathaniel
Giulio Romano
Golding, Arthur
Goslicius, Laurentius Grimalius
Gosson, Henry
Gosson, Stephen
Gough, Robert
Grafton, Richard
Granada, Luis de
Green, John
Greene, Robert
Greene, Thomas
Greville, Curtis
Greville, Fulke (Lord Brooke)
Griffin, Bartholomew
Gwinne, Matthew

Shakespeare's Works

Related Works

Mirror for Magistrates, A
Misery of Civil War, The (see Crowne, John)
Mucedorus
Passionate Pilgrim, The
Puritan, The
"Shall I Die?"
Sir John Oldcastle
Spread of the Eagle, The
Thomas Lord Cromwell
Traïson
Troublesome Raigne of King John, The
Ur-Hamlet
Ur-Shrew
Woodstock (Thomas of Woodstock)
Yorkshire Tragedy, A

Relatives of Shakespeare

Arden, Robert
Greene, Thomas
Hall, Elizabeth
Hall, John
Hathaway, Anne
Lambert, John
Nash, Thomas
Quiney, Thomas
Shakespeare, Anne
Shakespeare, Edmund
Shakespeare, Gilbert
Shakespeare, Hamnet
Shakespeare, Henry
Shakespeare, Joan
Shakespeare, Joan
Shakespeare, John
Shakespeare, Judith
Shakespeare, Mary Arden
Shakespeare, Richard
Shakespeare, Richard
Shakespeare, Susanna
Shakespeare, William

Scholars, Authors, Translators, Artists, Printers, and Publishers

Adams, Joseph Quincy
Adlington, William
Alexander, Peter
Allde, Edward
Amyot, Jacques
Apuleius, Lucius

Ariosto, Ludovico
Aristotle
Aspley, William
Auden, Wystan Hugh
Ayscough, Samuel
Bandello, Matteo
Barkstead, William
Barnes, Barnabe
Barnfield, Richard
Basse, William
Beaumont, Francis
Belleforest, François de
Benson, John
Berners, John Bourchier, Lord
Blount, Edward
Boas, Frederick S.
Boccaccio, Giovanni
Boece, Hector
Bonian, Richard
Boswell, James the younger
Bowdler, Thomas
Boydell, John
Bradley, Andrew Cecil
Bradock, Richard
Bright, Timothy
Brooke, Arthur
Buchanan, George
Bullough, Geoffrey
Burby, Cuthbert
Burnaby, William
Busby, John
Butter, Nathaniel
Camden, William
Capell, Edward
Carew, Richard
Castiglione, Baldassare
Caxton, William
Cervantes Saavedra, Miguel de
Chambers, Edmund Kerchever
Chapman, George
Chaucer, Geoffrey
Chester, Robert
Chettle, Henry
Cibber, Colley
Cicero, M. Tullius
Cinthio
Clarke, Charles Cowden
Clarke, Mary Cowden
Coleridge, Samuel Taylor
Collier, John Payne
Colonne, Guido delle

Craig, Hardin
Crane, Ralph
Creede, Thomas
Créton, Jean
Crowne, John
Cumberland, Richard
Daniel, Samuel
Danter, John
Davies, John of Hereford
Davies, Sir John
Davies, Richard
Day, John
Dekker, Thomas
Deloney, Thomas
Dennis, John
De Quincey, Thomas
Derby, William Stanley, Earl of
Dickens, Charles
Digges, Leonard
Dowden, Edward
Drayton, Michael
Droeshout, Martin
Dryden, John
Du Bartas, Guillaume de Sallust
Duffett, Thomas
Dumas, Alexandre
D'Urfey, Thomas
Eden, Richard
Edwards, Richard
Eld, George
Eliot, John
Eliot, Thomas Stearns
Elyot, Sir Thomas
Eschenburg, Johann Joachim
Fabyan, Robert
Fenton, Geoffrey
Fenton, Richard
Field, Richard
Fiorentino, Giovanni
Fisher, Thomas
Fleay, Frederick Gard
Fletcher, Giles
Fletcher, John
Florio, John
Ford, John
Foxe, John
French, George Russell
Froissart, Jean
Furness, Horace Howard
Furnivall, Frederick James
Gascoigne, George

Geoffrey of Monmouth
Gervinus, Georg Gottfried
Gide, Andre
Gildon, Charles
Giulio Romano
Goethe, Johann Wolfgang von
Golding, Arthur
Goslicius, Laurentius Grimalius
Gosson, Henry
Gosson, Stephen
Gower, John
Grafton, Richard
Granada, Luis de
Granville, George
Granville-Barker, Harley
Greene, Robert
Greg, Walter Wilson
Greville, Fulke (Lord Brooke)
Griffin, Bartholomew
Gwinne, Matthew
Hakluyt, Richard
Hall, Arthur
Hall, Edward
Hall, William
Halliwell-Phillips, James Orchard
Hanmer, Thomas
Harington, Sir John
Harris, Frank
Harrison, George Bagshawe
Harrison, John
Harrison, William
Harsnett, Samuel
Harvey, Gabriel
Hathway, Richard
Hayman, Francis
Hazlitt, William
Henryson, Robert
Heyes, Thomas
Heywood, John
Heywood, Thomas
Higgins, John
Hilliard, Nicholas
Hoby, Sir Thomas
Holinshed, Raphael
Holland, Hugh
Holland, Philemon
Homer
Hopkins, Richard
Hotson, Leslie
Hugo, Victor
Hugo, François-Victor

Hunnis, William
Ingleby, Clement Mansfield
Ireland, William Henry
Jackson, Roger
Jaggard, Isaac
Jaggard, William
Janssen, Cornelius
Janssen, Gheerart
Johnson, Arthur
Johnson, Charles
Johnson, Samuel
Jones, William
Jonson, Ben
Jourdain, Sylvester
Keats, John
Killigrew, Thomas
Kirkman, Francis
Kittredge, George Lyman
Knight, G. Wilson
Kyd, Thomas
Lacy, John
Lamb, Charles
Lamb, George
Langbaine, Gerard
Laplace, Pierre-Antoine de
Law, Matthew
Leake, William
Lee, Sidney
Legh, Gerard
Le Maçon, Antoine
Lennox, Charlotte
Leo Africanus
Lessing, Gotthold Ephraim
Le Tourneur, Pierre
Lillo, George
Ling, Nicholas
Lily, William
Livy
Lodge, Thomas
Lucian
Lupton, Thomas
Lydgate, John
Lyly, John
Mabbe, James
Malone, Edmond
Markham, Gervase
Marlowe, Christopher
Marsh, Henry
Marston, John
Massinger, Philip
Mayne, Jasper

Meres, Francis
Middleton, Thomas
Miller, James
Millington, Thomas
Milton, John
Montaigne, Michel de
Montemayer, Jorge de
More, Sir Thomas
Morgan, McNamara
Morgann, Maurice
Moseley, Humphrey
Munday, Anthony
Nashe, Thomas
North, Sir Thomas
Okes, Nicholas
Otway, Thomas
Ovid
Oxford, Edward de Vere, Earl of
Painter, William
Pasternak, Boris
Pater, Walter
Pavier, Thomas
Peele, George
Pepys, Samuel
Planché, James Robinson
Platter, Thomas
Plautus, Titus Maccius
Pliny the Elder
Plutarch
Pollard, Alfred William
Pope, Alexander
Porter, Henry
Pory, John
Preston, Thomas
Prynne, William
Puttenham, George
Puttenham, Richard
Raleigh, Sir Walter
Reed, Isaac
Reynolds, Frederick
Rich, Barnabe
Roberts, James
Robertson, John Mackinnon
Robinson, Richard
Rollins, Hyder
Rowe, Nicholas
Rowley, Samuel
Rowley, William
Ryther, Augustine
Sackville, Thomas
Sainte-Maure, Benoît de

Theatrical and Literary Terms

INDEX

moral uncertainty, 32
quotations, 963
resolution, providing, 28
sexual involvement, 27
social discipline, 28
sources, 30
synopsis, 24–27
text, 30
theatrical history, 30–31
Antony and Cleopatra
(opera) (Barber), 31
Antony and Cleopatra
(opera) (Malipiero), 31
Apemantus, 567–568
crude jokes, 563
Apocrypha, 667–668, 685,
733, 752, 924
Richard III, inclusion,
113
Apocrypha (Brooke), 118
Apollonius of Tyre, 460, 465,
469
Apologia (Apuleius), 668
Apology for Actors
(Heywood), 781
"Apology for Raimond de
Sebonde" (Sebonde), 836
Apolonius and Silla, 607
Apothecary, 521
Apparitions, 355, 737
prophecies, 355
apprentice piece, 70
Apuleius, Lucius, 667–668.
*See also Apologia; Golden
Ass; Metamorphoses*
Aquitaine, Eleanor of. *See*
Eleanor of Aquitaine
Arab League, 930
Aragon. *See* Arragon
Aragon, Catherine of. *See*
Katherine of Aragon
Arc, Jeanne d'. *See* Joan La
Pucelle
Arcadia (Sidney), 54, 326,
747, 838, 853
hero, 469
pastoral romance, 461
Archbishop of York,
Richard Scroop, 157,
186
Hastings, ally, 189
Henry IV, Part I, 162
Henry IV, Part II, 186
plans, 189–190
revolt, leading, 162

Archbishop of York, Thomas
Rotherham, 500–501
historical figure, 501
Archidamus, 647–648
Arcite, 630–631
comparison. *See* Palamon
personality, clarity
(absence), 631
Arden (Ardennes,
Anglicization), 668
Arden, Forest of, 49, 644,
668
armed march, 60
exile, 58
flight, 56–57, 63
paradise, misperception,
58
pastoral world, 52
Arden, Robert, 1, 668
Arden, Thomas, 669
Arden home, 685
Arden of Feversham,
668–669, 860
Areopagus poet group, 770
Argos, king of. *See* Diomedes
argument, 472, 475, 669
Ariel, 553–554
analogue. *See* Prospero
freedom (desire), 554
Ariosto, Ludovico, 669, 760,
894, 922. *See also I
Suppositi; Orlando Furioso*
aristocracy, fault, 81
aristocrats, compromise. *See*
Commoners
Aristotle, 669–670, 887,
896. *See also
Nichomachean Ethics;
Poetics*
exile, 670
Armada. *See* Spanish
Armada
Armado, Don Adriano de,
343
Armin, Robert, 670–671. *See
also Foole upon Foole;
Time Triumphant; Two
Maids of Moreclacke*
All's Well That Ends Well,
18
Cymbeline, 103
Dogberry, 671
joining. *See*
Chamberlain's Men
talents, 907

Twelfth Night, 608
As You Like It, 54, 56
Armstrong, Louis, 419
Arne, Thomas Augustine,
671
Tempest, 552
Winter's Tale (music), 646
Arnold, Matthew (biogra-
phy), 704
Arouet, François-Marie. *See*
Voltaire
Arragon (Aragon), 393
army, 831
caricature, 393
presentation, 389
Ars Amatoria (Arts of Love)
(Ovid), 849
Artemidorus, 291
Plutarch, account, 291
rhetoric professor, 291
Arte of English Poesie, The
(Puttenham), 646, 867
Arte of Navigation (Eden),
733
Artesius, 631
Arthur, Prince of England,
311–312
Archduke of Austria,
support, 311
death, 311–312
handling, 316
English crown, claim,
311
King Philip Augustus of
France, support, 311,
315
sources, ignoring, 311
artifacts, 1005
artists, 1007–1009
Art of the Theatre, The
(Craig), 718
Artois, Robert de
Beaumont-le-Roger,
Count of, 118
historical figure, 118
Arviragus, 101
fairy-tale figure, 101
Ascension Day, 318
Asche, Oscar, 56, 671
director. *See* Chu-Chin-
Chow
Measure for Measure, 378
Merry Wives of Windsor,
407
Othello, 448

Ashbourne portrait
(Kingston portrait), 671
Ashcroft, Peggy, 671
Antony and Cleopatra,
31
appearance. *See* tetralogy
As You Like It, 56
Cymbeline, 101
Desdemona, 877
King Lear, 328
Twelfth Night, 608
Asia Minor, 689, 855, 932
Asnath, 239, 247, 737
Aspinall, Alexander, 1,
671–672, 799, 901
Aspley, William, 672
partner. *See* Wise,
Andrew
Astor Place riot, 753, 825
Astrana Marín, Luis, 930
astrology, 753
Astrophel (Spenser), 903
Astrophel and Stella (Sidney),
519, 530
As You Like It
characters, 56–65
commentary, 51–54
date, 4
epilogue, 63
film, 721
First Folio appearance,
55
ideas/temperaments, jux-
taposition, 53
lovers, comparison,
52–53
plotting, 51–52
production. *See* National
Theatre
quotations, 963–964
roles, 5
rustic characters, con-
trast, 53
songs, quantity, 51
sources, 54
staging, 55–56
synopsis, 49–51
text, 54–55
theatrical history,
55–56
Athena, temple, 592
Athenian. *See* Old Athenian
Athens, 672. *See also Timon
of Athens*
study, 670

relief, Dauphin failure,
205
siege, 195, 201
Harington, Sir John, 430,
774, 797
translation. *See Orlando
Furioso*
"Hark, Hark, the Lark"
(translation), 894
Harlech Castle, 676
harlequin, popularization,
875
Harpy, 556
Harris, Frank (James
Thomas), 774–775. *See
also Man Shakespeare
and His Tragic Life Story;
My Life and Loves;
Shakespeare and His
Love; Women of
Shakespeare*
Harris, Henry, 775
Henry VIII, 270
Harrison, George Bagshawe,
775, 996. *See also
Elizabethan Journals;
England in Shakespeare's
Day; Jacobean Journals;
Shakespeare at Work*
Harrison, John, 775, 814
Rape of Lucrece publica-
tion, 474
Harrison, William, 775
collaborator. *See*
Holinshed
Harsnett, Samuel, 776. *See
also* Cambridge
University; *Declaration of
Egregious Popish Impostures*
Hart, Charles, 776, 835
Julius Caesar, 291
Othello, 447
Hart, Joan Shakespeare. *See*
Shakespeare, Joan
Hart, Lorenz, 71
Hart, William, 776
Henry IV, Part I, 161
Hartnoll, Phyllis, 996
Hart property, sale, 685
Harvey, 169
Peto, 175
name change,
Cobham insis-
tence, 169
origin, 169

Harvey, Gabriel, 3, 776
enmity, 842
quarrel. *See* Greene,
Robert; Nashe,
Thomas
Harvey, Laurence
Winter's Tale, 647
Henry V, 207
Harvey, William. *See* Hervey,
William
Hastings, Lord Ralph, 186,
189
Hastings, Lord William, 505
historical figure, 505
Hastings, Pursuivant, 505
Hathaway, Anne (Anne
Hathaway Shakespeare),
776–777
affair, 2, 3
cottage, 685
father, 762
hair, lock of, 792
handwriting, 746
house, 777
portrait, Adriana
(usage), 71
Hathway, Richard (Richard
Hathaway), 777–778
writer. *See* Admiral's Men
Haunted House, The
(Plautus), 536
Hawthornden, 801
Hayes, Helen, 743
Hayman, Francis, 768, 778
illustration, 774
Haymarket Theatre, 931
Hazlitt, William, 778. *See
also Characters in
Shakespeare's Plays;
Lectures on the English
Poets; Lectures on the
English Comic Writers;
Spirit of the Age; Life of
Napoleon*
King Lear restoration,
328
Merchant of Venice
review, 392
Headsman, 74
Heartbreak House (Shaw),
901
Hecate (Hecat, Heccat),
359–360
familiarity, 359–360
scenes, addition, 353, 359

supernatural character,
359
Hecatommithi (Cinthio), 377,
446
Whetstone version, 377
Hector, 594–595
chivalric norm, devia-
tions, 594
death, 595
Hecuba, 146–147
sorrowing woman,
model, 146–147
woes, recital, 139
Heicroft, Henry, 778, 915
Helen, 595
Cressida, relationship,
594
Helena (Helen)
All's Well That Ends Well,
19–21
focus, 13
appearance. *See* Florence
Coleridge comments,
19
energy, Parolles (influ-
ence), 23
initiative, establishment,
19–20
*Midsummer Night's
Dream*, 421
position, 23
positive characteristics,
14
romantic heroine,
20–21
virtue, paragon, 14–15,
19
Helenus, 595–596
Helicanus, 465–466
Heminge, John (John
Heminges), 686, 717,
778, 799
dedication, 836
Henry IV, Part I, 161
Henderson, John, 55, 778
Henry IV, Part I, 161
Othello, 447
Twelfth Night, 608
Henken, Elissa R., 996
*Henrici Quinti Angliae Regis
Gesta*, 200
Henri IV of France (king of
Navarre), 342
Henry, king of England
(Latin biographies), 200

Henry, Prince (King Henry
III of England), 315
historical figure, 315
Henry I, 778–779
Henry II, 778–779
Henry III. *See* Henry, Prince
Henry IV, King of England,
169–170
as Henry Bolingbroke,
484–485
monarch, strength, 858
reign, compression, 170
ruler, strength, 169–170
significance, 170
usurper, Hotspur percep-
tion, 170
weariness, 170
Henry IV, Part I
achievement, 160
characters, 162–179
commentary, 158–160
date, 161, 167
fair copy, 161
foul paper, 161
Holinshed information,
162
innovation, 158
involvement. *See* history
plays
popularity, decline,
161–162
Q editions, 161
Quarto editions, 161
quotations, 965–966
sources, 160–161
synopsis, 155–158
television productions,
162
text, 161
theatrical history,
161–162
Henry IV, Part II
animal imagery, 184
characters, 186–194
commentary, 182–185
date, 167
disease/death, references,
184
England, presentation,
182–183
First Folio publication,
185
handwritten copy. *See*
Dering manuscript
induction, 182

Olivier, Laurence, 694, 748,
845–846, 876. *See also
Confessions of an Actor;
On Acting*
Antony and Cleopatra, 31
Coriolanus, 84
Hamlet, 141
Henry IV, Part I, 161–162
Henry V, film, 201
Macbeth, 354
Merchant of Venice, 393
Moor, 442
renown, 761
Richard III, 509
Romeo and Juliet, 520
Titus Andronicus, 578
On Acting (Olivier), 846
One
Henry VI, Part II, 245
Troilus and Cressida, 597
One Within, 281
Onions, Charles Talbut, 997
onlie begetter, 780
*On Some of Shakespeare's
Female Characters*
(Faucit), 746
On Such a Night (Quayle),
869
"On the Knocking on the
Gate in *Macbeth*" (De
Quincey), 726
On the Russe Common Wealth
(Fletcher), 749
opera, 846–847. *See also
Comedy of Errors*
operatic masque, 762. *See
also Measure for Measure,
or Beauty the Best
Advocate*
Ophelia, 149–150, 903
affectionate nature, 150
death, conception, 139
drowning, 150
Hamlet
love, 138
love, denial, 145, 150
insanity, 150
rejection, 150
suicide, 150
wildflowers, wearing, *149*
*Orchestra, or a Poeme of
Dauncing* (Davies), 724
Orell, John, 997
Orff, Carl, 847–848
Orinoco River, 872

Orlando, 61–62
love, growth, 61
name, invocation, 54
servant, 56
Orlando Furioso (Ariosto),
54, 430, 669
Harington translation,
62
Orlando Furioso (Greene),
886
Orléans
La Pucelle, arrival, 848
Salisbury, death, 227
siege, 226, 755, 848
relief, 224
Orléans, Bastard of. *See
Bastard of Orléans*
Orléans, Charles, Duke of,
209–210
historical figure, 210
Orline, Lena Cowen, 998
Orphan, The (Otway), 848
Orsino, 613–614
emotions, misplacement,
614
love, translation, 606
reality, distortion, 613
Ortho-epia Gallica (Du
Bartas), 730, 734
Osberne of Northumber-
land. *See* Young Siward
Osric, 150
comic relief, 150
Ostler, 175
Ostler, William, 848
Benfield, replacement,
682
Oswald, 337
action-taking, 747
character. *See* Jacobean
drama
villain, 337
Otello (Rossini), 448, 847,
887
Otello (Verdi), 448, 690,
939
Othello, 454–455
race, impact, 455
racial element, 454–455
sanity, 455
suicide, 455
sympathetic figure, 445
Othello
Act 1, difference,
444–445

ballet, 448
characters, 448–456
commentary, 442–446
date, 5, 446–447
film versions, 448
Folio edition, 447
jealousy, motif,
443–444
Killigrew, Thomas, 807
marriages, parallelism,
443–444
morality play, 443
operas, 448
Quarto edition, 447
quotations, 972–973
society, rule (reestablishment), 446
sources, 446
synopsis, 440–442
television productions,
448
tension, increase, 446
text, 446–447
theatrical history,
447–448
trust, destruction
(motif), 443
Venice, racial bias, 445
willow scene, 445–446
Othello (Welles), 950
Other, 151
Other Clown, 151
Otway, Thomas, 848. *See
also History and Fall of
Caius Marius; Orphan;
Venice Preserved*
Barry rejection, 678
Outlaws, 622
*Outlines of the Life of
Shakespeare* (Halliwell-
Phillips), 774
Ovid (Publius Ovidius
Naso), 1, 476, 848–849.
*See also Amores; Ars
Amatoria; Fasti;
Metamorphoses*
erotic poetry, 637
rape/mutilation, tale. *See
Philomel*
Titus Andronicus, refer-
ences, 577
Oxford, Edward de Vere,
Earl of, 674, 849
Oxford, John de Vere, Earl
of, 261

Oxford English Dictionary, 68,
757
Oxford's Men, 849, 956
Oxford University, Lodge
(attendance), 819

P

Pacino, Al. *See Looking for
Richard*
Padua, 850
pagan religion, component.
See romances
Page
All's Well That Ends Well,
22
As You Like It, 62
diminutive stature, 190
Henry IV, Part II, 190
Richard III, 506
Romeo and Juliet, 525
Taming of the Shrew,
541
Timon of Athens,
570–571
Page, George, 410–411
*Painful Adventures of Pericles
Prince of Tyre, The*
(Wilkins), 953
Painter, 571
Painter, William, 850. *See
also Palace of Pleasure*
adaptation, 676
translation, 688
Palace of Pleasure (Painter),
116, 126, 565
Palamon, 634
Arcite, comparison,
630–631
prayer, 634
shallowness, 634
Palatine Electorate, recovery,
739
Palazzo del Tè, 763
Palmer, Alan, 997
Palmer, Veronica, 997
Palm Sunday, 926
Palsgrave's Men, 662, 728,
753, 850–851
change, 779
Gibborne, member, 761
Palsied-Eld, 718
Pandar, 468
Pandarus, 595, 597, 864
diction, exaggeration,
597